The Douglas Register

Being a detailed record of Births, Marriages and Deaths together with other interesting notes, as kept by the Rev. William Douglas, from 1750 to 1797.

* * * *

An Index of Goochland Wills.
Notes on the French-Huguenot Refugees who lived in Manakin-Town.

* * * *

Transcribed and Edited by
W. MAC. JONES

Director of the Genealogical Bureau of Virginia; Genealogist General, National Society, Sons of the American Revolution; Life Member Association for the Preservation of Virginia Antiquities; Member of the Virginia Historical Society, etc.

Southern Historical Press, Inc.
Greenville, South Carolina

This volume was reproduced
from a personal copy located in
the Publishers private library

Please direct all correspondence and book orders to:
SOUTHERN HISTORICAL PRESS, Inc.
PO Box 1267
Greenville, SC   29602-1267

Originally printed: Richmond, VA. 1928
ISBN #978-1-63914-110-4
Printed in the United States of America

Table of Contents

Richmond, Va., Nov. 7, 1892.

THIS IS TO CERTIFY that the "Parish Register of Goochland Parish, begun Anno 1756 by WILLIAM DOUGLASS, Minister" and contained in a large manuscript volume, bound in parchment, is my own property, having descended to me from the author, as follows: First: William Douglass' heir was his only child, Peggy Douglass, who married Nicholas Merriwether, by whom there were six children, of whom, Elizabeth Merriwether was the sixth, and my own father's mother. Nicholas Merriwether died Dec. 19th 1772, and his widow married Chiles Tyrril Feb. 20 1783. On Sept. 8 1784 they had a son, born to them, James Hunter Tyrril (or Terrell) who was the 7th child of Peggy Douglass, inherited this manuscript of his grandfather, and left it to his adopted son and heir James Hunter Minor, whose only daughter I married, and whose widow, Mary W. Minor, now of Charlottesville, Virginia, who was also his heir, gave the said manuscript to me, Robert W. Lewis.

The Rev. William Douglass was grandfather to my grandmother, Elizabeth Lewis, of Locust Grove, Charlottesville, Va. I inherited his library of several hundred volumes. Bishop Meade used this manuscript in composing his "Old Churches & Families of Virginia". I also own "The History of the House of Douglas" autograph copy of the Rev. Wm. Douglas, brought over from Scotland in 1750, showing him to be a lineal descendant of the Ducal House of Douglas (769 A. D.—1490 A. D.).

signed by me, ROBERT W. LEWIS.

(copy).

FOREWORD

For a great many years it has been the sincere desire of all those interested in the early records of Virginia to make the contents of the celebrated Douglas Register available to the public; but the owners, descendants of the Reverend Mr. Douglas, would not agree to its publication. It has been the good fortune of the writer to have succeeded in obtaining the consent of the present owner, Mr. Hunter Fielding Warner Lewis, to this publication.

In order to make the record more available for ready reference, the entries, under the various headings of Marriages, Births and Deaths, have been arranged alphabetically, after the manner of an index. This has been done without in any case changing the spelling, or phraseology, of the venerable recorder. It will be seen that in many instances the same name has been spelled in different ways, according to the manner of former days. The various forms of the same family name, wherever the editor was certain, have been placed together, regardless of the proper alphabetical place, in order to present the family grouping in a more comprehensive arrangement.

Some of the records of the early French settlers at Maniken Town, and a rough index of the Goochland County wills, inventories, etc., have been added to the publication, that the reader may understand better the origin of many of the family names that occur in the Register. Many marriages, of which there are now no available record, are indicated in the Birth Register, in which Mr. Douglas, very wisely, gives the maiden name of the mother, as well as the name of the father. These presumptive marriages have been set up from the Birth Registry and made into two alphabetical lists, one for the husbands and another for the wives.

The Reverend William Douglas came to St. James Northam Parish, in Goochland County, Virginia, (Dover Church), on the 12th of October, 1750. A memorandum in the Register shows that he had charge of St. James Northam Parish for twenty-seven years; Maniken Town (King William Parish), for nineteen years, and ministered to a charge in Buckingham County for four years.

There had been, according to his statement, no parish register kept up to the time that he took charge. He began, on the 15th of September, 1753, keeping a record of the marriages performed by him. The book in which the Register is kept, was procured by him at the beginning of the year 1756 and was kept from that time until near the time of his death, which occurred on the 7th of February, 1798. But he inserted many of the marriages performed by him before 1756, and in the matter of births the record goes back to 1705—including the names and dates of birth of children given him by their parents, who desired them recorded.

This book is known as "The Douglas Register" for the reason that it not only contains a record of Births, Christenings, Marriages, Deaths and Funerals in St. James Northam Parish and the county of Goochland, but in many instances in adjacent counties and others more remote. The record also is not only for the period he was in charge of St. James Northam Parish, but continues after he left that parish, on the 5th of September, 1777, and went to live in Louisa County. In fact he kept up the entries in the Register until 1797, and thus it covers a period of ninety-two years.

The book is made of the old Government stamped paper and is bound in calf and parchment. It is in a good state of preservation, though in some places the margin is worn or broken, and there are several pages missing.

The writer wishes to acknowledge the very efficient aid of the Hon. Charles M. Wallace in the preparation and editing of the manuscript; the intelligent co-operation of the publishers, Messrs J. W. Fergusson & Sons; and also to express his high appreciation of the endorsement of his effort by the following well-known authorities on Virginia records: Dr. Henry R. McIlwaine, State Librarian of Virginia; Dr. Lyon G. Tyler, historian and author; Dr. Wm. G. Stanard, Secretary of the Virginia Historical Society; Dr. Earl G. Swem, Librarian of William & Mary College; Dr. Joseph D. Eggleston, President of Hampden-Sydney College; and Dr. Robert A. Stewart, editor of the *Researcher*. He further wishes to acknowledge the generous response of the subscribers, whose names appear elsewhere in these pages.

With the ardent hope that this work will prove of interest and benefit to the public, W. MAC. JONES.

Richmond, Va., July 31, 1928.

ERRATA

P. 53, line 1.—The word "widow" should not be in brackets.
P. 104, line 3.—The words "alias Barclay" should not be in brackets.
P. 135, bottom line.—For "John Ingle" read "John Tugle."
P. 290, line 20.—For "Marriages p. 42 supra" read "p. 43 supra."
P. 351, bottom line.—Footnote will be found on p. 352.

THE DOUGLAS REGISTER

(BRIEF ACCOUNT OF DOVER CHURCH BY REV. WM. DOUGLAS)
(*From back of book—no paging*)

ffeb. 11 1720—

The Dover Church being the first Church in Goochland was appointed to be built which cost the Parish 54990 Lb tobacco: being 50 feet long & 24 wide. The Church Wardens that year were Mr. Tho: Randolph & John Woodson. Parish Levy 50 per poll. & having no Minr. They agreed with Mr. ffinney for to preach once in the month @ 500 lb tobacco a sermon & Cask. Tithables in all 326.

Dec: 2 1721

Whole tithables in Goochland this year are 407. Levy is 70 Lb. p Poll. Mr. ffinney continued to Preach once in the month. Whole charge in the Parish this year 54790 Lb tobacco.

Nov: 17 1722

Mr. ffinney Continued to preach once in the month per Agreement. 440 Tithables this year assessed at 80 per poll. Some alterations from the first agreement appointed to be made on Dover Church, for which Mr. Randolph is allowed 17000 Lb. tobacco & Cask. Whole charge on the parish this year 45503 Lb. tobacco.

Oct: 14. 1723.

Mr. ffinney continued Preacher as formerly. 519 Tithables this year are assessed at 68½ per poll. Whole charge of the parish 35668. Church Wardens William Womack & Noel Burton.

Sep: 1. 1724.

Mr. Randolph having finished the church according to Bargain, it was taken off his hands. Mr. ffinney continued Minr. by agreement. Mr. Randolph paid 7239 Lb. tobacco for church ornaments. 635 Tithables this year are assessed at 36½ per poll. Whole charge of the parish 23642 Lb. tobacco.

feb: 21. 1725

Mr. George Murdoch received Minister of this Parish & desired to preach at Rob: Carters on the south side the River & Major Bollings Quarter on the north side on the last Sunday in every moneth successively. Geor. Payne & Rob: Adams appointed Church Wardens.

Oct: 9 1725

Mr. George Murdoch Minr. 774 Tithables assessed at 36 Lb. tobacco per pole. Whole charge of the parish this year 27864 Lb. tobacco.

Nov: 14 1726.

Mr. George Murdoch Minr. 2612 Lb. tobacco levied to purchase a Glebe. This year were 872 tithables assessed at 40 per poll. A Reader appointed at Deep Creek is allowed 1000 Lb. tobacco yearly.

May 18. 1727.

Mr. Zachariah Brooks is hired to preach once a month for one year. A Reader is appointed to read prayers at John Sanders's & Mr. Ogilsbys on Licking hole on Sundays successively.

Oct: 21. 1727.

Mr. Brooks hired to preach monethly at 400 Lb. tobacco each time. Tho: Carter is appointed to Read prayers at Sam: Birks's. Mr. Randolph is appointed to Provide a surplice, two common Prayer books, two great Bibles, & Dr. Tillotsons Sermons for the use of the parish. John Huckaby appointed Sexton in room of Will: Roberts. Mr. paid 432 Lb. tobacco for preaching one sermon. 997 Tithables this year are assessed at 17 Lb. tobacco per poll. Total Charge of the Parish 16949 Lb. tobacco.

Nov: 12 1727

Mr. Becket is received Minr. of this Parish & is allowed 16000 Lb. tobacco & cask with allowance for conveniency per Annum.

Sep. 12 1750. The Revnd Will Douglas then was chosen Minr. of Goochland & continued till Nov: 1777 at wc time ye distractions commenced both in Church & State when I removed to my own in Louisa.

1752. Dec: 6   Tithables 1349 at 30 per pole 40366 Lb.
1753. Jan. 17   Tithes 1397 at 30 per pole 47116 Lb.
1754. Dec. 18   Tithes 1505 at 24 per pole 36120 Lb.
1755. Oct. 14   Tithes 1572 at 19 per pole 30118 Lb.
1756. Nov. 9   Tithes 1557 at 21 per pole 32865 Lb.
1757 Jan. 7   Tithes 1600 at 23 per pole 37378 Lb.
1758 Dec. 18   Tithes 1600 at 22 per pole 35596 Lb.
1759 Oct. 9   Tithes 1754 at 26 per pole 44521 Lb.
1760 Sep. 25   Tithes 1762 at 23 per pole 44050 Lb.
1761 Oct. 29   Tithes 1889 at 27 per pole 51003 Lb.
1762 Nov. 23   Tithes 1893 at 20 per pole 37860 Lb.
1763 Dec. 2   Tithes 1955 at 18 per pole 35190 Lb.
              100 Lb. tobacco levied for Col: Payne to buy church books.
1764. Dec. 10   Tithes 2028 at 19 per pole 38532 Lb.
1766. Feb: 4   Tithes 2061 at 22 per pole 45342 Lb.
1767. Feb: 6   Tithes 2077 at 21 per pole 43617 Lb.
              Jo: Payne charged cash for ye prayer Books.
              Jo: Payne appointed to build a Kitchen chimney to ye Glebe.

Mr. Gavine was Minr. here immediately before me, for Several years, whom I succeeded Sep: 15 1750, having been born in ye Shire of Galloway, near Wigton, Anno 1708, & educated by yt famous Christian & Scholar, the Rev. Mr. William McCulloch, afterwards Minr. of Cambusland near Glasgow, in ye learned Languages, Geography, Mathematicks & Chronology, till I went to ye College of Glasgow Nov. 6. 1725, to attend Mr. Gershom Carmichaels Lectures, on Logicks, Metaphysicks, Ethicks & oyr branches of Philosophy for 2 years. After wc I went to ye Colledge of Edinburgh, Governor to Mr. Ja. Gordon of Grange his son, where I attended Mr. Law on Moral Philosophy, Mr. Stewart on Physicks, Mr. Will Hamilton on Divinity, Mr. Crawford on Church History, Mr. Ker on French & Mr. ******* on Hebrew for 3 years & went to Glecairn in 1732.

Will: Douglas

Utensels belonging to Goochland Churches
Lickinghole has a Quart pewter Tankard
A Large Tablecloath & Napkin
A Delph plate for ye Sacrement bread
A Delph Bowl for Baptisms
A Crystal Cup
Dover Church has a large Tablecloth
A Quart pewter tankard
A Pewter Bason for Baptisms
A Delph Plate for Sacrament bread
A Crystal Cup.

PARISH REGISTER OF GOOCHLAND
begun
ANNO 1756 by WILLIAM DOUGLASS,
MINISTER—

I came to Goochland Decr. 12 1750, & preached for the first time in Dover Church, dec: 16th Sunday following; & have officiate as Minister since that time. But there being no Register in the Parish Since I came till now, is the cause why it has not been kept till this time.

The number of Marriages since I came till the time when this Register begins were 103 Couple after which a regular record is kept of all the subsequent Marriages from page 1st and of the Births & Christening from Page 48th. by me. . . . Will: Douglass, Minr.

Sep: 15. 50 preached first at Dover Church. Oct: 5 50. agreed for an year.

Oct. 2, 51. received by ye Vestry, as Parish Minister, by the then Vestry following, Viz: Stephen Sampson   Will: Holman   Will: Lewis   John Hopkins   Archer Payne.

List of the Vestry for the year 1756 when I got this book

Colo. Arthur Hopkins }
Cap. Will: Burton   } Church Wardens, 1756

Colo. Charles Lewis   Colo: Henry Wood   Colo. John Payne
Major John Smith   Major Josiah Payne   Cap: James Holman
George Payne   William Miller   Charles Jordan
John Woodson   Rob: Burton Oct: 1756   James Cole Oct: 1756
Cap: William Pryor dec: 1758   Capt Will: Stamps dec. 1758
Joseph Pollard. 1757   Capt Noel Burton 1761
Tho: Man: Randolph 1763.   Tho: Bolling 1764:
Jo: Bolling   Geo: Payne Junr.
Tho: Underwood   Joseph Woodson
                          * * * * * *

[Following notes made subsequent to original entries appear on this page.]

Two leaves are torn out at page 63. Very unjustly.

In ye Register of Baptisms are two leaves torn out wc contained 200 baptisms, viz: from Aug: 29. 1762 till March 31. 1763.

Out of this book were torn 30 clean leaves, & 5 written ones while it continued in Goochland Court House, & at Tuker Woodsons, after I had left it there.

                              Will: Douglass

MARRIAGES OF RECORD
(Male Index)

ADAMS, Ben:, & Nelly Coleman, both of Orange, 1781, Apl: 12. p. 21.

Adams, Ja: & Cecily Ford, in Goochland, 1751, ... pp. 26-32.

Adams, Wilson, & Molly Parish, both in Goochland 1771 Dec. 26 p. 13.

ADKINSON, Joseph, & Susannah Childers both in Hanover 1767, Feb: 25. p. 9.

AILSTOCK, Abra: & Isabel Ratcliff both of Louisa 1784, Dec: 23 p. 23.

AINSLEY, Benjamin, & Sarah Grayson, both of this parish 1769, Mar: 20 p. 11.

ALBRITAIN, John, & Mary Meanly, both of this parish 1768, Ap: 14 p. 10.

ALFORD, Anselm, & Ann Tony, both of Fluvanna, 1782 .... ---- p. 22.

Alford, Drury, & Bettie Cannon, of Louisa 1782, Mar: 13 p. 22.

ALLEN, Da: & Lucy Gardner, both of Louisa 1780, Dec: 25 p. 20.

Allen, James, & Patsy Woodfork, both of Orange 1787, Ap: 25 p. 24.

Allen, Joseph, & Ann Bailey, both of Goochland 1787, Oct: 19 p. 25.

Allen, Julius, in Henrico, & Mary Biggar in Hanover 1768, Oct: 11 p. 10.

Allen, Richard, & Anner Clements, both of ys parish 1777, Aug: 28 p. 18.

ALLEY, Isaiah, & Eliz: Watkins, both in ys parish 1775, Dec: 25 p. 17.

ALMOND, Jo: & Catie Falconer, both in Orange 1778, Oct: 7 p. 18.

ALSUP, John, & Jurya Potter, both in this parish 1762, May 23 p. 6.

ALVIS, Ashley, & Eliz: Knolling, both of Goochland 1772, Dec: 16 p. 13.

Alvis, David, & Mary Cauthon, both of this parish 1768, Aug: 20 p. 10.

Alvis, Shadrach, & Nansie Addison, both in Goochland 1773, Sep: 23 p. 14.

ANDERSON, Ben: & Sarah Johnson, both of Louisa 1773, Sep: 7 p. 14.

Anderson, Benjamin, & Judith Mims, both of this parish 1769, Jan: 27 p. 11.

Anderson, George, & Susannah Mims, both of this parish 1769, Mar: 23 p. 11.

Anderson, Col: Rich: & Catherine Fox, both of Louisa 1780, Ap: 24 p. 19

Anderson, Turner, & Susannah Daniel, in Louisa, asked only 1776, Jun: 12. p. 17.

ARMSTRONG, Lancelot, & Mary Brown, in Louisa 1778, Feb: 3 p. 18.

Armstrong, Will: & Mary Nichols, both in Louisa 1782, Nov. 14 p. 22.

ARNET, Da: & Mary Shuckleford, both of Louisa 1779, Oct: 28 p. 19.

Arnet, Lesly, & Francis Smith, both in this parish were married (17)92
.... p. 27.

Arnet, Will: & Molly Graves, both in Louisa 1781, Dec: 27 p. 21.

Arnet, Will: & Mary McGehee, both in Louisa 1791 ....
p. 27.

ARNOLD, Will: & Susan Tate, both of Louisa 1773, Oct: 11 p. 14.

Arnold, Will: & Judith Edwards, in Spot: 1784, Sep: 16 p. 23.

ASHLEY, William, & Hannah Pierce, both in this parish 1762, Mar: 9
p. 6.

ASKEW, Antony, & Jemima Childers, both in this parish 1759, Aug.
30 p. 4.

ATKINS, Edward, & Frances Wisdom, both of Orange 1780, Jan: 28
p. 19.

Atkins, Elkanak, & Sally Austine, both in Louisa 1771, Oct. 24 p. 12.

Atkins, Jo: & .... 1751 .... pp. 26-32.

Atkins, Jo: & Mary Groom, both of Spot: 1782, Aug: 1 p. 22.

Atkins, Lewis, & Judith Clark, both of Goochland, 1780, Nov: 28
p. 20.

ATKINSON, Henry, & Rach: Huchins (Houchens), both in this
parish 1756, Jan: 20 p. 2.

Atkinson, Lewis, & Martha Whitler, both of ys parish 1777, Sep: 4
p. 18.

Atkinson, Pleasants, & Obedience Whitloe, both of ys parish 1776,
Jun: 26 p. 17.

Atkinson, Stephen, & Ann Hanson, both in this parish 1762, May 15
p. 6.

Atkinson, Will: & Winnifred Clark, in Goochland 1784, June 22 p. 23.

AUSTIN, John, & Mary Holman, both in this parish 1765, Dec: 31
p. 8.

BAILIE, David, & Cecilia Stodghill, both of Albemarle, 1777, Jul: 1
p. 18.

Bailie, Tho: & Cloe May, both of Fluvanna 1780, Oct: 19 p. 20.

BAILEY, Callam, & Elizabeth Roundtree, both in this parish 1761, Jun:
4 p. 6.

Bailey, Callum, & Judith Guillam, both of ys parish 1776, Jul: 25 p. 17.

Bailey, James, in New Kent, & Ann Lawry in this parish 1762, Nov: 16
p. 7.

Bailey, John, & Angelany Thomas, both in this parish 1768, Mar: 8
p. 10.

Bailey, Tho: & Sarah Spalding, both in Maniken town 1757, feb: 13
p. 3.

Bailey, Tho: & Nancy Gentry, both of Louisa 1780, May 7 p. 20.

BAILY, Will: & Molly Alford, both in Goochland 1771, Dec. 26 p. 13.

BAKER, Jo: & Nancy Harris, both in Louisa [17]81, Feb: 12 p. 21.

Baker, John, & Susannah Perkins, both of this parish 1767, Jan: 5 p. 9.

Baker, Joseph, & Eliz: Herndon, both of ys parish 1773, Jul: 11 p. 16.

Baker, Overton, & Molley Green, both in Louisa 1780, Aug: 10 p. 20.

BALDOCK, Richard, & Elizabeth Clarkson, both in this parish 1761, Mar: 23 p. 5.

BALEW, John, & Mary Ripley, both in Albemarle, 1759, Mar: 21 p. 4.

BALLOW, Thomas, in Albemarle, & Cloe Battersby in Maniken town 1757, Mar: 17 p. 3.

BALL, Burgess, & Mary Chiechester, in Goochland 1770, July: 2 p. 12.

BALL, John, & Jean Kindred, both of ys parish 1775, Jan: 17 p. 16.

BANKS, Ralph, & Martha Venable, in Fluvanna, 1778; Dec: 9 p. 18.

Banks, Will: & Eliz: Martin 1753, Sep: 15 pp. 1-27-32.

BARCLAY, George, & Mary Cole, both of this parish 1766, Aug. 7 p. 9.

BARKER, Jo: & Eliz: Dyches, both in Goochland 1772, Oct: 24 p. 13.

Barker, Tho: & Mary Poor, both in Goochland 1772, Aug: 28 p. 13.

Barker, William, & Ann Evans, both in this parish 1769, Jul: 27 p. 11.

BARLOW, Ja: in Albemarle, & Lucy Edwards in Louisa 1780, Jan: 13 p. 19.

BARNARD, Rob: & Eliz: Ferrar, both in Goochland 1779, June 13 p. 19.

BARNER, Josh: in Goochland, & Frances Bowles in Hanover, 1772, Jun: 10 p. 13.

BARNES, John, & Mary Porter, in Maniken town 1755, Oct: 30 p. 2.

BARNET, Jos: & Lucy Wade, both in this parish 1754, Oct: 3 p. 1.

Barnet, Thomas, & Sarah Graves 1754, ffeb: 3 p. 1.

BARTLET, Ja: & Eliz: White, in Spot: 1783, Sep: 25 p. 23.

BASKET, Thomas, in this parish, & Mildred Martin in Cumberland 1761, Jan: 15 p. 5.

Basket, William, & Mary Pace, both in this parish 1761, Oct: 1 p. 6.

BATES, Ja: & Hithie Serjeant, both of Louisa 1783, Sep: 12 p. 23.

BATTLES, Shadrach, & Dolly Moss, both in Louisa 1780, Jul: 25 p. 20.

BEASLY, Cha: & Mary Partlow, of Spotsy: 1786, Jan: 18 p. 24.

BEGBIE, Will: & Drusilla Symes, both in Hanover 1770, Aug. 1 p. 12.

BELL, ..., & .... Strange, in Fluvanna 1781, Mar: 14 p. 21.

BELLAMY, Jo: & Eliz: Scrugs, both in Goochland, 1774, Sep: 13 p. 15.

BENNAUGH, David, & Anna Sandige, both in Spotsylvania 1787, Dec: 13 p. 25.

BENNET, Fisher-Rice, & Judith Hanson, both in Albemarle 1768, Dec: 13 p. 11.

Bennet, James, & Elizabeth Sampson, both of this parsih 1768, ... p. 10.

BENTLEY, Dan: & Rebecca Eadson, both of Fluvanna 1780, May 15 p. 20.

BEVER, Sam: & Eliz: Timberlick, both of Louisa 1782, Jun: 20 p. 22.

BIBB, Charles, & Annie Umbles, both of Louisa 1788, Ap: 29 p. 25.

Bibb, James, & Sarah ffarrer, both in this parish 1763, ffeb: 6 p. 7.

Bibb, John, & Sarah Thomason, both of Louisa 1779, Sep: 29 p. 19.

Bibb, Tho: & Eliz: Carpenter, both in Louisa 1787, Dec: 4 p. 25.

BIGGAR, Macon, & Christian Poindexter, both in Louisa 1779, Jul: 22 p. 19.

BILBOA, John, & Ann Walker, both in Maniken town 1760, Jun: 16 p. 5.

BIRKMYRE, William, & Hannah Brit, both in this parish 1768, Jun: 2 p. 10.

BLACK, Jonathan, & Judith Fairies, both of this parish 1775, Dec: 19 p. 16.

BLACKBURN, John, & Mary Griffin, both of ys parish 1776, Dec: 14 p. 17.

BLACKWEL, Jesse, & Mary Crow, both of ys parish 1776, Jan: 8 p. 17.

Blackwell, Jo: & Catie Wood, both of Orange 1782, Ap. 3 p. 22.

BLETSOE, Will: & Eliz: Craig, both of Spot: 1781, May 1 p. 21.

BLUNKHALL, William, & Rebekah Griffiths, both in this parish 1764, May 27 p. 8.

BLUNT, Charles, & Mary Waters, in Louisa 1787, Dec. 2 p. 25.

BOLDING, Will: & Ann Burgess, both from Albemarle 1772, Jul: 6 p. 13.

BOND, Geo: & Sarah Chace, both of Louisa 1785, June 10 p. 24.

Bond, Will: & Eliz: Cole, both of Louisa 1787, Aug: 23 p. 24.

Bond, Wright, & Frances Gready, both of Louisa 1788, July 6 p. 25.

BOWLES, Bartlet, & Ann Owen, both of this parish, 1766, Nov: 13 p. 9.

Bowles, Jesse, & Hannah Perkins, both in Goochland 1773, Mar: 3 p. 14.

Bowles, John, & Elizabeth Curd, in this parish 1764, Dec. 2 p. 8.

Bowles, John, & Mary Radford in Hanover 1768, Nov: 9 p. 10.

Bowles, Knight, & Sarah Curd, both in this parish 1767, Feb: 19 p. 9.

BOWMAN, John Sutton, in Prince Edward, & Sarah Cauthan in this parish, 1756, Dec. 27 p. 3.

Bowman, Rob: in Chesterfield, & Eliz: Craigwall in this parish 1765, Ap: 1 p. 8.

Bowman, Will: & Mary Cosby, both in Goochland 1779, Dec. 28 p. 19.

BOXLEY, Jo: & Mary Barclay, both of Louisa, 1789, Aprile 18 pp. 25-129.

BRADSHAW, Ben: & Ann McBride—in Goochland 1753, Ap: 8 pp. 27-32.

Bradshaw, Ben: & Hopey Poor, both in this parish 1778, Febr. 25 p. 18.

Bradshaw, Clayburn, & Eliz: Clements, both of Goochland 1779, Dec. 28 p. 19.

Bradshaw, Jo: & Lucy Sadler, both of Goochland 1771, Feb. 7 p. 12.

Bradshaw, Jo: & Eliz: Jordan, both of this parish 1758, ffeb: 14 p. 3.

Bradshaw, Will: & Mary Lad, both in this parish 1754, Jul: 7 p. 1.

BRET, Cha: & .... 1751 .... pp. 26-31.

Bret, John, & Susannah Holman, both in this 1770, May 30 p. 11.

Brit, Will: & Sarah Poor, both in Goochland 1784, Sep: 21 p. 23.

BRIERS, Edward, & Lucy Hawkins, both in Maniken town, 1761, Oct: 18 p. 6.

BROCK, Henry, & Calie Saunders, both of Spots: 1782, Mar: 7 p. 22.

Brock, John, & Judah Walker 1754, ffeb: 2 p. 1.

BROCKMAN, Jos: & Mary Page, both in Goochland 1773, Ap: 15 p. 14.

Brockman, Lewis, & Betsie Bletsoe, both in Orange 1779, Mar: 12 p. 18.

Brockman, Major, & Mary Paterson, both of Orange, 1779, Nov. 11 p. 19.

BROCKS, Will: & Susannah Williams, both in Henrico parish 1763, Mar: 24 p. 7.

BROMFIELD, Jo: & Annie Coleman, both in Goochland 1773, May 16 p. 14.

[BROOKS, James] & Eliz: Pollock, both in this parish 1764 .... p. 7.

BROOKS, Will: & Eliz: Jacobs, both in Louisa 1784, June 6 p. 23.

BROWN, Armistead, in Cumberland, & Sally Daniel in Louisa 1781, May 17 p. 21.

Brown, Charles, in Orange, & Henrietta Arnet in Louisa 1785, May 17 p. 24.

Brown, Jo: & Sarah Shoemaker, both in Goochland 1772, Nov: 1 p. 13.

Brown, Jo: & Molly Thomson, in Orange 1778, May 26 p. 18.

Brown, Reuben, & Susannah Napier, in this parish 1761, Jun: 11 pp. 5-6.

Brown, Will: & Dorothea Long, both in Louisa 1781, Oct: 30 p. 21.

BRYAN, Will: & Susannah Barret, both in this parish 1759, Dec. 24 p. 5.

BRYANT, Isaac, & Ann Williams, both in this parish 1766, Mar: 14 p. 9.

Bryant, James, & Jane Guerrant, both in Maniken town 1758, Jun: 11 p. 4.

Bryant, John, & Elizabeth Baker, both of this parish 1765, Jul: 22 p. 8.

Bryant, Will: & Mary Haris, both in Fluvana, 1780, May 26 p. 20.

BRYCE, Mr. Archibald, & Mary Mitchel, both in this parish were married 1769 Jul: 21 pp. 11-28.

BUGG, Billie, & .... 1751 .... pp. 26-32.

BULLOCK, Da: & Susannah More, in Louisa 1778, Feb: 4 p. 18.

Bullock, Da: & Jane Terry, both in Louisa 1782, Feb: 12 p. 21.

BUNCES, Tho: & Betsie Stevens, in Orange 1778, Dec: 26 p. 18.

BURGESS, Will: & Jane Pigg, from Albemarle 1770, Aug: 7 p. 12.

BURNLEY, Ja: & Eliz: Grant, both in Fluvanna 1779, Feb: 5 p. 18.

Burnley, Jo. & Susannah Crenshaw, both of Louisa 1785, Dec: 15 p. 24.

BURNSET, Tho: & Frances Woodfolk, both in Orange 1779, May 13 p. 19.

BURTON, Charles, & Mary Holland, both in this parish, 1763, Nov: 3 p. 7.

Burton, Julius, in Henrico, & Rebekah Clayton in this parish 1763, Mar: 10 p. 7.

Burton, Rob: & Judith Laforce, both in this parish 1757, Oct: 13 p. 3.

Burton, Walthall, & Sally Price, both in Goochland 1773, Feb: 13 p. 14.

BUSH, Philip, & Frances Vivian, both in Orange 1778, Oct. 6 p. 18.

Bush, Will: & Frances Tandy Bunces, both in Orange 1778, Dec: 9 p. 18.

BYERS, Ja: & Lovina Smith, in Louisa 1782, Dec: 19 p. 22.

CAIRDEN, Reu: & Ann Massie, both in Goochland 1771, Jun: 27 p. 12.

Cairden, Robert, & Molly Tugle, both in this parish 1767, Nov: 27 p. 10.

Cairden, Rob: & Eliz: Roberts, both of ys parish 1775, Nov. 26 p. 16.

CALDWELL, Tho: in Henrico & Sarah Crouch in this parish 1756, Aug: 30 p. 2.

CAMMOCK, Francis, & Clary Strange both of Spot: 1782, Nov: 6 p. 22.

CANNON, Jo: & Ann Whitlow, both in Goochland 1770, Dec: 29 p. 12.

CAREY, Wilson, & Jean Barbara Ker (Carr) in Goochland 1782, Jul: 21 p. 22.

CARLETON, Richard, & Lettitia Fairies, both of ys Parish 1777, Feb: 4 p. 17.

CARROL, Tho: & Mildred Walker, both in Louisa 1781, Oct. 4 p. 21.

CARTER, Charles in Cumberland, & Judith Carter in Lickinghole 1756, Jun: 24 p. 2.

Carter, Charles, & Bettie Pulham, both in Spotsylvania 1786, Oct: 19 p. 24.

Carter, Edward, & Eliz: Pleasants, both of ys parish 1777, May 20 p. 18.

Carter, Ja: in Cumberland, & Ann Merine, in Goochland 1771, Oct. 24 p. 12.

Carter, Jo: & Winifred Allen, both in Spots: 1784, Sep: 1 p. 23.

Carter, Rob: in Henrico, & Sus: Evans, in Goochland 1772, Ap: 15 p. 13.

Carter, Tho: & Mary Kilpatrick 1751 .... pp. 26-31.

Carter, Will: & Sarah Overstreet, both in Goochland 1773, Dec: 25 p. 14.

CASH, Will: & Ruth Walker, both of ys parish (Betw. 1750-1753) p. 31.

CATLET, Thomas, & ffrances fford, both in this parish 1759, Jan: 23 p. 4.

CAUTHON, James, & Sarah Bowles, both in this parish 1762, Sep: 28 p. 7.

Cauthon, John, & Margaret Hubbard, both in this parish 1766 Mar: .... p. 8.

Cauthon, Thomas, & Sarah Hubbard, both in this parish 1769, Oct: 31 p. 11. [See Cothan.]

CAWSON, Tho: & Nancy Day, both in Spot: 1784 Dec: 23 p. 23.

CESAR, Jo: & Mary Cosbie, both in Goochland 1773, Feb: 11 p. 14.

CHACE, Will: & Patience Goodrich, in Louisa (17)90 .... 4 p. 27.

CHANDLER, Carter, & Judith Young, both of Louisa 1788, July 24 p. 25.

CHEWNING, George, & Jeanie Bunch, both of Louisa 1783, May 29
p. 23.

CHILDERS, Jacob, & Mary Railey, both in Maniken town 1767, Ap:
23 p. 9.

Childers, John, & Maiden Loving [Lovel] both in this 1766, Nov. 10
p. 9.

Childers, Nicholas, & Isabel Harris, both in this parish 1756, Dec: 20
p. 2.

Childers, Philip, & Mary Green, both in Goochland 1773, Nov: 21 p. 14.

Childers, William, & Betty Nuchols, both in this parish 1767, Jan: 5
p. 9.

CHILDRES, Jo. & Lucy Woodrum, both in Goochland 1772, Jun: 14
p. 13.

CHILES, Ben: & Mildred Webber, both in Goochland 1774, May 20
p. 15.

Chiles, Malachie, & Eliz: Garton, both in Orange 1778, Nov: 29 p. 18.

CHRISTIAN, Drury, & Lucy Williams, both in Goochland 1751, ...
.... pp. 26-32.

Christian, Jo: & Judith Leek, both in Goochland 1771, May 9 p. 12.

CHRISTOPHER, Simon, & Ann Mitchel, both in Louisa 1782, Dec:
1 p. 22.

CHUMLY,* Richard, & Grace Milam, both in Maniken town 1756, May
9 p. 2.

CLAPTON, [Clopton], Richard, & Mary Davis, both in this parish
1759, Sep: 16 p. 4.

CLARK, Beverly, & Cary Hicks, both in this 1766. Nov: 17 p. 9.

Clark, Charles, & Sarah Cocke, both in Goochland 1773, Oct. 23 p. 14.

Clark, Dan: & Phebe Jordan, both in Goochland 1770, Aug: 23 p. 12.

Clark, Frank, & Ann Walker, both in this parish 1768, Sep: 22 p. 10.

Clark, Isaac, in Louisa, & Edee French in ys parish 1775, Feb: 7 p. 16.

Clark, Jac: & Sally Wood, both of Fluvanna 1780, May 11 p. 20.

Clark, James, in Amelia & Susannah Bib in this county 1762, May 20
p. 6.

Clark, Jo. in Louisa, and Eliz: Drumright in Goochland 1772, Ap: 16
p. 13.

Clark, Jo: & Sarah Manspoil, both in Orange 1780, Feb: 29 p. 19.

Clark, John, & Susannah Nicks, both in this 1767, Ap: 4 p. 9.

Clark, Jonathan, & Ann Bailey, both in Albemarle 1766, Jun: 4 p. 9.

Clark, Jos: & Hannah Hutcheson, both in this parish 1753, Dec: 25 p. 1.

Clark, Richard, & Mary Tony, both in Cumberland 1768, Dec: 6 p. 11.

Clark, Will: & Agnes Bailey, both in Fluvanna 1781, Feby. 1 p. 20.

Clark, William, & Agnes Williams, both in Albemarle 1766, Ap: 9 p. 9.

CLARKSON, Da: & Pattie Redman 1751 .... p. 26.

Clarkson, Da: & Ann Perkins, both in this parish 1760, Aug: 7 pp. 5-32.

Clarkson, John, in this parish & Judith Womack in Cumberland 1765,
Mar: 28 p. 8.

Clarkson, Will: & Martha Pledge, both in this parish 1761 Mar: 14 p. 5.

---

*Cholmonldly in Birth record.

CLAYTON, Dan: & Mary Barret, both in this parish 1758, Nov: 13 p. 4.

Clayton, Will: & Mary Rose, both of Spot: 1782, Oct: 15 p. 22.

CLEMENTS, James, & Mary Oliver, from King William 1757, Dec: 15 p. 3.

Clements, Jo: & Marianne England, both in Goochland 1771, Aug: 29 p. 12.

Clements, John, & Eliz: Hutchens [Houchens] both in this parish 1755, Jan: 28 p. 1.

Clements, Thomas, & Sarah Peace [Pace] both of this parish 1759, Jan: 10 p. 4.

CLOUGH, Rich: & Jean Woodson, in Goochland 1779, Sep: 23 p. 19.

CLOWDER, David, & Ann Thurston, both in this parish 1765, Sep: 29 p. 8.

COATS, Will, & Mildred Shepherd, both of ys Parish 1775, Sept: 28 p. 16.

COBB, Rob: & Ann Gizage Pondexter, in Louisa 1783, Nov: 19 p. 23.

COBBS, James, & Barbara Bibb, both in Albemarle 1760, Nov: 12 p. 5.

Cobbs, John, & Judith Cobbs, both in Albemarle 1763, Sep: 19 p. 7.

Cobbs, Tho: & Susannah Moon both in forks of James River, Albemarle, 1756, Jan: 27 p. 2.

COCKE, Benjamin, & Mary Johnson, both in this parish 1768, Jun: 23 p. 10.

Cocke, Ja: & Jean Johnson, both in Goochland 1773, Oct: 30 p. 14.

Cocke, Ja: & Martha Parish, both in Goochland 1774, Nov: 25 p. 15.

Cocke, Pleasants, & Elizabeth ffowler, both in this parish 1762, Jul: 1 p. 6.

COLBY, ...l, & Mildred Poor, both in this parish 1767 ....
p. 9.

COLE, James, & Fanny Cheeseman-Wells, both in Albemarle, 1776, Oct: 5 p. 17.

Cole, Rich: & Sarah Sansum, both of Louisa 1785 Dec: 29 p. 24.

Cole, Will: & Sally Byers, in Louisa 1789, Jan: 15 p. 25.

COLEMAN, Francis, & Mary Garret Brook of Louisa (17)91 ....
.... p. 27.

Coleman, Ja: & .... Leek 1751 .... pp. 26-32.

Coleman, John-Daniel, & Million Chamneys, both in this parish 1762 Feb: 12 p. 6.

Coleman, Sam: & Ann Wright, both of this parish 1756 Mar: 30 p. 2.

Coleman, Spencer, & Eliz: Goodwin, of Louisa 1787 May 22 p. 24.

Coleman, Tho: & Nancy Pemberton, both in Spotsylvania 1780, Dec. 3 p. 20.

Coleman, Tho: & Susanna Hawkins, of Orange 1781, Jul: 2 p. 21.

COLLEVAL, Benjamin, & Lucy ffenton, both in Henrico 1764, Dec: 13 p. 8.

COLLINS, Ed: & Ann Collins, both from Orange 1781, May 31 p. 21.

Collins, Mordecia, & Susannah Robbertson, both of Louisa 1790, ...
.... p. 27.

CONNERLY, [CONOLLY], Bryan & Jane Bassit, both on the Bird 1756, Jun: 22 p. 2.

Conoly, Bryan, & Sarah Davis, both of this parish 1767, Feb: 11 p. 9.

COOK, Will: & Susanna Garten, both of Orange 1785, June 13 p. 24.

COOPER, Dan: & Martha Branham, in Goochland 1779, Nov: 7 p. 19.

COPLAND, Henry, & Ann Martin, both in this parish 1761 Jul: 21 p. 6.

CORLEY, Nathaniel, & Annas Williams, both in this parish 1763, Ap: 9 p. 7.

COSBIE, Cha: & Eliz: Smith, both of Louisa 1785, Dec. 13 p. 24.

Cosbie, Garland, & Molly Poindexter, both of Louisa 1782, Jun: 27 p. 22.

Cosbie, Hickerson, & Ann Harris, in Louisa 1780, Oct: 13 p. 20.

COSBY, Fortunatus, & Mary Ann Fountain, in Louisa, were maried [17]95 Nov: 1 p. 28.

Cosby, Tho: & Eliz: Watkins, both of Louisa 1781 Ap. 20 p. 21.

COTHAN, George, & Diana Gentry, both of this parish 1761, Mar: 22 p. 5.

Cothan, Rob: & Zulima Laforce, both in this parish 1760, feb: 11 p. 5. [See Cauthon.]

COTTEREL, Charles W., & Mary Shepherd, both in Henrico 1777, Sep: 4 p. 18.

COX, Edward, & Cecily Guillam, both of this parish 1767, Dec. 10 p. 10.

Cox, George, in Louisa, & Elizabeth Howl in this county 1766, Oct: 31 p. 9.

Cox, John, & Elizabeth Fore, both in Maniken town 1766, Jun: 22 p. 9.

CRADOCK, Tho: & Lilly Ann Smith, both in Goochland 1771, Nov: 30 p. 13.

CRAWFORD, James, & Mary Perkins, both in this parish 1753, Nov: 27 p. 1.

Crawford, Peter, & Betsie Shilton, both in Louisa 1782, Ap: 11 p. 22.

CREELY, Jo: & Nancy Watkins, both of Goochland 1782, Jul: 25 p. 22.

CRENSHAW, Will: & Rietta Saunders, in Louisa 1779, Jul: 23 p. 19.

Crenshaw, Will: & Sarah Baker, both of Louisa 1783, Jan: 30 p. 22.

CROUCH, Stephen, & Elizabeth fferrar, both of this parish 1762, May 16 p. 6.

CROW, John, & Jean Whitlow, both in this parish 1758, Mar: 13 p. 3.

CROWDIS, Da: & Priscilla Lawrie, both in Goochland 1773, Ap: 10 p. 14.

CRUMPTON, Hen: & .... 1752 .... p. 32.

CURD, Edmund, & Mary Curd, both in this parish 1764, Mar: 18 p. 8.

Curd, James, & Mary Graves, both in this 1766, Nov: 20 p. 9.

Curd, John, & Ann Underwood, in Louisa 1775, Sep: 8 p. 16.

Curd, Joseph, in this parish, & Mary Warrin in St. Pauls* 1762, Sep: 28 p. 6.

CURLE, Julius, & Nancy Curd, in Goochland 1789, Mar: 7 p. 25.

*St. Pauls was in Hanover.

DAIR, Cha: & Eliz: Bradley, both in Orange 1782, Ap. 1 p. 22.

DALTON, Bradley, & Dolly Robertson, both of Louisa 1782, Oct: 31 p. 22.

Dalton, David, & Sarah Robinson, both in Louisa 1779, Sep. 27 p. 19.

DANDRIDGE, Nath: West, & Jean Pollard, in Goochland 1779, Aug: 3 p. 19.

DANIEL, Jo: & Sarah Chiles, both in Louisa 1780, Feb: 3 p. 19.

Daniel, John, & Sally Thurston, both ys parish 1776, Mar: 12 p. 17.

Daniel, Mosely, & Nanny Thurston, both of ys parish 1775, Oct: 12 p. 16.

Daniel, Will: & Mary Thomas, both in Louisa 1789, Mar: 30 p. 25.

DAVENPORT, Ja: & Mary Rutherford, both in Goochland 1781, Jan: 23 p. 20.

DAVIES, Abra: & Ann Johnson, both of Louisa 1779, Sep: 23 p. 19.

Davies, Charles, & Martha Slaten, both of this parish 1756, Jan: 7 p. 2.

Davies, David, & Sarah [Pore] Smith both widows in this parish 1755, Jun: 1 p. 1.

Davies, John, & Jurisha Parish, both in this parish 1754, Aug: 11 p. 1.

DAVIS, Joseph, & Glafre Cox, both in this parish 1759, Sep: 16 p. 4.

Davis, Thomas, & Susannah Hyat, in Orange 1783, May 1 p. 23.

DAWSON, Jos: & Judith Dudley, both in this parish 1753, Nov: 20 p. 1.

Dawson, Thomas, & Mary Carter, both in this parish 1756, Dec: 26 p. 3.

DAWSS, Tho: & Eliz: Wright, both in this parish 1754, Nov: 28 p. 1.

DAY, John, & Nancy Taylor, both in Spots: 1784, Mar: 20 p. 23.

Day, William, & Ann Tyrrie, both in Henrico 1760, Jun: 1 p. 5.

DEERING, Tho: & Mary Ramsay, both in Orange, 1783, June 20 p. 23.

DENTON, Jo: & Susan Thacker, both in Hanover 1773, Jan: 4 p. 13.

Denton, Will: & Eliz: Harris, both in Goochland 1779, Feb: 7 p. 18.

DEPEE, Jo: & .... 1751 .... pp. 26-31.

DEPRIEST, John, & Eliz: Rice, both in this parish 1759, Jun: 6 p. 4.

dePriest, Randolph, & Mary Mims, both in Goochland 1751, ... pp. 26-32.

Depriest, Will: & Tabitha Tony, both in this parish 1758, Ap: 6 p. 3.

DICKENS, Jo: & Catherine Sansum, both of Louisa 1783, Mar: 6 p. 22.

Dickens, Rich: & Eliz: Sansom, both of Louisa 1780, Oct. 20 p. 20.

DICKERSON, Elijah, & Susannah Smith, in Louisa 1782, Dec: 3 p. 22.

Dickerson, James, & Mary Nettles Betw: 1750-1753 .... p. 31.

Dickerson, Rich: & Ann Quarles, both in Spotsylvania 1779, Mar: 11 p. 18.

DIGGS, Thomas, in Louisa, & Ann Kent in Albemarle 1775, Jun: 9 p. 16.

DOSS, Jer: & Ursley Taylor, both in this county 1756, May 6 p. 2.

DOUGLASS, John, in Buckinghame, & Sarah Rue in this parish 1762, Dec: 6 p. 7.

Douglas, Will: in Petersburg, & Martha Taylor Selden aged 24 1786, Dec: 12 p. 25.

DOWDY, John, & Elizabeth Hubbert, both in this parish 1762, Jan: 7 p. 6.

DUDLEY, Edward, & Rosanna Smith, in Louisa 1788, Sep: 17 p. 25.

Dudley, John, in Albemarle, & Sarah Bromfield in this parish 1763, Ap: 7 p. 7.

DUKE, Hardin, & Betsie Swift, both of Louisa 1783, Ap: 15 p. 23.

Duke, Dr. Joseph, & Mary Quarles, both in Spotsylvania, maried them 1791, ... p. 27.

DURELL, Jo: & Martha Bibb, both of Louisa 1788, Nov: 20 p. 25.

DURHAM, Will: & Ann Swilley, both in Maniken town 1757, feb: 13 p. 3.

DYCHES, Henry, & Delany Haly, both in Louisa 1779, Jan: 10 p. 18.

Dyches, Ja: & Tabitha Haley, both in Louisa 1773, Nov: 8 p. 14.

Dyches, Will: & Sarah Haley, both in Louisa 1778, Sep: 28 p. 18.

EARNEST, Geo: in Hanover, & Catie White in Louisa 1782, May 17 p. 22.

EASLEY, Stephen, & .... Betw. 1750-1753 p. 31.

EAST, Ben: & Nancy Pruit, both in Goochland 1773, Aug: 26 p. 14.

East, Tho: & Winnifred Chapman, in Goochland 1751 .... pp. 26-31.

EASTON, Augustine, & Mary Ford, in Goochland 1772, Sep: 6 p. 13.

EDES, Tho: Bailey, & Eliz: Rutherford, both of ys parish 1775, Jan: 5 p. 16.

EDWARDS, Ambrose, & Olive Martin, both in Louisa 1774, Mar: 15 p. 15.

Edwards, Augustine, & Mary Watson, in Goochland 1770, May 30 p. 12.

Edwards, Charles, in this parish, & Hannah Moseby in Cumberland 1754, Jan: 27 p. 1.

Edwards, Geo: & Francis Dickerson, both in Louisa 1784, Jul: 22 p. 23.

Edwards, Gravet, & Eliz: Harris, both of Louisa, were maried (17)91, ... p. 27.

Edwards, Jesse, & Lucy East, both of this parish 1768, Mar: 5 p. 10.

Edwards, Jo: & Nancy Brasfud, both of Spot: 1781, Dec: 26 p. 21.

Edwards, Solomon, & Sarah Mathews, both of Louisa 1782, Dec: 27 p. 22.

Edwards, Tho: & Sarah Wright, both in this parish 1766, Oct: 17 p. 9.

Edwards, Will: & Eliz: Johnson, both in this parish 1756, May 19 p. 2.

ELLIOT, Richard, in Cumberland, & Philadelphia Guthrie there too 1768, Ap: 29 p. 10.

ELLIS, David, & Morning Harris, both of ys parish 1775, Dec: 29 p. 17.

Ellis, Jesse, in Henrico, & Sarah Woodson in this parish 1763, Mar: 9 p. 7.

Ellis, Jo: & Susanna DuVal, both in Henrico 1770, Nov: 25 p. 12.

Ellis, Jo: & Patty Wood, both in Henrico 1774, May 5 p. 15.

Ellis, Jos: of Henrico, & Mary Hughes of Goochland 1776, Nov: 4 p. 19.

Ellis, Joseph, & Christian fferrar, both of this parish 1769, Feb: 5 p. 11.

Ellis, Stephen, & Susan.: Smith, both in Henrico 1773, May 20 p. 14.

Ellis, Tho: & Mary Paterson, both in Henrico 1773, Jan: 21 p. 14.

Ellis, Tho: & Eliz: Hurt, [Hart] in Spotsylvania 1787, May 3 p. 24.

Ellis, Will; & Sarah Ragline, both in Goochland 1770, Dec: 30 p. 12.

EMMERSON, Sam: & Mildred Potter, of this parish 1756, Sep: 9 p. 2.

ENGLAND, Da: & Lucy Hodges, both in Goochland 1772, Nov: 12 p. 12.

England, James, & Mary Webber, both of this parish 1767, Oct. 1 p. 10.

England, William-Anderson, & Elizabeth Fairies, both of this parish 1765, Jan: 15 p. 8.

ESTIS, Abraham, & Sarah Timberlick both in Louisa 1787, Feb: 14 p. 24.

EUBANK, Stephen, & Lucy Jackson, both of this parish 1767, Sep: 24 p. 10.

EUSTACE, Joel, in Lunenburg, & Ann Harris in Maniken town 1770, Oct: 15 p. 12.

EVANS, John, & Frances Wade, both of this parish 1766, Aug: 3 p. 9.

Evans, Tho: & Marianne Web, both in Goochland 1771, Mar: 12 p. 12.

EVERIE, John, & Catherine Dowdy, both in ys parish 1776, Sep: 15 p. 17.

EWEL, Maxey, & Ann Mullins, both of this parish 1769, Jan: 5 p. 11.

FAIRIES, Will: & Sally Johnson, both in Louisa 1782, Nov: 24 p. 22.

Fairies, William & Judith Emmerson, both in this parish 1775, Ap: 27 p. 16.

Fairies, John, & .... Brian, both in Albemarle 1755, Jan: 12 p. 1.

ffairies, John, & Lucy Harlow, both in this parish 1762, Jul: 26 p. 6.

FAR, Edward, & Mary Perkins, both of Louisa 1779, Nov: 14 p. 19.

ffARMER, Isham, & Judith Moon, both in this parish 1760, Mar: 14 p. 5.

ffearne, John, & Eliz: Winfrey, in this parish 1759, May 9 p. 4.

FENWICK, Jo: & Mary Richardson, both in Goochland 1774, Dec: 24 p. 15.

FERGUSON, Will: & Marg: Vivian, in Orange 1779, Sep: 16 p. 19.

ffergusson, Abram, & Nannie Smith, in Louisa 1781, Nov: 8 p. 21.

ffergusson, Sam: & Eliz: Dunman, both of this parish 1759, Jan: 25 p. 4.

FERRAR, Barret, & Sarah Harris, both of Goochland, 1779, Mar: 15 p. 19.

fferrar, Jos: & Susannah Jordan, both in this parish 1755, Nov: 23 p. 2.

fferrar, Joseph-Royal, & Phebe Harris, in Maniken town 1762, Aug. 3 p. 6.

fferrar, Perrine, in this parish, & Sarah Lacy in St. Martins, Hanover, 1757, Dec. 30 p. 3.

fferrar, Peter, in Albemarle, & Trephenah Laforce in this Parish, 1766, Ap: 10 p. 9.

fferrar, William, & Eliz: Bib, both in this parish 1762, Mar: 17 p. 6.

Ferrar, Tho: & Bettie Martin, both in Goochland 1771, Oct. 24 p. 12.

Ferrar, Tho: & Susan: Hughes, both in Goochland 1772, Sep: 19 p. 13.

FIELDER, John, of Prince Edward, & Nanny Clark of ys parish 1774, Dec: 27 p. 16.

ffielder, Thomas, & Ann Woodhall, both of this Parish 1758, Dec: 28 p. 4.

FITZGERALD, Peter, & Lucy Johnson, both in Goochland 1774, Sep: 11 p. 15.

ffLEURNOY, Jac: & Eliz: Burner, in Maniken town 1755, Oct: 27 p. 2.

FLEMING, Jo: & Lovinah Clements, both in Louisa, 1783, Dec: 10 p. 23.

FLETCHER, ..., & Catie Elliott, in Spotsylvania .... p. 27.

FLEWELLING, Jonathan, & Ann Lawrence, both in Goochland 1772, Oct: 20 p. 13.

FORD, Bartlet, & Frankie Bowles, both in Goochland 1774, Mar: 20 p. 15.

Ford, Jo: & Angelica Lewis 1751, ... p. 26.

Ford, John, & Eliz: fferrar, both in this parish 1762, Jan: 22 p. 6.

ffOSTER, James, & Elizabeth Parish, both in this parish 1759, Oct: 28 p. 4.

FOWLER, Alex: & Magdalen Smith, both in Goochland 1780, Ap: 15 p. 19.

ffRANCIS, Thomas, & Hellender Basset, both in Maniken town 1760, Ap: 7 p. 5.

FULCHER, Jo: & Mary Clerk, both in Fluvanna, 1779, Feb: 4 p. 18.

FULLER, Bartholomer, & Christian Allen, in Orange were maried 1789, Nov: 11 p. 25.

FURBISH, Ja: & Mary Pace, both in Goochland 1774, Jul: 26 p. 15.

ffURLONG, John, & Jean Emmerson, both in this 1766, Oct: 17 p. 9.

Furlong, Rob: & Sar: Watkins, in Goochland 1753, Aug. 10 pp. 27-32.

FUZZIL, Moses, & Lucy Wilkinson, both in this 1770, May 1 p. 11.

GAINS, Humphrey, & Martha Bowles, in Goochland 1779, Feb: 18 p. 18.

Gains, Will: & Jeanie Pines, both in Spots: 1781, Mar: 11 p. 21.

GAMMON, Harrison, & Eliz: Horn, both in Goochland 1753, Jul: 10 pp. 27-32.

Gammon, Will: & Temperance Gardener, both in Louisa 1789, Dec: 26 p. 25.

GARLAND, Jo: & Lucy Gordon, both in Louisa, 1790, ... p. 27.

GARNET, Tho: & Susanna Holloday, both of Spotsyl: 1787, Aug. 9 p. 24.

GARRET, Peter, & Mary Perrue, both in Maniken town 1756, Nov:
25 p. 2.

Garret, Tho: & Suckie, Brockman, in Orange 1780, Nov: 16 p. 20.

GATHRY, Levi, & Betty Yamons, both of this parish 1764, Dec: 27
p. 8.

GEORGE, Anselm, & Nancy Huchins [Houchens], both of this parish
1775, May 7 p. 16.

George, James, & Mary Swift, both of this parish 1767, Nov: 28 p. 10.

George, Jo: & Mary Martin, both of Goochland 1779, Mar: 17 p. 19.

George, Leonard, & Jeanie Pore, both in this parish 1772, Jan: 18 p. 13.

GERRAND, [Guerrant] Dan: & Mary Porter, both in Maniken town
1770, Jul: 19 p. 12.

Gerrand, Jo: & Jean Hicks 1751, ... pp. 26-31.

Gerrand, Jo: & Mary Heath Powel, in Goochland 1782, Jul: 25 p. 22.

Gerrant, Jo: & Eliz: Hicks 175— .... pp. 27-32.

GIBSON, Benjamin & Priscilla Bradberry, both of Maniken town 1769,
Jan: 21 p. 11.

Gibson, Ja: & Sally Tally, both in Louisa 1779, Jan: 8 p. 18.

Gibson, Jo: & Mary Tally, both of Louisa 1783, Mar: 13 p. 22.

Gibson, Tho: in Prince Edward, & Martha Riddle in Goochland 1774,
Sep: 15 p. 15.

GIDDIN, Francis, & Mary White, both in Louisa 1782, Oct. 3 p. 22.

Giddin, Will: & Susanna West, both in Louisa 1780, Nov. 16 p. 20.

GILBERT, John, & Sarah Nichols, both in this parish 1768, Dec: 4 p.
11.

GILL, John, & Agnes Tony, both of ys parish 1777, Ap: 6 p. 18.

GILLAM, Jacob, & Sarah Horn, both of this parish 1769, Dec: 27 p. 11.

Gillam, James & Susannah Smith, both of Louisa [17]91 22
p. 27. [See Guillam.]

GLASS, James, & Eva Williams, both in this parish 1758, Oct: 9 p. 4.

Glass, John, & Sally Martin, both in this parish 1768, May 25 p. 10.

Glass, Tho: & Martha East, both in Goochland 1773, Mar: 23 p. 14.

Glass, William, & Elizabeth Megan, both in this parish 1766, May 15
p. 9.

GODSEY, John, & Ann Elam, both in Maniken town 1762, Nov: 14
p. 7.

GOFF, Zachariah, & Judith Mathews, both of ys parish 1775, Oct: 14
p. 16.

GOING, Henry, & Susannah ffreeson, both of this parish 1764, Jul: 22
p. 8.

GOLSON, Jo: & Frances Tourman, both in Cumberland 1770, Nov:
25 p. 12.

GOOCH, Clayborn, & Mildred Thomson, both of Louisa 1783, Mar:
13 p. 22.

Gooch, Liner, & Rhode Turner, both of Louisa 1780, Sp: 28 p. 19.

Gooch, Umphrey, & Mary Wagstaff, in Louisa 1783, Dec: 26 p. 23.

GOOD, John, & Frances Loftis, both in this parish 1765, Oct: 1 p. 8.

GOODMAN, Cha: & Rebekah Johnson of Albemarle 1774, Jan: 31 p. 14.

GORDON, Ja: in Lancaster, & Ann Payne in Goochland 1774, Jun: 30 p. 15.

Gordon, John, in this, & Judith Moracet in Maniken town parish 1758, Mar: 25 p. 3.

GOWEN, John, & Agnes Harlow, both of this parish 1758, Mar: 28 p. 4.

GRANGER, Ben: & Eliz: Edwards, both of ys parish Betw. 1750-1753 .... p. 31.

GRANT, Alex: & Agnes Jerat 1751, Dec: 20 p. 26.

GRASON, Ja: & Mary Christian, both in Goochland 1770, Dec: 19 p. 12.

GRAVES, Bartlet, & Frances Lane, both of Louisa 1787, Ap: 18 p. 24.

Graves, Adam, & Martha Holland, both in this 1769, May 4 p. 11.

Graves, Joel, & Sarah Graves, in Orange, were maried (17)90, ... 21 p. 27.

Graves, Rich: & Sally Arnet, both of Louisa 1780, Nov: 23 p. 20.

GRAY, Henry, & Phoebe Johnon, both of this parish 1776, Dec: 8 p. 17.

Gray, Jo: & Susan: Watkins, both in Goochland 1772, Dec: 23 p. 13.

Gray, Tho: & Kitty Young, both in county were maried (17)95, Nov: 4 p. 28.

GREEN, fforest, & Mary Rice, both of this parish 1761, Nov: 28 p. 6.

Green, Forest, & Martha Green, both of Louisa 1780, Jan: 28 p. 19.

Green, Jo: & Susannah Lawrence, of Goochland 1779, Oct: 4 p. 19.

GREGORY, James, & Sarah Thomson, both in this parish 1756, Nov: 28 p. 2.

GRIMES, Stephen, & Marg: England, in Goochland 1778, Oct: 18 p. 18.

GROOM, Rob: & Eliz: Bibb, both in Louisa 1788, Jan: 18 p. 25.

Groom, Will: & Dorothy Maddison (or, Mathison,) both in this Parish 1753, Sep: 25 p. 1.

GRUB, Dan: & Mary Hodges, both in this parish 1757, May 6 p. 3.

Grub, Mat: & Sally Shilton, both of Louisa 1783, Oct: 27 p. 23.

Grubs, Jesse, & Mary Younger, both of Goochland 1781, Jan: 24 p. 20.

GRUTHER, Will: & .... 1751, ... pp. 26-32.

GUILLAM, Ja: & Frances Hopkins, both in Goochland 1772, Dec: 16 p. 13.

Guillam, John, & Elizabeth Morell, both of this parish 1764, Sep: 27 p. 8.

Guillam, Jos: & Conney Parish, both of Goochland 1779, Nov: 6 p. 19. (See Gillam.)

GUIN, Alman, & Mary Evans, both of Goochland 1751, ... pp. 26-32.

GUNSTONE, John, & Susannah Paisly, both of this parish 1762, Sep: 30 p. 6.

HADEN, Anthony, & Drusilla Rowntree, both of this parish 1765, Jul:
14 p. 8.

Haden, Jos: & .... (Eliz: Handley) (see births) 175— ....
.... pp. 27-32.

Haden, Will: & Nancy Johnson, both of Albemarle 1775, Oct: 31 p. 16.

Haden, Zachariah, & Elizabeth Poor, both of this parish 1763, Jan: 27
p. 7.

HALES, John, in Henrico, & Elizabeth Miller in this parish 1760, feb:
20 p. 5.

Hales, Will: & Susanna Payne, in Goochland 1771, Jun: 26 p. 12.

HALEY, Ben: & Judith Dyches, both in Louisa 1779, Feb: 18 p. 18.

Haley, Jo: of Louisa, & Martha Fulcher of Fluvanna 1779, Mar: 17
p. 19.

Haley, Will: & Eliz: Clark, both of Louisa 1773, Nov: 1 p. 14.

HALKET, Tho: & Polly Johnson, in Spotsylvania 1785, Dec. 1 pp.
20-24.

HALL, David, & Dorcas Alley 1754, Nov: 20 p. 1.

Hall, Nathan, & Mary Wood, both of Louisa 1784, Oct: 12 p. 23.

Hall, Thomas, & Frances Williams, in this county 1765, Sep: 3 p. 8.

Hall, William, & Betty Page, both in this parish 1758, Mar: 12 p. 3.

HALLIDAY, Ben: & Sally Hampton, both in Louisa 1783, Oct: 26
p. 23.

HANCOKE, Austin, & Ann Nichols, both in Louisa 1781, Dec: 27
p. 21.

Hancoke, George, & Mary Whitloe, both of this parish 1763, Jan: 6 p. 7.

Hancocke, John, & Eliz: Maddox, both in this parish 1755, Oct: 16
p. 2.

Hancocke, Tho: & Mary Shoemaker, both in this parish 1758, Mar: 25
p. 3.

HANSON, John, in Albemarle & Elizabeth Pearse in this 1767, Ap:
3 p. 9.

Hanson, Will: & Mary Williams, both in this parish 1757, Dec: 26 p. 3.

HARDINE, Giles, & Amy Morris, in Louisa 1773, Jan: 30 p. 14.

Hardine, Will: & Biddy Houchins, both in Goochland 1773, Oct. 14
p. 14.

HARKINS, Joel, & Barbara Haris, both of Louisa 1781, Sep: 20 p. 21.

HARLOW, George, & ffrances Humphrey, both in this parish 1763,
Mar: 20 p. 7.

Harlow, Tho: & .... Betw. 1750-1753 p. 31.

HARPER, Joseph, & Ann Murphey, both in Louisa 1781, Nov: 25
p. 21.

HARIS (Harris) Job: & Mary Farmer, both of Louisa 1785, Sep: 5
p. 24.

Harris, Ben: & Priscilla Wager, both in Maniken town Betw. 1750-1753
p. 31.

Harris, Cornelius, & Keturah Webber, both in this parish 1759, Aug:
12 p. 4.

Harris, Cyrus, & Eliz: Bond, both in Louisa 1783, May 8 p. 23.

Harris, Dan: & Marg: Miller, both in Goochland 1779, June 19 p. 19.

Harris, David, & Elizabeth Rich, both in this parish 1760, Nov: 19 p. 5.

Harris, James, & Ursely fflournoy, both in Maniken town 1769, May 26 p. 11.

Harris, Jo: & ....* 1751, ... p. 26.

Harris, Joseph, in Cumberland & Rebekah Howard in this parish 1766, Feb: 6 p. 8.

Harris, Nat: & Mary Howard, both of Goochland 1782, Mar: 18 p. 22.

Harris, Nathaniel, & Martha Byers, both of Louisa 1788, May 29 p. 25.

Harris, Overton, & Jemima Harris, both in Louisa, were maried 1789, Sep: 16 p. 25.

Harris, Rob: & Mary Davis, both in Louisa 1784, Jul: 22 p. 23.

Harris, Sherard, & Hannah Page, both of this Parish 1761, Dec. 16 p. 6.

Harris, Tho: & Eliz: Woodhall, both in this parish 1758, Aug: 3 p. 4.

Harris, Tho: & Sarah Lacy, both in this parish 1764, Mar: 4 p. 8.

Harris, Tho: & Polly Gardener, in Spotsylvania were maried (17)93, ... p. 27.

Harris, Will: & Eliz: Cradock, both in this parish 1754, Aug: 28 p. 1.

Haris, Will: & Eliz: Evans, both in Cumberland 1770, Jun: 15 p. 12.

HARRISON, Carter Henry, in Cumberland & Susannah Randolph in this parish 1760, Nov: 9 p. 5.

Harison, Hen: & Nannie Groom, both in Spots: 1782, Jul: 18 p. 32.

Harrison, Tho: & Mary Kennon, both of this parish 1768, ffeb: 17 p. 10.

Harrison, ... [Capt. Wm.—see births] & Anna Payne, both of this parish 1763, ... p. 7.

Harrison, William, in this parish, & Mary Cobbs in Albemarle 1761, Jan: 1 p. 5.

HARVEY, Will: & Francis Dear, in this county (17)94, Nov: 6 p. 28.

HARWOOD, Will: & Nancie White, in Louisa (17)92 .... 8 p. 27.

HATCHER, Ben: & Mary Depee 1754, Ap: 25 p. 1.

Hatcher, Gideon, & Martha Leprade, both of this parish 1777, Sep. 4 p. 18.

Hatcher, Tho: & Sarah Porter, both in Maniken Town 1762, Jun: 3 p. 6.

Hatcher, Tho: & Lucy Curd, both in Goochland 1782, Sep: 16 p. 22.

HAWKINS, Elijah, & Ann Hill, both of Orange 1787, Jan: 30 p. 24.

Hawkins, Nic: & Ann Robinson, both of Spot: 1781, Nov: 14 p. 21.

HAWTHORN, Will: & Rebekah Woodward, both in Goochland 1782, May 12 p. 22.

HYAT, Lewis, & Barbara Allen, both of Spots: 1783, Dec: 23 p. 23.

HAYS, Rob: & Ruth Jones, 1754, Jan: 31 p. 1.

HENDERSON, George, & Ann Cobb, both of this parish 1761, Dec: 23 p. 6.

HENDRICK, John, & Sabrine Garret, both in Maniken Town 1757, Ap: 4 p. 3.

Hendrick, Will: & Ann Henderson, both of Louisa 1782, Dec: 19 p. 22.

*Eliz: Fergusson in Birth record.

HENLEY, Hez: & Keturah Ferrar, both in Goochland 1772, Aug: 4 p. 13.

HERNDON, Ben: & Rosana Wade, in Goochland 1771, Dec: 26 p. 13.

Herndon, Ja: & Ninnie Rice, both in Cumberland 1772, Oct: 4 p. 13.

Herndon, Jo: & Mary Clarkson, both of Goochland 1773, Dec: 27 p. 14.

HERON, James, & Sarah Taylor, married 1791, Sep: 11 p. 126.

HESTER, Jo: & Agnes Mayfield, both in Louisa 1779, Aug: 26 p. 19.

HICKS, Ja: & Ann Bellamy, both in Goochland 1773, May 17 p. 14.

Hicks, Meshack, & Ann Dawson, both in this parish 1765, May 5 p. 8.

Hicks, Sam: & Eliz: Woodlook, 1751, ... pp. 26-32.

Hicks, Stephen, & Agnes Hancock, both in this parish 1758, Aug. 24 p. 4.

HILL, Nathaniel, & Nanny Parish, both in this parish 1767, Sep: 3 p. 10.

Hill, Sam: & Nancy Tate, both of Louisa 1788, Dec: 25 p. 25.

Hill, Thomas, & Eliz: ffulcher, both of ys parish 1775, Nov: 25 p. 16.

HILLEY, Francis, & Sarah Dawson, both of ys parish 1753, Sep: .... p. 31.

HILTON, Ja: & Susannah Walton or Welton, in Goochland 175.., ..., pp. 27-33.

Hilton, John, & Obedient Coke [Cox] both in this parish 1757, Nov: 24 p. 3.

HODGES, Benjamin, & Elizabeth Stevenson, both in this parish 1762, Jan: 28 p. 6.

Hodges, David, & Elizabeth Page, both of this parish 1758, ffeb: 2 p. 3.

Hodges, Jo: & Judith Perkins, both of Goochland 1773, Dec: 27 p. 14.

Hodges, John, & Deborah Lee, both of this parish 1756, Nov: 11 p. 2.

Hodgses, Johnson, & Lucy Page, in Goochland .... p. 32.

Hodges, Jos: & Eliz: Harris, both in this parish 1756, Dec: 14 p. 2.

Hodges, Tho: & Sabra Horn, both in this parish 1759, Oct: 17 p. 4.

Hodges, Will: & Susannah Lovell, both in this parish 1758, May 27 p. 4.

Hodges, Will, & Eliz: Cocke, both in Goochland 1774, Jun: 2 p. 15.

HOGGAN, Jo: & Eliz: Pinax, both of Louisa 1781, Ap: 19 p. 21.

HOLEBROOK, Eddie, & Mary Tolben, both in this parish 1756, Oct: 17 p. 2.

HOLLAND, George of Louisa, & Susannah George of Goochland 1779, Nov: 7 p. 19.

Holland, Hezekiah, & Mary Walker, both of this parish 1765, Feb: 20 p. 8.

Holland, Jo: & Martha Williams, both in Goochland 1773, June 13 p. 14.

Holland, John, in this county & Joyce Baker in Albemarle 1759, ... p. 4.

Holland, Michael, & .... Betw. 1750-1753 p. 31.

Holland, Nat: & Jeanie Hutson, in Louisa 1776, May 23 pp. 17, 100.

HOLLADAY, Joseph & Agness Holladay 1787, Jan: 11 p. 24.

HOLLIDAY, Will: & Rebekah Rowling of Louisa 1788, Jul: 31 p. 25.

HOLYDAY, Joseph, & Martha Holyday, both of Spotsylvania 1785, Nov: 10 p. 24.

HOLMAN, James, in Maniken Town, and Sarah Miller in Goochland 1769, Oct: 30 p. 11.

Holman, John, & Eliz: Burton, both in this 1770, May 20 p. 11.

HOPPER, Jo: & Mary Horn, both in Goochland 1770, May 27 p. 12.

Hopper, John, & Milley Rice, both of this parish 1775, Mar: 26 p. 16.

Hopper, Luther, & Eliz: Nash, both in this parish 1756, Dec: 20 p. 2.

HORN, Jesse, & Susan: Milton, both in Goochland 1773, Dec: 22 p. 14.

Horn, Jo: Christopher, & Sally Thomson, both in Louisa 1784, Sep: 23 p. 23.

HOUCHENS, Cha: & Lucy Clements, both in this parish 1753, Sep: 20 p. 1.

Houchins, Cha: & Ann Britt, both in Goochland 1782, Mar: 28 p. 22.

Houchins, ffrancis, & Joice Clements, both in this parish 1758, Jan: 10 p. 3.

Houchins. Ja: & Marg: Johnson, both of Goochland 1780, Apr. 18 p. 19.

HOWARD, David in Bedford, & Judith Lane in Fluvanna (17)81 Feb: 26 p. 21.

Howard, Drury, & Mary Lane, both of this parish 1759, Jan: 25 p. 4.

Howard, James, in this parish, & Jean Bourn in Trinity Parish 1767, Jun: 11 p. 9.

Howard, Jo: & Ann: Massie, both in Goochland 1779, Aug: 11 p. 19.

HOWEL, Isaac, & Judith Banks, both of ys parish 1775, Feb: 23 p. 16.

HUBBARD, John, & Elizabeth Clark, both in this parish 1763, May 31 p. 7.

Hubbard. Thomas, & Rachel Street, both in ys parish 1775, Mar: 31 p. 17.

HUDLESTONE, Benjamin, & Elizabeth Pankie, both in Maniken Town 1762, Sep: 23 p. 6.

Hudlestone, David, in Henrico, & Sarah Easly in this parish 1757, Mar: 17 p. 3.

HUDNEL, Will: & ffrances Smith, both in this parish 1757, Dec: 15 p. 3.

HUGHES, Benjamin, & Rebekah Cothan, both in this parish 1756, Aug. 30 p. 2.

Hughes, Jo: & Ann Merriwether, in Louisa 1783, June 18 p. 23.

Hughes, William, & Susannah Bowles, both of Hanover 1775, Ap: 10 p. 16.

HUMBER, John, in St. Pauls Parish, & Eliz: Christian in this parish 1757, Mar: 30 p. 3.

HUMPHREYS, Jo: & Sarah Young, both in Louisa 1782, Jan: 3 p. 21.

Humphreys, Will: & Sarah Statham, both in Louisa 1774, Dec: 12 p. 15.

HUNTER, And: & Ann Lane, both in Louisa 1770, Oct: 25 p. 12.

HUTSON, David, & Mary Clapton, in Louisa 1788, June 26 p. 25.

Hutson, Reuben, & Nancy Micham, both of Spot: 1782, Jan: 10 p. 21.

HUTTON, Tho: & Susan: Green, both in Goochland 1772, Sep: 29 p. 13.

HYAT, Asa, & Mary Sale, both in Orange, 1779, Aug: 29 p. 19.

IMBREY, Jos: & .... p. 32.

Imbrey, Thomas, & Ann Jackson, both in this parish 1757, Oct. 20 p. 3.

INGRAM, Will: & Ann Hawkins, both of Spot: 1782, Oct: 8 p. 22.

INNES, Will: & .... 175.. .... pp. 27-32.

ISABEL, Christopher, & Winnifred Johnson, both of Goochland 1780, Oct. 12 p. 20.

Isabel, James, & Eliz: Coleman, both of ys parish 1776, Feb: 20 p. 17.

Isabel, Lewis, & Ann Anderson, in Hanover, 1775, Nov: 17 p. 16.

Isabel, Will: & Mary Crenshaw, both in Goochland 1774, Jun: 5 p. 15.

JACKSON, John, & Elizabeth Hodges, both of this parish 1761, Ap: 19 p. 5.

Jackson, Joseph, & Susannah Carter, both of this parish 1760, Aug: 28 p. 5.

JAMES, Jo: & Francis Morris, both in Hanover 1774, Dec: 1 p. 15.

James, Spencer, & Frances Davis, both in Orange 1780, Aug: 22 p. 20.

James, Will: & Mary Hinds, both in Hanover 1774, Jul: 14 p. 15.

JAMISON, Andrew, & Martha Stephenson, both in this parish 1762, Jul: 22 p. 6.

JENKINS, Is: & Ann Holland, both of Louisa 1781, Ap: 15 p. 21.

JENNINGS, Daniel, & Mary Conway, both in Henrico 1767, Jul: 5 p. 9.

JERRAT, Devreux, & Joanna Wade, both of ys parish 1775, Jan: 26 p. 16.

JOHNSON, Ben: & Marg: Johnson, both of Goochland 1779, Oct: 21 p. 19.

Johnson, Benjamin, & Susannah Peace, both in this parish 1759, Jul: 22 p. 4.

Johnson, Benjamin, & Martha Hughes in St. Martin's Parish 1766, Mar: 6 p. 8.

Johnson, Charles, & Elizabeth Edwards, both in Goochland 1768, Oct: 18 p. 10.

Johnson, Cha: & Keziah Henly, both in Goochland 1771, Dec: 8 p. 13.

Johnson, Christopher, & Elizabeth Dabney, both of Hanover 1777, Feb: 22 p. 17.

Johnson, David, in this, & Lucy Ellis in Henrico 1762, Ap: 13 p. 6.

Johnson, Drury, & Hannah Clark, both of ys parish 1751, Oct: 14 pp. 26-31.

Johnson, George, & Jean Rowe, both in Louisa 1784, Oct: 22 p. 23.

Johnson, Henry, & Ann Meekie, both of Louisa 1785, Jan: 20 p. 23.

Johnson, Jacob, & Sarah Knowling, both of ys parish 1775, Dec: 25 p. 17.

Johnson, Ja: & Eliz: Clarkson, both of Louisa 1779, Jan: 28 p. 18.

Johnson, James, & Sarah Bettesworth, both in Louisa 1783, May 15 p. 23.

Johnson, James, & Mildred Mims, 1751 .... pp. 26-32.

Johnson, James, in St. Pauls, & Rach: Haddon, in this parish 1755, dec: 15 p. 2.

Johnson, James, & Rebekah Martin, both of this parish 1766, Feb: 27 p. 8.

Johnson, James, & Sarah Parish, both in Goochland 1768, Nov: 3 p. 10.

Johnson, James, & Eliz: Glass, both of ys parish 1776, Nov: 3 p. 17.

Johnson, Jeremiah, & Susannah Cauthon, both in this parish 1759, ffeb: 26 p. 4.

Johnson, Jeremiah, & Eliz: Thomson, both of ys parish 1777, Feb: 23 p. 17.

Johnson, John, & Martha Perry, both of this parish 1760, feb: 20 p. 5.

Johnson, John, & Annie Webber, both of ys parish 1776, Jan: 27 p. 17.

Johnson, John, & Judith Martin, both of ys parish 1777, Feb: 22 p. 17.

Johnson, Joseph, & Sarah Johnson, both of Louisa 1789, June 25 p. 25.

Johnson, Lewis, & Barbara Garland, both in Louisa 1788, Jan: 5 p. 25.

Johnson, Phil: in Caroline, & Eliz: Taylor in Goochland 1771, Nov: 7 p. 12.

Johnson, Rich: & Dolly Powers, both of this parish 1769, Nov: 14 p. 11.

Johnson, Richard, & Ann Nichols, both in this parish 1764, Dec: 23 p. 8.

Johnson, Stephen, & Susannah Pace, both of this parish 1765, Oct. 1 p. 8.

Johnson, Walter, & Marg: Johnson, both of Goochland 1773, Dec: 21 p. 14.

Johnson, Will: & Eliz: Mills, both in this parish 1755, feb: 4 p. 1.

Johnson, Will: & Mary Weaver, both in Maniken Town 1770, Aug: 20 p. 12.

Johnson, Will: & Ann Smith, both in Goochland 1771, Dec: 10 p. 13.

Johnson, Will: & Judith Johnson, both of ys parish 1775, Oct: 27 p. 16.

Johnson, William, & Eleanor Depp, both in Maniken Town 1776, Sep: 17 p. 17.

JOHNSTON, John, & Helen Thompson, both in this parish 1754, Sep. 23 p. 1.

JONES, Godfrey, & Mary McBride, both in this parish 1766, Jul: 1 p. 9.

Jones, Harrison, & Ruth Addison, both in this parish 1759, Aug: 24 p. 4.

Jones, Henry, in Louisa, & Lucy Parish of this parish 1760, Aug: 28 p. 5.

Jones, Stephen, & Massey Thurston, both of ys parish 1776, Sep: 1 p. 17.

Jones, Will: of Cumberland, & Elizabeth Cosby of this parish 1774, Dec: 27 p. 16.

Jones, Will: & Sally Thomas, both in Louisa 1780, Aug. 1 p. 20.

JORDAN, James, & Sarah Stodghill, both of this parish 1761, ffeb. 27 p. 5.

Jordan, Jeremiah, in Caroline, & Louisa Walton in Albemarle 1759, ffeb: 22 p. 4.

Jordan, Matthew, & Mary Stodghill, both in this parish 1763, Oct: 1 p. 7.

Jordan, Sam: & Frances Periere of Henrico 1774, Jan: 27 p. 14.
Jordan, Will: & Eliz: Woodson, both in Goochland 1771, Nov: 19 p. 12.

KAY, John, & Nancy Ford, both of ys county 1776, Oct: 19 p. 17.
KEEN, Jo: & Hithy Williams, both of Spotsylvania 1781, Jul: 18 p. 21.
KENNEDY, James, in Augusta, & Sarah Hodges in this parish 1763, Jan: 12 p. 7.
KID, James, & Mourning Parish, both in this parish 1755, Oct: 19 p. 2.
Kidd, Moses, & Milly Clark, both in Albemarle 1768, Sep: 29 p. 10.
KIMBROW (Kimbrough) Jos: & Eliz: Yauncey, both of Louisa 1785, Jan: 6 p. 23.
Kimbro, Rob: & Sarah Smith, both of Louisa 1786, Jan: 11 p. 24.
KING, Thomas, & Mary Mask, both of this parish 1760, Ap: 3 p. 5.
KNIGHT, Ephraim, & Mildred Coaker, both in Louisa 1780, Oct: 15 p. 20.
Knight, Jonathan, in Lunenburgh, & Judith Woodson in this parish 1757, Feb: 24 p. 3.
KNIGHTEN, Will: & Eliz: Paterson both of Louisa. 1782 Feb: 24 p. 22.
KNIGHTON, Tho: & Eliz: Row, both in Louisa 1785, Mar: 24 p. 24.
KNOWLING, James, & Sarah Webster both of ys parish. Mar: 10 1776 p. 17.

LACY, Ben: & Judith Christian, both in Goochland 1774, Oct: 25 p. 15.
Lacy, Cha: & Eliz: Hudson, both in Louisa 1774, Jul: 28 p. 15.
Lacy, Elkanah, & Mary Brown, both in Maniken town 1756, Jan: 18 p. 2.
Lacy, Jesse, & Mary Johnson, both in Louisa 1774, Sep: 6 p. 15.
Lacy, Math: & Sus: Rutherford, both in Goochland 1772, Ap: 8 p. 13.
LAD, Const: & .... 1753, ... pp. 27-32.
LAMBERT, Joseph, & Jean Poore, both of ys parish 1775, Oct. 1 p. 16.
LANCASTER, Nathaniel, in Henrico, & Hope Walker in this parish 1758, Ap: 19 p. 3.
Lancaster, Rob: & Lucy Dair, both of Orange 1780, Nov: 7 p. 20.
LANDRUM, James, & Peany Waukins, both of Louisa 1788, May 15 p. 25.
Landrum, John, & Elizabeth Landrum, in Richmond County 1763, May 1 p. 7.
Landrum, Samuel, & Elizabeth Taylor, both of Maniken town 1769, Feb: 11 p. 11.
Landrum, Thomas, & Molly Hawkins, both in Maniken town 1759, Oct: 1 p. 4.
LANE, Aires, & Mary Woodson, both in this parish 1759, Ap: 15 p. 4.
Lane, Henry, widower, & Sarah Logan, both in this parish 1759, Jan: 21 p. 4.
Lane, Jac: & Mary Bradshaw 1751, ... pp. 26-31.
Lane, Jo: & Ann Garland, both of Louisa (17)81, Feb: 6 p. 21.
Lane, Jo: & Mary Owen, both of Goochland 1781, Mar: 20 p. 21.

Lane, Larkin, & Sarah Price, both of Spotsylvania 1787, Ap: 26 p. 24.

Lane, Rich: & Sarah Yauncey, both of Louisa 1781, Aug: 9 p. 21.

Lane, Tho: & Molly Groom, both in Goochland 1773, Jul: 31 p. 14.

LAURENCE, Henry, & Eliz: Parish, both of ys 1775, Jul: 26 p. 16.

Laurence, Jo: & Maryanne Powers, both in Goochland 1771, Jul: 8 p. 12.

LAURY, Jesse, & Ann Weldy, both of ys parish 1776, Jan: 21 p. 17.

Lawry, Edward, & Ann Grub, both in this parish 1757, feb: 21 p. 3.

LAYNE, David, & Elizabeth Bowdery, both of this parish 1768, Mar: 17 p. 10.

Layne, William & Ruth Taylor, both of this parish 1764, Oct: 25 p. 8.

LEE, Benjamin, & Mary Richardson, both in Goochland 1766, Sep: 18 p. 9.

Lee, John, & Betty Page, both in this parish 1755, Sep: 11 p. 1.

Lee, Stephen, & Ann Pore, both in this parish 1763, Nov: 3 p. 7.

Lee, Will: in Northumberland, & Jean Payne in Goochland 1780, Sep: 28 p. 20.

LEAK, Elisha, & Joyce Thomson, both in this parish 1760, Ap: 20 p. 5.

Leek, Jo: & Nancy Fleming, both of Louisa 1789, Mar: 9 p. 25.

Leak, Josiah, in this parish, & Ann ffenton in Henrico 1759, Jan: 1 p. 4.

Leek, Mask, & Patience Morris, in Hanover county 1758, Nov: 22 p. 4.

Leek, Peter, & Hannah Wade, both of this parish 1775, Ap: 19 p. 16.

Leek, Walter, & Winnifred Johnson, both in Goochland 1773, Aug: 1 p. 14.

LILLY, Armiger, & .... 1751, ... pp. 26-32.

LEPRADE, John, & Susannah Wadley, both of this parish 1760, Aug: 10 p. 5.

LETCHER, Stephen, & Elizabeth Perkins, both in this 1767, Jan: 22 p. 9.

LEWIS, Howel, & Betsie Coleman, both of Goochland 1780, May 3 p. 19.

Lewis, John, & Judith Crouch, both of this parish 1762, Aug: 22 p. 6.

Lewis, John, & Eliz: McBride, both of this parish 1758, May 30 p. 4.

Lewis, John, in Carolina & Eliz: Cannon in ys parish 1776, Feb: 8 p. 17.

Lewis, Joseph, & Ann Porter, both of ys parish 1777; Mar: 16 p. 18.

Lewis, Mr. Rob: & Jean Woodson, both of this parish 1760, feb: 20 p. 5.

Lewis, Rob: of Louisa, & ffrances Lewis of this parish 1760, Sep: 3 p. 5.

Lewis, Tho: & Susannah Ellis, both in Henrico 1758, Jun: 1 p. 4.

Lewis, Tho: & Eliz: Merriwether, both in Albemarle 1788, June 24 p. 25.

Lewis, Will: & Sally Man, both of Goochland 1774, Feb: 24 p. 14.

LILLY, Tho: & Mary Smith, both in this parish 1759, Dec: 26 p. 5.

LINDSAY, Caleb & Sally Stevens, both in Orange 1785, Mar: 10 p. 23.

Lindsay, Will: & Nancy Shepherd, both of Orange 1781, Oct: 3 p. 21.

LOCK, James, & Susannah DePee in Maniken Town 1753, Sep: 20 p. 1.

LOGAN, Antony, & Agnes Curry, both in this parish 1759, Dec: 9 p. 4.

Logan, Antony, & Judith Bellamy, both in Goochland 1771, Dec: 16 ·p. 13.

LOOKADOO, John, & Susannah Spalden, both in Maniken Town 1762, Jan: 24 p. 6.

*[LOVE]L, [George] & Betty Burford, both in this parish 1764, ... p. 7.

LOVEL, John, & Mary Smith, both in this parish 1759, Dec: 20 p. 5.

(Lovel, William), in Amelia & Mary Lovel in this parish 1764 .... p. 7.

LOYD, Nicholas, & Sarah Napper, both in this parish 1756, Dec: 14 p. 2.

LUCK, Rich: & Mary Fleming, both of Louisa, Ja: Sandige, Surety 1788, Mar: 14 p. 25.

LUSTER, Jacob, & Elizabeth Britt, both in this parish 1768, Aug: 11 p. 10.

LYON, Peter, in Albemarle, & Bettie Norvil in Goochland 1771, Oct: 8 p. 12.

LYONS, Benjamin, & Jeanie Hunter, both of Louisa 1777, Feb: 23 p. 17.

McALISTER, Alexr., & Eliz: Smith, both of Louisa 1783, Feb: 20 p. 22.

McAlister, Ben: & Lucy Faukener, both of Louisa 1788, Aug: 19 p. 25.

McCallister, Nath: & Martha Johnston, both in Louisa were maried 1790, Mar: 22 p. 25.

McBRIDE, Rich: & Frances Moss, both of Goochland 1780, Sep: 28 p. 20.

McCAWL, Stokes, & Mary Radford, widow, in this parish 1754, Jul: 23 p. 1.

MACOMACK, John, & Susannah Bullington, both in this parish 1763, Jan: 9 p. 7.

McCORMACK, Thomas, & Lucy Proffit, both in this parish 1754, ffeb: 3 p. 1.

McCOY, Jo: & Martha Humphreys, both in Louisa 1780, Feb: 17 p. 19.

McCRAW, Will: & ....? Betw. 1750 & 1753, ... p. 31.

McGEEHEE, Augustine, & Sarah Thompson, were married 1790, Feby. 4 p. 25.

McGhee, Will: & Ann Swiddy, both of Louisa 1787, May 10 p. 24.

McKENZIE, Ben: & Agnes Broadfoot, both in Goochland 1771, Jun: 26 p. 12.

McNEAL, Arch: & Sally Chandler, both of Orange 1782, Feb: 14 p. 22.

MADDOX, David, & Sally Perkins, both in this parish 1768, Sep: 11 p. 10.

Maddox, Jacob, & Susannah Clarkson, both in this parish 1758, Jan: 9 p. 3.

(*Name torn out, but supplied from birth records.)

Mattox, James, & Nanny Webster, both in this parish 1761, Mar: 13 p. 5.

Maddox, John, & Mary Boyd, both in this parish 1755, Sep: 5 p. 1.

Maddox, Will: & Mary Sampson, both in ys parish Betw. 1750-1753 p. 31.

Maddox, William, & Mary Ellis, in Henrico 1765, Mar: 7 p. 8.

Mattox, William, & Aggie Foster, both of Buckingham 1775, Dec: 10 p. 16.

MADLOCK, John, & Judah Witt, both of this parish 1756, Nov: 22 p. 2.

Matlock, Zachariah, & Lucy Wash, both in Louisa 1780, Dec: 7 p. 20.

MALLORY, Henry & Lucy Long, both in Orange 1781, Dec: 27 p. 21.

Mallory, Thomas, & Constance Davis, both in Louisa 1781, Oct: 4 p. 21.

Mallery, William, & Mary Tuggle, both in Goochland 1768, Oct: 20 p. 10.

MARKHAM, Barnard, & Mary Harris, both in Maniken town 1767, May 14 p. 9.

MARTIN, Antony, & Sarah Holman, both in Maniken town 1758, Dec: 21 p. 4.

Martin, Ben: in Albemarle, & Diana Harrison in this parish 1766, Aug: 21 p. 9.

Martin, Gideon, & Susanna Bryant, both of Albemarle 1767, Oct: 19 p. 10.

Martin, Ja: & Eliz: Clarkson, both of Fluvanna 1779, Feb: 4 p. 18.

Martin, Job, & Mary Clarkson, both in this parish 1765, Sep: 24 p. 8.

Martin, Jo: & Lucy Lane, both of Goochland 1779, Mar: 16 p. 19.

Martin, John, & Mary Rogers, both of ys parish 1751, Oct: 2 pp. 26-31.

Martin, John, & Rachel Peace (Pace) both in this parish 1757, Jan: 3 p. 3.

Martin, John, & Barbara Lewis, both in this parish 1763, Aug: 7 p. 7.

Martin, Mathew, & Mary Bullock, both in this parish 1763, Nov: 2 p. 7.

Martin, Sam: & Ann Pleasants, both in Goochland 1771, Jul: 4 p. 12.

Martin, Stephen, & Rebekah Bryant, in Albemarle county 1768, Jan: 2 p. 10.

Martin, Tho: & Susan: Walker, both in Goochland 1772, Oct: 24 (27) p. 13.

Martin, Valentine, & Ann Scot of Cumberland 1769, Jan: 28 p. 11.

Martin, Will: & Jean Holman, both in Maniken town 1759, Dec: 20 p. 5.

Martin, Will: & Sarah Barnet, both of Albemarle 1774, Feb: 7 p. 14.

Martin, Will: & Susannah England, both of ys parish 1776, Dec: 19 p. 17.

Martin, William, & Eliz: Lockram, both on the Bird 1757, May 3 p. 3.

MASSIE, Nath: in this parish, & Ann Clark in Albemarle 1776, Aug: 24 p. 17.

Massie, Sylvanus, & Hannah Raglin, both in this parish 1757, Oct: 3 p. 3.

Massie, Tho: in this parish, & Mary Williams in Louisa 1766, May 20 p. 9.

Massie, Thomas, & Eliz: Massie, both of ys parish 1776, Jun: 28 p. 17.

MASTERS, Edward, & Betty Furcran, both in Cumberland 1761, Mar: 12 p. 5.

Masters, Will: & .... Betw. 1750-1753 p. 31.

MATHEWS, Edward, in this parish, & Tabitha Hopson in Henrico 1758, May 1 p. 4.

Mathews, Edward, & Jean Watkins, both in Goochland 1772, Ap: 21 p. 13.

Mathews, Sherard, & Jean Byers, both of Louisa 1779, Jan: 9 p. 18.

MAXEY, John, & Marianne fforsey, both in Maniken town 1758, Jan: 19 p. 3.

MAY, Ambrose, & Eliz: Bailey, both in Goochland 1771, Feb: 3 p. 12.

MAYO, Jacob, & Susannah Isabel, both in this parish 1768, Jan: 2 p. 10.

Mayo, James, in Goochland, & Mary Plant in Hanover 1758, Sep: 28 p. 4.

Mayo, Jos: & Jeanie Richardson, in Goochland 1773, Jan: 1 p. 13.

Mayo, Stephen, & Ann Isabel, both of Goochland 1783, Feb: 6 p. 22.

MEAD, Henry, & Frances Young, both of Louisa 1781, May 3 p. 21.

Mead, Jo: & Eliz: Meekie, in Louisa 1784, Mar: 24 p. 23.

Mead, Thornton, & Mary Garland, both of Louisa 1788, Jan. 24 p. 25.

MEECHUM, Paul, & Susannah Meeks, both in Goochland 1772, Jan: 2 p. 13.

MELDON, Absalom, & Ann Freeman were maried (17)97, Feb: 3 p. 28.

Melton, Silas & .... 1751, ... pp. 26-31.

MERRIT, Ben: & Judah Gilchrist, both in this parish 1755, Nov: 10 p. 2.

MERRIWETHER, George, & Martha Merriwether, both in Goochland 1768, Nov: 2 p. 10.

Merriwether, James, & Eliz: Pollard, in this parish 1762, Sep: 10 p. 6.

Merriwether, Nicholas, & Margaret Douglass, in this parish 1760, Dec: 31. She's my child. p. 5.

Merriwether, Nicholas Hunter, & Beckie Tyrrel, both of Louisa 1787, Feb: 26 p. 24.

Merriwether, Tho: & Ann Minor, both in this, were maried (17)91, ... p. 27.

Merriwether, Will: in Hanover, & Martha Wood in ys parish Betw. 1750-1753 p. 31.

Merriwether, Will: Douglas, & Betsie Lewis, both of Albemarle 1788, Feb. 29 p. 25.

MICHAUX, Jacob, & Sally Nevils, both in Cumberland 1765, Mar: 21 p. 8.

MILLER, Will: & Joana Leprade, both in Goochland 1772, Mar: 19 p. 13.

MIMS, John, & Sarah Horn, both of this parish 1756, Mar: 7 p. 2.

Mims, John, & Mary Moss, both of this parish 1761, Oct: 8 p. 6.

Mims, Shadrach, & Maty Allen, both in this Parish 1754, ffeb: 3 p. 1.

Mims, Shadrach, & Eliz: Woodson, both in this parish 1760, May 24 p. 5.

Mims, Thomas, & Mary Wright, both in this parish 1756, Dec. 23 p. 3.

MINTER, Richard, & Martha Scrugs, both in this parish 1757, Jun: 27, p. 3.

Minto, Richard, & Eliz: Perkins, both in this parish 1754, Oct: 6 p. 1.

MITCHEL, Benjamin, in New Kent, & Ann Holland, widow in this parish 1756, Mar: 29 p. 2.

Mitchel, Robert, in Richmond. & Judith Hughes in Cumberland 1776, Mar: 11 p. 17.

Mitchel, Tho: & Eliz: Ogilsvy, both of ys parish 1775, Feb: 21 p. 16.

Mitchel, Will: & Sarah Letcher, both of this parish 1769, Dec: 19 p. 11.

MOOR, John, & Patty Moor, both of ys parish 1776, Jan: 15 p. 17.

MORE, Amos Lad, & Ann Rogers, both of ys parish 1775, Dec: 21 p. 17.

MORELAND, John & Ann Ogilsvy, both of ys parish 1775, Nov: 16 p. 16.

MORELL, Drury, & Judith Sampson, both in this parish 1758, ffeb: 7 p. 3.

Morell, Drury, & Dorcas Rowntree, both in this parish 1763, Sep: 29 p. 7.

MORRIS, Geo: & Sally Biggars, both of Louisa 1783, Sep: 11 p. 23.

Morris, Is: & Ann Dickerson Smith, in Louisa 1783, Dec: 23 p. 23.

Morris, Jo: of Louisa, & Sarah Periere, of Goochland 1779, Sep: 30 p. 19.

Morris, John, & Mary Harris, both of this parish 1756, Aug. 2 p. 2.

Morris, Jos: & Mary Ferrar, both in Goochland 1771, May 12 p. 12.

Morris, Nathaniel Gersdean, & Mary R. Woodson, both of this Parish 1778, Augt. 8 p. 18.

Morris, Sam: in Hanover, & Susannah Wasem in this parish 1766, Oct: 16 p. 9.

Morris, Sam: & Martha Biggars, both in Louisa 1791, ... p. 27.

Morris, Tho: & Mary Russel, both of Louisa 1782, Aug: 18 p. 22.

MORTON, Will Jordan, & Martha Pryor, both of Goochland 1779, Mar: 16 p. 19.

MOSEBY, Robert, & Ann Lewis, both of this parish 1769, May 4 p. 11.

Moseby, Samuel in Carolina, & Jean Roberts in Goochland 1773, Mar: 4 p. 14.

MOSELY, John, & Ann Williams, both of ys parish 1751, Dec: 27 pp. 26-31.

Mosely, Joseph, & Ann Graves, both of this parish 1768, Mar: 17 p. 10.

Mosely, Rob: & Magdalen Garrat, both in Maniken town 1756, Sep: 23 p. 2.

Mosely, Samuel, & Martha Hodges, both in this parish 1761, May 12 p. 6.

Mosely, Will: & Keziah Overstreet, both in Goochland 1772, Nov: 28 p. 13.

Mosely, William, & Ann Lewis, both of ys parish 1775, ... p. 17.

MOSS, Alexr. & Ann Thurmond, both of this parish 1760, Dec: 27 p. 5.

Moss, Gideon, & Susannah Richardson, both in this parish 1762, Jan: 1 p. 6.

Moss, Capt. Hugh, & Jeane fford, both in this parish 1768, Jun: 4 p. 10.

Moss, John, & Charity Hughes, in Hanover 1761, Nov: 20 p. 6.

Moss, Nat: & Joanna Johnson, both of Goochland 1780, Dec: 31 p. 20.

Moss, Samuel, & Susannah Powel, both of ys parish 1776, Jan: 3 p. 17.

MULLEN, Will: & Eliz: Hutton, both of ys parish 1775, Jan: 24 p. 16.

Mullins, Anthony, & Ann Lewis, both in Goochland 1779, June 14 p. 19.

Mullins, Henry, & Frances Walton, both in this parish 1762, Dec: 29 p. 7.

MUSICK, Ephraim, & Winny Clasbie, in Albemarle 1786, Oct: 3 p. 24.

NAPIER, Arch: & Mary Hubard, both in this parish 1766, Jan: 6 p. 8.

Napier, Rene, in this parish, & Rebekah Hurt in Drisdale Parish 1765, Mar: 28 p. 8.

Napier, Patrick, & Eliz: Woodson, in this parish 1776, Sep: 29 p. 17.

Napier, Rich: & Molly Wells, both in Albemarle 1772, Oct: 22 p. 13.

Napier, Stephen, & .... 1751, ... pp. 23-32.

NASH, Arthur, & Sarah Abrey, widow, both in this parsih 1755, Mar: 17 p. 1.

Nash, John, & Mary Basket, both of this parish 1761, Dec: 24 p. 6.

Nash, Marvel, & Agnes Hodges, both in this parish 1762, Oct: 26 p. 7.

NETHERLAND, Jo: of Powhatan, & Mary Thurston of Spot: 1781, Aug. 22 p. 21.

NICHOLS, Pouncey, & Susan Knight in Hanover 1774, Jun: 25 p. 15.

Nichols, Sam: in this, & Eleanor Knight in Hanover 1776, Aug: 25 p. 17.

Nichols, Sam: & Sar: Garland, both in Louisa 1789, Feb: 29 p. 25.

Nichols, Will: & Eliz: Woody, both in Goochland 1774, Mar: 6 p. 15.

Nichols, Will: & Henrietta Terry, both in Louisa 1782, Sep: 26 p. 22.

Nickols, Francis, & Eleazor Williams, both in Goochland 1773, Jun: 20 p. 14.

Nicols, Charles, & Mary Hicks, in ys parish 1775, Jan: 5 p. 16.

NICHOLSON, John, & Susannah Williams 1753, Dec: 8 p. 1.

NIGHTINGALE, Math: & Lucy Cauthon, both in this parish 1759, Dec: 26 p. 5.

NILSON, (Nelson), Ja: & Lucy Robinson, both in Spots: 1781, May 3 p. 21.

Nilson, Jo: & Agathy Winslow, both of Spots: 1784, Jul: 6 p. 23.

NORTH, ..., in Buchingham, & Eliz: Thornhill in this parish 1763, ... p. 7.

NORVIL, Spencer, & Frances Hill, both of this parish 1770, Feb: 22 p. 11.

Norvil, Tho: & Judith Parish, both in Goochland 1779, Feb: 4 p. 18.

Norvil, Tho: & Mary Dawson, both in this parish 1768, Jan: 7 p. 10.

NUCKOLDS, Tho: & Nanny Riddy, both in this parish 1778, Febr. 25 p. 18.

OGILSBY, Jacob, & Ann Bailey, both of this parish 1760, feb: 14 p. 5.
Ogilsby, Richard, & Elizabeth Price, both in this Parish 1758, Sep: 3 p. 4.
Ogilsvy, Will: & Martha Ellis, in Henrico 1771, Dec: 29 p. 13.
ORFORD, Ja: & Eliz: Taylor, both in Albemarle 1771, May 30 p. 12.
Orford, Jacob, in Fluvanna, & Nancy Hunter in Louisa 1779, Mar: 4 p. 18.
OSEBURN, Michael, & Mary Hanson 1751, Dec: 20 pp. 26-31.
OVERSTREET, James, & Frances Hewbanks [Eubank] both in this county 1767 May 31 p. 9.
Overstreet, Will: & Eliz: Overstreet 1777, May 22 p. 18.
OWEN, Barnet, & Rachel Horton, both in Goochland 1771, Nov: 21 p. 12.
Owen, James, & Eliz: Russel, both of ys parish 1776, Oct: 23 p. 17.
Owen, Joel, & Mary Wilkerson, both of this parish 1765, Aug. 29 p. 8.
Owen, William, & Ageia Wilkerson, both of this Parish 1766, Oct: 28 p. 9.
OWL, Absalom, & Ann Holland, both of this parish 1769, Aug. 13 p. 11.

PACE, Edward, & Susannah Johnston, both in Goochland 1784, Sep: 21 p. 23.
Pace, Jesse, & Frances Hall, both of ys parish 1776, Jan: 29 p. 17.
Pace, Jo: & Ann Pace, both of Goochland 1774, Feb: 1 p. 14.
Pace, Joseph, & Mary Ann Page, both of this parish 1762, Oct: 26 p. 7.
Pace, Murray, & Mary Ashley, both in ys- 1775, Sep: 15 p. 16.
PAGE, Ben: & Anna Wright, both in Goochland 1771, Dec: 3 p. 13.
Page, Billie, & .... 1753, ... pp. 27-32.
Page, James, & Mary England, both of this parish 1765, May 16 p. 8.
Page, James, & Sarah Welburn, both of this parish 1768, Ap: 16 p. 10.
Page, John, & Unity Harris, both in this parish 1756, Nov: 14 p. 2.
Page, John, & Eadith Cauthan, both in this parish 1761, Oct: 31 p. 6.
Page, Jos: & Eliz: Steventon, both in this parish 1758, Ap: 13 p. 3.
Page, Rob: in this parish & Winnifred Patty in Bedford 1759, Mar: 20 p. 4.
Page, Rob: & Rachel Brockman, both of Goochland 1773, Dec: 26 p. 14.
Page, Rob: & Eliz: Welburn, both in Goochland 1779, Aug: 11 p. 19.
Page, Will: & Agnes Houchins, both in this parish 1757, Dec: 2 p. 3.
Page, Will: & Ann England, both in this parish 1764, Dec: 11 p. 8.
Page, Will: & Mary Wetherspoon, both in Goochland 1770, Sep: 24 p. 12.
PARISH, Aaron, & Sarah Barns, in Westover 1762, Jan: 18 p. 6.
Parish, Abram, & Sarah Clark, both in this parish 1767, Oct: 8 p. 10.
Parish, Anderson, & Mary Tate, in Orange 1778, Dec: 5 p. 18.
Parish, Anselm, & Mildred Atkins, both in this parish 1758, ffeb: 20 p. 3.
Parish, Booker, & Constancy Massie, both in this 1767, Jan: 29 p. 9.
Parish, Charles, & .... 1751, ... pp. 26-31.

Parish, Davie, & Judith Holland, both in this parish 1758, Jan: 4 p. 3.

Parish, Henry, & Margaret Oden, both in this parish 1765, Sep: 16 p.8

Parish, Humphreh, & Mary Ann Raine, in Goochland 1783, Sep: 16 p. 23.

Parish, Humphry, & Eliz: Lane, both in ys parish 1751, ... pp. 26-32.

Parish, Isham, & Elizabeth Atkins, both of this parish 1764, Jun: 5 p. 8.

Parish, Ja: & Sarah Timberlick, both in Louisa 1780, Oct: 11 p. 20.

Parish, Jo: & .... 1751, ... pp. 26-31.

Parish, Joel, & Eliz: Hill, both in this parish 1757, Dec: 26 p. 3.

Parish, Joseph, & Charity Atkinson, both of this parish 1767, Sep: 22 p. 10.

Parish, Moses, & Mary Hill, both in this parish 1761, Jan: 29 p. 5.

Parish, Nathaniel, & Mary Williams, both of ys parish 1777, June 2 p. 18.

Parish, Nelson, & Molly Parish, both in this parish 1763, Feb: 8 p. 7.

Parish, Sherard, & Mildred Blackwell, both of this parish 1764, Oct: 2 p. 8.

PARKER, Harry, & Joanna Thomas, both in Spotsylvania 1786, Jul: 25 p. 24.

PARROT, Tyree, & Olney Bowe, both of Louisa 1783, Jan: 2 p. 22.

PAULET, Rich: & Catherine Smith, both of Louisa 1781, Jan: 10 p. 20.

PAYNE, George, & Agatha George, both in this parish 1754, Dec: 26 p. 1.

Payne, George, & Betty McCartey-Morton, in James City Parish 1765, Dec: 31 p. 8.

Payne, Jesse, & Sally Lewis, both in Goochland 1779, Jan: 8 p. 18.

Payne, Josias, & Eliz: ffleming, both in this parish 1755, Aug: 23 p. 1.

Payne, Math: & Sally Pryor, both in Goochland 1773, May 4 p. 14.

Payne, Rob: & Ann Burton, both in this parish 1762, Jul: 22 p. 6.

Payne, Rob: Burton, & Mary Sydenham Morton both in Goochland 1773, Dec: 22 p. 14.

Payne, Will: & Mary Barret, both in this parish 1755, Mar: 6 p. 1.

PEARSON, Richmond, & Sarah Haden, both in Albemarle 1772, Nov: 5 p. 13.

PEATROSS, Rich: & Agnes Hurt, in Spotsylvania 1787, May 3, p. 24.

PEERS, Anderson, & Judith Leprade, both of Goochland 1780, Oct: 24 p. 20.

PENDLETON, Edmund, & Milley Pollard, in Goochland 1764, Aug: 16 p. 8.

PEMBERTON, Richard, & ffrances Bradley, both in Maniken Town 1757, Sep: 1 p. 3.

Pemberton, Will: & Joanna Howard, in Maniken Town 1771, May 12 p. 12.

PERRIERE, Hezekiah, & Mary Ellis, both in Henrico 1764, Aug: 16 p. 8.

Perriere, Hezekiah, & Ann Ellis, both in Henrico 1773, Dec: 17 p. 14.

Periere, Obadiah, in Henrico, & Mary Miller in Goochland 1779, Mar: 14 p. 18.

Periere, Sam: & Eliz: Henley, both of ys parish 1775, Nov: 24 p. 16.

PERKINS, Abram, & Eliz: Williams, both of ys 1775, Jul: 29 p. 16.

Perkins, Antony, & Aggie Pulham, both of Louisa 1780, Dec: 25 p. 20.

Perkins, Archelaus, & Ann Mitchel, both of Goochland 1784, Sep: 2 p. 23.

Perkins, Benjamin, & Mary Curd, both in this parish 1768, Dec: 18 p. 11.

Perkins, Constant, & Mary Allen, both in this parish 1761, May 31 p. 6.

Perkins, [Const]ant, & Ann Walker, both in this parish 1763 .... p. 7.

Perkins, Constant, & Judith Poor, both in Goochland 1780, Nov: 9 p. 20.

Perkins, James, & Judith Whitlow, both of this parish 1764, Nov: 1 p. 8.

Perkins, Joel, & Ann Bailey, both of this parish 1767, Dec: 24 p. 10.

Perkins, John, in Goochland, & Ursley Richardson in Henrico, 1768, Oct: 12 p. 10.

Perkins, Joseph, & Betsey Price, both in ys parish 1775, Dec: 21 p. 16.

Perkins, Stephen, & Sarah Bowles, both in Goochland 1772, Dec: 13 p. 13.

Perkins, Will: in New Kent, & Susannah Massie, widow in this parish, 1756, ffeb: 24 p. 2.

Perkins, Will: & Sarah Walker, both in Goochland 1772, Dec: 17 p. 13.

Perkins, Will: & Martha Hunter, both of Louisa 1785, Aug: 17 p. 24.

PERRY, Bartlet, & Mary Simson, both in Louisa 1784, Oct: 12 p. 23.

Perry, Samuel, & Agnes Johnson, both of this parish 1760, Ap: 20 p. 5.

PHILIPS, Capt. Rich: & Eliz: Waddy, both of Louisa 1785, Nov: 20 p. 24.

PHILPOT, John, & Elizabeth Man, both in this parish 1769, Jun: 24 p. 11.

PIERCE, Thomas, & Edeth East, both in this parish 1760, Nov: 22 p. 5-.

PLEASANTS, Archibald, & Jean Woodson, both of ys- 1775, Aug: 5. She was baptized by me. p. 16.

Pleasants, Is: & Jean Pleasants, both in Goochland 1782, Aug: 22 p. 22.

Pleasants, John, in Cumberland, & Ann Randolph in Goochland 1759, Jun: 14 p. 4.

Pleasants, Jos: & Mary Gerrand [Guerrant] both in Goochland 1772, Ap: 23 p. 13.

Pleasants, Richard, & Ann Leprade, both in this parish 1762, Jul: 1 p. 6.

Pleasants, Rob: & Fanny Clark, both in Goochland, 1773, Dec: 4 p. 14.

Pleasants, Tho: & Nancy Parsons, both in Goochland 1772, Jan: 2 p. 13.

PLEDGE, Arch: in Goochland, & Christian Ferrar in Henrico 1774, Feb: 17 p. 14.

Pledge, Archer, & Nancy Woodson, both of ys parish 1775, Mar: 2 p. 16.

Pledge, Will: & Ann Clarkson, both in Goochland 1773, Feb: 16 p. 14.

Pledge, William, & Ursley Woodson, both of ys parish 1775, May 28 p. 16.

POINDEXTER, Jo: & Eliz: Thornton, both in Louisa 1781, Dec: 26 p. 21.

Poindexter, Jo: & Frances Arnet, both of Louisa, 1785, Jul: 14 p. 24.

Pindexter, Tho: & Eliz: Pledge, both of this parish 1760, feb: 13 p. 5.

Poindexter, Will, & Polly McGehee, both in Louisa (17)91, ... p. 27.

POLLARD, Thomas, & Sarah Hardine, both of this parish 1763, Jan: 30 p. 7.

POLLOCK, John, & Margaret Jones, both in this parish 1767, Ap: 8 p. 9.

Pollock, Peter, & Mary Poor, both of Goochland 1779, Nov: 26 p. 19.

Pollock, Will: & Ann Ballow, both in Cumberland 1770, Mar: 23 p. 11.

POOR, Jo: in Goochland, & Mary Kent in Albemarle 1774, Feb: 3 p. 14.

Poor, Thomas, & Mary Ann Jones, both in this parish 1767, Dec: 29 p. 10.

Poor, Will: & Molly Sampson, both in Goochland 1771, Sep: 24 p. 12.

POPE, Tho: in ys parish, & Mary Snead in Albemarle 1776, Dec: 8 p. 17.

PORTER, Will: & Sarah Johnson, both of Louisa 1782, Jun: 20 p. 22.

Porter, William, & Magdalene Chastain, both of Maniken Town 1765, Feb: 13 p. 8.

POTTER, Thomas, & Diana Alsup, both in this parish 1763, Jul: 31 p. 7.

POVALL, Robert, in Henrico, & Winifred Jones Miller in this parish 1760, Jun: 14 p. 5.

POWERS, David, & Eliz: Laurence, both in Louisa 1775, Jul: 18 p. 16.

Powers, Will: in Goochland, & Eliz: Johnson in Hanover 1774, Nov: 29 p. 15.

PRICE, Barret, in Henrico, & Sally Graves, in Goochland 1771, Aug: 25 p. 12.

Price, Jo: & Mary Johnson, in Goochland 1779, Aug: 3 p. 19.

Price, Leonard, & Judith Eldridge, both in Goochland 1770, Nov: 10 p. 12.

PRIDDY, Will: & Jean Hunter 1755, feb: 5 p. 1.

Priddy, Will: & Ann Harlow, both in Hanover 1771, Ap: 25 p. 12.

PROFIT, Da: & Eliz: Smith, both of this parish 1757, Ap: 7 p. 3.

Profit, John, & Susannah Arrington, both in this parish 1757, Mar: 10 p. 3.

Proffit, Will: & Sarah Thurstane, both in this parish Im.... 1762, Sep: 12 p. 6.

PRYOR, Samuel, in Amelia & ffrances Morton of this parish 1760, Aug: 27 p. 5.

Pryor, Will: in ys parish, & Eliz: Hughes in Cumberland 1776, May 16 p. 17.

PUGH, Thomas, & Nancie Tiller, both of Maniken Town 1769, Jan: 22 p. 11.
PULHAM, Tho: & Jean Ray, in Louisa 1778, Jul: 19 p. 18.
Pulham, Zach: & Sarah Black, both in Louisa 1782, Feb: 14 p. 21.

QUARLES, John, & Becky Minor, of Louisa (17)91, ... p. 27.
Quarles, Rob: & Patsy Minor, of Louisa (17)91, ... p. 27.
Quarles, Will: & Francis Vivian, in Orange 1779, Sep: 16 p. 19.
QUISSENBERRY, Geo: & Jeanie Daniel, both of Orange 1783, June 4 p. 23.

RADFORD, Edward, & Ann Curd, both in this parish 1762, Jul: 22 p. 6.
Radford, Milner, & Sarah Lewis, both in this— 1766, Dec: 25 p. 9.
RAGLINE, Jacob, & Martha Loftus, both in Goochland 1773, Jul: 18 p. 14.
Raglin, Sam: & Eliz: Meekie, both of Louisa 1788, Dec: 12 p. 25.
RAILY, Jo: & Betty Randolph, both in Goochland Betw. 1750-1753 p. 31.
RAIN, John, & Susannah Mitchel, both in this parish 1754, Aug. 3 p. 1.
Raine, Nath: & Judith Blackwel, both of Louisa 1779, Dec: 19 p. 19.
RAWLINES, Ben: & Betty Holyday, both of Spotsyl: 1785, Dec: 25 p. 24.
RAWLINGS, Jo: & Nancy Hollowday, both in Spot: 1783, Ap: 1 p. 23.
RAWSON, Jos: & Mildred Edwards, both in Spot: 1782, Jul: 4 p. 22.
REALY, Shilton, & .... 1753, ... pp. 27-32.
REDMAN, Abra: & Eliz: Slater, both in Louisa 1785, Mar: 17 p. 23.
Redman, Abram, & Catie [Brown] 1787, Oct: 23 p. 25.
REID, Jo: & Frances Morton, both in Goochland 1773, Mar: 1 p. 14.
RENOLDS, Benjamin, & Eliz: Fleming, in Louisa 1789, Feb: 5 p. 25.
RICE, Cha: & Mary Tony, both in Albemarle 1774, Nov: 4 p. 15.
Rice, Clayburn, & Molly Smith, both in Goochland 1773, Mar: 25 p. 14.
Rice, Tandy, & Sarah Sampson, of this parish 1761, Nov: 28 p. 6.
Rice, Will: & Ann Smith, both in Goochland 1772, Sep: 10 p. 13.
RICH, Timothy, & Mary Johnson (Johnston) both of ys parish 1751, Sep: 18 pp. 26-31.
RICHARDS, Charles, & Susannah Ryan, both in this parish, 1758, Aug: 6 p. 4.
RICHARDSON, George, & Elizabeth Miller, both in this— 1766, Nov: 15 p. 9.
Richardson, Will: & Frances Harrison, both in this— 1770, May 23 p. 11.
RICKET, James, in Amelia, & Martha Wade in this parish 1768, Aug: 7 p. 10.
RIDDEL, James, & Eliz: Costilla, both of ys parish 1776, Mar: 17 p. 17.
Riddle, Math: & Jean Caddel, both in Goochland 1779, Jan: 9 p. 18.
Riddle, Tho: & Agnes Mims, both in this parish 1755, Oct: 13 p. 2.

Riddle, Tho: Eadith Watkins, both in Goochland 1773, Jul: 11 p. 14.
RIGSBY, William, & Susannah Adams, in Louisa 1776, Feb: 22 p. 17.
ROBARDS, Jo: & Sar: Marshall, both in Goochland 1772, Jul: 9 p. 13.
Robards, Will: & Eliz: Lewis, both of Goochland 1781, Sep: 7 p. 21.
ROBERTS, Ja: & Mary Massie, both in Goochland 1774, Dec. 2 p. 15.
Roberts, Jo: .... 175— .... pp. 27, 32.
Roberts, Will: & Sarah Hutson, both of Louisa 1779, Ap: .... p. 19.
Roberts, William, & Elizabeth Lewis, both in this parish 1758, Jan: 5
   p. 3.
Roberts, Will: & Eliz: Pleasants-Cocke, both in Goochland 1774, Jan:
   3 p. 14.
ROBERTSON, John, & Mary Creasy, both in Albemarle 1762, Oct:
   13 p. 7.
ROBINSON, Ben: & Catherine Parker, both of Spot: 1783, Feb: 18
   p. 22.
Robinson, Is: .... 1751 .... pp. 26, 31.
Robinson, John, & Elizabeth Parish, both of this parish 1761, Dec: 23
   p. 6.
RODGERS, John, & Ann Lewis, both of this parish 1769, Feb: 23
   p. 11.
Rodgers, Will: & Mary Johnson, both in Goochland 1770, Sep: 8 p. 12.
Rogers, Jo: & .... 1751, ... pp. 26-31.
Rogers, Jo: & Eliz: Epperson, both in Goochland 1771, Oct: 26 p. 12.
ROSS, Alexr. & Mourning Woody, both in Goochland 1772, Nov: 6
   p. 13.
Ross, James, & Jean Loving, both in this parish 1766, Feb: 17 p. 8.
ROWE, Moses, & Rebecca Manteloe, both in Louisa (17)92, ...
   .... p. 27.
ROWNTREE, Thomas, & Letitia Barnard, in Albemarle 1767, (July)
   6 p. 9.
Rowntree, Turner, & Sarah Woodson, both of Goochland 1766, Aug:
   26 p. 9.
Rowntree, Will: & Jean ffenton, in Henrico 1759, Nov: 4 p. 4.
RYAN, Philip, & Jean Bullinton 1751, ... pp. 26-31.
Ryan, Philip, & Elizabeth Mills, both in this parish 1766, Mar: 7 p. 8.
Ryan, Will: in Albemarle, & Mary Chancellor in Goochland 1773, Dec:
   2 p. 14.
Ryan, William, & Sarah Swanson, both in this parish 1760, Ap: 13 p. 5.

SADLER, Will: & Ann Brown, both in Goochland 1770, Aug: 5 p. 12.
SALLEY, (SALLEE) Abram, & Eliz: Woodson 1753, Aug: 24 pp.
   27-32.
Sallie, Isaac, & Eliz: Bryan, both in Maniken Town 1759, May 6 p. 4.
SALMON, James, & Patty Clarkson, both of ys parish 1776, Dec: 5
   p. 17.
SAMPSON, Charles, in this & Ann Porter in Maniken Town 1767,
   Nov: 3 p. 10.
Sampson, Richard, & Ann Curd, both in Goochland 1771, Nov: 24
   p. 13.

Sampson, Stephen, & Sarah Johnson, both in this parish 1753, Sep: 20 p. 1.
Sampson, William, & Mary McGuire 1751, ... pp. 26-31.
SANDERS, Geo: & Martha Rice, both in Goochland 1771, Dec: 17 p. 13.
Sanders, Ja: & Mary Jones 1753, Sep: 20 p. 1.
Sanders, John, & Eliz: Hancock, both in this parish 1758, Oct: 23 p. 4.
Sanders, Will: & Judith Lane, both in Goochland 1771, Jan: 10 p. 12.
SANDAGE, Jos: & Eliz: Wright, both of Louisa 1782, Feb: 14 p. 22.
Sandidge, Austin, & Mary Holladay, in Spotsylvania 1786, Sep: 28 p. 24.
Sandidge, Ja: & Patsy Benaugh, both in Spotsylvania 1787, Jan: 24 p. 24.
Sandige, James, in Hanover, & Judith Lock in this parish 1757, Nov: 3 p. 3.
SASSEEN, Alexr. & Sally Bantam, both in Maniken Town 1767, ... p. 9.
Sasseen, David, & Eliz: Parish, both in Maniken town 1768, Dec: 10 p. 11.
SCOT, Arthur, & Frances Ker, both in Goochland 1773, Sep: 5 p. 14.
Scot, Dan: & Ann Randolph, in ys parish 1751, Nov: 28 pp. 26-31.
Scot, James, & Judith Parish, both in this parish 1763, ffeb: 17 p. 7.
Scot, James, & Anna Gray, both of Louisa: my overseer 1777, Sep: 8 p. 18.
Scot, John, & Judith Atkinson, both of this parish 1767, Sep: 29 p. 10.
Scot, Robert, & Judith Chastain, both in Maniken Town 1762, Oct: 30 p. 6.
Scot, Will: & Mary Wilkerson, both in Cumberland 1773, Oct: 21 p. 14.
SCRUGS, James, & Susan Pore, both in this parish 1762, Sep: 28 p. 6.
Scrugs, Richard, & Rachel Wright, both in this parish 1763, ... p. 7.
SCURRY, ..., & .... 1753, Aug: 5 pp. 27-32.
SHELTON, Da: & Henrietta Thomason, both in Louisa 1786, Nov: 7 p. 24.
Shelton, John, & Eliz: Lawson, both in this parish 1760, Jul: 30 p. 5.
Shilton, Jo: & Mary Payne, both in Goochland 1772, Sep: 1 p. 13.
Shilton, Tho: & Cecily Dabney, both of Louisa 1782, Feb: 20 p. 22.
SHEPHERD, Philip, & Susanna Thomson, both of Spot:* 1786 [or] 1785, Dec: 23 pp. 20-24.
Shepherd, Robert, & Sarah Clark, both of ys parish 1777, Feb: 23 p. 17.
SHIP, Tho: in Goochland, & Jedidiah More in Carolina 1774, Feb: 20 p. 14.
SHOEMAKER, John, & Sarah Jerrat, both of this parish 1755, Nov: 9 p. 2.
SHORT, John, & Olive Sasseen, both in Maniken town 1766, Sep: 18 p. 9.

*Spot: in one entry, Louisa in the other.

Short, Thomas, & Ann Payne, both in Maniken Town 1762, Jan: 10 p. 6.

Short, Young, & Mary Bilboa, in Maniken Town 1756, ffeb: 3 p. 2.

SIMMONS, Jo: & .... Betw. 1750-1753 p. 31.

SLADEN, John, & Susannah Hodges, both in this parish 1756, Dec: 20 p. 2.

Sladon, Jo: & Judith Garlan, in Louisa 1788, Oct: 4 p. 25.

Slaydon, Dan: & Sally Isabel, both in Goochland 1782, Oct: 2 p. 22.

Slaydon, Will: & Sar: Groom, both in Goochland 1770, Aug: 16 p. 12.

SLAUGHTER, Cha: in Culpeper, & Eliz: Poindexter in Louisa 1780, Feb: 3 p. 19.

Slaughter, Jo: & Ann Lewis Thomason, of Louisa was maried 1790, Mar: 26 p. 25.

SMITH, Absalom, & Esther Chandler, both of Orange 1781, Oct: 26 p. 21.

Smith, Cha: & Nancy Johnson, both of Louisa 1783, Nov: 20 p. 23.

Smith, Champness, & Eliz: Hubbard, both in Louisa 1782, Jan: 4 p. 21.

Smith, Christopher, & Mary Anderson, both of Louisa 1786, Nov: 21 p. 24.

Smith, Edward, in Albemarle & Sally Rice in this parish 1762, Dec: 3 p. 7.

Smith, George, & Caroline Trabue, both in Maniken Town 1758, Jun: 4 p. 4.

Smith, Guy, & .... Hopkins, 1751, ... pp. 26-31.

Smith, James, & Mary Worley, both in Maniken Town 1760, Oct: 2 p. 5.

Smith, Joseph, & Eliz: Edwards, of Louisa 1789, Jan: 8 p. 25.

Smith, Patrick, & Sarath Nowlin, both in this parish 1778, Febr. 25 p. 18.

Smith, Payton, in Henrico, & Judith Wadley in this parish 1763, Mar: 17 p. 7.

Smith, Rhodes, & Unity Thomson, of Louisa 1787, Sep: 10 p. 24.

Smith, Rob: & Eliz: Carrol, both in Goochland 1771, Ap: 28 p. 12.

Smith, Rob: & Mary Jerrat, both in Goochland 1774, Aug: 11 p. 15.

Smith, Rob: & Susannah Woodrum, both in Louisa 1780, Jul: 8 p. 20.

Smith, Shilton, & Dianah Moss, both of Louisa 1788, Ap: 3 p. 25.

Smith, Tho: & Magdalen Garret, both in Maniken Town 1756, Oct: 15 p. 2.

Smith, Will: in Louisa, & Sarah Pryor in Goochland 1784, Jul: 28 p. 23.

SNEAD, Charles, in Henrico, & Mary Guillam in this parish 1767, Dec: 22 p. 10.

Snead, John, & Sarah Woodrum, both in this parish 1763, Ap: 6 p. 7.

SOUTHERLAND, Sanders, & Martha Davis, in Albemarle 1758, Dec: 22 p. 4.

SPENCER, Sion, in Charlotte county, & Mary Harison in Maniken town 1769, May 20 p. 11.

STANFORD, David, & Eliz: ffurkerant, both in Maniken Town 1759, Dec: 16 p. 5.

STANLEY, John, & Eliz: Howard 1755, Ap: 20 p. 1.

Stanley, Maddox, in Hanover, & Ann Miller in ys parish 1776, Dec: 19 p. 17.

Stanley, Maddox, & Sarah Bunch, both in Louisa 1784, Jul: 22 p. 23.

STARKIE, Jos: & Eliz: Leprade in Goochland 1753, Aug: 9 pp. 27-32.

STEPENS, Tho: & .... in Albemarle 1759, Jan: 30 p. 4.

STEVENS, John, & Mary Smith, in Spotsylvania 1787, Dec: 18 p. 25.

STEWART, Cha: & Mildred Stewart, both of Louisa 1781, Sep: 14 p. 21.

STODGHILL, Ambrose, & Susannah Denton, in Hanover 1763, Jan: 24 p. 7.

STOKES, Sylvanus, in Cumberland, & Cat: Hicks in this parish 1755, Sep: 21 p. 2.

STONE, Caleb, & Sarah Ashlen, both in Albemarle 1776, May 16 p. 17.

STRAITON, Henry, widower, in Cumberland & Sarah Hampton in this parish 1753, Dec: 26 p. 1.

Stratton, Abraham, & Nannie Tony, both of Goochland 1773, Jul: 12 p. 14.

STREET, Billie, & .... 1751 .... pp. 26-31.

SUBLET, Benjamin, & Eliz: Jordan, both in this parish 1762, Jun: 24 p. 6.

SULLIVAN, Michael, & Biddy Wilson, both of this parish 1775, Dec: 21 p. 16.

SWIFT, Jo: & Sarah Swift, both in Louisa 1783, Feb: 6 p. 22.

SYMES, Lewis, & Peggie Leonard, both in Louisa 1784, Sep: 10 p. 23.

TALLY, Geo: & Sally Cole, in Louisa, maried 1793, Dec: 26 p. 28.

Tally, Mich: & Barbara Cole, both in Louisa [179]3 .... p. 27.

Tally, Reuben, & Martha Dyer, both of Louisa 1773, Oct: 7 p. 14.

Tally, Will: & Lydia Cole, both of Louisa 1791 [Mar]ch p. 27.

TAILOR, Moses, & Obedience Smith, both in this— 1767, Jan: 23 p. 9.

TATE, Rob: & Susanna Bibb, both of Louisa 1780, Dec: 21 p. 20.

Tate, Will, & Marg: Tate, both of Louisa 1779, Dec: 25 p. 19.

TAYLOR, Char: & .... Betw. 1750-1753 p. 31.

Taylor, John ffoster, & Eliz: Woodhal, both in this parish 1755, Oct: 9 p. 2.

Taylor, Mathew, & Sally Cram, both of ys parish married by Mr. Tod irregularly 1776, Nov: 7 p. 17.

Taylor, Tho: & Milley Barker, both of Goochland 1774, May 29 p. 15.

Taylor, Will: & .... Betw. 1750-1753 p. 31.

TELFORD, Jo: & Marg: King, both of Louisa 1780, Dec: 6 p. 20.

TERRELL, Richard, & Lucy Carr, maried 1792, Oct: 5 p. 127.

Terrill, Tho: & Sarah Shilton, both of Louisa 1780, Oct: 23 p. 20.

Terril, Will: & Ann Daniel, both in Orange 1780, Nov: 26 p. 20.

Terrill, Richmond, & Cecilia Darracot, in Louisa 1782, Ap: 25 p. 22.

TERRY, Emmanuel, & Eliz: Thomson, both in Louisa 1784, Oct: 14 p. 23.

THACHER, Archelaus, & Ann Chace, both of Louisa 1781, Jul: 31 p. 21.

Thacker, Benjamin, & Neffeny Emmerson, both in this parish 1767, Nov: 5 p. 10.

Thacker, John, & Eliz: Thacker, both of this parish 1758, Nov: 5 p. 4.

Thacker, Will: & Eliz: Smith, both in Louisa 1784, Dec: 3 p. 23.

THACKSTON, David, & Sarah Shepherd, both of ys parish 1777, Mar: 16 p. 18.

Thactson, Ja: & Eliz: Clark, both in this parish 1753, Sep: 20 p. 1.

THOMAS, Benjamin, & Rebekah Hurst, both in this parish 1769, Jun: 13 p. 11.

Thomas, Daniel & Salley Welday, both of ys 1775, Sep: 7 p. 16.

Thomas, Jesse, in Cumberland, & Jane Bowles in Goochland 1781, Feb: 15 p. 21.

Thomas, Nathan, & Mary Jones, both in Goochland 1774, Dec: 18 p. 15.

Thomas, Thomas, & Rebekah Lookadoe, both in Maniken Town 1765, Sep: 1 p. 8.

Thomas, William, & Rebekah Upton, 1754, Dec: 26 p. 1.

THOMASON, Byares, & Sarah White, both in Louisa 1784, Ap: 15 p. 23.

Thomason, Jo: & Frances Cook, both of Louisa 1780, Dec: 23 p. 20.

Thomason, Rich: & Sarah Terry, both of Louisa (18 miles) 1786, Ap: 25 p. 24.

Thomason, Tho: & Eliz: Weldie, both of Goochland 1770, Nov: 19 p. 12.

Thomason, Will: & Unity Hix, of Louisa, both—4 miles—1786, Ap: 18 p. 24.

THOMPKINS, Will: in Hanover, & Mary Meekie in Louisa 1786, Dec: 26 p. 24.

THOMSON, Clifton, & Mary Raglane, both of Louisa 1788, Feb: 26 p. 25.

Thomson, David, & Eleanor Thomson, both of Louisa 1779, Nov: 30 p. 19.

Thomson, Ja: & Tempe Mooney, both in Louisa 1783, Jul: 6 p. 23.

Thomson, Jo: & Sally Ragline, both in Louisa 1789, Mar: 31 p. 25.

Thomson, Waddy, & Eliz: Anderson, in Louisa 1787, Aug: 8 p. 24.

Thomson, Will: & Frances Quarles, in Spot: 1781, Dec: 20 p. 21.

THORNWELL, & Lucy Coleman, both in this parish 1757, Dec: 5 p. 3.

THURMOND, Benjamin, & Susannah Moss, both in this parish 1758, Jan: 11 p. 3.

Thurmond, [Philip], & Judith Tucker, both in Albemarle 1764, ... p. 7.

Thurmond, William, & Mackie Norvil, both in this parish 1766, Ap: 10 p. 9—.

THURSTON, Jo: & Patty Wetherspoon, both in Goochland 1772, May 18 p. 13.

Thurston, Reu: & Marianne Lawry, both in Goochland 1772, Dec: 24 p. 13.

Thurston, Will: & Jean Jones, both in this parish 1763, Sep: 12 p. 7.

TIGNOR, Aquila, & Ann Lucas, both of this parish 1765, Aug: 29 p. 8.

TIMBERLICK, Rich: & Mary Curd, both in this parish 1759, Dec: 22 p. 5.

TOD, John, in Cumberland, & Mary Williams in this parish 1764, Mar: 9 p. 8.

TOLLIVER, Will: & Mary Hopper, both of this parish 1770, Feb: 27 p. 11.

TOMSON, Richard, & Mary Abstent, both in this parish 1758, Jul: 4 p. 4.

TONY, Alex: & Ann Ashline, both of ys parish 1777, Mar: 16 p. 18.

Tony, Charles, & Ann Steventon, both in this parish 1761, ffeb: 1 p. 5.

Tony, Sherwood, & Lory England, both of this parish 1765, Feb: 7 p. 8.

TOOLY, James, in Buckingham, & Elizabeth Maddox in this parish 1767, Dec: 20 p. 10.

TOURMAN, Tho: & Eliz: Mitchel, in Goochland 1778, Oct: 20 p. 18.

TRAINHAM, Sam: & Mary Ogilsvy, both of Orange 1782, Mar: 25 p. 22.

TRENT, Alexr: & .... Scot, in Maniken 175—, ... pp. 27-32.

TRIBUE, David, & Mary Sallee, both in Maniken Town 1760, May 7 p. 5.

TRICE, Ja. & Polly Smith, both of Louisa 1787, Feb: 22 p. 24.

Trice, Jo: & Pattie Smith, in Louisa 1783, Sep: 9 p. 23.

Trice, William, in Amherst, & Molly Rice in this parish 1768, Dec: 13 p. 11.

Trice, William, & Ann Nelson, both in Louisa 1790, ... 15 p. 27.

TROTMAN, Sam: & Catherine Barnet, both of Louisa 1783, Oct: 7 p. 23.

TUCKER, Obadiah, & Eliz: Kent, both of Albemarle 1769, Dec: 11 p. 11.

TUGGLE, Henry, & Hellender Conolly, both in Goochland 1751, ... pp. 26-32.

Tuggle, Jo: & Ann Cawley, both in Goochland 1770, Jul: 29 p. 12.

Tuggle, Joshua, & Eliz: Pace, both of Goochland 1780, Dec: 26 p. 20.

Tuggle, William, & Ann Nash, both in this parish 1765, Sep: 25 p. 8.

TURNER, Bartholomew, & Mary Johnson, both in this parish 1763, ... p. 7.

TURPINE, Thomas, & Martha-Ward Gains, in Maniken Town 1767, Ap: 9 p. 9.

UNDERWOOD, George, & Elizabeth Curd, both in this parish 1768, Dec: 25 p. 11.

UTLEY, Jo: & Nancy Clarkson, both in Goochland 1772, Dec: 23, p. 13.

UTLEY, William, & Mary Ragline, both in this 1766, Dec: 13 p. 9.

VASS, Vincent, & Elizabeth Mannin, both in Orange, 1783, Aug: 29 p. 23.

VAUGHAN, James, & Amelia Brumfield, both in this parish 1757, feb: 27 p. 3.

Vaughan, Ja: & Mary Harris, both of ys parish 1777, Jan: 20 p. 17.

Vaughan, Ja: & Judith Hopkins, both of Goochland 1783, Feb: 27 p. 22.

Vaughan, Jo: & Mary Barnes 1754, ffeb: 3 p. 1.

Vaughan, Littleberry, & Juliana Brown, both in Henrico 1774, May 22 p. 15.

Vaughan, Shadrach, & Mary Merriwether, both in Goochland 1770, Jun: 19 p. 12.

VENABLE, Hugh Lewis, & Mary Martin, both in this parish 1757, Jun: 14 p. 3.

VIE, Gideon, & Isabel .... both in Albemarle 1759, Mar: 21 p. 4.

WADE, Daniel, & Mary Neves, both in this parish 1776, May 30 p. 17.

Wade, Jo: & Susanna Bowles, both in Goochland 1770, Oct. 15 p. 12.

Wade, John Utley, & Elles Woodrum, both in this parish 1763, Oct: 21 p. 7.

Wade, Rich: & Judith Hancoke, both in Goochland 1772, Nov: 8 p. 13.

Wade, Richard, & Eliz: Barker, both in this parish 1755, feb: 5 p. 1.

Wade, Rob: & Rebekah Rowntree, both in Goochland 1771, Feb: 7 p. 12.

WADLEY, William, & Mary Womack, both of this parish 1768, Ap: 15 p. 10.

WALDEN, Sam: & Rachel Shepherd, both in this parish 1756, Jan: 22 p. 2.

WALDY, Will: & Ann Baily, both of Fluvanna 1781, Oct: 22 p. 21.

WALES, John, in Charles City, & Elizabeth Laumox, both in this parish 1760, Jan: 26 p. 5.

WALKER, Da: & Eliz: Gilbert, both in Goochland 1770, Oct: 13 p. 12.

Walker, David, & Sarah Slaydon, both in this parish 1758, Ap: 6 p. 3.

Walker, Ja: & Fanny Cannon, both in Goochland 1774, Jun: 26 p. 15.

Walker, Joel, & Sarah Bowen, both of Goochland 1774, Jan: 13 p. 14.

Walker, John, & Lydia Gilbert, both of this parish 1769, Mar: 2 p. 11.

Walker, John, & Hannah Hollinshead, both in ys parish 1776, Mar: 15 p. 17.

Walker, Peter, & Eliz: Harris, both in Cumberland 1756, Dec: 23 p. 3.

[Walker, Peter] & Sarah Harris, in Maniken town 1764, ... p. 7.

Walker, Peter, & Sarah Wadley, both in this parish 1766, Nov: 6 p. 9.

Walker, Philip, & Agnes Watson, both in this parish 1763, Aug: 25 p. 7.

Walker, Philip, & Mary Smith, both in this parish 1769, May 25 p. 11.

WALTON, William, & Eliz: Tilman, both in this parish 1758, Dec: 1 p. 4.

WARE, John, in Caroline, & Ann Harrison on the Byrd in this County 1756, May 27 p. 2.

Ware, John, in Maniken town, & Mary Watson in Henrico 1762, Ap: 6 p. 6.

WASH, Tho:, & Susannah Fox, both of Louisa, by Mr. Tod 1785, Jan: 4 p. 23.

WATKINS, Cha: & Lucy Curd, in Goochland 1772, Dec: 23 p. 13.

Watkins, John, & Sarah Turner, both in this parish 1763, Jan: 12 p. 7.

WATSON, Ja: & Eliz: Shilton, both in Louisa 1773, Jan: 1 p. 13.

Watson, Ninian, & Sar: Quissenberry, both of Louisa 1783, Sep: 30 p. 23.

Watson, Thomas, & Hannah Hemus, both in this parish 1757, Ap: 11 p. 3.

Watson, William in Hanover, & Martha Pleasants in this—1767, Feb: 17 p. 9.

WAYFORD, Tho: & Eliz: Hodges, both in Goochland 1774, May 1 p. 15.

WEAVER, Ben: in Maniken town, & Mary Woodson in this parish 1758, Ap: 27 p. 3.

Weaver, Dan: & Sarah Durham, both in Maniken town 1756, Nov: 11 p. 2.

Weaver, David, & Massinbad Shoemaker, both in this—1769, Dec: 24 p. 11.

Weaver, Sam: widower, & Eliz: Williams, both in this parish 1755, Mar: 19 pp: 26-31.

WEB, Is: & Ann Farmer, both in Goochland 1770, Oct: 25 p. 12.

Web, Jo: & .... in Albemarle Betw. 1750-1753— p. 31.

Web, Will: & Mary Farmer, both in Goochland 1770, Nov: 25 p. 12.

Webb, Geor: & Mrs. Hannah ffleming in this parish, but Mr. Webb in Hanover, 1756, Ap: 15 p. 2.

Webb, James, & Agnes Hughes, both in this parish 1770, Mar: 1 p. 11.

WEBBER, Augustine, in ys, & Naomi Jones in Hanover 1775, May 30 p. 16.

Webber, Jo: in Goochland, & Eliz: Wiglesworth in Spotsylvania 1773, Aug: 8- p. 14.

Webber, Philip, & Tahpenes Ward, 1751, Oct: 14 p. 26.

Webber, Will: & Mary Woodford, both in Caroline 1773, Jan: 23 p. 14.

WEBSTER, David, & Judith Carter, both in this— 1770, Ap: 10 p. 11.

Webster, Henry, & Anna Richards, both in Louisa 1784, Jul: 8 p. 23.

Webster, John, & Ann Knowline, both in this parish 1762, Aug: 26 p. 6.

WELBURN, Thomas, & Hannah Lambkin, both in this parish 1769, Oct: 23 p. 11.

WHARTON, Sam: & Letty Hutchison, both in Spotsyl: 1786, Mar: 8 p. 24.

WHITE, Jo: & Ann Jackson, both of Louisa 1783, Dec: 25 p. 23.

White, Jo: & Jeanie Crank, both in Louisa 1790, Jan: 21 p. 25.

White, Will: & Ann Overstreet, both of this parish 1769, Dec: 21 p. 11.

White, Will, & Susannah Davis, both in Louisa 1782, May 9 p. 22.

White, Will: & Mary Brockman, in Orange 1782, Sep: 12 p. 22.

WHITEFIELD, Will: & Mary Towler, both in Goochland 1772, Dec: 14 p. 13.

WHITLOCK, John, & Ann Logan, both in this parish 1754, Oct: 6 p. 1.

Whitlock, Nathan, & Diana Hicks, both of this parish 1756, Sep: 7 p. 2.

Whitlock, Robert, & Aggie Alford, both in this parish 1764, Ap: 17 p. 8.

Whitlock, Thomas, & Sally Henderson, both of ys parish 1776, Jun: 9 p. 17.

Whitlock, William, & Mary Rowntree, both in this parish 1767, Dec: 22 p. 10.

WHITLOW, Henry, & Martha Radford, both of this parish 1767, Dec: 3 p. 10.

WILBURN, Rob: & Ann Mims, both in this parish 1755, Oct: 9 p. 2.

Wilburn, Thomas, & Christian Page, both of this parish 1759, Oct: 22 p. 4.

WILKERSON, Gerard, & Ann Perkins, both in Goochland 1774, May 9 p. 15.

Wilkerson, Will: & Lorana Perkins, in Goochland, Betw. 1750-1753 p. 31.

Wilkerson, Will, & Sarah ffranklin, both in this parish 1761, Jul: 11 p. 6.

Wilkerson, Wyat, & Mary Britt, both in this parish 1765, Dec: 26 p. 8.

WILLIAMS, Elias, & Agatha Mosely, both in this parish 1757, Mar: 10 p. 3.

Williams, Jo: & Eliz: Ailestock, in this parish 1793 .... p. 27.

Williams, John, of ys, & Susannah Ellis of Henrico 1775, Jan: 12 p. 16.

Williams, Nathan, & Sarah Brown, in Henrico 1775, Dec: 21 p. 16.

Williams, Will: & Elizabeth Comber, both of this parish 1762, Dec: 30 p. 7.

Williams, Zach: & Mary Poor, both in this parish 1755, Nov: 20 p. 2.

WILLIAMSON, Tho: & Afarillah Corley, both in this parish 1762, Feb: 18 p. 6.

Williamson, William, & Ann Mayo, both in this parish 1763, Oct: 25 p. 7.

WILLIS, Edward, & Calis Barker, both of this parish 1765, Jun: 30 p. 8.

Willis, Pleasants, & Sally Read, both in Henrico 1774, Dec: 10 p. 15.

WILSON, Peter, in Pittsylvania, & Sally Ellis in Henrico 1775, Ap: 18 p. 16.

WINGFIELD, Mathew, & Sarah Hinds, both in Hanover 1775, Dec: 21 p. 17.

Wingfield, Robert, & Frances Jordan, both of this parish 1765, Jun: 11 p. 8.

WINSTON, Is: & Lucy Cole, both in Hanover 1770, Jun: 2 p. 12.

Winston, Jo: & Mary Johnson, both in Louisa 1780, Dec: 7 p. 20.

WITHER, John, & Eliz: Barnet 1755, feb: 21 p. 1.

WOMACK, Henry, & Mary Terry, in Louisa 1778, Jul: 31 p. 18.

WOOD, Ja: & Ann Lipscomb both in Louisa 1785, Oct: 12 p. 23.

Wood, Samuel, & Elizabeth Merian, both in this parish 1762, Dec: 23 p. 7.

Wood, Tho: & Helender Johnson, in Goochland 1781, Mar: 19 p. 21.

WOODFOLK, Jos: & Betsey Barnet both of Louisa 15 miles 1786, Jul: 6 p. 24.

WOODHAL, John, & Jemima Willis, both in this parish 1757, Oct: 13 p. 3.

WOODHALL, Cha: & Elizabeth Black, both of this parish 1765, Oct: 1 p. 8.

Woodhall, John, & Dorothy Pledge, both in this parish 1756, Aug: 12 p. 2.

Woodhall, William, widower, & Marianne Hancock both in this parish 1758, Dec: 3 p. 4.

Woodhall, William, & Mary ffielder, both of this parish 1759, Ap: 12 p. 4.

WOODRUM, David, & Susannah Barnet, both in this parish 1765, Sep: 22 p. 8.

Woodrum, John, & Mary Baze, both in this parish 1761, Nov: 15 p. 6.

Woodrum, Will: & Aggie Webster, both of Goochland 1782, Dec: 16 p. 22.

WOODSON, Ben: & Sally Johnson, both in Goochland 1779, Mar: 14 p. 18.

Woodson, James, & Eliz: Whitlock, both in this parish 1754, Jul: 23 p. 1.

Woodson, Jo: & Mary Lightfoot Anderson, in Hanover 1786, Mar: 30 pp. 24, 129, 137.

Woodson, Jo: Stephen, & Anna Woodson, in Goochland 1778, Oct: 12 pp. 18, 137.

Woodson, John, & Thea [Dorothea] Randolph, both in ys parish 1751, Oct: 14 pp. 26-31-129.

Woodson, John, & Eliz: Bailey, both in this parish 1754, Dec: 24 p. 1.

Woodson, John, in Albemarle, & Mary Mims in this parish 1760, Mar: 20 p. 5.

Woodson, Jos: in Goochland, & Sarah Hughes in Cumberland 1779, Nov: 24 p. 19.

Woodson, Joseph, & Mildred Radford, both of this parish 1770, Jan: 2 p. 11.

Woodson, Josias, & Eliz: Woodson, both in Goochland 1778, Nov: ......* p. 18.

Woodson, Mat: in this parish, and Betty Villain, in Maniken town 1753, Novr: 28 p. 1.

Woodson, Rene, in Albemarle, & Martha Johnson in Louisa 1775, Feb: 2 p. 16.

Woodson, Samuel, & Eliz: Payne, both of ys parish 1777, June 19 p. 18.

Woodson, Shadrach, in Buckingham, & Sus: Walker in this parish 1766, Aug: 14 p. 9.

---

*Decr. 3, 1778, on p. 129 of the original.

Woodson, Stephen, & Lucy fferrar, both of this parish 1758, May 9 p. 4.

Woodson, Tho: & Mary Woodson, both in Goochland 1751 .... pp. 26-31.

Woodson, Tuck: & Mary Netherland, 1751 .... pp. 26-31.

WOODWARD, John, & Susannah Tilman, both in this parish 1756, ffeb: 29 p. 2.

Woodward, Will: & Sarah Hall, both of Louisa 1784, Oct: 12 p. 23.

WOODY, Henry, & Susannah Martin, both in this parish 1761, Jan: 13 p. 5.

WOOLBANKS, Will: & Nancy Weatherspoon, both of Louisa 1778, Dec: 29 p. 18.

WRIGHT, Cha: & Sally Purvis, both of this County were maried 1792, ... p. 27.

Wright, Francis, & Mercy Goldsmith, both in Goochland 1771, May 30 p. 12.

Wright, Jo: & Fanny Thomason, both in Louisa 1783, Feb: 5 p. 22.

Wright, John, & Mary Pierce, both in this parish 1756, Jan: 14 p. 2.

Wright, Joseph, & Eliz: Gouch, both in Louisa were maried 1790, ... 25 p. 27.

Wright, Roderick, & Hannah Cawley, both in this parish 1769, Oct: 31 p. 11.

Wright, William, & Martha Cawley, both in this parish 1769, Oct: 5 p. 11.

YARBORROUGH, Alsop, in Hanover, & Sarah Macnemara, in Albemarle 1768, Ap: 16 p. 10.

Yarborough, John, & Barsheba Harris, both in this parish 1762, Oct: 22 p. 7.

YAUNCEY, Stephen, & Jean Bond, both of Louisa 1779, Oct: 12 p. 19.

YEARGAN, Andrew, & Oney Bowles, both in this parish 1757, Jan: 3 p. 3.

YOUNG, Daniel, & Elizabeth Wafer, both in ys parish 1777, June 19 p. 18.

Young, Jo: & .... 1751 .... p. 26.

Young, Jo: & Sarah Martin, in Louisa 1781, Aug: 8 p. 21.

Young, Lewis, Eliz: Smith, both in Louisa 1781, Sep: 27 p. 21.

YOUNGER, John, & Ann Moss, both in this parish 1757, Nov: 30 p. 3.

MARRIAGES

(Female Index)

ABREY, Sarah [widow] & Arthur Nash, both in this Parish Mar: 17 1755 p. 1.

ABSTENT, Mary & Richard Tomson, both in this Parish Jul: 4, 1758 p. 4.

ADAMS, Susannah & William Rigsby, in Louisa Feb: 22, 1776 p. 17.

ADDISON, Ruth & Harrison Jones, both in this Parish Aug: 24 1759 p. 4.

Addison, Nansie & Shadrach Alvis, both in Goochland Sep: 23 1773 p. 14.

AILESTOCK, Eliz: & Jo. Williams .... 1793 p. 27.

ALFORD, Aggie & Robert Whitlock, both in this parish Ap: 17 1764 p. 8.

Alford, Molly & Will: Baily, both in Goochland Dec. 26 1771 p. 13.

ALLEN, Mary & Shadrach Mims, both in this parish ffeb: 3 1754 p. 1.

Allen, Mary & Constant Perkins, both in this parish May 31 1761 p. 6.

Allen, Barbara & Lewis Hayat, both of Spots: Dec: 25 1783 p. 23.

Allen, Winifred & Jo: Carter, both in Spots: Sep: 1 1784 p. 23.

Allen, Christian, in Orange & Bartholomew Fuller Nov. 11 1789 p. 25.

ALLEY, Dorcas & David Hall Nov. 20 1754 p. 1.

ALSUP, Diana, & Thomas Potter, both in this parish Jul: 31 1763 p. 7.

ANDERSON, Ann, & Lewis Isabel, in Hanover Nov: 17 1775 p. 16.

Anderson, Mary Lightfoot & Jo: Woodson, in Hanover Mar: 30 1786 p. 24.

Anderson, Mary & Christopher Smith, both of Louisa Nov: 21 1786 p. 24.

Anderson, Eliz: & Waddy Thomson, in Louisa Aug: 8 1787 p. 24.

ARNET, Sally, & Rich: Graves, both of Louisa Nov: 23 1780 p. 20.

Arnet, Henrietta in Louisa & Charles Brown in Orange, May 17 1785 p. 24.

Arnet, Frances, & Jo: Poindexter, both of Louisa Jul: 14 1785 p. 24.

ARRINGTON, Susannah & John Profit, both in this parish Mar: 10 1757 p. 3.

ASHLEN, Sarah, & Caleb Stone, both in Albemarle, May 16 1776 p. 17.

ASHLINE, Ann, & Alex: Tony, both in ys parish Mar: 16 1777 p. 18.

ASHLEY, Mary, & Murray Pace, both in ys— Sep: 15 1775 p. 16.

ATKINS, Mildred & Anselm Parish, both in this parish ffeb: 20 1758 p. 3.

Atkins, Elizabeth, & Isham Parish, both of this parish June 5 1764 p. 8.

ATKINSON, Charity & Joseph Parish, both of this parish Sep: 22, 1767 p. 10.

Atkinson, Judith & John Scot, both of this parish Sep: 29, 1767 p. 10.

AUSTINE, Sally & Elkanak Atkins, both in Louisa Oct: 24 1771 p. 12.

BAKER, Joyce, in Albemarle & John Holland in this county ....
   1759 p. 4.

Baker, Elizabeth & John Bryant, both of this parish Jul: 22 1765 p. 8

Baker, Sarah, & Will: Crenshaw, both of Louisa Jan: 30 1783 p. 22.

BAILEY, Eliz: & John Woodson, both in this parish Dec. 24 1754 p. 1.

Bailey, Ann, & Jacob Ogilsby, both of this parish feb: 14 1760 p. 5.

Bailey, Ann, & Jonathan Clark, both in Albemarle Jun: 4 1766 p. 9.

Bailey, Ann, & Joel Perkins, both in this parish Dec. 24 1767 p. 10.

Bailey, Eliz: & Ambrose May, both in Goochland Feb: 3 1771 p. 12.

Bailey, Ann, & Joseph Allen both in Goochland Oct. 19 1787 p. 25.

Bailey, Agnes, & Will: Clark, both in Fluvanna Feb. 1 1781 p. 20.

Baily, Ann & Will: Waldy, both of Fluvanna Oct. 22 1781 p. 21.

BALLOW, Ann, & Will: Pollock, both in Cumberland Mar: 23, 1770
   p. 11.

BANKS, Judith & Isaac Howel, both of ys parish Feb: 23 1775 p. 16.

BANTAM, Sally, & [A]lexr. Sasseen, both in Manikentown ....
   .... 1767 p. 9.

BARCLAY, Mary & Jo: Boxley, both of Louisa April 18 1789 p. 25.

BARKER, Eliz: & Richard Wade, both in this parish feb: 5 1755 p. 1.

Barker, Calis, & Edward Willis, both of this parish Jun: 30 1765 p. 8.

Barker, Milley, & Tho: Taylor, both in Goochland May 29 1774 p. 15.

BARNARD, Letitia, & Thomas Rowntree, in Albemarle, (Jul:) 6
   1767 p. 9.

BARNES, Mary & John Vaughan ffeb: 3 1754 p. 1.

Barns, Sarah, in Westover, & Aaron Parish Jan: 18 1762 p. 6.

BARNET, Eliz: & John Wither feb: 21 1755 p. 1.

Barnet, Susannah, & David Woodrum, both in this parish Sep: 22 1865
   p. 8.

Barnet, Sarah, & Will: Martin, both of Albemarle, Feb: 7 1774 p. 14.

Barnet, Catherine & Sam: Trotman, both of Louisa, Oct: 7 1783 p. 23.

Barnet, Betsey, & Jos: Woodfolk, both of Louisa—15 miles—(J)ul:
   6 1786 p. 24.

BARRET, Mary, & Will: Payne, both in this parish Mar: 6 1755 p. 1.

Barret, Mary, & Dan: Clayton, both in this parish Nov: 13 1758 p. 4.

Barret, Susannah, & Will: Bryan, both in this parish Dec. 24, 1759 p. 5.

BASKET, Mary, & John Nash, both of this parish Dec: 24 1761 p. 6.

BASSET, Hellender, & Thomas ffrancis, both in Manikentown Ap: 7
   1760 p. 5.

BASSIT, Jane, & Bryan Connerly, both on the Bird Jun: 22 1756
   p. 2.

BATTERSBY, Cloe, in Manikentown & Thomas Ballow in Albemarle,
   Mar: 17 1757 p. 3.

BAZE, Mary, & John Woodrum, both in this parish Nov: 15 1761
   p. 4.

BELLAMY, Judith, & Antony Logan, both in Goochland Dec. 16
   1771 p. 13.

Bellamy, Ann, & Ja: Hicks, both in Goochland May 17 1773 p. 14.

BENAUGH, Patsy, & Ja: Sandidge, both in Spotsylvania Jan: 24 1787 p. 24.

BETTESWORTH, Sarah, & Ja: Johnson, both of Louisa May 15 1783 p. 23.

BIB, Eliz: & William fferrar, both in this parish Mar: 17 1762 p. 6.

Bibb, Eliz: & Rob: Groom, both in Louisa Jan: 18 1788 p. 25.

Bibb, Martha, & Jo: Durell, both of Louisa Nov: 20 1788 p. 25.

Bib, Susannah, in this county & James Clark in Louisa May 20 1762 p. 6.

Bibb, Barbara, & James Cobbs, both in Albemarle Nov. 12 1760 p. 5.

Bibb, Susannah, & Rob: Tate both of Louisa Dec: 21 1780 p. 20.

BIGGAR, Mary, in Hanover, & Julius Allen, in Henrico Oct. 11 1768 p. 10.

BIGGARS, Martha, & Sam: Morris, both in Louisa .... 1791 p. 27.

BILBOA, Mary, & Young Short, in Manikentown ffeb: 3 1756 p. 2.

BLACK, Elizabeth, & Charles Woodhall, both of this parish Oct: 1 1765 p. 8.

Black, Sarah, & Zack: Pulham, both in Louisa Feb: 14 1782 p. 21.

BLACKWELL, Mildred, & Sherard Parish, both of this parish Oct: 2 1764 p. 8.

BLACKWAL, Judith & Nath: Raine, both of Louisa Dec: 19 1779 p. 19.

BLETSOE, Betsie, & Lewis Brockman, both in Orange Mar: 12 1779 p. 18.

BOND, Jean, & Stephen Yauncey, both of Louisa Oct: 12 1779 p. 19.

Bond, Eliz: & Cyrus Harris, both in Louisa May 8 1783 p. 23.

BOURN, Jean in Trinity Parish & James Howard in this parish, Jun: 11 1767 p. 9.

BOWDERY, Elizabeth & David Layne, both of this parish, Mar: 17 1768 p. 10.

BOWE, Olney, & Tyree Parrot, both of Louisa Jan: 2 1783 p. 22.

BOWEN, Sarah, & Joel Walker, both of Goochland Jan: 13 1774 p. 14.

BOWLES, Oney, & Andrew Yeargan, both in this parish Jan: 3 1757 p. 3.

Bowles, Sarah, & James Cauthon, both in this parish Sep: 28 1762 p. 7.

Bowles, Susanna, & Jo: Wade, both in Goochland Oct: 13 1770 p. 12

Bowles, Frances, in Hanover, & Josh: Barner in Goochland, Jun: 10 1772 p. 13.

Bowles, Sarah, & Stephen Perkins, both in Goochland Dec: 13 1772 p. 13.

Bowles, Frankie, & Bartlet Ford, both in Goochland Mar: 20 1774 p. 15.

Bowles, Susannah, & William Hughes, both of Hanover Ap: 10 1775 p. 16.

Bowles, Martha & Humphrey Gains, in Goochland Feb: 18 1779 p. 18

Bowles, Jane, in Goochland & Jesse Thomas in Cumberland Feb: 1£ (17) 81 p. 21.

BOYD, Mary, & John Maddox, both in this parish Sep: 5 1755 p. 1.

BRADBERRY, Priscilla, & Benjamin Gibson, both of Manikentown Jan: 21, 1769 p. 11.

BRADLEY, ffrances & Richard Pemberton, both of Manikentown Sep: 1 1757—p. 3.

Bradley, Eliz: & Cha: Davis, both in Orange Ap: 1 1782 p. 22.

BRADSHAW, Mary & Jac: Lane .... 1751—pp. 26, 31.

BRANHUM, Martha, & Dan: Cooper, in Goochland Nov: 7 1779 p. 19.

BRASFUD, Nancy, & Jo: Edwards, both of Spots: Dec. 26 1781 p. 21.

BRIT, Hannah, & William Birkmyre, both in this parish Jan: 2 1768 p. 10.

Britt, Mary, & Wyat Wilkerson, both in this parish Dec. 26 1765 p. 8.

Britt, Elizabeth, & Jacob Luster, both in this parish Aug: 11 1768 p. 10.

Britt, Ann, & Cha: Houchins, both in Goochland Mar: 28 1782 p. 22.

BROADFOOT, Agnes, & Ben McKenzie, both in Goochland Jun: 26 1771 p. 12.

BROCKMAN, Rachel, & Rob: Page, both of Goochland Dec. 26 1773 p. 14.

Brockman, Sukie, & Tho: Garret, in Orange Nov. 16 1780 p. 20.

Brockman, Mary, & Will: White, in Orange Sep: 12 1782 p. 22.

BROOKS, Mary Garret, & Francis Coleman, of Louisa .... (17) 91—p. 27.

BROWN, Mary, & Elkanah Lacy, both in Manikentown Jan: 18 1756 p. 2.

Brown, Ann, & Will: Sadley, both in Goochland Aug. 5 1770 p. 12.

Brown, Juliana, & Littleberry Vaughan, both in Henrico May 22 1774 p. 15.

Brown, Sarah, & Nathan: Williams, both in Henrico Dec. 21 1775 p. 16.

Brown, Mary, & Lancelot Armstrong, in Louisa Feb: 3 1778 p. 18.

BRUMFIELD, Amelia, & Thomas Vaughan, both in this parish feb: 27 1757 p. 3.

Bromfield, Sarah, in this parish & John Dudley in Albemarle, Ap: 7 1763 p. 7.

BRIAN, ..., & John ffairies, both in Albemarle Jan: 12 1755 p. 1.

BRYAN, Eliz: & Isaac Sallie, both in Manikentown May 6 1759 p. 4.

BRYANT, Susanna, & Gideon Martin, both of Albemarle, Oct. 19 1767 p. 10.

Bryant, Rebekah, & Stephen Martin, in Albemarle county Jan. 2 1768 p. 10.

BULLOCK, Mary, & Mathew Martin, both in this parish Nov: 2 1763—p. 7.

BULLINGTON, Susannah, & John Macomack, both in this parish Jan. 9 1763 p. 7.

BULLINTON, Jean & Philip Ryan .... 1751 pp 26, 31.

BUNCES, Frances Tandy, & Will Bush, both in Orange Dec. 9 1778 p. 18.

BUNCH, Jeanie, & Geo. Chewning, both of Louisa May 29 1783 p. 23.

Bunch, Sarah, & Mattox Stanley, both in Louisa Jul: 22 1784 p. 23.

BURFORD, Betty, & [George Love]L, [torn] both in this parish 1764 p. 7.

BURGESS, Ann, & Will Bolding, both from Albemarle Jul: 6 1772 p. 13.

BURNER, Eliz: & Jac: ffleurnoy, in Maniken Town Oct. 27 1755 p. 2.

BURTON, Ann, & Rob: Payne, both in this parish Jul: 22 1762 p. 6.

Burton, Eliz: & John Holman, both in this May 20 1770 p. 11.

BYERS, Jean, & Sherard Mathews, both of Louisa Jan. 7 1779 p. 18.

Byers, Martha & Nathaniel Harris, both of Louisa May 29 1788 p. 25.

Byers, Sally, & Will: Cole, in Louisa Jan: 15 1789 p. 25.

CADDEL, Jean, & Math: Riddle, both of Goochland Jan: 9 1779 p. 18.

CANNON, Fanny, & Ja: Walker, both in Goochland Jun: 26 1774 p. 15.

Cannon, Eliz: in ys. parish & John Lewis in Carolina Feb. 8 1776 p. 17—

Cannon, Betsie, & Drury Alford, in Louisa Mar: 13 1782 p. 22.

CARPENTER, Eliz: & Tho: Bibb, both in Louisa Dec: 4 1787— p. 25.

CARROL, Eliz: & Rob: Smith, both in Goochland Ap: 28 1771 p. 12.

CARTER, Judith on Lickinghole, & Charles Carter in Cumberland, Jun: 24 1756 p. 2.

Carter, Mary, & Thomas Dawson, both in this parish Dec. 26 1756 p. 3.

Carter, Susannah, & Joseph Jackson, both of this parish Aug. 28 1760 p. 5.

Carter, Judith, & David Webster, both in this Ap: 10 1770 p. 11.

CAUTHAN, Sarah, in this parish, & John Sutton-Bowman, in Pr. Edward, Dec. 27 1756—p. 3.

Cauthan, Susannah, & Jeremiah Johnson, both in this parish ffeb: 26 1759 p. 4.

Cauthon, Lucy, & Math: Nightingale, both in this parish Dec. 26 1759 p. 5.

Cauthan, Eadith, & John Page, both in this parish Oct. 31 1761 p. 6.

Cauthon, Mary, & David Alvis, both of this parish Aug. 20 1768 p. 10.

CAWLEY, Martha, & William Wright, both in this parish Oct. 5 1769 p. 11.

Cawley, Hannah, & Roderick Wright, both in this parish Oct. 31 1769 p. 11.

Cawley, Ann, & Jo: Tuggle, both in Goochland Jul: 29 1770 p. 12.

CHACE, Ann, & Archelaus Thacher, both of Louisa, Jul: 31 1781 p. 21.

Chace, Sarah, & Geo: Bond, both of Louisa, June 10 1785 p. 24.

CHAMNEYS, Million, & John-David Coleman, both in this parish, Feb: 12 1762 p. 6.

CHANCELLOR, Mary, in Goochland & Will: Ryan in Albemarle Dec: 2 1773 p. 14.

CHANDLER, Esther, & Absalom Smith, both of Orange, Oct 26 1781 p. 21.

Chandler, Sally, & Arch: McNeal, both of Orange Feb: 14 1782 p. 22.

CHAPMAN, Winnifred, & Tho: East, in Goochland .... 1751— pp. 26, 31.

CHASTAIN, Judith, & Robert Scot, both in Manikentown 30 Oct: 1762 p. 6.

Chastain, Magdalene, & William Porter, both of Manikentown 13 Feb: 1765 p. 8.

CHIECHESTER, Mary, & Burgess Ball, in Goochland Jul: 2 1770 p. 12.

CHILDERS, Jemima, & Anthony Askew, both in this parish Aug: 30 1759 p. 4.

CHILDRES, Susannah, & Joseph Adkinson, both in Hanover, Feb. 25 1767 p. 9.

CHILES, Sarah, & Jo: Daniel, both in Louisa Feb. 3 1780 p. 19.

CHRISTIAN, Eliz: in this parish; & John Humber in St. Pauls Par. Mar: 30 1757 p. 3.

Christian, Mary, & Ja: Grason, both in Goochland Dec. 19 1770 p. 12.

Christian, Judith, & Ben: Lacy, both in Goochland Oct. 25 1774 p. 15.

CLAPTON, Mary, & David Hutson, in Louisa June 26 1788—p. 25.

CLARK, Hannah, & Drury Johnson (or Johnston) both of ys parish, Oct: 14 1751 pp. 26, 31.

Clark, Eliz: & Ja: Thackston, both in this parish Sep: 20 1753 p. 1.

Clark, Elizabeth, & John Hubbard, both in this parish May 31 1763 p. 7.

Clark, Sarah, & Abram Parish, both in this parish Oct. 8 1767 p. 10.

Clark, Milly, & Moses Kidd, both in Albemarle Sep: 29 1768 p. 10.

Clark, Eliz: & Will: Haley, both in Louisa Nov. 1 1773 p. 14.

Clark, Fanny, & Rob: Pleasants, both in Goochland Dec. 4 1773 p. 14.

Clark, Nanny, of ys Parish, & John Fielder of Prince Edward, Dec. 27 1774 p. 16.

Clark, Ann, in Albemarle, & Nath: Massie, of this Parish Aug. 24 1776 p. 17.

Clark, Sarah, & Robert Shepherd, both of ys parish Feb. 23 1777 p. 17.

Clark, Mary, & Jo: Fulcher, both of Fluvanna Feb: 4 1779 p. 18.

Clark, Judith, & Lewis Atkins, both of Goochland Nov. 28 1780 p. 20.

Clark, Winnifred, & Will Atkinson, in Goochland June 22 1784 p. 23.

CLARKSON, Susannah, & Jacob Maddox, both in this parish, Jan: 9 1758 p. 3.

Clarkson, Elizabeth, & Richard Baldock, both in this parish, Mar: 23 1761 p. 5.

Clarkson, Mary, & Job Martin, both in this parish Sep: 24, 1765 p. 8.

Clarkson, Nancy, & Jo: Utley, both in Goochland Dec. 23 1772 p. 13.

Clarkson, Ann, & Will: Pledge, both in Goochland, Feb. 16 1773 p. 14.

Clarkson, Mary, & Jo: Herndon, both of Goochland, Dec. 27 1773 p. 14.

Clarkson, Patty & James Salmon, both of ys parish Dec. 5 1776 p. 17.

Clarkson, Eliz: & Ja: Johnson, both of Louisa Jan: 28 1779 p. 18.

Clarkson, Eliz: & Ja: Martin, both of Fluvanna Feb. 4 1779 p. 18.

CLASBIE, Winny, & Ephraim Musick, in Albemarle Oct. 3 1786— p. 24.

CLAYTON, Rebekah, in this parish & Julius Burton in Henrico Mar: 10 1763 p. 7.

CLEMENTS, Lucy, & Charles Houchens, both in this parish Sep: 20 1753 p. 1.

Clements, Joice, & ffrancis Houchins, both in this parish Jan: 10 1758 p. 3.

Clements, Anner, & Richard Allen, both of ys parish Aug. 28 1777 p. 18.

Clements, Eliz: & Clayburn Bradshaw, both of Goochland Dec. 28 1779 p. 19.

Clements, Lovinah, & Jo: Fleming, both in Louisa Dec. 10 1783 p. 23.

COAKER, Mildred, & Ephraim Knight, both in Louisa Oct. 15 1780 p. 20.

COBBS, Mary, in Albemarle & William Harrison in this parish, Jan: 1 1761 p. 5.

Cobb, Ann, & George Henderson, both of this parish Dec. 23 1761 p. 6.

Cobbs, Judith, & John Cobbs, in Albemarle Sep: 19 1763 p. 7.

COCKE, Sarah, & Charles Clark, both in Goochland, Oct. 23 1773 p. 14.

Cocke, Eliz: Pleasants, & Will: Roberts, both in Goochland Jan.: 3 1774 p. 14.

Cocke, Eliz: & Will: Hodges, both in Goochland Jun: 2 1774 p. 15.

COKE, Obedient, & John Hilton, both in this parish Nov. 24 1757 p. 3.

COLE, Mary, & George Barclay, both of this parish Aug. 7 1766 p. 9.

Cole, Lucy, & Is. Winston, both in Hanover Jun: 2 1770 p. 12.

Cole, Eliz: & Will: Bond, both of Louisa Aug. 23 1787 p. 24.

Cole, Lydia, & Will: Tally, both of Louisa [Mar]ch 1791 p. 27.

Cole, Barbara, & Mich: Tally, both in Louisa .... 1793 p. 27.

Cole, Sally, & Geo: Tally, in Louisa maried Dec: 26 1793 p. 28.

COLEMAN, Lucy, & Will: Thornwell, both in this parish Dec. 5 1757 p. 3.

Coleman, Annie, & Jo: Bromfield, both in Goochland May 16 1773 p. 14.

Coleman, Eliz: & James Isabel, both of ys parish Feb. 20 1776 p. 17.

Coleman, Betsie, & Howel Lewis, both of Goochland May 3 1780 p. 19.

Coleman, Nelly, & Ben: Adams, both of Orange Ap: 13 1781 p. 21.

COLLINS, Ann, & Ed. Collins, both from Orange May 31 1781 p. 21.

COMBER, Elizabeth, & Will: Williams, both of this parish Dec. 30 1762 p. 7.

CONOLLY, Helender & Henry Tuggle, both in Goochland .... 1751 pp. 26, 32.

CONWAY, Mary, & Daniel Jennings, both in Henrico Jul: 5 1767 p. 9.

COOK, Frances, & Jo: Thomason, both of Louisa Dec. 23 1780 p. 20.

CORLEY, Afarillah, & Tho: Williamson, both in this parish Feb: 18 1762 p. 6.

COSBIE, Mary, & Jo: Cesar, both in Goochland Feb: 11 1773 p. 14.

Cosby, Eliz: of this parish & Will Jones of Cumberland, Dec. 27 1774 p. 16.

Cosby, Mary, & Will: Bowman, both of Goochland Dec. 28 1779 p. 19.

COSTILLA, Eliz: & James Riddle, both of ys Parish Mar: 17 1776 p. 17.

COTHAN, Rebekah, & Benjamin Hughes, both in this parish, Aug. 30 1756 p. 2 [see Cauthon].

COX, Glafre, & Jos: Davis, both in this parish Sep: 16 1759 p. 4.

CRADOCK, Eliz: & Will: Harris, both in this parish Aug. 28 1754 p. 1.

CRAIG, Eliz: & Will: Bletsoe, both of Spots. May 1 1781 p. 21.

CRAIGWALL, Eliz: in this parish & Rob: Bowman in Chesterfield, Ap: 1 1765 p. 8.

CRAM, Sally & Mathew Taylor, both of ys parish, Nov. 7 1776 p. 17. married by Mr. Todd irregularly.

CRANK, Jeanie & Jo: White, both in Louisa Jan: 21 1790 p. 25.

CREASY, Mary, & John Robertson, both in Albemarle, Oct. 13 1762 p. 7.

CRENSHAW, Mary, & Will: Isabel both in Goochland Jun: 5 1774. p. 15.

Crenshaw, Susanna & Jo: Burnley, both of Louisa Dec. 15 1785 p. 24.

CROUCH, Sarah, in this parish, & Tho: Caldwell in Henrico Aug. 30 1756 p. 2.

Crouch, Judith & Jo: Lewis, both of this parish Aug. 27 1762 p. 6.

CROW, Mary, & Jesse Blackwel, both of ys parish Jan: 8 1776 p. 17.

CURD, Ann, & Edward Radford, both in this parish Jul: 22 1762 p. 6.

Curd, Mary, & Edmund Curd, both in this parish Mar: 18 1764 p. 8.

Curd, Elizabeth, & John Bowles, in this parish Dec. 2 1764 p. 8.

Curd, Sarah, & Knight Bowles, in this parish Feb. 19 1767 p. 9.

Curd, Mary, & Benjamin Perkins, both in this parish Dec. 18 1768 p. 11.

Curd, Elizabeth, & George Underwood, both in this parish Dec. 25 1768 p. 11.

Curd, Ann, & Richard Sampson, both in Goochland Nov. 24 1771 p. 13.

Curd, Lucy, & Cha: Watkins, in Goochland Dec. 23 1772 p. 13.

Curd, Lucy, & Tho: Hatcher, both in Goochland Sep. 16 1782 p. 22.

Curd, Nancy, & Julius Curle, both in Goochland Mar: 7 1789 p. 25.

CURRY, Agnes, & Antony Logan, both in this parish Dec. 9 1759 p. 4.

DABNEY, Elizabeth, & Christopher Johnson, both of Hanover, Feb. 22 1777 p. 17.

Dabney, Cecily & Tho: Shilton, both of Louisa Feb. 20 1782 p. 22.

DAIR, Lucy & Rob: Lancaster, both of Orange Nov: 7 1780 p. 20.

DANIEL, Susannah, & Turner Anderson, in Louisa (asked only) Jun: 12 1776 p. 17.

Daniel, Ann, & Will: Terril, both in Orange Nov. 26 1780 p. 20.

Daniel, Sally, in Louisa, & Armistead Brown in Cumberland May 17 1781 p. 21.

Daniel, Jeanie, & Geo. Quisenberry, both of Orange June 4 1783 p. 23.

DARRACOT, Cecelia, & Richmond Terrill, in Louisa Ap: 25 1782 p. 22.

DAVIS, Martha, & Sanders Southerland, in Albemarle Dec. 22 1758 p. 4.

Davis, Mary, & Rich: Clopton both in this parish Sep: 16 1759 p. 4.

Davis, Sarah, & Bryan Conoly, both of this parish Feb. 11 1767 p. 9.

Davis, Frances & Spencer James, both in Orange Aug. 22 1780 p. 20.

Davis, Constance & Tho: Mallory, both in Louisa Oct. 4 1781 p. 21.

Davis, Susannah, & Will White, both in Louisa May 9 1780 p. 22.

Davis, Mary, & Rob: Harris, both in Louisa Jul. 22 1784 p. 23.

DAWSON, Sarah, & Francis Hilley, both of ys parish .... 1753 p. 31.

Dawson, Ann, & Meshack Hicks, both in this parish May 5 1765 p. 8.

Dawson, Mary, & Thomas Norvil, both of this parish Jan. 7 1768 p. 10.

DAY, Nancy, & Tho: Cawson, both in Spots: Dec. 23 1784 p. 23.

DEAR, Frances, & Will: Harvey, in this county Nov: 6 1794 p. 28.

DENTON, Susannah, & Ambrose Stodghill, in Hanover Jan: 24 1763 p. 7.

DePEE, Susannah, & James Lock, in Maniken Town Sep: 20 1753 p. 1.

Depee, Mary, & Ben: Hatcher Ap: 25 1754 p. 1.

DEPP, Eleanor, & William Johnson, both in Maniken Town Sep: 17 1776 p. 17.

DICKERSON, Francis & Geo: Edwards, both in Louisa Jul: 22 1784 p. 23.

DOUGLAS, Margaret, & Nicholas Merriwether in this parish Dec: 31 1760 p. 5. She's my child.

DOWDY, Catherine, & John Everie, both in ys parish Sep: 15 1776 p. 17.

DRUMRIGHT, Eliz: in Goochland, & Jo: Clark in Louisa Ap: 16
1772 p. 13.

DUDLEY, Judith, & Jos: Dawson, both in this parish Nov. 20 1753
p. 1.

DUNHAM, Eliz: & Sam: fferguson, both of this parish Jan: 25
1759 p. 4.

DURHAM, Sarah, & Dan: Weaver, both in Maniken-Town Nov. 11
1756 p. 2.

DU VAL, Susanna, & Jos. Ellis, both in Henrico Nov. 25 1770 p. 12.

DYCHES, Eliz: & Jo: Barker, both in Goochland Oct. 24 1772 p. 13.

Dyches, Judith, & Ben: Haley, both in Louisa Feb. 18 1779 p. 18.

DYER, Martha & Reuben Tally, both of Louisa, Oct. 7 1773 p. 14.

EADSON, Rebecca, & Dan: Bentley, both of Fluvanna, May 15 1780
p. 20.

EASLY, Sarah, in this parish, & David Hudlestone in Henrico Mar:
17 1757 p. 3.

EAST, Edeth, & Thomas Pierce, both in this parish Nov: 22 1760 p. 5.

East, Lucy, & Jesse Edwards, both of this parish Mar: 5 1768 p. 10.

East, Martha, & Tho: Glass, both in Goochland Mar: 23 1773 p. 14.

EDWARDS, Eliz: & Ben: Granger, both of ys parish Betw. 1750-53
p. 31.

Edwards, Elizabeth, & Charles Johnson, both in Goochland Oct. 18
1768 p. 10.

Edwards, Lucy, in Louisa, & Ja: Barlow in Albemarle Jan: 13 1780
p. 19.

Edwards, Mildred, & Jos: Rawson, both in Spots: Jul: 4 1782 p. 22.

Edwards, Judith, & Will Arnold, in Spots: Sep: 16 1784 p. 23.

Edwards, Eliz: & Joseph Smith, of Louisa Jan: 8 1789 p. 25.

ELAM, Ann, & John Godsey, both in Manikentown Nov. 14 1762 p. 7.

ELDRIDGE, Judith, & Leonard Price, both in Goochland Nov: 10
1770 p. 12.

ELLIOT, Catie & .... Fletcher, in Spotsylvania ....
p. 27.

ELLIS, Susannah, & Tho: Lewis, both in Henrico Jun: 1 1758 p. 4.

Ellis, Lucy, in Henrico, and Davis Johnson, in this Ap: 13 1762 p. 6.

Ellis, Mary, & Hezekiah Perriere, both in Henrico Aug. 16 1764 p. 8.

Ellis, Mary & William Maddox, in Henrico Mar: 7 1765 p. 8.

Ellis, Martha & Will: Ogilsvy, in Henrico Dec. 29 1771 p. 13.

Ellis, Ann, & Hezekiah Periere, both in Henrico Dec. 17 1773 p. 14.

Ellis, Susannah, of Henrico & John Williams of ys Jan: 12 1775 p. 16.

Ellis, Sally, in Henrico & Peter Wilson in Pittsylvania Ap: 18 1775
p. 16.

EMMERSON, Jean, & John ffurlong, both in this Oct. 17 1766 p. 9.

Emmerson, Neffeny, & Benjamin Thacker, both in this parish Nov. 5
1767 p. 10.

Emmerson, Judith, & William Fairies, both of this parish Ap: 27
1775 p. 16.

ENGLAND, Ann, & Will: Page, both in this parish Dec. 11 1764 p. 8.

England, Lory & Sherwood Tony, both in this parish Feb: 7 1765 p. 8.

England, Mary, & James Page, both of this parish May 16 1765 p. 8.

England, Marianne, & Jo: Clements, both in Goochland Aug: 29 1771 p. 12.

England, Susannah, & Will: Martin, both of ys parish Dec. 19 1776 p. 17.

England, Marg: & Stephen Grimes, in Goochland Oct. 18 1778 p. 18.

EPPERSON, Eliz: & Jo: Rogers, both in Goochland Oct. 26 1771 p. 12.

EVANS, Mary & Alman Guin, both in Goochland .... 1751 pp. 26, 32.

Evans, Ann, & William Barker, both in this parish Jul: 27 1769 p. 11.

Evans, Eliz: & Will: Harris, both in Cumberland Jun: 15 1770 p. 12.

Evans, Sus: in Goochland, & Rob: Carter in Henrico Ap: 15 1772 p. 13.

FAIRIES, Elizabeth, & William Anderson England, both of this parish Jan: 15 1765 p. 8.

Fairies, Judith, & Jonathan Black, both of ys parish Dec. 19 1775 p. 16.

Fairies, Lettitia, & Richard Carleton, both of ys parish Feb: 4 1777 p. 17.

FALCONER, Catie, & Jo: Almond, both in Orange Oct. 7 1778 p. 18.

FARMER, Ann, & Is: Web, both in Goochland Oct. 25 1770 p. 12.

Farmer, Mary & Will: Web, both in Goochland Nov. 25 1770 p. 12.

Farmer, Mary, & Job: Harris, both of Louisa Sep. 5 1785 p. 24.

FAUKENER, Lucy & Ben: McAlister, both of Louisa Aug: 19 1788 p. 25.

FFENTON, Ann in Henrico, & Josiah Leak in this parish Jan 1 1759 p. 4.

ffenton, Jean, & Will: Rowntree, in Henrico Nov: 4 1759 p. 4.

ffenton, Lucy & Benjamin Collevel, both in Henrico Dec. 13 1764 p. 8.

FFERRAR, Lucy, & Stephen Woodson, both of this parish May 9 1758 p. 4.

fferrar, Eliz: & John fford, both in this parish Jan: 22 1762 pp. 6, 32.

fferrar, Elizabeth & Stephen Crouch, both of this parish May 16 1762 p. 6.

fferrar, Sarah, & James Bibb, both of this parish ffeb: 6 1763 p. 7.

fferrar, Christian, & Joseph Ellis, both of this parish Feb: 5 1769 p. 11.

Ferrar, Mary, & Jos: Morris, both in Goochland May 12 1771 p. 12.

Ferrer, Keturah, & Hez: Henley, both in Goochland Aug. 4 1772 p. 13.

Ferrar, Christian, in Henrico & Arch: Pledge, in Goochland Feb: 17 1774 p. 14.

Ferrar, Eliz: & Rob: Barnard, both in Goochland June 13 1779 p. 19.

FIELDER, Mary, & John Craigwall, both in this parish May 10 1756 p. 2.

ffielder, Mary & William Woodhall, both of this parish Ap: 12 1759 p. 4.

FFLEMING, Eliz: & Josias Payne, both in this parish Aug. 23 1755 p. 1.

ffleming, Mrs. Hannah, in this parish, & Geor: Webb, in Hanover Apl. 15 1756 p. 2.

Fleming, Mary, & Rich: Luck both of Louisa, Ja: Sandidge, Surety Mar: 14 1788 p. 25.

Fleming, Eliz: & Benjamin Renolds, in Louisa Feb. 5 1789 p. 25.

Fleming, Nancy, & Jo: Leek, both of Louisa Mar: 9 1789 p. 25.

FFLOURNOY, Ursley, & James Harris, both in Manikentown May 26 1769 p. 11.

FORD, Molly & .... Oct: 14, 1751 pp. 26-31.

Ford, Cecily, & Ja: Adams, in Goochland .... 1751 pp. 26, 32.

fford, Jeanie, & Capt. Hugh Moss, both in this parish Jun: 4 1768 p. 10.

fford, ffrances, & Thomas Catlett, both in this parish Jan: 23 1759 p. 4.

Ford, Mary, & Augustine Easton, both in Goochland Sep: 6 1772 p. 13.

Ford, Nancy, & John Kay, both of ys county Oct. 19 1776 p. 17.

FORE, Elizabeth, & John Cox, both in Manikentown Jun: 22 1766 p. 9.

FFORSEY, Marianne, & John Maxey, both in Manikentown Jan. 19 1758 p. 3.

FOSTER, Aggie, & William Mattox, both of Buckingham Dec. 10 1775 p. 16.

FOUNTAINE, Mary Ann, & Fortunatus Cosby, in Louisa Nov: 1 (17)95 p. 28.

FFOWLER, Elizabeth, & Pleasants Cocke, both in this parish Jul: 1 1762 p. 6.

FOX, Catherine, & Col. Rich: Anderson, both of Louisa Ap: 24, 1780 p. 19.

Fox, Susannah, & Tho: Wash, both of Louisa (by Mr. Tod) Jan. 4 1785 p. 23.

FFRANKLIN, Sarah, & Will: Wilkerson, both in this parish Jul: 11 1761 p. 6.

FREEMAN, Ann & Absalom Meldon, Feb: 3 [17]97 p. 28.

FFREESON, Susannah, & Henry Going, both of this parish Jul: 22 1764 p. 8.

FRENCH, Edee, in this parish & Isaac Clark, in Louisa, Feb: 7 1775 p. 16.

FFULCHER, Eliz: & Thomas Hill, both of ys parish Nov. 25 1775 p. 16.

Fulcher, Martha of Fluvanna & Jo: Haley of Louisa Mar: 17 1779 p. 19.

FURCRAN, Betty, & Edward Masters, both in Cumberland Mar: 12 1761 p. 5.

ffurkerant, Eliz: & David Stanford, both in Maniken-town Dec. 16 1759 p. 5.

GAINS, Martha-Ward, & Thomas Turpin, in Manikentown Ap: 9 1767 p. 9.

GARDENER, Temperance & Will: Gammon both in Louisa Dec. 26 1789 p. 25.

Gardener, Lucy, & Da: Allen, both of Louisa Dec. 25 1780 p. 20.

Gardener, Polly & Tho: Harris, in Spotsylvania were maried ....⌐ 1793 p. 27.

GARLAND, Ann, & Jo: Lane, both of Louisa Feb: 6 1781 p. 21.

Garland, Barbara, & Lewis Johnson, both in Louisa Jan: 5 1788 p. 25.

Garland, Mary, & Thornton Mead, both of Louisa Jan: 24 1788 p. 25.

Garlan, Judith & Jo: Sladon, in Louisa Oct: 4 1788 p. 25.

Garland, Sar: & Sam: Nichols, both in Louisa Feb: 29 1789 (sic) [1788] p. 25.

GARRAT, Magdalen, & Rob: Moseley, both in Manikentown Sep: 23 1756 p. 2.

Garret, Magdalen & Tho: Smith, both in Manikentown Oct. 15 1756 p. 2.

Garrot, Sabrine, & John Hendrick, both in Maniken Town Ap: 4 1757 p. 3.

GARTEN, Susanna, & Will: Cook, both of Orange June 13 1785 p. 24.

Gorton, Eliz: & Malachie Chiles, both in Orange Nov. 29 1778 p. 18.

GENTRY, Diana, & George Cothan, both in this parish Mar: 22 1761 p. 5.

Gentry, Nancy & Tho: Bailey both in Louisa May 7 1780 p. 20.

GEORGE, Agatha, & George Payne, both in this parish Dec. 26 1754 p. 1.

George, Susannah, of Goochland, & Geo: Holland of Louisa, Nov. 7 1779 p. 19.

GILBERT, Lydia, & John Walker, both of this parish Mar: 2 1769 p. 11.

Gilbert, Eliz: & Da: Walker, both in Goochland Oct. 13 1770 p. 12.

GILCHRIST, Judah, & Ben: Merrit, both in this parish Nov. 10 1755 p. 2.

GLASS, Eliz: & James Johnson, both of ys parish Nov: 3 1776 p. 17.

GOLDSMITH, Mercy, & Francis Wright, both in Goochland May 30 1771 p. 12.

GOOD, Mary, & Rich: Timberlick, both in this parish Dec. 22 1759 p. 5.

GOODRICH, Patience & Will: Chace, in Louisa .... (17)90 p. 27.

GOODWIN, Eliz: & Spencer Coleman of Louisa May 22 1787 p. 24.

GORDON, Lucy & Jo: Garland, both in Louisa .... 1790 p. 27.

GOUCH, Eliz: & Joseph Wright, both in Louisa .... 25 1790 p. 27.

GRANT, Eliz: & Ja: Burnley, both in Fluvanna Feb. 5 1779 p. 18.

GRAY, Anna, & James Scot, both of Louisa my overseer Sep: 8 1777 p. 18.

GRAYSON, Sarah, & Benjamin Ainsley, both of this parish Mar: 20 1769 p. 11.

GRAVES, ..., & Thomas Barnet ffeb. 3 1754 p. 1.

Graves, Mary, & James Curd, both in this Nov. 20 1766 p. 9.

Graves, Ann & Joseph Mosely, both of this parish Mar: 17 1768 p. 10.

Graves, Sally, in Goochland & Barret Price in Henrico Aug. 25 1771 p. 12.

Graves, Molly, & Will: Arnet, both in Louisa Dec. 27 1781 p. 21.

Graves, Sarah & Joel Graves in Orange .... 21 (17)90—p. 27.

GREADY, Frances & Wright Bond both of Louisa Jul: 6 1788 p. 25.

GREEN, Susan & Tho: Hutton, both in Goochland Sep: 29 1772 p. 13.

Green, Mary, & Philip Childers, both in Goochland Nov. 21 1773 p. 14.

Green, Martha, & Forest Green, both of Louisa Jan. 28 1780 p. 19.

Green, Molley, & Overton Baker, both in Louisa Aug. 10 1780 p. 20.

GRIFFIN, Mary, & John Blackburn, both of ys parish Dec. 14 1776 p. 17.

GRIFFITHS, Rebekah, & William Blunkhall, both in this parish, May 27 1764 p. 8.

GROOM, Sar: & Will: Slaydon, both in Goochland, Aug. 16 1770 p. 12.

Groom, Molly, & Tho: Lane, both in Goochland Jul: 31 1773 p. 14.

Groom, Nannie, & Hen: Harrison, both in Spots. Jul. 18 1782 p. 22.

Groom, Mary, & Jo: Atkins, both of Spots: Aug. 1 1782. p. 22.

GRUB, Ann, & Edward Lawry, both in this parish feb. 21 1757 p. 3.

GUERRANT, Jane, & James Bryant, both in Manikentown Jun: 11 1758 p. 4.

Gerrand, Mary & Jos. Pleasants, both in Goochland Ap: 23 1772 p. 13.

GUILLAM, Cecily, & Edward Cox, both in this parish Dec. 10 1767 p. 10.

Guillam, Mary of this parish & Charles Snead in Henrico, Dec. 22 1767 p. 10.

Guillam, Judith & Callum Bailey, both of ys parish Jul: 25 1776 p. 17.

GUTHRIE, Philadelphia, & Richard Elliot, in Cumberland Ap: 29 1768 p. 10.

HADDEN, Rach: in this parish & James Johnson in St. Pauls Dec. 15 1755 p. 2.

HADEN, Sarah, & Richmond Pearson, both in Albemarle Nov. 5 1772 p. 13.

HALEY, Tabitha, & Ja: Dyches, both in Louisa Nov. 8 1773 p. 14.

Haley, Sarah, & Will: Dyches, both in Louisa Sep. 28 1778 p. 18.

Haly, Delany, & Henry Dyches, both in Louisa Jan. 10 1779 p. 18.

HALL, Frances & Jesse Pace, both of ys parish Jan: 29 1776 p. 17.

Hall, Sarah, & Will: Woodward, both of Louisa Oct. 12 1784. p. 23.

HAMPTON, Sarah, in this Parish & Henry Straiton, in Cumberland, Dec. 26 1753 p. 1.

Hampton, Sally, & Ben: Holliday, both in Louisa Oct. 26 1783 p. 23.

HANCOCK, Agnes, & Stephen Hicks, both in this parish Aug: 24 1758 p. 4.

Hancock, Eliz: & John Sanders, both in this parish Oct. 23 1758 p. 4.

Hancock, Marianne, & William Woodhall, both in this parish, Dec. 3 1758 p. 4.

HANCOKE, Judith & Rich: Wade, both in Goochland Nov. 8 1772 p. 13.

HANSON, Mary & Michael Oseburn Dec: 20 1751 pp. 26-31.

Hanson, Ann, & Stephen Atkinson, both in this parish May 15 1762 p. 6.   L

Hanson, Judith & Fisher-Rice Bennet both in Albemarle Dec. 13 1768 p. 11.

HARDINE, Sarah, & Thomas Pollard, both of this parish Jan: 20 1763 p. 7.

HARLOW, Agness, & John Gowen, both of this parish Mar: 28 1758 p. 4.

Harlow, Lucy, & John ffaries, both in this parish Jul: 26 1762 p. 6.

Harlow, Ann, & Will: Priddy, both in Hanover Ap: 25 1771 p. 12.

HARRIS, Eliz: & Jos. Hodges, both in this parish Dec. 14 1756 p. 2.

Harris, Mary, & John Morris, both in this parish Aug. 2 1756 p. 2.

Harris, Isabel, & Nicholas Childers, both in this parish Dec. 20 1756 p. 2.

Harris, Eliz: & Peter Walker, both in Cumberland Dec. 23 1756 p. 3.

Harris, Phoebe, & Joseph-Royal fferrar, in Manikentown Aug. 3 1762 p. 6.

Harris, Barsheba, & John Yarborough, both in this parish Oct. 22 1762 p. 7.

Harris, Sarah & [Peter Walker]* [torn] in Manikentown .... 1764 p. 7.

Harris, Mary, & Barnard Markham, both in Manikentown May 14 1767 p. 9.

Harris, Mary, in Manikentown, & Sion Spencer in Charlotte county, May 20 1769 p. 11.

Harris, Ann, in Manikentown, & Joel Eustace in Lunenburg Oct. 15 1770 p. 12.

Harris, Morning, & David Ellis, both of ys parish Dec. 29 1775 p. 17.

Harris, Mary, & Ja: Vaughan, both of ys parish Jan. 20 1777 p. 17.

Harris, Sarah, & Barret Ferrar, both of Goochland Mar: 15, 1779 p. 19.

Harris, Eliz: & Will: Denton, both in Goochland Feb: 7 1779 p. 18.

Haris, Mary, & Will: Bryant, in Fluvanna May 26 1780 p. 20.

Harris, Ann, & Hickerson Cosbie, in Louisa Oct. 13 1780 p. 20.

Harris, Nancy, & Jo: Baker, both of Louisa Feb. 12 (17)81 p. 21.

Haris, Barbara, & Joel: Harkins, both of Louisa Sep: 20 1781 p. 21.

Harris, Jemima & Overton Harris, both in Louisa Sep: 16 1789 p. 25.

Harris, Eliz: & Gravet Edwards both of Louisa .... (17)91 p. 27.

*From birth entries.

HARRISON, Ann on the Byrd in this county, & John Ware, in Caroline, May 27 1756 p. 2.

Harrison, Dianna, in this parish, & Ben: Martin in Albemarle Aug: 21 1766 p. 9.

Harrison, Frances, & Will: Richardson, both in this May 23 1770 p. 11.

HAWES, Unity & John Page, both in this parish Nov; 14 1756 p. 2.

HAWKINS, Matty, & Thomas Landrum, both in Manikentown Oct. 1 1759 p. 4.

Hawkins, Lucy, & Edward Briers, both in Manikentown Oct. 18 1761 p. 6.

Hawkins, Susanna, & Tho: Coleman, of Orange Jul: 2 1781 p. 21.

Hawkins, Ann, & Will: Ingram, both of Spots: Oct. 8 1782 p. 22.

HEMUS, Hannah, & Thomas Watson, both in this parish Ap: 11 1757 p. 3.

HENDERSON, Sally, & Thomas Whitlock, both of ys parish Jun: 9, 1776 p. 17.

Henderson, Ann, & Will: Hendrick, both of Louisa Dec. 19 1782 p. 22.

HENLY, Keziah, & Cha: Johnson, both in Goochland Dec. 8 1771 p. 13.

Henley, Eliz: & Sam: Periere, both of ys parish Nov. 24 1775 p. 16.

HERNDON, Eliz: & Joseph Baker, both of ys parish Jul: 11 1773 p. 16.

HEWBANKS, Frances, & James Overstreet, both in this county May 31, 1767 p. 9.

HICKS, Cat: in this parish & Sylvanus Stokes in Cumberland Sep: 21 1755 p. 2.

Hicks, Diana, & Nathan Whitlock, both of this parish Sep. 7 1756 p. 2.

Hicks, Cary, & Beverly Clark, both in this Nov: 17 1766 p. 9.

Hicks, Mary & Charles Nicols, in ys parish Jan: 5 1775 p. 16.

Hicks, Eliz: & Jo: Gerrant .... 175.... pp. 27-32.

Hicks, Jean & Jo: Gerrand .... 1751 pp. 26-31. [See Hix.]

HILL, Eliz: & Joel Parish, both in this parish Dec. 26 1757 p. 3.

Hill, Mary, & Moses Parish, both in this parish Jan. 29 1761 p. 5.

Hill, Frances & Spencer Norvil, both of this parish Feb. 22 1770 p. 11.

Hill, Ann, & Elijah Hawkins, both of Orange Jan: 20 1787 p. 24.

HINDS, Mary, & Will: James, both in Hanover, Jul: 14 1774 p. 15.

Hinds, Sarah & Mathew Wingfield, both in Hanover Dec. 21 1775 p. 17.

HIX, Unity, & Will: Thompson, of Louisa—4 miles—Ap: 18 1786 p. 24. [See Hicks.]

HODGES, Susannah, & John Sladen, both in this parish Dec. 20 1756 p. 2.

Hodges, Mary, & Dan: Grub, both in this parish May 6 1757 p. 3.

Hodges, Elizabeth, & John Jackson, both in this parish Ap. 9 1761 p. 5.

Hodges, Martha & Samuel Mosely, both in this parish May 12 1761 p. 6.

Hodges, Agnes, & Marvel Nash, both in this parish Oct. 26 1762 p. 7.

Hodges, Sarah, & James Kennedy, in this parish Jan: 12 1763 p. 7.

Hodges, Lucy, & Da: England, both in Goochland Nov: 12 1772 p. 12.

Hodges, Eliz: & Tho: Wayford, both in Goochland May 1 1774 p. 15.

HOLLOWDAY, Nancy, & Jo: Rawlings, both in Spot: Ap: 1 1783. p. 23.

Holyday, Martha & Jo: Holyday, both of Spotsylvania Nov. 10 1785 p. 24.

Holyday, Betty, & Ben: Rawlines, both of Spotsyl: Dec. 25 1785 p. 24.

Holladay, Mary, & Austin Sandidge, in Spotsylvania Sep: 28 1785 p. 24.

Holladay, Susannah, & Tho: Garnet, both of Spotsyl: Aug. 9 1787 p. 24.

Holladay, Agness, & Joseph Holladay, in Spotsylvania Jan: 11 1787 p. 24.

HOLLAND, Ann, widow in this parish & Benjamin Mitchell, in New Kent, Mar: 29 1756 p. 2.

Holland, Judith, & Davie Parish, both in this parish Jan: 4 1758 p. 3.

Holland, Mary, & Charles Burton, both in this parish Nov. 3 1763 p. 7.

Holland, Martha & Adam Graves, both in this May 4 1769 p. 11.

Holland, Ann, & Absalom Owl, both of this parish Aug: 13 1769 p. 11.

Holland, Ann, & Is: Jenkins, both of Louisa Ap: 15 1781 p. 21.

HOLLINSHEAD, Hannah, & John Walker, both in this parish Mar: 15 1776 p. 17.

HOLMAN, Sarah, & Antony Martin, both in Manikentown, Dec. 21 1758 p. 4.

Holman, Jean, & Will: Martin, both in Manikentown Dec. 20 1759 p. 5.

Holman, Mary, & John Austine, both in this parish Dec. 31 1765 p. 8.

Holman, Susannah, & John Bret, both in this May 23, 1770 p. 11.

HOPSON, Tabitha, in Henrico, & Edward Mathews in this parish, May 1 1758 p. 4.

HOPKINS, Molly & .... 1751 pp. 26-32.

Hopkins, ... & Guy Smith Jul: 10 1753 pp. 26, 31.

Hopkins, Frances, & Ja: Guillam, both in Goochland Dec. 16 1772 p. 13.

Hopkins, Judith, & Ja: Vaughan, both of Goochland Feb. 27 1783 p. 22.

HOPPER, Mary, & Will: Tolliver, both of this parish Feb: 27 1770 p. 11.

HORN, Eliz: & Harrison Gammon Jul: 10 1753 pp. 27-32.

Horn, Sarah, & John Mims, both of this parish Mar: 7 1756 p. 2.

Horn, Sabra, & Thomas Hodges, both in this parish Oct: 17 1759 p. 4.

Horn, Sarah, & Jacob Gillam, both of this parish Dec. 27 1769 p. 11.

Horn, Mary, & Jo: Hopper, both in Goochland May 27 1770 p. 12.

HORTON, Rachel, & Barnet Owen, both in Goochland Nov: 21 1771 p. 12.

HOUCHINS, Agnes, & Will: Page, both in this parish Dec. 2 1757 p. 3.

Houchins, Biddy, & Will: Hardine, both in Goochland Oct. 14 1773 p. 14.

HOWARD, Eliz: & John Stanley, Ap: 20 1755 p. 1.

Howard, Rebekah, in this parish & Joseph Harris in Cumberland Feb: 6 1766 p. 8.

Howard, Joanna, & Will: Pemberton in Manikentown, May 12 1771 p. 12.

Howard, Mary, & Nat: Harris, both of Goochland, Mar: 18 1782 p. 22.

HOWL, Elizabeth, in this county, & George Cox in Louisa, Oct: 31 1766 p. 9.

HUBBARD, Elizabeth, & John Dowdy, both in this parish Jan: 7 1762 p. 6.

Hubard, Mary, & Arch: Napier, both in this parish Jan: 6 1766 p. 8.

Hubbard, Margaret, & John Cauthon, both in this parish Mar: .... 1766 p. 8.

Hubbard, Sarah, & Thomas Cauthon, both in this parish Oct: 31 1769 p. 11.

Hubbard, Eliz: & Champness Smith, both in Louisa Jan: 4 1782 p. 21.

HUDSON, Eliz: & Cha: Lacy, in Louisa Jul: 28 1774 p. 15.

HUCHINS, Rach: & Henry Atkinson, both in this parish Jan: 20 1756 p. 2.

Huchins, Nancy, & Anselm George, both of this parish May 7 1775 p. 16.

HUGHES, Charity, & John Moss in Hanover Nov: 20 1761 p. 6.

Hughes, Martha, & Benjamin Johnson, in St. Martins parish Mar: 6 1766 p. 8.

Hughes, Agnes, & James Webb, both of this parish Mar: 1 1770 p. 11.

Hughes, Susan, & Tho: Ferrar, both in Goochland Sep: 19 1772 p. 13.

Hughes, Judith in Cumberland, & Robert Mitchel in Richmond Mar: 11 1776 p. 17.

Hughes, Eliz: in Cumberland, & Will: Pryor in ys parish May 16 1776 p. 17.

Hughes, Mary, of Goochland & Jos. Ellis of Henrico Nov: 4 1776 p. 19.

Hughes, Sarah in Cumberland, & Jos: Woodson in Goochland Nov. 24 1779 p. 19.

HUMPHREY, ffrances, & George Harlow, both in this parish Mar: 20 1763 p. 7.

Humphreys, Martha, & Jo: McCoy, both in Louisa Feb. 17 1780 p. 19.

HUNTER, Jean, & Will: Priddy feb: 5 1755 p. 1.

Hunter, Jeanie, & Benjamin Lyons, both of Louisa Feb. 23, 1777 p. 17.

Hunter, Nancy, in Louisa, & Jacob Orford in Fluvanna Mar: 4 1779 p. 18.

Hunter, Martha, & Will: Perkins both of Louisa Aug: 17 1785 p. 24.

HURT, Rebekah, in Drisdale Parish & Rene Napier in this parish, Mar: 28 1765 p. 8.

Hurt, Eliz: in Spotsylvania & Tho: Ellis May 3 1787 p. 24.

Hurt, Agnes & Rich: Peatross in Spotsylvania May 3 1787 p. 24.

HURST. Rebekah, & Benjamin Thomas both of this parish Jun: 13 1769 p. 11.

HUTCHENS, Eliz: & John Clements both in this parish Jan: 28 1755 p. 1.

HUTCHESON, Hannah, & Jos. Clark both in this parish Dec. 25 1753 p. 1.

HUTCHISON, Letty, & Sam: Wharton in Spotsyl: Mar: 8 1786 p. 24.

HUTSON, Jeanie, & Nat: Holland in Louisa May 23 1776 pp. 17, 100.

Hutson, Sarah, & Will: Roberts, both of Louisa Ap: .... 1779 p. 19.

HUTTON, Eliz: & Will Mullen, both of ys parish Jan: 24 1775 p. 16.

HYAT, Susanna, & Tho: Davis, in Orange May 1, 1783 p. 23.

ISABEL, Susannah, & Jacob Mayo, both in this parish Jan: 2 1768 p. 10.

Isabel, Sally, & Dan: Slaydon, both in Goochland, Oct: 2 1782 p. 22.

Isabel, Ann, & Stephen Mayo, both of Goochland, Feb. 6 1783 p. 22.

JACKSON, Ann, & Thomas Imbrey, both in this parish Oct. 20 1757 p. 3.

Jackson, Lucy, & Stephen Eubank, both of this parish Sep. 24 1767 p. 10.

Jackson, Ann, & Jo: White, both of Louisa Dec. 25 1783 p. 23.

JACOBS, Eliz: & Will: Brooks, both in Louisa June 6 1784 p. 23.

JERAT, Agnes, & Alex: Grant Dec. 20 1751 p. 26.

Jerrat, Sarah, & John Shoemaker, both of this parish Nov: 9 1755 p. 2.

Jerrat, Mary, & Rob: Smith, both in Goochland Aug. 11 1774 p. 15.

JOHNON, Phoebe, & Henry Gray, both of ys parish Dec. 8 1776 p. 17.

JOHNSON, Sarah, & Steph: Sampson, both in this parish Sep: 20 1753 p. 1.

Johnson, Eliz: & Will: Edwards, both in this parish May 19 1756 p. 2.

Johnson, Agnes, & Samuel Perry, both of this parish Ap: 20 1760 p. 5.

Johnson, Mary, & [B]artholomew Turner, both in this parish .... 1763 p. 7.

Johnson, Mary, & Benjamin Cocke, both in this parish Jun: 23 1768 p. 10.

Johnson, Mary, & Will: Rodgers, both in Goochland Sep: 8 1770 p. 12.

Johnson, Winnifred, & Walter Leek, both in Goochland Aug. 1 1773 p. 14.

Johnson, Sarah, & Ben: Anderson, both of Louisa Sep: 7 1773 p. 14.

Johnson, Marg: & Walter Johnson, both of Goochland Dec. 21 1773, p. 14.

Johnson, Rebekah, & Cha. Goodman, of Albemarle Jan: 31 1774 p. 14.

Johnson, Mary, & Jesse Lacy, both in Louisa Sep: 6 1774 p. 15.

Johnson, Lucy, & Peter Fitzgerald, both of Goochland Sep: 11 1774 p. 15.

Johnson, Eliz: in Hanover, & Will: Powers in Goochland Nov: 29 1774 p. 15.

Johnson, Martha, in Louisa, & Rene Woodson in Albemarle Feb: 2 1775 p. 16.
Johnson, Nancy, & Will Haden, both of Albemarle Oct. 31 1775 p. 16.
Johnson, Judith, & Will: Johnson, both of ys parish Oct. 27 1775 p. 16.
Johnson, Sally, & Ben: Woodson, both in Goochland Mar: 14 1779 p. 18.
Johnson, Mary, & Jo: Price, in Goochland Aug. 3 1779 p. 19.
Johnson, Ann, & Abra: Davies, both of Louisa Sep. 23 1779 p. 19.
Johnson, Marg: & Ben: Johnson, both of Goochland Oct. 21 1779 p. 19.
Johnson, Marg: & Ja: Houchins, both of Goochland Apr: 18 1780 p. 19.
Johnson, Winnifred, & Christopher Isabel, both of Goochland Oct. 12 1780 p. 20.
Johnson, Mary, & Jo: Winston, both of Louisa Dec: 7 1780 p. 20.
Johnson, Joanna, & Nat: Moss, both of Goochland Dec. 31 1780 p. 20.
Johnson, Helender, & Tho: Wood, in Goochland Mar: 19 1781 p. 21.
Johnson, Sarah, & Will: Porter, both of Louisa Jun: 20 1782 p. 22.
Johnson, Nancy, & Cha: Smith, both of Louisa Nov. 20 1782 p. 23.
Johnson, Polly, & Tho: Halket in Spotsylvania Dec. 1 1785 p. 20 also p. 24.
Johnson, Mary, & Timothy Rich, both of ys parish Sep: 18 1751 p. 31.
Johnson, Sarah & Joseph Johnson, both of Louisa Jun: 25 1789 p. 25.
JOHNSTON, Martha & Nath: McCallister both in Louisa Mar: 22 1790 p. 25.
Johnston, Jean, & Ja: Cocke, both in Goochland Oct. 30 1773 p. 14.
Johnston, Eliz: Thornton, & Jo: Poindexter, both in Louisa Dec. 26 1781 p. 21.
Johnston, Sally, & Will: Fairies, both in Louisa Nov: 24 1782 p. 22.
Johnston, Susannah, & Edward Pace, both in Goochland Sep: 21 1784 p. 23.
JONES, Mary, & Ja: Sanders Sep: 20 1753 p. 1.
Jones, Ruth, & Rob: Hays Jan: 31 1754 p. 1.
Jones, Jean, & Will: Thurston, both in this parish Sep: 12 1763 p. 7.
Jones, Margaret, & John Pollock, both in this parish Apl: 8 1767 p. 9.
Jones, Mary Ann, & Thomas Poor, both in this parish Dec: 29 1767 p. 10.
Jones, Mary, & Nathan Thomas, both in Goochland Dec. 18 1774 p. 15.
Jones, Naomi, in Hanover, & Augustine Webber, in this May 30 1775 p. 16.
JORDAN, Susannah, & Jos: fferrar, both in this parish Nov: 23 1755 p. 2.
Jordan, Eliz: & John Bradshaw, both of this parish ffeb: 14 1758 p. 3.
Jordan, Eliz: & Benjamin Sublet, both in this parish Jun: 24 1762 p. 6.
Jordan, Frances, & Robert Wingfield, both of this parish Jun: 11 1765 p. 8.
Jordan, Phebe, & Dan: Clark, both in Goochland Aug: 23 1770 p. 12.

KENNON, Mary, & Thomas Harrison, both of this parish ffeb: 17 1768 p. 10.
KENT, Eliz: & Obadiah Tucker, both of Albemarle Dec: 11 1769 p. 11.

Kent, Mary, in Albemarle, & Jo: Poor in Goochland, Feb. 3 1774 p. 14.
Kent, Ann, in Albemarle, & Thomas Diggs in Louisa Jun: 9 1775 p. 16.
KER, Frances, & Arthur Scot, both in Cumberland Sep: 5 1773 p. 14.
Ker, Jean Barbara, & Wilson Carey, in Goochland Jul: 21 1782 p. 22.
KINDRED, Jean, & John Ball, both of ys parish Jan: 17'1775 p. 16.
KING, Marg: & Jo: Telford, both of Louisa Dec. 6 1780 p. 20.
KNIGHT, Susan, & Pouncy Nichols, in Hanover Jun: 25 1774 p. 15.
Knight, Eleanor, in Hanover, & Sam: Nichols in this Aug: 25 1776
    p. 17.
KNOLLING, Eliz: & Ashley Alvis, both of Goochland Dec. 16 1772
    p. 13.
KNOWLINE, Ann, & John Webster, both in this parish Aug. 26 1762
    p. 6.
KNOWLING, Sarah, & Jacob Johnson, both of ys parish Dec. 25 1775
    p. 17.

LACY, Sarah, in St. Martins, Hanover, & Perrine fferrar in this parish,
    Dec. 30 1757 p. 3.
Lacy, Sarah, & Tho: Harris, in this parish Mar: 4 1764 p. 8.
LAD, Mary, & Will: Bradshaw, both in this parish Jul: 7 1754 p. 1.
LAFORCE, Judith, & Rob: Burton, both in this parish Oct: 13 1757
    p. 3.
Laforce, Zulima, & Rob: Cothan, both in this parish Feb: 11 1760 p. 5.
Laforce, Trephenah, in this parish, & Peter fferrar in Albemarle, Ap:
    10 1766 p. 9.
LAMBKIN, Hannah, & Thomas Welburn, both in this parish Oct. 23
    1769 p. 11.
LANDRUM, Elizabeth, & John Landrum, in Richmond county May 1
    1763 p. 7.
LANE, Eliz: & Humphrey Parish, both in ys parish 1751
    pp. 26-32.
Lane, Mary, & Drury Howard, both of this parish Jan: 25 1759 p. 4.
Lane, Ann, & And: Hunter, both in Louisa Oct: 25 1770 p. 12.
Lane, Judith, & Will: Sanders, both in Goochland Jan: 10 1771 p. 12.
Lane, Lucy, & Jo: Martin, both of Goochland Mar: 16 1779 p. 19.
Lane, Judith, in Fluvanna, & David Howard in Bedford Feb: 26 1781
    p. 21.
Lane, Frances, & Bartlet Graves, both of Louisa Ap: 18 1787 p. 24.
LAUMOX, Elizabeth & John Wales in Charles City—both in this
    parish— Jan: 26 1760 p. 5.
LAURENCE, Ann, & Jonathan Flewelling, both in Goochland Oct: 20
    1772 p. 13.
Laurence, Eliz: & David Powers, both in Louisa Jul: 18 1775 p. 16.
Laurence, Susannah, & Jo: Green, of Goochland Oct: 4 1779 p. 19.
LAWRIE, Marianne, & Reu: Thurston, both in Goochland Dec: 24
    1772 p. 13.
Lawrie, Priscilla, & Da: Crowdis, both in Goochland Ap: 10 1773 p. 14.
LAWSON, Eliz: & John Shelton both in this parish Jul: 30 1760 p. 5.

LEE, Deborah, & John Hodges, both in this parish Nov: 11 1756 p. 2.
LEEK, ... & Ja. Coleman .... 1751 pp. 26-32.
Leek, Judith, & Jo: Christian, both in Goochland May 9 1771 p. 12.
LEPRADE, Eliz: & Jos: Starkie, in Goochland Aug. 9 1753 pp. 27-32.
Leprade, Ann, & Richard Pleasants, both in this parish Jul: 1 1762 p. 6.
Leprade, Joana, & Will: Miller, both in Goochland Mar: 19 1772 p. 13.
Leprade, Martha, & Gideon Hatcher, both of ys parish Sep: 4 1777
    p. 18.
Leprade, Judith, & Anderson Peers, both of Goochland Oct: 24 1780
    p. 20.
LEONARD, Peggie, & Lewis Symes, both of Louisa Sep: 10 1784
    p. 23.
LETCHER, Sarah, & Will: Mitchel, both of this parish Dec: 19 1769
    p. 11.
LEWIS, Angelica & Jo: Ford .... 1751 p. 26.
Lewis, Elizabeth, & William Roberts, both in this parish Jan: 5 1758
    p. 3.
Lewis, ffrances, of this parish, & Rob: Lewis of Louisa, Sep: 3 1760
    p. 5.
Lewis, Barbara, & John Martin, both in this parish Aug. 7 1763 p. 7.
Lewis, Sarah, & Milner Radford, both in this Dec: 25 1766 p. 9.
Lewis, Ann, & John Rodgers, both of this parish Feb. 23 1769 p. 11.
Lewis, Ann, & Robert Moseby, both in this parish May 4 1769 p. 11.
Lewis, Ann, & William Mosely, both of ys parish .... 1775 p. 17.
Lewis, Sally, & Jesse Payne, in Goochland Jan: 8 1779 p. 18.
Lewis, Ann, & Anthony Mullins, both in Goochland June 14 1779 p. 19.
Lewis, Eliz: & Will: Robards, both of Goochland Sep: 7 1781 p. 21.
LIPSCOMB, Ann, & Ja: Wood, both in Louisa Oct. 12 1784 p. 23.
LOCK, Judith, in this parish, & James Sandige, in Hanover Nov. 3
    1757 p. 3.
LOCKRAM, Eliz: & William Martin, both in this parish May 3 1757
    p. 3.
LOFTIS, Frances, & John Good, both in this parish Oct. 1 1765 p. 8.
Loftus, Martha, & Jacob Ragline, both in Goochland July: 18 1773 p. 14.
LOGAN, Ann, & John Whitlock, both in this parish Oct. 6 1754 p. 1.
Logan, Sarah, & Henry Lane, widower, both of this parish Jan: 21
    1759 p. 4.
LOOKADOE, Rebekah, & Thomas Thomas, both in Manikentown
    Sep: 1 1765 p. 8.
LONG, Dorothea, & Will: Brown, both in Louisa Oct: 30 1781 p. 21.
Long, Lucy, & Henry Mallory, both in Orange Dec: 27 1781 p. 21.
LOVEL, Susannah, & Will: Hodges, both in this parish May 27 1758
    p. 4.
Lovel, Mary in this parish & (William Lovel) in Amelia ....
    1764 p. 7.
LOVING, Jean, & James Ross, both in this parish Feb: 17 1766 p. 8.
Loving*, Maiden, & John Childers, both in this Nov: 10 1766 p. 9.

---

*Spelled Lovel elsewhere.

LOWRY, Ann, in this parish, & James Bailey in New Kent Nov: 16 1762 p. 7.

LUCAS, Ann, & Aquila Tignor, both of this parish Aug: 29 1765 p. 8.

McBRIDE, Ann & Ben: Bradshaw, in Goochland Ap: 8 1753 pp. 27-32.

McBride, Eliz: & John Lewis, both of this parish May 30 1758 p. 4.

McBride, Mary, & Godfrey Jones, both in this parish Jul: 1 1766 p. 9.

McGEHEE, Mary & Will: Arnet both in Louisa .... 1791 p. 27.

McGehee, Polly & Will: Poindexter both in Louisa .... (17)91 p. 27.

McGUIRE, Mary & William Sampson Oct. 8 1751 pp. 26-31.

MacNEMARA, Sarah, in Albemarle, & Alsop Yarborrough in Hanover Ap: 16 1768 p. 10.

MADDISON, [or, Mathison] Dorothy, & Will: Groom, both in this parish Sep: 25 1753 p. 1.

MADDOX, Eliz: & John Hancocke, both in this parish Oct: 16 1755 p. 2.

Maddox, Eliz: in this parish & James Tooly in Buckingham Dec. 20 1767 p. 10.

MAN, Elizabeth, & John Philpot, both in this parish Jan: 24 1769 p. 11.

Man, Sally, & Will: Lewis, both of Goochland Feb: 24 1774 p. 14.

MANNIN, Eliz: & Vincent Vass, both in Orange Aug. 29 1783 p. 23.

MANSPOIL, Sarah, & Jo: Clark, both in Orange Feb. 29 1780 p. 19.

MANTELOE, Rebecca & Moses Rowe, both in Louisa .... (17)92 p. 27.

MARSHALL, Sar: & Jo: Robards, both in Goochland Jul: 9 1772 p. 13.

MARTIN, Eliz: & Will Banks Sep: 15 1753 p. 1.

Martin, Mary, & Hugh Lewis Venable, both in this parish Jun: 14 1757 p. 3.

Martin, Susannah, & Henry Woody, both in this parish Jan: 13 1761 p. 5.

Martin, Mildred, in Cumberland, & Thomas Basket in this parish, Jan: 15 1761 p. 5.

Martin, Ann, & Henry Copland, in this parish Jul: 21 1761 p. 6.

Martin, Rebekah, & James Johnson, both of this parish Feb: 27 1766 p. 8.

Martin, Sally, & John Glass, both in this parish May 25 1768 p. 10.

Martin, Bettie, & Tho: Ferrar, both in Goochland Oct: 24 1771 p. 12.

Martin, Olive, & Ambrose Edwards, both in Louisa Mar: 15 1774 p. 15.

Martin, Judith, & John Johnson, both of ys parish Feb: 22 1777 p. 17.

Martin, Mary, & Jo: George, both of Goochland Mar: 17 1779 p. 19.

Martin, Sarah, & Jo: Young, in Louisa Aug: 8 1781 p. 21.

MASK, Mary, & Thomas King, both of this parish Apr: 3 1760 p. 5.

MASSIE, Susannah, widow in this parish & Will: Perkins in New Kent, ffeb: .... 1756 p. 2.

Massie, Constancy, & Booker Parish, both in this Jan: 29 1767 p. 9.

Massie, Ann, & Reu: Cairden, both in Goochland Jun: 27 1771 p. 12.

Massie, Mary, & Ja: Roberts, both in Goochland Dec: 2 1774 p. 15.

Massie, Eliz: & Thomas Massie, both of ys parish Jun: 28 1776 p. 17.

Massie, Ann, & Jo: Howard, both in Goochland Aug: 11 1779 p. 19.

MATHEWS, Judith, & Zachariah Goff, both of ys parish Oct: 14 1775 p. 16.

Mathews, Sarah, & Solomon Edwards, both of Louisa Dec: 27 1782 p. 22.

MAY, Cloe, & Tho: Bailie, both of Fluvanna Oct: 19 1780 p. 20.

MAYFIELD, Agnes, & Jo: Hester, both in Louisa Aug: 26 1779 p. 19.

MAYO, Ann, & William Williamson, both in this parish Oct. 25 1763 p. 7.

MEANLY, Mary, & John Albrittain, both of this parish Ap: 14 1768 p. 10.

MEEKS, Susanna, & Paul Meecham, both in Goochland Jan: 2 1772 p. 13.

MEEKIE, Eliz: & Jo: Mead in Louisa Mar: 24 1784 p. 23.

Meekie, Ann, & Henry Johnson, both of Louisa Jan: 20 1785 p. 23.

Meekie, Mary, in Louisa, & Will: Thompkins in Hanover, Dec: 26 1786 p. 24.

Meekie, Eliz: & Sam: Raglin, both of Louisa Dec: 12 1788 p. 25.

MEGAN, Elizabeth, & William Glass, both in this parish May 13 1766 p. 9.

MERIAN, Elizabeth, & Samuel Wood, both in this parish Dec: 23 1762 p. 7.

MERINE, Ann, in Goochland, & Ja: Carter in Cumberland Oct: 24 1771 p. 12.

MERRIWETHER, Martha, & George Merriwether, both in Goochland Nov: 2 1768 p. 10.

Merriwether, Mary, & Shadrach Vaughan, both in Goochland Jun: 19 1770 p. 12.

Merriwether, Ann, & Jo: Hughes, in Louisa June 18 1783 p. 23.

Merriwether, Eliz: & Tho: Lewis both in Albemarle June 24 1788 p. 25.

MICHAM, Nancy, & Reuben Hutson, both of Spots: Jan: 10 1782 p. 21.

MILAM, Grace, & Richard Chumly, both in Maniken town May 9 1756 p. 2.

MILTON, Susan, & Jesse Horn, both in Goochland Dec: 22 1773 p. 14.

MILLER, Elizabeth, in this parish, & John Hales in Henrico Feb: 20 1760 p. 5.

Miller, Winifred-Jones, in this parish, & Robert Povall in Henrico Jun: 14 1760 p. 5.

Miller, Elizabeth, & George Richardson, both in this Nov: 13 1766 p. 9.

Miller, Sarah, in this parish, & James Holman in Manikentown Oct: 30 1769 p. 11.

Miller, Mary, of Goochland, & Obadiah Periere in Henrico Mar: 14 1779 p. 18.

Miller, Marg: & Dan: Harris, both in Goochland June 19 1779 p. 19.

MILLS, Eliz: & Will: Johnson, both in this parish feb: 4 1755 p. 1.

Mills, Elizabeth & Philip Ryan, both in this parish Mar: 7 1766 p. 8.

MIMS, Mildred & James Johnson, ... 1751 pp. 26-32.

Mims, Mary & Randolph de Priest, both in Goochland .... 1751 pp. 26-32.

Mims, Ann, & Rob: Wilburn, both in this parish Oct: 9 1755 p. 2.

Mims, Agnes, & Tho: Riddle, both in this parish Oct: 13 1755 p. 2.

Mims, Mary, in this parish, & John Woodson in Albemarle Mar: 20 1760 p. 5.

Mims, Judith, & Benjamin Anderson, both of this parish Jan: 27 1769 p. 11.

Mims, Susannah, & George Anderson, both of this parish Mar: 23 1769 p. 11.

MINOR, Patsy, & Rob: Quarles, of Louisa .... (17)91 p. 27.

Minor, Becky, & John Quarles, of Louisa .... (17)91 p. 27.

Minor, Ann & Tho: Merriwether, both in this .... (17)91 p. 27.

MITCHEL, Susannah, & John Rain, both in this parish Aug: 3 1754 p. 1.

Mitchel, Mary, & Mr. Archibald Bryce, both in this parish Jul: 21 1769 p. 11.

Mitchel, Eliz: & Tho: [or The:] Tourman, in Goochland Oct: 20 1778 p. 18.

Mitchel, Ann, & Simon Christopher, both in Louisa Dec. 1 1782 p. 22.

Mitchel, Ann, & Archelaus Perkins, both of Goochland Sep: 2 1784 p. 23.

MOON, Susannah, & Tho: Cobbs, both in fforks of James River, Albemarle Jan: 27 1756 p. 2.

Moon, Judith, & Isham ffarmer, both in this parish Mar: 14 1760 p. 5.

MOONEY, Tempe, & Ja: Thomson, both in Louisa Jul: 15 1783 p. 23.

MOOR, Patty, & John Moor, both of ys parish Jan: 15 1776 p. 17.

MORACET, Judith, in Manikentown, & John Gordon in this parish Mar: 25 1758 p. 3.

MORE, Jedidiah, in Caroline, & Tho: Ship in Goochland, Feb: 20 1774 p. 14.

More, Susannah, & Da: Bullock in Louisa Feb: 4 1778 p. 18.

MORELL, Elizabeth, & John Guillam, both of this parish Sep: 27 1764 p. 8.

MORRIS, Patience, & Mask Leek, in Hanover county Nov: 22 1758 p. 4.

Morris, Amy, & Giles Hardine, in Louisa Jan: 30 1773 p. 14.

Morris, Frances, & Jo: James, both in Hanover Dec. 1 1774 p. 15.

MORTON, ffrances, of this parish, & Samuel Pryor in Amelia, Aug: 27 1760 p. 5.

Morton, Betty-McCartey, & George Payne, in James City Parish Dec: 31 1765 p. 8.

Morton, Frances, & Jo: Reid, both in Goochland Mar: 1 1773 p. 14.

Morton, Marg: Sydenham, & Rob: Burton Payne, both in Goochland, Dec: 22 1773 p. 14.

MOSEBY, Hannah, in Cumberland, & Charles Edwards in this parish, Jan: 27 1754 p. 1.

MOSELY, Agatha, & Elias Williams, both in this parish Mar: 10 1757 p. 3.

MOSS, Ann, & John Younger, both in this parish Nov: 30 1757 p. 3.

Moss, Susannah, & Benjamin Thurmond, both in this parish Jan: 11 1758 p. 3.

Moss, Mary, & John Mims, both of this parish Oct: 8 1761 p. 6.

Moss, Dolly, & Shadrach Battles, in Louisa Jul: 25 1780 p. 20.

Moss, Frances, & Rich: McBride, both of Goochland Sep: 28 1780 p. 20.

Moss, Dianah & Shilton Smith both of Louisa Ap: 3 1788 p. 25.

MULLINS, Ann, & Maxey Ewel, both of this parish Jan: 5 1769 p. 11.

MURPHEY, Ann, & Jos: Harper, both in Louisa Nov: 25 1781 p. 21.

NAPIER, Susannah, & Reuben Brown, in this parish Jun: 11 1761 p. 6.

NAPPER, Sarah, & Nicholas Loyd, both in this parish Dec: 14 1756 p. 2.

NASH, Eliz: & Luther Hopper, both in this parish Dec: 20 1756 p. 2.

Nash, Ann, & William Tuggle, both in this parish Sep: 25 1765 p. 8.

NELSON, Ann & William Trice both in Louisa .... 15 1790 p. 27.

NETHERLAND, Mary & Tucker Woodson .... 1751 pp. 26-31.

NETTLES, Mary, & James Dickerson Betw. 1750-53 p. 31.

NEVES, Mary, & Daniel Wade, both in this parish May 30 1776 p. 17.

NEVILS, Sally, & Jacob Michaux, in Cumberland Mar: 21 1765 p. 8.

NICHOLS, Ann, & Richard Johnson, both in this parish Dec: 23 1764 p. 8.

Nichols, Sarah, & John Gilbert, both in this parish Dec: 4 1768 p. 11.

Nichols, Ann, & Austine Hancoke, both in Louisa Dec. 27 1781 p. 21.

Nichols, Mary, & Will: Armstrong, both in Louisa Nov: 14 1782 p. 22.

NICKS, Susannah, & John Clark, both in this Ap: 4 1767 p. 9.

NORVIL, Mackie, & William Thurmond, both in this parish Ap: 10 1766 p. 9.

Norvil, Bettie, in Goochland & Peter Lyon, in Albemarle Oct. 8 1771
p. 12.

NOWLIN, Sarah, & Patrick Smith, both in this parish Feb. 25 1778
p. 18.

NUCKOLS, Betty, & William Childers, both in this parish Jan: 5
1767 p. 9.

ODEN, Margaret, & Henry Parish, both in this parish Dec. 24
1765 p. 8.

OGILVY, Ann, & John Moreland, both of ys parish Nov: 16 1775
p. 16.

OGILSVY, Eliz: & Tho: Mitchel, both of ys parish Feb: 21 1775
p. 16.

Ogilsvy, Mary, & Sam: Trainham, both of Orange Mar: 25 1782
p. 22.

OLIVER, Mary, & James Clements, from King William Dec: 15 1757
p. 3.

OVERSTREET, Ann, & Will; White, both of this parish Dec. 21
1769 p. 11.

Overstreet, Keziah, & Will: Mosely, both in Goochland Nov: 28
1772 p. 13.

Overstreet, Sarah, & Will: Carter, both in Goochland Dec. 25 1773
p. 14.

Overstreet, Eliz: & Will Overstreet May 22 1777 p. 18.

OWEN, Ann, & Bartlet Bowles, both of this parish Nov: 13 1766
p. 9.

Owen, Mary, & Jo: Lane, both of Goochland Mar: 20 1781 p. 21.

PACE, Mary, & William Basket, both in this parish Oct: 1 1761 p. 6.

Pace, Susannah, & Stephen Johnson, both in this parish Oct. 1 1765
p. 8.

Pace, Ann, & Jo: Pace, both of Goochland, Feb: 1 1774 p. 14.

Pace, Mary, & Ja: Furbish, both in Goochland Jul: 26 1774 p. 15.

Pace, Eliz: & Joshua Tuggle, both of Goochland Dec: 26 1780 p. 20.
(See Peace)

PAGE, Betty, & John Lee, both in this parish Sep: 11 1755 p. 1.

Page, Elizabeth, & David Hodges, both of this parish ffeb: 2 1758
p. 3.

Page, Betty, & William Hall, both in this parish Mar: 12 1758 p. 3.

Page, Christian, & Tho: Wilburn, both in this parish Oct: 22 1759
p. 4.

Page, Hannah & Sherard Harris, both of this parish Dec: 16 1761
p. 6.

Page, Mary-Ann, & Joseph Pace, both in this parish Oct: 26 1762
p. 7.

Page, Mary, & Jos: Brockman, both in Goochland Ap: 15 1773 p. 14.

Page, Lucy & Johnson Hodgses, in Goochland .... p. 32.

PAISLY, Susannah, & John Gunstone, both of this parish Sep: 30 1762 p. 6.

PANKIE, Elizabeth, & Benjamin Hudlestone, both in Manikentown Sep: 23 1762 p. 6.

PARISH, Jurisha, & John Davies, both in this parish Aug: 11 1754 p. 1.

Parish, Mourning, & James Kid both in this parish Oct: 19 1755 p. 2.

Parish, Elizabeth, & James ffoster, both of this parish Oct: 28 1759 p. 4.

Parish, Lucy, in this parish, & Henry Jones in Louisa Aug: 28 1760 p. 5.

Parish, Elizabeth, & John Robinson, both of this parish Dec. 23 1761 p. 6.

Parish, Judith, & James Scot, both in this parish ffeb: 17 1763 p. 7.

Parish, Molly, & Nelson Parish, both in this parish Feb: 8 1763 p. 7.

Parish, Nanny, & Nathaniel Hill, both in this parish Sep: 3 1767 p. 10.

Parish, Sarah, & James Johnson, both in Goochland Nov: 3 1768 p. 10.

Parish, Eliz: & David Sasseen, both in Manikentown Dec. 10 1768 p. 11.

Parish, Molly, & Wilson Adams, both in Goochland Dec. 26 1771 p. 13.

Parish, Martha, & Ja: Cooke, both in Goochland Nov. 25 1774 p. 15.

Parish, Eliz: & Henry Laurence, both in ys Jul: 26 1775 p. 16.

Parish, Judith, & Tho: Norvil, both in Goochland Feb: 4 1779 p. 18.

Parish, Conney, & Jos: Guillam, both of Goochland, Nov: 6 1779 p. 19.

PARKER, Catherine & Ben: Robinson, both of Spots: Feb: 18 1783 p. 22.

PARSONS, Nancy, & Tho: Pleasants, both in Goochland Jan: 2 1772 p. 13.

PARTLOW, Mary, & Cha: Beasley, of Spotsy: Jan: 18 1786 p. 24.

PATERSON, Mary, & Tho: Ellis, both in Henrico Jan: 21 1773 p. 14.

Paterson, Mary, & Major Brockman, both of Orange Nov: 11 1779 p. 19.

Paterson, Eliz: & Will Knighten, both of Louisa Feb: 24 1782 p. 22.

PATTY, Winnifred, in Bedford, & Rob: Page in this parish, Mar: 20 1759 p. 4.

PAYNE, Ann, & Thomas Short, both in Manikentown Jan: 10 1762 p. 6.

Payne, Anna, & .... Harrison, both in this parish .... 1763 p. 7.

Payne, Susanna & Will Hales, in Goochland Jun: 26 1771 p. 12.

Payne, Mary, & Jo: Shilton, both in Goochland Sep. 1 1772 p. 13.

Payne, Ann, in Goochland & Ja: Gordon in Lancaster Jun: 30 1774 p. 15.

Payne, Eliz: & Samuel Woodson, both of ys parish June 19 1777 p. 18.

Payne, Jean, in Goochland & Will: Lee in Northumberland 28 Sep: 1780 p. 20.

PEACE, Rachel & John Martin, both in this parish Jan: 3 1757 p. 3.

Peace, Sarah, & Thomas Clements, both of this parish Jan: 10 1759 p. 4.

Peace, Susannah, & Benjamin Johnson, both in this parish Jul: 22 1759 p. 4.
            (See Pace)

PEARSE, Elizabeth, in this, & John Hanson in Albemarle Ap: 3 1767 p. 9.

PEMBERTON, Nancy, & Tho: Coleman, both in Spotsylvania Dec: 3 1780 p. 20.

PERRIRE, Mary, & Peter Garret, both in Manikentown Nov: 25 1756 p. 2.

Periere, Frances, & Sam: Jordan, of Henrico Jan: 27 1774 p. 14.

Periere, Sarah of Goochland, & Jo: Morris of Louisa Sep: 30 1779 p. 19.

PERKINS, Mary, & James Crawford, both in this parish Nov: 27 1753 p. 1.

Perkins, Eliz: & Richard Minto, both in this parish Oct: 6 1754 p. 1.

Perkins, Ann, & David Clarkson, both in this parish Aug. 7 1760 p. 5.

Perkins, Susannah, & John Baker, both of this parish Jan: 5 1767 p. 9.

Perkins, Elizabeth, & Stephen Letcher, both in this Jan: 22 1767 p. 9.

Perkins, Sally, & David Maddox, both in this parish Sep: 11 1768 p. 10.

Perkins, Hannah, & Jesse Bowles, both in Goochland Mar: 3 1773 p. 14.

Perkins, Judith, & Jo: Hodges, both of Goochland Dec. 27 1773 p. 14.

Perkins, Ann, & Gerard Wilkerson, both of Goochland May 9 1774 p. 15.

Perkins, Mary, & Edward Far, both of Louisa Nov: 14 1779 p. 19.

Perkins, Lorana, & Will: Wilkerson, in Goochland Between 1750 and 1753 p. 31.

PERRY, Martha, & John Johnson, both in this parish feb: 20 1760 p. 5.

PIERCE, Mary & John Wright, both in this parish Jan: 14 1756 p. 2.

Pierce, Hannah, & William Ashley, both in this parish, Mar: 9 1762 p. 6.

PIGG, Jane, & Will: Burgess, from Albemarle Aug: 7 1770 p. 12.

PINAX, Eliz: & Jo: Hoggan, both of Louisa Ap: 19 1781 p. 21.

PINES, Jeanie, & Will Gains, both in Spots: Mar: 11 1781 p. 21.

PLANT, Mary, in Hanover, & James Mayo in Goochland, Sep: 28 1758 p. 4.

PLEASANTS, Martha, in this, & William Watson in Hanover, Feb:
17 1767 p. 9.

Pleasants, Ann, & Sam: Martin, in Goochland Jul: 4 1771 p. 12.

Pleasants, Eliz: & Edward Carter, both in ys parish May 20 1777
p. 18.

Pleasants Jean, & Is: Pleasants, both in Goochland Aug: 22 1782
p. 22.

PLEDGE, Dorothy, & John Woodhall, both in this parish Aug: 12
1756 p. 2.

Pledge, Eliz: & Tho: Pindexter, both of this parish feb: 13 1760
p. 5.

Pledge, Martha, & Will: Clarkson, both in this parish Mar: 14
1761 p. 5.

POINDEXTER, Christian, & Macon Biggar, in Louisa Jul: 22 1779
p. 19.

Poindexter, Molly, & Garland Cosbie, both of Louisa Jun: 27 1782
p. 22.

Poindexter, Eliz: in Louisa, & Cha: Slaughter in Culpeper, Feb: 3
1780 p. 19.

Poindexter, Ann Gizage, & Rob: Cobb in Louisa Nov: 19 1783
p. 23.

POLLARD, Eliz: & James Merriwether, in this parish Sep: 10 1762
p. 6.

Pollard, Milly, & Edmund Pendleton, in Goochland Aug: 16 1764
p. 8.

Pollard, Jean & Nat: West Dandridge, in Goochland Aug: 3 1779
p. 19.

POLLOCK, Eliz: & [James Brooks]* [torn] both in this parish
········ 1764 p. 7.

POOR, Mary, & Zach: Williams, both in this parish Nov: 20 1755
p. 2.

Poor, Elizabeth, & Zachariah Haden, both in this parish Jan: 27 1763
p. 7.

Poor, Mildred, & ················l Colby, both in this parish ········ ···· 1767
p. 9.

Poor, Jeanie, & Leonard George, both in this parish Jan: 18 1772
p. 13.

Poor, Mary, & Tho: Barker, both in Goochland Aug: 28 1772 p. 13.

Poor, Jean, & Joseph Lambert, both of ys parish Oct: 1 1775 p. 16.

Poor, Hopey, & Ben: Bradshaw, both in this parish Feb: 25 1778
p. 18.

Poor, Mary & Peter Pollock, both of Goochland Nov: 26 1779 p. 19.

Poor, Judith, & Constant Perkins, both in Goochland Nov: 9 1780
p. 20.

Poor, Sarah, & Will: Brit, both in Goochland Sep: 21 1784 p. 23.

PORE, Susan & James Scrugs, both in this parish Sep. 28 1762 p. 6.

Pore, Ann, & Stephen Lee, both in this parish Nov: 3 1763 p. 7.

*From birth entries.

PORTER, Mary & John Barnes, in Manikentown Oct: 30 1755 p. 2.

Porter, Sarah, & Tho: Hatcher, in Manikentown Jun: 3 1762 p. 6.

Porter, Ann in Manikentown, & Charles Sampson, in this, Nov: 3 1767 p. 10.

Porter, Mary, & Dan: Gerrand, both in Manikentown Jul: 19 1770 p. 12.

Porter, Ann, & Joseph Lewis, both in ys parish Mar: 16 1777 p. 18.

POTTER, Mildred & Sam: Emmerson, of this parish Sep: 9 1756 p. 2.

Potter, Jurga, & John Alsup. both in this parish May 23 1762 p. 6.

POWEL, Susannah, & Samuel Moss, both of ys parish Jan: 3 1776 p. 17.

Powel, Mary Heath, & Jo: Gerrand, in Goochland Jul: 25 1782 p. 22.

POWERS, Dolly, & Rich: Johnson, both of this parish Nov: 14 1769 p. 11.

Powers, Maryanne, & Jo: Laurence, both in Goochland Jul: 8 1771 p. 12.

PRICE, Elizabeth, & Richard Ogilsby, both in this Parish Sep: 3 1758 p. 4.

Price, Sally, & Walthall Burton, both in Goochland Feb: 13 1773 p. 14.

Price, Betsey, & Joseph Perkins, both in ys parish Dec: 21 1775 p. 16.

Price, Sarah, & Larkin Lane, both of Spotsylvania Ap: 26 1787 p. 24.

PROFFIT, Lucy, & Thomas McCormack, both in this parish ffeb: 3 1754 p. 1.

PRUIT, Nancy, & Ben: East, both in Goochland Aug: 26 1773 p. 14.

PRYOR, Sally & Math: Payne, both in Goochland May 4 1773 p. 14.

Pryor, Martha & Will: Jordan, both of Goochland Mar: 16 1779 p. 19.

Pryor, Sarah, in Goochland, & Will Smith in Louisa, Jul: 28 1784 p. 23.

PULHAM, Aggie, & Antony Perkins, both of Louisa Dec: 25 1780 p. 20.

Pulham, Bettie, & Cha: Carter, both in Spotsylvania Oct: 19 1786 p. 24.

PURVIS, Sally & Cha: Wright both of this county were maried .... 1792 p. 27.

QUARLES, Ann & Rich. Dickerson, both in Spotsylvania Mar: 11 1779 p. 18.

Quarles, Frances, & Will: Thompson, in Spots: Dec. 20 1781 p. 21.

Quarles, Mary, & Dr. Joseph Duke, both in Spotsylvania .... 1791 p. 27.

QUISSENBERRY, Sar: & Ninian Watson, both of Louisa Sep: 30 1783 p. 23.

RADFORD, Mary, widow, & Stokes McCawl, in this parish Jul: 23 1754 p. 1.

Radford, Martha, & Henry Whitlow, both of this parish Dec: 3 1767 p. 10.

Radford, Mary, & John Bowles, in Hanover Nov: 9 1768 p. 10.

Radford, Mildred, & Joseph Woodson, both of this parish Jan: 2 1770 p. 11.

RAGLIN, Hannah, & Sylvanua Massie, both in this parish Oct: 3 1757 p. 3.

Ragline, Mary, & William Utley, both in this Dec: 13 1766 p. 9.

Ragline, Sarah, & Will Ellis, both in Goochland Dec: 30 1770 p. 12.

Raglane, Mary & Clifton Thomson, both in Louisa Feb: 26 1788 p. 25.

Ragline, Sally & Jo: Thomson, both in Louisa Mar: 31 1789 p. 25.

RAILEY, Mary, & Jacob Childers, both in Manikentown Apl: 23 1767 p. 9.

RAINE, Mary Ann, & Humphrey Paris, in Goochland Sep: 16 1783 p. 23.

RAMSAY, Mary, & Tho: Deering, both in Orange June 30 1783 p. 23.

RANDOLPH, Ann in Goochland, & John Pleasants in Cumberland Jun: 14 1759 p. 4.

Randolph, Susannah, in this parish, & Carter Henry Harrison in Cumberland Nov: 9 1760 p. 5.

Randolph, Betty & Jo: Raily, both in Goochland Betw. 1750-53 p. 31.

Randolph, Thea & John Woodson, both in ys parish Oct: 14 1751 pp. 26-31.

Randolph, Ann & Dan: Scot in ys parish Nov: 28 1751 pp. 26-31.

RATCLIFF, Isabel, & Abra: Ailstock, both of Louisa Dec: 23 1784 p. 23.

RAY, Jean, & Tho: Pulham, in Louisa Jul: 19 1778 p. 18.

READ, Sally, & Pleasants Willis, both in Henrico Dec: 10 1774 p. 15.

REDMAN, Pattie & Da: Clarkson .... 1751 p. 26.

RICE, Eliz: & John Depriest, both in this parish Jun: 6, 1759 p. 4.

Rice, Mary, & fforest Green, both of this parish Nov: 28 1761 p. 6.

Rice, Sally, in this parish, & Edward Smith in Albemarle, Dec: 3 1762 p. 7.

Rice, Molly, in this parish, & William Trice in Amherst Dec: 13 1768 p. 11.

Rice, Martha, & Geo. Sanders, both in Goochland Dec: 17 1771 p. 13.

Rice, Nannie, & Ja. Herndon, both in Goochland Oct: 4 1772 p. 13.

Rice, Milley, & John Hopper, both of this parish Mar: 26 1775 p. 16.

RICH, Elizabeth, & David Harris, both of this parish Nov: 19 1760 p. 5.

RICHARDS, Anna, & Henry Webster, both in Louisa Jul: 8 1784 p. 23.

RICHARDSON, Susannah, & Gideon Moss, both in this parish Jan: 1 1762 p. 6.

Richardson, Mary, & Benjamin Lee, both in Goochland Sep: 18 1766 p. 9.

Richardson, Ursley, in Henrico, & John Perkins in Goochland Oct: 12 1768 p. 10.

Richardson, Jeanie, & Jos: Mayo, in Goochland Jan. 1 1773 p. 13.

Richardson, Mary, & Jo: Fenwick, both in Goochland Dec: 24 1774 p. 15.

RIDDLE, Martha, in Goochland, & Tho: Gibson in Prince Edward Sep: 15 1774 p. 15.

RIDDY, Nanny, & Tho: Nuckolds, both in this parish Feb: 25 1778 p. 18.

RIPLEY, Mary, & John Balew, both in Albemarle Mar: 21 1759 p. 4.

ROBARDS, Susannah, & David Martin, both in this Feb: 22 1767 p. 9.

ROBERTS, Jean, in Goochland & Samuel Moseby in Caroline Mar: 4 1773 p. 14.

Roberts, Eliz: & Rob: Cairden, both of ys parish Nov: 26 1775 p. 16.

ROBERTSON, Dolly, & Bradley Dalton, both in Louisa Oct: 31 1782 p. 23.

ROBBERTSON, Susannah & Mordecia Collins both of Louisa .... 1790 p. 27.

ROBINSON, Sarah, & David Dalton, both in Louisa Sep: 27 1779 p. 19.

Robinson, Lucy, & Ja: Nilson, both of Spots: May 3 1781 p. 21.

Robinson, Ann, & Nic: Hawkins, both of Spots: Nov: 14 1781 p. 21.

ROGERS, Mary, & John Martin, both of ys parish Oct. 2 1751 pp. 26-31.

Rogers, Ann, & Amos Lad More, both of ys parish Dec. 21 1775 p. 17.

ROSE, Mary, & Will: Clayton, both of Spots: Oct. 15 1782 p. 22.

ROUNDTREE, Elizabeth, & Callam Bailey, both in this parish Jun: 4 1761 p. 6.

ROWNTREE, Dorcas, & Drury Morell, both in this parish Sep: 29 1763 p. 7.

Rowntree, Drusilla, & Anthony Haden, both of this parish Jul: 4 1765 p. 8.

Rowntree, Mary, & William Whitlock, both in this parish Dec. 22 1767 p. 10.

Rowntree, Rebekah, & Rob: Wade, both in Goochland Feb: 7 1771 p. 12.

ROWLINGS, Rebeccah & Will Holliday, of Louisa Jul: 31 1788 p. 25.

ROW, Eliz: & Tho: Knighton, both in Louisa Mar: 24 1785 p. 24.

Rowe, Jean & Geo: Johnson, both in Louisa Oct: 22 1784 p. 23.

RUE, Sarah, in this parish & John Douglass, in Buckinghame Dec: 6 1762 p. 7.

RUSSEL, Eliz: & James Owen, both of this parish Oct: 23 1776 p. 17.

Russel, Mary, & Tho: Morris, both of Louisa Aug: 18 1782 p. 22.

RUTHERFORD, Eliz: & Tho: Bailey, Both of ys parish Jan: 5 1775 p. 16.

Rutherford, Sus: & Math: Lacy, both in Goochland Ap: 8 1772 p. 13.

Rutherford, Mary & Ja: Davenport, both in Goochland Jan: 23 1781 p. 20.

RYAN, Susannah, & Charles Richards, both in this parish Aug: 6 1758 p. 4.

SADLER, Lucy, & Jo: Bradshaw, both in Goochland Feb: 7 1771 p. 12.

SALE, Mary, & Asa Hyat, both in Orange Aug: 29 1779 p. 19.

SALLEE', Mary, & Daniel Tribue, both in Manikentown May 7 1760 p. 5.

SAMPSON, Mary & Will: Maddox both in ys parish Betw. Sep. 12 1750 & Sep. 25 1753 p. 31.

Sampson, Judith, & Drury Morell, both in this parish ffeb: 7 1758 p. 3.

Sampson, Sarah, & Tandy Rice, both of this parish Nov: 28 1761 p. 6.

Sampson, Elizabeth, & James Bennet, both of this parish .... 1768 p. 10.

Sampson, Molly, & Will: Poor, both in Goochland Sep: 24 1771 p. 12.

SANDIDGE, Anna & David Bennaugh, both in Spotsylvania Dec. 13 1787 p. 25.

SANSOM, Eliz: & Rich: Dickens, both of Louisa Oct: 20 1780 p. 20.

SANSUM, Catherine & Jo: Dickens, both of Louisa Mar: 6 1783 p. 22.

Sansum, Sarah, & Rich: Cole, both of Louisa Dec: 29 1785 p. 24.

SASSEEN, Olive, & John Short, both in Manikentown Sep: 18 1766 p. 9.

SAUNDERS, Rietta, & Will: Crenshaw, in Louisa Jul: 23 1779 p. 19.

Saunders, Calie, & Henry Brock, both of Spots: Mar: 7 1782 p. 22.

SCOT, ... & Alexr. Trent, in Manakin .... 175.... pp. 27-32.

Scot, Ann, & Valentine Martin, of Goochland Jan: 28 1769 p. 11.

SELDEN, Mary Taylor & Will: Douglas in Petersburg Dec. 12 1786 p. 25.

SERGEANT, Hithie, & Ja: Bates, both of Louisa Sep: 12 1783 p. 23.

SCRUGS, Martha, & Richard Minter, both in this parish Jun: 27 1757 p. 3.

Scrugs, Eliz: & Jo: Bellamy, both in Goochland Sep: 13 1774 p. 15.

SHEPHERD, Rachel, & Sam: Walden, both in this parish Jan: 22 1756 p. 2.

Shepherd, Mildred, & Will: Coats, both of ys parish Sep: 28 1775 p. 16.

Shepherd, Sarah, & David Thackston, both of ys parish Mar: 16 1777 p. 18.

Shepherd, Mary, & Charles W. Cotterel, both in Henrico Sep: 4 1777 p. 18.

Shepherd, Nancy, & Will: Lindsay, both of Orange Oct: 3 1781 p. 21.

SHILTON, Eliz: & Ja: Watson, both in Louisa Jan: 1 1773 p. 13.

Shilton, Sarah, & Tho: Terril, both of Louisa Oct: 23 1780 p. 20.

Shilton, Betsie, & Peter Crawford, both in Louisa Ap: 11 1782 p. 22.

Shilton, Sally, & Mat: Grub, both of Louisa Oct: 27 1783 p. 23.

SHOEMAKER, Mary, & Tho: Hancocke, both in this parish Mar: 25 1758 p. 3.

Shoemaker, Massinbard, & David Weaver, both in this Dec: 24 1769 p. 11.

Shoemaker, Sarah, & Jo: Brown, both in Goochland Nov: 1 1772 p. 13.

SHUCKLEFORD, Mary, & Da: Arnet, both of Louisa Oct: 28 1779 p. 19.

SIMSON, Mary, & Bartlet Perry, both in Louisa Oct: 12 1784 p. 23.

SLATEN, Martha, & Charles Davies, both of this parish Jan: 17 1756 p. 2.

SLATER, Eliz: & Abra: Redman, both in Louisa Mar: 17 1785 p. 23.

SLAYDON, Sarah, & David Walker, both in this parish Ap: 6 1758 p. 3.

SMITH, Sarah, & David Davies, both widows in this parish Jun: 1 1755 p. 1.

Smith, Eliz: & Da. Profit, both of this parish Ap: 7 1757 p. 3.

Smith, ffrances, & Will: Hudnel, both in this parish Dec: 15 1757 p. 37.

Smith, Mary, & John Lovel, both in this parish Dec. 20 1759 p. 5.

Smith, Mary, & Tho: Lilly, both in this parish Dec: 26 1759 p. 5.

Smith, Obedience, & Moses Tailor, both in this Jan: 23 1767 p. 9.

Smith, Mary, & Philip Walker, both in this parish May 25, 1769 p. 11.

Smith, Lilly Ann, & Tho: Cradock both in Goochland Nov: 30 1771 p. 13.

Smith, Ann, & Will: Johnson, both in Goochland Dec. 10 1771 p. 13.

Smith, Ann, & Will: Rice, both in Goochland Sep: 10 1772 p. 13.

Smith, Molly, & Clayburn Rice, both in Goochland Mar: 25 1773 p. 14.

Smith, Susan: & Stephen Ellis, both in Henrico May 20 1773 p. 14.

Smith, Magdalen, & Alex: Fowler, both of Goochland Ap: 15 1780 p. 19.

Smith, Catherine, & Rich: Paulet, both of Louisa Jan: 10 1781 p. 20.

Smith, Eliz: & Lewis Young, both in Louisa Sep: 27 1781 p. 21.

Smith, Nannie, & Abram ffergusson, in Louisa Nov: 8 1781 p. 21.

Smith, Susannah, & Elijah Dickerson, in Louisa Dec: 3 1782 p. 22.

Smith, Lovina, & Ja: Byers, in Louisa Dec: 19 1782 p. 22.

Smith, Eliz: & Alexr. McAlister, both of Louisa Feb: 20 1783 p. 22.

Smith, Pattie, & Jo: Trice, in Louisa Sep: 9 1783 p. 23.

Smith, Ann Dickerson, & Is: Morris in Louisa Dec. 23 1783 p. 23.

Smith, Eliz: & Will: Thacker, both in Louisa Dec: 3 1784 p. 23.

Smith, Eliz: & Cha: Cosbie, both of Louisa Dec: 13 1785 p. 24.

Smith, Sarah, & Rob: Kimbro, both of Louisa Jan: 11 1786 p. 24.

Smith, Polly, & Ja: Trice, both of Louisa Feb: 22 1787 p. 24.

Smith, Mary & John Stevens in Spotsylvania Dec: 18 1787 p. 25.

Smith, Rosanna, & Edward Dudley, in Louisa Sep. 17 1788 p. 25.

Smith, Susanna, & James Gillam, both of Louisa .... 22 1791 p. 27.

Smith, Frances & Lesly Arnet both in this parish 1792
p. 27.

SNEAD, Mary, in Albemarle, & Tho: Pope in ys parish Dec: 8 1776
p. 17.

SPALDING, Sarah, & Tho: Bailey, both in Manikentown feb: 13
1757 p. 3.

SPALDEN, Susannah, & John Lookadoe, both in Manikentown Jan:
24 1762 p. 6.

STATHAM, Sarah, & Will: Humphreys both in Louisa Dec: 12
1774 p. 15.

STEPHENSON, Martha, & Andrew Jamison, both in this parish,
Jul: 22 1762 p. 6.

STEVENS, Betsie, & Tho: Bunces, in Orange Dec: 26 1778 p. 18.

Stevens, Sally & Caleb: Lindsay, in Orange Mar: 10 1785 p. 23.

STEVENSON, Elizabeth, & Benjamin Hodges, both in this parish
Jany. 28 1762 p. 6.

STEVENTON, Eliz: & Jos: Page, both in this parish Ap: 13 1758
p. 3.

STEVENTOWN, Ann, & Charles Tony, both in this parish ffeb: 1
1761 p. 5.

STEWART, Mildred, & Cha: Stewart, both of Louisa Sep: 14 1781
p. 21.

STODGHILL, Sarah, & James Jordan, both in this parish ffeb: 27
1761 p. 5.

Stodghill, Mary, & Mathew Jordan, both in this parish Oct. 1 1763
p. 7.

Stodghill, Cecelia, & David Bailie, both of Albemarle Jul: 1 1777
p. 18.

STRANGE, ... & .... Bell, in Fluvanna Mar: 14
1781 p. 21.

Strange, Clary, & Francis Cammock, both of Spots: Nov: 6 1782
p. 22.

STREET, Rachel, & Thomas Hubbard, both in ys parish Mar: 31 1775
p. 17.

SWANSON, Sarah, & William Ryan, both in this parish Ap: 13 1760
p. 5.

SWIDDY, Ann, & Will: McGhee, both of Louisa May 10 1787
p. 24.

SWIFT, Mary, & James George, both of this parish Nov: 28 1767
p. 10.

Swift, Sarah, & Jo: Swift, both in Louisa Feb: 6 1783 p. 22.

Swift, Hardine & Betsie Swift, both of Louisa Ap: 15 1783 p. 23.

SWILLEY, Ann, & Will: Durham, both in Manikentown feb: 13
    1757 p. 3.
SYMES, Drusilla, & Will Begbie, both in Hanover Aug: 1 1770 p. 12.

TATE, Susan: & Will Arnold, both of Louisa Oct: 11 1773 p. 14.
Tate, Mary, & Anderson Parish, in Orange Dec. 5 1778 p. 18.
Tate, Marg: & Will Tate, both of Louisa Dec. 25 1779 p. 19.
Tate, Nancy & Sam: Hill both of Louisa Dec: 25 1788 p. 25.
TAYLOR, Ursley, & Jer: Doss, both in this county May 6 1756 p. 2.
Taylor, Ruth, & William Layne, both of this parish Oct: 25 1764 p. 8.
Taylor, Elizabeth, & Samuel Landrum, both of Manikentown Feb:
    11 1769 p. 11.
Taylor, Eliz: & Ja: Orford, both in Albemarle May 30 1771 p. 12.
Taylor, Eliz: in Goochland & Phil: Johnson in Caroline, Nov: 7 1771
    p. 12.
Taylor, Nancy, & Jo: Day, both in Spots. Mar: 20 1784. p. 23.
TALLY, Sally, & Ja: Gibson, both in Louisa Jan: 8 1779 p. 18.
Tally, Mary, & Jo: Gibson, both of Louisa Mar: 13 1783 p. 22.
TERRY, Nancy, & Henry Womack, in Louisa Jul: 31 1778 p. 18.
Terry, Jane, & Da: Bullock, both in Louisa Feb: 12 1782 p. 21.
Terry, Henrietta, & Will: Nichols, both in Louisa Sep: 26 1782 p. 22.
Terry, Sarah, & Rich: Thomason, both of Louisa (18 miles) Ap: 25
    1786 p. 24.
THACKERS, Eliz: & John Thackers, both of this parish Nov: 5
    1758 p. 4.
Thacker, Susan: & Jo: Denton, both in Hanover Jan: 4 1773 p. 13.
THOMAS, Angelany, & John Bailey, both of this parish Mar: 8
    1786 p. 10.
Thomas, Sally, & Will: Jones, both in Louisa Aug: 1 1780 p. 20.
Thomas, Joanna, & Harry Parker, both in Spotsylvania Jul: 25 1786
    p. 24.
Thomas, Mary, & Will: Daniel both in Louisa Mar: 30 1789 p. 25.
THOMASON, Sarah, & John Bibb both of Louisa Sep: 29 1779
    p. 19.
Thomason, Fanny, & Jo: Wright, both in Louisa Feb: 5 1783 p. 22.
Thomason, Henrietta, & Da: Shelton, both in Louisa Nov: 7 1786
    p. 24.
Thomason, Ann Lewis & Jo: Slaughter of Louisa Mar: 26 1790 p. 25.
THOMSON, Sarah, & James Gregory, both in this parish Nov: 28
    1756 p. 2.
Thomson, Joyce, & Elisha Leak, both of this parish Ap: 20 1760 p. 5.
Thomson, Eliz: & Jeremiah Johnson, both of ys parish Feb: 23 1777
    p. 17.
Thomson, Molly, & Jo: Brown, in Orange May 26 1778 p. 18.
Thomson, Eleanor, & David Thomson, both of Louisa Nov: 30 1779
    p. 19.

Thomson, Mildred, & Clayborn Gooch, both of Louisa Mar: 13 1783 p. 22.

Thomson, Sally, & Christopher Horn, both in Louisa Sep: 23 1784 p. 23.

Thomson, Eliz: & Emmanuel Terry, both in Louisa Oct: 14 1784 p. 23.

Thomson, Susanna, & Philip Shephord, both of Spot Dec: 23 1785 p. 20. *

Thomson, Susannah & Philip Shepherd, both of Louisa Dec. 23 1786 p. 24.*

Thomson, Unity, & Rhodes Smith, of Louisa Sep: 10 1787 p. 24.

THOMPSON, Helen, & John Johnston, both in this parish Sep: 23 1754 p. 1.

Thompson, Sarah, & Augustine McGehee Feb: 4 1790 p. 25.

THORNHILL, Eliz: in this parish & .... North in Buckingham .... 1763 p. 7.

THURMOND, Ann, & Alexr. Moss, both of this parish Dec: 27 1760 p. 5.

THURSTANE, Sarah, & Will: Proffit, both in this parish Sep: 12 1762 p. 6.

THURSTON, Ann, & David Clowder, both in this parish Sep: 29 1765 p. 8.

Thurston, Nanny, & Mosely Daniel, both of ys parish Oct: 12 1775 p. 16.

Thurston, Sally, & John Daniel, both ys parish Mar: 12 1776 p. 17.

Thurston, Massey, & Stephen Jones, both of ys parish Sep: 1 1776 p. 17.

Thurston, Mary, of Spot: & Jo: Netherland of Powhatan Aug: 22 1781 p. 21.

TILLER, Nancie, & Thomas Pugh, both of Manikentown Jan: 22 1769 p. 11.

TILMAN, Susannah, & John Woodward, both in this parish ffeb: 29 1756 p. 2.

Tilman, Eliz: & William Walton, both in this parish Dec: 1 1758 p. 4.

TIMBERLICK, Sarah, & Ja: Parish, both in Louisa Oct: 11 1780 p. 20.

Timberlick, Eliz: & Sam: Bever, both of Louisa Jun: 20 1782 p. 22.

Timberlick, Sarah, & Abraham Estis, both in Louisa Feb: 14 1787 p. 24.

TOLBEN, Mary & Eddie Holebrook, both in this parish Oct: 17 1756 p. 2.

TONY, Tabitha, & Will: Depriest, both in this parish Ap: 6 1758 p. 3.

Tony, Mary, & Richard Clark, both in Cumberland Dec: 6 1768 p. 11.

Tony, Nannie, & Abraham Stratton, both in Goochland Jul: 12 1773 p. 14.

*Seems to be a double entry.

Tony, Mary, & Cha: Rice, both in Albemarle Nov: 4 1774 p. 15.
Tony, Agnes, & John Gill, both of this parish Ap: 6 1777. p. 18.
Tony, Ann, & Anselm Alford, both of Fluvanna May 19 1782 p. 22.
TOURMAN, Frances, & Jo: Gibson, both in Cumberland Nov: 25
   1770 p. 12.
TOWLER, Mary, & Will: Whitefield, both in Goochland Dec: 14
   1772 p. 13.
TRABUE, Caroline, & George Smith, both in Manikentown Jun: 4
   1758 p. 4.
TUCKER, Judith, & .... Thurmond, both in Albemarle
   .... 1764 p. 7.
TUGLE, Molly, & Robert Cairden, both in this parish Nov: 27 1767
   p. 10.
TUGGLE, Mary, & William Mallery, both in Goochland Oct. 20 1768
   p. 10.
TURNER, Sarah, & John Watkins, both in this parish Jan: 12 1763
   p. 7.
Turner, Rhoda, & Liner Gooch, both of Louisa Ap: 28 1780 p. 19.
TYRRIE, Ann, & William Day, both in Henrico Jun: 1 1760 p. 5.
TYRREL, Beckie, & Nicholas Hunter Merriwether, both of Louisa
   Feb: 26 1787 p. 24.

UMBLES, Annie & Charles Bibb, both of Louisa Ap: 29 1788 p. 25.
UNDERWOOD, Ann, in Louisa, & John Curd in ys. Sep: 8 1775
   p. 16.
UPTON, Rebekah, & William Thomas Dec: 26 1754 p. 1.

VENABLE, Martha & Ralph Banks, in Fluvanna Dec. 9 1778 p. 18.
VILLAIN, Betty, in ManikenTown & Mat: Woodson in this parish
   Nov: 28 1753 p. 1.
VIVIAN, Frances, & Philip Bush, both in Orange, Oct: 6 1778 p. 18.
Vivian, Marg: & Will: Ferguson, in Orange Sep: 16 1779 p. 19.
Vivian, Frances, & Will: Quarles, in Orange Sep: 16 1779 p. 19.

WADDY, Eliz: & Capt. Rich: Philips, both of Louisa Nov: 20 1785
   p. 24.
WADE, Lucy, & Jos. Barnet, both in this parish Oct: 3 1754 p. 1.
Wade, Frances, & John Evans, both of this parish Aug: 3 1766 p. 9.
Wade, Martha, in this parish, & James Ricket in Amelia Aug. 7 1768
   p. 10.
Wade, Rosana, & Ben: Herndon, in Goochland Dec: 26 1771 p. 13.
Wade, Joanna, & Devreux Jerrat, both of ys parish Jan: 26 1775
   p. 16.
Wade, Hannah, & Peter Leek, both of this parish Ap: 19 1775 p. 16.
Wade, Ann, in this parish, & Maddox Stanley in Hanover Dec: 19
   1776 p. 17.
WADLEY, Susannah, & John Leprade, both of this parish Aug: 10
   1760 p. 5.

Wadley, Judith, in this parish, & Payton Smith in Henrico Mar: 17 1763 p. 7.

Wadley, Sarah, & Peter Walker, both in this parish Nov: 6 1766. p. 9.

WAFER, Elizabeth, & Daniel Young, both in ys parish June 19 1777 p. 18.

WAGER, Priscilla & Ben: Harris both in Maniken-town Betw. 1750-53 p. 31.

WAGSTAFF, Mary, & Umphrey Gooch, in Louisa Dec: 26 1783 p. 23.

WALKER, Ruth & Will: Cash, both of ys parish Betw. 1750-53 p. 31.

Walker, Judah, & John Brock ffeb: 2 1754 p. 1.

Walker, Hope, in this parish, & Nathaniel Lancaster in Henrico Ap: 19 1758 p. 3.

Walker, Ann, & John Bilboa, both in ManikenTown Jun: 16 1760 p. 5.

Walker, Ann, & (Const)ant Perkins, both in this parish, ... 1763 p. 7. (margin torn)

Walker, Mary, & Hezekiah Holland, both of this parish Feb: 20 1765 p. 8.

Walker, Sus: in this parish, & Shadrach Woodson in Buckingham, Aug: 14 1766 p. 9.

Walker, Ann, & Frank Clark, in this parish Sep: 22 1768 p. 10.

Walker, Sus: & Tho: Martin, both in Goochland Oct: 24 1772 p. 13.

Walker, Susan, & Tho: Martin, both in Goochland Oct: 27 1772 p. 13.

Walker, Sarah, & Will: Perkins, both in Goochland Dec: 17 1772 p. 13.

WALLER, Mildred, & Tho: Carrol, both in Louisa Oct: 4 1781 p. 21.

WALTON [or Welton] Susanna & Ja. Hilton, in Goochland .... 175.... pp. 27-34.

Walton, Louisa, in Albemarle & Jeremiah Jordan in Caroline ffeb: 22 1759 p. 4.

Walton, Frances, & Henry Mullins, both in this parish Dec: 29 1762 p. 7.

WARD, Tahpenes & Philip Webber Oct: 14 1751 p. 26.

WARRIN, Mary, in St. Pauls, & Joseph Curd in this parish Sep: 28 1762 p. 6.

WASEM, Susannah, in this parish, & Sam: Morris, in Hanover, Oct: 16 1766 p. 9.

WASH, Lucy, & Zachariah Matlock, both in Louisa Dec 7 1780 p. 20.

WATERS, Mary & Charles Blunt in Louisa Dec. 2 1787 p. 25.

WATSON, Mary, in Henrico, and John Ware in Manikentown Ap: 6 1762 p. 6.

Watson, Agnes, & Philip Walker, both in this parish Aug. 25 1763 p. 7.

Watson, Mary, & Augustine Edwards, in Goochland May 30 1770 p. 12.

WATKINS, Sar: & Rob: Furlong in Goochland Aug. 10 1753 pp. 27-32.

Watkins, Jean, & Edward Mathews, both in Goochland Ap: 21 1772 p. 13.

Watkins, Susan: & Jo: Gray, both in Goochland Dec. 23 1772 p. 13.

Watkins, Eadith, & Tho: Riddle both in Goochland Jul: 11 1773 p. 14.

Watkins, Eliz: & Isaiah Alley, both of ys parish Dec: 25 1775 p. 17.

Watkins, Eliz: & Tho: Cosby, both of Louisa Ap: 20 1781 p. 21.

Watkins, Nancy, & Jo: Creely, both of Goochland Jul: 22 1782 p. 22.

Watkins, Peany & James Landrum, both of Louisa May 15 1788 p. 25.

WEATHERSPOON, Nancy, & Will: Woolbanks, both of Louisa Dec: 29 1778 p. 18.

Wetherspoon, Mary, & Will: Page, both in Goochland Sep: 24 1770 p. 12.

Wetherspoon, Patty, & Jo: Thurston, both in Goochland May 18 1772 p. 13.

WEAVER, Mary, & Will Johnson, both in Manikentown Aug: 20 1770 p. 12.

WEB, Marianne, & Tho: Evans, both in Goochland Mar: 12 1771 p. 12.

WEBBER, Keturah, & Cornelius Harris, both in this parish Aug: 12 1759 p. 4.

Webber, Mary, & James England, both in this parish Oct: 1 1767 p. 10.

Webber, Mildred, & Ben: Chiles, both in Goochland May 20 1774 p. 15.

Webber, Annie & John Johnson, both of ys parish Jan: 27 1776 p. 17.

WEBSTER, Nany, & James Mattox, both in this parish Mar: 13 1761 p. 5.

Webster, Sarah, & James Knowling, both of ys parish Mar: 10 1776 p. 17.

Webster, Aggie, & Will: Woodrum, both of Goochland Dec: 16 1782 p. 22.

WELBURN, Sarah, & James Page, both of this parish Ap: 16 1768 p. 10.

Welburn, Eliz: & Rob: Page, both in Goochland Aug: 11 1779 p. 19.

WELDIE, Eliz: & Tho: Thomason, both in Goochland Nov: 19 1770 p. 12.

WELDAY, Salley, & Daniel Thomas, both of ys Sep: 7 1775 p. 16.

WELDY, Ann, & Jesse Laury, both of ys parish Jan: 31 1776 p. 17.

WELLS, Molly & Rich: Napier, in Albemarle Oct: 22 1772 p. 13.

Wells, Fanny Cheesman, & James Cole, both in Albemarle Oct: 5 1776 p. 17.

WHITE, Catie, in Louisa, & Geo: Earnest in Hanover May 17 1782 p. 22.

White, Mary, & Francis Giddin, both in Louisa Oct: 3 1782 p. 22.

White, Eliz: & Ja: Bartlet both in Spot: Sep: 25 1783 p. 23.

White, Sarah, & Byars Thomason, both in Louisa Ap: 15 1784 p. 23.

White, Nancie & Will: Harwood in Louisa .... 1792 p. 27.

WHITLER, Martha, & Lewis Atkinson, both of ys parish Sep: 4 1777 p. 18.

WHITLOCK, Eliz: & James Woodson, both in this parish Jul: 23 1754 p. 1.

WHITLOW, Jean, & John Crow, both in this parish Mar: 13 1758 p. 3.

Whitloe, Mary, & George Hancoke, both of this parish Jan: 6 1763 p. 7.

Whitlow, Judith, & James Perkins, both of this parish Nov: 1 1764 p. 8.

Whitlow, Ann, & Jo: Cannon, both in Goochland Dec: 29 1770 p. 12.

Whitloe, Obedience, & Pleasants Atkinson, both of ys parish Jun: 26 1776 p. 17.

WIGLESWORTH, Eliz: in Spotsylvania & Jo: Webber, in Goochland Aug: 8 1773 p. 14.

WILKERSON, Mary, & Joel Owen, both of this parish Aug: 29 1765 p. 8.

Wilkerson, Ageia, & William Owen, both of this parish Oct: 28 1766 p. 9.

Wilkerson, Lucy, & Moses Fuzzil, both in this May 1 1770 p. 11.

Wilkerson, Mary, & Will: Scot, both in Cumberland Oct. 21 1773 p. 14.

WILLIAMS, Susannah, & John Nicholson Dec. 8 1753 p. 1.

Williams, Eliz: & Sam: Weaver, widower, both in this parish Mar: 19 1755 p. 1.

Williams, Mary, & Will: Hanson, both in this parish Dec: 26 1757 p. 3.

Williams, Eva, & James Glass, both in this parish Oct: 9 1758 p. 4.

Williams, Susannah, & Will: Brocks, both in Henrico parish Mar: 24 1763 p. 7.

Williams, Annas, & Nathaniel Corley, both in this parish Ap: 9 1763 p. 7.

Williams, Mary, in this parish, & John Tod in Cumberland Mar: 9 1764 p. 8.

Williams, Frances, & Thomas Hall, in this county Sep: 3 1765 p. 8.

Williams, Ann, & Isaac Bryant, both in this Parish Mar: 14 1766 p. 9.

Williams, Agnes, & William Clark, both in Albemarle Ap: 9 1766 p. 9.

Williams, Mary, in Louisa, & Tho: Massie in this parish May 20 1766 p. 9.

Williams, Martha, & Jo: Holland, both in Goochland June 13 1773 p. 14.

Williams, Eleazor, & Francis Nickols, both in Goochland Jun: 20 1773 p. 14.

Williams, Eliz: & Abram Perkins, both of ys Jul: 29 1775 p. 16.

Williams, Mary, & Nathaniel Parish, both of ys parish June 2 1777 p. 18.

Williams, Hithy, & Jo: Keen, both of Spotsylvania Jul: 18 1781 p. 21.

Williams, Lucy & Drury Christian both in Goochland .... 1751 pp. 26-32.

Williams, Ann & John Mosely both of ys parish Dec. 27 1751 pp. 26-31.

WILLIS, Jemima, & John Woodhal, both in this parish Oct: 13 1757 p. 3.

WILSON, Biddy, & Michal Sullivan, both of ys parish Dec. 21 1775 p. 16.

WINFREY, Eliz: & John ffearne, in this parish May 9 1759 p. 4.

WINSLOW, Agathy, & Jo: Nilson, both of Spots: Jul: 6 1784 p. 23.

WISDOM, Frances, & Edward Atkins, both of Orange Jan: 28 1780 p. 19.

WITT, Judah, & John Madlock, both in this parish Nov: 22 1756 p. 2.

WOMACK, Judith in Cumberland, & John Clarkson, in this parish Mar: 28 1765 p. 8.

Womack, Mary, & William Waddey, both of this parish Ap: 15 1768 p. 10.

WOOD, Martha & Will Merriwether in ys parish Betw. 1750-53 p. 31.

Wood, Patty, & Jo: Ellis, both in Henrico May 5 1774 p. 15.

Wood, Sally, & Jac: Clark, both of Fluvanna May 11 1780 p. 20.

Wood, Susanna, & Will: Giddin, both in Louisa Nov: 16 1780 p. 20.

Wood, Catie, & Jo: Blackwell, both of Orange Ap: 3 1782 p. 22.

Wood, Mary, & Nathan Hall, both of Louisa Oct: 12 1784 p. 23.

WOODFORD, Mary, & Will Webber, both in Caroline Jan: 23 1773 p. 14.

WOODFOLK, Frances & Tho: Burnset, both in Orange May 13 1779 p. 19.

WOODFORK, Patsy, & James Allen, both of Orange Ap: 25 1787 p. 24.

WOODHAL, Eliz: & John ffoster Taylor, both of this parish Oct: 9 1755 p. 2.

Woodhall, Eliz: & Tho: Harris, both in this parish Aug. 3 1758 p. 4.

Woodhall, Ann, & Thomas ffielder, both of this parish Dec. 28 1758 p. 4.

WOODLOOK, Eliz: & Sam: Hicks .... 1751 pp. 26-32.

WOODDRUM, Sarah, & John Snead, both in this parish Ap: 6 1763 p. 7.

Woodrum, Elles, & John Utley Wade, both in this parish Oct: 21 1763 p. 7.

Woodrum, Lucy & Jo: Childres, both in Goochland Jun: 14 1772 p. 13.

Woodrum, Susannah, & Rob: Smith both in Louisa Jul: 8 1780 p. 20.

WOODSON, Mary & Tho: Woodson, both in Goochland .... 1751 pp. 26-31.

Woodson, Eliz: & Abram Salley (or Sallee) Aug. 24 1753 pp. 27-32.

Woodson, Judith in this parish, & Jonathan Knight in Lunenburg Feb: 24 1757 p. 3.

Woodson, Mary in this parish, & Ben: Weaver in Manikentown Ap: 27 1758 p. 3.

Woodson, Mary, & Aires Lane in this parish Ap: 15 1759 p. 4.

Woodson, Jean, & Mr. Rob: Lewis, both in this parish feb: 20 1760 p. 5.

Woodson, Eliz: & Shadrach Mims, both in this parish May 24 1760 p. 5.

Woodson, Sarah, in this parish & Jesse Ellis in Henrico Mar: 9 1763 p. 7.

Woodson, Sarah, & Turner Rowntree, both of Goochland Aug: 26 1766 p. 9.

Woodson, Eliz: & Will: Jordan, both in Goochland Nov: 19 1771 p. 12.

Woodson, Nancy, & Archer Pledge, both of this parish Mar: 2 1775 p. 16.

Woodson, Ursley, & William Pledge both of ys parish May 28 1775 p. 16.

Woodson, Jean, & Archibald Pleasants, both of ys. Aug. 5 1775. She was baptized by me. p. 16.

Woodson, Eliz: & Patrick Napier, in this parish Sep. 29 1776 p. 17.

Woodson, Mary R. & Nathaniel Garsdean Morris, both of this parish, Aug. 8 1778 p. 18.

Woodson, Anna, & Jo: Stephen Woodson, in Goochland Oct. 12 1778 p. 18.

Woodson, Eliz: & Josias Woodson, both in Goochland Nov: ...... 1778* p. 18.

Woodson, Jean, & Rich: Clough, in Goochland Sep: 23 1779 p. 19.

WOODWARD, Rebekah, & Will: Hawthorn, both in Goochland May 12 1782 p. 22.

WOODY, Mourning, & Alexr. Ross, both in Goochland Nov: 6 1772 p. 13.

Woody, Eliz: & Will: Nichols, both in Goochland Mar: 6 1774 p. 15.

WORLEY, Mary, & James Smith, both in Maniken Town Oct: 2 1760 p. 5.

WRIGHT, Eliz: & Tho: Dawss, both in this parish Nov: 28 1754 p. 1.

Wright, Ann, & Sam: Coleman, both of this parish Mar: 30 1756 p. 2.

Wright, Mary, & Thomas Mims, both in this parish Dec. 23 1756 p. 3.

Wright, Rachel, & Richard Scrugs, both in this parish .... 1763 p. 7. (margin torn)

Wright, Rachel, & Tho: Edwards, both in this parish Oct: 17 1766 p. 9.

Wright, Anna, & Ben: Page, both in Goochland Dec. 3 1771 p. 13.

Wright, Eliz: & Jos: Sandage, both of Louisa Feb: 14 1782 p. 22.

YAMONS, Betty & Levi Gathry both of this parish—1764—Dec. 27 p. 8.

---

*Decr. 3 1778, on pp. 129, 137 of the original

YAUNCEY, Sarah & Rich: Lane, both of Louisa 1781—Aug: 9
   p. 21.
Yauncey, Eliz: & Jos: Kimbrow, both of Louisa 1785—Jan: 6, p. 23.
YOUNG, Frances & Henry Mead, both of Louisa 1781—May 3,
   p. 21.
Young, Sarah & Jo: Humphreys, both in Louisa 1782—Jan: 3, p. 21.
Young, Judith, & Carter Chandler both of Louisa Jul: 24 1788 p. 25.
Young, Kitty & Tho: Gray both in this county Nov. 4 1795 p. 28.
YOUNGER, Mary & Jesse Grubs, both of Goochland 1781—Jan: 24,
   p. 20.

MARRIAGES NOT RECORDED BY REV. WM. DOUGLAS

BUT INDICATED BY THE BIRTH REGISTRY.

Date here given, unless otherwise specified, is birth date of first child shown in this register.

MALE INDEX

ADAMS, Samuel, & Susannah Jones Apl. 1764.
ALCOCK, John, & Patty Wood 20 Feb. 1777.
ALFORD, Jacob, & Ann Hunter 10 Dec. 1779.
ALLEN, George, & Mary Thurstone 11 Sep. 1766.
Allen, Clifton, & Susannah Jones 30 Jan. 1774.
Allen, James, & Sarah Crowder 14 Dec. [1755].
Allen, John, & Jean Tandie 26 June 1784.
Allen, Richard, & Eliz: Richardson 29 June 1782.
ALLISON, Jarret, & Frances Moody, 9 Jany. 1762.
*ALMOND, Thomas, & Mary Sanson ....
ALPHINE, John, & Frances Shepherd 5 Apl. 1767.
ALSTOCK, William, & Susanna Couper 10 Sept. 1785.
ANDERSON, George, & Frances Woodson 22 Sept. 1758.
Anderson, Col. James, & Susannah Daniel 3 May 1786.
Anderson, Nathan, & Martha Periere 4 Feb. 1784.
Anderson, Richard, & Ann Merriwether 3 Aug. 1782.
ANTONY, Nathaniel, & Fanny Jacobs — June, 1780.
Antony, Thomas, & Elizabeth Martin 26 Aug. 1764.
APPLEBY, William, & Elizabeth Milton 1 Dec. 1767.
†ARESKIN, Charles, & Sarah Currie 18 Aug. 1764.
ARMSTRONG, John, & Sarah Poindexter 31 Mar. 1783.
ARMSTEAD, William, & Mary Knucles 11 Jany. 1788.
ARNOT, James, & Sally Burroughs 4 Sep. 1784.
ARRINGTON, Knaves, & Priscilla Goddart 17 Apl. 1756.
ASHLINE [Ashley], John & Frances Shepherd 29 Mar. [1758].
†ASKEW, Charles, & Sarah Curry 20 Oct. 1780.
ASKRIDGE, George & Mary White 29 Jul: 1758.
ATKINS, Joseph, & Mildred James 29 Feb. 1779.
Atkins, Joseph, & Ann Atkins 29 Jul: 1789.
Atkins, Spencer, & Rebecca Yancey 14 Jul: 1796.
ATKINSON, Henry, & Rachel Potter 19 Dec. 1756.
Atkinson, William, & Mary Perkins 6 Feb. 1757.
*AULMAN, Thomas, & Mary Samson, 18 Sep. 1787.
AUSTINE, William, & Hannah Glin 10 Mch. 1758.
†AYSCOUGH, Charles & Sarah Currie 12 Jan. 1756.
BACON, Lyddel, & Ann Apperson 19 Mch. 1771.
Bacon, Thomas, & Milley Edwards 12 Aug. 1792.

*Almond—Evidently same people.
†Erskine—Evidently same people.

BAILEY, David, & Elizabeth Ryan 14 Oct. 1759.
Bailey, Philip, & Mary Smith 27 May 1769.
Bailey, William, & Molly Groom 26 Sep. 1768.
BAKER, Francis, & Mary Ashley 6 Dec. 1765.
Baker, Joshua, & Susanna Freeman, 31 June 1790 [sic.]
Baker, Overton, & Molley Lankford 21 Jany. 1795.
Baker, Will: & Mary Walton 5 Nov. 1783.
BALL, Lewis, & Rebekah Hughes 25 Jany. 1768.
BALLARD, Benjamin, & Jemima Harris 1 Sep. 1757.
BANTAM, John, & Jean Nichols 10 Apl. 1765.
BARKER, George, & Eliz: Brown 1 Dec. 1766.
Barker, John, & Nancy Harris 18 July 1786.
BARLEY, Will: & Molly Orford 25 Sep. 1776.
BARNET, Isaac, & Aggie Stokes 24 Aug. 1761.
BARNARD, (Barnet) John, & Agnes Allington [Arrington] 26 Apl.
    1757.
BARNET, Joseph, & Lucy Red 26 Apl. 1757.
Barnet, Will: & Hannah Fenton—26 June 1761.
BARRET, Charles, & Eliz: Clough 7 Feb. 1787.
Barret, Lewis, & Jane Price 23 Nov. 1781.
BARTLET, James, & Betsey White 12 Dec. 1784.
BATES, James, & Winifred Hix 22 Nov. 1747.
Bates, Moses, & Rebekah Fleming 1 Jany. 1787.
BAUGH, Burwell, & Ann Williams 2 Jany. 1776.
BEADLES, [Beigle] John, & Susanna West 15 Nov. 1784.
Beadles, Will, & Ann Yauncey 14 Oct: 1784.
BEEKLY, [Beckly], John, & Henrietta Raglin 29 Aug. 1782.
BELLAMY, Ben: & Dorothy Ham 23 Jan. 1779.
BENNET, Richard, & Ann Lee 15 Apl. 1763.
Bennet, Fisher-Richard, & Judith Amos 23 Aug. 1780.
Bennet, William, & Sarah Harris 20 Dec. 1767.
Bennet, William, & Mary Fleming 18 Mch. 1767.
BETHEL, Valentine, & Sarah Brooks 26 May 1768.
BEGBY, Richard, & Sarah Kimbro 29 Apl. 1764.
BIBB, Henry, & Sarah Mead 2 May 1781.
Bibb, John, & Sarah Thomas 7 Jan. 1782.
Bibb, Robert, & Sarah Mead 29 Apl. 1792.
Bibb, Will: & Elizabeth Biggars 2 May 1783.
BIGGARS, David, & Eliz: Fergusson 2 Mch. 1781.
Biggar, Will: & Martha Richardson 13 Oct. 1781.
BIRD, John, & Ann Bond 11 Dec. 1785.
BLACKLOCK, Jeremiah, & Eliz: Gentry 9 Dec. 1764.
BLOCKLY, Edward, & Martha Basket 12 Nov. 1744.
BOLLING, John, & Mary Jefferson 24 Mch. 1762.
Bolling, Thomas, & Elizabeth Gay 31 Jan. 1761.
BOLTON, Charles, & Elizabeth Hickins 11 Jul: 1757.
BOWLES, Gideon, & Ann Hughes 2 Dec. 1757.

Bowles, Patrick, & Nannie Owen 22 Nov. 1770.

Bowles, Philip, & Sarah Bacon 29 Dec. 1773.

BRADBURN, Will: & Mary Johnson 23 Dec. 1782.

BRADSHAW, John, & Sarah McBride 4 Nov. 1759.

Bradshaw, Lardner, & Ann Bradshaw 20 Apl. 1782.

BRAGS, John, & Frances Marks 26 Dec. 1781.

BRANCH, Daniel, & Eliz: Porter 18 Nov. 1762.

Branch, Gernat, & Eliz: Branch 2 May 1762.

BRENTHAM, David, & Frances Basket 25 Apl. 1762.

BRANSFORD, John, & Judith Ominet 5 Apl. 1767.

BRITT [Brett] Obadiah, & Ann Thomson 28 Mch. 1753.

BRETT, John, & Winifred Conolly 9 Oct. 1756.

BRET, William, & Hannah Conolly 12 Feb. 1759.

BRICKEN, George, & Elizabeth Adams 14 Aug. 1775.

BROADFOOT, Pat: & Agnes Broadfoot 8 Apl. 1762.

BROADHEAD, Jonathan, & Axie Esther 29 Jan. 1784.

BROCKMAN, Will: & Mary Lindsay 1 Jul: 178—

BRODIE, Archibald, & Eve Weesiger 10 Apl. 1763.

BROOKS, Thomas, & Judith Bow 15 Aug: 1767.

BROOMFIELD, Moses, & Ruth Patrick 31 Dec. 1758.

BROWN, Ludlow, & Elizabeth Hinds 5 Jan. 1772.

BROWNLEY, James, & Elizabeth Grant 19 Jan. 1782.

BRYAN, John, & Catherine Cashine 5 Sept. 1764.

Bryan, John, & Elizabeth Hamlet 11 Nov. 1766.

Bryan, John, & Obedience Burton 27 Nov. 1766.

Bryan, Thomas, & Christian Woolam 27 Jul. 177—.

BRYANT, John, & Elizabeth Hanson 18 Apl. 1762.

Bryant, Sylvanus, & Ann Hamlet 3 June 1767.

BRYCE, Archibald, & Mary Mitchel 31 Jul: 1770.

BULLINGTON, John, & Mary Witt 4 Sep: 1757.

BULLOCK, William, & Mary Bullock 14 Dec. 1773.

BURESS, Charles, & Sarah Woodfork 3 Sep. 1763.

BURFORD, Miles, & Ann Holman 13 Apl. 1765.

BURGESS, Edward, & Ann Francis 24 Dec. 1766.

Burgess, John, & Elizabeth Sanders 17 Nov. 1780.

BURKS, Obediah, & Mary Burks 13 Nov. 1758.

Burks, Matthew, & Eliz: Halfpenny 19 Nov. 1780.

BURNS, John, & Jean Travis 28 Apl. 1757.

BURNLEY, James, & Elizabeth Mills 13 Oct. 1785.

BURROWS [Burroughs] John, & Mary Harris 3 Jul. 1790.

BURTON, Charles, & Mary Hunt 10 Mch. 1781.

Burton, John, & Susannah Garret 27 Aug. 1785.

Burton, Noel, & Lucy Barret 9 Apl. 1756.

Burton, Capt: William, & Rebekah Cobbs 27 Jan. 1758.

Burton, Robert, & Priscilla .... 12 Aug. 1725.

BUSBY, Edward, & Mildred Smith 10 Apl. 1782.

BUTLER, Nathan, & Priscilla Antony 8 Sep. 1783.

BYBIE, John, & Jean Giles 24 Mch. 1760.

CAID, James & Morning Parish, 11 Jan. 1759.
CAIRDEN, John, & Mary Snugs 18 Jun: 1772.
Cairden, Robert, & Phyllis Woolbank [Wilbank] 1 Jan: 1764.
CALLIS, Will: & Martha Winston 28 Jan. 1786.
CAMM, [Camp] Joseph, & Eliz: Thomas 22 Apl. 1758.
Camp, John, & Mary Craighill 28 Sep. 1767.
Camp, Will: & Keziah Gentry 28 Feb. 1772.
CARR, [Ker] Dabney, & Martha Jefferson 7 Mar. 1768.
CARROL, Will: & Eliz. Jewel 13 Jul: 1753.
CARTER, Edward, & Mary Bullington 11 June 1748.
Carter, Elijah, & Ursley Parlow [Partlow] 13 Dec. 1782.
Carter, John, & Nancy Tugg 18 Jany. 1783.
Causeby (Cosby) Samuel, & Elizabeth Four 24 Jan. 1765.
CAUTHEN, John, & Agnes Harris 8 May 1769.
CAUTHON, Will: & Sarah Fairies 30 Nov. 1769.
CAVE, Reuben, & Mary Ramsay .... Jan: 1781.
CAWLEY, Nathaniel, & Ann Williams 10 Jan. 1760.
CAWLAH, [Corley] Will: & Morning Byers 19 Apl. 1787.
CESAR, Bartholomew, & Elizabeth Jones 19 Jul. 1775.
Cesar, David & Mary Henderson 29 Mch. 1762.
Cesar, George, & Elizabeth Watkins 10 Dec. 1767.
CHANDLER, Joseph & Ann Atkinson 20 Dec. 1757.
Chandler, Richard & Elizabeth Carter 17 Sep. 1770.
CHANCELLOR, Thomas, & Sarah King 12 Mch. 1757.
CHAPEL, Abraham, & Ann Drake, 29 Jany. 1768.
Chapel, Edward, & Frances Williams 22 Oct. 1760.
CHASTINE, John, & Elizabeth Logwood 23 June 1765.
CHEEK, William, & Jeanie Raglin 15 June 1776.
CHILDERS, Abraham, & .... 1746.
Childers, Major, & Eliz: Hampton 4 Oct. 1772.
Childers, Mathew, & Eliz: Turner 9 Jul: 1772.
Childers, Sam: & Elizabeth Clark 20 Oct. 1772.
Childers, Will: & Ann Childers 25 Nov. 1764.
CHILES, Henry, & Judith Daniel 3 Sep. 1781.
Chiles, James, & Susannah Graves 29 Jan. 1787.
CHOWNING, George, & Hannah Rogers 4 Jan. 1762.
CHRISTIAN, Charles, & Sarah Duke 18 Nov. 1770.
Christian, Turner, & Anna Payne 17 Jany. 1781.
Christian, Will: & Martha Evans 28 Aug. 1783.
CHRISTMAS, Thomas, & Mary Chisholm .... 1782.
CLAPTON, [Clopton] Benjamin, & Agnes Morgan 26 Dec. 1756.
CLARK, Charles, & Marianne Salley [Salle] 3 Dec. 1763.
Clark, Christopher, & Milley Tyrrell ....
Clark, Francis & Catherine Hunly [Hundley] 11 June 1767.
Clark, Jeffery, & Ruth Harris 19 Oct: 1756.
Clark, John, & Eliz. Ellis 2 Feb. 1766.
Clark, Turner & Jean Edwards 27 Dec. 1758.
CLARKSON, James & Elizabeth Abray 13 Sep. 1768.

CLAYTON, Richard, & Susannah Coleman 14 Jul: 1766.
CLEMENTS, John & Elizabeth Hugens [Houchins] 2 Aug. 1756.
Clements, Stephen & Susannah Tony 6 Apl. 1757.
Clements, William, & Mary Wright 24 Sep. 1757.
Clements, William & Isabella Halley 2 Dec. 1768.
CLIFF, George, & Marg: Nelson 30 Oct. 1772.
CLOE, John, & Frances Crane 9 Dec. 1773.
COATS, Isaac, & Rebekah Griffiths 29 Oct. 1760.
COBB, Robert, & Ann Given [Gisage] Poindexter 27 May 1785.
COCK, James, & Mary Lewis 9 Nov. 1757.
COCKE, James, & Jane Johnson 3 Feb. 1775.
Cocke, James, & Martha Holland Parish 23 Apl. 1776.
Cocke, John, & Elizabeth Richardson 23 Feb. 1768.
COKE, [Cocke], Thomas, & Ann Johnson 21 Jan. 1754.
COLBARD, [Colvard] William, & Mercy Holland 2 Jan. 1759.
COLE, Capt. James, & Mary Willis 19 Dec. 1747.
Cole, James, & Fannie Willis 3 June 1781.
Cole, Sam: & Elizabeth Cosbie [married] 29 Apl. 1777.
Cole, William, & Sarah Clayborn 10 Nov. 1775.
Cole, William, & Sarah Woodson 10 Jan. 1781.
COLEMAN, James, & Sarah Taylor 27 Feb. 1782.
Coleman, James, & Betty Coleman 27 Nov. 1782.
Coleman, John, & Hannah Hutchison 15 Mch. 1781.
Coleman, John Daniel, & Million Shamble 22 Feb. 1764.
Coleman, Robert Edward, & Catie Robinson 9 Mch. 1781.
CONNOR, John, & Mary Merriwether 27 Oct. 1787.
COOK, William, & Ann Nelson 12 Dec. 1782.
COOPER, Antony, & Easter Burdel, 9 Aug. 1783.
COPLAND, David, & Susan Skelton, 7 Jany. 1772.
CORNELIUS, George, & Susan Nelson 10 Feb. 1780.
CORLEY, Will, & Mourning Byers 26 Mar. 1783.
COSBIE [Cosby] Charles, & Elizabeth Sydnor [married] 14 Dec. 1759.
Cosby, Charles, & Barbara Byers 1 May 1784.
Cosby, David, & Mary Johnston 26 Jany. 1757.
Cosbie, John, & Jemima Yauncey 2 June 1781.
Cosby, Samuel & Elizabeth Ford, 5 Sep: 1761.
Cosby, Samuel, & Mildred Poor 5 Dec. 1774.
Cosbie, Thomas, & Elizabeth Watkins 16 Jul: 1782.
Cosby, Wingfield, & Mary Morris 18 Dec. 1772.
Cosbie, Wingfield, & Ann Baker, 29 Apl. 1782.
Cosbie, Zaccheus, & Morning Jackson 27 Jany. 1782.
COTHAN [Cauthon] James, & Mary Ferrar 17 Nov. 1755.
Cothan, John, & Agnes Harris 12 June 1756.
COTTEREL, Richard, & Martha Pimble 15 May 1757.
CREALY, John, & Nancy Watkins 15 Mar. 1787.
CRAIGWELL, Will: & Mary Burgess 11 Aug. 1756.
CRANKS, Thomas, & Elizabeth Richardson, 25 Apl. 1765.
CRANK, Henry, & Mildred Chewning 7 Mar. 1767.

CRAWFORD, John, & Jean Byers 7 Jul: 1783.

CRANE, John, & Frances Pawn 28 Dec. 1775.

CROSBIE, Will: & Elizabeth Hall 20 May 1780.

CROUCH, John, & Susannah Ellis 29 Nov. 1764.

Crouch, John, & Lucy Ferrar 14 Aug. 1788.

Crouch, Richard, & Judith Sampson 12 Feb. 1733.

Crouch, Stephen, & Elizabeth Ferrar 20 Mch. 1763.

CROWDAS [Crowder] David, & Priscilla Laury 10 Nov. 1782.

CRUTCHFIELD, Will: & Betty Sutton 21 Mar. 1766.

CURD, Edmond, & Elizabeth Crogwall 10 Jul: 1786.

Curd, John, & Lucy Brent 24 June 1759.

Curd, Richard, & Sarah Downer 11 Jul: 1762.

Curd, Will: & Mary Watkins 11 Oct. 1764.

CURL, Jeremiah, & Mary McGeary 24 Mch. 1760.

CURRIERE, John, & Elizabeth Runnels 23 Nov. 1774.

CURRIER, Robert, & Ann Thomson 11 Dec. 1784.

DABNEY, James, & Judith Anderson 27 Jan. 1777.

Dabney Sam: & Jean Merriwether 1 Jul: 1781.

DAILY, Tho: & Ann Gentry 20 Dec. 1782.

DALTON, John, & Maty Branham 28 Dec. 1777.

DANDRIDGE, Col. Nathaniel West, & Dorothea Spotswood 12 Sep: 1764.

DANIEL, Charles & Sarah Tate 8 Dec. 1773.

Daniel, James & Elizabeth Montague 17 Dec. 1775.

Daniel, Jesse & Frances Nelson 18 Dec. 1791.

Daniel, Obadiah, & Sarah Mosely 10 Aug. 1756.

Daniel, Thomas & Eliz: Stith 28 Sep: 1776.

Daniel, Will: & Patsie Red ....

DARNOLD, Abram, & Marianne Nelson 24 Aug. 1781.

DAVID, Ben: & Eliz: Jones 17 Sep: 1784.

DAVIES, David, & Sarah Pore 30 May 1756.

DAVIE, Peter, & Elizabeth Moracet 8 Jul: 1763.

DAVIS, Abram, & Ann Johnson 10 Apl. 1781.

Davis, David & Catie Blackie 1 Oct: 1779.

Davis, Jeremiah, & Ursley Taylor 16 feb. 1767.

Davis, ... & Mary Cole 14 Jul: 1772.

Davis, James, & Sarah Blackie (or Blakey) 21 Mar: 1781.

Davis, James, & Mary Williams 11 Jan: 1771.

Davis, John & Ann Tinsley 13 Mar: 1767.

Davis, John Lewis, & Jean Edmondson 16 Apl. 1766.

Davis, Robert & Rebekah Martin 26 Mch. 1782.

Davis, Stephen, & Eliz. Bow, 1 Feb. 1776.

DAY, Henry & Sarah Shortly 23 Jan: 1785.

Day, John, & Dorothy Henly, 15 Jan: 1762.

DELANY, John, & Mildred Groom .... 1775.

DENNISON, John, & Eliz: Smith 2 May 1781.

DENTON, Thomas, & Mary Faries, 1 Oct. 1771.

DEPP, Peter, & Susannah Harris 3 Apl. 1763.

DEPRIEST, Robert, & Martha Baily 15 Oct: 1766.
DESPERATE, [or Desphire] Thomas, & Mary Pulham 14 Apl. 1782.
DICKERSON, James, & Mary Cole [alias Barclay,]* were married
    Feb: 1778.
DICKINSON, Thomas & Mary McNemar 2 Sept. 1786.
DICKS, James & Henrietta Reevis 3 May 1758.
DICKSON, John, & Susannah Hooker 4 Sept. 1774.
DOUGLALS, Robert, & Cat: .... 1741.
DRAKE, Thomas, & Lucy .... 1761.
Drake, Will & Mary Watts 3 Mch. 1761.
DRUINE, James, & Mary Weaver 5 Jun: 1757.
DRUMRIGHT, Thomas, & Sarah Crafton 27 Jan. 1764.
Drumright, Will: & Eliz: Jones 27 Aug. 178—.
DUKE, Clevish & Nancy Brouken 7 Sep. 1783.
DUNCAN, Robert, & Sarah Turner 15 Mch. 1776.
DUVAL, Benjamin, & Ann Kay 24 Jan: 1765.
Duval, Joseph & Eliz: Shepherd 24 Sep. 1773.
DYCHES, James & Henrietta Reeves 20 Apl. 1760.
Dyches, John, & Judith Lewis 7 Dec. 1746.

EADS, Isaac, & Eliz: Allen 2 Dec. 1757.
EAST, Thomas, & Winnifred Champion 23 Oct. 1757.
EASTIS, Richard, & .... Ealcot 25 Sept. 1784.
EDMONDSON, John, & Mary Norman 28 Dec. 1782.
EDMONDSTON, Will: & Hannah Walden 10 Nov. 1785.
EDWARDS Charles, & Mary Daniel 9 June 1767.
Edwards, Joseph, & Mary Bibb 4 Apl. 1790.
Edwards, Reuben, & Mary Clements 7 Dec. 1783.
Edwards, Zachariah, & Susannah Thomas .... 1771.
ELDRIDGE, Thomas, & Winnifred Millar 20 Feb. 1776.
ELLIS, Joseph, & Eliz: Perkins .... 175—.
ENGLAND, John & Ann Newbanks [Eubank] 15 Dec. 1764.
EUBANKS, Richard, & Sylla Hewit 22 May 1770.
EVANS, Joseph & Susannah Lacy 22 Jany. 1744.

FAGG, Charles, & Ann Mare 15 Apl. 1786.
FAG, John, & Lucy Talford 3 Oct. 1787.
FARMER [or FARMBROUGH] Thomas, & Mary Anderson 10 Jan:
    1757.
Farmer, Thomas, & Anna Pitts 23 Mch. 1783.
FERGUSSON, Abram, & Nanny Smith 1 Dec. 1782.
FFERRAR, John & Mary Wadlaw 30 Nov: 1755.
fferrar, Joseph-Royal, & Phebe Harris 18 Jul: 1763.
fferrar, Richard, & Eliz: Sanders 20 Mch. 1756.
fferrar, Thomas, & Elizabeth: fferrar 23 Nov. 1756.
fferrar, Will: & Mary Williams 2 Dec. 1755.
FFERRIS, William, & Martha Trueman 11 Oct. 1758.
FERROL, Charles, & Sarah Williams, 29 June 1767.

*She m. 1st, George Barclay.

FFIELD, Richard, & Elizabeth Morrell .... Oct. 1757.

FFIELDER, Bartholomew, & Ann Shoemaker, 22 May 1756.

ffielder, Thomas, & Judith Craigwall 26 Apl. 1757.

FFINCH, Blagden, & Elizabeth Barnet 1 Aug. 1763.

ffinch, John, & Mary Williamson 1 Oct. 1757.

FINNICK, John, & Mary Richardson, 8 Apl. 1775.

FITZPATRICK, Peter, & Mary Perkins .... 1771.

FFIRMAN, Benjamin, & Susannah Moss 8 Jan: 1759.

FFLEMING, Tarleton, & Mary Randolph 18 Jul: 1763.

ffleming, Will: & Betty Champ 29 Apl. 1776.

FFLOURNOY, Samuel, & Elizabeth Harris 30 Sep. 1763.

FOP, [Phop] Benjamin, & Mary Reeves 4 Oct. 1782.

FORD, Thomas, & Keturah Winn 15 Jany. 1758.

FORE, John, & Winifred Alvison 9 June 1782.

FONTAINE, Aaron, & Barbara Tyrrel, (married) 19 May 1773.

FOSTER, Edmond, & Sarah Taylor 3 Oct. 1783.

ffoster, John, & Eliz: Woodhall .... Aug. 1756.

Foster, Richard, & Eliz: Spencer 5 Sept. 1780.

Foster, Thomas, & Susannah Foster 30 Oct. 1782.

FFOWLER, Alexr. & Sarah Bugg 2 Jan. 1759.

Fowler, John, & Rebekah Archer 30 Sept. 1768.

FOX, John, & Grace Young 10 Nov. 1782.

FRANCIS, Reuben, & Frances Napier .... 1766.

FFREEMAN, Holman, & .... Cox 13 June 1756.

ffreeman, Isaac & Barbara Gray 29 Mar. 1783.

freeman, John & Christian Rory 8 Apl. 1771.

Freeman, Robert, & Sarah Hill 28 Dec. 1780.

FFRETWELL, John, & Mary Bullock 1 Dec. 1770.

FFULCHER,-John, & Susannah George 17 Apl. 1771.

Fulcher, Samuel, & Leadia Hopkins 8 Jany. 1786.

FFURBUSH, William, & Sarah Richardson 7 Jan. 1765.

FFURLONG, Robert, & Sarah Watkins 9 May 1756.

GAINS, James, & Agnes Rollins 15 Mch. 1782.

Gaines, Richard, & Mildred Hollinger 1 Jan: 1761.

Gains, William, & Mary Strawn 11 Oct. 1787.

GALDEN, Samuel, & Elizabeth Turner 28 Dec. 1764.

GAMBIL, Henry, & Charlotte Juet, 21 June 1777.

GARLANDS, Thomas, & Eliz: Garlands 6 May 1782.

GARNER, Henry, & Jane Gatly 4 Aug. 1788.

GARET, Will: & Ann Johnson 27 Feb. 1782.

Garret, Henry, & Mary Johnson 10 Feb. 1781.

GARTH, David, & Frances Snead 23 Nov. 1781.

GARTHWRIGHT, Will, & Jean Ann Garthwright 14 Ap: 1769.

GAY, Charles & Ann Adkins 24 Jan: 1768.

GEDDY, Gerard, & Mary Bright, 2 feb. 1765.

GENTRY, John, & Milley Edwards 18 May 1781.

Gentry, Nathaniel, & Marianne Black 15 Mch. 1781.

Gentry, Nicholas, & Sarah Dickin 8 Jul: 1781.
GEORGE, James, & Agatha Watts 11 Nov. 1738.
GERRANT, John, & Eliz: Porter 11 Oct. 1770.
GIBSON, Gideon, & Susanna Branham .... Nov. 1772.
Gibson, James, & Sally Williams 27 May 1787.
Gipson, Thornton, & Eliz: Watkins 18 June 1784.
GLEN, John, & Mary Thomas 12 June 1782.
Glen, John, & Mary Bolton 30 May 1785.
Glen, Tyree, & Sarah Shilton 17 May 1764.
GOING, Aaron, & Mary Going 31 July 1763.
Going, Philip, & Judith Potter 4 Mar. 1770.
GOLSON, John, & Frances Strueman (Tourman) 12 Sept. 1771.
GOUGE [Gooch] Thomas, & Lucy Higgins 20 June 1773.
Gooch, Will: & Lovinah Clements 16 Feb: 1769.
GOODMAN, John, & Jeannie Lawrie 26 Mar: 1781.
Goodman, Overton, & Mary Camp 7 feb. 1765.
GORDON, Will: & Catherine Mitchel 24 Feb. 1773.
GOWAN, Will: & Anna Stacia Sullivan 17 Sep. 1756.
GRADY, George, & Fannie Biglow 30 Dec. 1795.
GRAVES, Henry, & Mary Cussins .... 1770.
Graves, Isaac, & Betty Coward [Cowherd] 28 Jan: 1781.
Graves, Ralph, & Judith Womack 1 Sept. 1756.
GRAY, Henry, & Ruth Mutrie 4 June 1768.
Gray, Thomas, & Letty Harris 8 Feb. 1759.
GRAYDY, James, & Eliz: Jennings 17 Jan. 1782.
GRAYSON, James, & Eliz: Williams .... 1756.
GREEN, John, & Mary Parish 24 Oct. 1757.
Green, John, & Sarah Griffiths 20 Jan. 1763.
Green, Thomas, & Susanna Hall 1 Dec. 1783.
Green, Thomas, & Mary Clark 3 Nov. 1781.
Green, Billie, & Lucy Sexton 5 Feb. 1780.
GROOM, Will: & Dorothy Mathison 29 Aug. 1757.
GILLAM, John, & Sarah Faris 27 Apl. 1761.
Guillam, Will: & Ann Symes 14 Apl. 1782.
GUNTER, John, & Susannah Harris .... 1783.
GWIN, Alman, & Mary Evans 30 Nov. 1755.
Gwin, Bartley, & Catherine ffembrag 3 Mar. 1757.

HADEN, George, & Elizabeth Taylor 7 Mch. 1775.
Haden, John, & Jean Moseley 10 Dec. 1757.
Haden, Joseph, & Eliz: Handley, or Hundley 3 Feb. 1764.
Haden, Joseph, & Mary Peatross 30 Apl. 1774.
HAINES, John, & Frances Yarbrough 16 June 1783.
HALEY, Bartlett, & Jean Streatum 16 Aug. 1770.
HAMMOND, James, & Mary Hargiss 29 Jan. 1760.
HANCOKE, Major, & Ann Thomas 18 June 1786.
Hancoke, Major, & Mary Moreland 5 Sep. 1782.
Hancoke, Stephen, & Catherine Merchant 29 Aug. 1766.

HANKINS, Joseph, & Hannah Aggin 20 Feb. 1781.
HANSON, John, & Judith ffields 4 Jany. 1760.
Hanson, Richard, & Mary Milton 16 June 1781.
HARDINE, Groves, & Sarah Williamson 18 Dec. 1767.
Hardine, Thomas, & Jean Ferrar 3 Jany. 1783.
Hardine, William, & Eliz: Lockrum 2 Oct. 1763-4.
HARPER, Joseph, & Anna Harris 28 Jan. 1782.
HARRIS, Edward, & Jerusha Davis 14 Nov. 1785.
Harris, Frederick, & Eliz. Tyrril 13 Dec. 1784.
Haries, Jacob, & Lucy Granger 15 Sept. 1776.
Harris, John, & Obedience Turpine 20 May 1763.
Harris, Nathan, & Sally Knight 25 Oct. 1782.
Harris, Robert, & Peeny Walton 12 Oct. 1782.
Harris, Will: & Mary Hudson 29 Jany. 1758.
Harris, Will: & Sarah Steefe 23 Jany. 1762.
HARRISON, Andrew & Jean Dillard .... 1757.
Harrison, Benjamin, & Sarah Bullard 17 Jany. 1756.
Harrison, Charles, & Frances Hughland 20 Jany. 1762.
HART, John, & Rachel Gray 23 May 1782.
HARTON, Will: & Unity Lane 19 Feb. 1757.
HAWKINS, John, & Anna Gabriella Jones 16 Sept. 1783.
HEAD, Isaac, & Rachel Long 15 Dec. 1783.
Head, David, & Isabel Jones 8 Aug. 1785.
HEALE, Will, & Susannah Payne 11 Jul. 1772.
HEARD, Thomas, & Eliz: Fitzpatrick 2 Aug. 1767.
HELMS, Thomas, & Sally Powers 28 Oct. 1783.
HEMUS, Will: & Lucy Woodward 16 Jany. 1750.
Hemus, Nicolas & Mary Massey, 7 Jany. 1761.
HENDERSON, David, & Hannah Symes 8 Nov. 1785.
Henderson, Thomas, & Mary Wheeler 8 Feb. 1786.
HENDRICK, James, & Lucretia Gardener 17 Jany. 1782.
HENLEY, Leonard, & Eliz: Jude 1 Oct. 1768.
Henley, Richard, & Lucy Bowles 8 Jany. 1782.
Henley, Will, & Marianne Smith 22 Jany. 1773.
HARNDON, [Herndon] Lewis, & Frances Thomson 1 Jul: 1767.
Herndon, Edward, & Bettie Minor 12 Sept. 1784.
HESTEN, Austin, & Susanna Freeman .... 1796.
HICKS, Absolom, & Mary Haris 20 Apl. 1760.
Hicks, David, & Sarah Lee 5 Oct. 1772.
Hicks, Henry, & Betty Willis 24 Oct. 1756.
Hicks, Jesse, & Mary Grubs 4 Mar. 1770.
HILL, David, & Ann Thomson, 17 Jany. 1782.
Hill, Joshua & Caroline Singer 23 Sep. 1783.
Hill, John & Tabitha Bailey 22 May 1757.
Hill, John, & Peggie French 6 June 1763.
Hill, John, & Peggie Tolliver 23 Jul: 1769.
HILTON, James, & Mary Hall 28 Jul: 1763.
Hilton, John, & Mary Ligton 15 June 1787.

HINDS, Richard, & Mary Brown .... 1759.

HODGES, Edmund, & Nathana Walker 13 June 1757.

Hodges, John & Martha Price 27 June 1769.

HOGAN, William, & Susannah Williams 16 Jan. 1784.

Hoggan, John, & Helener Couts 4 Dec. 1781.

HOGES, David, & Mary Alsop 5 Apl. 1764.

HOLLADAY, Ben: & Sally Hampton 9 June 1786.

Holliday, James, & Sophie Sandidge 4 Sep. 1785.

HOLLAND, George, & Mary Coleman 15 Feb. 1762.

Holland, John, & Marth: Weeks 16 Jany. 1735.

HOLMAN, William, & Jean Martin 30 Nov. 1763.

Holman, William, & Susannah Thomson 31 Aug. 1766.

Holman, Will: & Becky Woodward .... 1776.

HOLLOWAY, Major, & Sarah Paterson 21 June 1780.

HOLT, John, & Jeanie Dudley 18 Feb. 1768.

HOOTEN, Thomas, & Susannah Green 28 Jany. 1773.

HOPE, Jac: & Eliz: Shorer 5 Nov. 1779.

HOPKINS, John, & Mary Martin 11 Feb. 1763.

Hopkins, Joseph, & Eliz. Timberlick 15 Jany. 1781.

HOPPER, John, & Agnes Toney 2 Dec. 1757.

Hopper, Thomas, & Eliz: Profit 19 May 1757.

HOPSON, Henry, & Martha Nevils 13 Sep. 1756.

HORN, John, & Sarah Perkins 30 Dec. 1755.

Horn, John Christopher, & Sally Thomson 5 Jul: 1785.

HOUCHINS, Charles & Ann Towler 4 May 1782.

HOWARD, John, & Eliz: Stanley 14 Nov. 1765.

Howard, Will: & Rebekah Morgan 19 Oct. 1761.

Howard, Will: & Judith Amos 13 Mch. 1756.

HOWEL, Absolom, & Ann Holland 11 Jul: 1770.

HOWGENS, John, & Martha Orford 14 June 1763.

HOWLE, Richard, & Ann Walker 16 Jany. 1775.

HOWARTON, Will, & Bathsheba Perry 8 June 1782.

HUBBARD, Daniel, & Sarah Pasture 26 Mch. 1781.

Hubbard, Thomas, & Margaret Kirk 17 Nov. 1756.

HUCKABEE, John, & Ellis Camp 4 Mch. 1769.

HUCKSTEP, James, & Eliz: Dobb 7 May 1784.

Huckstep, Sam: & Nanny Harris 14 Oct. 1771.

HUDLESEY, [or Hulsey] Charles & Hannah [or Anna] Witt 2 Jul:
    1756.

HUGHES, John, & Judith Nevil 3 Apl. 1758.

Hughes, John, & Mary Grant 15 Dec. 1763.

Hughes, Joshua, & Caroline Stringer 31 Mch. 1781.

Hughes, Rice, & Lucy Gardner 16 May 1766.

Hughes, Rice, & Christian Terrie 21 Apl. 1781.

Hughes, Sim: & Martha Biggars 22 June 1783.

Hughes, Will: & Sarah Murray 26 Aug. 1784.

HULCHER, John, & Susannah George 22 Jul: 1776.

HUMPHREY, David, & Jean Taylor 18 Dec. 1765.

HUNTER, George, & Mildred Miller 6 June 1761.
Hunter, George, & Mildred Austine 25 Nov. 1763.
Hunter, Peter, & Ann Cash 3 Jul: 1765.
Hunter, Stephen, & Mary Steatum 7 Nov. 1766.
Hunter, Will: & Charity Loftus 16 Jun: 1760.
HUTCHISON, John, & Mary Steers 26 Jul. 1783.
Hutchison, Robert, & Phebe Carter 13 Sept. 1782.
Hutchison, Will: & Sarah Reid [or Red] 20 Dec. 1780.

INGLE, John, & Mary Huchins, [Houchens] 10 May 1758.
Ingle, William, & Ann Nash 20 Oct. 1766.
INGLIS, Alexr., & Mary Kavanaugh 5 Mch. 1760.
ISABEL, William, & Ann Dillard 5 Mch. 1757.

JACKSON, Charles, & Jean Anderson 20 Jan. 1783.
Jackson, Jarvis, & Helena Lee 21 Aug. 1758.
Jackson, Will: & Susan Goodwin 13 Sep. 1781.
JAMES, Richard, & Mary Turpine 30 Dec. 1761.
JOHNS, Philip, & Elizabeth Wright 22 Apl. 1760.
JOHN, John, & Lucy Mallory 24 Jan. 1761.
JOHNSTON, Charles, & Agnes Thomson 30 Mch. 1757.
JOHNSON, Charles, & Mary Ann Ferrar 16 Dec. 1783.
Johnson, Daniel, & Hannah Edwards 5 Nov. 1756.
Johnson, David, & Mary Berryman 11 Jany. 1769.
Johnson, George, & Jean Roe (Rowe) 16 Mch. 1786.
Johnson, James, & Rachel Street 30 June 1758.
Johnson, Jonathan, & Ann Castle 24 Dec. 1787.
Johnson, Joseph, & Sarah Harris 21 Nov. 1757.
Johnson, Joseph, & Sarah Freeman, 17 Jany. 1790.
Johnson, Richard, & Dolly Powis (Powers) 7 Oct. 1772.
Johnson, Richard, & Susan Garret 1 Nov. 1780.
Johnson, Thomas, & Elizabeth Merriwether 30 Aug. 1763.
Johnson, Thomas, & Ursely Green 21 Jan. 1774.
Johnson, Maj. Thomas, & Urcila Row 14 Jul: 1781.
Johnson, Townell, & Jean Woodie 28 June 1760.
Johnson, Will: & Christian Leek (Leake) 13 Apl. 1751.
Johnson, Will: & Elizabeth Huchison 9 Oct. 1756.
JONES, David, & Betty Golson 12 Feb. 1782.
Jones, James, & Mary Golstone 13 Apl. 1782.
Jones, John, & Lucy Mallory 7 Jany. 1764.
Jones, John, & Susanna Timberlick 28 Dec. 1783.
Jones, Philip, & Elizabeth Wright 14 Mch. 1758.
Jones, Thomas, & Esther Thomas 17 May 1769.
Jones, Thomas, & Sarah Partlow .... 1784.

KER, John, & Elizabeth Henderson 23 Jany. 1758.
KILL, James, & Morning Parish 6 Aug. 1756.
KID, John, Ruth Parish 19 Sep. 1758.
Kid, Lewis, & Obedience Kid, 10 Aug. 1759.

KIE, Martin, & Ann Bibb 17 Feb. 1768.
KILSHAW, John, & Sally Parish 8 Feb. 1785.
KIMBRO [Kimbrough] Micajah, & Eliz. McNamara 7 Oct. 1770.
Kimbro, Thomas, & Bettie Forster 21 Feb. 1786.
KING, Ambrose, & Sarah Brown 11 Dec. 1773.
King, James, & Winnifred Stokes 14 Mch. 1776.
King, John, & Mary Lipscum (Lipscomb) 6 Apl. 1766.
King, Martin, & Martha Guillam 21 Apl. 1756.
KIRBY, John, & Sarah Morton 4 Nov. 1757.
Kirby, Will: & Alley Seay 28 Apl. 1781.
KNIGHTON, James, & Barbara Hall 17 Nov. 1796.
Knighton, James, & Molly Freeman .... Sept. 1795.
Knighten, Will: & Elizabeth Paterson ....
KNOWLING, Christopher, & Mary Emmerson 28 Oct. 175—.
Knowling, David, & Mary Fergusson 8 May 1758.
Knowling, James, & Sarah Webster .... 1776.
Knowling, John, & Mary Paterson 22 Nov. 1765.

LACY, Alexr. & Lucy Chetwood 5 Oct. 1765.
Lacy, Elliott, & Elizabeth Young 20 Aug. 1757.
Lacy, Nathaniel & Mary Bootle 2 May 1764.
LAD, Noble, & Judah Damarel .... Jan. 1753.
LADD, Will: & Sarah Chowning 6 Nov. 1785.
LOYD, Will: & Sarah Chowning 6 Nov. 1782.
LAFORCE, Rene, & Agnes Moseby 27 Aug. 1756.
LANCASTER, John, & Susan Singleton 20 Jan: 1781.
LANDRUM, Samuel, & Hannah Hawkins 17 Nov. 1765.
LANE, David, & Elizabeth Pryor 30 Mch. 1757.
Lane, David, & Elizabeth Philpots 5 Oct. 1770.
Lane, David, & Cat: Fairies 10 Jany. 1782.
Lane, Dumas, & Mary Dickson .... 1781.
Lane, Henry, & Frances Spiller 18 Jul: 1781.
Lane, James, & Mary Craigwall 22 Aug. 1756.
Lane, John, & Sarah Reems 5 Jany. 1769.
Lane, John, & Susanna Jones 10 Jul: 1787.
LANSDOWN, John, & Frances Whirley 5 Dec. 1761.
LAUNDERS, Kimbrock, & Mary Branham 24 Jul. 1782.
LAURENCE, Henry, & Elizabeth Stanley 11 Mch. 1765.
LAWRENCE, John, & Mary Ann Powers 2 July 1788.
LAURY, Aaron, & Ann Weldy 28 Oct. 1776.
Laury, Joseph, & Priscilla Fowler 10 June 1765.
Laury, William, & Mary Pulleing 14 Mch. 1763.
Lawrie, Aaron & Penelope White 30 Jany. 1757.
Lawry, John, & Elizabeth Davis 4 June 1757.
Lawrie, Mathew, & Elizabeth Goss 31 Jan. 1759.
Lawrie, Moses, & Elizabeth Clark 7 Sept. 1756.
LAWLESS, Thomas, & Sarah Jones 30 Dec. 1760.
LAWSON, David, & Ann Harvey 31 Jul: 1760.

Lawson, Jonas, & Mary Nash 3 Aug. 1767.
LAWYER, John, & Mary Mallory 16 Jul: 1781.
LE MAY, John, & Annas Branham 14 May 1776.
LEE, Joseph, & Molly Knight ....
LENTHICUM, Thomas, & Jean Geather 6 June 1786.
LEONARD, John, & Mary Price 13 Jul: 1775.
LEPRADE, John, & Temperance Ferrar 12 Jany. 1749.
Leprade, John, & Anna Williams 10 Feb. 1753.
LEWIS, Edward, & Ann Meuse 4 Apl. 1764.
Lewis, Joseph, & Sarah Williamson 13 Nov. 1764.
Lewis, William, & Sarah McBride .... May 1756.
Lewis, William, & Hannah Underwood 22 Apl. 1760.
Lewis, William, & Lucy Merriwether 31 Oct. 1772.
Lewis, William, & Sally Man 28 Dec. 1774.
Lewis, Zachariah, & Ann Tyrril 25 Feb. 1784.
Lewis, Waller, & Sarah Lewis 6 Oct. 1786.
LIGG, William, & Elizabeth Webster 6 June 1758.
LILLY, Thomas, & Susannah Smith 21 Nov. 1764.
Lilly, William, & Elizabeth Pollet 26 Sep. 1764.
LILSWORTH, Thomas, & Betsey .... 3 July 1783.
LINDSAY, Landie, & Cat: Quarles 1 Feb. 1782.
LIPSCOMB, Joseph, & Frances Tandie 24 Dec. 1774.
Lipscomb, Joseph, & Mary Kimbro 26 Apl. 1782.
LIVELY, Joseph, & Sarah Taylor 15 Oct. 1773.
LONGMIRE, George, & Frances .... 23 Nov. 1765.
Longmyre, Will: & Hannah Britt 6 Apl. 1769.
LUCAS, George, & Lucy Gerrard 18 June 1764.

McALISTER, David, & Abigail Tate 5 May 1784.
McAlister, William, & Elizh. Bib 29 June 1780.
McBRIDE, Edward, & Elizh. Williams 10 Apl. 1757.
McBride, John, & Mary Crouch 26 Sep. 1726.
McBride, Richard, & Frances Moss 25 Feb. 1782.
McCAWL, Stokes, & Mary Stratton 15 Mch. 1756.
McCawl, Stokes, & Agnes Williamson 29 Dec. 1767.
McCRAE, Roderick, & Mary Dudley 26 Sep. 1771.
MACKGHEE, Austin, & Mary Harris 19 Jany. 1786.
McGHEE, Augustine, & Sarah Wyatt 11 Nov. 1790.
McGhee, James, & Lydia Hansford Mullins .... Mch. 177—.
McGhee, John, & Mary Stewart 25 Oct. 1782.
McGhee, Joseph, & Ann Merriwether 5 Aug. 1786.
McGhee, William & Levina Smith 31 Oct. 1783.
McGUIRE, Francis, & Hannah Jackson 4 Jany. 1760.
McGuire, William, & Ann Mallory 11 Feb. 1758.
McKAY, David, & Helen McClure 10 Mch. 1768.
McKIE, Hugh, & Mary Lamkin 14 Jul: 1760.
MACON, William, & Sally Woodson 2 Mch. 1782.
MADDISON, John, & Mary Biggar 16 Aug. 1785.

MALLORY, Henry, & Sarah Dabney .... June 1786.
Mallory, John, & Lucy Sutherland 25 Sep. 1786.
Mallory, William, & Ann Hoggan 21 Nov. 1783.
MAN, James, & Betty Thomason 2 Dec. 1769.
Man, John, & Elizabeth Davies [or Davis] 21 Dec. 1755.
MARKS, John, & Ann Collier 17 Mch. 1766.
Marks, John, & Lucy Merriwether 6 Jany. 1786.
Marks, Peter, & Joanna Sydnor 12 Sep. 1769.
MARLOW, Charles, & Sarah Brewer 16 Jany. 1760.
MARTIN, Austine, & Ann Forsee 9 Dec. 1765.
Martin, James, & Ann Ogilsvy 8 Apl. 1763.
Martin, Joseph, & Sarah Hinds 11 Aug. 1781.
Martin, John, & Mary Cairden 7 Jany. 1769.
Martin, Mitchel, & Mary Martin 6 Jul: 1783.
Martin, Samuel, & Susanna Thomas Jones 14 Jul: 1765.
Martin, William, & Judith Hemus 3 Sep. 1756.
MASON, Joseph, & Sarah Downman 5 Jul: 1753.
Mason, Peter, & Elizabeth McKoy 14 Aug: 1756.
MASSIE, Nathaniel, & Elizabeth Watkins 2 Jan. 1772.
Massie, William, & Frances Adams 5 Aug. 1766.
MATHEWS, Edward, & Tabither Hopson, 11 Apl. 1759.
Mathews, Richard, & Agnes Farmer 12 Jan. 1762.
Mathews, William, & Mary Holman 27 Apl. 1787.
MATHISON, John, & Mary Mathison 11 Feb. 1759.
Mathison, John, & Mary Biggars, 24 May 1776.
MATTOX [Maddox] Benjamin, & Mary Moore 24 Sep. 1756.
Mattox, Jacob, & Susanna Clarkson 25 Oct. 1758.
MAY, Ambrose, & Ann Chisholm 3 Jany. 1781.
May, John, & Chloe Chisom 2 Mch. 1779.
MAYO, James, & Martha Williamson 3 Mch. 1764.
Mayo, Robert, & Mary Richardson 30 Jan. 1771.
Mayo, Valentine, & Ann Peterson 2 June 1760.
MAYDWELL, James, & Sarah Arp 26 Nov. 1756.
MEANLEY, Isaac, & Elizabeth Dennet 19 Jany. 1758.
MEEKIE, George, & Elizabeth Meekie 15 May 1783.
MEREDITH, Samuel [or James] & Mildred Bagby 15 May 1760.
Meredith, William, & Ann Burns [or Bonds] 9 Sep: 1765.
MERRIL, William, & Sally Haden 31 Apl. 1778.
MERRIN, Richard, & Ann Conolly 21 Apl. 1756.
MERRIWETHER, James, & Sally Merriwether 14 May 1785.
Merriwether, Nicholas, & Elizabeth Merriwether 4 Aug. 1772.
Merriwether, Nicholas, & Sarah Ragline 15 Mch. 1787.
Merriwether, Will Douglas, & Elizh. Lewis .... 1788.
MEYHIM, James, & Martha Hatcher 31 Jul: 1765.
MICKLEROY, Aventoun, & Sarah Dawson 6 Feb. 1773.
MILLS, Nathaniel, & Frances Thomson 31 Oct. 1785.
Mills, William, & Peggie Swift 7 Feb. 1782.
Mills, William, & Elizabeth Fountain 11 Apl. 1782.

MILLER, William, & Mary Heath 22 May 1743.

MILTON, David, & Constant Hog 16 Apl. 1765.

Milton, William, & Keziah Lyne 22 June 1781.

MIMS, Drury, & Elizabeth Woodson 5 Apl. 1761.

MINOR, Garret, & Mary Overton Tyrrell 2 Feb. 1775.

Minor, Thomas Carr, & Ann Redd 27 May 1787.

MITCHEL, Archer, & Hannah Kirby 8 Nov. 1761.

Mitchel, Archelaus, & Mary Gregory 8 Mch. 1766.

Mitchel, Barnet, & Nancy Lane .... 1782.

Mitchell, David, & Sarah Moss 5 Dec. 1756.

Mitchel, John, & Marianne Sinclair 7 Sep. 1775.

Mitchel, John, & Elizabeth Snelson 2 Jan. 1782.

Mitchel, Thomas, & Judith Moss 13 Mch. 1759.

Mitchel, Thomas, & Mildred Merriwether 6 Dec. 1775.

Mitchel, Thomas, & Isabella Jordan 10 Mch. 1784.

MORE, Charles, & Ann Wylie 3 Jul: 1768.

More, Warren, & Anne Seay 5 Sep. 1779.

Moore, William, & Sarah Perkins 27 Dec. 1758.

MORACET, David, & Jean Baker 29 Dec. 1768.

Moracet, John, & Elizabeth Blankenship 22 Jul: 1757.

Moracet, John, & Fanny Ford [or Fore] 4 Apl. 1763.

MORELAND, Wright, & Ann Wilson 8 Sep. 1764.

MORGAN, John, & Mary Rogers 21 Dec. 1758.

Morgan, Gerard, & Elizabeth Milton .... Oct. 1772.

MORRIS, David, & Elizabeth Guthry 20 Jany. 1784.

Morris, John, & Linney Brown 12 Oct. 1786.

Morris, Joseph, & Annie Potter 24 May 1771.

Morris, Samuel, & Mary Jones 18 Oct. 1783.

Morris, William, & Sarah McComack 25 Mch. 1765.

MORTON, John, & Mary Tandie 28 Mar. 1789.

MOSEBY, David, & Ann Coke 3 Apl. 1781.

Moseby, Samuel, & Jerusha Bowles 2 Oct. 1755.

MOSELY, Arthur, & Martha Camp 31 Jul: 1763.

Mosely, Elijah, & Nivine Garner 14 June 1768.

Mosely, John & Sarah Walker 14 June 1764.

Mosely, Robert, & Magdalen Gerrand 7 Nov. 1760.

MOSS, Samuel, & Elizabeth Tisdale 23 May 1764.

MULLINS, Harry, & Mary Tony 3 Oct. 1760.

Mullins, John, & Betty Conolly 16 May 1756.

Mullins, William, & Elizabeth Hutton 24 Nov. 1775.

MUNDAY, Abram, & Molly Burrows 3 Apl. 1786.

MYLOM, Samuel, & Sarah Kemp 28 Feb. 1764.

NAPIER, Booth, & Christian Norvil 19 Oct. 1765.

Napier, John, & Mary Champion 1 May 1764.

Napier, Rene, & Rebekah Hurt 19 June 1766.

NASH, Arthur, & Sarah Abrey 31 Dec. 1755.

Nash, Henry, & Alice Holland 23 May 1773.

NELSON, John, & Rebekah Woodley 3 Nov. 1781.
Nelson, John & Susanna Coleman .... 1784.
Nelson, Joseph, & Lucy Tate 18 May 1783.
NETHERLAND, Wade, & Ann Williamson 21 Oct. 1765.
NEVES, William, & Christian Mask 16 Apl. 1759.
NEWS, Edward, & Susannah Rogers 3 Jul: 1763.
NEWTON, Samuel, & Agnes Chiles 3 Jul. 1781.
NICHOLS, William, & Mary Peek 16 May 1760.
NOON, Jacob, & .... 26 Jan. 1739.
NORDEN, Christopher, & Mary Emmerson 13 June 1754.
NORMAN, Joseph, & Elizabeth Sled* 7 Dec. 1785. Baptized Sep: 12
    1785 [sic].
NORMAND, Joshua, & Eliz. Slate* 3 Apl. 1786.

OAKES, Isaac & Rachel Crane 17 Feb. 1775.
OGILSBY, Richard, & Sarah Fergusson 17 Dec. 1756.
Ogilsby, William, & Ann Perkins 6 May 1756.
Ogilsby, William, & Martha Ellis 4 Feb. 1774.
OMINET, Charles, & Dianah Hudson 2 Feb. 1763.
OLIVER, John, & Ann Sharp 15 May 1758.
Oliver, Thomas, & Agnes Boyd 20 May 1765.
Oliver, Thomas, & Agnes Rollins 16 Mar. 1758.
ORFORD, James, & Lucy Bailey 1 Aug. 1756.
OSBURN, Michael, & Mary Hanson 18 Jul: 1759.
OVERSTREET, James, & Frances Eubank 1 Jul: 1768.
Overstreet, James, & Nancy Lewis 18 May 1786.
Overstreet, Thomas, & Zillas Yearnie 19 Oct. 1784.
OWEN, Barnet & Mary Walker 22 Mch. 1757.
Owen, William, & Agnes Wilkerson, 29 Jul: 1769.

PACE, Jesse, & Frances Hall 15 Mch. 1777.
Pace, John, & Susannah Huchins [Houchins] 3 May 1759.
PAGE, Axelheath, & Christian Page 22 Apl. 1756.
Page, James, & Mary England 26 Mch. 1766.
Page, William, & Jeanie Stevens 23 Dec. 1755.
PANKIE, Samuel, & Betsey Belford 16 Feb. 1763.
PARISH, Abraham, & Martha Holland 4 Nov. 1764.
Parish, Booker, & Constancy Massie 13 Nov. 1767.
Parish, John, & Susannah Green 18 May 1770.
Parish, Jolly, & Ann Powis 8 Dec. 1767.
Parish, John, & Mary Parish 26 Jan. 1769.
Parish, Joseph, & Mary Pretty 6 May 1777.
Parish, Moses, & Sarah Martin 28 Jan. 1759.
Parish, Nimrod, & Ann Williams 2 June 1787.
Parish, Robert, & Sarah Beaks 17 Apl. 1785.
Parish, Robert, & Sarah Bowles 21 Aug. 1788.
PARKER, Richard, & Hannah Cave 2 June 1781.

*Probably the same people.

Parker, Winslow or Winston, & Mary Thomas 22 Apl. 1782.

Parker, William, & Susanna Winslow 10 Aug. 1785.

PAYNE, Archer, & Martha Dandridge 20 Nov. 1770.

Payne, George, & Mary Woodson 30 Oct. 1705.

Payne, George, & Judith Burton 23 Mar. 1758.

Payne, George, & Agatha George 18 Apl. 1756.

Payne, George, & Elizabeth Morton 17 Jany. 1784.

Payne, Jesse, & Frances Morton 28 June 1768.

Payne, Col. John, & Jean Smith 7 Oct. 1758.

Payne, John, & Mary Chichester 5 Feb. 1767.

Payne, John, & Mary Jones 5 June 1782.

Payne, Tarleton, & Elizabeth Winston 28 June 1784.

Payne, William, & Mary Thomson 24 Jany. 1768.

PEACOCK, Edward, & Molly Underwood 9 Mar. 1774.

PEIK, John, & Sally Sneed 19 Dec. 1785.

PEY, George, & Mary Eubank 28 Mch. 1767.

PEERS, Anderson, & Ann Powers 17 Aug. 1772.

PENDLETON, Henry, & Ailcy Ann Winston 24 Oct. 1786.

PERRIERE, Thomas, & Mary Bowles 27 Jul: 1767.

PERKINS, Abraham, & Sicily Turpine 28 Nov. 1756.

Perkins, Hardine, & Sarah Price 15 Aug. 1756.

Perkins, John, & Rachel Fergusson 6 Sep. 1757.

Perkins, John, & Mary Anthony 13 Oct. 1765.

Perkins, John, & Lucy Mitchel 2 Sep. 1766.

Perkins, John, & Sarah Sned 15 Jul: 1788.

Perkins, Joseph, & Hellender Taylor 29 Jun. 1765.

Perkins, Michael, & Winifred Rae 8 June 1781.

Perkins, Richard, & Jane .... 29 Sep. 1725.

Perkins, Richard, & Susannah Coleman 30 Nov. 1756.

Perkins, Samuel, & Jean Johnson 27 Nov. 1784.

Perkins, William, & Susannah Holland 7 Aug. 1757.

PERRY, Edmond, & Elizabeth Lockinton 29 Sep. 1780.

Perrie, James, & Nansie Tandy 18 Feb. 1792.

Perry, Larkin, & Isabel Collins, 11 Jan. 1782.

Perry, Roderick, & Jean Randolph 10 Mar. 1783.

Perry, William, & Ann Beazly 8 Oct. 1783.

PHILIPS, Richard & Ann Johnson 15 June 1782.

Philips, Richard, & Elizabeth Waddy, 20 Jany. 1788.

PHOP [Fop] Ben: & Mary Reeve 15 Dec. 1780.

PIERCE [Pearse] Joseph, & Marianne Page 19 Oct. 1763.

Pierce, Josias, & Elizabeth Britt 7 Mch. 1759.

Pierce, Muray, & Mary Bragg 27 Jul: 1785.

Pierce, William, & Hannah Bowden 21 Sept. 1756.

PLEDGE, Francis, & Eliz: Poindexter .... Sept. 1769.

POINDEXTER, Nimrod, & Ann Rocket 17 Sep. 1769.

Poindexter, William, & Margaret Daniel 9 June 1782.

POINTER, John, & Dolly Davis 27 Jany. 1767.

POLLOCK, Thomas, & Susannah Curd 6 Sep. 1784.

POOR, Abraham, & Judah Gardener 19 Apl. 1756.
PORE, Robert, & Judith Walker 5 Jany. 1762.
Pore, Thomas, & Elizabeth Mosely 23 Dec. 1756.
PORTER, John, & Sarah Watkins 26 Apl. 1765.
POUCKEET, Thomas, & Mary Franklin 12 Aug. 1766.
POWERS, Daniel, & Ann Lawrence 22 Oct. 1781.
POWIS, Major, & Dorothea Mathison 9 Aug. 1767.
Powis, Thomas, & Mary Trammel 13 May 1767.
Powis, William, & Judah Mattison 20 Mar. 1758.
POWELL, John, & Eliz. .... 21 Feb. 1756.
Powell, Samuel, & Sarah Nuckols 2 Feb. 1774.
Powell, William, & Elizabeth Liggins 2 Jul: 1767.
PRETTY, Thomas, & Elizabeth Harlow 21 June 1768.
Pretty, William, & Jean Hunter 27 Apl. 1764.
PRICE, Meredith, & Elizabeth Fox 31 May 1764.
Price, Samuel, & Elizabeth Perriere 31 May 1763.
Price, William, & Susannah Burton 7 Mar. 177—.
PRIDDY, George, & Penelope Davis 19 Jany. 1774.
PRUIT, David, & Rachel Vinninghame 5 Feb. 1763.
Pruit, John, & Ellis Addison 9 Aug. 1758.
PRYOR, Richard, & Mary Mooney 11 Dec. 1763.
Pryor, Capt. William, & Sara Wood 10 Feb. 1757.
PUGH, Willoughby, & Martha Landrum 2 Nov. 1763.
PULHAM, David, & Bettie Dickerson 7 Sep. 1786.
Pulham, James, & Agnes Matlock 5 Mch. 1781.
Pulham, Joseph, & Betty Holyday 26 Sep. 1785.

QUARLES, Tunstal, & Susannah Edwards 11 May 1781.
Quarles, William, & Frances Evans 10 Sep. 1782.
QUISSENBURY, Aaron, & Rachel Shilton 28 Mch. 1781.

RAE, David, & Elizabeth Rice 20 Dec. 1768.
RAGLIN, Isaac, & Elizabeth Thomson 23 May 1757.
RAILY, Isham, & Susanna Woodson 18 Jul: 1785.
RANDOLPH, Col: Thomas, & Ann Carey 16 June 1770.
Randolph, Isham, & Jane Rogers 25 Sept. 1738.
RATCLIFF, William, & Elizabeth Harrison 14 Jan. 1764.
REES, John, & Judith Watson 10 Jany. 1749.
RICE, Charles, & Mary Holman 3 Apl. 1756.
Rice, Edward, & Ann Ryan 16 Jul: 1758.
Rice, Hezekiah, & Mary Saunders 16 Mar. 1783.
Rice, John, & Mary Johnson 22 Sep. 1780.
RICH, Jeremiah, & Mary Hunter 24 Nov. 1758.
RICHARDS, John, & Ursley Rutherford 2 Jul: 1781.
Richards, Will: & Sarah Smith 14 Nov. 1780.
RICHARDSON, Landy, & Sarah Underwood 17 Mch. 1759.
Richardson, Robert, & Sarah Furbish 4 Sep. 1758.
Richardson, Robert, & Mary Bibb 3 Dec. 1784.
Richardson, Samuel, & Susannah Hales 20 Dec. 1767.

Richardson, Turner, & Ann Allen 22 Nov. 1766.
Richardson, William, & Nancy Arnot 10 Mch. 1785.
ROACH, James, & Mary Hardine 19 Jul: 1763.
ROBERTSON, John, & Judah Brier 7 Dec. 1758.
Robertson, Thomas, & Agnes Hill 19 Feb. 1769.
ROBISON, John, & Ann Ford 11 June 1758.
Robinson, William, & Agnes Smith 28 Oct. 1781.
ROGERS, George, & Frances Pollard 12 Jul: 1764.
Rogers, William, & Judah Bradshaw 25 Sep. 1755.
Rogers, William, & Mary Callifax 10 Jany. 1772.
ROUNTREE, Turner, & Sarah Woodson 23 Aug. 1771.
ROYSTER, William, & Prudence Watkins 12 Feb. 1761.
RUSSEL, Thomas, & Mary Gardner .... 1769.
RUTHERFORD, Larkin, & Rachel Morgan 22 Jan. 1758.
Rutherford, William, & Ursley Parish 14 Aug. 1766.
RYAN, Edward, & Susan Whit 22 Sep. 1774.
Ryan, Whitehead, & Elizabeth Fulcher 29 Mar. 1757.

SADLER, Benjamin, & Ann Taylor .... 1756.
Sadler, John, & Susanna Atkinson 18 Sep. 1769.
SAGE, Pater, & Elizabeth Stewart 25 May 1782.
SALMONS, Benjamin & Priscilla Potter 6 Aug. 1756.
Salmons, John, & Naomie Depriest 6 June 1759.
Salmons, John, & Judith Cairden 26 July 1783.
SAMPSON, Stephen, & Mary Woodson 16 August 1729.
SAUNDERS, John, & Mercy .... 13 Feby. 1783.
SANDERS, Julius, & Jemima Woodward .... Oct. 1755.
Sanders, Nathaniel, & Sally Patty 15 Nov. 1781.
SANDIFORD, Abram, & Joanna Branch 5 Aug. 1764.
SCOT, Walter, & Agnes Martin 21 Feb. 1767.
SCRIMJOUR, John, & Ann Lyon 24 May 1762.
SCRUGGS, Julius, & Sarbery Frinch .... 1766.
SEA, Abraham, & Naomi Lovine 25 Dec. 1759.
SEAY, Josiah, Prudence Utley, 1 May 1778.
Seay, John, & Rebekah More 28 Feb. 1781.
Seay, Stephen, & Ann Ryan 3 Dec. 1780.
SHAKINE, Roger, & Ann Carter 13 Nov. 1770.
SHAMBLES, Thomas, & Million Wells 13 May 1757.
SHARP, William, & Susannah Childers 24 Feb. 1767.
Sharp, Thomas, & Judith Sharp 13 Dec. 1781.
SHASTINE [Chastain] John, & Frances Branch 10 June 1762.
Shasteen, John, & Elizabeth Logwood 16 July 1768.
SHEETS, Samuel, & Susannah Langford 21 Jul: 1773.
SHILTON, Peter, & Frances Nichols 23 Jul. 1763.
SHIP, Thomas, & Jediah Moore 15 Oct. 1776.
SHODOANG [Chadouin], Francis, & Sarah Weaver 16 Nov. 1761.
SHEPHERD, Augustine, & Sarah Shilton 21 Dec. 1760.
Shepherd, John, & Mary Lilly 9 June 1761.

Shepherd, Robert, & Elizabeth Baxter 15 Nov. 1766.

Shepherd, Robert, & Elizabeth Blackstone 9 Apl. 1769.

Shepherd, William, & Martha Arrington 7 Apl. 1762.

SHOEMAKER, Evans, & Judith Burks 2 Oct. 1756.

Shoemaker, Thomas, & Sarah Hicks 30 Jan. 1756.

SHORT, John, & Olive Sassine 29 Feb. 1768.

SIMS, James, & Elizabeth Saunders 1 Apl. 1767.

SMITH, Childers, & Frances Field 25 Dec. 1763.

Smith, David, & Mary Byers 15 Apl. 1784.

Smith, David, & Frances Dickinson 5 Dec. 1789.

Smith, George, & Ann Caroline Tribue 7 Feb. 1762.

Smith, George, & Judith Gerran [Gerrand] 16 Apl. 1767.

Smith, Jesse, & Molly Henley 11 Feb. 1774.

Smith, John, & Susannah Raison 7 Oct. 1736.

Smith, John, & Elizabeth Hopkins 4 Apl. 1758.

Smith, John, & Caroline Short 17 Oct. 1764.

Smith, John, & Mary Storey .... Apl. 1764.

Smith, Leonard, & Elizabeth Hollinhead 7 Oct. 1774.

Smith, Michael, & Judith Rice 15 June 1759.

Smith, Moses, & Biddy Alexander, 12 Apl. 1764.

Smith, Nathan, & Unity Dickerson 30 Nov. 1780.

Smith, Obadiah, & Mary Burk 23 Aug. 1744.

Smith, Obadiah, & Lucy Poor 30 Aug. 1775.

Smith, Robert, & Susan Barnet 22 Jul. 1780.

Smith, William, & Elizabeth Watkins 4 May 1762.

Smith, William, & Sarah Pryor 2 Feb. 1785.

Smith, William, & Mary Rose (Rhodes) 23 July 1773.

Smith, William, & Elizabeth Young 15 Mch. 1774.

Smith, William, & Frances McGhee 7 Apl. 1782.

Smith, William & Catharine Bibb .... 1782.

SMITHY, Robert, & Rebekah Shepherd 6 Oct. 1756.

SNEED, Arch: & Sally Pope 24 Jul: 1780.

SNEAD, John, & Sarah Johnson 10 Jan. 1784.

Snead, William, & Catherine Sharp 6 Apl. 1748.

SNELSON, Nathaniel, & Sarah Spier 22 Mch. 1788.

SOUTHALL, Turner, & Martha Vandeval 27 Apl. 1765.

Southall, Stephen, & Martha Wood 9 Apl. 1787.

SPIER, David, & Elizabeth Wash 15 Nov. 1784.

STAMPS. Capt. William, & Elenor Brent 17 Oct. 1757.

STAPLES, David, & Christian Ford 14 Sept. 1757.

STARK, Benjamin, & Ann Chace 11 Oct. 1782.

Stark, Capt. Thomas, & Jean Williams 15 Feb. 1757.

Stark, Thomas, & Martha Price 27 Apl. 1763.

STEERS, William, & Sara Halliday, 7 Oct. 1783.

STEVENS, Henry, & Elizabeth Davis 13 Nov. 1786.

STEWART, Robert, & Jean Wright 27 June 1788.

STRANGE, Abram, & Mary More 12 Jul. 1780.

Strange, John, & Ann Mitchell 22 Sep. 1756.

STREET, William, & Judith Bryant 12 Mch. 1764.
STRONG, Nathan, & Catherine Callichan 10 Dec. 1776.
Strong, William, & Frances Johnson 22 Apl. 1764.
STUART, Joseph, & Ann Stuart 12 May 1788.
STUBBLEFIELD, Henry, & Frankie Smith 19 Oct. 1786.
Stubblefield, Robert, & Susanna Parker 11 Mch. 1783.
SUBLET, Lewis, & Frances Hillason 28 May 1763.
SUMMERS, Thomas, & Martha Wetherspoons 23 Sep. 1782.
SUMPTER, Christopher, & Elizabeth Farmer 29 Apl. 1762.
SUTHERLAND, Joseph, & Judith Appleberry 12 Apl. 1761.
SUTTON, William, & Tabitha Wisdom 18 March 1786.
SWANSON. William, & Mary McGuire 7 Oct. 1757.
SWIFT, Richard, & Elizabeth Rice 16 Mch. 1783.
Swift, William, & Frances Waddy 30 Dec. 1756.
SYMES, James, & Elizabeth Sanders, 18 Oct. 1770.
Symes, Fenton, & Keziah Hill 20 Oct. 1782.
SYMENS, Moses & .... 1770.

TALIFERRAR, Nich. & Ann Taliferrar 6 Aug. 1782.
TALES, Will: & Mary Tales 29 Sep. 1788.
TALLY, Story, & Ann Hagart [Harger] 10 Nov. 1784.
Tally, Will: & Lydia Cole 18 Jan. 1792.
TANDIE, Henry, & Ann Mills 6 Nov. 1781.
TATE, Ja, & Frances Hutson 8 May 1781.
Tate, Ja: & Rebekah Hutson 18 Ap. 1782.
Tate, Will, & Eliz. Hutson 17 Feb. 1782.
Tate, Zimri, & Martha Mayfield 6 Aug. 1782.
TAYLOE, And: Mintellet, & Lucy Fletcher 25 Ap. 1787.
TAYLOR, Absolom, & Sarah East 1 Feb. 1769.
Taylor, Edward, & Judith Coleman 13 Feb. 1776.
Taylor, John, & .... 1768?
TERREL, Joel, & Lucy Ragline 24 Aug. 1781.
TYRRILL, Chiles, & Margt. Douglas 8 Sep. 1784.
TYRRIL, Will, & Martha Winston 14 May 1781.
TERRY, Da: & Nelly Biggar 24 Feb. 1777.
THACKER, Benjamin, & Ruth Bowls 2 Jul. 1757.
Thacker, Nathaniel, & Kesiah Evans 27 Feb. 1767.
Thacker, William, & Mary Evans 12 Sep. 1756.
THOMAS, Charles, & Frances Amson [Anson] [Armstead] 26 Feb. 1781.
Thomas, Geo. & Mary White 9 Dec. 1775.
Thomas, Geo. & Sarah Payne 14 Dec. 1771.
Thomas, James, & Mary White 4 Jul. 1769.
Thomas, Rowland Sr. & Jane Thurston 22 Ap. 1782.
Thomas, Rowland, & Mary Parker 3 June 1782.
THOMASON, Fleming, & Ann Smith 18 Ap. 1785.
Thomason, George, & Mary Pollard 27 Feb. 1735.
Thomason, Geo: & Eliz: Timberlick .... Aug. 1782.

Thomason, Jo: & Susanna............ 24 Sep. 1785.
Thomason, Jo: & Frances Cook 17 Dec. 1782.
Thomason, Nath: & Patty Wood 28 Dec. 1782.
Thomason, Sam, & Ann Payne 4 Sep. 1774.
Thomason, Thomas, & Eliz. Lodan 28 May 1758.
Thomason, Tho: & Mary Wright 10 May 1777.
Thomason, Will, & Basset Umphrah [Humphrey] 23 Dec. 1781.
Thomason, Will, & Eliz. Hallom 2 Dec. 1783.
THOMSON, Anderson, & Ann Anderson 24 Dec. 1785.
Thomson, Cha. & Agnes Wood 11 Feb. 1783.
Thomson, Da: & Hellender Thomson 28 Sep. 1780.
Thomson, Jo: & Lucy Epperson 8 June 1777.
Thomson, Math: & Sarah Wyat 3 Oct. 1783.
Thomson, Rodger, & Ann Crenshaw 19 Sep. 1785.
Thomson, Stephen, & Mary Armstead 4 Aug. 1785.
Thomson, Waddy, & Mary Lewis 21 Sept. 1775.
THURLEY, Will, & Eliz. Applebery 1 Ap. 1781.
THURMOND, John, & Mally Dickerson 1 Jan. 1761.
THURSTONE, Francis, & Hester Richards 4 Jan. 1757.
TIMBERLICK, Jo: & Christina Thomason 22 Dec. 1782.
Timberlick, Philip, & Jean Fears [Feers] 29 Dec. 1782.
TINSLEY, Philip, & Kesiah Stodghill 4 Oct. 1765.
TODD, John, & Mary Williams 7 Aug. 1775.
TOLLIVER, John, & Eliz. Symer 23 May 1768.
TONY, Aaron, & Ann Weildy 20 Jan. 1782.
Tony, Bishop, & Sarah Ashly 20 Mar. 1756.
TOWLER, Cornelius, & Nanny Grubs 10 Nov. 1775.
Towler, Geo: & Fannie Bourns 3 Sep. 1787.
Towler, James, & Mary Jones 29 Sep. 1768.
Towler, John, & Sarah Thomas 2 Jan. 1762.
Towler, Limmard, & Hellender Churchill 21 Dec. 1767.
TOWLES, Stokely, & Elizabeth Downman 3 Jan. 1777.
TRIBUE, John, & Ollan Dupuy 23 Feb. 1766.
TRUE, Henry, & Jane Hatter 10 Dec. 1785.
True, Joseph, & Sarah Wheeler 1 Dec. 1785.
True, Martin, & Betsie Snead 17 Jan. 1784.
TUCKER, Simpson, decd. & Mary Kent 3 Jan. 1757.
TUGGLE, John, & Mary Huchen [Houchens] 19 Sep. 1756.
TURNER, Bartholomew, & Mary Johnston 18 Jul. 1765.
Turner, Henry, & Susannah Johnson 4 Oct. 1756.
Turner, Henry, & Jane Godby 25 Aug. 1787.
TYRRIE, Da. & Hellender Biggar 14 Jany. 1786.
TYRIE, Rich: & Tamar Hilliard 1 Jan. 1772.

UNDERWOOD, Thomas, & Ann Taylor 2 Oct. 1765.
UTLEY, Jacob, & Dinah Hillsman 28 Aug. 1775.
Utley, John, & Alice Woodrum 8 June 1770.
Utley, John, & Ann Lewis 26 Dec. 1755.
Utley, Josiah, & Elizabeth Gordon 3 Apl. 1778.

VAUGHAN, Joseph, & Ann Payne 9 May 1770.
Vaughan, Mathew, & Mary Martin 23 Jul: 1767.
Vaughan, Hugh-Lewis, & Mary Martin 27 May 1760.
Vaughan, William, & Ann Clark 12 Mch. 1767.
VEST, John, & Lucy Chandler 27 Sept. 1784.

WADE, Dan, & Delphe Green 4 Mar. 1782.
Wade, David, & Eliz. Price 18 Jan. 1771.
Wades, Nath. & Mary Taylor 27 Ap. 1782.
Wade, Will: & Ann Cothan 23 Jun. 1757.
Wade, Will: & Ann Baily 17 Feb. 1784. (See Will: Weldie, below.)
WADDY, Samuel, & Mary Cook 15 Sep. 1783.
WALKER, David, & Ann Horn 16 Aug. 1767.
Walker, Joseph, & Mary Howard 23 Sep. 1764.
Walker, Philip, & Susannah Hilton 26 Sep. 1759.
Walker, Shadrach, & Hannah Shepherd 12 Ap. 1783.
Walker, Tho: & Mildred Thornton 22 Jun. 1764.
WALDROP, [WARDROP] Sam: & Jean Foster 14 Oct. 1784.
*WARE, ..., & Betsy Brown 20 Feb. 1783.
*Ware, Malachi, & Bettie Brown 22 Aug. 1785.
WASH, Tho: & Henleey Wash 14 Nov. 1786.
WATKINS, Geo. & Eliz. Watkins 13 Feb. 1782.
Watkins, Joel, & Barbara Overton Harris 12 Jan. 1784.
Watkins, Thomas, & Dorothy Dickson 27 May 1761.
WATSON, John, & Ann Jones 5 Ap. 1773.
Watson, Jo: & Nancy Anderson 20 June 1781.
*WAUGH, Malachi, & Betty Brown 20 Feb. 1781.
WEBB, Will: & Mourning Pruit 12 Ap. 1756.
WEBBER, William, & Anne Winn 1 Aug. 1764.
WEBSTER, Geo: & Ann Humphreys 8 May 1787.
Webster, Luke, & Sally Begbie 13 Oct. 1772.
Webster, Nath: & Marg. Steel 19 Jul. 1756.
WEISEGER, Daniel, & Mary Bell 17 May 1763.
WELDIE, Will: & Ann Baily 4 June 1782. [See Will: Wade, above.]
WELBURN, Gunnery, & Judith Owen 14 Sep. 1771.
WELLBURN, Lewis, & Mary Ship 23 Ap. 1760.
WELBURN, Will: & Jane Alsome 15 Dec. 1773.
WHARTON, Jo: & Rachel Schooler 6 Sep. 1785.
Wharton, Sam: & Lucy Schouler 12 May 1785.
WHEELER, Mark, & Frances Hutson 22 Oct. 1781.
WHITE, George, & Marg: Adrian [Orren] 13 Sep. 1763.
White, Rich: & Lucy Richardson 29 Oct. 1773.
White, Will: & Cattie Chapman 20 Oct. 1785.
WHITEHEAD, Joseph, & Grisheld Rogers 8 May 1751.
WHITLOE, Henry, & Martha Radford 6 Jan. 1769.
WHITLOCK, John, & Catherine Barnet 1 Aug. 1756.
Whitlock, John, & Sarah Edwards 28 Oct. 1774.

*Same people.

Whitlock, Tho. & Mary Williamson 6 May 1756.

Whitlock, Will: & Mildred Gentry 23 June 1783.

WILKERSON, Richard, & Mary Worsham 3 Aug. 1759.

WILKISON, Townsend, & Mally Carter 13 Oct. 1771.

WILLIAMS, Drury, & Tabitha Marshal 8 Nov. 1771.

Williams, Eliezer, & Martha Strong 30 Sep. 1767.

Williams, Henry, & Ann Lightfoot 2 Dec. 1769.

Williams, Ja. & Eliz. Mullins 21 Dec. 1783.

Williams, John, & Eliz: Fickland 24 Nov. 1769.

Williams, John, & Mary Marshal 17 May 1780.

Williams, Philip, & Frances Taylor 17 Aug. 1759.

Williams, Philemon, & Ann Lancaster 22 Feb. 1757.

Williams, Powel, & Lucy Haines 23 Mar. 1760.

Williams, Solomon, & Lucy Holland 20 May 1782.

Williams, Will: & Elizabeth Comber 7 Feb. 1764.

Williams, William, & Ann Mayo 7 Dec. 1768.

Williams, Zach: & Mary Pore 1 Oct. 1756.

WILLIAMSON, John, & Lucy Hog 26 May 1765.

Williamson, Pat, & Nannie Champion 8 Aug. ....

WILLIS, Henry, & Mary Watkins 3 Nov. 1755.

Willis, Rob. & Hellender Nailine 12 Jul. 1756.

Willis, William, & Susannah Freeman 31 Aug. 1764.

WILLOUGHBY, Henry, & Jean Lipscomb 1 Feb. 1788.

WILSON, Jonathan, & Marg. Stewart 13 Nov. 1773.

WILEY, Jo: & Jean Johnson 12 Nov. 1783.

WINDROW, Rich. & Millender Antony 17 Oct. 1781.

WIMPHREY, Peter, & Betty Moon 30 Dec. 1759.

WINFREY, John, & Mary Turpine 13 Feb. 1762.

WINGFIELD, Tho: & Eliz. Nelson 13 Ap. 1784.

WINN, Tho: & Eliz. Dabney Anderson 9 Mar. 1781.

WINSTON, Ja: & Sarah Marks 20 Aug. 1783.

Winston, John, & Tabitha Cocke 14 May 1761.

Winston, Tarleton, & Eliz. Winston 14 July 1788.

Winston, William, & Marianne Curd 4 Sep. 1770.

WITT, John, & Mary Bullington .... 1753?

WOOD, John, & Sarah Byrd 23 Jan. 1762.

Wood, Tho. & Mary Hope 9 June 1781.

Wood, Major Valentine, & Lucy Henry 7 Feb. 1765.

Wood, William, & Martha Cate 27 Jul. 1760.

Wood, Will, & Sarah Hall 28 Oct. 1785.

WOODHALL, Jacob, & Agnes Hicks 5 Oct. 1763.

Woodhal, Sampson, & Sarah Steel 24 Mar. 1756.

WOODIE, William, & Lucy Barnet 21 Jan. 1765.

WOODRUM, John, & Mary Bays 24 Mar. 1764.

Woodrum, John & Mary Barker, 3 Jany. 1776.

Woodram, William, & Martha More 4 Mar. 1756.

WOODSON, Benjamin, & Rebekah Cock 4 Dec. 1757.

Woodson, James, & Eliz. Whitlock 10 Mar. 1758.

Woodson, John, & Ann Harris 25 Dec. 1764.
Woodson, Jos: & Sarah Crouch 12 Oct. 1783.
Woodson, Pat, & Nancy Cloof [Clough] 25 Jul. 1771.
Woodson, Rene, & Mary Thomson 16 Feb. 1759.
Woodson, Samuel, & Sar: Mills 30 Jan. 1783.
Woodson, Tho: & Elizabeth Woodson 19 Nov. 1763.
Woodson, Tucker, & Sarah Knolling 29 Dec. 1774.
WOODWARD, Jer: & Elizabeth Morris 7 Jun. 1770.
Woodward, Warwick, & Ann Hamler 21 Oct. 1773.
WOOLAMS, John, & Eliz. Cawley 2 Feb. 1774.
WOOLBANKS, Richard, & Priscilla Hewet 14 Mar. 1767.
WOOTON, John, & Ann Harris 14 Mar. 1769.
WORD, Tho: & Frances Henderson 11 May 1783.
WORTHY, Tho. & Sar: Gannoway 12 Dec. 1771.
Worthy, Tho. & Sarah Gentry 13 June 1774.
WRIGHT, Augustine, & Mary Pucket 15 Feb. 1757.
Wright, Cha: & Sallie Jarvis .... 1793?
Wright, John, & Judith Barns 22 Mar. 1759.
Wright, John & Judah Easley .... Feb. 1756.
Wright, Jo: & Eliz: Frazer 11 Sep. 1777.
Wright, John, & Mary Pace 14 Nov. 1765.
Wright, Tho: & Betsie Groom 19 Jan. 1779.

YARBORROUGH, Thomas Griggs, & Mary Spurlock 15 June 1756.
YATES, Will, & Sarah Harris 11 Nov. 1786.
YAUNCEY, Cha: & Mary Crawford 13 Oct. 1784.
Yauncey, Jo: & Eliz. Cosbie 25 June 1783.
YOUNG, Hakely, & Susanna Lane 8 Oct. 1787.
Young, [Younger] John, & Ann Moss 29 Jul. 1760.

MARRIAGES—*Not recorded by Rev. Wm. Douglas, but indicated by Birth Registry. Date Here Given, Unless Otherwise Specified, Is Birth Date of First Child Shown in This Register*

FEMALE INDEX

ABRAY, Elizabeth, & James Clarkson 13 Sep. 1768.
Abrey, Sarah, & Arthur Nash 31 Dec. 1755.
ADAMS, Elizabeth, & George Bricken 14 Aug. 1775.
Adams, Frances, & William Massie 5 Aug. 1766.
ADDISON, Ellis, & John Pruit 9 Aug. 1758.
ADKINS, Ann, & Charles Gay 24 Jan. 1768.
AGGIN, Hannah, & Joseph Hankins 20 Feb. 1781.
ALEXANDER, Biddy, & Moses Smith 12 Apl. 1764.
ALLEN, Ann, & Turner Richardson 22 Nov. 1766.
Allen, Eliz: & Isaac Eads 2 Dec. 1757.
ALSOME, Jane, & Will Welburn 15 Dec. 1773.
ALSOP, Mary, & David Hoges 5 Apl. 1764.
ALVISON, Winnifred, & John Fore 9 June 1782.
AMOS, Judith, & Will: Howard 13 Mch. 1756.
Amos, Judith, & Fisher-Richard Bennet 23 Aug. 1780.
ANDERSON, Ann, & Anderson Thomson 24 Dec. 1785.
Anderson, Elizabeth Dabney, & Thomas Winn, 9 March 1781.
Anderson, Jean, & Charles Jackson 20 Jan. 1783.
Anderson, Judith, & James Dabney 27 Jan. 1777.
Anderson, Mary, & Thomas Farmer [or Farmbrough] 10 Jan. 1757.
Anderson, Nancy, & John Watson 20 June 1781.
ANTHONY, Mary, & John Perkins 13 Oct. 1765.
ANTONY, Millender, & Richard Windrow 17 Oct. 1781.
Antony, Priscilla, & Nathan Butler 8 Sep. 1783.
APPERSON, Ann, & Lyddel Bacon 19 Mch. 1771.
APPLEBERY, Elizabeth, & William Thurley 1 Apl. 1781.
Applebery, Judith, & Joseph Sutherland 12 Apl. 1761.
ARCHER, Rebekah, & John Fowler 30 Sept. 1768.
ALLINGTON [Arrington], Agnes, & John Barnard [Barnet] 26 Apl. 1757.
ARRINGTON, Martha, & William Shepherd 7 Apl. 1762.
ARP, Sarah, & James Maydwell 26 Nov. 1756.
ARMSTEAD, [Amson] [Anson], Frances, & Charles Thomas 26 Feb 1781.
Armstead, Mary, & Stephen Thomson 4 Aug. 1785.
ARNOT, Nancy, & William Richardson 10 Mch. 1785.
ASHLEY, Mary, & Francis Baker 6 Dec. 1765.
ASHLY, Sarah, & Bishop Tony 20 Mch. 1756.
ATKINS, Ann, & Joseph Atkins 29 Jul: 1789.

ATKINSON, Ann, & Joseph Chandler 17 Sep. 1770.
Atkinson, Susanna, & John Sadler 18 Sep. 1769.
AUSTINE, Mildred, & George Hunter 25 Nov. 1763.

BACON, Sarah, & Philip Bowles 29 Dec. 1773.
BAGBY, Mildred, & Samuel [or James] Meredith 15 May 1760.
BAILEY, Ann, & Will Weldie 4 June 1782.
Baily, Ann, & William Wade 17 Feb. 1784.
Bailey, Lucy, & James Orford 1 Aug. 1756.
Baily, Martha, & Robert Depriest 15 Oct. 1766.
Bailey, Tabitha, & John Hill 22 May 1757.
BAKER, Ann, & Wingfield Cosbie 29 Apl. 1782.
Baker, Jean, & David Moracet 29 Dec. 1788.
BARKER, Mary, & John Woodrum 3 Jany. 1776.
BARNES, Judith, & John Wright 22 Mch. 1759.
BARNET, Catherine, & John Whitlock 1 August 1756.
Barnet, Elizabeth, & Blagden ffinch 1 Aug. 1763.
Barnet, Lucy, & William Woodie 21 Jan 1765.
Barnet, Susan, & Robert Smith 22 Jul. 1780.
BARRET, Lucy, & Noel Burton 9 Apl. 1756.
BASKET, Frances, & David Brentham 25 Apl. 1762.
Basket, Martha, & Edward Blockly 12 Nov. 1744.
BAXTER, Elizabeth, & Robert Shepherd 15 Nov. 1766.
BAYS, Mary, & John Woodrum 24 Mch. 1764.
BEAKS, Sarah, & Robt. Parish 17 Apl. 1785.
BEAZLEY, Ann, & William Perry 8 Oct. 1783.
BEGBIE, Sally, & Luke Webster 13 Oct. 1772.
BELFORD, Betsey & Samuel Pankie 16 Feb. 1763.
BELL, Mary, & Daniel Weiseger 17 May 1763.
BERRYMAN, Mary, & David Johnson 11 Jany. 1769.
BIBB, Ann, & Martin Kie 17 Feb. 1768.
Bibb, Catherine, & Wm. Smith .... 1782.
Bibb, Mary, & Joseph Edwards 4 Apl. 1790.
Bib, Elizabeth, & William McAllister 29 June 1780.
Bibb, Mary, & Robert Richardson 3 Dec. 1784.
BIGGARS, Elizabeth, & Will: Bibb 2 May 1783.
Biggar, Hellender, & David Tyrrie 14 Jany. 1786.
Biggars, Martha, & Sim: Hughes 22 June 1783.
Biggars, Mary, & John Mathison 24 May 1776.
Biggar, Mary, & John Maddison 16 Aug. 1785.
Biggar, Nelly, & David Terry 24 Feb. 1777.
BIGLOW, Fannie, & George Grady 30 Dec. 1795.
BLACK, Marianne, & Nathaniel Gentry 15 Mch. 1781.
BLACKIE, Catie, & David Davis 1 Oct. 1779.
Blackie [or Blakey], Sarah, & James Davis 21 Mar: 1781.
BLACKSTONE, Elizabeth, & Robert Shepherd 9 Apl. 1769.
BLANKENSHIP, Elizabeth, & John Moracet 22 July 1757.
BOLTON, Mary, & John Glen 30 May 1785.

BOND, Ann, & John Bird 11 Dec. 1785.

BOOTLE, Mary, & Nathaniel Lacy 2 Nov. 1764.

BOURNS, Fannie, & George Towler 3 Sep. 1787.

BOW, Eliz: & Stephen Davis 1 Feb. 1776.

Bow, Judith, & Thomas Brooks 15 Aug: 1767.

BOWLS, Ruth, & Benjamin Thacker 2 Jul: 1757.

Bowles, Jerusha, & Samuel Moseby 2 Oct. 1755.

Bowles, Lucy, & Richard Henley 8 Jany. 1782.

Bowles, Mary, & Thomas Perriere 27 July 1767.

Bowles, Sarah, & Robt. Parish 21 Aug. 1788.

BOWDEN, Hannah, & William Pierce 21 Sept. 1756.

BOYD, Agnes, & Thomas Oliver 20 May 1765.

BRADSHAW, Ann, & Lardner Bradshaw 20 Apl. 1782.

Bradshaw, Judah, & William Rogers 25 Sept. 1755.

BRAGG, Mary, & Muray Pierce 27 Jul: 1785.

BRITT, Elizabeth, & Josias Pierce 7 Mch. 1759.

BRANCH, Eliz: & Gernat Branch 2 May 1762.

Branch, Frances, & John Shastine [Chastain] 10 June 1762.

Branch, Joanna, & Abram Sandiford 5 Aug. 1764.

BRANHAM, Annas, & John LeMay 14 May 1776.

Branham, Maty, & John Dalton 28 Dec. 1777.

Branham, Mary, & Kimbrock Launders, 24 Jul. 1782.

Branham, Susanna, & Gideon Gibson .... Nov. 1772.

BRENT, Elenor, & Capt. Wm. Stamps 17 Oct. 1757.

Brent, Lucy, & John Curd 24 June 1759.

BREWER, Sarah & Charles Marlow 16 Jany. 1760.

BRIER, Judah & John Robertson 7 Dec. 1758.

BRIGHT, Mary, & Gerrard Geddy 2 feb. 1765.

BRITT, Hannah, & Will Longmyre 6 Apl. 1769.

BROADFOOT, Agnes, & Pat: Broadfoot 8 Apl. 1762.

BROOKS, Sarah, & Valentine Bethel 26 May 1768.

BROUKEN, Nancy, & Clevish Duke 7 Sep. 1783.

BROWN, Betty, & Malachi Waugh 20 Feb. 1781.

Brown, Betsy, & .... Ware 20 Feb. 1783.

Brown, Bettie, & Malachi Ware 24 Aug. 1785.

Brown, Eliz: & George Barker 1 Dec. 1766.

Brown, Linney, & John Morris 12 Oct. 1786.

Brown, Mary, & Richard Hinds .... 1759.

Brown, Sarah, & Ambrose King 11 Dec. 1773.

BRYANT, Judith, & William Street 12 Mch. 1764.

BUGG, Sarah, & Alexr. ffowler 2 Jan. 1759.

BULLARD, Sarah, & Benjamin Harrison 17 Jany. 1756.

BULLOCK, Mary, & John ffretwell 1 Dec. 1770.

Bullock, Mary, & William Bullock 14 Dec. 1773.

BULLINGTON, Mary, & Edward Carter 11 June 1748.

Bullington, Mary, & John Witt .... 1753.

BURDEL, Easter, & Antony Cooper 9 Aug. 1783.

BURGESS, Mary, & Will: Craigwell 11 Aug. 1756.

BURKS, Judith, & Evan Shoemaker 2 Oct. 1756.

Burk, Mary, & Obadiah Smith 23 Aug. 1744.

BURKS, Mary, & Obediah Burks 13 Nov. 1758.

BURNS [or BONDS], Ann, & William Meredith 9 Sep. 1765.

BURROUGHS, Sally, & James Arnot 4 Sept. 1784.

BURROWS, Molly, & Abram Munday 3 Apl. 1786.

BURTON, Judith, & George Payne 23 March 1758.

Burton, Obedience, & John Bryan 27 Nov. 1766.

Burton, Susannah, & William Price 7 March 177...

BYERS, Barbara, & Charles Cosby 1 May 1784.

Byers, Jean, & John Crawford 7 Jul: 1783.

Byars, Mary, & David Smith 15 Apl. 1784.

Byers, Mourning, & Will: Corley [see Cawlah] 26 Mar. 1783.*

Byers, Morning, & Will: Cawlah [Corley] 19 Apl. 1787.*

BYRD, Sarah, & John Wood 23 Jany. 1762.

CAIRDEN, Mary, & John Martin 7 Jany. 1769.

CALLICHAN, Catherine, & Nathan Strong 10 Dec. 1776.

CALLIFAX, Mary, & William Rogers 10 Jany. 1772.

CAMP, Ellis, & John Huckabee 4 Mch. 1768.

Camp, Mary, & Overton Goodman 7 feb: 1765.

Camp, Martha, & Arthur Mosely 31 July 1763.

CAREY, Ann, & Col. Thomas Randolph 16 June 1770.

CARTER, Elizabeth, & Richard Chandler 17 Sep. 1770.

Carter, Ann, & Roger Shamine 13 Nov. 1757.

Carter, Mally, & Townsend Wilkison 13 Oct. 1771.

Carter, Phebe, & Robert Hutchison 13 Sept. 1783.

CASH, Ann, & Peter Hunter 3 Jul: 1765.

CASHINE, Catherine, & John Bryan 5 Sep. 1764.

CASTLE, Ann, & Jonathan Johnson 24 Dec. 1787.

CATE, Martha & William Wood 27 July 1760.

CAVE, Hannah, & Richard Parker 2 June 1781.

CAWLEY, Elizabeth, & John Woolams, 2 Feb. 1774.

CHACE, Ann, & Benjamin Stark 11 Oct. 1782.

CHAMP, Betty, & Will: ffleming 29 Apl. 1776.

CHAMPION, Mary, & John Napier 1 May 1764.

Champion, Nannie, & Pat. Williamson 8 Aug. ....

Champion, Winnifred, & Thomas East 23 Oct. 1757.

CHAPMAN, Cattie, & William White 20 Oct. 1785.

CHANDLER, Lucy, & John Vest 27 Sept. 1784.

CHETWOOD, Lucy, & Alexr. Lacy 5 Oct. 1765.

CHEWNING, Mildred, & Henry Crank 7 Mar. 1767.

CHICHESTER, Mary, & John Payne 5 Feb. 1767.

CHILDERS, Ann, & Will: Childers 25 Nov. 1764.

Childers, Susannah & Wm. Sharp 24 Feb. 1767.

CHILES, Agnes, & Samuel Newton 3 July 1781.

*Evidently the same people.

CHISHOLM, Ann, & Ambrose May 3 Jany. 1781.

Chisom, Chloe, & John May 2 Mch. 1779.

Chisholm, Mary, & Thomas Christmas .... 1782.

*CHOWNING, Sarah, & William Ladd 8 Nov. 1785.

*Chowning, Sarah, & Will Loyd 6 Nov. 1782.

CHURCHILL, Hellender, & Limmard Towler 21 Dec. 1767.

CLARK, Ann, & William Venable 12 March 1767.

Clark, Elizabeth & Moses Lawrie 7 Sep. 1756.

Clark, Elizabeth, & Sam: Childers 20 Oct. 1772.

Clark, Mary, & Thomas Green 3 Nov. 1781.

CLARKSON, Susanna, & Jacob Mattox [Maddox] 25 Oct. 1758.

CLEMENTS, Lovinah, & Will: Gooch 16 Feb: 1769.

Clements, Mary, & Reuben Edwards 7 Dec. 1783.

CLOOF [Clough] Nancy, & Pat: Woodson 25 Jul: 1771.

CLOUGH, Eliz:, & Charles Barret, 7 Feb. 1787.

CLAYBORN, Sarah, & William Cole 10 Nov. 1775.

COBBS, Rebekah, & Capt: William Burton 27 Jan. 1758.

COCK, Rebekah & Benjamin Woodson 4 Dec. 1757.

COCKE, Tabitha, & John Winston 14 March 1761.

COKE, Ann, & David Moseby 3 Apl. 1781.

COLE, Lydia, & William Tally 18 Jany. 1792.

Cole [alias Barclay,] Mary, & James Dickerson were married Feb: 1778.

Cole, Mary, & .... Davis 14 Jul: 1772.

COLEMAN, Betty, & James Coleman 27 Nov. 1782.

Coleman, Judith, & Edward Taylor 13 Feb. 1776.

Coleman, Mary, & George Holland 15 Feb. 1762.

Coleman, Susannah, & Richard Clayton 14 Jul: 1766.

Coleman, Susanna, & John Nelson .... 1784.

Coleman, Susannah, & Richard Perkins 30 Nov. 1756.

COLLIER, Ann, & John Marks 17 Mch. 1766.

COLLINS, Isabel, & Larkin Perry 11 Jan. 1782.

COMBER, Elizabeth, & William Williams 7 Feb. 1764.

CONOLLY, Ann, & Richard Merrin 21 Apl. 1756.

Conolly, Betty, & John Mullins 16 May 1756.

Conolly, Hannah, & William Bret 12 Feb. 1759.

Conolly, Winifred, & John Brett 9 Oct. 1756.

COOK, Frances, & John Thomason 17 Dec. 1782.

Cook, Mary, & Samuel Wade 15 Sep. 1783.

COSBIE, Elizabeth, & Sam: Cole [married] 29 Apl. 1777.

Cosbie, Elizabeth, & John Yauncey 25 June 1783.

COTHAN, Ann, & William Wade 23 June 1757.

COUPER, Susanna, & Will: Alstock 10 Sept. 1785.

COUTS, Hellener, & John Hoggan, 4 Dec. 1781.

COWARD [Cowherd], Betty & Isaac Graves 28 Jan: 1781.

COX, ..., & ffreeman Holman 13 June 1756.

*Evidently the same.

CRAFTON, Sarah, & Thomas Drumright 27 Jan. 1764.
CRAIGHILL, Mary, & John Camp 28 Sep. 1767.
CRANE, Frances, & John Cloe 9 Dec. 1773.
Crane, Rachel, & Isaac Oakes 17 Feby. 1775.
CRAIGWALL, Judith, & Thomas ffielder 26 Apl. 1757.
CRAIGSWALL, Mary, & James Lane 22 Aug. 1756.
CROGWALL, Elizabeth, & Edmond Curd 10 Jul: 1786.
CRAWFORD, Mary, & Charles Yauncey 13 Octo. 1764.
CRENSHAW, Ann, & Rodger Thomson 19 Sep. 1785.
CROUCH, Mary, & John McBride 26 Sep. 1726.
Crouch, Sarah, & Joseph Woodson 12 Oct. 1783.
CROWDER, Sarah, & James Allen 14 Dec. [1755].
CURD, Marianne, & William Winston 4 Sept. 1770.
Curd, Susannah, & Thomas Pollock 6 Sep. 1784.
CURRIE, Sarah, & Charles Ayscough* 12 Jan 1756.
Currie, Sarah, & Charles Areskin* 18 Aug. 1764.
CURRY, Sarah, & Charles Askew* 20 Octo. 1780.
CUSSINS, Mary, & Henry Graves .... 1770.

DABNEY, Sarah, & Henry Mallory .... June 1786.
DAMAREL, Judah, & Noble Lad .... Jan. 1753.
DANDRIDGE, Martha & Archer Payne 20 Nov. 1770.
DANIEL, Judith, & Henry Chiles 3 Sep: 1781.
Daniel, Mary, & Charles Edwards 9 June 1767.
Daniel, Margaret, & William Poindexter 9 June 1782.
Daniel, Susannah, & Col: James Anderson 3 May 1786.
DAVIS, Dolly, & John Pointer 27 Jany. 1767.
DAVIES [or Davis] Elizabeth, & John Man 21 Dec. 1755.
DAVIS, Elizabeth, & John Lawry 4 June 1757.
Davis, Elizabeth, & Henry Stevens 13 Nov. 1786.
Davis, Jerusha, & Edward Harris 14 Nov. 1785.
Davis, Penelope, & George Priddy 19 Jany. 1774.
DAWSON, Sarah, & Aventoun Mickleroy 6 Feb. 1773.
DENNETT, Elizabeth, & Isaac Meanly 19 Jany. 1758.
DICKERSON, Bettie, & David Pulham 7 Sep. 1786.
Dickerson, Mally, & John Thurmond 1 Jan 1761.
Dickerson, Unity, & Nathan Smith 30 Nov. 1780.
DICKIN, Sarah, & Nicholas Gentry 8 Jul: 1781.
DICKINSON, Frances, & David Smith 5 Dec. 1789.
DICKSON, Dorothy, & Thomas Watkins 27 May 1761.
Dickson, Mary, & Dumas Lane .... 1781.
DILLARD, Ann, & William Isabel 5 Mch. 1757.
Dillard, Jean, & Andrew Harrison .... 1757.
DOBB, Eliz: & James Huckstep 7 May 1784.
DOUGLAS, Margaret, & Chiles Tyrrill 8 Sep. 1784.
DOWNER, Sarah, & Richard Curd 11 Jul: 1762.

*Erskine—The same people.

DOWNMAN, Elizabeth, & Stokely Towles 3 Jany. 1777.
Downman [Dunman] Sarah, & Joseph Mason 5 July 1753.
DRAKE, Ann, & Abraham Chapel 29 Jany. 1768.
DUDLEY, Jeanie, & John Holt 18 Feb. 1768.
Dudley, Mary, & Roderick McCrae 26 Sep. 1771.
DUKE, Sarah, & Charles Christian 18 Nov. 1770.
DUPUY, Ollan, & John Tribue [Trabue] 23 Feby. 1766.

EALCOT, ..., & Richard Eastis 25 Sept. 1784.
EASLEY, Judith, & John Wright .... Feb. 1756.
EAST, Sarah, & Absolom Taylor 1 Feb. 1769.
EDMONDSON, Jean, & John Lewis David 16 Apl. 1766.
EDWARDS, Hannah, & Daniel Johnson 5 Nov. 1756.
Edwards, Jean, & Turner Clarke 27 Dec. 1756.
Edwards, Milley, & John Gentry 18 May 1781.
Edwards, Milley, & Thomas Bacon 12 Aug. 1792.
Edwards, Sarah, & John Whitlock 28 Oct. 1774.
Edwards, Susannah, & Tunstal Quarles 11 May 1781.
ELLIS, Martha, & William Ogilsby 4 Feb. 1774.
Ellis, Eliz: & John Clark 2 Feb. 1766.
Ellis, Susannah, & John Crouch 29 Nov. 1764.
EMMERSON, Mary, & Christopher Knowling 28 Oct. 175...
Emmerson, Mary, & Christopher Norden 13 June 1754.
ENGLAND, Mary, & James Page 26 Mch. 1766.
EPPERSON, Lucy, & John Thomson 8 June 1777.
ESTHER, Axie, & Jonathan Broadhead 29 Jan. 1784.
[EUBANK] Newbanks, Ann, & John England 15 Dec. 1764.
Eubank, Frances, & James Overstreet, 1 July 1768.
Eubank, Mary, & George Pey 28 Mch. 1767.
EVANS, Frances, & William Quarles 10 Sept. 1782.
Evans, Kesiah, & Nathaniel Thacker 27 Feb. 1767.
Evans, Mary, & Gwin Alman 30 Nov. 1755.
Evans, Mary, & William Thacker 12 Sep. 1756.
Evans, Martha, & Will: Christian 28 Aug. 1783.

FAIRIES, Cat: & David Lane 10 Jany. 1762.
Fairies, Sarah, & Will: Cauthon 30 Nov. 1769.
Faries, Mary, & Thomas Denton 1 Oct. 1771.
Faris, Sarah, & John Gillam 27 Apl. 1761.
FARMER, Agnes, & Richard Mathews 12 Jan. 1762.
Farmer, Elizabeth, & Christopher Sumpter 29 Apl. 1762
FFEMBRAG, Catherine, & Bartley Gwin 3 Mar: 1757.
FENTON, Hannah, & Will: Barnet, 26 June 1761.
FFERRAR, Elizabeth, & Thomas fferrar 23 Nov. 1756.
Ferrar, Elizabeth, & Stephen Crouch 20 Mch. 1763.
Ferrar, Jean, & Thomas Hardine 3 Jany. 1783.
Ferrar, Lucy, & John Crouch 14 Aug: 1788.
Ferrar, Mary, & James Cothan [Cauthon] 17 Nov. 1755.

Ferrar, Mary Ann, & Charles Johnson 16 Dec. 1783.
Ferrar, Temperance, & John Leprade 12 Jany. 1749.
FERGUSSON, Eliz: & David Biggars 2 Mch. 1781.
Fergusson, Mary, & David Knowling 8 May 1758.
Fergusson, Rachel, & John Perkins 6 Sep. 1757.
Fergusson, Sarah, & Richard Ogilsby 17 Dec. 1756.
FICKLAND, Elizabeth, & John Williams 24 Nov. 1769.
FIELD, Frances & Childers Smith 25 Dec. 1763.
FFIELDS, Judith, & John Hanson 4 Jany. 1760.
FITZPATRICK, Eliz: & Thomas Heard 2 Aug. 1767.
FLEMING, Mary, & William Bennet 18 Mch. 1767.
Fleming, Rebekah, & Moses Bates 1 Jany. 1787.
FLETCHER, Lucy, & And: Mintellet Tayloe 25 Apl. 1787.
FORD, Ann, & John Robison 11 June 1758.
Ford, Christian, & David Staples 14 Sept. 1757.
Ford, Elizabeth, & Samuel Cosbie 5 Sep. 1761.
FOUR, Elizabeth, & Samuel Causeby [Cosby] 24 Jan. 1765.
FORD, [Fore] Fanny, & John Moracet 4 April 1763.
FORSEE, Ann, & Austine Martin 9 Dec. 1765.
FORSTER, Bettie, & Thomas Kimbro 21 Feb. 1786.
Foster, Jean, & Samuel Waldrop [Wardrop] 14 Oct. 1784.
Foster, Susannah, & Thomas Foster 30 Oct. 1782.
FOUNTAIN, Elizabeth, & William Mills 11 Apl. 1782.
FOWLER, Priscilla, & Joseph Laury 10 June 1765.
FOX, Elizabeth & Meredith Price 31 May 1764.
FRANCIS, Ann, & Edward Burgess 24 Dec. 1766.
FRANKLIN, Mary, & Thomas Pouckeet 12 Aug. 1766.
FRAZER, Elizabeth, & John Wright 11 Sept. 1777.
FREEMAN, Molly, & James Knighton .... Sept. 1795.
Freeman, Sarah, & Joseph Johnson 17 Jany. 1790.
Freeman, Susannah, & William Willis 31 Aug. 1764.
Freeman, Susanna, & Joshua Baker 31 June 1790.
Freeman, Susanna, & Austin Hesten .... 1796.
French, Peggie, & John Hill 6 June 1763.
FRINCH [French] Sarbery, & Julius Scruggs .... 1766.
FULCHER, Elizabeth, & Whitehead Ryan 29 Mch. 1757.
FURBISH, Sarah, & Robert Richardson 4 Sept. 1758.

GANNOWAY, Sarah, & Thomas Worthy 12 Dec. 1771.
GARDENER, Judah, & Abraham Poor 19 Apl. 1756.
Gardener, Lucretia, & James Hendrick 17 Jany. 1782.
GARDNER, Lucy, & Rice Hughes 16 May 1766.
Gardner, Mary, & Thomas Russel .... 1769.
GARLANDS, Eliz: & Thomas Garlands 6 May 1782.
GARNER, Nivine, & Elijah Mosely 14 June 1768.
GARRET, Susan, & Richard Johnson 1 Nov. 1780.
GARRET, Susannah, & John Burton 27 Aug: 1785.
GARTHWRIGHT, Jean-Ann, & Will: Garthwright 14 Ap: 1769.

GATLY, Jane, & Henry Garner 4 Aug. 1788.
GAY, Elizabeth, & Thomas Bolling 31 Jan. 1761.
GEATHER, Jean, & Thomas Lenthicum 6 June 1766.
GENTRY, Eliz: & Jeremiah Blacklock 9 Dec. 1764.
Gentry, Keziah, & Will: Camp 28 Feb. 1772.
Gentry, Sarah, & Thomas Worthy 13 June 1774.
Gentry, Ann, & Tho: Daily 20 Dec. 1782.
Gentry, Mildred, & William Whitlock 23 June 1783.
GEORGE, Agatha, & George Payne 18 Apl. 1756.
George, Susannah, & John ffulcher 17 Apl. 1771.
George, Susannah, & John Hulcher 22 Jul: 1776.
GERRAN, [Gerrand] Judith, & Geo. Smith 16 Apl. 1767.
Gerrand, Magdalen, & Robert Mosely 7 Nov. 1760.
GERRARD, Lucy, & George Lucas 18 June 1764.
GILES, Jean, & John Bybie 24 Mch. 1760.
GLIN, Hannah, & Will: Austine 10 Mar: 1758.
GODBY, Jane, & Henry Turner 25 Aug. 1787.
GODDART, Priscilla, & Knaves Arrington 17 Ap: 1756.
GOING, Mary, & Aaron Going 31 July 1763.
GOLSON, Betty, & David Jones 12 Feb. 1782.
GOLSTONE, Mary, & James Jones 13 Apl. 1782.
GOODWIN, Susan, & William Jackson 13 Sept. 1781.
GORDON, Elizabeth, & Josiah Utley 3 Apl. 1778.
GOSS, Elizabeth, & Mathew Lawrie 31 Jany. 1759.
GRANGER, Lucy, & Jacob Haries 15 Sept. 1776.
GRANT, Elizabeth, & James Brownley 19 Jan. 1782.
Grant, Mary, & John Hughes 15 Dec. 1763.
GRAVES, Susannah, & James Chiles 29 Jan. 1787.
GRAY, Barbara, & Isaac ffreeman 29 Mar. 1783.
Gray, Rachel, & John Hart 23 May 1782.
GREGORY, Mary, & Archelaus Mitchel 8 Mch. 1766.
GREEN, Delphe, & Dan. Wade 4 Mch. 1782.
Green, Susannah, & John Parish 18 May 1770.
Green, Susannah, & Thomas Hooten 28 Jany. 1773.
Green, Ursely, & Thomas Johnson 21 Jan. 1774.
GRIFFITHS, Rebekah, & Isaac Coats 29 Oct. 1760.
Griffiths, Sarah, & John Green 20 Jan. 1763.
GROOM, Bessie, & Thomas Wright 19 Jany. 1779.
Groom, Mildred, & John Delany .... 1775.
Groom, Molly, & William Bailey 26 Sep. 1768.
GRUBS, Mary, & Jesse Hicks 4 Mar: 1770.
Grubs, Nanny, & Cornelius Towler 10 Nov. 1775.
GUILLAM, Martha, & Martin King 21 Apl. 1756.
GUTHRY, Elizabeth, & David Morris 20 Jany. 1784.

HADEN, Sally, & William Merril 31 Apl. 1778.
HAINES, Lucy, & Powel Williams 23 Mch. 1760.
HAGART [Harger], Ann, & Story Tally 10 Nov. 1784.

HALES, Susannah, & Samuel Richardson 20 Dec. 1767.

HALFPENNY, Eliz:, & Matthew Burks 19 Nov. 1780.

HALL, Barbara, & James Knighton 17 Nov. 1796.

Hall, Elizabeth, & Will: Crosbie 20 May 1780.

Hall, Frances, & Jesse Pace 15 Mch. 1777.

Hall, Mary, & James Hilton 28 Jul: 1763.

Hall, Sarah, & William Wood 28 Oct. 1785.

Hall, Susanna, & Thomas Green 1 Dec. 1783.

HALLEY, Isabella, & William Clements 2 Dec. 1768.

HALLOM, Elizabeth, & William Thomason 2 Dec. 1783.

HAM, Dorothy, & Ben: Bellamy 23 Jan. 1779.

HAMLER, Ann, & Warwick Woodward 21 Oct. 1773.

HAMLET, Ann, & Sylvanus Bryant 3 June 1767.

Hamlet, Elizabeth, & John Bryan 11 Nov. 1766.

HAMPTON, Eliz: & Major Childers 4 Oct. 1772.

Hampton, Sally, & Ben: Holladay 9 June 1786.

HANSON, Elizabeth, & John Bryant 18 Apl. 1762.

Hanson, Mary, & Michael Osburn 18 July 1759.

HARDINE, Mary, & James Roach 19 July 1763.

HARGISS, Mary, & James Hammond 29 Jan. 1760.

HARLOW, Elizabeth & Thomas Pretty 21 June 1768.

HARRIS, Agnes, & John Cothan [Cauthen] 12 June 1756.

Harris, Ann, & John Woodson 25 Dec. 1764.

Harris, Ann, & John Wooton 14 Mch. 1769.

Harris, Anna, & Joseph Harper 28 Jan. 1782.

Harris, Barbara Overton, & Joel Watkins 12 Jan. 1784.

Harris, Elizabeth, & Samuel fflournoy 30 Sep. 1763.

Harris, Jemima, & Benjamin Bullard 1 Sep. 1757.

Harris, Letty, & Thomas Gray 8 Feb. 1759.

Haris, Mary, & Absolom Hicks 20 Apl. 1760.

Harris, Mary, & Austin Mackghee 19 Jany. 1786.

Harris, Mary, & John Burrows [Burroughs] 3 Jul. 1790.

Harris, Nancy, & John Barker 18 July 1786.

Harris, Phebe, & Joseph-Royal fferrar 18 Jul: 1763.

Harris, Ruth, & Jeffery Clark 19 Oct: 1756.

Harris, Sarah, & Joseph Johnson 21 Nov. 1757.

Harris, Sarah, & William Bennet 20 Dec. 1767.

Harris, Sarah & William Yates 11 Nov. 1786.

Harris, Susannah, & Peter Depp 3 Apl. 1763.

Harris, Susannah, & John Gunter .... 1783.

HARRISON, Elizabeth, & William Ratcliff 14 Jany. 1764.

HARRY, Nanny, & Sam: Huckstep 14 Oct. 1771.

HARVEY, Ann, & David Lawson 31 July 1760.

HATCHER, Martha, & James Meyhim 31 July 1765.

HATTER, Jane, & Henry True 10 Dec. 1785.

HAWKINS, Hannah, & Samuel Landrum 17 Nov. 1765.

HEATH, Mary, & William Miller 22 May 1743.

HEMUS, Judith, & William Martin 3 Sep. 1756.

HENDERSON, Elizabeth & John Ker 23 Jany. 1756.

Henderson, Frances & Thomas Word 11 May 1783.

Henderson, Mary, & David Cesar 29 Mch. 1762.

HENLY, Dorothy, & John Day 15 Jan: 1762.

HENLEY, Molly, & Jesse Smith 11 Feb. 1774.

HENRY, Lucy, & Maj. Valentine Wood 7 Feb. 1765.

HEWET, Priscilla, & Richard Woolbanks 14 Mch. 1767.

Hewit, Sylla, & Richard Eubanks 22 May 1770.

HICKS, Agnes & Jacob Woodhall 5 Oct. 1763.

Hicks, Sarah, & Thomas Shoemaker 30 Jany. 1756.

Hix [Hicks] Winifred, & James Bates 22 Nov. 1747.

HICKINS, Elizabeth, & Charles Bolton 11 Jul: 1757.

HIGGINS, Lucy, & Thomas Gouge [Gooch] 20 June 1773.

HILL, Agnes, & Thomas Robertson 19 Feb. 1769.

Hill, Keziah, & Fenton Symes 20 Oct. 1782

Hill, Sarah, & Robert Freeman 28 Dec. 1780.

HILLASON, Frances, & Lewis Sublet 28 May 1763.

HILLIARD, Tamar, & Richard Tyrie 1 Jan. 1772.

HILLSMAN, Dinah, & Jacob Utley, 8 Jany. 1770.

HILTON, Susannah, & Philip Walker 26 Sep. 1759.

HINDS, Elizabeth, & Ludlow Brown 5 Jan. 1772.

Hinds, Sarah, & Joseph Martin 11 Aug. 1781.

HOG, Constant, & David Milton 16 Apl. 1765.

Hog, Lucy, & John Williamson 26 May 1765.

HOGGAN, Ann, & William Mallory 21 Nov. 1783.

HOLLAND, Alice, & Henry Nash 23 May 1773.

Holland, Ann, & Absolom Howel 11 Jul: 1770.

Holland, Lucy, & Solomon Williams 20 May 1782.

Holland, Martha & Abraham Parish 4 Nov. 1764.

Holland, Mercy, & William Colbard [Colvard] 2 Jan. 1759.

Holland, Susannah, & William Perkins 7 Aug. 1757.

HOLLINGER, Mildred, & Richard Gains 1 Jan: 1761.

HOLLINHEAD, Elizabeth, & Leonard Smith 7 Oct. 1774.

HOLMAN, Ann, & Miles Burford 13 Apl. 1765.

Holman, Mary, & Charles Rice 3 Apl. 1756.

Holman, Mary, & William Mathews 27 Apl. 1787.

HOLYDAY, Betty, & Joseph Pulham 26 Sept. 1785.

HALLIDAY [Holliday] Sara, & William Steers 7 Oct. 1783.

HOOKER, Susannah, & John Dickson 4 Sept. 1774.

HOPE, Mary, & Thomas Wood 9 June 1781.

HOPKINS, Elizabeth & John Smith 4 Apl. 1758.

Hopkins, Leadia, & Samuel Fulcher 8 Jany. 1786.

HOPSON, Tabitha, & Edward Mathews 11 Apl. 1759.

HORN, Ann, & David Walker 16 Aug. 1767.

HOWARD, Mary, & Joseph Walker 23 Sep. 1764.

HUGENS [Houchens], Elizabeth, & John Clements 2 Aug. 1756.

HUCHEN, [Houchens] Mary, & John Tuggle 19 Sep. 1756.

HUCHINS, [Houchens] Mary, & John Ingle 10 May 1758.

Huchins [Houchens] Susannah, & John Pace 3 May 1759.
HUDSON, Mary, & Will: Harris 29 Jany. 1758.
Hudson, Dianah, & Charles Ominet 2 Feb. 1763.
HUTSON, Frances, & Mark Wheeler 22 Oct. 1781.
Hutson, Frances, & James Tate 8 May 1781.
Hutson, Rebekah, & James Tate 18 Apl. 1782.
HUGHES, Ann, & Gideon Bowles 2 Dec. 1757.
Hughes, Rebekah, & Lewis Ball 25 Jany. 1768.
HUGHLAND, Frances, & Charles Harrison 20 Jany. 1762.
HUMPHREYS, Ann, & Geo. Webster 8 May 1787.
Humphrey [Umprah], Basset, & William Thomason 23 Dec. 1781.
HUNLY [Hundley], Catherine, & Francis Clark 11 June, 1767.
HANDLEY [or Hundley], Eliz: & Joseph Haden 3 Feb. 1764.
HUNT, Mary, & Charles Burton 10 Mch. 1781.
HUNTER, Ann, & Jacob Alford 10 Dec. 1779.
Hunter, Jean, & William Pretty 27 Apl. 1764.
Hunter, Mary, & Jeremiah Rich 24 Nov. 1758.
HUCHISON, Elizabeth, & William Johnson 9 Oct. 1756.
HUTCHISON, Hannah, & John Coleman 15 Mar: 1781.
HUTSON, Elizabeth, & William Tate 17 Feb. 1782.
HUTTON, Elizabeth, & William Mullins 24 Nov. 1775.

JACOBS, Fanny, & Nathaniel Antony June .... 1780.
JACKSON, Hannah, & Francis McGuire 4 Jany. 1760.
Jackson, Morning, & Zaccheus Cosbie 27 Jany. 1782.
JAMES, Mildred, & Joseph Atkins 29 Feb: 1779 [sic.] [1778.]
JARVIS, Sallie, & Charles Wright .... 1793.
JEFFERSON, Mary, & John Bolling 24 Mch. 1762.
Jefferson, Martha, & Dabney Carr [or Ker] 7 Mar. 1768.
JENNINGS, Eliz: & James Graydy 17 Jan. 1782.
JEWEL, Eliz: & Will: Carrol 13 Jul: 1753.
JOHNSON, Ann, & Thomas Coke [Cocke] 21 Jan. 1754.
Johnson, Ann, & Abram Davis 10 Apl. 1781.
Johnson, Ann, & Will: Garet 27 Feb. 1782.
Johnson, Ann, & Richard Philips 15 June 1782.
Johnson, Frances, & Wm. Strong 22 Apl. 1764.
Johnson, Jane, & James Cocke 3 Feb. 1775.
Johnson, Jean, & John Wiley 12 Nov. 1783.
Johnson, Jean, & Samuel Perkins 27 Nov. 1784.
Johnston, Mary, & David Cosby 26 Jany. 1757.
Johnston, Mary, & Bartholomew Turner 18 July 1765.
Johnson, Mary, & John Rice 22 Sep. 1780.
Johnson, Mary, & Henry Garret 10 Feb. 1781.
Johnson, Mary, & Will: Bradburn 23 Dec. 1782.
Johnson, Sarah, & John Snead 10 Jan. 1784.
Johnson, Susannah, & Henry Turner 4 Oct. 1756.
JONES, Ann, & John Watson 5 April 1773.
Jones, Anna Gabriella, & John Hawkins 16 Sept. 1783.

Jones, Elizabeth, & Bartholomew Cesar 19 Jul. 1775.
Jones, Eliz: & Ben: David 17 Sep: 1784.
Jones, Eliz: & Will: Drumright 27 Aug. 178...
Jones, Isabel, & David Head 8 Aug. 1785.
Jones, Mary, & James Towler 29 Sep. 1768.
Jones, Mary, & John Payne 5 June 1782.
Jones, Mary, & Samuel Morris 18 Oct. 1783.
Jones, Sarah, & Thomas Lawless 30 Dec. 1760.
Jones, Susannah, & Samuel Adams Apl. 1764.
Jones, Susanna Thomas, & Samuel Martin 14 July 1765.
Jones, Susannah, & Allen Clifton 30 Jan: 1774.
Jones, Susanna, & John Lane 10 Jul: 1787.
JORDAN, Isabella, & Thomas Mitchel 10 Mch. 1784.
JUDE, Eliz: & Henry Leonard 1 Oct. 1768.
JUET, Charlotte, & Henry Gambil 21 June 1777.

KAY, Ann, & Benjamin Duval, 24 Jan: 1765.
KAVANAUGH, Mary, & Alexr. Inglis 5 Mch. 1760.
KEMP, Sarah, & Samuel Mylom 28 Feb. 1764.
KENT, Mary, & Simpson Tucker, decd. 3 Jany. 1757.
KID, Obedience, & Lewis Kid 10 Aug. 1759.
KILL, (Kid) James, & Morning Parish 6 Aug. 1756.
KIMBRO, Sarah, & Richard Begby 29 Apl. 1764.
Kimbro, Mary, & Joseph Lipscomb 26 Apl. 1782.
KING, Sarah, & Thomas Chancellor 12 Nov. 1757.
KIRBY, Hannah, & Archer Mitchel 8 Nov. 1761.
KIRK, Margaret, & Thomas Hubbard 17 Nov. 1756.
KNIGHT, Sally, & Nathan Harris 25 Oct. 1782.
Knight, Molly, & Joseph Lee .... See p. 237, infra.
KNOLLING, Sarah, & Tucker Woodson 29 Dec. 1774.
KNUCLES, Mary, & Will: Armstead 11 Jany. 1788.

LACY, Susannah, & Joseph Evans 22 Jany. 1744.
LANCASTER, Ann, & Philemon Williams 22 Feb. 1757.
LANGFORD, Susannah, & Samuel Sheets 21 Jul: 1773.
LANKFORD, Molley, & Overton Baker 21 Jany. 1795.
LAMKIN, Mary, & Hugh McKie 14 Jul. 1760.
LANDRUM, Martha, & Willoughby Pugh 2 Nov. 1763.
LANE, Nancy & Barnet Mitchel .... 1782.
Lane, Susanna, & Young Hakely 8 Oct. 1787.
Lane, Unity, & Will: Harton 19 Feb. 1757.
LAWRENCE, Ann, & Daniel Powers, 22 Oct. 1781.
LAWRIE, Jeannie, & John Goodman 26 Mar: 1781.
LAURY, Priscilla, & David Crowdas [Crowder] 10 Nov. 1782.
LEE, Ann, & Richard Bennet 15 Apl. 1763.
Lee, Helena, & Jarvis Jackson 21 Aug. 1758.
Lee, Sarah, & David Hicks 5 Oct. 1772.
LEEK, [Leake] Christian, & William Johnson 13 Apl. 1751.

LEWIS, Ann, & John Utley 26 Dec. 1755.
Lewis, Elizabeth, & Will: Douglas Merriwether .... 1788.
Lewis, Judith, & John Dyches 7 Dec. 1746.
Lewis, Mary, & James Cock 9 Nov. 1757.
Lewis, Mary, & Waddy Thomson 21 Sept. 1775.
Lewis, Nancy, & James Overstreet 18 May 1786.
Lewis, Sarah, & Waller Lewis 6 Oct. 1786.
LIGHTFOOT, Ann, & Henry Williams 2 Dec. 1769.
LIGGINS, Elizabeth, & William Powell 2 July 1767.
LIGTON, Mary, & John Hilton 15 June 1787.
LILLY, Mary, & John Shepherd 9 June 1761.
LINDSAY, Mary, & Will: Brockman 1 Jul: 178—.
LIPSCUM [Lipscomb] Mary, & John King 6 Apl. 1766.
Lipscomb, Jean, & Henry Willoughby 1 Feb. 1786.
LOCKINGTON, Elizabeth, & Edmond Perry 29 Sep. 1780.
LOCKRUM, Eliz: & William Hardine 2 Oct. 1763-4.
LODAN, Elizabeth, & Thomas Thomason 28 May 1758.
LOFTUS, Charity, & Will: Hunter 16 Jun: 1760.
LOGWOOD, Elizabeth, & John Chastine 23 June 1765.
LOGWOOD, Elizabeth, & John Chasteen [Chastain] 16 July 1768.
LONG, Rachel, & Isaac Head 15 Dec. 1783.
LOVINE, Naomi, & Abraham Sea 25 Dec. 1759.
LYNE, Keziah, & William Milton 22 June 1781.
LYON, Ann, & John Scrimjour 24 May 1762.

McBRIDE, Sarah, & William Lewis .... May 1756.
McBride, Sarah, & John Bradshaw 4 Nov. 1759.
McCOMACK, Sarah, & William Morris 13 Mch. 1765.
McCLURE, Helen, & David McKay 10 Mch. 1768.
McGEARY, Mary, & Jeremiah Curl 24 Mch. 1760.
McGHEE, Frances, & William Smith 7 Apl. 1782.
McGUIRE, Mary, & William Swanson 7 Oct. 1757.
McKOY, Elizabeth, & Peter Mason 14 Aug. 1756.
McNAMARA, Elizabeth, & Micajah Kimbro 7 Oct. 1770.
McNEMAR, Mary, & Thomas Dickinson 2 Sept. 1786.
MALLORY, Ann, & William McGuire 11 Feb. 1758.
Mallory, Lucy, & John Jones 24 Jan. 1761.
Mallory, Mary, & John Lawyer 16 July 1781.
MAN, Sally, & William Lewis 28 Dec. 1774.
MARKS, Frances, & John Brags 26 Dec. 1781.
Marks, Sarah, & James Winston 20 August 1783.
MARTIN, Agnes, & Walter Scot 21 Feb. 1767.
MARSHAL, Mary, & John Williams 17 May 1780.
Marshal, Tabitha, & Drury Williams, 8 Nov. 1771.
MARTIN, Alizabeth, & Thomas Antony 26 Aug: 1764.
Martin, Jean, & William Holman 30 Nov. 1763.
Martin, Mary, & Hugh Lewis Vaughan 27 May 1760.
Martin, Mary, & John Hopkins 11 Feb. 1763.

Martin, Mary & Matthew Vaughan 23 Jul: 1767.
Martin, Mary, & Mitchel Martin 6 July 1783.
Martin, Rebekah, & Robert Davis 26 Mar: 1782.
Martin, Sarah, & Moses Parish 28 Jan. 1759.
MASK, Christian, & William Neves 16 April 1759.
MASSIE, Constancy, & Booker Parish 13 Nov. 1767.
Massey, Mary, & Nicolas Hemus 7 Jany. 1761.
Mathison, Dorothea, & Major Powis 9 Aug. 1767.
MATTISON, Judah, & William Powis (Powers) 20 Mch. 1758.
Mathison, Mary, & John Mathison 25 Oct. 1759.
MATLOCK, Agnes, & James Pulham 5 Mch. 1781.
MAYFIELD, Martha, & Zimri Tate 6 Aug. 1782.
MAYO, Ann, & William Williams 7 Dec. 1768.
MEAD, Sarah, & Henry Bibb 2 May 1781.
Mead, Sarah, & Robert Bibb 29 Apl. 1792.
MEEKIE, Elizabeth, & George Meekie 15 May 1783.
MERRIWETHER, Elizabeth, & Thomas Johnson 30 Aug. 1763.
Merriwether, Elizabeth, & Nicholas Merriwether 4 Aug. 1772.
Merriwether, Lucy, & William Lewis 31 Oct. 1772.
Merriwether, Mildred, & Thomas Mitchel 6 Dec. 1775.
Merriwether, Jean, & Sam: Dabney 1 Jul: 1781.
Merriwether, Ann, & Richard Anderson 3 Aug: 1782.
Merriwether, Sally, & James Merriwether 14 May 1785.
Merriwether, Lucy, & John Marks 6 Jany. 1786.
Merriwether, Ann, & Joseph McGhee 5 Aug. 1786.
Merriwether, Mary, & John Connor 27 Oct. 1787.
MERCHANT, Catherine, & Stephen Hancoke 29 Aug. 1766.
MEUSE, Ann, & Edward Lewis 4 Apl. 1764.
MILLS, Ann, & Henry Tandie 6 Nov. 1781.
Mills, Eliz: & Ja: Burnley 13 Oct. 1785.
Mills, Sarah, & Samuel Woodson 30 Jan. 1783.
MILLER, Mildred, & George Hunter 6 June 1761.
MILLAR, Winnifred, & Thomas Eldridge 20 Feb. 1776.
MILTON, Eliz: & William Appleby 1 Dec: 1767.
Milton, Elizabeth, & Gerald Morgan .... Oct. 1772.
Milton, Mary, & Richard Hanson 16 June 1781.
MINOR, Bettie, & Edward Herndon 1 Jul: 1767.
MITCHELL, Ann, & John Strange 22 Sep. 1756.
Mitchel, Catherine, & Will: Gordon 24 Feb. 1773.
Mitchel, Lucy, & John Perkins 2 Sep. 1766.
Mitchel, Mary, & Archibald Bryce 31 Jul: 1770.
MONTAGUE, Elizabeth, & James Daniel 17 Dec. 1775.
MOODY, Frances, & Jarrat Allison 9 Jany. 1762.
MOON, Betty, & Peter Wimphrey 30 Dec. 1759.
MOONEY, Mary, & Richard Pryor 11 Dec. 1763.
MORACET, Elizabeth, & Peter Davie 8 Jul: 1763.
MARE, Ann, & Charles Fagg 15 Apl. 1786.
MORE, Jediah, & Thomas Ship 15 Oct. 1776.

More, Martha, & William Woodram 4 Mch. 1756.
MOORE, Mary, & Benjamin Mattox [Maddox] 24 Sep. 1756.
MORE, Mary, & Abram Strange 12 Jul: 1780.
More, Rebekah, & John Seay 28 Feb. 1781.
MORELAND, Mary, & Major Hancoke 5 Sep. 1782.
MORGAN, Agnes, & Benjamin Clapton [Clopton] 26 Dec. 1756.
Morgan, Rachel, & Larkin Rutherford 22 Jan. 1758.
Morgan, Rebekah, & Will: Howard 19 Oct. 1761.
MORRELL, Elizabeth, & Richard ffield .... Oct. 1757.
MORRIS, Elizabeth, & Jer: Woodward 7 June 1770.
Morris, Mary, & Wingfield Cosby 18 Dec. 1772.
MORTON, Elizabeth, & George Payne 17 Jany. 1784.
Morton, Frances, & Jesse Payne 28 June 1768.
Morton, Sarah, & John Kirby 4 Nov. 1757.
MOSEBY, Agnes, & Rene Laforce 27 Aug. 1756.
MOSELY, Elizabeth, & Thomas Pore 23 Dec. 1756.
Moseley, Jean, & John Haden 10 Dec. 1757.
Mosely, Sarah, & Obadiah Daniel 10 Aug. 1756.
MOSS, Ann, & John Young or Younger 29 July 1760.
Moss, Frances & Richard McBride 25 Feb. 1782.
Moss, Judith, & Thomas Mitchel 13 Mch. 1759.
Moss, Sarah, & David Mitchel 5 Dec. 1756.
Moss, Susannah, & Benjamin ffirman 8 Jan: 1759.
MULLINS, Elizabeth, & James Williams 31 Aug. 1781.
Mullins, Lydia Hansford & James McGhee .... Mch. 177—.
MURRAY, Sarah, & Will: Hughes 26 Aug. 1784.
MUTRIE, Ruth, & Henry Gray 4 June 1768.

NAILINE, Hellender, & Robert Willis 12 July 1756.
NAPIER, Frances, & Reuben Frances .... 1766.
NASH, Ann, & William Ingle 20 Oct. 1766.
Nash, Mary, & Jonas Lawson 3 Aug. 1767.
NELSON, Ann, & William Cook, 12 Dec. 1782.
Nelson, Elizabeth, & Thomas Wingfield 13 April 1784.
Nelson, Frances, & Jesse Daniel 18 Dec. 1791.
Nelson, Marianne, & Abram Darnold 24 Aug. 1781.
Nelson, Marg: & George Cliff 30 Oct. 1772.
Nelson, Susan, & George Cornelius 10 Feb. 1780.
NEVIL, Judith, & John Hughes 3 Apl. 1758.
Nevils, Martha, '& Henry Hopson 13 Sep: ·1756.
NICHOLS, Frances, & Peter Shilton 23 Jul. 1763.
Nichols, Jean, & John Bantam 10 Apl. 1765.
NORMAN, Mary, & John Edmondson 28 Dec. 1782.
NORVIL, Christian, & Booth Napier 19 Oct. 1765.
NUCKOLS, Sarah, & Samuel Powell 2 Feb. 1774.

OGILSVY, Ann, & James Martin 8 Apl. 1763.
OMINET, Judith, & John Bransford 5 Apl. 1767.

ORFORD, Martha, & John Howgens 14 June 1763.
Orford, Molly, & Will: Barley 25 Sep. 1776.
ORREN, Margaret, & George White 13 Sep. 1763.
OWEN, Judith, & Gunnery Welburn 14 Sep. 1771.
Owen, Nannie, & Patrick Bowles 22 Nov. 1770.

PACE, Mary, & John Wright 14 Nov. 1765.
PAGE, Christian, & Axelheath Page 22 Apl. 1756.
Page, Marianne, & Joseph Pierce 19 Oct. 1763.
PARKER, Mary, & Rowland Thomas 3 June 1782.
Parker, Susanna, & Robt. Stubblefield 11 Mch. 1783.
PARISH, Martha Holland, & James Cocke 23 Apl. 1776.
Parish, Mary, & John Green 24 Oct. 1757.
Parish, Mary, & John Parish 26 Jan. 1769.
Parish, Morning, & James Caid 11 Jan. 1759.
Parish, Ruth & John Kid 19 Sept. 1758.
Parish, Sally, & John Kilshaw 8 Feb. 1785.
Parish, Ursley & William Rutherford 14 Aug. 1766.
PARTLOW, Sarah, & Thomas Jones .... 1784.
PARLOW [Partlow], Ursley, & Elijah Carter 13 Dec. 1782.
PASTURE, Sarah, & Daniel Hubbard 17 Nov. 1756.
PATERSON, Elizabeth, & William Knighton .... 1782.
Paterson, Sarah, & Major Holloway 21 June 1780.
PATRICK, Ruth, & Moses Broomfield 31 Dec. 1758.
PATTY, Sally, & Nathaniel Sanders 15 Nov. 1781.
PAWN, Frances, & John Crane 28 Dec. 1775.
PAYNE, Ann, & Joseph Vaughan 9 May 1770.
Payne, Ann, & Sam: Thomason 4 Sep. 1774.
Payne, Anna, & Christian Turner 17 Jany. 1781.
Payne, Sarah, & George Thomas 14 Dec. 1771.
Payne, Susannah, & Will: Heale 11 Jul: 1772.
PEATROSS, Mary, & Joseph Haden 30 Apl. 1774.
PEEK, Mary, & William Nichols 16 May 1760.
PEERS, (Fears), Jean, & Philip Timberlick 29 Dec. 1782.
PERKINS, Ann, & William Ogilsby 6 May 1756.
Perkins, Eliz: & Joseph Ellis .... 175—.
Perkins, Mary, & William Atkinson 6 Feb: 1757.
Perkins, Mary, & Peter Fitzpatrick .... 1771.
Perkins, Sarah, & John Horn 30 Dec. 1755.
Perkins, Sarah, & William Moore 27 Dec. 1758.
PERRIERE, Elizabeth, & Samuel Price 31 May 1763.
Periere, Martha, & Nathan Anderson 4 Feb. 1784.
PERRY, Bathsheba, & Will: Howarton 8 June 1782.
PETERSON [Paterson] Ann, & Valentine Mayo 2 June 1760.
Peterson, Mary, & John Knowling 22 Nov. 1765.
PHILPOTS, Elizabeth, & David Lane 5 Oct. 1770.
PIMBLE, Martha, & Richard Cotterel 15 May 1757.
PITTS, Anna, & Thomas Farmer 23 Mch. 1783.

POINDEXTER, Ann Given [Gisage], & Robert Cobb 27 May 1785.
Poindexter, Elizabeth, & Francis Pledge .... Sept. 1769.
Poindexter, Sarah, & John Armstrong 31 Mar. 1783.
POLLARD, Frances, & George Rogers 12 July 1764.
Pollard, Mary, & George Thomason, 27 Feb. 1735.
POLLET, Elizabeth & William Lilly 26 Sep. 1764.
POPE, Sally, & Arch. Sneed 24 Jul: 1780.
POOR, Lucy, & Obadiah Smith 30 Aug. 1775.
Pore, Mary, & Zach: Williams 1 Oct. 1756.
Poor, Mildred, & Samuel Cosby 5 Dec. 1774.
Pore, Sarah, & David Davies 30 May 1756.
PORTER, Eliz: & Daniel Branch 18 Nov. 1762.
Porter, Eliz: & John Gerrant 11 Oct. 1770.
POTTER, Annie, & Joseph Morris 24 May 1771.
Potter, Judith, & Philip Going 4 Mar. 1770.
Potter, Priscilla, & Banjamin Salmons 6 Aug. 1756.
Potter, Rachel, & Henry Atkinson 19 Dec: 1756.
POWERS, Ann, & Anderson Peers 17 Aug. 1772.
Powers, Mary Ann, & John Lawrence 2 July 1788.
Powers, Sally, & Thomas Helms 28 Oct. 1783.
POWIS, Ann, & Jolly Parish 8 Dec. 1767.
Powis [Powers] Dolly, & Richard Johnson 7 Oct. 1772.
PRETTY, Mary, & Joseph Parish 6 May 1777.
PRICE, Elizabeth, & David Wade 18 Jany. 1771.
Price, Jane, & Lewis Barret 23 Nov. 1781.
Price, Martha & Thomas Stark 27 Apl. 1763.
Price, Martha, & John Hodges 27 June 1769.
Price, Mary, & John Leonard 13 July 1775.
Price, Sarah, & Hardine Perkins 15 Aug. 1756.
PROFIT, Eliz: & Thomas Hopper 19 May 1757.
PRUIT, Mourning, & William Webb 12 Apl. 1756.
PRYOR, Elizabeth & David Lane 30 Mch. 1757.
Pryor, Sarah, & William Smith 2 Feb. 1785.
PUCKET, Mary, & Augustine Wright 15 Feb. 1757.
PULHAM, Mary, & Thomas Desperate [or Desphire] 14 Apl. 1782.
PULLEING, Mary, & William Laury 14 Mch. 1763.

QUARLES, Cat: & Landie Lindsay 1 Feb. 1782.

RADFORD, Martha, & Henry Whitloe 6 Jan. 1769.
RAE, Winifred, & Michael Perkins 8 June 1781.
RAISON, Susannah & John Smith 7 Oct. 1736.
RAGLIN, Henrietta, & John Beekly, [Beckly] 29 Aug. 1782.
RAGLIN, Jeanie, & William Cheek 15 June 1776.
RAGLINE, Lucy, & Joel Terrell 24 Aug. 1781.
Ragline, Sarah, & Nicholas Merriwether 15 Mch. 1787.
RAMSAY, Mary, & Reuben Cave .... Jan: 1781.
RANDOLPH, Jean, & Roderick Perry, 10 Mch. 1783.

Randolph, Mary, & Tarleton ffleming 18 Jul: 1763.
REDD, Ann, & Thomas Carr Minor 27 May 1787.
Red, Lucy, & Joseph Barnet 26 Apl. 1757.
Red, Patsy, & Will: Daniel ....
REID [or Red], Sarah, & Will: Hutchison 20 Dec. 1780.
REEMS, Sarah, & John Lane 5 Jany. 1769.
REEVIS, Henrietta, & James Dicks 3 May 1758.
REEVES, Henrietta, & James Dyches 20 Apl. 1760.
Reeve [Reeves] Mary, & Benjamin Phop [Fop] 15 Dec. 1780.
RHODES [Rose] Mary, & William Smith 23 July 1773.
RICE, Elizabeth, & David Rae 20 Dec. 1768.
Rice, Elizabeth, & Richard Swift 16 Mch. 1783.
Rice, Judith, & Michael Smith 15 June 1759.
RICHARDS, Hester, & Francis Thurstone 4 Jan. 1757.
RICHARDSON, Elizabeth, & Thomas Cranks 25 Apl. 1765.
Richardson, Elizabeth, & John Cocke 23 Feb. 1768.
Richardson, Eliz: & Richard Allen 29 June 1782.
Richardson, Lucy, & Richard White 29 Oct. 1773.
Richardson, Martha, & Will: Biggar 13 Oct. 1781.
Richardson, Mary, & Robert Mayo 30 Jany. 1771.
Richardson, Mary, & John Finnick 8 Apl. 1775.
Richardson, Sarah, & William ffurbish 7 Jan. 1765.
ROBINSON, Catie, & Robert Edward Coleman 9 Mch. 1781.
ROCKET, Ann, & Nimrod Poindexter 17 Sept. 1769.
ROE, (Rowe) Jean, & Geo. Johnson 16 Mch. 1786.
ROGERS, Grisheld, & Joseph Whithead 8 May 1751.
Rogers, Hannah, & George Chowning 4 Jan. 1762.
Rogers, Jane, & Isham Randolph 25 Sep. 1738.
Rogers, Mary, & John Morgan 21 Dec. 1758.
Rogers, Susannah, & Edward News 3 July 1763.
ROLLINS, Agnes, & Thomas Oliver 16 Mar. 1758.
Rollins, Agnes, & James Gains 15 Mch. 1782.
RORY, Christian, & John ffreeman 8 Apl. 1771.
ROW, Urcila, & Thomas Johnson 21 Jany. 1774.
RUNNELS, Elizabeth, & John Curriere 23 Nov. 1774.
RUTHERFORD, Ursley, & John Richards 2 July 1781.
RYAN, Ann, & Edward Rice 16 July 1758.
Ryan, Ann, & Stephen Seay 3 Dec. 1780.
Ryan, Elizabeth, & David Bailey 14 Oct. 1759.

SALLEY [Salle], Marianne, & Charles Clark 3 Dec. 1763.
SAMPSON, Judith, & Richard Crouch 12 Feb. 1733.
Samson [Sanson], Mary, & Thos. Aulman [Almond] 18 Sep: 1787.
SANDERS, Eliz: & Richard fferrar 20 Mch. 1756.
SAUNDERS, Elizabeth, & James Sims 1 Apl. 1767.
SANDERS, Elizabeth, & James Symes 18 Oct. 1770.
Sanders, Elizabeth, & John Burgess 17 Nov. 1780.
Saunders, Mary, & Hezekiah Rice 16 Mch. 1783.

SANDIDGE, Sophie, & James Holliday 4 Sep: 1785.
SASSINE, Olive, & John Short 29 Feb. 1768.
SCHOOLER, Rachel, & John Wharton 6 Sep. 1785.
SCHOULER, Lucy, & Samuel Wharton 12 May 1785.
SEAY, Anne, & Warren More 5 Sep. 1779.
Seay, Alley, & William King 28 Apl. 1781.
SEXTON, Lucy, & Billie Green 5 Feb. 1780.
SHAMBLE, Million, & John Daniel Coleman 22 Feb. 1764.
SHARP, Ann, & John Oliver 15 May 1758.
Sharp, Catherine, & Wm. Snead 6 Apl. 1748.
Sharp, Judith, & Thomas Sharp 13 Dec. 1768.
SHEPHERD, Eliz: & Joseph Duval 24 Sep. 1773.
Shepherd, Frances, & John Ashline [or Ashley] 29 Mar: [1758].
Shepherd, Frances, & John Alphine 5 Apl. 1767.
Shepherd, Hannah, & Shadrach Walker 12 Apl. 1783.
Shepherd, Rebekah & Robt. Smithey 6 Oct. 1756.
SHILTON, Rachel, & Aaron Quissenbury 28 Mch. 1781.
Shilton, Sarah, & Augustine Shepherd 21 Dec. 1760.
Shilton, Sarah, & Tyree Glen 17 May 1764.
SHIP, Mary & Lewis Welburn 23 Apl. 1760.
SHOEMAKER, Ann, & Bartholomew ffielder, 22 May 1756.
SHORT, Caroline, & John Smith 17 Oct. 1764.
SHORTLY, Sarah, & Henry Day 23 Jan: 1785.
SHORER, Eliz: & Jac: Hope 5 Nov. 1779.
SINCLAIR, Marianne, & John Mitchel 7 Sep. 1775.
SINGER, Caroline, & Joshua Hill, 23 Sep: 1783.
SINGLETON, Susan, & John Lancaster 20 Jan. 1781.
SKELTON, Susan, & David Copland 7 Jany. 1772.
*SLED, Elizabeth, & Joseph Norman 7 Dec. 1785. Baptized Sep: 12 1785 [sic].
*SLATE, Elizabeth, & Josua Norman 3 Apl. 1766.
SMITH, Agnes, & William Robinson 28 Oct. 1781.
Smith, Ann, & Fleming Thomason 18 Apl. 1785.
Smith, Eliz: & John Dennison 2 May 1781.
Smith, Frankie, & Henry Stubblefield 19 Oct. 1786.
Smith, Jean, & Col. John Payne 7 Oct. 1758.
Smith, Levina, & Wm. McGhee 31 Oct. 1783.
Smith, Mary, & Philip Bailey 27 May 1769.
Smith, Marianne, & Will: Henley 22 Jany. 1773.
Smith, Mildred, & Edward Busby 10 Apl. 1782.
Smith, Nanny, & Abram Fergusson 1 Dec. 1782.
Smith, Sarah, & William Richards 14 Nov. 1780.
Smith, Susanna, & Thomas Lilly 21 Nov. 1764.
SNEAD, Betsie, & Martin True 17 Jany. 1784.
Snead, Frances, & David Garth 23 Nov. 1781.
SNEED, Sally, & John Peik 19 Dec. 1785.
SNED, Sarah, & John Perkins 15 July 1788.

*Probably the same people.

SNELSON, Elizabeth, & John Mitchel 2 Jan. 1782.
SNUGS, Mary, & John Cairden 18 Jun: 1772.
SPENCER, Eliz: & Richard Foster 5 Sept. 1780.
SPIER, Sarah, & Nathl. Snelson 22 Mch. 1788.
SPILLER, Frances, & Henry Lane 18 July 1781.
SPOTSWOOD, Dorothea, & Col. Nathaniel West Dandridge 12 Sep
  1764.
SPURLOCK, Mary, & Thomas Griggs Yarborough 15 June 1756.
STANLEY, Elizabeth, & Henry Laurence 11 Mch. 1765.
Stanley, Eliz: & John Howard 14 Nov. 1765.
STEEFE, Sarah, & Will: Harris 23 Jany. 1762.
STEEL, Margaret, & Nathaniel Webster 19 July 1756.
Steel, Sarah, & Sampson Woodhall 24 Mar. 1756.
STEERS, Mary, & John Hutchison 26 Jul: 1783.
STEVENS, Jeanie & William Page 23 Dec. 1755.
STEWART, Elizabeth, & Peter Sage 25 May 1782.
Stewart, Margaret, & Jonathan Wilson 13 Nov. 1773.
Stewart, Mary, & John McGhee 25 Oct. 1782.
STITH, Eliz: & Thomas Daniel 28 Sep: 1776.
STODGHILL, Kesiah, & Philip Tinsley 4 Oct. 1765.
STOKES, Aggie, & Isaac Barnet 24 Aug. 1761.
Stokes, Winnifred & James King 14 Mch. 1776.
STOREY, Mary, & John Smith .... Apl. 1764.
STRATTON, Mary, & Stokes McCawl 15 Mch. 1756.
STRAWN, Mary, & William Gains 11 Oct. 1787.
STEATUM, Mary, & Stephen Hunter 7 Nov. 1766.
STREATUM, Jean, & Bartlett Haley 16 Aug. 1770.
STRUEMAN [Tourman], Frances, & John Golson 12 Sept. 1771.
STREET, Rachel, & James Johnson 30 June 1758.
STRINGER, Caroline, & Joshua Hughes 31 Mch. 1781.
STRONG, Martha, & Eliezer Williams, 30 Sep. 1767.
STUART, Ann, & Joseph Stuart 12 May 1788.
SULLIVAN, Anna Stacia, & Will: Gowan 17 Sep. 1756.
SUTHERLAND, Lucy, & John Mallory 25 Sep. 1786.
SUTTON, Betty, & Will: Crutchfield 21 Mar: 1766.
SWIFT, Peggie, & William Mills 7 Feb. 1782.
SYDNOR, Elizabeth, & Charles Cosbie [Cosby] marries 14 Dec. 1759.
Sydnor, Joanna, & Peter Marks 12 Sep. 1769.
SYMES, Ann, & Will: Guillam 14 Apl. 1782.
Symes, Hannah, & David Henderson 8 Nov. 1785.
SYMER, Elizabeth, & John Tolliver 23 May 1768.

TALES, Mary, & Will Tales 29 Sep. 1788.
TALFORD, Lucy, & John Fag 3 Oct. 1787.
TALIFERRAR, Ann, & Nicholas Taliferrar 6 Aug. 1782.
TANDIE, Frances, & Joseph Lipscomb 24 Dec. 1774.
Tandie, Jean, & John Allen 26 June 1784.
Tandie, Mary, & John Morton 28 Mch. 1789.

TANDY, Nansie, & James Perrie, 18 Feb. 1792.

TATE, Abigail, & David McAlister 5 May 1784.

Tate, Lucy, & Joseph Nelson 18 May 1783.

Tate, Sarah, & Charles Daniel 8 Dec. 1773.

TAYLOR, Ann, & Benjamin Sadler .... 1756.

Taylor, Ann, & Thomas Underwood 2 October 1765.

Taylor, Elizabeth, & George Haden 7 Mch. 1775.

Taylor, Frances, & Philip Williams 17 Aug. 1759.

Taylor, Hellender, & Joseph Perkins 29 June 1765.

Taylor, Jean, & David Humphrey 18 Dec. 1765.

Taylor, Mary, & Nathaniel Wade 27 Apl. 1782.

Taylor, Sarah, & Joseph Lively 15 Oct. 1773.

Taylor, Sarah, & James Coleman 27 Feb. 1782.

Taylor, Sarah, & Edmond Foster 3 Oct. 1783.

Taylor, Ursley, & Jeremiah Davis 16 feb. 1767.

TERRIE, Christian, & Rice Hughes 21 Apl. 1781.

THOMAS, Ann, & Major Hancoke 18 June 1786.

Thomas, Eliz: & Joseph Camm [or Camp] 22 Ap. 1758.

Thomas, Esther, & Thomas Jones 17 May 1769.

Thomas, Mary, & John Glen 12 June 1782.

Thomas, Mary, & Winslow or Winston Parker 22 Apl. 1782.

Thomas, Sarah, & John Towler 2 Jan. 1762.

Thomas, Sarah, & John Bibb 7 Jan. 1782.

Thomas, Susannah, & Zachariah Edwards .... 1771.

THOMASON, Betty, & James Man 2 Dec. 1769.

Thomason, Christina, & John Timberlick 22 Dec. 1782.

THOMSON, Ann, & Obadiah Britt [Brett] 28 Mch. 1753.

Thomson, Ann, & David Hill 17 Jany. 1782.

Thomson, Ann, & Robert Curriere 11 Dec. 1784.

Thomson, Agnes, & Charles Johnston 30 Mch. 1757.

Thomson, Elizabeth, & Isaac Raglin 23 May 1757.

Thomson, Frances, & Lewis Harndon [Herndon] 1 Jul: 1767.

Thomson, Frances, & Nathaniel Mills 31 Oct. 1785.

Thomson, Hellender & David Thomson 28 Sep. 1780.

Thomson, Mary, & Rene Woodson 16 Feb. 1759.

Thomson, Mary, & William Payne 24 Jany. 1768.

Thomson, Sally, & John Christopher Horn 5 Jul: 1785.

Thomson, Susannah, & William Holman 31 Aug. 1766.

THORNTON, Mildred, & Thomas Walker 22 June 1764.

Thurston, Jane, & Rowland Thomas Sr. 22 Apl. 1782.

THURSTONE, Mary, & George Allen 11 Sep: 1766.

TIMBERLICK, Eliz: & Joseph Hopkins 15 Jany. 1781.

Timberlick, Elizabeth, & George Thomason .... Aug. 1782.

Timberlick, Susanna, & John Jones 28 Dec. 1783.

TINSLEY, Ann, & John Davis 13 Mar: 1767.

TISDALE, Elizabeth, & Samuel Moss 23 May 1764.

TOLLIVER, Peggie, & John Hill 23 Jul: 1769.

TONEY, Agnes, & John Hopper 2 Dec. 1757.

Tony, Mary, & Harry Mullins 3 Oct. 1760.
Tony, Susannah, & Stephen Clements 6 Apl. 1757.
TOWLER, Ann, & Charles Houchins 4 May 1782.
TRAMMEL, Mary, & Thomas Powis 13 May 1767.
TRAVIS, Jean, & John Burns 28 Apl. 1757.
TRIBUE [Trabue] Ann Caroline, & Geo. Smith 7 Feb. 1762.
TRUEMAN, Martha, & William fferris 11 Oct. 1758.
TUGG, Nancy, & John Carter 18 Jany. 1783.
TURNER, Elizabeth, & Samuel Galden 28 Dec. 1764.
Turner, Eliz: & Mathew Childers 9 Jul: 1772.
Turner, Sarah, & Robert Duncan 15 Mch. 1776.
TURPINE, Mary, & Richard James 30 Dec. 1761.
Turpine, Mary, & John Winfrey 13 Feb. 1762.
Turpine, Obedience, & John Harris 20 May 1763.
Turpine, Sicily, & Abraham Perkins 28 Nov. 1756.
TYRRIL, Ann, & Zachariah Lewis 25 Feb. 1794.
Tyrrel, Barbara, & Aaron Fontaine (married) 19 May 1773.
TYRRIL, Eliz: & Frederick Harris 13 Dec. 1784.
TYRRELL, Mary Overton & Garret Minor 2 Feb. 1775.
Tyrrell, Milley, & Christopher Clark ....
TYRY, Ann, & William Day 8 Aug: 1767.

UNDERWOOD, Hannah, & William Lee 22 Apl. 1760.
Underwood, Molly & Edward Peacock 9 Mch. 1774.
Underwood, Sarah, & Landy Richardson 17 Mch. 1759.
UTLEY, Prudence, & Josiah Seay 1 May 1778.

VANDEVAL, Martha, & Turner Southall 27 Apl. 1765.
VINNINGHAME, Rachel, & David Pruit 5 Feb. 1763.

WADDY, Frances, & William Swift 30 Dec. 1756.
Waddy, Elizabeth, & Richard Philips 20 Jany. 1788.
WADLAW, Mary, & John Fferrar 30 Nov. 1755.
WALDEN, Hannah, & Will: Edmondson 10 Nov: 1785.
WALKER, Ann, & Richard Howle 16 Jany. 1775.
Walker, Sarah, & John Mosely 14 June 1764.
Walker, Judith, & Robert Pore 5 Jany. 1762.
Walker, Nathana, & Edmund Hodges 13 June 1757.
Walker, Mary, & Barnet Owen 22 Mch. 1757.
WALTON, Mary, & Will: Baker 5 Nov. 1783.
Walton, Peeny, & Robert Harris 12 Oct. 1782.
WARD, Tahpenes, & Philip Webber 24 May 1756.
WASH, Elizabeth, & David Spier 15 Nov. 1784.
Wash, Henleey & Thomas Wash 14 Nov. 1786.
WATKINS, Elizabeth, & George Cesar 10 Dec. 1767.
Watkins, Elizabeth, & Thomas Cosbie 16 Jul: 1782.
Watkins, Elizabeth, & William Smith 4 May 1762.
Watkins, Elizabeth & George Watkins, 13 Feb. 1782.

Watkins, Elizabeth, & Nathaniel Massie 2 Jan. 1772.

Watkins, Eliz: & Thornton Gipson 18 June 1784.

Watkins, Mary, & Will Curd 11 Oct. 1764.

Watkins, Mary, & Henry Willis 3 Nov. 1755.

Watkins, Nancy, & John Crealy 15 Mar. 1787.

Watkins, Prudence, & William Royster 12 Feb. 1761.

Watkins, Sarah, & Robert ffurlong 9 May 1756.

Watkins, Sarah, & John Porter 26 Apl. 1765.

WATSON, Judith, & John Rees 10 Jany. 1749.

WATTS, Agatha, & James George 11 Nov. 1738.

Watts, Mary, & Will Drake 3 Mch. 1761.

WEAVER, Mary, & James Druine 5 Jun: 1757.

Weaver, Sarah, & Francis Shodoang (Chadowin) 16 Nov. 1761.

WEBSTER, Elizabeth, & William Ligg 6 June 1758.

Webster, Sarah, & James Knowling .... 1776.

WEEKS, Marth: & John Holland 16 Jany. 1735.

WEESIGER, Eve, & Archibald Brodie 10 Apl. 1763.

WELDY, Ann, & Aaron Laury 28 Oct. 1776.

WEILDY, [WELDY] Ann, & Aaron Tony 20 Jany. 1782.

WELLS, Million, & Thomas Shambles (Chambliss) 13 May 1757.

WEST, Susanna, & John Beadles [Beigle] 15 Nov. 1784.

WETHERSPOONS, Martha, & Thomas Summers 23 Sep. 1782.

WHEELER, Mary, & Thomas Henderson 8 Feb. 1786.

Wheeler, Sarah, & Joseph True 1 Dec. 1785.

WHIT, Susan, & Edward Ryan 22 Sept. 1774.

WHITE, Betsey, & James Bartlet 12 Dec. 1784.

WHITLOCK, Elizabeth, & James Woodson 10 Mch. 1758.

WHITE, Mary, & George Askridge 29 July 1758.

White, Mary, & James Thomas 4 Jul: 1769.

White, Mary, & George Thomas 9 Dec. 1775.

White, Penelope & Aaron Laurie 30 Jany. 1757.

WHIRLEY, Frances, & John Lansdown 5 Dec. 1761.

WILKERSON, Agnes, & William Owen 29 July 1769.

WILLIAMS, Anna, & John Leprade 10 Feb. 1753.

Williams, Ann, & Nathaniel Cawley 10 Jan. 1760.

Williams, Ann, & Burwell Baugh 2 Jany. 1776.

Williams, Ann, & Nimrod Parish 2 June 1787.

Williams, Eliz: & James Grayson .... 1756.

Williams, Elizabeth, & Edward McBride 10 Apl. 1757.

Williams, Frances, & Edward Chapel 22 Oct. 1760.

Williams, Jean, & Capt. Thos. Stark 15 Feb. 1757.

Williams, Mary, & Will: fferrar 2 Dec. 1755.

Williams, Mary, & James Davis 11 Jan: 1771.

Williams, Mary, & John Todd 7 Aug. 1775.

Williams, Sarah, & Charles Ferrol 29 June 1767.

Williams, Sally, & James Gibson 27 May 1787.

Williams, Susannah, & William Hogan 16 Jan. 1784.

WILLIAMSON, Agnes, & Stokes McCawl 29 Dec. 1767.

Williamson, Ann, & Wade Netherland 21 Oct. 1765.

Williamson, Martha, & James Mayo 3 Mch. 1764.

Williamson, Mary, & Thomas Whitlock 6 May 1756.

Williamson, Mary, & John ffinch 1 Oct. 1757.

Williamson, Sarah, & Joseph Lewis 13 Nov. 1764.

Williamson, Sarah, & Hardine Groves 18 Dec. 1767.

WILLIS, Betty, & Henry Hicks 24 Oct. 1756.

Willis, Fannie, & James Cole 3 June 1781.

Willis, Mary, & Capt. James Cole 19 Dec. 1747.

WILSON, Ann, & Wright Moreland 8 Sept. 1764.

WINN, Keturah, & Thomas Ford 15 Jany. 1758.

Winn, Anne, & William Webber 1 Aug. 1764.

WINSLOW, Susanna, & Wm. Parker 10 Aug. 1785.

WINSTON, Ailcy Ann, & Henry Pendleton 24 Oct. 1786.

Winston, Elizabeth, & Tarleton Payne 28 June 1784.

Winston, Elizabeth, & Tarleton Winston 14 July 1788.

Winston, Martha & William Tyrril 14 May 1781.

Winston, Martha, & Will: Callis 28 Jan. 1786.

WISDOM, Tabitha, & William Sutton 18 Mch. 1786.

WITT, Hannah, [or Anna] & Charles Huddlesey [or Hulsey] 2 Jul:
1756.

Witt, Mary, & John Bullington 4 Sep: 1757.

WOMACK, Judith, & Ralph Graves 1 Sept. 1756.

WOOD, Agnes, & Charles Thomson 11 Feb. 1783.

Wood, Martha & Stephen Southall 9 Apl. 1787.

Wood, Patty, & John Alcock 20 Feb. 1777.

Wood, Patty, & Nathaniel Thomason 28 Dec. 1782.

Wood, Sarah, & Capt. William Pryor 10 Feb. 1757.

WOODIE, Jean, & Townell Johnson 28 June 1760.

WOODLEY, Rebekah, & John Nelson 3 Nov. 1781.

WOODFORK, Sarah, & Charles Buress 3 Sep: 1763.

Woodhall, Eliz: & John ffoster .... Aug. 1756.

WOODRUM, Alice, & John Utley 8 Jany. 1770.

WOODSON, Elizabeth, & Thomas Woodson 19 Nov. 1763.

Woodson, Elizabeth, & Drury Mims 5 Apl. 1761.

Woodson, Frances, & George Anderson 22 Sept. 1758.

Woodson, Mary, & George Payne 30 Oct. 1705.

Woodson, Sarah, & Turner Rountree 23 Aug. 1771.

Woodson, Sarah, & William Cole 10 Jan. 1781.

Woodson, Sally, & William Macon 2 Mch. 1782.

Woodson, Susanna, & Isham Raily 18 July 1785.

WOODWARD, Becky, & Will: Holman .... 1776.

Woodward, Jemima, & Julius Sanders .... Oct. 1755.

Woodward, Lucy, & Will: Hemus 16 Jany. 1750.

WOOLAM, Christian, & Thomas Bryan 27 Jul. 177...

WOOLBANK, [Wilbank] Phyllis, & Robert Cairden 1 Jan: 1764.

WORSHAM, Mary, & Richard Wilkerson 3 Aug. 1759.

WRIGHT, Elizabeth, & Philip Jones 14 Mch. 1758.

Wright, Elizabeth, & Philip Johns 22 April 1760.
Wright, Jean, & Robert Stewart 27 June 1788.
Wright, Mary, & William Clements 24 Sep. 1757.
Wright, Mary, & Thomas Thomason 10 May 1777.
WYAT, Sarah, & Mathew Thomson 3 Oct. 1783.
Wyatt, Sarah, & Augustine McGhee 11 Nov. 1790.
WYLIE, Ann, & Charles More 3 July 1768.

YAUNCEY, Ann, & Will: Beadles 14 Oct: 1784.
Yauncey, Jemima, & John Cosbie 2 June 1781.
YANCEY, Rebecca, & Spencer Atkins 14 Jul: 1796.
YARBROUGH, Frances, & John Haines 16 June 1783.
YEARNIE, Zillas, & Thomas Overstreet 19 Oct. 1784.
YOUNG, Elizabeth, & Elliott Lacy 20 Aug. 1757.
Young, Elizabeth, & William Smith 15 Mch. 1774.
Young, Grace, & John Fox 10 Nov. 1782.

BIRTHS *and* BAPTISMS

James Adams & Cecily fford a son named Robert born May 9, 1757. Baptized Jun: 1 1757. p. 51.

James Adams & Cecily fford a Daughter named Nannie born dec: 28 1763. Baptized Jul: 29 1764. p. 68.

James Adams & Sally fford a Daughter named Sally fford born Jul: 20 1768. Baptized Aug: 20 1769. p. 85.

James Adams & Cicily Ford a Daughter named Milly born Jun: .... 1770. Baptized Oct: 14 1770. p. 88.

Joseph Adkinson & Judith Childers a Daughter named Dolly born Jan: 31 1769. Baptized Mar: 5 1769. p. 83.

Benjamin Ainsly & Sarah Grayson a Daughter named Ann born May 20 1770. Baptized Jun: 17 1770. p. 87.

Jo: Albritain & Mary Meanly a son named Richard born May 29 1769. Baptized Jul: 16 1769. p. 85.

John Albrittian & Mary Meanly a daughter named Sarah born May 2, 1774. Baptized Sep. 18, 1774. p. 97.

John Alcock & Patty Wood a daughter named Frances born Feb. 20, 1777. Baptized May 7, 1777. p. 101.

Jo: Alcox & Patty Wood a child named Patty born Dec. 1781. Baptized Ap. 7 1782. p. 106.

Jo: Alcox & Pattie Wood a son John born Dec. 25 1783. Baptized June 16 1785. p. 114.

Jacob Alford & Ann Hunter a child Ann-Hunter, Dec 10, 1779. Baptized May 19, 1782. p. 106.

Jacob Alford & Ann Hunter a Son named John born Feb. 5, 1782. Baptized May 19, 1782. p. 106.

Ja: Alford & Nansie Hunter a child Lucy born Sep: 21 1783. Baptized June 26 1785. p. 114.

Ja: Alford & Nansie Hunter a son Payton, born Feb. 6 1785. Baptized June 26 1785. p. 114.

Clifton Allen & Susannah Jones a son named James born Jan. 30, 1774. Baptized Ap. 10, 1774. p. 96.

George Allen & Mary Thurstone a Daughter named Rachel born Sep: 11 1766. Baptized Oct: 2 1766. p. 75.

Ja: Allen & Sar: Crowder on the little Byrd had a son born decr. 14. Named Richard. Baptized Jan: 11 1756. p. 48.

James Allan & Sarah Crowders a Daughter named Elizabeth born Jan: 6, 1759. Baptized ffeb: 4 1759. p. 54.

James Allen & Sarah Crouthers a Daughter named Susannah born Jun: 4 1761. Baptized Jul: 19 1761. p. 60.

James Allen & Sarah Cloudas a Daughter named Mary born Oct: 16 1763. Baptized Nov: 20 1763. p. 66.

James Allen & Sarah Clouder a son named George born Nov: 29 1766. Baptized Feb: 15 1767. p. 76.

James Allen & Sarah Crowders a son named James born Mar: 28 1769. Baptized Ap: 23 1769. p. 84.

James Allen & Sarah Crowder a son named William born Ap. 29 1772. Baptized May 31, 1772. p. 92.

James Allan & Sarah Crowdis a daughter named Martha born Jan. 22, 1775. Baptized Mar. 5, 1775. p. 98.

James Allen & Sarah Crowther a Daughter called Sally born Ap. 14, 1777. Baptized June 1, 1781. p. 102.

Ja: Allan & Patsy Woodfolk a son John born Jul: 10 1788. Baptized Sep: 10 1788. p. 121.

Jo: Allen & Jean Tandie a son Will: Savage born June 26 1784. Baptized Nov. 10 1784. p. 113.

Rich: Allen & Eliz. Richardson a child Patsy born June 29, 1782. Baptized Nov. 24, 1782. p. 108.

Rich: Allen & Anna Clements twins, Jo: & James born Jan: 31 1783. Baptized Ap: 19 1783. p. 109.

Isaiah Alley & Eliz: Watkins a daughter named Peggy born Feb. 17, 1777. Baptized Ap. 13, 1777. p. 101.

Jarrat Allison & ffrancis Moody a Daughter named Phenie [?] born Jan: 9 1762. Baptized May 30 1762. p. 63.

Gerrard Allison & ffrances Moodie a Daughter called Menie born Dec: 28 1763. Baptized Ap: 15 1764. p. 67.

Jo: Almond & Cat Faukner a child Nancy born May 27, 1781. Baptized Sep. 7, 1782. p. 107.

Tho: Almond & Mary Sanson, a son Sam-Sanson, born Jul: 29 1785. Baptized Sep: 12 1785. p. 115.

John Alphine & Frances Shepherd a son named William born Ap: 5 1767. Baptized Jun: 11 1767. p. 77.

Will; Alstock & Susanna Couper, Rebekah born Sep. 10 1785. Baptized June 4 1786. p. 116.

John Alsup & Jurya Potter a Daughter named Sarah born Jul: 1, 1763. Baptized Aug: 28 1763. p. 65.

John Alsop & Jeroyal Potter a son named William born Oct: 12, 1764. Baptized Nov: 18 1764. p. 69.

John Alsop & Juriah Potter a Daughter named Fanny born Sep. 28 1766. Baptized Nov: 2 1766. p. 75.

David Alvis & Mary Cauthon a son named Harris born Dec: 9 1769. Baptized Dec: 21 1770. p. 86.

David Alvis & Mary Cauthon a daughter named Aggie born Oct. 22, 1775. Baptized Nov. 12, 1775. p. 99.

Shadrach Alvis & Nanny Addison a daughter named Eliz. born Sep. 30, 1774. Nov. 20, 1774. p. 97.

Shadrack Alvis & Ann Addison a daughter named Nansy born Oct. 5, 1775. Baptized Jul. 21, 1776. p. 100.

Shadrack Alvis & Nannsey Addison a son named Meredith born Ap. 20, 1777. Baptized Jul. 13, 1777. p. 102.

George Anderson & ffrances Woodson in Albemarle a Daughter named Susannah born Sep: 22, 1758. Baptized May 2 1759. p. 55.

Geo: Anderson & Susannah Mims a Daughter named Sally born Mar: 1 1770. Baptized May 27 1770. p. 87.

Col: Ja. Anderson & Susannah Daniel, a son Jo: Daniel May 3 1786. Baptized June 4 1786. p. 116.

Nathan Anderson & Martha Periere, Tho: Periere Feb. 4 1784. Baptized Ap: 11 1785. p. 114.

Rich: Anderson & Ann Merriwether, Ann Merriwether born Aug 3, 1782. Baptized Sep. 18, 1782. p. 107.

Rich: Anderson & Catie Fox a son Chandy born May 7 1781. Baptized Mar: 30 1786. p. 116.

Rich: Anderson & Catie Fox a child Susanna born Oct. 1 1782. Baptized Mar: 30 1786. p. 116.

Rich: Anderson and Catie Fox a son Joseph born Aug: 17 1784. Baptized Mar: 30 1786. p. 116.

Rich: Anderson & Catie Fox a child Nansy born Nov: 22 1785. Baptized Mar: 30 1786. p. 116.

Turner Anderson & Susanna Daniel, Nathaniel Spotswood, Sep. 7 1783. Baptized Jany. 1 1786. p. 116.

Nathaniel Antony & Fanny Jacobs, a son Randolph, June 1780. Baptized June 10 1785. p. 114.

Nathaniel Antony & Fanny Jacobs, Cela, born Ap: 1785. Baptized June 10 1785. p. 114.

Thomas Antony & Elizabeth Martin a son named David born Aug: 26 1764. Baptized Dec: 24 1767. p. 79.

Thomas Antony & Elizabeth Martin a daughter named Sarah born Jul: 11 1767. Baptized Dec: 24 1767. p. 79.

William Appleby & Eliz: Milton a Daughter named Maybie born Dec. 1 1767. Baptized Oct: 16 1768. p. 82.

Charles Areskine* & Sarah Currie a Daughter named Frankie-Currie born Aug: 18 1764. Baptized Oct: 7 1764. p. 69.

Jo: Armstrong & Sarah Poindexter a child Sally born Mar: 31 1783. Baptized Oct. 28 1783. p. 110.

Lancelot Armstrong & Mary Bond a son David born Nov. 7 1782. Baptized Oct. 28 1783. p. 110.

Will: Armstrong & Mary Nichols a son Rich: Ellis born Nov. 8 1783. Baptized Ap: 25 1784. p. 111.

Will: Armstead & Mary Knucles Rebecca Jan: 11 1788. Baptized Ap: 13 1788. p. 120.

Ja: Arnot & Sally Burroughs a son Burrows born Sep: 4 1784. Baptized May 17 1785. p. 114.

Will Arnot & Mary Graves, a Son James born Oct. 17, 1782. Baptized Mar. 15, 1783. p. 108.

Will: Arnet & Polly Graves a son Billie born Sep: 1 1785. Baptized June 4 1786. p. 116.

Knaves Arrington & Priscilla Goddart a Son named William born Ap: 17, 1756. Baptized Jul: 27 1757. p. 51.

---

*Erskine.

John Ashline & ffrances Shepherd a Daughter named Sarah born Mar: 29. Baptized Ap: 4 1758. p. 52.

John Ashley & ffrances shepherd a Son named John born Jul: 30 1761. Baptized Ap: 12 1762. p. 62.

John Ashlan & ffrances Shepherd a Daughter named ffrances born Oct: 5 1763. Baptized Mar: 31 1764. p. 67.

Will: Ashley & Hannah Pierce a Daughter named Ann born Jan: 11 1763. Baptized Ap: 1 1763. p. 64.

Will: Ashley & Hannah Pace a Daughter named Mary born Ap: 28 1765. Baptized Feb: 23 1766. p. 73.

Will Ashley & Hannah Pace a daughter named Hannah born Ap. 16, 1771. Baptized 1772. p. 91.

Charles Askew & Sarah Curry a child named Rebecca born Oct. 20, 1780. Baptized Aug. 26 1781. p. 104.

George Askridge & Mary White a Daughter named Mary born Jul: 29 1758. Baptized Aug: 20 1758. p. 53.

Jo: Atkins & Sarah Brockman in Orange were maried Mar. .... 1753.

Ap: 4. 54 their son Frankie was born. now maried.
May 27 55 yr son Joseph was born. now maried.
Feb: 4. 57 yr son John was born. maried.
Mar: 3. 59 Susannah was born.
Sep. 18. 60 yr son Jonathan was born. died in ye war.
Jul: 4. 62 Ann was born.
May 17 64 yr son Hezekiah was born. maried.
May 12. 67 Mary was born.
May 11. 69 Sarah was born.
May 17. 71 Marthah was born.
June 27. 73 Lydia was born.
July 4. 75 Rhodie was born.
Aug: 23. 78 Rebekah was born.
In all thirteen children. p. 135.

Jos: Atkins & Mildred James a child Sarah born Feb. 29 1779. Baptized Aug. 5 1784. p. 112.

Jos: Atkins & Mildred James a son Jonathan born Ap: 25 1782. Baptized Aug. 5 1784. p. 112.

Jos: Atkins & Ann Atkins a son Parham born July 29 89. Baptized Aug. 21 1790. p. 126.

Jos: Atkins & Ann Atkins a son Davis born Ap: 3 1790. Baptized Aug. 21 1790. p. 126.

Lewis Atkins & Judith Clark a child Betsy born May 3 1784. Baptized June 22 1784. p. 112.

Spencer Atkins & Rebecca Yancey a girl named Elizabeth born July 14 1796. Baptized June 18 1797. p. 130.

Stephen Atkins & Annie Hanson a daughter in fornication named Mildred born Jun: 22 1762 [sic]. Baptized 1762 feb: 10. p. 61.

Stephen Atkinson & Ann Hanson a Daughter named Martha born Jan: 26 1764. Baptized Mar: 18 1764. p. 67.

Stephen Atkinson & Ann Hanson a son named William born May 1st 1766. Baptized Jun: 27 1766. p. 74.

Stephen Atkins & Annie Hanson a Daughter named Charity born Nov: 13 1768. Baptized Dec: 10 1768 p. 83.

Stephen Atkins & Annie Hanson a daughter named Sarah born Jan. 28, 1773. Baptized May 9, 1773. p. 94.

Stephen Atkinson & Ann Hanson a daughter named Elizabeth born Dec. 25. 1775. Baptized Mar. 24, 1776 p. 99.

Henry Atkinson & Rachel Potter a Son named Bartlet born Dec: 19 1756. Baptized 1757 Jan: 23. p. 50.

Henry Atkinson & Rachel Houchins a son named Moseby born Sep: 29 1758. Baptized 1758 Oct: 29. p. 53.

Henry Atkinson & Rachel Houchins a son named Jesse born Mar. 12 1762. Baptized 1762 Ap: 12. p. 62.

William Atkinson & Mary Perkins a Daughter named Elizabeth born feb: 6 1757. Baptized 1757 Ap: 9. p. 50.

Thos: Aulman & Mary Samson Martha Chandler Sep: 18 1787. Baptized March 10 1788. p. 120.

James Austine & Mary Holman a son named William born Sep: 10 1766. Baptized Oct: 12 1766. p. 75.

James Austin & Mary Holman a Daughter named Susannah born Oct: 10 1768. Baptized Dec: 13 1768. p. 83.

James Austin & Mary Holman a son Reuben born Nov. 17 1770. Baptized Dec: 6 1770. p. 88.

James Austin & Mary Holman a son named James born Dec. 8, 1772. Baptized Jan. 17, 1773. p. 93.

Will: Austine & Hannah Glin a Daughter named Ann born Mar: 10 1758. Baptized 1758 Ap: 16. p. 52.

Will: Austine & Hannah Glen a son named James born decr. 1, 1760. Baptized 1761 feb: 19. p. 59.

Charles Ayscough & Sarah Currie at Christians Miln a son born Jan: 12 1756 named Obadiah. Baptized 1756 Ap: 4. p. 48.

Lyddel Bacon & Ann Apperson a Daughter named Anne Apperson born Mar: 19 1771. Baptized Ap: 3 1771. p. 89.

Tho: Bacon & Milley Edwards a son Thomie born Aug. 12 1790. Baptized Mar: 18 1792. p. 126.

Callam Bailey & Eliz. Rountree a daughter named Fanny born Feb. 17, 1774. Baptized Mar. 3, 1774. p. 95.

David Bailey & Elizabeth Ryan a son named James born Oct: 14 1759. Baptized 1760 Ap: 4. p. 57.

John Baily & Angelina Thomas a son named Park born feb: 6 1769. Baptized Feb: 23 1769. p. 83.

John Baily & Angellany Thomas a daughter named Elizabeth born Jul 1, 1773. Baptized Dec. 26, 1773. p. 95.

Philip Baily & Mary Smith a Daughter named Sally born May 27 1769. Baptized Aug: 27 1769. p. 86.

Philip Bailey & Mary Smith a son named Charles born Dec. 24, 1770. Baptized Jul. 21, 1771. p. 90.

Tho: Baily & Chloe Chisholm a child Martha Ryan Jan: 3, 1782. Baptized May 26, 1782. p. 106.

Tho: Baily & Chloe Chisholm a son Augustine born Ap: 11 1783. Baptized June 1 1783. p. 109.

William Baily & Molly Groom a son named John born Sep: 26 1768. Baptized Oct: 20 1768. p. 82.

William Baily & Mary Alford a daughter named Sarah Holman born Nov. 26 1773. Baptized Jan. 22, 1774. p. 95.

Francis Baker & Mary Ashley a son named John born Dec. 6 1745. Baptized Ap: 23 1765. p. 71.

ffrancis Baker & Mary Ashlin a son named Joseph born decr. 3, 1753. Baptized 1756 Jun: 13. p. 48.

ffrancis Baker & Mary Ashly a Daughter named Mally born Nov: 26 1758. Baptized 1759 ffeb: 21. p. 54.

John Baker & Susannah Perkins a son named Jesse born Oct: 10 1767. Baptized Mar: 8 1768. p. 80.

Jo: Baker & Nancy Harris a child named Mary born Dec: 17, 1781. Baptized Feb. 12, 1782. p. 105.

Joshua Baker & Susanna Freeman a daughter Eliz-Jones June 31 1790. Baptized Aug. 15 1790. p. 126.

Joshua Baker & Susanna Freeman a son Joshua born Mar: 14 1792. Baptized May 1 1792. p. 126.

Overton Baker and Molley Lankford a daughter named Salley, born January 21 1795. p. 138. [Different hand writing.]

Thomas Baker and Mildred Edwards a son named Reubin born December 14th 1794. p. 138. [Different hand writing.]

Will Baker & Mary Walton a child Mary June 18, 1780. Baptized Jan. 30, 1783. p. 108.

Will Baker & Mary Walton a child Elizabeth born Nov. 5, 1782. Baptized Jan. 30, 1783. p. 108.

Burgess Ball & Mary Chicester a daughter named Eliz: Burgess born—[margin torn]. Baptized Mar. 29, 1772. p. 92.

Lewis Ball & Rebekah Hughes a Daughter named Elizabeth born Jan: 25 1768. Baptized Jun: 6 1768. p. 81.

Lewis Ball & Rebekah Hughes a daughter named Betsy born Jan. 1, 1773. Baptized Ap. 4, 1773. p. 94.

Benjamin Ballard & Jemima Harris a Daughter named Susannah born Sep: 1, 1757. Baptized 1757 Nov: 13. p. 51.

Ralph Banks & Martha Venable a son William born Sep. 24, 1781. Baptized May 26, 1782. p. 106.

Will: Banks & Eliz: Martin a son named William born dec: 6, 1755. Baptized 1756 June 26. p. 49.

Will: Banks & Eliz: Martin a Daughter named Betty born Mar: 8 1758. Baptized 1758 Ap: 4. p. 52.

Will: Banks & Eliz: Martin a son named Ralph born Jun: 1, 1759. Baptized 1759 Sep: 16 & Nov: 11. pp. 55-56.

Will: Banks & Eliz: Martin a Daughter named Mildred born Jan: 14 1762. Baptized 1762 Ap: 12. p. 62.

John Bantam & Jean Nichols a son named Samuel born Ap: 10 1765. Baptized Ap: 23 1765. p. 71.

George Barclay & Mary Cole a Daughter named Mary: Willis born Oct: 5 1767. Baptized Nov: 15 1767. p. 79.

George Barclay & Mary Cole a Daughter named Eliz: Martin born Jul: 14 1769. Baptized Aug. 1 1769. p. 85.

George Barker & Eliz: Brown a Daughter named Ann born Dec: 1 1766. Baptized Mar: 29 1767. p. 76.

Jo: Barker & Nancy Harris a child Cattie born Jul: 18 1786. Baptized Sep: 23 1787. p. 120.

Tho. Barker & Mary Poor a daughter named Cat: Gardner born Mar. 22, 177—. Baptized Jul. 25, 1773. p. 94.

Thomas Barker & Mary Poor a daughter named Judith born Oct. 15, 1774. Baptized Jan. 22, 1775. p. 97.

Thomas Barker & Mary Poor a son named John born Mar. 19, 1776. Baptized May 19, 1776. p. 100.

Will Barker & Ann Evans a daughter named Nancy born Feb. 12, 1773.

Will Barker & Ann Evans anoyr daughter named Susan-Lacy born Jul: 29 1775. Baptized May 30, 1776. p. 100.

Will Barley & Mally Orford a daughter named Sallie born Sep. 25, 1776. Baptized Ap. 26, 1777. p. 101.

Isaac Barnet & Aggie Stokes a Daughter named susannah born Aug: 24 1761. Baptized 1762 feb: 5. p. 61.

John Barnard & Agnes Allington a Daughter named Mary: Howard born Ap: 26, 1757. Baptized 1757 Aug: 28. p. 51.

John Barnet & Agnes Arrington a Son named Daniel born Jul: 14, 1759. Baptized 1759 Sep: 23. p. 55.

Joseph Barnet & Lucy Red a son named Joseph Royal born Oct: 10, 1758. Baptized 1758 Dec: 3. p. 53.

Joseph Barnet & Lucy Wade a son named Micajah born May 13, 1760. Baptized 1760 Jun: 24. p. 57.

Tho: Barnet & Sarah Graves a Son named John born Ap: 13 1762. Baptized 1762 May 16. p. 63.

Will: Barnet & Hannah ffenton a Son named John born Jun: 26, 1761. Baptized 1761 Jul: 26. p. 60.

Will: Barnet & Hannah Fenton a son named William born May 15 1769. Baptized Jun: 3 1769. p. 85.

Will Barnet & Hannah Fenton a daughter named Nansy born Oct. 1, 1771. Baptized 1772. p. 91.

William Barnet & Hannah Ffenton a son named Thomas born Jan 21, 1774. Baptized Mar. 28, 1774. p. 96.

William Barnet & Hannah Fenton a daughter named Cecily born Feb. 12, 1776. Baptized Oct. 15, 1776. p. 100.

Ch. Barret & Eliz: Clough, Will Torrence born Feb: 7 1787. Baptized Ap: 15 1787. p. 118.

Lewis Barret & Jane Price a child Mary born Nov. 23, 1781. Baptized Ap. 14, 1782. p. 106.

Lewis Barret & Jean Price a son Lewis born Jan. 17 1784. Baptized June 11 1784. p. 112.

Ja: Bartlet & Betsey White a child Nansy Foster, Dec. 12 1784. Baptized Oct. 23 1785. p. 115.

Tho: Basket & Mildred Martin a son named Martin born dec: 6, 1761. Baptized 1762 Ap: 25. p. 62.

Thomas Basket & Mildred Martin a Daughter named Sarah born Mar: 16 1764. Baptized May 13 1764. p. 67.

Will: Basket & Mary Pierce a Daughter named susannah born Jun: 21, 1762. Baptized 1762 Jul: 18. p. 63.

William Baskit & Mary Pierce a Daughter named Mary born Mar: 11 1764. Baptized Mar: 12 1764. p. 67.

William Basket & Mary Pierce a son named Thomas born Jan: 6 1768. Baptized May 1 1768. p. 80.

James Bates & Winifred Hix had a son born Nov: 22 1747. named ffleming. p. 40.

James Bates & Winifred Hix had a son born Nov: 23 1749. named William. p. 40.

James Bates & Winifred Hix anoyr son born May 29 1752. named Samuel. p. 40.

James Bates & Winifred Hix anoyr son born Mar: 24 1754. named Stephen. p. 40.

James Bates & Winnifred Hicks a son named Daniell born Jul: 6 1756. Baptized 1756 Aug: 29. p. 49.

Moses Bates & Rebekah Fleming, Rebeckah Jan: 1 '87. Baptized Dec. 12 '88. p. 122.

Burwell Baugh & Ann Williams a daughter named Betty born Jan. 2, 1776. Baptized May 15. p. 100.

Jo: Beadle & Susanna West a child Mary West born Nov. 15 1784. Baptized Dec. 8 1784. p. 113.

Ja: Beigle & Sucky West a son John born Aug: 15 1786. Baptized Nov: 15 1786. p. 118.

Ja: Beadle & Suckie West a child Letitia born Sep: 8 1790. Baptized Oct: 4 1790. p. 126.

Will: Beadle & Ann Yauncey a son William born Oct. 14 1784. Baptized Nov. 10 1784. p. 113.

Will: Beigle & Ann Yauncey a child Ann born Ap: 12 1786. Baptized Nov. 15 1786. p. 118.

Jo: Beekly & Henrietta Raglin a son William born Aug. 29, 1782. Baptized Nov. 14, 1782. p. 108.

Jo: Beckly & Henrietta Raglin a son John born Ap: 19 1787. Baptized Jul: 1 1787. p. 119.

Ben Bellamy & Dorothy Ham a child named Elizabeth born Jan. 23, 1779. Baptized Oct 20, 1781. p. 104.

Fisher Bennet & Judith Hanson a son named John born Aug. 16, 1773. Baptized Nov. 14, 1773. p. 95.

Fisher Rich: Bennet & Judith Amos a Son named Richard born Aug 23, 1780. Baptized Oct 21, 1781. p. 104.

James Bennet & Eliz: Sampson a son named Richard born feb: 8 1769. Baptized Mar: 19 1769. p. 83.

James Bennet & Eliz: Sampson a son named Stephen born Oct: 18 1770. Baptized Nov: 18 1770. p. 88.

James Bennet & Eliz. Sampson a son named James born Feb. 14, 1773. Baptized Mar. 13, 1773. p. 93.

Richard Bennet & Ann Lee a son named Millender born Ap: 15, 1763. Baptized 1763 Aug: 25. p. 65.

William Bennet & Sarah Harris a Daughter named Elizabeth born dec: 20 1767. Baptized Jan: 30 1768. p. 79.

William Bernard & Mary Fleming a son named Richard-Fleming born Mar: 18 1767. Baptized Jun: 10 1767. p. 77.

Valentine Bethel & Sarah Brooks a son named Samuel born May 26 1768. Baptized Oct: 16 1768. p. 82.

Rich: Begby & Sar: Kimbro a child Sarah, Ap: 29 1784. Baptized Ap: 9 1787. p. 118.

Rich: Begby & Sar: Kimbro a son Sylvanus Morris born Sep: 29 1786. Baptized Ap: 9 1787. p. 118.

REGISTER OF HENRY BIBB & SARAH MEED maried 1. Robert; 2. Mary; 3. John; 4. Minor; 5. Ann; 6. Susannah; 7. Henry; 8. Hartwell; 9. Sarah; 10. David; 11. Patsy; 12. Elizabeth. p. 144.

Henry Bibb & Sarah Mead a son named Minor born May 2, 1781. Baptized Oct 24 1781. p. 105.

Hen: Bibb & Sar: Mead a child Ann born Sep. 20, 1782. Baptized Sep. 30, 1782. p. 107.

Henry Bibb & Sarah Mead, twins, Henry & Hartwell born May 12 1784. Baptized Jul: 12 1784. p. 112.

Henry Bibb & Sarah Mead, Susanna born .... Baptized June 18 1786. p. 117.

Henry Bibb & Sarah Mead a son David born May 2 1788. Baptized June 8 1788. p. 121.

Henry Bibb & Sarah Meed a daughter Sarah Mar: 6 1790. Baptized Sep: 29 1790. p. 126.

Henry Bibb & Sarah Meede a girl named Elizabeth born Jan. 11 1795. Baptized May 22 1796. p. 127.

James Bibb & Sarah ffarrar a son named John born Jan: 18 1764. Baptized Mar: 4 1764. p. 66.

Jo: Bibb & Sarah Thomas a child Patsie born Jan: 17, 1782. Baptized May 5, 1782. p. 106.

Jo: Bibb & Sally Thomason a son Tho: Chew born Ap: 7 1787. Baptized May 22 1787. p. 119.

Rob: Bibb & Sarah Mead a child Martha born Ap: 29 1792. Baptized Aug. 12 1792. p. 126.

Will: Bibb & Eliz: Biggars a son Biggars born May 2 1783. Baptized Sep: 11 1783. p. 110.

Da: Biggars & Eliz: Ferguson, a son Ferguson, Mar: 2 1781. Baptized Sep: 11 1783. p. 110.

Da: Biggars & Eliz: Fergusson a son Miles Spotswood Feb. 4 1786. Baptized Feb: 4 1787. p. 118.

Macon Biggars & Christian Gissage a child Huldah born May 17 1783. Baptized Sep: 3 1785. p. 115.

Macon Biggars & Christian Gissage a child Betsie Smith born Apl: 22 1785. Baptized Sep: 3 1785. p. 115.

Will Biggar & Martha Richardson, Polly Richardson born Oct 13, 1781. Baptized Aug. 9, 1782. p. 107.

Will: Biggar & Martha Richardson a son Landie, Sep: 20 1785. Baptized Apl. 23 1786. p. 116.

John Bilboa & Ann Walker a Daughter named Susannah born Ap: 29 1764. Baptized July 8 1764. p. 68.

John Bilboa & Ann Walker a son named John born Oct: 7 1766. Baptized Mar: 22 1767. p. 76.

Jo: Bird & Ann Bond, a son William born Dec: 11 1785. Baptized Jul: 23 1786. p. 117.

Jeremiah Blacklock & Eliz: Gentry a Daughter named Sarah-Cade born dec: 9 1764. Baptized Jan: 13 1764. p. 69.

Jeremiah Blacklock & Eliz: Gentry, a son named Hezekiah born May 2 1771. Baptized Oct: 6 1771. p. 90.

Jeremiah Blacklock & Eliz. Gentry a daughter named Patty born Sep. 4, 1773. Baptized Aug. 28, 1774. p. 97.

Ed: Blockly & Martha Basket, a Daughter born Nov: 12 1744. named Mary. p. 40.

Ed: Blockly & Martha Basket a Daughter born Aug: 13 1747. named Martha. p. 40.

Ed: Blockly & Martha Basket a Daughter born Aug: 3 1750. named Sarah. p. 40.

Ed: Blockly & Martha Basket a Son born June 17 1753. named Edward. p. 40.

William Blunkhall & Rebekah Griffiths a Daughter named Ann born Mar: 11 1765. Baptized Ap: 7 1765. p. 70.

Will: Blunkhall & .... a son Will: Smith born Feb. 28 1784. Baptized Nov. 25 1784. p. 113.

John Bolling & Mary Jefferson a son named John born Mar: 24 1762. Baptized 1762 May 8. p. 62.

Mr: John Bolling & Mrs. Mary Jefferson a son named Thomas born feb: 11 1764. Baptized Mar: 6 1764. p. 67.

John Bolling & Mary Jefferson a Daughter named Jane born Sep: 17 1765. Baptized Mar: 2 1766. p. 73.

John Bolling & Mary Jefferson a Daughter named Ann born Jul: 20 1767. Baptized Aug: 28 1767. p. 78.

John Bolling & Mary Jefferson a Daughter named Martha born .... 1769. Baptized Nov: 24 1769. p. 86.

John Bolling & Mary Jefferson a son named Edward born Sep. 17, 1772. Baptized Dec. 15, 1772. p. 93.

Mr. Tho: Bolling & Eliz: Gay a son named John born Jan: 31, 1761. Baptized 1761 feb: 15. p. 59.

Mr. Tho: Bolling & Elizabeth a Daughter named Rebekah born Aug: 19, 1763. Baptized 1763 Sep: 25. p. 65.

Mr. Thomas Bolling & Betty Gay a Daughter named Mary born Jan: 27 1765. Baptized feb: 12 1765. p. 70.

Charles Bolton & Eliz: Hickins a son named John born Jul: 11, 1757. Baptized 1758 Ap: 3. p. 52.

Bartlet Bowles & Ann Owen a Daughter named Cecily-Owen born Sep: 13 1768. Baptized Oct: 16 1768. p: 82.

Gideon Bowls & Ann Hughes a Daughter named Jean born dec: 2 1757. Baptized 1758 ffeb: 19. p. 52.

Gideon Bowles & Ann Hughes a son named Hughes born feb: 7 1760. Baptized 1760 Ap: 27. p. 57.

Gideon Bowles & Ann Hughes a son named Nathan born Jan: 21 1762. Baptized 1762 Ap: 12. p. 62.

Gideon Bowles & Ann Hughes a son named Anderson born May 3 1764. Baptized Jun: 25 1764. p. 68.

Gideon Bowles & Ann Hughes a Daughter named Mary born May 27 1767. Baptized Oct: 25 1767. p. 79.

Gideon Bowles & Ann Hughes a Daughter named Elizabeth born Nov: 2 1769. Baptized May 6 1770. p. 87.

Gideon Bowles & Charity [Ann?] Hughes a son named Clayburn Hughes born Mar 23, 177—. Baptized Jul. 4, 1773. p. 94.

Gideon Bowles & Ann Hughes a daughter named Judith born Jan. 11, 1775. Baptized Aug. 1, 1775. p. 98.

Gideon Bowles & Ann Hughes a son named William born Ap. 10, 1777. Baptized Oct 16, 1777. p. 102.

Jesse Bowles & Hannah Perkins a son named David born Feb. 26, 1776. Baptized Ap. 14, 1776. p. 100.

Jesse Bowles & Hannah Perkins had a son named Stephen born Oct 15, 1777. Baptized Ap. 19, 1778. p. 103.

John Bowles & Elizabeth Curd a son named Benjamin born Oct: 5 1765. Baptized Dec: 16 1765. p. 72.

John Bowles & Eliz: Curd a Daughter named Sarah-Waddie born feb: 1769. Baptized Ap: 9 1769. p. 84.

John Bowles & Eliz. Curd a daughter named Nansy born Oct 18, 1771. Baptized Nov. 1771. p. 91.

Jo: Bowles & Eliz: Curd a child named Betsy Price born Dec. 22, 1781. Baptized Mar. 17, 1782. p. 105.

John Bowles & Mary Radford a daughter named Martha born Dec. 19, 1773. Baptized Feb. 14, 1774. p. 95.

Knight Bowles & Sarah Curd a daughter named Molly born Dec 13 1767. Baptized Jan: 24 1768. p. 79.

Knight Bowles & Sarah Curd a Daughter named Nansy born May 7 1770. Baptized Jun: 3 1770. p. 87.

Patrick Bowles & Nannie Owen a daughter named Nannie Jones born Nov 22 1770. Baptized Mar: 17 1771. p. 89.

Philip Bowles & Sarah Bacon a son named Thomas born Dec. 29, 1773. Baptized Feb. 14, 1774. p. 95.

John Sutton: Bowman & Sarah Cothan a Son named Nathaniel born Jun: 10, 1758. Baptized 1758 Sep: 24. p. 53.

John Sutton: Bowman & Sarah Cothan a Daughter named Rebekah born Jan: 4, 1760. Baptized 1760 ffeb: 10. p. 56.

Will Bradburn & Mary Johnson, Sally Johnson born dec. 23, 1782. Baptized Mar. 15, 1783. p. 108.

Benjamin Bradshaw & Ann mcBride a son born Jan: 20 1756 named William. Baptized 1756 feb: 29. p. 48.

Benjamin Bradshaw & Ann mcBride a son named Edward born Oct: 31 1758. Baptized 1758 Nov: 28. p. 53.

Benjamin Bradshaw & Ann mcBride a Daughter named Mary-Curd born feb: 16 1761. Baptized 1761 May 17. p. 59.

John Bradshaw & Eliz: Jordan a Son named Larner born Mar: 10, 1759. Baptized 1759 Jul: 7. p. 55.

John Bradshaw & Eliz: Jordan a son named Robert born Nov: 14, 1760. Baptized 1761 feb: 9. p. 59.

John Bradshaw & Elizabeth Jordan a son named John born Ap: 18, 1763. Baptized 1763 Sep: 4. p. 65.

John Bradshaw & Elizabeth Jordan a son named Jordan born Mar: 9 1767. Baptized May 17 1767. p. 77.

John Bradshaw & Sarah mcBride a son named Clayburn born Nov: 4, 1759. Baptized 1760 Jan: 14. p. 56.

John Bradshaw & Sarah mcBride a Daughter named Mary born Jan: 29 1763. Baptized 1763 May 21. p. 64.

John Bradshaw & Sarah McBride a son named John born Nov: 23 1764. Baptized Jan: 26 1765. p. 69.

John Bradshaw & Sarah McBride a son named Shadrach born Aug: 16 1766. Baptized Oct: 1 1766. p. 75.

John Bradshaw & Sarah McBride a son named Benjamin born May 3 1768. Baptized Jun: 12 1768. p. 81.

John Bradshaw & Sarah McBride a son named Brice born Mar: 20 1770. Baptized May 27 1770. p. 87.

John Bradshaw & Sarah McBride a daughter named Sarah born Sep. 3, 1772. Baptized Dec. 6, 1772. p. 93.

John Bradshaw & Lucy Sadler a son named William born Oct 9, 1771. Baptized Jan. 14, 1772. p. 91.

John Bradshaw & Lucy Sadler a son named Benjamin born Mar. 24, 1775. Baptized May 14, 1775. p. 98.

Lardner & Ann Bradshaws, a child Elizabeth born Ap. 20, 1782. Baptized July 21, 1782. p. 107.

Will: Bradshaw & Mary Lad a Son named William born Mar: 31 1756. Baptized 1756 May 29. p. 48.

Will: Bradshaw & Mary Lad 2 sons Joseph & Benjamin born May 28 1758. Baptized 1758 Oct: 23. p. 53.

Jo: Brags & Francis Marks a Son Marks born Dec 26, 1781. Baptized May 26, 1782. p. 106.

Jo: Bragg & Francis Marks a son Elias born Sep: 12 1784. Baptized May 14 1787. p. 118.

Jo: Bragg & Francis Marks a daughter Susanna born July 8 1786. Baptized May 14 1787. p. 118.

Daniel Branch & Eliz: Porter in Maniken a Daugh: named Mary born Nov: 18, 1761. Baptized 1762 Jan: 10. p. 61.

Daniel Branch & Elizabeth Porter a son named Mathew born Mar: 30 1764. Baptized May 6 1764. p. 67.

Dan: Branch & Eliz: Porter a Daughter named Eliz: Barbara born Mar: 27 1766. Baptized May 11 1766. p. 73.

Dan: Branch & Eliz: Porter a Daughter named Frances born Sep: 15 1768. Baptized Nov: 20 1768. p. 82.

Gernat Branch & Eliz: Branch a son named Jonathan born May 2 1762. Baptized 1762 Jul: 25. p. 63.

David Branham & ffrances Basket a Daughter named Judith born Ap: 25, 1762. Baptized 1762 Jun: 6. p. 63.

David Branham & Frances Basket a Daughter named Patty born Ap: 18 1766. Baptized Aug: 2 1767. p. 78.

John Bransford & Judith Ominet a son named Thomas born Ap: 5 1767. Baptized May 3 1767. p. 77.

John Bransford & Judith Ammonet a son named Francis born Jun: 30 1768. Baptized Aug: 7 1768. p. 81.

Obadiah Britt & Ann Thomson a son named William born Mar: 28 1753. Baptized Sep: 29 1765. p. 72.

Obadiah Britt & Ann Thomson a Daughter named Patty born Jul: 19 1765. Baptized Sep: 29 1765. p. 72.

Obadiah Brett & Ann Thompson on the Bird a Daughter born Mar: 19 1756 named Annie. Baptized 1756 Ap: 19. p. 48.

Obadiah Brett & Anna Thompson a Daughter named Lucy born Jan: 12 1758. Baptized 1758 ffeb: 19. p. 52.

Obadiah Brett & Ann Thomson a Son named John born Sep: 10, 1759. Baptized 1759 Oct: 14. p. 56.

Obadiah Britt & Nanny Thomson a Daughter named Elizabeth born Jan: 20 1761. Baptized 1761 Mar: 1. p. 59.

Obadiah Britt & Ann Thomson a son named Obadiah born Mar: 15 1763. Baptized 1763 Ap: 24. p. 64.

Obadiah Bret & Ann Thomson a Daughter named Sally born Dec. 22 1766. Baptized Aug: 2 1767. p. 78.

Obediah Brit & Mary Smith a child Elizabeth born Jan: 17 1784. Baptized May 30 1784. p. 111.

John Brett & Winifred Conolly a Daughter named Nannie born Oct: 9, 1756. Baptized 1756 Nov: 28. p. 49.

John Brett & Winifred Conolly a son named James born Jul: 9 1758. Baptized 1758 Aug: 20. p. 53.

John Britt & Winifred Conolly a son named Daniel born Aug: 14 1760. Baptized 1760 Sep: 28. p. 58.

John Britt & Winnifred Conolly a Daughter named Milley born July 19 1763. Baptized 1763 Sep: 11. p. 65.

John Bret & Winnifred Conolly a Daughter named Molly born Jan: 10 1766. Baptized Mar: 31 1766. p. 73.

Jo: Bret & Susan Holman a daughter named Mary born Sep: 4 1771. Baptized Sep: 22 1771. p. 90.

John Brett & Susannah Holman a son named Will Holman born Sep. 4, 1773. Baptized Oct. 17, 1773. p. 95.

Jo: Bret & Susanna Holman a son Obed born Oct. 19 1783. Baptized June 20 1784. p. 112.

Jo: Brit & Ann Adams a son named Obediah born Dec: 27, 1780. Baptized Ap. 12, 1781. p. 103.

William Bret & Hannah Conolly a son named Obed born feb: 12, 1759. Baptized 1759 Ap: 1. p. 54.

William Bret & Hannah Conolly a son named Jesse born May 12 1761. Baptized 1761 Jun: 21. p. 60.

Will: Brett & Hannah Conolly a Daughter named Jeanie born Aug: 21, 1763. Baptized 1763 Sep: 25. p. 65.

William Bret & Hannah Conolly a son named William born Aug: 9 1766. Baptized Oct: 14 1766. p. 75.

Will: Bret & Winefred [Hannah?] Conoly a son named William born Jul: 29 1768. Baptized Sep: 4 1768. p. 82.

George Bricken & Eliz. Adams a son named Will. George born Aug. 14, 1775. Baptized Oct 1, 1775. p. 99.

Pat: Broadfoot & Agnes Broadfoot a Daughter named Margaret born Mar: 25 1762. Baptized 1762 Ap: 8. p. 62.

Jonathan Broadhead & Axie Esther, twins Tho: & Will: born Jan. 29 1784. Baptized May 30 1784. p. 111.

Joseph Brockman & Mary Page a son named Robert born Jul. 8, 1775. Baptized Oct 1, 1775. p. 99.

Will Brockman & Mary Lindsay a son named Caleb Lindsay born Jul 1, 178—. Baptized Oct 3 1781. p. 104.

Will: Brockman & Mary Lindsay, Joshua Lindsay, Jany. 1783. Baptized Apl: 23 1786. p. 116.

Archibald Brodie & Eve Weesiger a son named John born Ap: 10, 1763. Baptized 1763 May 30. p. 64.

James Brooks & Elizabeth Pollock a Daughter named Nansie born Mar: 31 1765. Baptized May 1 1765. p. 71.

Thomas Brooks & Judith Bow a daughter named Sarah born Jun: 26 1767. Baptized Aug: 15 1767. p. 78.

.... Brooks & .... Baptized feb: 25 1770. p. 87.

Will Brooks & Eliz: Jacobs, Frankie, born Sep. 8 1784. Baptized June 10 1785. p. 114.

Moses Broomfield & Ruth Patrick a Daughter named Martha born Dec: 21 1758 [sic]. Baptized 1758 Mar: 25. p. 52.

Armstead Brown & Sally Daniel a child named Betty Born, Sep 5, 1782. Baptized Oct 16, 1782. p. 108.

Armstead Brown & Sally Daniel a son Henry born May 10 1786. Baptized Aug: 6 1786. p. 117.

Armistead Brown & Sally Daniel a son John, Oct: 12 1789. Baptized Feb: 17 89(90). p. 122.

Armistead Brown & Sally Daniel a child Sally Beverly born Oct 31 1792. Baptized Augt. 4, 1793. p. 122.

Armistead Brown & Sally Daniel a son Edwin Jones born July 23 1794. Baptized Nov: 8 1796. p. 127.

Cha: Brown & Ardler Cornet a child Lucy born Ap: 1 1786. Baptized June 4 1786. p. 116.

Ludlow Brown & Eliz: Hinds a son named William born Jan. 5, 1772. Baptized Jan. 15 1772. p. 91.

Reuben Brown & Susannah Napier a son named Tarlton born May 7 1764. Baptized Jul: 19 1764. p. 68.

Reuben Brown & Susannah Napier a daughter named Sarah born Mar 18 .... Baptized May 1, 1774. p. 96.

Reuben Brown & Susannah Napier a son Reuben born Sep. 26, 1771. Baptized May 1, 1774. p. 96.

Reuben Brown & Susannah Napier a son Skelton born Feb 23 1774. Baptized May 1, 1774. p. 96.

Ja: Brownley & Eliz: Grant a child Agnes born Jan. 19, 1782. Baptized May 26, 1782. p. 106.

Isaac Bryan & Ann Williams a son named John born Mar: 6 1767. Baptized May 10 1767. p. 77.

Isaac Bryan & Ann Williams a son named David born Jan: 10 1769. Baptized Sep: 14 1769. p. 86.

Is: Bryan & Ann Williams a son named Williams born May 27, 1781. Aug. 25 1781. p. 104.

Is: Bryan & Ann Williams a son Thomas born Sep: 29 1784. Baptized June 26 1785. p. 114.

John Bryan & Catherine Cashine a son named James born Sep: 5 1764. Baptized Sep: 9 1764. p. 69.

John Bryan & Eliz: Hamlet son named John born Nov: 11 1766. Baptized May 10 1767. p. 77.

John Bryan & Obedience Burton a son named Benjamin born Nov: 27 1766. Baptized Ap: 24 1767. p. 77.

Tho: Bryan & Christian Woolam a Daughter named Mary: Woolam born Jul: 27, 177—. Baptized Aug. 10, 1777. p. 102.

James Bryant & Jean Gerrand a son named William born Dec: 30 1765. Baptized Jan: 25 1766. p. 73.

James Bryant & Jean Gerrand a Daughter named Jean-Gerrand born Jan: 10 1769. Baptized Mar: 4 1769. p. 83.

John Bryant & Eliz: Hanson a son named William born Ap: 18, 1762. Baptized 1762 Aug: 29. p. 63.

Sylvanus Bryant & Ann Hamlet a son named Martin born June 3 1767. Baptized Sep: 6 1767. p. 78.

Sylvanus Bryant & Ann Hamlet a Daughter named Nansie born Aug. 23 1769. Baptized Oct: 29 1769. p. 86.

Arch: Bryce & Mary Mitchel a Daughter named Mary Gilcrist born Jul: 31 1770. Baptized Ap 22 1771. p. 89.

Arch: Bryce & Mary Mitchel were married July 21, 1769. p. 28.

Arch. Bryce & Mary Mitchel a child, Mary Gilchrist baptized by Do......la...... July 31, 1770. p. 28.

Arch: Bryce & Mary Mitchel a child Agnes bap: by Mr. Coats, died .... Baptized Jan: 3, 1773. p. 28.

Arch: Bryce & Mary Mitchel a son Will Mitchel by Mr. Selden, di...... .... Baptized Mar: 14, 1775. p. 28.

Arch: Bryce & Mary Mitchel a child Ann baptized by Mr. Dougla.. Baptized Feb: 3, 1780. p. 28.

Arch: Bryce & Mary Mitchel a child Eliz: baptized by Mr. Dougla.. Baptized Mar: 19, 1782. p. 28.

Arch: Bryce & Mary Mitchel a son John baptized by Mr. Buch-.anan. Baptized May 3, 1784. p. 28.

Arch: Bryce & Mary Mitchel a child Charlotte bap. by Mr. Buchana....... Baptized June 15, 1786. p. 28.

Arch: Bryce & Mary Mitchel a child Elizabeth born Mar: 19, 1782. Baptized July 21, 1782. p. 107.

Edward Bryers & Lucy Hawkins a Daughter named Nanny born Aug: 3, 1763. Baptized 1763 Oct: 16. p. 65.

John Bullington & Mary Witt a Son named John born Sep: 4 1757. Baptized 1757 Nov: 13. p. 51.

William & Mary Bullocks a daughter called Nansie born Dec. 14, 1773. Baptized Feb. 27, 1774. p. 95.

Da: Bullock & Jane Terry a child Sally Terry born Dec. 21 1782. Baptized June 3 1783. p. 109.

Da. Bullock & Jeanie Terry a child Nancy Born Ap: 25 1784. Baptized Sep: 26 1784. p. 112.

Charles Buress & Sarah Woodfork a Daughter named Fanny born Sep: 3 1763. Baptized Dec: 23 1763. p. 66.

Miles Burford & Ann Holman a son named Tandie born Ap: 13 1765. Baptized May 26 1765. p. 71.

Edward Burges & Ann Francis a son named Garland born Dec: 24 1766. Baptized Jun: 11 1767. p. 78.

Jo: Burges & Eliz: Sanders a child named Patsie Woodward born Nov. 17, 1780. Baptized Oct. 21, 1781. p. 104.

Obadiah & Mary Burks a son named Charles born Nov: 13 1758. Baptized 1759 Jan: 15. p. 54.

Mat: Burks & Eliz: Halfpenny a Son named James born Nov. 19. Baptized Nov. 19, 1781. p. 105.

John Burns & Jean Travis a Daughter named Patty born Ap: 28 1757. Baptized 1757 May 29. p. 51.

John Burns & Jean Travis a Daughter named Rhoda born Jan: 26 1760. Baptized 1760 Mar: 15. p. 57.

John Burns & Jean Travis a Daughter named Elizabeth born Ap: 1, 1763. Baptized 1763 Jun: 4. p. 64.

Ja: Burnley & Eliz: Grant a son named Alexander born Oct. 28, 1781. Baptized Aug. 25, 1781. p. 104.

Ja: Burnley & Eliz: Mills a son Abner born Oct. 13 1785. Baptized Dec. 15 1785. p. 115.

Jo: Burrows & Mary Harris a child Nancy born July 3 1790. Baptized Sep: 5 1790. p. 126.

Jo: Burroughs & Mary Harris a child Lucy born June 17 1792. Baptized Aug: 9 1792. p. 122.

Jo: Burroughs & Mary Harris a son John born Sep 23 1794. Baptized Nov: 30 1794. p. 127.

Jo: Burroughs & Mollie Harris a boy named James born May 25 1797. Baptized July 24 1797. p. 130.

Charles Burton & Mary Holland a son named George born Jul: 3 1764. Baptized Sep: 9 1764. p. 69.

Charles Burton & Mary Holland a son named Edmond born Sep: 22 1765. Baptized Sep: 28 1765. p. 72.

Cha: Burton & Mary Hunt a child Mary born May 10 1781. Baptized Jan: 14 1785. p. 113.

Cha: Burton & Mary Hunt a child Nancy born Oct. 14 1784. Baptized Jan: 14 1785. p. 113.

John Burton & Susannah Garret a Daughter named Sarah born Aug: 27 1765. Baptized Sep: 22 1765. p. 72.

Noel Burton & Lucy Barret a Son named Robert born Ap: 9, 1756. Baptized 1756 May 9. p. 48.

Noel Burton & Lucy Barret a Daughter named Priscilla born dec: 26 1757. Baptized 1758 Jan: 1. p. 51.

Capt Noel Burton & Lucy Barret a Daughter named Elizabeth born Nov: 11 1759. Baptized 1759 Dec: 25. p. 56.

Noel Burton & Lucy Barret a son named William-Barret born Ap: 2 1765. Baptized Ap: 28 1765. p. 71.

Noel Burton & Lucy Barret a Daughter named .... born feb: 20 1768. Baptized Ap: 3 1768. p. 80.

Rob: Burton & Priscilla .... a Daugh: born Aug: 12, 1725 named Ann. p. 40.

Rob: Burton & .... a Daugh: born Sep: 24, 1738 named Elizabeth. p. 40.

Capt: Rob: Burton & Judith Laforce a Daughter named Sarah born Jul: 16 1758. Baptized 1758 Jul: 29. p. 53.

Capt: Rob: Burton & Judith Laforce a Daughter named Priscilla born May 29 176—* Baptized 1761 Jul: 12. p. 60.

Robert Burton & Judith Laforce a Daughter named Jean born Mar: 29 1765. Ap: 27 1765. p. 71.

Robert Burton & Judith Laforce a Daughter named Lucy born May 13 1767. Baptized Jul: 5 1767. p. 78.

Cap: Will: Burton & Rebekah Cobbs a Son named John: Cobbs born Jan: 27 1758. Baptized 1758 May 27. p. 52.

Ed. Busby & Mildred Smith a Son Francis born Ap: 10, 1782. Baptized Mar. 17, 1782. p. 106.

Nathan Butler & Priscilla Antony a child Rhodie born Sep: 8 1783. Baptized Ap: 12 1784. p. 111.

---

*Margin torn.

Ja: Byers & Louvina Smith a child Sally, Jan: 3 1786. Baptized Jul: 9 1786. p. 117.

John Bybie & Jean Giles a son named Thomas born Mar: 24, 1760 Baptized 1761 Sep: 8. p. 61.

James Caid & Morning Parish a Daughter named Mary born Jan: 11 1759. Baptized 1759 ffeb 18. p. 54.

John Cairden & Mary Snugs a daughter named Mary born Jun. 18, 1772. Baptized Jul. 12, 1772. p. 92.

Reuben Cairden & Ann Massie a son named David born Nov. 24, 1772. Baptized Feb. 28, 1773. p. 93.

Reuben Cairden & Ann Massie a son named Thomas born Oct 20, 1774. Baptized Nov. 25, 1774. p. 97.

Reuben Cairden & Ann Massie a daughter named Mary born Feb. 22, 1776. Baptized Ap. 7, 1776. p. 99.

Reuben Carden & Anna Massie a child Anna born Ap: 28 1782. Baptized Ap: 26 1783. p. 109.

Robert Cairden & Phyllis Woolbank a Daughter named Betty born Jan: 1 1764. Baptized Feb: 19 1764. p. 66.

Robert Cairden & Phyllis Wilbank a Daughter named Sally born Nov: 12 1765. Baptized Dec: 22 1765. p. 72.

Robert Cairden & Phyllis Woolbanks a Daughter named Patty born Mar: 23 1768. Baptized May 1 1768. p. 80.

Robert Cairden & Phyllis Woolbank a Daughter named ffanny born Jun: 24 1770. Baptized Jul: 29 1770. p. 88.

Rob: Cairden & Phyllis Woolbanks a son named Archie born Jan. 3, 1773. Baptized Ap. 11, 1773. p. 94.

Robert Cairden & Mary Tuggle a son named James born Nov: 17 1769. Baptized Feb: 11 1770. p. 86.

Rob: Cairden & Mally Tuggle a son named Jesse born Nov. 22, 1771. Baptized 1772. p. 91.

Robert Carden & Eliza: Robards had a daught. named Dicey, born June 12, 1788. Baptized Aug. 2, 1788. p. 103.

Thomas Caldwell & Sarah Crouch in Henrico a Daughter named Lilias born Oct: 2, 1757. Baptized 1757 Oct: 23. p. 51.

Thomas Caldwell & Sarah Crouch a Son named William born Sep: 12, 1759. Baptized 1759 Sep: 23. p. 55.

Tho: Caldwell & Sarah Crouch a Daughter named Sarah born Aug: 11 1761. Baptized 1761 Aug: 23. p. 61.

Will: Callis & Martha Winston a son Cleon born Jan: 28 1786. Baptized Apl: 18 1786. p. 116.

Joseph Camm & Eliz: Thomas a Daughter named Elizabeth born Ap: 22, 1758. Baptized 1758 Oct: 29. p. 53.

Joseph Camp & Elizabeth Thomas a Daughter named susannah Born Aug: 10, 1763. Baptized 1763 Sep: 12. p. 65.

John Camp & Mary Craighill a son named William born Sep: 28 1767. Dec: 19 1767. p. 79.

Will Camp & Keziah Gentry a daughter named Martha born Feb. 28, 1772. Baptized Jun. 2, 1772. p. 92.

Rich: Carleton & Letitia Fairies a Son named Martin: King born
Nov: 18, 1777. Baptized Nov: 30 1777. p. 103.

Rich: Carleton & Letitia Fairies a child Henrietta born Nov. 3
1782. Baptized May 18 1783. p. 109.

Dabney Ker & Martha Jefferson, twins named Mary & Lucy, born
Mar: 7 1768. Baptized Jul: 9 1768. p. 81.

Dabney Carr & Martha Jefferson a son named Peter born Jan: 2
1770. Baptized Ap: 12 1770. p. 87.

Dabney Carr & Martha Jefferson a son named Samuel born Oct.
9, 1771. Dec. 16, 1771. p. 91.

Dabney Carr & Martha Jefferson a son named Dabney born Ap.
27, 1773. Baptized May 21, 1773. p. 94.

Tho: Carrol & Patty [Mildred] Waller a son William born Aug.
7 1784. Baptized Jun: 8, 1785. p. 114.

Tho: Carrel & Polly Waller, a son Sam-Adams born June 8 1786.
Baptized Aug. 6 1786. p. 117.

Will: Carrol & Eliz: Jewel a son named Thomas born July 16,
1753. Baptized 1756 June 26. p. 49.

Will: Carrol & Eliz: Dewil a Son named Spencer born May 5,
1756. Baptized 1756 Jun: 13. p. 48.

William Carrol & Elizabeth Jewel a Daughter named Jeanie born
Oct: 5 1758. Baptized 1759 ffeb: 18. p. 54.

Charles Carter & Judith Carter a son named Martin born Ap: 7
1763. Baptized Mar: 11 1764. p. 67.

Charles Carter & Judith Carter a Daughter named Judith born
Jan: 30 1765. Baptized May 5 1765. p. 71.

Charles & Judith Carters a son named Jacob born Oct: 9 1766.
Baptized May 7 1767. p. 77.

Charles & Judith Carters a Daughter named Patty born Dec: 23
1768. Baptized Jun: 25 1769. p. 85.

Edward Carter & Mary Bullington a Son named Edward born
Jun: 11 1748. p. 41.

Elijah Carter & Ursley Parlow a child Adcocke born dec. 13, 1782.
Baptized Mar: 25, 1783. p. 108.

Elijah Carter & Ursley Partlow a son George born June 9 1784.
Baptized Oct. 23 1785. p. 115.

Jo: Carter & Nancy Tugg a child Milley born Jan: 18 1783. Baptized Oct. 19 1786. p. 118.

Jo: Carter & Winifrede Allen a son Garland born Dec. 18 1785.
Baptized Mar: 8 1786. p. 116.

Thomas Carter & Mary Kilpatrick a son named Jesse born Mar: 4
1756. Baptized 1759 ffeb: 18. p. 54.

Thomas Carter & Mary Kilpatrick a son named Abraham born
Ap: 9 1758. Baptized 1759 ffeb: 3. p. 54.

Will Carter & Sarah Overstreet a son named James born Dec. 23,
1774. Baptized Aug 3, 1775. p. 98.

William Cash & Ruth Walker a son named Howard born Aug: 6,
1757. Baptized 1759 Mar: 4. p. 54.

William Cash & Ruth Walker a Daughter named Susannah born Nov. 1 1758. Baptized 1759 Mar: 4. p. 54.

Will: Cash & Ruth Walker a son named William born Nov: 7 1760. Baptized 1761 Ap: 26. p. 59.

Will: Cash & Ruth Walker a Daughter named Eliz: born feb: 9 1762. Baptized 1762 Ap: 11. p. 62.

Thomas Catlet & ffrances fford a son named William born Nov: 11 1759. Baptized 1760 ffeb: 17. p. 56.

Thomas Catlet & ffrances fford a Son named John born Nov: 25, 1762 [sic]. Baptized 1762 Jan: 2. p. 61.

Samuel Causeby & Elizabeth Four a Daughter named Elizabeth born Jan: 24 1765. Baptized Ap: 14 1765. p. 71.

John Cauthen & Agnes Harris a son named Nathan born May 8 1769. Baptized Jun: 25 1769. p. 85.

Will: Cauthon & Sarah Fairies a Daughter named Betty born Nov: 30 1769. Baptized Ap: 23 1770. p. 87.

Reuben Cave & Mary Ramsay a child named Pamela born Jan. 1781. Baptized May 13, 1781. p. 103.

Nathaniel Cawley & Ann Williamson a son named Richard born Jan: 10 1760. Baptized 1760 Mar: 19. p. 57.

Nathaniel Cawley & Annas Williams a son called William born Aug: 16 1768. Baptized Sep: 4 1768. p. 82.

Will: Cawlah & Morning Byers a son Pleasant Ap: 19 1787. Baptized June 10 1787. p. 119.

Bartholomew Cesar & Eliz: Jones a daughter named Nancy born July: 18, 1775. Baptized May 18, 1777. p. 102.

David Cesar & Mary Henderson a Daughter named Mary born Mar: 29 1762. Baptized 1762 Jun: 3. p. 63.

David Cesar & Mary Henderson a Daughter named Sally-Rollins, born May 28 1768. Baptized Jul: 17 1768. p. 81.

George Cesar & Elizabeth Watkins a son named Will: Watkins born dec. 10 1767. Baptized Ap: 30 1768. p. 80.

John Casar & Mary Cosby a daughter named Nansy born Feb. 29, 1774. Baptized Dec. 27, 1774. p. 97.

Joseph Chandler & Ann Atkinson a Daughter named Eliz: born dec: 20 1757. Baptized 1758 ffeb: 5. p. 52.

Joseph Chandler & Ann Atkinson a son named John born Jun: .... 1759. Baptized 1759 Jun: 20. p. 55.

Richard Chandler & Eliz: Carter a Daughter named Sarah Smith born Sep: 17 1770. Baptized Nov: 11 1770. p. 88.

Rich: Chandler & Eliz. Carter a son named Rich: Carter born Nov. 9, 1771. Baptized Jan. 26, 1772. p. 91.

Thomas Chancellor & Sarah King a Daughter named Ann born Mar: 12, 1757. Baptized 1757 Ap: 24. p. 50.

Tho: Chancellor & Sarah King a son named Thomas born dec: 9 1758. Baptized 1759 Jan: 15. p. 54.

Tho: Chancellor & Sarah King a son named Robert born Mar: 1, 1761. Baptized 1761 Ap: 5. p. 59.

Tho: Chancellor & Sarah King a son named Julius born Dec: 24 1764. Baptized Jan: 13 1764. p. 69.

Thomas Chancellor & Sarah King a son named John born May 5 1767. Baptized Jun: 14 1767. p. 78.

Abraham Chapel & Ann Drake a Daughter named Ann born Jan: 29 1768. Baptized Ap: 3 1768. p. 80.

Edward Chapell & ffrances Williams a Daughter named Sarah born Oct: 22, 1760. Baptized 1761 Nov: 22. p. 61.

John Chastine & Elizabeth Logwood a son named John born Jun: 23 1765. Baptized Jul: 21 1765. p. 72.

John Chastain & Eliz: Logwood a son named Lewis born Dec: 2 1766. Baptized Jan: 17 1767. p. 76.

Will: Cheek & Jeanie Raglin a son named Burwell born Jan. 15, 1776. Baptized Feb. 4, 1776. p. 99.

Abram Childers & .... a Son named Creed born about 17 years agoe. Baptized 1763 May 6. p. 64.

Jacob Childers & Mary [Railey] a Daughter named Elizabeth born Ap: 1 1768. Baptized Jul: 17 1768. p. 81.

John Childers & Lucy Woodrum a son named James born Jul 16, 1773. Baptized Aug. 22, 1773. p. 94.

John Childers & Maiden Lovel a Daughter named Nansy born Ap: 23 1769. Baptized [June] 3 1769. p. 84.

Major Childers & Eliz. Hampton a daughter named Molly born Oct. 4, 1772. Baptized May 16, 1773. p. 94.

Mathew Childers & Eliz. Turner a daughter named Sally born July 9, 1772. Baptized May 16, 1773. p. 94.

Nicholas Childers & Isabel Harris a Daughter named Isabel born Sep: 30 1757. Baptized 1757 Nov: 6. p. 51.

Nicolas Childers & Eliz: Harris a Daughter named Ann born Sep: 1, 1759. Baptized 1759 Oct: 7. p. 56.

Sam Childers & Eliz: Clark a son named Samuel born Oct 20, 1772. Baptized Jan 24, 1773. p. 93.

Samuel Childers & Eliz. Clark a son named Daniel born Oct 27, 1774. Baptized Feb. 5, 1775. p. 97.

Will: Childers & Ann Childers a son named Joseph born Nov: 25 1764. Baptized Ap: 28 1765. p. 71.

Will: & Ann Childers a son named William born Ap: 5 1766. Baptized May 11 1766. p. 73.

William Childers & Ann Childers a Daughter named Elizabeth born Ap: 9 1768. Baptized May 15 1768. p. 81.

Will: Childers & Ann Childers a son named Benjamin born Ap: 15 1771. Baptized Oct 27 1771. p. 90.

Will Childers & Ann Childers a daughter named Ann born Mar. 19, 1773. Baptized May 16, 1773. p. 94.

Will & Ann Childers twins viz Salley & Jesse born Jan. 30, 1776. Baptized Mar. 10, 1776. p. 99.

William Childers & Betty Nuckols a son named Richard born May 8 1767. Baptized May 23 1767. p. 77.

Will: Childers & Betty Nuckolds a son named Richard born Dec: 2 1768. Baptized Jan: 22 1769. p. 83.

Hen Chiles & Judith Daniel a Son James born Sep: 3, 1781. Baptized Ap. 9, 1782. p. 106.

James Chiles & Susannah Graves a child Jeanie Jan: 29 1787. Baptized Dec. 8 1787. p. 120.

Rich: *Cholmonldly & Grace Mylam a son named David born Jun 16 1768. Baptized Jul: 17 1768. p. 81.

George Chowning & Hannah Rogers a son named William born Jan: 4, 1762. Baptized 1762 feb: 7. p. 61.

George Chowning & Hannah Rogers a Son named Chatwin born Jun: 27, 1763. Baptized 1763 Jul: 10. p. 65.

Charles Christian & Sarah Duke a son named Charles: Hunt born Nov: 18 1770. Baptized Dec 23 1770. p. 89.

Drury Christian & Lucy Williams a son named James born this day. Baptized 1758 Ap: 23. p. 52.

Drury Christian & Lucy Williams a son named Gideon born Aug: 16 1760. Baptized 1760 Sep: 28. p. 58.

Drury Christian & Lucy Williams a Daughter called Ann born Mar: 3 1764. Baptized Ap: 8 1764. p. 67.

Drury Christian & Lucy Williams a son named Drury born Aug: 18 1766. Baptized Oct: 12 1766. p. 75.

Turner Christian & Anna Payne a Son named Billie Payne born Jan 17, 1781. Baptized Sep 6, 1781. p. 104.

Turner Christian & Annie Payne a Son Jesse George bo.................. Baptized Dec. 17, 1782. p. 108.

Will: Christian & Martha Evans a son John born Aug: 28 1783. Baptized Nov: 6 1783. p. 110.

Tho: Christmas & Mary Chisholm a Son Archer born 1782. Baptized Ap. 26, 1782. p. 106.

John Clac [or Clae] & Frances Crane a son called William born Dec. 9, 1773. Baptized Jun. 5, 1774. p. 96.

Benjamin Clapton & Agnes Morgan a Son named Walter born dec: 26 1756. Baptized 1757 Mar. 20. p. 50.

Benjamin Clapton & Aggie Morgan a Daughter named Elizabeth born May 5, 1760. Baptized 1761 Oct: 6. p. 61.

Benjamin Clopton & Agnes Morgan a Daughter named Olave Judith born Jul: 5 1762. Baptized Jul: 15 1764. p. 68.

Benjamin Clopton & Agnes Morgan anoyr Daughter named Mary born Ap: 27 1764. Baptized Jul: 15 1764. p. 68.

Benjamin Clopton & Agnes Morgan a Daughter named Susannah born Jul: 23 1766. Baptized Oct: 22 1766. p. 75.

Benjamin Clopton & Aggie Morgan a son named Ben-Michaux born Aug: 19 1768. Baptized Nov: 27 1768. p. 82.

Ben: Clopton & Aggie Morgan a son named Antony born Jun: 28 1770. Baptized Dec. 25 1770. p. 89.

---

*Chumly in Marriage Records.

Richard Clapton & Mary Davis a daughter named susannah born Jun: 27 1760. Baptized 1760 Sep: 28. p. 58.

Charles Clark & Marianne Salley a son named John born dec: 3 1763. Baptized Mar: 3 1764. p. 66.

Charles Clarke & Marianne Sallee a son named John born Ap: 24 1766. Baptized Jun: 1 1766. p. 74.

Christopher Clark, once in Louisa, now in Georgia. An account of his family June 1791: Milley Tyrrell his wife, Micajah oldest son maried, Christopher his 2d age 30, David age 28, Mourning age 26 has 5 daughters, Judith maried has 1 child age 24, Rachel about 22 has 3 boys, a widow now, Agathy about 20, ...nally about 18 maried, Samuel 16, Joshuah 14, Milley 12, Chiles Tyrel died age 2 moneths, Suckie 9, Lucy 5. p. 138.

Daniel Clark & Phebe Jordan a daughter named Milley born Sep. 22, 1773. Baptized Jun. 1, 1774. p. 96.

Dan Clark & [Phebe Jordan] a son named Ja: Jordan born Feb. 7, 1781. Baptized Nov. 19, 1781. p. 105.

Francis Clark & Catherine Hunly a daughter named Dolly born Oct: 20 1766. Baptized Jun: 11 1767. p. 78.

Francis Clark & Catherine Hundley a Daughter named Lucy born Sep: 21 1768. Baptized Oct: 1 1768. p. 82.

Jacob Clark & Sally Wood a Son named Abraham born Sep 15, 1781. Baptized Oct 22, 1781. p. 105.

James Clark & Susannah Bib a son named John born Ap: 23 1768. Baptized June 13 1768. p. 81.

James Clark & Susanna Bib a son named Richard born Jun: 5 1765. Baptized Dec: 15 1770. p. 89.

James Clark & Susanna Bib a son named Thomas born Sep: 5 1770. Baptized Dec: 15 1770. p. 89.

Jeffery Clark & Ruth Harris a Son named John born Oct: 19, 1756. Baptized 1757 Ap: 9. p. 50.

Jeffery Clark & Ruth Harris a Daughter named Judith born Ap: 29, 1759. Baptized 1759 Sep: 9. p. 55.

Jeffery Clark & Ruth Harris a son named Stephen born Mar: 22 1762. Baptized 1762 May 22. p. 63.

Jeffery Clark & Ruth Harris a Daughter named Winniefred born Jan: 29 1764. Ap: 29 1764. p. 67.

Jeffery Clark & Ruth Harris a Daughter named Jeanie born Oct: 10 1766. Baptized Mar: 15 1767. p. 76.

Jeffery Clark & Ruth Harris a Daughter named Mildred born Jan: 29 1769. Baptized May 21 1769. p. 84.

Geoffry Clark & Ruth Harris a daughter named Huldah born Mar. 10, 1772. Baptized Ap. 17, 1772. p. 92.

John Clark & Susannah Nicks a Daughter named Lydia born Jul: 20 1767. Baptized Aug: 30 1767. p. 78.

John Clark & Susannah Nicks a Daughter named Patty born May 24 1769. Baptized Jul: 23 1769. p. 85.

John Clark & Susannah Nicks a daughter named Elizabeth born Jul. 8, 1771. Baptized Ap. 26, 1772. p. 92.

John Clark & Eliz: Ellis, Twins named Joseph & Zachariah born feb: 2 1766. Ap: 20 1766. p. 73.

Jonathan Clark & Ann Bailey a son named James born Jun: 8 1767. Baptized Ap: 11 1768. p. 80.

Jos: Clark & Hannah Hutchison a son named Micajah born Ap: 19, 1754. Baptized 1759 Ap: 7. p. 54.

Joseph Clark & Hannah Hutchison a Daughter named Susannah born Sep: 23 1756. Baptized 1757 Ap: 9. p. 50.

Jos: Clark & Hannah Hutchison a Daughter named Mally born Nov: 13 1758. Baptized 1759 Ap: 7. p. 54.

Joseph Clark & Hannah Hutchison a Daughter named Nelly born Ap: 19 1761. Baptized 1761 Jun: 6. p. 60.

Joseph Clark & Hannah Hutchison a son named Mathew born feb: 7, 1763. Baptized 1763 Sep: 4. p. 65.

Joseph Clark & Hannah Hutchison a Daughter named Elizabeth born Dec. 17 1764. Baptized Jan: 26 1766. p. 73.

Joseph Clark & Hannah Hutchison a son named Elisha born Dec: 5 1768. Baptized Sep: 10 1769. p. 86.

Turner Clark & Jean Edwards a son named Turner born decr. 27 1758. Baptized 1759 Ap: 7. p. 54.

Turner Clark & Jean Edwards a Daughter named Sarah born Nov: 23 1749. Baptized 1759 Ap: 7. p. 54.

Turner Clark & Jean Edwards a Daughter named ffanney born Nov: 28 1752. Baptized 1759 Ap: 7. p. 54.

Turner Clark & Jean Edwards a Son named Charles born dec: 29 1754. Baptized 1759 Ap: 7. p. 54.

Turner Clark & Jean Edwards a son named Isham born Mar: 15 1762. Baptized 1762 May 22. p. 63.

William Clark & Agnes Williams a Daughter named Nanny born Dec. 1 1767. Baptized Ap: 11 1768. p. 80.

Will Clark & Agnes Baily a child Betsy born Mar. 2, 1782. Baptized May 26, 1782. p. 106.

David Clarkson & Eliz: Redmond a son named Jesse born Nov: 20 1760. Baptized 1761 Jan: 31. p. 58.

David Clarkson & Patty Redmond a Daughter named Patty born Jul: 5, 1763. Baptized 1763 Aug: 21. p. 65.

David Clarkson & Elizabeth Redman a Daughter named Lucy born Ap: 27 1766. Baptized Jun: 22 1766. p. 74.

David Clarkson & Eliz: Redman a son named John born Ap: 27 1769. Baptized Jul: 30 1769. p. 85.

David Clarkson & Eliz: Redman a daughter named Judith born Oct 14, 1771. Baptized Jan. 3. 1775. p. 97.

[David Clarkson & Eliz: Redman] Ditto Likewise a son named William born Sep: 25 1774. Baptized Jan: 3 1775. p. 97.

Da: Clarkson & Eliz: Redman, a son David born Jun: 27, 1779. Baptized Nov. 24, 1782. p. 108.

David Clarkson & Ann Perkins a Daughter named ffrances born Jul: 8, 1761. Baptized 1761 Aug: 7. p. 60.

David Clarkson & Ann Perkins a son named John born .... Baptized Sep: 25 1765. p. 72.

James Clarkson & Elizabeth Abray a Daughter named Sally born Sep: 13 1768. Baptized Jun 26 1769. p. 85.

Will: Clarkson & Martha Pledge a Daughter named Mary born June 15, 1761. Baptized 1761 Nov: 8. p. 61.

Richard Clayton & Susannah Coleman a Daughter named Rebekah born Jul: 14 1766. Baptized Oct: 16 1766. p. 75.

James Clements & Mary Oliver a son named .... born dec: 7, 1758. Baptized 1759 Jan: 21. p. 54.

James Clements & Mary Oliver a Daughter called Jean born Sep: 13 1760. Baptized 1760 Oct: 12. p. 58.

James Clements & Mary Oliver a Daughter named Mary born Aug: 23 1765. Baptized Dec: 25 1765. p. 72.

James Clements & Mary Oliver a Daughter named Nancy born Mar: 13 1767. Baptized Ap: 19 1767. p. 77.

James Clements & Mary Oliver a son named James born Dec: 23 1768. Baptized Jan: 29 1769. p. 83.

Jo: Clements & Eliz: Hugens a Daughter named Annie born Aug: 2, 1756. Baptized 1756 Sep: 5. p. 49.

John Clements & Eliz: Houchins a son named James born Jan: 15, 1758. Baptized 1758 Ap: 30. p. 52.

John Clements & Eliz: Huchins a son named John born Jun: 14 1759. Baptized 1759 Sep: 16 & Nov: 11. pp. 55-56.

John Clements & Eliz: Huchins a Daughter named Elizabeth born Jan: 23 1761. Baptized 1761 Mar: 15. p. 59.

John Clements & Elizabeth Huchins a Daughter named Rachel born Jun: 15 1764. Baptized Aug: 5 1764. p. 68.

Jo: Clements & Eliz: Houchins a son named Stephen born feb: 12 1766. Baptized Ap: 27 1766. p. 73.

Stephen Clements & Susannah Tony a Son named Benjamin born Ap: 6 1757. Baptized 1757 May 1. p. 50.

Stephen Clements & Susannah Tony a Son called Charles born Aug: 23 1760. Baptized 1760 Oct: 12. p. 58.

Tho: Clements & Sarah Pace a Son named Stephen born May 11, 1761. Baptized 1761 Jun: 7. p. 60.

Tho: Clements & Sarah Pierce a son named John born Mar: 7 1763. Baptized 1763 Ap: 1. p. 64.

Thomas Clements & Sarah Pace a son named James born Mar: 2 1765. Baptized Ap: 14 1765. p. 70.

Thomas Clements & Sarah Pace a son named Benjamin born Dec: 10 1766. Baptized Mar: 29 1767. p. 76.

Thomas Clements & Sarah Pace a son named Thomas born Ap: 19 1769. Baptized Jun: 4 1769. p. 85.

Tho: Clements & Sarah Pace a daughter named Ann born Jul: 11 1771. Baptized Sep: 22 1771. p. 90.

William Clements & Mary Wright a son named Thomas born Sep: 24 1757. Baptized 1757 Nov: 13. p. 51.

Will Clements & Mary Wright a son named Jesse born Ap: 14, 1760. Baptized 1760 May 25. p. 57.

Will: Clements & Mary Wright a Daughter named Joyce born Nov: 18, 1762. Baptized 1763 Ap: 10. p. 64.

Will: Clements & Isabella Halley a Daughter named Mary born dec. 2 1768. Baptized Feb: 19 1769. p. 83.

Geo. Cliff & Mary Nilson a son named James born Oct 30, 1772. Baptized Jan. 30, 1773. p. 93.

Rich: Clough & Jane Woodson a child Mary born Mar. 9, 1782. Baptized June 16, 1782. p. 107.

Isaac Coats & Rebekah Griffiths a son named John born Oct: 29, 1760. Baptized 1760 Nov: 17. p. 58.

Rob: Cobb & Ann Given [Gisage] Poindexter; Jo: Poindexter born May 27 1785. Baptized Feb. 9 1786. p. 116.

Rob: Cobb & Ann Given [Gisage] Poindexter a child Polly Lewis. Baptized Nov: 7 1787. p. 120.

Rob: Cobb & Nancy Poindexter a child born dec: 25 1789. Baptized Sep: 5 1790. p. 126.

Rob: Cobbs & Ann Poindexter a son William born Mar: 2 1792. Baptized June 28 1792. p. 126.

Benjamin Cocke & Mary Johnson a daughter called Ann, born May 24 1769. Baptized Jul: 23 1769. p. 85.

James Cock & Mary Lewis a Son named John born Nov: 9 1757. Baptized 1758 Jan: 5. p. 51.

James Coke & Mary Lewis a Daughter named Sarah: Lewis born feb: 5, 1760. Baptized 1760 Jun: 5. p. 57.

James Cocke & Mary Lewis a Daughter named Susannah born Aug: 5 1764. Baptized Mar: 21 1765. p. 70.

James Cocke & Jane Johnson a daughter named Elizabeth born Feb. 3, 1775. Baptized Mar. 3, 1775. p. 98.

Ja: Cocke & Martha Holland Parish a daughter named David [sic] born Ap. 23, 1776. Baptized May 23, 1776. p. 100.

Ja: Cocke & Martha Parish a son named William born Aug 1, 1777. Baptized Oct 13, 1777. p. 102.

Ja: Cocke & Martha Parish a son named Jack Fleming born Jan: 4, 1782. Baptized Mar. 17, 1782. p. 105.

Ja: Cocke & Martha Parish a child Mary Lewis born Aug. 11 1783. Baptized Ap: 18 1784. p. 111.

John Cocke & Elizabeth Richardson a Daughter named Rebekah born feb: 23 1768. Baptized Ap: 11 1768. p. 80.

Pleasant Cocke & Elizabeth Fowler a son named William born dec. 21 1766. Baptized Feb: 22 1767. p. 76.

Pleasants Cocke & Elizabeth ffowler a son named Robert born feb; 14 1769. Baptized Mar: 19 1769. p. 84.

Tho: Coke (Cocke) & Ann Johnson a Son named Samuel born Jan: 21, 1754. Baptized 1756 Aug: 28. p. 49.

Tho: Coke [Cocke] & Ann Johnson a Son named John born Jul: 27, 1756. Baptized 1756 Aug: 28. p. 49.

Thomas Coke & Ann Johnston a Daughter named Mary born Oct: 24, 1758. Baptized 1759 ffeb: 14. p. 54.

Tho: Cocke & Ann Johnston a Daughter named Nansie born Oct: 1 1760. Baptized 1761 Jun: 6. p. 60.

Thomas Cocke & Ann Johnson a Daughter named Agnes born Mar: 29 1765. Baptized Sep: 15 1765. p. 72.

William Colbard & Mercy Holland a Daughter named Elizabeth' born Jan: 2, 1759. Baptized 1759 June: 16. p. 55.

Will: Colbert & Massey Holland a son named Neil, born Oct: 12 1760. Baptized 1761 Ap: 27. p. 59.

William Colbert & Massey Holland a son named William born Nov: 1st 1762. 1763 May 25. p. 64.

William Colbert & Meray Holland a Daughter named Betty born May 25 1765. Sep: 25 1765. p. 72.

Will Colvard & Mary Holland a Daughter named Nancy born Ap; 6 1767. Baptized Jan: 15 1768. p. 79.

William Colvard & Mercy Holland a Daughter named Damaris born Mar: 25 1769. Baptized Ap: 10 1770. p. 87.

Capt: Ja. Cole & Mary Willis had a child Mary. Baptized Dec: 19. 1747. p. 129.

Geo: Barclay & Mary Cole were married Aug: 17. 1766. p. 129.

Geo: Barclay & Mary Cole had a son Patrick. Baptized Oct: 18. 1770. p. 129.

Geo: Barclay & Mary Cole had a child Catie Cole. Baptized Jul: 22. 1772. p. 129.

Geo: Barclay & Mary Cole had a child Lucy Martin. Baptized Mar: 15 1776. p. 129.

Capt: Ja: Cole died aged 42. Baptized Mar: 1767. p. 129.

Mrs. Mary Cole died aged 47. Baptized Jul: 1770. p. 129.

Cap: James Cole & Mary Wills [Willis] a Daughter named Mary born Dec: 19 1747. p. 41.

Cap: James Cole & Mary Wills a son named James born Sep: 26 1751. p. 41.

Cap: James Cole & Mary Wills a Son named William born May 31 1753. p. 41.

Cap: James Cole & Mary Wills a Daughter named Cathrine born May 2 1755. p. 41.

James Cole & Mary Wills a son named John born May 9 1757. Baptized 1757 Jun: 12. p. 51.

Capt Ja: Cole & Mary Willis a Daughter named Jeanie born Ap: 2 1760. Baptized 1760 Ap: 30. p. 57.

James Cole & Mary Willis a son named Rascow born Mar: 9 1762. Baptized 1762 Ap: 11. p. 62.

Major James Cole & Mary Willis a son named Dudley born May 7 1764. Baptized May 11 1764. p. 67.

James Cole & Mary Willis a Daughter named Susannah born Aug: 19 1766. Baptized Aug: 20 1766. p. 75.

Ja: Cole & Fannie Willis a child Lucy born June 3, 1781. Baptized Aug 26, 1781. p. 104.

Ja: Cole & Fanny Willis a son Roscow born Jan: 28 1783. Baptized Sep: 28 1783. p. 110.

Rich: Cole & Sarah Sansum a son William born Oct: 5 1786. Baptized Dec. 25 1786. p. 118.

Sam: Cole & Eliz: Cosbie a son named Jo: Cosbie born May 24 1781. Baptized Aug. 4, 1781. p. 103.

Sam Cole & Eliz: Cosby a son Richard born Sep: 8 1782. Baptized Ap: 25 1784. p. 111.

Sam Cole & Eliz: Cosby a child Mary Hickerson born Feb. 20 1784. Baptized Ap: 25 1784. p. 111.

Sam: Cole & Eliz: Cosbie, a son William born Nov. 9 1785. Baptized Dec. 29 1785. p. 115.

Sam Cole & Eliz: Cosby a child Lydia born Ap: 15 1787. Baptized May 11 1788. p. 121.

Accompt of Mr. Sam: Cole & Ez: Cosbies Children—they were maried Ap: 29 1777. Barbarah, Elizabeth, John, Richard, Mary, William, Lydia, Sally, Thomas, Rebekah, Louisa, Samuel. p. 129.

William Cole & Sarah Clayborn a daughter named Mary born Nov. 10, 1775. Baptized Mar. 18, 1776. p. 99.

Will Cole & Sarah Woodson a child Sarah born Jan. 10, 1781. Baptized Aug. 26, 1781. p. 104.

Ja: Coleman & Sarah Taylor a child Polly Wade born Feb. 27, 1782. Baptized Aug. 5, 1782. p. 107.

Ja. & Betty Colemans a child Sarah born Nov. 27, 1782. Baptized Mar. 25, 1783. p. 108.

Jo: Coleman & Hannah Hutchison a child named Cattie-Waggoner born Mar. 15, 1781. Baptized May. 13, 1781. p. 103.

John Daniel Coleman & Million Shamble a Daughter called Betty born feb: 22 1764. Baptized Mar: 17 1764. p. 67.

John Daniel Coleman & Millener Chambles a Daughter named Ann born Mar: 3 1766. Baptized Ap: 23 1766. p. 73.

John-Daniel Coleman & Million Shambles a son named Jesse born Oct: 4 1768. Baptized Jan: 28 1769. p. 83.

Robert Coleman & Nanny Grayson a Daughter named Betty born Nov: 11 1766. Baptized Feb: 3 1767. p. 76.

Rob: Ed: Coleman & Catie Robinson a child named Martha born Mar. 9, 1781. Baptized May. 13, 1781. p. 103.

Rob: Edward Coleman & Cat: Robinson a child Lucretia Mar: 24 1782. Baptized Jul: 20 1783. p. 110.

Rob: Edward Coleman & Catherine Robison, Sarah Reeves, born Apl. 17 1786. Baptized Aug: 13 1786. p. 117.

Samuel Coleman & Ann Wright a Daughter named Jeanie born Jul: 18, 1756. Baptized 1757 Mar. 6. p. 50.

Sam: Coleman & Ann Wright a Daughter named Jeanie born Jun: 22, 1759. Baptized 1762 May 10. p. 63.

Sam: Coleman & Ann Wright a Son named David born Jan: 6, 1762. Baptized 1762 May 10. p. 63.

Jo: Connor & Mary Merriwether, Sally born Oct. 27 1787. Baptized Dec. 2 1787. p. 120.

Bryan Conolly & Sarah Davis a son named James born Aug: 1 1762. Baptized Feb: 11 1767. p. 76.

Bryan Conolly & Sarah Davis a Daughter named Jean born Jan: 28 1767. Baptized Feb: 11 1767. p. 76.

Bryant Conolly & Sarah Davis a Daughter named Mary born dec: 13 1768. Baptized Feb: 19 1769. p. 83.

Bryan Conolly & Sarah Davies a daughter named Betty born Oct. 5, 1771. Baptized Dec. 15, 1771. p. 91.

Will Cook & Ann Nelson a Son Mordecai born dec. 12, 1782. Baptized Jan. 30, 1783. p. 108.

Will: Cook & Ann Nelson a son Edward Nelson born Dec. 7 1784. Baptized Mar: 31 1785. p. 113.

Will: Cook & Ann Nelson a child Elizabeth born June 16 1787. Baptized Sep: 23 1787. p. 120.

Antony Cooper & Easter Burdel a son Thomas born Aug: 9 1783. Baptized Oct. 26 1783. p. 110.

Dan: Cooper and Martha Branham a child Hannah born Mar: 15 1784. Baptized June 20 1784. p. 112.

Dan: Cooper and Martha Branham a son Billie born Oct. 25 1779. Baptized June 20 1784. p. 112.

Dan: Cooper and Martha Branham a son Imanuel born Dec. 7 1781. Baptized June 20 1784. p. 112.

David Copland & Susan Skelton a daughter named Susan: Skelton born Jan 7, 1772. Baptized Jan. 23, 1772. p. 91.

Henry Copland & Ann Martin a Daughter named Dycie born Jun: 29 1764. Baptized Aug: 26 1764. p. 69.

Geo: Cornelius & Susan Nelson a child named Rebekah born Feb. 10, 1780. Baptized Oct 14, 1781. p. 104.

Nathaniel Corley & Annas Williams a son named Nathaniel born Jul: 7 1764. Baptized Aug: 12 1764. p. 68.

Wil: Corley & Mourning Byers a sun Wil: Byers born Mar: 26 1783. Baptized May 18 1783. p. 109.

Mr. Charles Cosbie once here in Louisa, now in Georgia, account of his family. Charles Cosby the father Eliz: Sydnor his wife married dec. 14 1759. Sydnor Cosby his oldest son maried born Oct. 7, '62. Robert Cosby 2d son was born Sep. 26, '65. Fortunatus his 3d son born dec: 30 '67. Richmond his 4th son was born dec: 14, '72. James his 5th son was born Oct: 20, '74. David his 6th son. Charles Scot his 7th son. Patsy his 1st daughter was born feb: 13 '64. Judith his 2d daughter was born Oct: 12 '69. Polly his 3d daughter was born Mch. 16, '71. Barbarah his 4th daughter. Lucy his 5th daughter born Mar: 5, '83. p. 138.

Charles Cosbie & Eliz. Sydnor a son named James Overton born Oct. 20, 1774. Baptized Feb. 14, 1775. p. 97.

Cha: Cosbie & Eliz: Sydnor a child Lucy Hawkins born Mar: 5 1783. Baptized 21 June 1783. p. 109.

Cha: Cosby & Barbara Byers a son Ja: Douglas born May 1 1784. Baptized Sep: 26 1784. p. 112.

David Cosby & Mary Johnston a Daughter named Winnifred born Jan: 26, 1757. Baptized 1757 May 8. p. 50.

David Cosbie & Mary Johnston a son named William born feb: 14, 1759. Baptized 1759 May 6. p. 55.

David Cosbie & Mary Johnson a son named Jeremiah born Oct:· 11. 1761. Baptized 1762 feb: 7. p. 61.

David Coseby & Mary Johnston a son named James born Mar 28 1765. Baptized May 19 1765. p. 71.

David Cosbie & Mary Johnson a son named Pleasants born .... 1769. Baptized Nov: 13 1769. p. 86.

Garland Cosbie & Molly Poindexter, Stith Poindexter, born Nov: 27 1783. Baptized Oct: 2 1784. p. 112.

Garland Cosbie & Molly Poindexter a child Nicholas, Feb. 22 1785. Baptized Nov: 3 1785. p. 115.

Hickerson Cosbie & Nancy Harris a Son named Garland born May 2, 1781. Baptized Ap. 8 1781. p. 103.

Hickerson Cosbie & Nancy Harris a child Mary born Jun: 23, 1782. Baptized Aug. 4, 1782. p. 107.

Jo: Cosbie & Jemima Yauncey a child named Patsie born June 2, 1781. Baptized Sep. 27, 1781. p. 104.

Jo: Cosbie & Jemima Yauncey a child Amadia born Feb. 17 1783. Baptized May 12 1783. p. 109.

Jo: Cosbie & Jemima Yauncey, Archelaus Yauncey born Sep. 27 1784. Baptized Jan: 1 1785. p. 113.

Jo: Cosby & Jemima Yauncey a son William born Aug. 17 1786. Baptized Sep: 17 1786. p. 117.

Jo: Cosbie & Jemima Yauncy a son Nathan born Nov. 13 1788. Baptized Jan: 1 1789. p. 122.

Sam: Cosbie & Eliz. fford a Daughter named Mary born Sep: 5, 1761. Baptized 1761 Nov: 8. p. 61.

Samuel Cosbie & Elizabeth ffore a son named William born feb: 7, 1763. Baptized 1763 Jun: 5. p. 64.

Sam Cosby & Mildred Poor a daughter named Patty: Mosely born Dec. 5, 1774. Baptized Mar. 11, 1774. p. 96.

Tho: Cosbie & Eliz: [Watkins] Cosbie a son William born July 16, 1782. Baptized Oct 19, 1782. p. 108.

Tho: Cosbie & Eliz: Watkins a son John, Dec. 18 1784. Baptized Jan: 14 1786. p. 116.

Wingfield Cosby & Mary Morris a son named Wingfield born Dec. 18, 1772. Baptized Jan. 30. 1773. p. 93.

Wingfield Cosbie & Ann Baker a child Mally born: Ap 29, 1782. Baptized Sep. 9, 1782. p. 107.

Wingfield Cosbie & Ann Baker a child Ann Winkfield born Aug.
10 1783. Baptized Sep: 28 1783. p. 110.

Wingfield Cosbie & Ann Baker, a son, Tho: Baker, born June 28
1784. Baptized Mar: 31 1785. p. 114.

Wingfield Cosbie & Ann Baker, Overton-Martin Feb. 10 1787.
Baptized Jul: 1 1787. p. 119.

Zacheus Cosbie & Morning Jackson a child Mary born Jan 27,
1782. Baptized May 5, 1782. p. 106.

James Cothan & Mary fferrar a Daughter named Temperance born
Nov: 17 1755. Baptized 1756 May 9. p. 48.

Jo: Cothan & Agnes Harris a son named Jesse born Jun: 12,
1756. Baptized 1756 Jul: 28. p. 49.

John Cothan & Agnes Haris a son named Nathan born dec: 10
1758. Baptized 1759 Jan: 7. p. 54.

John Cothan & Agnes Harris a Daughter named Suckie born Nov:
17. 1761. Baptized 1762 Mar: 14. p. 62.

John Cothan & Agnes Harris a Daughter named Annie born Jun:
30 1764. Baptized Jul: 15 1764. p. 68.

Rob: Cothan & Zulima Laforce a Daughter named Keturah born
Dec: 1 1760. Baptized 1761 Ap: 5. p. 59.

Robert Cothan & Zulima Laforce a son named Richard born Mar:
17 1764. Baptized Sep: 9 1764. p. 69.

Richard Cotterel & Martha Pimble a Daughter named Judah:
Smith born May 15, 1757. Baptized 1757 Jul: 3. p. 51.

Edward Cox & Cecily Guilliam a Daughter named Elizabeth born
Oct: 10 1768. Baptized Oct: 23 1768. p. 82.

Edward Cox & Cecily Gillam a Daughter named Sally born May
11 1770. Baptized Aug: 19 1770. p. 88.

Edward Cox & Cecily Gillam a daughter named Mary born Ap.
25, 1772. Baptized May 31, 1772. p. 92.

Edward Cox & Cecily Guilam a daughter named Ann born May
20, 1776. Baptized Aug. 10, 1776. p. 100.

Ed: Cox & Cecily Guillam a Son Jesse born Sep. 27, 1781. Baptized July 21, 1782. p. 107.

John Cox & Elizabeth Fore a Daughter named Mary born Sep:
18 1767. Baptized Feb: 20 1768. p. 79.

Thomas Craddock & Lilly Ann Smith a daughter named Eliz:
Smith born June 177—. Baptized Jul: 20, 1777. p. 102.

Jo: Crealy & Nancy Watkins, Will: Watkins, Mar: 15 1787.
Baptized Oct: 17 1787. p. 120.

John Craigwell & Marianne ffielder a Daughter named Martha
born Sep: 18. 1756. Baptized 1757 feb: 13. p. 50.

Will: Craigwell & Mary Burgess a Daughter named Sally born
Aug: 11 1756. Baptized 1756 Sep: 12. p. 49.

Will: Craigwall & Mary Burgess a son named John born Oct: 18
1758. Baptized 1759 Sep: 29. p. 56.

Will: Craigwall & Mary Burgess a Daughter named Ursley born
Aug: 4, 1761. Baptized 1761 Aug: 9. p. 60.

Will: Craigwall & Mary Burgess a son named David born feb: 23 1766. Baptized May 11 1766. p. 73.

Thomas Cranks & Elizabeth Richardson a son named Mathew born Ap: 25 1765. Baptized Jul: 6 1765. p. 71.

Thomas Crank & Eliz: Richardson a son named Thomas born Sep: 9 1767. Baptized Nov: 15 1767. p. 79.

Tho: Crank & Eliz: Richardson, a Daughter named Mary, born Oct: 16 1770. Baptized Ap: 8 1771. p. 89.

Tho: Crank & Eliz. Richardson a son named William born Sep: 18, 1772. Baptized Jun. 6, 1774. p. 96.

Henry Crank & Mildred Chewning a son named George born Mar: 7 1767. Baptized May 10 1767. p. 77.

Henry Crank & Mildred Chowning a Daughter named Betty born Jul: 23 1768. Baptized Sep: 24 1768. p. 82.

Henry Crank & Mildred Chowning a son named Henry born May 28 1769. Baptized feb: 22 1770. p. 87.

John Crane & Francis Pawn a daughter named Isabel born Dec 28, 1775. Baptized June 30, 1776. p. 100.

Jo: Crawford & Jean Byers a son John born Jul: 7 1783. Baptized Oct. 12 1783. p. 110.

Will Crosbie & Eliz: Hall a child Barbara born May 20, 1780. Baptized Ap. 26, 1782. p. 106.

John Crouch & Susannah Ellis a Daughter named Sarah born Nov: 29 1764. Baptized Dec: 23 1764. p. 69.

John Crouch & Susannah Ellis a Daughter named Susannah born Sep: 25 1766. Baptized Jan: 11 1767. p. 75.

John Crouch & Susannah Ellis a son named Hardine born Jun. 16, 1772. Baptized Aug. 16, 1772. p. 92.

John Crouch & Susannah Ellis a son named Richard born Mar 23, 1774. Baptized Jun. 12, 1774. p. 96.

John Crouch & Susannah Ellis a son named Stephen born Nov. 29, 1776. Baptized Ap. 13, 1777. p. 101.

Jo: Crouch & Lucy Ferrar a son Tho: Harris born Aug. 14 1788. Baptized Oct. 24 1788. p. 121.

Rich: Crouch & Judith Sampson a son born feb: 12 1733. named Richard. p. 40.

Richard Crouch & Judith Sampson a Daughter born Jul: 5 1738. named Martha. p. 40.

Stephen Crouch & Eliz: fferrar a Daughter named Nansie born Mar: 20, 1763. Baptized 1763 May 15. p. 64.

Stephen Crouch & Elizabeth fferrar a Daughter named Judith born Jul: 19 1764. Baptized Sep: 9 1764. p. 69.

Stephen Crouch & Elizabeth fferrar a Daughter named Sarah born Dec: 15 1765. Baptized Jan: 26 1766. p. 73.

Stephen Crouch & Eliz: Ferrar a Daughter named Nancy born Sep: 9 1768. Baptized Oct: 7 1768. p. 82.

Stephen Crouch & Eliz: ffarrar a son named Stephen, born .... 1770. Baptized Jan: 8 1771. p. 89.

David Crowthers [Clowder] & Ann Thurston a Daughter named Sally born Aug: 2 1766. Baptized Aug: 31 1766. p. 75.

David Crowder & Nannie Thurston a Daughter named Betty born Mar: 11 1769. Baptized May 14 1769. p. 84.

David Crowder [Clowder] & Nanny Thurston a daughter named Susannah born Oct 1, 1772. Baptized Nov. 15, 1772. p. 93.

David Crowdis & Priscilla Laury a daughter named Lucy born Jun. 25, 1774. Sep 18, 1774. p. 97.

David Crouthers & Prisalla Laury a son named John born Feb. 17, 1776. Baptized Ap. 28, 1777. p. 100.

Da: Crowdas & Priscilla Laury a child Patsie born Mar. 10, 1782. Baptized Nov. 24, 1782. p. 108.

Will: Crutchfield & Betty Sutton a son named Thomie-Elliot born Mar: 21 1766. Baptized Jul: 24 1768. p. 81.

Will Crutchfield & Betty Sutton a daughter named Mary born Ap. 8, 1770. Baptized Mar. 29, 1772. p. 92.

Will Crutchfield & Betty Sutton a daughter named Betsey born Mar. 27, 1773. Baptized Nov. 3, 1774. p. 97.

Will Crutchfield & Betty Sutton a daughter named Jeanie born Dec. 12, 1775. Baptized Feb. 18, 1777. p. 101.

Edmund Curd & Mary Curd a Daughter named Jeanie born Jul: 12 1765. Baptized Aug: 4 1765. p. 72.

Edmond Curd & Mary Curd a Daughter named Peggy born Jun: 22 1767. Baptized Jul: 19 1767. p. 78.

Edmund & Mary Curds a son named Edward born May 20 1769. Baptized Jun: 11 1769. p. 85.

Edmund & Mary Curds a son named Richard born feb: 23 1771. Baptized Mar: 24 1771. p. 89.

Edmond & Mary Curds a daughter named Elizabeth born Mar. 5, 1773. Baptized Mar. 28, 1773. p. 94.

Edmond & Mary Curds a son named Charles born Feb. 18, 1777. Baptized Mar. 28, 1777. p. 101.

Edmond Curd & Eliz: Crogwall, Sam: Hawes, Jul: 10 1786. Baptized Aug: 22 1786. p. 117.

James Curd & Mary Graves a son named Jesse born Dec: 7 1767. Baptized Jan: 10 1768. p. 79.

James Curd & Mary Graves a Daughter named Betsy born Jul: 18 1769. Baptized Jul: 27 1769. p. 85.

James Curd & Mary Graves a daughter named Nansy born Jun. 12, 1774. Baptized Jul. 31, 1774. p. 97.

John Curd & Lucy Brent a son named James born Jun: 24, 1759. Baptized 1759 Jul: 4. p. 55.

John Curd & Lucy Brent a son named John born Nov: 23 1760. Baptized 1761 Jan: 16. p. 58.

John Curd & Lucy Brent a Daughter named Elizabeth born feb: 25 1762. Baptized 1762 May 22. p. 63.

John Curd & Lucy Brent a Daughter named Nannie born Mar: 5 1764. Baptized May 20 1764. p. 67.

John Curd & Lucy Brent a Daughter called Catherine born Jan:
29 1766. Baptized Mar: 2 1766. p. 73.

John Curd & Lucy Brent a son named Newton born Nov: 31
[sic] 1767. Baptized Dec: 13 1767. p. 79.

John Curd & Lucy Brent a Daughter named Mary born Sep: 10
1769. Baptized Dec: 17 1769. p. 86.

John Curd & Lucy Brent a son named Price born Aug: 14 1771.
Baptized Aug 18 1771. p. 90.

John Curd & Lucy Brent a son named Daniel born Oct 14, 1773.
Baptized Dec. 5, 1773. p. 95.

John Curd & Lucy Brent a son named Woodford born Dec. 15,
1775. Baptized Dec. 26, 1775. p. 99.

Jo: Curd & Ann Underwood a .... born June 5
1783. Baptized Ap: 18 1784. p. 111.

Jo: Curd & Ann Underwood in Goochland a son Thomas born Jan:
25 1786. Baptized June 17 1787. p. 119.

Joseph Curd & Mary Warren a Daughter named Elizabeth born
Jul: 24, 1763. Baptized 1763 Aug: 25. p. 65.

Joseph Curd & Mary Warran a daughter named Martha born
Sep. 5, 1771. Baptized 1772. p. 91.

Richard Curd & Sarah Downer a Daughter named Nannie: Williams born Jul: 11 1762. Baptized 1762 Jul: 22. p. 63.

Will: Curd & Mary Watkins a Daughter named Susannah born
Oct: 11 1764. Baptized Nov: 25 1764. p. 69.

William Curd & Mary Watkins a Daughter named Mary born
Oct: 10 1767. Baptized Oct: 23 1768. p. 82.

Jeremiah Curl & Mary McGeary a son named Dudley born Mar:
24 1760. Baptized 1760 Ap: 13. p. 57.

John Curriere & Eliz. Runnels a daughter named Dianah born
Nov. 23, 1774. Baptized Feb 23, 1775. p. 98.

Rob: Currier & Ann Thomason a child Christian born Dec. 11
1784. Baptized Sep: 20 1785. p. 115.

James Dabney & Judith Anderson a daughter named Mary born
Jan. 27, 1777. Baptized Ap. 10, 1777. p. 101.

Sam Dabney & Jean Merriwether a son named Francis born Jul:
1, 1781. Baptized Feb. 20, 1782. p. 105.

Tho: Daily & Ann Gentry a son Jo: Hubbard born Dec. 20 1782.
Baptized Sep: 8 1783. p. 110.

Jo: Dalton & Mary Branham a son William born Dec. 28 1777.
Baptized Oct. 5 1784. p. 113.

Jo: Dalton & Mary Branham a child Fanny born Jul: 8 1779.
Baptized Oct. 5 1784. p. 113.

Col: Nathaniel West Dandridge & Dorothea Spotswood a Daughter named Elizabeth born Sep: 12 1764. Baptized Sep: 28 1764.
p. 69.

Nat: West Dandridge & Dorothea Spotswood a daughter named
Mary: Clayburn born Jan. 14, 1772. Baptized 1772. p. 91.

Charles Daniel & Sarah Tate a daughter named Sally born Dec. 8, 1773. Baptized Jan. 12, 1774. p. 95.

Charles Daniel & Sarah Tate a son named Robert born Jun. 15 1776. Baptized Jul. 10, 1776. p. 100.

Charles Daniel & Sar: Tate a child Susan born Sep. 8, 1781. Baptized Nov. 4, 1781. p. 105.

Cha: Daniel & Sarah Tate a child Mary born May 5 1784. Baptized June 15 1784. p. 112.

Cha: Daniel & Sarah Tate a child Lucy born Ap: 20 1787. Baptized Sep: 10 1787. p. 119.

James Daniel & Elizabeth Montague a .... named Bat...... born Dec. 17, 1775. Baptized Ap. 10 1776. p. 100.

Ja: Daniel & Eliz: Montague a son named James born. Baptized May 17, 1781. p. 103.

Ja: Daniel & Eliz: Montague a child Nancy born Mar: 19 1783. Baptized May 25 1783. p. 109.

Ja: Daniel & Eliz: Montague a son Harry born Oct. 16 1785. Baptized Feb: 9 1786. p. 116.

Jesse Daniel & Frances Nelson a son Jo: Nelson born Dec. 18 1791. Baptized Sep: 23 1792. p. 122.

John Daniel & Sarah Thurston a daughter named Massie: Thurston born Feb. 18, 1777. Baptized Mar. 23, 1777. p. 101.

Jo: Daniel & Sally Thurston a child Susan Nicholas. Baptized Feb. 27, 1783. p. 108.

Nicholas Daniel & Susannah Howlet a daughter named Patty born. Baptized May 14, 1775. p. 98.

Obadiah Daniel & Sarah Mosely a son named Ichabod born Aug: 10, 1756. Baptized 1756 Oct: 17. p. 49.

Tho: Daniel & Eliz: Stith.................... a daughter named Elizabeth born Sep. 28, 1776. Baptized Nov. 5, 1777. p. 101.

Tho: Daniel & Eliz: Stith a son Garret born Oct 2, 1782. Baptized Oct 16, 1782. p. 108.

Will: Daniel & Patsie Red a son Thomas, Dec. 12 1784. Baptized Oct. 23 1785. p. 115.

Abram Daniel [Darnold] & Marianne Nelson a child Lucy born Aug 24. Baptized Oct. 11, 1781. p. 104.

Abram Darnold & Marianne Nelson a child Francis Nelson born. Baptized Aug. 12 1785. p. 114.

David Davies & Sarah Pore a son named David born May 30, 1756. Baptized 1756 June 27. p. 49.

Peter Davie & Elizabeth Moracet a son named Abraham born Jul: 8, 1763. Baptized 1763 Aug: 21. p. 65.

Abram Davis & Ann Johnson a child named Nancy born Ap. 10, 1781. Baptized Sep. 23, 1781. p. 104.

Abram Davis & Ann Johnson a child Polly Anderson born Nov. 6, 1782. Baptized Jan. 5, 1783. p. 108.

Ben: Davis & Eliz: Jones, Rich: Jones, born Sep: 17 1784. Baptized June 16 1785. p. 114.

Da: Davis & Catie Blackie a son Crispin born Oct. 1 1779. Baptized Ap: 26 1783. p. 109.

Da: Davis & Catie Blackie a child Catie born Aug. 1 1782. Baptized Ap: 26 1783. p. 109.

Jeremiah Daws* & Ursley Taylor a son named Elijah born Dec: 16 1761. Baptized 1762 Ap: 11. p. 62.

Jeremiah Davis* & Ursley Taylor a son named Clayburn born feb. 16 1767. Baptized May 31 1767. p. 77.

............†Davis & Mary Cole a daughter named Betsie born July 14, 1772. Baptized Aug. .... 1772. p. 93.

Ja: Davis & Sarah Blackie a Son named James born Mar. 21, 1781. Baptized May 13, 1781. p. 103.

Ja: Davis & Sar: Blakey a son William born Dec. 28 1782. Baptized June 16 1785. p. 114.

Ja: Davis & Mary Williams a son named Walter Meeks born Jan: 11 1771. Baptized Ap: 8, 1771. p. 89.

John Davis & Jerusha Parish a Daughter named Tabitha born dec: 2 1756. Baptized 1757 Ap: 11. p. 50.

John Davis & Jerusha Parish a son named William born Jul: 14, 1760. Baptized 1760 Aug: 17. p. 58.

John Davis & Jerusha Parish a son named James born Oct: 23, 1762. Baptized 1763 Jul: 31. p. 65.

John Davis & Jerusha Parish a Daughter named Winney born Jan: 26 1765. Baptized Ap: 14 1765. p. 71.

John Davis & Ann Tinsley a son named William born Mar: 13 1767. Baptized Dec: 16 1767. p. 79.

Jo: Lewis Davis & Jean Edmondson a Daughter named Axia born Ap: 16 1766. Baptized Jul: 14 1766. p. 74.

Joseph Davis & Glaphery Cockes a Daughter named Betty born July: 16, 1762. Baptized 1762 Aug: 15. p. 63.

Joseph Davis & Glapher Cox a son named John born Nov: 17 1764. Baptized Mar: 3 1765. p. 70.

Joseph Davies & Glaffry Cocke a son named Jesse born Jul: 21 1768. Baptized Sep: 4 1768. p. 82.

Rob: Davis & Rebekah Martin a son Austine Martin born March 26, 1782. Baptized Nov. 24, 1782. p. 108.

Stephen Davis & Eliz: Bow a daughter named Sally-Bedford born Feb. 1, 1776. Baptized Ap. 6, 1777. p. 101.

Tho: Dawson & Mary Carter a Daughter named Martha born Jan: 1, 1758. Baptized 1758 Mar: 19. p. 52.

Thomas Dawson & Mary Carter a Daughter named susannah born Mar: 3, 1759. Baptized 1759 May 13. p. 55.

Thomas Dawson & Mary Carter a son named William born Dec: 3, 1760. Baptized 1761 Jan: 24. p. 58.

Thomas Dawson & Mary Carter a son named John born Ap: 16 1762. Baptized 1762 Jun: 6. p. 63.

*See Doss.
†Margin torn.

Thomas Dawson & Mary Carter a son named Martin born Mar: 15 1764. Baptized Ap: 22 1764. p. 67.

Thomas Dawson & Mary Carter a Daughter named Elizabeth born Mar: 26 1766. Baptized Jun: 29 1766. p. 74.

Henry Day & Sar: Shortly a child Susannah, Jan: 23 1785. Baptized June 16 1785. p. 114.

Jo: Day & Dorothy Henley a Son named Ransom born Jan: 15, 1762. Baptized 1762 Ap: 12. p. 62.

Jo: Day & Ann Taylor a son Overton born Mar: 19 1784. Baptized June 16 1785. p. 114.

John Delany & Mildred Groom a son named Prettiman born. Baptized Oct 3, 1775. p. 99.

John Delaney & Mildred Groom a daughter named Margaret born Sep. .... 1776. Baptized May 8, 1777. p. 101.

Jo: Dennison & Eliz: Smith a child named Sarah born May 2, 1781. Baptized May 20, 1781. p. 103.

Tho: Denton & Mary Ffaries a son named Jo.: Ffaries born Oct 1, 1771. Baptized Jan. 5 1772. p. 91.

Thomas Denton & Mary Faries a daughter named Nansy: Denton born Jul. 21, 1773. Baptized Nov. 5, 1773. p. 95.

Peter Depp & Susannah Harris a Daughter named Elizabeth born Ap: 3, 1763. Baptized 1763 May 1st. p. 64.

Randolph Depriest & Mary Mims a son named Robert born Nov: 5 1763. Baptized Jan: 28 1764. p. 66.

Randolph Depriest & Mary Mims a Daughter named ffrances born Mar: 7 1767. Baptized Jul: 5 1767. p. 78.

Rob: Depriest & Martha Bailey a Daughter named Mary born Oct: 15 1766. Baptized May 10 1767. p. 77.

Rob: Depriest & Martha Baily a Daughter named Judith born feb: 27 1768. Baptized Jul: 3 1768. p. 81.

Will: Depriest & Tabitha Tony a son named John born Mar: 14 1761. Baptized 1761 Ap: 26. p. 59.

Will: Depriest & Tabitha Tony a Daughter named Annie born Mar: 1 1768. Baptized Jul: 3 1768. p. 81.

Tho: Desperate & Mary Pulham a child Betsy born Ap. 14, 1782. Baptized May 26, 1782. p. 106.

Tho: Desphire & Mary Pulham a son Augustine born Nov. 18 1783. Baptized Apl. 12 1784. p. 111.

Benjamin Deval [Duval] & Ann Kie a Daughter named Sally born May 15, 1761. Baptized 1761 Jun: 3. p. 60.

William Dey [Day] & Ann Tyry a son named Thomas born Aug: 8 1767. Baptized June 6 1768. p. 81.

Rich: Dickens & Eliz: Sansom a child Nancy born June 12 1784. Baptized Ap: 11 1785. p. 114.

Rich: Dickens & Eliz: Samson a son John born Aug: 10 1787. Baptized Nov: 12 1787. p. 120.

Elijah Dickinson & Susanna Smith a son Edmund born Aug. 13 1783. Baptized Dec. 2 1783. p. 110.

Elijah Dickinson & Susanna Smith a son Ballard Smith, Jan: 19 1786. Baptized Mar: 20 1786. p. 116.

Elijah Dickinson & Susanna Smith a child Ann Smith June 1 1788. Baptized Sep: 17 1788. p. 121.

Elijah Dickinson & Susanna Smith a child Elizabeth C. born April 20. Baptized Sept. 5 1791. p. 126.

James Dickerson & Marg: Nettles a son named John born Nov: 19 1759. Baptized 1760 ffeb: 3. p. 56.

James Dickerson & Marg: Nettles a Daughter named Rachel born feb: 2, 1762. Baptized 1762 Mar: 14. p. 62.

Ja: Dickison & Mary Cole a Son Ja: Cole born Dec. 24, 1781. Baptized Ap. 10, 1782. p. 106.

Ja. Dickerson & Mary Cole alias Barclay were married. Feb: 1778. p. 129.

Ja: Dickerson & Mary Cole had a child Susanna Robinson. Baptized Mar: 21. 1779. p. 129.

Ja: Dickerson & Mary Cole had a child Nansie Roscow. Baptized May 31 1780. p. 129.

Ja: Dickerson & Mary Cole had a son Ja: Cole. Baptized Dec: 24 1781. p. 129.

Rich: Dickason & Ann Quarles a Son Nathaniel born Jan 9, 1782. Baptized Ap. 28, 1782. p. 106.

Rich: Dickerson & Ann Quarles a son Richard born Oct. 22 1783. Baptized Ap: 26 1784. p. 111.

Rich: Dickinson & Ann Quarles a child Charles, June 24 1785. Baptized Oct. 11 1785. p. 115.

Rich: Dickenson & Ann Quarles a child Bettie Mar: 21 1788. Baptized June 22 1788. p. 121.

Tho: Dickinson & Mary McNemar, Eliz: Johnson, Sep: 2 1786. Baptized Ap: 29 1787. p. 118.

James Dicks & Henrietta Reevis a son named John born May 3 1758. Baptized 1758 Jun: 25. p. 52.

John Dickson & Susannah Hooker a son named John born Sep. 4, 1774. Baptized Aug. 7, 1775. p. 99.

Tho: Diggs & Ann Kent a son John born Aug. 25 1783. Baptized Oct. 5 1783. p. 110.

Jeremiah Doss & Ursley Taylor a Daughter named Nanny born Ap: 11 1757. Baptized 1757 Jun: 12. p. 51.

Jeremiah Doss & Ursley Taylor a Daughter named Sarah born Aug: 27 1759. Baptized 1760 Ap: 13. p. 57.

Jeremiah Doss & Ursley Taylor a son named Israel born Dec: 15 1768. Baptized Ap: 2 1769. p. 84.

See also Daws.

Rob: Douglass & Cat: .... a Daugh: born Jul: 24 1741. named Elizabeth. p. 40.

Revnd Will: Douglass & Nicholas Hunter a Daughter born on tuesday Aug. 30 1737. named Margaret. p. 40.

John Dowdy & Eliz: Hubbard a Daughter named ffrances born Dec: 19 1762. Baptized 1763 Ap: 17. p. 64.

John Dowdy & Elizabeth Hubbard a son named Clayburn born Mar: 4 1765. Baptized May 12 1765. p. 71.

John Dowdy & Eliz: Hubbard a Daughter named Mary born Oct: 7 1767. Baptized May 29 1768. p. 81.

John Dowdy & Eliz: Hubbard a Daughter named Sally born Jan: 15 1770. Baptized Ap: 23 1770. p. 87.

Tho: Drake & Lucy .... in Cumberland a son named Thomas born .... 1761. Baptized 1762 Jan: 10. p. 61.

Will: Drake & Mary Watts a son named Martin born Mar: 3 1761. Baptized 1761 Jun: 21. p. 60.

William Drake & Mary Watts a Daughter named Anna born Ap: 7, 1763. Baptized 1763 May 8. p. 64.

James Druine & Mary Weaver a Son named Samuel born Jun: 5 1757. Baptized 1757 Jul: 17. p. 51.

James Druine & Mary Weaver a Daughter named Mary born May 6, 1759. Baptized 1759 Jun: 17. p. 55.

James Druine & Mally Weaver a Daughter named Lucy born May 27, 1761. Baptized 1761 Jun: 3. p. 60.

Tho: Drumright & Sarah Crafton a son named George born 1764 Jan: 27. Baptized Ap: 1 1764. p. 67.

Tho: Drumright & Sarah Crafton a son named James born Mar: 27 1766. Baptized Aug: 16 1766. p. 74.

Thomas Drumright & Sarah Crichton a son named John born Jan: 10 1768. Baptized Mar: 17 1768. p. 80.

Tho: Drumright & Sarah Crafton a son named Bennet born Jan 1770. Baptized Sep. 7, 1770. p. 88.

Tho: Drumright & Sarah Crafton a daughter named Sally born Jan 7, 1772. Baptized Ap. 16, 1772. p. 92.

Tho. Drumright & Sarah Crafton a daughter named Nanney born Nov. 20, 1774. Baptized May 28, 1775. p. 98.

Will: Drumright & Eliz: Jones a son Dabney-Harrison, Aug. 27 178—. Baptized Oct: 20 1789. p. 122.

Will: Drumright & Eliz: Jones a child Judith born Ap: 1 1783. Baptized Oct: 20 1789. p. 122.

Ed: Dudley & Roxana Smith, a son Ballard Smith born Sep: 11 1789. Baptized Dec: 22 1789. p. 122.

G. Dudley & Roxana Smith a child Ann Meriwether Sept. 27 1791. Baptized June 23 1792. p. 126.

Clevish Duke & Nancy Brouken a child Amie Dyer born Sep: 7 1783. Baptized Oct: 28 1783. p. 110.

Clevas Duke & Ann Brekun a child Nancy born Feb. 9 1787. Baptized July 1 1787. p. 119.

Robert Duncan & Sarah Turner a daughter named Mary: Turner born Mar. 15, 1776. Baptized Dec. 14, 1776. p. 101.

Benjamin Duval & Ann Kay a son named Benjamin born Jan: 24 1765. Baptized Ap: 28 1765. p. 71.

Joseph Duval & Eliz. Shepherd a daughter named Nansie born Sep 24, 1773. Baptized Oct. 31, 1773. p. 95.

James Dyches & Henrietta Reeves a Daughter named Mary born Ap: 20 1760. Baptized 1760 May 25. p. 57.

John Dyches & Judith Lewis a Daughter named Elizabeth born dec: 7th 1746. p. 41.

John Dyches & Judith Lewis a Daughter named Judith born Mar: 1 1749. p. 41.

John Dyches & Judith Lewis a Son named John born Ap: 19, 1751. p. 41.

John Dyches & Judith Lewis a Son named Henry born Oct: 17, 1753. p. 41.

John Dyches & Judith Lewis a Son named William born Jan: 21, 1757. Baptized 1757 Mar. 13. p. 50.

Isaac Eads & Eliz: Allen a Daughter named Marianne born dec: 2, 1757. Baptized 1758 May 14. p. 52.

Tho: Eades & Eliz: Rutherford a son named Thomas born Jan: 10, 1782. Baptized Mar. 17, 1782. p. 105.

Ben. East & Nansy Pruit a daughter named Mary born May 24, 1774. Baptized Aug. 7, 1774. p. 97.

Benjamin East & Nannie Pruit a son named John born June 11, 1775. Baptized Sep 29, 1775. p. 99.

Ben East & Nancy Pruit a son named Benjamin born Aug: 1, 1776. Baptized June 1, 1777. p. 102.

Ben: East & Nancy Pruit a child Betsie born Aug. 29 1783. Baptized Sep: 21 1784. p. 112.

Tho: East & Winnifred Champion a son named James born Oct: 23, 1757. Baptized 1757 Dec: 15. p. 51.

Rich: Eastis & Ealcot a child Elizabeth born Sep: 25 1784. Baptized Oct. 13 1784. p. 113.

Jo: Edmondson & Mary Norman, Jo: Pleasants, Dec. 28 1782. Baptized Jul: 20 1783. p. 110.

Will: Edmonton & Hannah Walden a son William, Nov: 19 1785. Baptized Mar: 17 1786. p. 116.

Charles Edwards & Mary Daniel a Daughter named Jean born Jun: 9 1767. Baptized Aug: 23 1767. p. 78.

Charles Edwards & Mary Daniel a .... named .... born May 21 1769. Baptized Jun: 25 1769. p. 85.

Jesse Edwards & Lucy East a Daughter named Judith born Sep: 22 1768. Baptized [May] 23 1769. p. 84.

Jos: Edwards & Mary Bibb a child Sally Hardine Ap: 4 1790. Baptized Jul: 8 1790. p. 125.

Reu: Edwards & Mary Clements a child Milley born Dec. 7 1783. Baptized Mar: 28 1784. p. 111.

Tho: Edwards & Sarah Wright a son named William born May 29 1768. Baptized Jul: 3 1768. p. 81.

Thomas Edwards & Sarah Wright a Daughter named Betty born Mar: 19 1770. Baptized May 6 1770. p. 87.

Tho: Edwards & Mary Wright, a son named Thomas born Jun: 27 1771. Baptized Aug 11 1771. p. 90.

William Edwards & Eliz: Johnson a son named Thomas born Nov: 2, 1756. Baptized 1757 May 22. p. 51.

William Edwards & Eliz: Johnson a son named William born Jul: 25 1758. Baptized 1759 ffeb: 25. p. 54.

William Edwards & Eliz: Johnson a son named Rob: born May 10, 1760. Baptized 1760 Sep: 7. p. 58.

William Edwards & Elizabeth Johnston a son named Benjamin born Mar: 29 1764. Baptized May 27 1764. p. 67.

Will: Edwards & Eliz: Johnson a Daughter named Mary born feb: 29 1766. Baptized May 11 1766. p. 73.

Will: Edwards & Eliz: Johnson a Daughter named Betty born Ap: 2 1768. Baptized Aug: 28 1768. p. 82.

Zachariah Edwards & Susannah Thomas a daughter named Eliz. Thomas born .... Baptized Jun. 30, 1771. p. 90.

Zach. Edwards & Susannah Thomas a daughter named Matilda: Becky born Jan 7, 1774. Baptized Mar. 13, 1774. p. 96.

Tho: Eldridge & Winnifred Millar a daughter named Winnifred born Feb. 20, 1776. Baptized Feb. 22, 1777. p. 101.

Jesse Ellis & Sally Woodson a Daughter named Nansy born Oct: 25 1769. Baptized Jan: 2 1770. p. 86.

John Ellis & Polly Wood a son named Josiah born Jul 6, 1775. Baptized Oct 15, 1775. p. 99.

John Ellis & Patty Wood a Daughter named Bathsheba born May 21, 1777. Baptized June 29, 1777. p. 102.

Jo: Ellis & Patsie Wood a child Sally born June 19 1787. Baptized Oct. 17, 1787. p. 120.

John Ellis & Susannah Duval a daughter named Annie born Mar: 7, 1777. Baptized June 29, 1777. p. 102.

Joseph Ellis & Eliz: Perkins in Hnerico a Daughter named Elizabeth born .... 175... Baptized 1757 Ap: 9. p. 50.

Joseph Ellis & Elizabeth Perkins a son named Charles born Oct: 13 1764. Baptized Mar: 7 1765. p. 70.

Joseph Ellis & Eliz: Perkins a son named Samuel born Mar: 18 1766. Baptized Ap: 10 1766. p. 73.

Joseph Ellis & Christian fferrar, a son named Robert born Jan 14 1770. Baptized Sep: 2 1770. p. 88.

Stephen Ellis & Susanah Smith had a son named Samuel born Nov 11, 1777. Baptized Ap. 26 1778. p. 103.

Tho: Ellis & Eliz: Hart a girl Rebelka born May 1 1789. Baptized Jul: 24 97. p. 130.

Tho: Ellis & Elizabeth Hart a Son John born Ap: 26 1791. Baptized Ap: 26 91. p. 130.

Tho. Ellis & Eliz: Hurt a son James born feb: 5 1793. p. 130.

Thomas Ellis & Elizabeth Hart a son William born Aug: 11 1794. p. 130.

Tho: Ellis & Eliz: Hart a girl Elizabeth born Mar: 28. 1796. p. 130.

Thomas Ellis & Eliz: Paterson a daughter named Sally born Jul: 22, 1777. Baptized Sep. 4, 1777. p. 102.

Tho: Ellis & Eliz: Patterson a child Suckie Dec. 27 1786. Baptized 17 Oct. 1787. p. 120.

Tho: Ellis & Eliz: Paterson a daughter named Nancy born Aug. 1, 1775. Baptized Oct 15, 1775. p. 99.

Samuel Emmerson & Mildred Potter a Son named David born Mar: 14, 1758. Baptized 1758 May 14. p. 52.

Samuel Emmerson & Mildred Potter a Daughter named Elizabeth born Jan: 25, 1763. Baptized 1763 Sep: 12. p. 65.

David England & Lucy Hodges a son named Stephen born Jan 12, 1774. Baptized Mar. 13, 1774. p. 96.

James England & Mary Webber a Daughter named Betty born Nov: 26 1768. Baptized Feb: 5 1769. p. 83.

John England & Ann Newbanks a Daughter named Elizabeth born Dec: 15 1764. Baptized Mar: 3 1765. p. 70.

John England & Ann Eubank a daughter named Sarah born Jun. 23, 1773. Baptized Jul: 25, 1773. p. 94.

John England & Ann Eubank a son named Dabney born Nov. 25, 1775. Baptized Mar. 3, 1776. p. 99.

Will: Anderson England & Eliz: Fairies a son named John born Ap: 1 1767. Baptized May 31 1767. p. 77.

Will: England & Eliz: Fairies a Daughter named Mary born Jan: 28 1769. Baptized Ap: 9 1769. p. 84.

Will England & Eliz. Fairies a daughter named Ann born May 11, 1771. Baptized Jul. 7, 1771. p. 90.

Will England & Eliz. Faries a son named William born May 15, 1773. Baptized Jul. 11, 1773. p. 94.

Will England & Eliz. Fairies a daughter named Patty born Jun. 15, 1775. Baptized Aug. 20, 1775. p. 99.

Abram Estis & Sarah Timberlick a son John born Jan: 3 1788. Baptized Ap: 14 1788. p. 120.

Abram Estis & Sarah Timberlake a son named Will born May 13 1791. Baptized Sep. 17 1791. p. 122.

Abraham Ester & Sar: Timberlick a son Joel born feb: 16 93. Baptized Nov: 19. 1793. p. 127.

Rich: Ewbanks & Sylla Hewit a son named John born May 22 1770. Baptized July 29 1770. p. 88.

John Evans & Frances Wade a son named Archie born Jun: 7 1770. Baptized Aug: 12 1770. p. 88.

Joseph Evans & Susannah Lacy. Twins called Frances & John born Jan: 22 1744. pp. 40, 41.

Joseph Evans & Susannah Lacy a Daughter called Ann born ffeb: 23 1746. pp. 40, 41.

Joseph Evans & Susannah Lacy a Son named Thomas born ffeb: 23 1749. pp. 40, 41.

Joseph Evans & Susannah Lacy a Daughter named Susannah born Jan: 16 1753. pp. 40, 41.

Jos: Evans & Susannah Lacy a Son named Joseph born May 17, 1756. Baptized 1756 Jun: 20. pp. 41, 49.

Joseph Evans & susannah Lacy a Daughter named Sarah born Aug: 13, 1759. Baptized 1759 Sep: 9. p. 55.

Joseph Evans & Susannah Lacy a Daugh: named Martha born Mar: 6 1762. Baptized 1762 Ap: 4. p. 62.

Maxey Ewel & Ann Mullins a son named Thomas born Oct: 27 1769. Baptized Dec: 19 1769. p. 86.

Cha: Fagg & Ann Mare a child Sarah born Ap: 15 1786. Baptized Ap: 26 1787. p. 118.

Jo: Fag & Lucy Talford a son James-Rankin born Oct: 3 1787. Baptized Ap: 27 1788. p. 120.

Edward Fair [Far] & Mary Perkins a son Edward born Ap: 12 1783. Baptized June 1 1783. p. 109.

Ed: Far & Mary Perkins a son William born Nov: 5 1785. Baptized April 10 1786. p. 116.

Thomas ffarmer & Mary Anderson in Albemarle a Son named Anderson Jan: 10th. Baptized 1757 Mar. 20. p. 50.

Tho: ffarmbrough & Mary Anderson & son named John born Ap: 3, 1759. Baptized 1761 Nov: 22. p. 61.

Tho: ffarmbrough & Mary Anderson a Daughter named Sarah born Oct: 23 1760. Baptized 1761 Nov: 22. p. 61.

Tho: Farmer & Anna Pitts a child Sally born Mar: 23 1783. Baptized Ap: 26 1783. p. 109.

Abram Fergusson & Nanny Smith a child Mally born dec. 1, 1782. Baptized Jan. 2, 1783. p. 108.

Abram Fergusson & Nancy Smith a child Betsey born Nov: 18 1784. Baptized June 13 1784. p. 112.

Will: ffergusson & Mary Bevens [Marg: Vivian] a son Bevens born Aug. 30 1784. Baptized Nov: 11 1784. p. 113.

John fferrar & Mary Wadlaw a Daughter named Jenye born Nov: 30, 1755. Baptized 1756 Aug: 30. p. 49.

John fferrar & Mary Wadlow a Daughter named Malley born Jul: 13 1758. Baptized 1759 Jan: 15. p. 54.

Jos: fferrar & Susanna Jordan a Daughter named Susanna born Oct: 10 1756. Baptized 1756 Oct: 24. p. 49.

Jos: fferrar & Susannah Jordan a son named Charles born dec: 6 1758. Baptized 1759 Jan: 15. p. 54.

Joseph: Royal fferrar & Phebe Harris a Daughter named Sarah born Jul: 1763. Baptized 1763 Sep: 18. p. 65.

Joseph Royal fferrar & Phoebe Harris a Daughter named Sarah born feb: 10 1765. Baptized Mar: 16 1765. p. 70.

Joseph Royal Ferrar & Phebe Harris a Daughter named Mary born Jan: 27 1767. Baptized Feb: 28 1767. p. 76.

Joseph Royal Ferrar & Phebe Harris a Daughter named Lucy born Feb. 19 1769. Baptized May 11 1769. p. 84.

Perrine fferrar & Sarah Lacy a Daughter called Ann born Oct: 9, 1758. Baptized 1758 Dec: 3. p. 53.

Perrine fferrar & Sarah Lacy a Son named Mathew born Oct: 29, 1760. Baptized 1760 Dec: 14. p. 58.

Perrine fferrar & Sarah Lacy a Daughter named Sally born feb: 2 1765. Baptized Mar: 17 1765. p. 70.

Perrine ffarrar & Sarah Lacy a Daughter named Lucy born Aug: 4 1767. Baptized Sep: 6 1767. p. 78.

Perrine Ferrar & Sarah Lacy a daughter named Elizabeth born Oct: 14 1769. Baptized Ap: 8 1770. p. 87.

Richard fferrar & Eliz: Sanders a Son named Stephen born Mar: 20 1756. Baptized 1756 May 9. p. 48.

Rich: fferrar & Eliz: Sanders a son named Shadrach born Sep: 5 1757. Baptized 1758 Mar: 26. p. 52.

Richard fferrar & Elizabeth Sanders a Daughter named Priscilla born Ap: 8 1759. Baptized 1759 Jun: 17. p. 55.

Richard fferrar & Elizabeth Sanders a son named Rene born Mar: 22, 1761. Baptized 1761 Jun: 28. p. 60.

Tho: & Eliz: fferrar a Daughter named Mary Ann born Nov: 23, 1756. Baptized 1757 Jan: 2. p. 49.

Thomas fferrar, & Elizabeth fferrar a son named John born Aug: 1, 1758. Baptized 1758 Aug: 27. p. 53.

Will: fferrar & Mary Williams had a son baptised, being born dec: 2d Nathaniel. Baptized 1756 Jan: 18. p. 48.

William fferrar & Mary Williams a Daughter named Nansie born Mar: 24 1760. Baptized 1760 Ap: 20. p. 57.

Will: fferrar & Mary Williamson a Daughter named Sally born Mar: 22 1762. Baptized 1762 Jun: 13. p. 63.

Will: fferrar & Eliz: Bibb a son named Robert born Aug: 15, 1763. Baptized 1763 Sep: 18. p. 65.

William fferrar & Elizabeth Bibb a Daughter named Jean born Sep: 6 1765. Baptized Jan: 4 1766. p. 72.

William fferrar & Elizabeth Bib a Daughter named Annie born Feb: 7 1768. Baptized Mar: 13 1768. p. 80.

William fferrar & Eliz: Bibb a Daughter named Elizabeth born Dec. 9 1770. Baptized feb: 26 1770. p. 87.

William fferris & Martha Trueman a Daughter named Elizabeth born Oct: 11 1758. Baptized 1759 Ap: 1. p. 54.

Charles Ferrol & Sarah Williams a Daughter named Mary born Jun: 29 1767. Baptized Ap: 3 1768. p. 80.

Richard ffield & Elizabeth Morroll a Daughter named Ann born Oct: 1757. Baptized 1758 Jan: 5. p. 51.

Thomas ffields [Fielder] & Ann Woodhall a Daughter named Judith born feb: 23 1761. Baptized 1761 Jun: 6. p. 60.

Bartholomew ffielder & Ann Shoemaker upon Janito a Son born .... Named Dennis. Baptized 1756 May 22. p. 48.

Thomas ffielder & Judith Craigwall a son named John ffielder born Ap: 26, 1757. Baptized 1759 Sep. 29. p. 56.

[Thomas Fielder &] Judith Craigwall a Daughter named Eliz: Ann Craigwal born Aug: 20 1763. Baptized Sep. 3, 1777. p. 102.

[Thomas Fielder &] Judith Craigwall a son named Sam: Knolling born. Baptized Nov. 2 1777. p. 103.

Blagden ffinch & Elizabeth Barnet a Daughter named ffanney born A[ug] 1. 1763. Baptized 1763 Oct: 16. p. 65.

Blagden ffinch & Elizabeth Barnet a Daughter named Patty born dec. 1 1765. Baptized Mar: 8 1766. p. 73.

John ffinch & Mary Williamson a son named Robert born Oct: 1 1757. Baptized 1758 Jan: 30. p. 51.

John ffinch & Mary Williamson a son named George born Oct: 20, 1759. Baptized 1760 ffeb: 11. p. 56.

John ffinch & Mary Williamson a Daughter named Lucy born Ap: 1, 1761. Baptized 1761 Jul: 26. p. 60.

Jo: Finnick & Mary Richardson a Son Samuel born Apl. 8 1775. Baptized July 21, 1782. p. 107.

Peter Ffitsgerald & Lucy Johnson a daughter named Mary born Oct 29, 1775. Baptized Dec. 30, 1775. p. 99.

Ben: Fitzpatrick & Mary Perkins a son named Constantine: Perkins born Jun: Baptized Aug 18 1771. p. 90.

Ben Fitzpatrick & Mary Perkins a son named Benjamin born Sep: 15, 1780. Baptized May 19, 1781. p. 103.

Benjamin ffirman & Susannah Moss a Son named John born Jan: 8 1759. Baptized 1759 Ap: 15. p. 54.

Jo: Fleming & Lovina Coleman (Clements) a child Jeany Martin, Sep: 22 1786. Baptized Jan: 30 1787. p. 118.

Tarlton ffleming & Mary Randolph a son named Tarlton born Jul: 18, 1763. Baptized 1763 Aug: 23. p. 65.

Tarlton ffleming & Mary Randolph a son named William-Randolph born Ap: 14 1765. Baptized May 3 1765. p. 71.

Tarlton ffleming & Mary Randolph a son named Thomas-Man born feb: 15 1767. Baptized Mar: 19 1767. p. 76.

Tavlton Ffleming & Mary Randolph a daughter named Judith born Jul 4, 1769. Baptized Aug 30, 1772. p. 93.

Will: Fleming & Betty Champ a Daughter named Lucy: Champ born Ap. 29, 1776. Baptized May 22, 1776. p. 100.

Samuel fflournoy & Elizabeth Harris a son named Jordan born Sep: 30 1763. Baptized Jan: 7 1764. p. 66.

Samuel fflournoy & Elizabeth Harris a Daughter named Elizabeth-Julie born Nov: 25 1765. Baptized Mar: 8 1766. p. 73.

Sam: Fleurnoy & Elizabeth Harris a Daughter named Martha born feb: .... 1768. Baptized Ap: 2 1768. p. 80.

Ben Fop & Mary Reeves a son John born Oct. 4 1782. Baptized June 22 1784. p. 112.

Ben Fop & Mary Reeves a son William born Mar: 10 1784. Baptized June 22 1784. p. 112.

John fford & Angelica Lewis a Daughter named Sally born dec: 31 1756. Baptized 1757 Ap: 11. p. 50.

John fford & Elizabeth ffarrar a son named William born Nov: 6 1763. Baptized Jan: 8 1764. p. 66.

John fford & Elizabeth fferrar a Daughter named Mary born Sep: 18 1766. Baptized Nov: 16 1766. p. 75.

John fford & Eliz: ffarrar a Daughter named Jeanie born Dec: 31 1768. Baptized Jul: 23 1769. p. 85.

Thomas fford & Keturah Winn a Daughter named Nannie born Jan: 15 1758. Baptized 1758 Mar: 12. p. 52.

Jo: Fore & Winifred Alvison a child Hellender born June 9, 1782. Baptized Nov. 24, 1782. p. 108.

[Record of Aaron Fontaine's Family]
Mrs. Barbara Tyrel, Mrs. Fountain, was born Sep. 3, 1756.
Mr. Aaron Fontaine was born Nov: 30 1753 & maried May 19, 1773. p. 144.
Register of Mr. Aaron Fountain & Barbara Tyrryll their Children & family Jan: 12, 1797.
Peter born dec: 15. 1774.
James Tyrel Nov: 19. 1776.
Mary Anne born Oct: 14. 78.
Elizabeth born Sep: 5. 80.
Matilda born Sep: 13. 82.
Patsie Minor Mar: 14. 85.
Sallie Sarah Mar: 17. 87.
Mariah feb: 16. 89.
America Mar: 10. 91.
Will Maury Jan: 16. 93.
Barbara Ker dec: 25. 94.
Ann Overton Ap: 19. 96. p. 144.
Aaron Fontaine & Barbara Terril, Patsy Minor, Mar. 14 1785. Baptized Ap: 16 1785. p. 114.
Aaron Fountain & Barbara Terrill a child Sarah, Mar 17 1787. Baptized Mar: 30 1787. p. 118.
Aaron Fountain & Babie Tyrel a child Moriah, Feb. 16 1789. Baptized Mar: 29 1789. p. 122.
Aaron Fontaine & Barbara Terrell his wife a son born 16 January 1793, Wm. Maury Fontaine. Baptized 1793 Mch. 19. p. 127.
Aaron Fountain & Barbara Terrell a child Barbarah Carr born 25 Dec. 1794. Baptized Mar: 5 1795. p. 127.
Aaron Fountain & Barbarah Tyrrel a daughter Ann Overton born Ap: 19 96. Baptized June 3 1796. p. 127.

Edmond Foster & Sarah Taylor a child Catherine born Oct. 3 1783. Baptized Dec: 8 1783. p. 110.

James ffoster & Elizabeth Parish a Daughter named susannah born Oct: 11 1760. Baptized 1760 Nov: 22. p. 58.

Ja: ffoster & Eliz: Parish a Son named James born Mar: 23 1762. Baptized 1762 Jun: 6. p. 63.

James ffoster & Elizabeth Parish a son named Bartlet born Jun: 8, 1763. Baptized 1763 Jul: 17. p. 65.

James ffoster & Elizabeth Parish a Daughter named Judith born Oct: 22 1764. Baptized Nov: 18 1764. p. 69.

James Foster & Elizabeth Parish a son named Anthony born May 5 1766. Baptized Jun: 29 1766. p. 74.

James ffoster & Elizabeth Parish a Daughter named Elizabeth born May 23 1767. Baptized Jun: 21 1767. p. 78.

John ffoster & Eliz: Woodhall a Daughter named Agness born Aug: 1756. Baptized 1756 Sep: 12. p. 49.

Rich: Foster & Eliz: Spencer a child named Mary born Sep. 5, 1780. Baptized Apl. 8, 1781. p. 103.

Tho: & Susannah Fosters a child Cat: Graves born Oct: 30 1782. Baptized Ap: 14 1783. p. 109.

Tho: & Susanna Fosters a son James born Ap: 4 1785. Baptized May 9 1786. p. 114.

Tho: & Susanna Foster a son Billie gustavus, Dec. 29 1788. Baptized Apl: 13 1789. p. 122.

Alexr Fowler & Magdalen Smith a Son William born Sep 2, 1782. Baptized Feb. 9, 1783. p. 108.

Alexr: Fowler & Magdalen Smith a son Jacob born Mar: 21 1782. Baptized Ap: 18 1784. p. 111.

Alexr. ffowler & Sarah Bugg a son named Sherwood born Jan: 2 1759. Baptized May 2, 1759. p. 55.

Alexr. ffowler & Sarah Bug a son named Edmund born Aug: 14, 1761. Baptized 1762 Ap: 9. p. 62.

John Fowler & Rebekah Archer a son named Jesse born Sep: 30 1768. Baptized Nov: 3 1768. p. 82.

Jo: Fox & Grace Young a child Ann born Nov. 10, 1782. Baptized Feb. 9, 1783. p. 108.

Jo: Fox & Grace Young a child Grace born Feb. 1785. Baptized Mar: 14 1785. p. 113.

Reuben Francis & Frances Napier a child named Frances born .... 1766. Baptized Aug. 26, 1781. p. 104.

Reuben Francis & Frances Napier a son named Rob: Napier born Jul: 4, 176... Baptized Oct. 20, 1781. p. 104.

Reuben Francis & Frances Napier a son named Charles born July 4, 1770. Baptized Oct. 20, 1781. p. 104.

Holman ffreeman & .... Cox in Amelia a Daughter named ffrances born Jun: 13, 1756. Baptized 1756 Oct: 24. p. 49.

Isaac Freeman & Barbara Gray a son William born Mar: 29 1783. Baptized May 18 1783. p. 109.

Is: Freeman & Barbara Gray a son Alexr. born Nov. 24 1785. Baptized Dec. 27 1785. p. 115.

Is. Freeman & Barbara Gray a son John born Jan 23, 1781. Baptized Nov. 11, 1782. p. 108.

Isaac Freeman & Barbarah Gray, Rachel Gray born Aug. 30 1788. Baptized Jul: 27 1789. p. 125.

Isaac Freeman & Babbie Grey a daughter called Sally born May 5 1791. Baptized Mar: 24 1792. p. 126.

Is: Freeman & Barbara Gray a child Lucy born May 18 1793. Baptized Jul: 29 1794. p. 127.

Is: Freeman & Barbara Gray a girl Barbarah born Jan. 5 1795. Baptized March 13 1796. p. 127.

Jo: Freeman & Christian Rory a Daughter named Ann born Ap. 8 1771. Baptized Ap: 10 1771. p. 89.

John Freeman & Christian Rory a daughter named Frances born Jun. 16, 1773. Baptized Oct 9, 1773. p. 95.

John Freeman & Christian Rory a son named Josiah born Oct 3, 1775. Baptized June 11, 1776. p. 100.

Rob: Freeman & Sarah Hill a son named Wyat born Dec: 28, 1780. Baptized Ap. 9, 1781. p. 103.

Rob: Freeman & Sarah Hill a son Thomas born Sep: 9 1784. Baptized Ap: 11 1785. p. 114.

Rob: Freeman & Sarah Hill a son George born Oct. 8 1786. Baptized Aug. 13 1787. p. 119.

William ffrench & Ann Howard a Daughter in fornication named Edie ffrench born Ap: 19. Baptized 1758 Oct: 29. p. 53.

John ffretwell & Mary Bullock a son named Muscow born Dec: 1 1770. Baptized Mar: 3 1771. p. 89.

John Ffretwell & Mary Bullock a son named John born Jul. 13, 1772. Baptized Sep. 20, 1772. p. 93.

John Fretwell & Mary Bullock a daughter named Nansie born Sep. 22 1774. Baptized Jan. 8, 1775. p. 97.

John ffulcher & Susannah George a Daughter named Catie born Ap: 17 1771. Baptized May 19 1771. p. 89.

John Ffulcher & Susannah George a son named William born May 23, 1773. Baptized Jul. 4, 1773. p. 94.

Sam: Fulcher & Leadia Hopkins a son Ezekiel, born Jan: 8 1786. Baptized June 4 1786. p. 116.

William ffurbush & Sarah Richardson a son named John born Jan: 7 1765. Baptized Jul: 6 1765. p. 71.

John ffurlong & Jean Emmerson a son named Hubbard, born Jun: 13 1768. Baptized Aug: 20 1768. p. 81.

Rob: ffurlong & Sarah Watkins a Daughter named ffrances born May 9 1756. Baptized 1756 Jun: 13. p. 48.

Rob: ffurlong & Sarah Watkins a Daughter born feb: 16 1759 named Marg. Baptized 1759 Mar: 23. p. 54.

Ja: Gains & Agnes Rollins a son James born Mar: 15, 1782. Baptized Ap. 21, 1782. p. 106.

Rich: Gaines & Mildred Hollinger a Daughter named Milly born Jan: 1, 1761. Baptized 1761 Mar: 15. p. 59.

Richard Gaines & Mildred Hollanger a Daughter named Elizabeth born Ap: 15, 1763. Baptized 1763 Sep: 18. p. 65.

Will: Gains & Mary Strawn, Priestley born Oct. 11 1787. Baptized Dec. 2, 1787. p. 120.

Samuel Galden & Elizabeth Turner a Daughter called Elizabeth born Dec: 28 1764. Baptized Ap: 7 1765. p. 70.

Samuel Galden & Elizabeth Turner a Daughter named Kesiah born Dec: 13 1766. Baptized Feb: 8 1767. p. 76.

Henry Gambil & Charlotte Juet a son named Henry: Juet born June 21, 1777. Baptized Aug. 10, 1777. p. 102.

Harrison Gammon & Eliz: Horn a Daughter named Suckie born Oct: 7 1760. Baptized 1761 Ap: 26. p. 59.

Harrison Gammon & Eliz: Horn a Daughter named Sally born Oct: 25 1764. Baptized Mar: 30 1767. p. 77.

Harrison Gammon & Elizabeth Horn a son named William born Mar: 6 1768. Baptized Ap: 11 1768. p. 80.

Harrison Gammon & Eliz: Horn a son named Anderson born Mar: 13 1770. Baptized Jul. 29 1770. p. 88.

Tho: & Eliz: Garlands, a child Sally born May 6, 1782. Baptized June 27, 1782. p. 107.

Tho: & Elizabeth Garlands a child Overton Nov: 7 1788. Baptized Mar: 31 1789. p. 122.

Henry Garnar & Jane Gatly a son Patrick Henry born Aug. 4 1788. Baptized July 13 1789. p. 125.

Will: Garet & Ann Johnson a child Ann born Feb. 27, 1782. Baptized June 27, 1782. p. 107.

Henry Garret & Mary Johnson a child named Elizabeth born Feb. 10, 1781. Baptized Oct 19, 1781. p. 104.

Henry Garret & Mary Johnson a child Mary born Oct. 26 1782. Baptized June 1 1783. p. 109.

Harry Garrit & Mary Johnson a son Richard born Aug. 31 1784. Baptized Jan. 1 1785. p. 113.

Henry Garret & Mary Johnson a son Peter Nobins June 11 1787. Baptized July 8 1787. p. 119.

Da: Garth & Frances Snead a Son William born Nov. 23, 1781. Baptized Ap. 14, 1782. p. 106.

Da: Garth & Frances Sneed a son John born Feb. 26 1784. Baptized Jul: 18 1784. p. 112.

Will: Garthwright & Jean-Ann Garthwright a daughter named Nansy born Ap. 14, 1769. Baptized 1772. p. 91.

Will: Garthwright & Jean-Ann Garthwright a Daughter named .... born Nov. 11, 1771. Baptized 1772. p. 91.

Charles Gay & Ann Adkins a son named Daniel born Jan: 24 1768. Baptized Ap: 3 1768. p. 80.

Gerard Geddy & Mary Bright a Daughter named Mary born feb: 2 1765. Baptized Mar: 15 1765. p. 70.

Jo: Gentry & Milley Edwards a Son named Basil: Wagstaff born May 18, 1781. Baptized July 15, 1781. p. 103.

Jo: Gentry & Mildred Edwards a child Elizabeth born Aug. 14 1783. Baptized Sep: 8 1783. p. 110.

Jo: Gentry & Milly Edwards, a son William Gravil born Jan: 23 1786. Baptized April 10 1786. p. 116.

Nath: Gentry & Marianne Black a Son named Wyat born Mar: 15, 1781.   Ap. 9, 1781. p. 103.

Nic. Gentry & Sarah Dickin a child Sarah Perrine born July 8, 1781. Baptized Sep. 30, 1781. p. 104.

Nicholas Gentry & Sarah Dickens a son Bobbie born Ap: 3 1784. Baptized June 14 1784. p. 112.

Nicholas Gentry & Sar: Dicken, Benajah Brooks, May 22 1786. Baptized June 12 1786. p. 116.

Anselm George & Ann Houchins a daughter named Susannah: Watts born Feb. 17, 1776. Baptized May 30, 1776. p. 100.

Anselm George & Ann Hutchins a son named Rob: Price born Jan. 20, 1780. Baptized May 18, 1781. p. 103.

Ja: George & Agatha Watts a Daughter born Nov: 11 1738. named Agathy. p. 40.

Ja: George & Agatha Watts a Son named Anselm born Sep: 28 1751. p. 40.

Ja: George & Agatha Watts a Son named Jesse born Ap: 19 1756. p. 40.

James George & Agatha Watts a Son named Robert born Oct: 26 1756. Baptized 1756 Oct: 31. p. 49.

James George & Agatha Watts a daughter named Susannah born Sep: 13 1758. Baptized 1759 Jan: 7. p. 54.

James George & Mary Swift a Daughter named Elizabeth born Mar: 10 1768. Baptized Mar: 20 1768. p. 80.

James George & Mary Swift a Daughter named Mary-Watts born May 15 1770. Baptized Jun: 4 1770. p. 87.

James George & Mary Swift a daughter named Nancy born Feb. 4, 1773. Baptized May 14, 1773. p. 94.

James George & Mary Swift a son named James born Feb. 20, 1775. Baptized May 14, 1775. p. 98.

James George & Mary Swift a daughter named Frances born Mar: 22, 1777.   May 31, 1777. p. 102.

Jeames George & Mary Swift a sun Robert born Aug: 16 1783. Baptized Dec: 2 1786. p. 118.

Jo: George & Mary Martin a son Robert born Oct. 9 1783. Baptized June 20 1784. p. 112.

Leonard George & Jeanie Poor a daughter named Elz: Watts born Oct 27 1772. Baptized Nov. 15, 1772. p. 93.

Jo: Gerrant & Eliz. Porter a daughter named Elizabeth born Oct 11, 1770. Baptized Jul. 30, 1771. p. 90.

John Guerrant & Eliz: Porter twins Jeanie and Judith born June 21, 1777. Baptized Nov. 2, 1777. p. 103.

Jo: Gerrand & Mary Heath a son Robert born Jul: 16 1783. Baptized Ap: 18 1784. p. 111.

Gideon Gibson & Susanna Branham a son Ambrose born Nov. 1772. Baptized Oct. 5 1784. p. 113.

Gideon Gibson & Susanna Branham a son Malachi born Jul: 31 1775. Baptized Oct. 5 1784. p. 113.

Ja: Gibson & Sally Williams a child .... born May 27 1787. Baptized July 1 1787. p. 119.

Jo: Gipson [Gibson] & Mary Tally a son Will: Spencer born Ap: 7 1784. Baptized June 6 1784. p. 111.

Jo: Gibson & Mary Tally a son John, born Dec. 2 1785. Baptized Nov. 15 1786. p. 118.

Jo: Gibson & Mary Tally a child Cecily born Jan: 21 1788. Baptized Ap: 27 1788. p. 121.

Thornton Gipson & Eliz: Watkins, Barbara Overton, June 18 1784. Baptized Dec. 1 1785. p. 115.

Will: Giddin & Susannah Wood a son Ja: Wood born Aug. 11 1784. Baptized Oct. 11 1784. p. 113.

John Gilbert & Sarah Nichols a son named William born Oct: 9 1769. Baptized Nov: 26 1769. p. 86.

Jo: Gill & Aggie Tony a child Ritta born Ap. 2, 1782. Baptized May 19, 1782. p. 106.

James Glass & Eve Williams a Son named William born Nov: 25 1760. Baptized 1761 Aug: 30. p. 61.

James Glass & Eve Williams a son named David born Sep: 21 1764. Baptized Jun: 25 1768. p. 68.

James Glass & Eve Williams a son named John born Dec: 22 1765. Baptized May 17 1766. p. 74.

James Glass & Eve Williams a Daughter named Molly born Jun: 11 1768. Nov: 3 1768. p. 82.

James Glass & Eve Williams a son named James born Jun. 14, 1772. Baptized Ap. 22, 1772. p. 92.

James Glass & Eve Williams a son named Archer born May 25, 1774. Baptized Nov. 13, 1774. p. 97.

John Glass & Sally Martin a son named David born May 27 1769. Baptized Sep: 14 1769. p. 86.

John Glass & Sally Martin a son named John born Jun. 8, 1771. Baptized Ap. 22, 1772. p. 92.

John Glass & Sally Martin a son named James born Sep 27, 1774. Baptized Nov. 3, 1774. p. 97.

John Glass & Sally Martin a son named William born Oct 20, 1776. Baptized Mar. 23, 1777. p. 101.

William Glass & Elizabeth Megaen a son named Thomas born Ap: 22 1767. Baptized Jun: 11 1767. p. 77.

William Glass & Eliz: Megain a Daughter named Molly born Ap: 10 1769. Baptized Sep: 14 1769. p. 86.

Will Glass & Eliz. McGan a daughter named Nancy born Nov. 4, 1771. Baptized Ap. 22, 1772. p. 92.

Jo: Glen & Mary Thomas a Son Simeon born June 12, 1782. Baptized Sep. 18, 1782. p. 107.

Jo: Glen & Mary Bolton a child Polly born May 30 1785. Baptized Oct. 2 1785. p. 115.

Tyree Glen & Sarah Shilton a Daughter named Jeannie born May 17 1764. Baptized Jun: 25 1764. p. 68.

John Godsey & Ann Elam a Daughter named Mary born Jan: 1 1766. Baptized Mar: 8 1766. p. 73.

John Godsey & Ann Elam a Daughter named Ann born Nov: 16 1767. Baptized Dec: 19 1767. p. 79.

Aaron Going & Mary Going a son named John born Jul: 31, 1763. Baptized 1763 Aug: 28. p. 65.

Philip Going & Judith Potter a Daughter named Molly born Mar: 4 1770. Baptized May 27 1770. p. 87.

John Golson & ffrances Strueman [Tourman] a daughter named Lucie born Sep: 12 1771. Baptized Oct: 6 1771. p. 90.

Clayburn Gooch & Mildred Thomson a son Thomson born Jan: 28 1784. Baptized Ap: 12 1784. p. 111.

Claiburn Googe & Milley Thomson a child Unie born Sep: 14 1787. Baptized May 12 1788. p. 121.

Pomphrey [Humphrey] Gooch & Mary Thomson a son John born Nov. 2 .... Baptized Apl. 11 1785. p. 114.

Humphey Gough & Mary Thomson a son Rollin Oct. 31 1787. Baptized May 12 1788. p. 121.

Liner Gouge & Rhodie Turner, a son Dabney born Feb. 22 1786. Baptized Apl: 23 1786. p. 116.

Tho: Gouge & Lucy Higgins a son named Gideon born Jun. 20, 1773. Baptized Aug. 15 1773. p. 94.

Will: Gooch & Lovinah Clements a child Sally born Feb: 16 1769 Baptized Dec. 10 1783. p. 110.

Will Gouge & Luvina Clements a daughter named Jemima born Dec 29 177—. Baptized Mar. 15, 1774. p. 96.

John Good & Frances Loftus a son named William born Sep: 8 1766. Baptized Oct. 19 1766. p. 75.

John Good & Frances Loftus a Daughter named Sarah born Oct: 23 1768. Baptized Dec: 25 1768. p. 83.

Jo: Goodman & Jeanie Lawrie a son George born Mar: 26 1781. Baptized Oct. 5 1784. p. 113.

Overton Goodman & Mary Camp a son named William born feb: 7 1765. Baptized Jul: 6 1765. p. 72.

John Gordon & Judith Moracet a Daughter named Elizabeth born May 31, 1759. Baptized 1759 Jul: 1. p. 55.

John Gordon & Judith Moracet a Daughter named Mary born Mar: 10 1761. Baptized 1761 Ap: 5. p. 59.

John Gordon & Judith Moracet a Daughter named Judith born Aug 3 1770. Baptized Sep: 2 1770. p. 88.

Will Gordon & Catherine Mitchel a daughter named Mary born Feb. 24, 1773. Baptized Ap. 4, 1773. p. 94.

Will: Gowan & Anna Stacia Sullivan a Daughter named Anna Statia born Sep: 17, 1756. Baptized 1757 Mar. 6. p. 50.

William Gouven & Honesty Sullivan a son named James born Nov: 28 1758. Baptized 1759 ffeb: 18. p. 54.

Geo: Grady & Fannie Biglow a girl named Nansie born dec: 30 1795. Baptized July 24 1797. p. 130.

Benjamin Granger & Eliz: Edwards a son named Benjamin born May 26, 1758. Baptized 1758 Jul: 9. p. 53.

Alex: Grant & Agnes Gerard a Daughter named Judith born Oct. 1 1769. Baptized feb: 21 1770. p. 87.

Alexn Grant & Agnes Jarrat a son named William born Feb. 17, 1772. Baptized Ap. 22, 1772. p. 92.

Henry Graves & Mary Cussins .... Baptized feb: 25 1770. p. 87.

Henry Graves & Mary Cussins a daughter called Mary born Feb. 20, 1774. Baptized Ap. 17, 1774. p. 96.

Henry Graves & Mary Cusons a son named John born Nov. 22, 1772. Baptized Jan 10, 1773. p. 93.

Is: Graves & Betty Coward a child named Drusilla born Jan: 28, 1781. Baptized May 6, 1781. p. 103.

Is: Graves & Betty Cowherd a son Francis born May 22 1783. Baptized Jul: 13 1783. p. 110.

Is: Graves & Bettie Cowherd a child Bettie born Aug. 15 1785. Baptized Oct. 22 1785. p. 115.

Is: Graves & Bettie Cowherd a child Isaac born June 8 1787. Baptized Sep: 16 1787. p. 119.

Isaac Graves & Bettie Coward a son Colby born Mar: 5 1789. Baptized Aug. 23 1789. p. 125.

Ralph Graves & Judith Womack a Daughter named Sally born Sep: 1, 1756. Baptized 1756 Oct: 10. p. 49.

Henry Gray & Ruth Mutrie a son named William born June 4 1768. Baptized Nov: 13 1768. p. 82.

Henry Gray & Phebe Johnson a son Dan: Begby born Dec. 12 1782. Baptized Ap: 20 1783. p. 109.

Henry Gray & Phebe Johnson a son Will: Henry born Feb. 19 1786. Baptized Oct: 17 1787. p. 120.

Tho: Gray & Letty Harris a child named Mary: Bib born Feb. 8, 1759. Baptized May 29 1781. p. 103.

Tho: Gray & Letty Harris a son named Charles: Haris born May 7, 1781. Baptized May 29, 1781. p. 103.

Tho: Gray & Lettie Harris a son David born June 18 1783. Baptized Ap: 3 1784. p. 111.

Tho: Gray & Letty Harris a son William born June 2 1786. Baptized Aug. 12 1786. p. 117.

Tho: Gray & Letitia Harris, Sallie Bibb, born Nov. 4 1788. Baptized Jul: 8 1790. p. 125.

Tho: Gray & Cath: Young a son John born Ap: 19 1796. Baptized Aug: 25 1796. p. 127.

Ja: Graydy & Eliz: Jennings a child Nancy, Jan: 17 1782. Baptized Oct. 23 1785. p. 115.

Ja: Graydy & Eliz: Jennings a child Jo: Jennings born Oct: 17 1784. Baptized Oct. 23 1785. p. 115.

James Grayson & Eliz: Williams a Son born .... 1756 named Thomas. Baptized 1756 May 2. p. 48.

James Grayson & Elizab: Williams a son named John born Jan: 24 1759. Baptized 1759 Mar: 4. p. 54.

Forest & Patsie Greens a son Joseph born Augt. 11 1782. Baptized Dec. 14 1783. p. 109.

John Green & Mary Parish a son named William born Oct: 24, 1757. Baptized 1757 Dec: 11. p. 51.

John Green & Mary Parish a Daughter named Judith born dec: 13 1760. Baptized 1761 Mar: 29. p. 59.

John Green & Mary Parrish a son named Thomas born May 31, 1763. Baptized 1763 Jul: 17. p. 65.

John Green & Mary Parish a son named Edward born Nov: 30 1765. Baptized May 17 1766. p. 74.

John Green & Mary Parish a Daughter named Frankie born Jun: 21 1768. Baptized Jul: 24 1768. p. 81.

John Green & Mary Parish a Daughter named Mary born June 30 1770. Baptized Sep: 30 1770. p. 88.

John Green & Mary Parish a daughter named Lucy born Jan. 29, 1773. Baptized May 2, 1773. p. 94.

John Green & Mary Parish a son named James born Feb. 13, 1775. Baptized May 28, 1775. p. 98.

John Green & Sarah Griffiths a son named Joseph born Mar: 5. 1760. Baptized 1760 Ap: 20. p. 57.

John Green & Sar: Griffiths a Daughter named Rebekah born Jan: 20 1763. Baptized 1763 Ap: 3. p. 64.

Tho: Green & Susanna Hall a son William born Dec. 1 1783. Baptized June 20 1784. p. 112.

Tho: Green & Mary Clark, Sammin Williams, Ap: 23 1787. Baptized Oct: 17 1787. p. 120.

Tho: Green & Mary Clark, a child, Nancy born Nov: 3 1781. Baptized Oct: 17 1787. p. 120.

Tho: Green & Mary Clark, Thomas, born May 26 1783. Baptized Oct: 17 1787. p. 120.

Billie Green & Lucy Sexton a son named James born Feb: 5 1780. Baptized May 18, 1781. p. 103.

Will: Green & Lucy Sexton a child Sally born Aug. 14 1782. Baptized Ap: 26 1783. p. 109.

Will: Green & Lucy Sexton a child Juggie born Dec. 9 1783. Baptized June 20 1784. p. 112.

Will: Green & Lucy Saxton a child Patsy Sept. 21 1785. Baptized Dec: 3 1786. p. 118.

James Gregory & Sarah Thompson a son named William born Aug: 11. 1758. Baptized 1758 Dec: 3. p. 53.

Will: Groom & Dorothy Mathison a Son named Henry: Mathison born Aug: 29 1757. Baptized 1757 Oct: 30. p. 51.

William Groom & Dorothea Mathison a Daughter named Nansie born Ap: 9, 1759. Baptized 1759 Aug: 5. p. 55.

William Groom & Dorothy Mathison a son named William born Mar: 6 1761. Baptized 1761 Jul: 19. p. 60.

Will: Groom & Dorothea Mattison a son named Robert born Jul: 27, 1763. Baptized 1763 Sep: 12. p. 65.

John Gillam & Sarah Faris a son named Jacob born Ap: 27 1761. Baptized 1761 Jul: 5. p. 60.

John Guillam & Sarah Fairies a Daughter named Elizabeth Mar: 1 1763. Baptized 1763 Jun: 5. p. 64.

John Guillam & Sarah Fairies a Daughter named Martha born Mar: 3 1766. Baptized Jun: 29 1766. p. 74.

John Guillam & Sarah Faries a son named Taylor born Jul: 23 1768. Baptized Oct: 23 1768. p. 82.

John Guillam & Sarah Fairies a Daughter named Susannah born Jan: 31 1771. Baptized Mar: 29 1771. p. 89.

Jo: Guillam & Conny Parish a child named Elizabeth born Nov. 20, 1780. Baptized Mar. 16, 1782. p. 105.

Jo: Guillam & Annie Parish, a Son Robert born Jul: 6, 1782. Baptized Sep. 30, 1782. p. 107.

Will: Guillam & Ann Symes a son James born Ap. 14, 1782. Baptized June 16, 1782. p. 107.

Jo: Gunter & Susannah Harris a son Charles born. Baptized May 19 1783. p. 109.

Thomas Guthry & Eliz. Garden a daughter named Polly born Jan. 12, 1773. Baptized Feb. 14, 1773. p. 93.

Tho: Guthrie & Eliz: Gardener a son named James born Ap. 18, 1777. Baptized Oct. 21, 1777. p. 102.

[Thomas,] Guthry & Eliz: Gardener a child Elizabeth born .... 1782. Baptized Aug. 18, 1782. p. 107.

Alman Gwin & Mary Evans had a daughter named Elizabeth born Nov. 30, 1755. p. 105.

Alman Gwin & Mary Evans near Dover had a Daughter baptised, born Nov: 30th Nam: Eliz: Baptized 1756 Jan: 4. p. 48.

Bartley Guin & Catherine ffembrag a Son named Benjamin born Mar: 5 1757. Baptized 1757 May 22. p. 51.

Bartlet Gwine & Catherine ffermbra a Daughter named Mary born Jun: 1, 1759. Baptized 1759 Jun: 17. p. 55.

Antony Haden & Drusilla Rountree a Daughter named Jeannie born Jan: 9 1768. Baptized Feb: 16 1768. p. 79.

Antony Haden & Eliz: Pore a son named James born Jan: 6 1771. Baptized Ap: 10 1771. p. 89.

Anthony Haden & Drusilla Rountree a son named John Jan. 20, 1772. Baptized Ap. 22, 1772. p. 92.

Geor. Haden & Eliz. Taylor a son named Isaiah born Mar. 7, 1775. Baptized Aug. 7, 1775. p. 98.

Geo: Haden & Eliz: Taylor, Geo: Washinton born Jan. 3, 1782. Baptized Mar. 24, 1782. p. 106.

John Haden & Jean Mosely a Daughter named Jeanie born dec: 10 1757. Baptized 1757 Dec: 26. p. 51.

John Haden & Jeanie Mosely a Daughter named Mildred born Ap: 14 1760. Baptized 1760 Ap: 30. p. 57.

John Haden & Jean Mosely a son named Benjamin born May 26, 1762. Baptized 1762 Jun: 20. p. 63.

John Haden & Joan Mosely a Daughter named Rachel born Ap: 25 1764. Baptized May: 11 1764. p. 67.

Joseph Haden & Elizabeth Handley a Daughter named Elizabeth born feb: 3 1764. Baptized Ap: 22 1764. p. 67.

Joseph Haden & Eliz. Hundley a daughter named Judith born May 19, 1772. Baptized Nov. 5, 1772. p. 93.

Joseph Haden & Mary Patross a son named Nilson born Ap. 30, 1774. Baptized Dec. 17, 1775. p. 97.

Jos: Haden & Mary Parrol & child named Polly born Feb: 1781. Baptized Oct 22, 1781. p. 105.

Joseph Haden & Mary Peatross a son Joseph, Sep: 23 1783. Baptized July 8 1787. p. 119.

Joseph Haden & Mary Peatross a child Jeanie born Oct .... 1785. Baptized July 8 1787. p. 119.

Joseph Haden & Mary Peatross a child Rhode born Sep: .... 1786. Baptized July 8 1787. p. 119.

Zachariah Haden & Eliz: Pore a son named Robert born Aug: 10 1765. Baptized Jul: 16 1767. p. 78.

Zachariah Haden & Eliz: Pore a son named Thomas-Pore born Jun 16 1767. Baptized Jul: 16 1767. p. 78.

Zachariah Haden & Eliz: Pore a Daughter named Susannah born Sep: 29 1768. Baptized Nov: 3 1768. p. 82.

Zach. Haden & Eliz: Poor a daughter named Elizabeth born Jun. 18, 1773. Baptized Jul. 25, 1773. p. 94.

Zachariah Haden & Eliz. Pore a son named Jesse born Sep. 6, 1776. Baptized Oct 23, 1776. p. 100.

Jo: Haines & Francis Yarbrough twins, Jemima & Ann, June 16 1783. Baptized Oct. 28 1783. p. 110.

Bartlett Haly & Jean Steatum a son Charles born Aug: 16 1770. Baptized Dec: 3 1770. p. 88.

Tho: Hall & Frances Williams a son named Justance born Aug: 10 1770. Baptized Nov 18 1770. p. 88.

William Hall & Betty Page a Daughter named Hannah born Jan: 10 1758. Baptized 1758 ffeb: 19. p. 52.

Will: Hall & Betty Page a Daughter named Betty born Ap: 23, 1760. Baptized 1760 May 25. p. 57.

William Hall & Betty Page a Daughter named Rebekah born Mar:
27 1765. Baptized May 26 1765. p. 71.

Will: Hall & Ann Yamons a child Adie Lane born June 2 1783.
Baptized Apl: 12 1784. p. 111.

James Hammond & Mary Hargiss a Son named John born Jan:
29 1760. Baptized 1760 Jun: 8. p. 59.

George Hancoke & Mary Whitlock [Whitloc] a son named Mathew
born Dec: 22 1763. Baptized Ap: 8 1764. p. 67.

Major Hancoke & Ann Thomas a son named John born Jun:
18 1766. Baptized Jul: 27 1766. p. 74.

Major Hancoke & Ann Thomas a Daughter named Judith born
May 11 1768. Baptized Jun: 12 1768. p. 81.

Major Hancoke & Ann Thomas a Daughter named Molly born
Jun: 11 1769. Baptized Jul: 16 1769. p. 85.

Major Hancocke & Ann Thomas a Daughter named Susannah
born Aug 27 1770. Baptized Nov. 11 1770. p. 88.

Major Hancoke & Ann Thomas a son named Major born Feb.
8, 1772. Baptized 1772. p. 91.

Major Hancoke & Ann Thomas a daughter named Betsy born
Jan 4, 1774. Baptized Mar. 13, 1774. p. 96.

Major Hancoke & Ann Thomas a daughter Sarah born Oct 20,
1775. Baptized Jan. 1, 1776. p. 99.

Major Hancoke & Ann Thomas a daughter named Nancy born
Dec 10, 1776. Baptized Feb. 16, 1777. p. 101.

Major Hancoke & Mary Moreland a son Lewis born Sep: 5 1782.
Baptized Ap: 19 1783. p. 109.

Stephen Hancoke & Catherine Merchant a Daughter named Ruth
born Aug: 29 1766. Baptized Sep: 7 1766. p. 75.

Tho: Hancock & Mary Shoemaker a Daughter named Ann born
Nov: 26 1758. Baptized 1759 ffeb: 11. p. 54.

Tho: Hancoke & Mary Shoemaker two Sons, Benjamin & John
born Nov: 13, 1760. Baptized 1761 Jan: 26. p. 58.

Thomas Hancoke & Mary Shoemaker a Daughter named Mary
born Jun: 3 1763. Baptized 1763 Sep: 26. p. 65.

Tho: Hancoke & Mary Shoemaker a Daughter named Obedience
born May 14 1764. Baptized Sep: 2 1764. p. 69.

Thomas Hancoke & Mary Shoemaker a son named Stephen born
Jun: 6 1766. Baptized Sep: 7 1766. p. 75.

Jos: Hankins & Hannah Aggin a son named William born Feb
20, 1781. Baptized Ap. 9, 1781. p. 103.

John Hanson & Judith ffields a Daughter named Mildred born
Jan: 4 1760. Baptized 1760 Ap: 13. p. 57.

John Hanson & Eliz: Pace* a son named William born Sep:
21 1767. Baptized Nov: 20 1767. p. 79.

John Hanson & Eliz: Pace a son named Joseph Pace born Mar:
20 1769. Baptized Jun: 4 1769. p. 85.

*Pearse in Marriage records.

Rich: Hanson & Mary Milton a child named Sele born June 16, 1781. Baptized Sep. 2, 1781. p. 104.

Giles Harding & Amidiah Morris a son named George born Dec: 17, 1773. Baptized Mar. 6, 1774. p. 95.

Giles Hardine & Amy Morris a .... Baptized Feb. 9, 1777. p. 101.

Giles Hardine & Amie Morris a child Mary born Dec. 2, 1781. Baptized June 16, 1782. p. 107.

Giles Hardine & Amie Morris, a son Giles, June 3 1784. Baptized April 1 1786. p. 116.

Giles Hardine & Amie Morris a child Patsy born Jan: 19 1786. Baptized April 1 1786. p. 116.

Groves Hardine & Sarah Williamson a daughter named Sally born Dec 18, 1767. Baptized May 6, 1774. p. 96.

Groves Hardine & Sarah Williamson a daughter named Lucy born Sep. 11, 1770. Baptized May 6, 1774. p. 96.

Groves Hardine & Sarah Williamson a son John born Jun 20 1773. Baptized May 6, 1774. p. 96.

Tho: Hardine & Jean Ferrar a child Eliz: Bibb born Jan: 3 1783. Baptized Ap: 25 1783. p. 109.

Tho: Hardine & Jeany Ferrar a son Thomas born Sep: 2 1787. Baptized Oct: 17 1787. p. 120.

William Hardine & Eliz: Lockrum a Daughter named Mary born Oct: 2 1764 (sic). Baptized Jun: 25 1764. p. 68.

Jos: Harper & Anna Harris a son John born Jan: 28 1782. Baptized Jan: 6 1788. p. 120.

Jos: Harper & Anna Harris a child Sarah born Oct: 28 1783. Baptized Jan: 6 1788. p. 120.

Jos: Harper & Anna Harris a child Dudley born Dec. .... 1785. Baptized Jan: 6 1788. p. 120.

Ben: Haris & Priscilla Wager a Daugh: named Priscilla: Wager born .... Baptized 1761 Ap: 5. p. 59.

Ben: Harris & Priscilla Wager a Daughter named Ann-Hanson born Nov: 19 1764. Baptized Dec: 22 1764. p. 69.

Cornelius Harris was baptised the day of his marriage being formerly a Quaker. Baptized 1759 Aug: 12. p. 55.

Cyrus Harris & Betsy Bond a son Robbie born June 23 1784. Baptized Sep: 10 1784. p. 112.

Edward Harris & Jerusha Davis, Lancelot, Nov. 14 1785. Baptized Ap: 29 1787. p. 118.

Frederick Harris & Eliz: Tyrril, Eliz: Burnet, born Dec. 13 1784. Baptized Mar: 31 1785. p. 113.

Jacob Haries & Lucy Granger a son named Nat: Dabney born Sep. 15, 1776. Baptized Mar 6, 1777. p. 101.

Ja: Harris & [Ursley Flournoy] in Manikentown a son named ffrancis born Jan. 10 1762. Baptized 1762 Jan: 10. p. 61.

John Harris & Eliz: ffergusson a son named Peter born Sep: 21, 1758. Baptized 1758 Dec: 3. p. 53.

John Harris & Obedience Turpine a son named Jordan born May 20, 1763. Baptized 1763 Jul: 25. p. 65.

Jo: Harris & Obediance Turpine a Daughter named Caroline Matilda born Dec. 1 1765. Baptized May 11 1766. p. 73.

John Harris & Obedience Turpine a son named Francis born May 7 1768. Baptized Oct: 9 1768. p. 82.

Joseph Harris & Rebekah Howard a Daughter named Elizab: born Ap: 16 1767. Baptized May 26 1767. p. 77.

Nathan Harris & Sally Knight a son Edward born Oct: 25 1782. Baptized Sep: 10 1784. p. 112.

Nathan Harris & Sally Knight a son Samuel born Ap: 22 1784. Baptized Sep: 10 1784. p. 112.

Nathan Haris & Sally Knight a child Jeany born Oct: 22 1787. Baptized May 11 1788. p. 121.

Nathan Harris & Martha Byers a child Polly born Ap: 1 1788. Baptized 29 May 1788. p. 121.

Bob: Harris & Peeny Walton a child Martha Burnet born Oct 12, 1782. Baptized Jan 30, 1783. p. 108.

Rob: Harris & Mary Davis, Maria Cookson born June 4 1786. Baptized Oct: 1 1786. p. 117.

Rob: Harris & Mary Davis, Benjamin Burnet, born Nov. 10 1787. Baptized May 4 1788. p. 121.

Sherard Harris & Hannah Page a son named John born Ap: 3 1765. Baptized May 26 1765. p. 71.

Sherard Harris & Hannah Page a Daughter named Hannah born Jan: 19 1768. Baptized Mar: 27 1768. p. 80.

Thomas Harris & Eliz: Woodhal a son named David born May 13 1759. Baptized 1759 Sep: 23. p. 55.

Will: Harris & Mary Hudson a Daughter named Susannah born Jan: 29 1758. Baptized 1758 Mar: 19. p. 52.

Will: Harris & Mary Hudson Twins named Abner & Jesse born Jun: 22, 1762. Baptized 1762 Aug: 15. p. 63.

Will: Harris & Sarah Steefe a son named Henry born Jan: 23 1762. Baptized 1762 May 30. p. 63.

Andrew Harrison & Jean Dillard a Daughter named Mally born .... 1757. Baptized 1757 Dec: 26. p. 51.

Andrew Harrison & Joan Dillard a son named Andrew born Mar: 24 1764. Baptized Ap: 22 1764. p. 67.

Benjamin Harrison & Sarah Bullard a Daughter born Jan: 17 1756 named Mary. Baptized 1756. feb: 22. p. 48.

Benjamin Harrison & Sarah Bullard a Daughter named Nelly born dec: 11 1758. Baptized 1759. ffeb: 4. p. 54.

Benjamin Harrison & Sarah Bullard a Daughter named Betty born Jul: 15 1764. Baptized Aug: 26 1764. p. 69.

Carter Henry Harrison & Susannah Randolph a Daughter named Betty born Mar: .... Baptized May 14 1764. p. 67.

Charles Harrison & ffrances Hughland a Daughter named Nansie born Jan: 20, 1762. Baptized 1762 Mar: 14. p. 62.

Capt: William Harrison & Anna Payne a son named Robert born Jun: 29 1766. Baptized Jul: 20 1766. p. 74.

William Harrison & Anne Payne a Daughter named Susannah born Jan: 22 1768. Baptized Feb: 17 1768. p. 79.

Jo: Hart & Rachel Gray a son Alexander, born May 23, 1782. Baptized Nov 11, 1782. p. 108.

Will: Harton & Unity Lane a son named Jeremiah born feb: 19, 1757. Baptized 1757 Ap: 17. p. 50.

Gid: Hatcher & Martha Leprade a child Jo: Leprade born, Mar. 27, 1781. Baptized June 16, 1782. p. 107.

Gideon Hatcher & Martha Laprade a child Ann Eliz: born Aug. 10 1782. Baptized Dec. 17 1783. p. 110.

Gideon Hatcher & Martha Laprade a child sarah born Nov: 18 1783. Baptized Dec. 17 1783. p. 110.

Thomas Hatcher & Sarah Porter a Daughter named Phebe born Jul: 23 1764. Baptized Sep: 9 1764. p. 69.

Thomas Hatcher & Sarah Porter a Daughter named Sarah born Dec. 6 1767. Baptized Jan: 30 1768. p. 79.

Tho: Hatcher & Sarah Porter a daughter named Eliz: Porter born Aug: 1777. Baptized Sep. 21, 1777. p. 102.

Tho: Hatcher & Lucy Curd in Goochland a son Thomas born Dec. 9 1786. Baptized June 17 1787. p. 119.

Elijah Hawkins & Nancy Hill, Jo: Byars Dec: 5 1788. Baptized Dec. 25 1788. p. 122.

Jo: Hawkins & Anna Gabriella Jones a son Tho: Wyat born Sep: 16 1783. Baptized Nov: 28 1783. p. 110.

Isaac Head & Rachel Long a child Betsie born Dec. 15 1783. Baptized Nov. 1 1784. p. 113.

Da: Head & Isable Jones a child Frankie Stot [or Scot] born Aug. 8 1785. Baptized Oct: 19 1786. p. 117.

Will Heale & Susannah Payne a daughter named Sarah born Jul 11, 1772. Baptized Aug. 2, 1772. p. 92.

William Heale & Susannah Payne a son named John born Jany. 1st 1775. Baptized Mar: 5 1775. p. 98.

Thomas Heard & Eliz: Fitzpatrick a daughter named Catherine born Aug: 2 1767. Baptized Jun: 20 1768. p. 81.

Thomas Herd & Eliz: ffitzpatrick a son named Abraham born feb: 26 1769. Baptized Jun: 10 1769. p. 85.

Tho: Helms & Sally Powers-, Jo: Rufus Powers Oct: 28 1783. Baptized May 21 1787. p. 119.

Tho: Helms & Sally Powers-, Mary Ann Swinney, Aug: 20 1786. Baptized May 21 1787. p. 119.

Will: Hemus & Lucy Woodward had a daughter named Susannah born Jan: 16, 1750. p. 40.

Will: Hemus & Lucy Woodward a Daugh: named Elizabeth born May 29, 1752. p. 40.

Will: Hemus & Lucy Woodward a Daugh: named Lucy born Aug: 5, 1755. p. 40.

Will: Hemus & Lucy Woodward a Daughter named Mally born Ap: 30 1756. Baptized 1756 June 26. p. 49.

Nicolas Hemus & Mary Massey a Daughter named Sally born Jan: 7 1761. Baptized 1761 Mar: 22. p. 59.

Da: Henderson & Hannah Symes, Sar: Thomson, Nov: 8 1785. Baptized Mar: 30 1786. p. 116.

Tho: Henderson & Mary Wheeler a child Delphie born Feb: 8 1786. Baptized Oct: 19 1786. p. 117.

Ja. Hendrick & Lucretia Gardener, Temperance Gardener, born Jan. 17 1782. Baptized June 6 1784. p. 112.

Ja. Hendrick & Kersey Gardener a child, Mary Ford born Sep: 10 1784. Baptized Oct: 1 1786. p. 117.

Ja. Hendrick & Kersey Gardener a child, Martha-Duke born June 20 1786. Baptized Oct: 1 1786. p. 117.

Leonard Henley & Eliz: Jude a son named Leonard born Oct: 1 1768. Baptized Nov: 21 1768. p. 82.

Rich: Henley & Lucy Bowles a son Tarleton born Jan. 8 1782. Baptized Ap. 14, 1782. p. 106.

Will Henley & Marianne Smith a daughter named Nancy born Jan 22, 1773. Baptized May 16, 1773. p. 94.

Lewis Harndon [Herndon] & Frances Thomson a son named James born Jul: 1 1767. Baptized Aug: 23 1767. p. 78.

Edward Herndon & Bettie Minor, a son George born Sep. 12 1784. Baptized Jan. 28 1785. p. 113.

James Heron & Sarah Taylor a son William Douglas born then. Baptized June 8 1791. p. 126.

Austin Hesten & Susannana Freeman a child Betsey born. Baptized May 11 1796. p. 138.

Absalom Hicks & Mary Haris a Daughter named Jeanie born Ap: 20, 1760. Baptized 1760 Jun: 1. p. 57.

Absalom Hicks & Mary Harris a Daughter named Diana born dec: 5 1761. Baptized 1762 Mar: 7. p. 62.

David Hicks & Sarah Lee a daughter named Nansy born Oct 5, 1772. Baptized Ap. 11, 1773. p. 94.

David Hicks & Sarah Lee a daughter named Elizabeth born Feb. 18, 1775. Baptized May 7, 1775. p. 98.

David Hicks & Sarah Lee a daughter named Abba-Lee Reeves born Mar 26, 1777. May 11, 1777. p. 103.

Henry Hicks & Betty Willis a Son named Henry born Oct: 24 1756. Baptized 1757 feb: 27. p. 50.

Henry Hicks & Betty Willis a son named Harman born Mar: 5 1760. Baptized 1760 May 4. p. 57.

Harry Hicks & Eliz: Willis a Daughter named Eliz: born Jan: 21, 1762. Baptized 1762 Aug: 15. p. 63.

Jesse Hicks & Mary Grubs a Daughter named Nansie born Mar: 4 1770. Baptized Mar: 22 1770. p. 87.

Jesse Hicks & Mary Grubs a daughter named Sally born Mar. 13, 1772. Baptized Ap. 26, 1772. p. 92.

Jesse Hicks & Mary Grub a daughter called Susannah born May 20, 1774. Baptized Jul. 3, 1774. p. 97.

Jesse Hicks & Mary Grubs a son named John: Casie born May 11, 1776. Jul. 21, 1776. p. 100.

Meshack Hicks & Ann Dawson a Daughter named Betsey born Dec. 25 1766. Baptized Ap: 19 1767. p. 77.

Meshack Hicks & Ann Dawson a daughter named Nancy born Oct: 27 1769. Baptized Mar: 25 1770. p. 87.

Sam: Hix & Eliz: Woodlock a Son named ffrederick born Mar: 12, 1756. Baptized 1756 Jun: 7. p. 48.

Stephen Hicks & Agnes Hancock a Son named Nathaniel born May 5, 1759. Baptized 1759 Jul: 1. p. 55.

Stephen Hicks & Agnes Hancock a Daughter named Winifred born Sep: 1, 1760. Baptized 1760 Oct: 5. p. 58.

Stephen Hicks & Agnes Hancoke a Daughter named Edith born Jan: 24 1762. Baptized 1762 Ap: 9. p. 62.

Stephen Hicks & Agnes Hancoke a Daughter named Mary born May 9, 1763. Baptized 1763 Jun: 26. p. 64.

Da: Hill & Ann Thomson a child Patsy Byers born Jan. 17, 1782. Baptized May 19, 1782. p. 106.

Joshua Hill & Caroline Singer a child Nancy born Sep. 23 1783. Baptized May 2 1784. p. 111.

John Hill & Tabitha Bailey a son named Samuel: Parks born May 22 1757. Baptized 1757 Oct: 30. p. 51.

John Hill & Peggie French a Daughter named Taboth born Jun: 6 1763. Baptized Jun: 14 1764. p. 68.

John Hill & Peggie Tolliver a Daughter named Betty born Jul: 23 1769. Baptized feb: 22 1770. p. 87.

ffrances Hilley & Sarah Dawson a Daughter named Susannah born Sep: 8 1757. Baptized 1757 Dec: 11. p. 51.

Francis Hilley & Sarah Dawson a Daughter named Jean born Mar: 12 1765. Baptized Aug: 18 1765. p. 72.

Francis Hilley & Sarah Dawson a son named Francis born Jun: 29 1767. Baptized Aug: 23 1767. p. 78.

James Hilton & Susannah Welton a Son named George born feb: 12 1758. Baptized 1758 Mar: 17. p. 52.

James Hilton & Susannah Walton a son named John born Jan: 3, 1760. Baptized 1760 May 6. p. 57.

Ja: Hilton & Mary Hall a Daughter named Susan Hilton born July 28 1763. Baptized Dec: 23 1763. p. 66.

John Hilton & Obedience Cox a son named George born May 20 1761. Baptized 1761 Sep: 13. p. 61.

Jo: Hilton & Mary Ligton a child Rebecca Philips on June 15 1787. Baptized Nov: 1 1787. p. 120.

Richard Hinds & Mary Brown a son named Dudley: Brown born ---- .... 1759. Baptized 1759 Dec: 16. p. 56.

Rich: Hinds & Mary Brown a Daughter named Mary born Jan: 12 1762. Baptized 1762 Mar: 7. p. 62.

Richard Hinds & Mary Brown a son named Tarlton born Ap: 18 1765. Baptized Jun: 9 1765. p. 71.

Richard Hinds & Mary Brown a Son named Richard born Mar: 28 1770. Baptized Ap: 29 1770. p. 87.

Edmund Hodges & Nathana Walker a Son named Jesse born Jun: 13 1757. Baptized 1757 Aug: 7. p. 51.

John Hodges & Deborah Lee a Daughter named Lucy born May 26, 1757. Baptized 1757 Jul: 24. p. 51.

John Hodges & Deborah Lee a son named Jesse born Nov: 10 1760. Baptized 1760 Dec: 7. p. 58.

John Hodges & Deborah Lee a daughter named Mary born Sep. 30, 1773. Baptized Nov. 7, 1773. p. 95.

John Hodges & Martha Price a Daughter called Sarah born Jun: 27 1769. Baptized Sep: 21 1769. p. 86.

John Hodges & Martha Price a son named James born Jun. 11, 1775. Baptized Sept 20, 1775. p. 99.

John Hodges & Judith Perkins a daughter named Elizabeth born Aug. 17, 1777. Oct. 19, 1777. p. 102.

Johnson Hodges & Lucy Page a Daughter born dec: 21 1755 named Nannie. Baptized 1756 Jan: 25. p. 48.

Johnson Hoges & Lucy Page a Son named William born Oct: 1, 1757. Baptized 1757 Nov: 13. p. 51.

Johnson Hodges & Lucy Page a Daughter named Annie born Sep: 17 1759. Baptized 1759 Dec: 9. p. 56.

Johnson Hodges & Lucy Page a Daughter named Lucy born Jul: 20, 1763. Baptized 1763 Aug: 23. p. 65.

Johnson Hodges & Lucy Page a daughter named Christian born Sep 26, 1771. Baptized Nov. 30, 1771. p. 91.

Joseph Hodges & Elizabeth Harris a Daughter named Nanny born June 15: 1757. Baptized 1757 Jul: 24. p. 51.

Joseph Hodges & Eliz: Haris a Daughter named Elizabeth born Sep: 29 1759. Baptized 1759 Dec: 23. p. 56.

Joseph Hodges & Eliz: Harris a son named Sherrard born Mar: 1 1762. Baptized 1762 May 9. p. 62.

Joseph Hodges & Elizabeth Harris a Daughter named ffrances born dec: 15 1763. Baptized Ap: 1 1764. p. 67.

Joseph Hodges & Elizabeth Harris a son named William born Mar: 10 1765. Baptized Jun: 16 1765. p. 71.

Tho: Hodges & Sabrah Horn a Daughter named Sally born dec: 28 1760. Baptized 1761 Mar: 15. p. 59.

Thomas Hodges & Sabra Horn a Daughter named Ann born Oct: 11 1764. Baptized Mar: 3 1765. p. 70.

Thomas Hodges & Sabra Horn a Daughter named Betty born May 2 1767. Baptized Jun: 21 1767. p. 78.

Tho: Hodges & Sabrah Horn a Daughter named Jeanie born May 31 1769. Baptized Jul: 16 1769. p. 85.

Wiliam Hodges & Susannah Lovel a son named John born Mar: 27 17 1759. Baptized 1759 Ap: 29. p. 55.

Will: Hodges & susannah Lovel a Son named George born Mar: 27 1762. Baptized 1762 Ap: 25. p. 62.

William Hodges & Susannah Lovel a Daughter named Mary born Ap: 9 1764. Baptized May 13 1764. p. 67.

Will: Hodges & Susannah Lovel a son named Christian born Ap: 12 1766. Baptized May 18 1766. p. 74.

Will: Hodges & Susannah Lovel a Daughter named Ann born Nov: 12 1768. Baptized Jan: 29 1769. p. 83

Will Hodges & Susannah Lovel a son called David born Jul. 15, 1774. Baptized Aug. 28, 1774. p. 97.

Will: Hogan & Susannah Williams a child Peggie Thomson, Jan: 16 1784. Baptized Nov. 25 1784. p. 113.

Jo: Hoggan & Helener Couts a child named Rebekah born Dec 4. 1781. Baptized Feb. 21, 1782. p. 105.

David Hoges & Mary Alsop a son named William born Ap: 5 1764. Baptized Aug: 5 1764. p. 68.

Ben: Holladay & Sally Hampton a son Benjamin born June 9 1786. Baptized Sep: 28 1786. p. 117.

Ben: Holladay & Sally Hampton a son George born Jan: 24 1788. Baptized Ap: 28 1788. p. 121.

Ja: Holliday & Sophia Sandidge, Anna, born Sep. 4 1785. Baptized Nov. 10 1785. p. 115.

Ja: Holladay & Suffier Sandidge Elizabeth born July 25 1787. Baptized Aug. 9 1787. p. 119.

Ja: Holladay & Martha Holladay, Patty Lewis June 8 1787. Baptized Aug. 9 1787. p. 119.

Joseph Holladay & Agnes Holladay a son Edward born Mar: 12 1788. Baptized 28 Apl. 1788. p. 121.

Geor: Holland & Mary Coleman a Son named Rich: Anderson born feb: 15. 1762. Baptized 1762 Ap: 12. p. 62.

George Holland & Mary Coleman a Daughter named Salley born Ap: 26 1764. Baptized Jun: 24 1764. p. 68.

George Holland & Mary Coleman a Daughter named Frankie born Ap: 8 1766. Baptized May 17 1766. p. 74.

George Holland & Mary Coleman a son named Michael born Mar: 30 1768. Baptized Ap: 10 1768. p. 80.

Geo: Holland & Susannah George a child Keturah born Jul: 1 1783. Baptized Dec. 25 1783. p. 111.

Hezekiah Holland & Mary Walker a Daughter named Sally born Sep: 8 1765. Baptized Ap: 27 1766. p. 73.

Hezekiah Holland & Mary Walker a Daughter named Rachel born Aug. 3 1767. Baptized Nov: 15 1767. p. 79.

Hezek: Holland & Mary Walker a son named John born Jul: 11 1769. Baptized Oct: 8 1769. p. 86.

John Holland & Martha Weeks a Son named John born Jun: 16 1735. p. 41.

John Holland and Martha Weeks a son named Michael born dec: 29 1737. p. 41.

John Holland & Martha Weeks a Daughter named Judith born Nov: 4 1739. p. 41.

John Holland & Martha Weeks a Son named Hezekiah born Jun: 14 1742. p. 41.

John Holland & Martha Weeks a son named Richard born feb: 3 1743 [Sic]. p. 41.

John Holland & Martha Weeks a Daughter named Martha born Ap: 8 1745. p. 41.

John Holland & Martha Weeks a Son named Nathaniel born Ap: 1 1748. p. 41.

John Holland & Martha Weeks a Daughter named Alie born dec: 12 1752. p. 41.

John Holland & Martha Meeks a Daughter named Mary born Jul: 27 1756. Baptized 1756 Oct: 31. p. 49.

John Holland & Martha Meeks a Daughter named Lucy born Mar: 31, 1758. Baptized 1758 Jul: 28. p. 53.

John Holland & Martha Williams a daughter named Nansey born Sep. 10, 1774. Baptized Nov. 3, 1774. p. 97.

John Holland & Martha Williams a daughter named Sally born Feb. 17, 1776. Baptized June 28 1776. p. 100.

Major Holloway & Sar: Paterson a child Betsy born June 21 1780. Baptized Ap: 24 1783. p. 109.

Major Holloway & Sar: Paterson twins, Tho: & Obediah born Dec. 26 1782. Baptized Ap: 24 1783. p. 109.

James Holman & Sarah Miller a Daughter named Peg: Martin born Jul: 26, 17—. Baptized Oct: 14 1770. p. 88.

James Holman & Sarah Miller a son named Will: Miller born Nov. 15, 1772. Baptized Jan. 31, 1773. p. 93.

William Holman & Jean Martin a son named James born Nov: 30 1763. Baptized Jan: 8 1764. p. 66.

William Holman & Susannah Thomson a son named George born Aug: 31 1766. Baptized Oct: 14 1766. p. 75.

William Holman & Susanna Thompson a Daughter named Sarah born Jul: .... Baptized Aug: 1 1769. p. 85.

Will Holman & Becky Woodward a child named Nancy born 1776. Baptized Feb, 21, 1782. p. 105.

Will Holman & Becky Woodward a child named Catherine born Ap. 23, 1781. Baptized Feb. 21, 1782. p. 105.

John Holt & Jeanie Dudley a son named William born feb: 18 1768. Baptized Ap: 11 1768. p. 80.

Tho. Hooten & Susannah Green a son named John born Jan. 28, 1773. Baptized Ap. 11, 1773. p. 94.

Jac: Hope & Eliz: Shorer a son named William born Nov. 5, 1779. Baptized Aug. 25, 1781. p. 104.

John Hopkins & Mary Martin a Daughter named Judith born feb: 11. 1763. Baptized 1763 May 4. p. 64.

John Hopkins & Mary Martin a Daughter named Jeanie born Aug: 9 1767. Baptized Nov: 16 1767. p. 79.

John Hopkins & Mary Martin a son named Arthur born Sep: 19 1769. Baptized Oct: 8 1769. p. 86.

John Hopkins & Mary Martin a son named John born Mar. 31, 1772. Baptized May 11, 1772. p. 92.

John Hopkins & Mary Martin a son named Henry born Feb. 6, 1775. Baptized Ap. 16, 1775. p. 98.

John Hopkins & Mary Martin a daughter named Mally born Feb. 22, 1777. Baptized Mar. 23, 1777. p. 101.

Jo: Hopkins & Mary Martin a Son James born Dec. 25, 1781. Baptized July 21, 1782. p. 107.

Jo: Hopkins & Mary Martin a son William born Feb. 26 1784. Baptized Ap: 17 1784. p. 111.

Jo: Hopkins & Mary Martin in Goochland, Bettie Pettit, born Jan: 1 1786. Baptized June 18 1787. p. 119.

Jos: Hopkins & Eliz: Timberlick, Mary Timberlick born Jan. 15, 1781. Baptized June 20, 1782. p. 107.

John Hopper & Agnes Tony a Son named James born dec: 2 1757. Baptized 1758 Jan: 8. p. 51.

John Hopper & Agnes Tony a Daughter named Agnes born May 11. 1760. Baptized 1760 May 11. p. 57.

John Hopper & Mary Horn a son named Paterson: Brandel born Mar. .... Baptized Jul. 21, 1771. p. 90.

John Hopper & Mary Horn a son named Anderson born Jan. 29, 1773. Jun. 13, 1773. p. 94.

John Hopper & Milley Rice a daughter named Milley born Feb. 5, 1776. Baptized Mar. 17, 1776. p. 99.

Luther Hopper & Eliz: Nash a Son named Robert born feb: 10 1759. Baptized 1759 Ap: 15. p. 59.

Luther Hopper & Eliz: Nash a Daughter named Milly born feb: 8 1761. Baptized 1761 Mar: 29. p. 59.

Luther Hopper & Elizabeth Nash a Daughter named Rachel born Mar: 31, 1763. Baptized 1763 May 8. p. 64.

Luther Hopper & Elizabeth Nash a Daughter named Mary born Mar: 26 1765. Baptized May 26 1765. p. 71.

Tho: Hopper & Eliz: Profit a Daughter named Jane born May 19. 1757. Baptized 1757 Jul: 3. p. 51.

Thomas Hopper & Eliz: Profit a son named John born Ap: 16. 1759. Baptized 1759 May 13. p. 55.

Tho: Hopper & Elizabeth Prophet a son named Thomas born Mar: 4 1761. Baptized 1761 Mar: 19. p. 59.

Tho: Hopper & Elizabeth Profit a Daughter named Susannah born May 17 1764. Baptized Jun: 24 1764. p. 68.

Thomas Hopper & Elizabeth Prophet a Daughter named Annie born Jul: 5 1766. Baptized Aug: 10 1766. p. 74.

Henry Hopson a married man was christened this day himself. Baptized Mar: 15 1765. p. 70.

Henry Hopson & Martha Nevils a son named Henry born Sep. 13 1756. Baptized Mar: 15 1765. p. 70.

Henry Hopson & Martha Nevils also a son named Joseph born feb: 25 1758. Baptized Mar: 15 1765. p. 70.

Henry Hopson & Martha Nevils also a son named William born Dec: 2 1759. Baptized Mar: 15 1765. p. 70.

Henry Hopson & Martha Nevils also a Daughter named Elizabeth born Oct: 19 1761. Baptized Mar: 15 1765. p. 70.

Henry Hopson & Martha Nevils also a son named Samuel born Nov 5 1762. Baptized Mar: 15 1765. p. 70.

Henry Hopson & Martha Nevils also a daughter named Lucy born May 16 1764. Baptized Mar: 15 1765. p. 70.

John Horn & Sarah Perkins a Daughter named Mary born decr. 30 1755. Baptized 1756 May 30. p. 48.

John Horn & Sarah Perkins a Daughter called Massie born Aug: 3. 1760. Baptized 1760 Oct: 12. p. 58.

John Horn & Sarah Perkins a son named Nicholas born Nov: 25 1762. Baptized 1763 Mar: 31. p. 64.

Jo: Christopher Horn & Sally Thomson, a child Nancy-Sally born Jul: 5 1785. Baptized Sep: 3 1785. p. 115.

Charles Houchins & Lucy Clements a son named Jesse born feb: 27 1758. Baptized 1758 May 14. p. 52.

Char: Houchins & Lucy Clements a son named Charles born Nov: 22 1759. Baptized 1759 Dec: 9. p. 56.

Charles Hugens & Lucy Clements a Daughter named Anna born Jul: 12. 1762. Baptized 1762 Aug: 15. p. 63.

Charles Houchins & Lucy Clements a son named John born Jun: 20 1765. Baptized Jul: 28 1765. p. 72.

Charles Houchins & Lucy Clements a Daughter named Elizabeth born Jan: 26 1768. Baptized Ap: 1 1768. p. 80.

Charles Houchins & Lucy Clement a son named William born Sep: 17, 1770. Baptized Nov. 11 1770. p. 88.

Charles Houchins & Lucy Clements a daughter named Mary born Ap. 16, 1773. Baptized Jun. 13, 1773. p. 94.

Charles Huchins & Lucy Clements a son named Joshua born Jan. 1, 1776. Baptized Ap. 28, 1777. p. 100.

Cha: Houchins & Lucy Clements a Son Edward born Nov. 14, 1781. Baptized Mar. 28, 1782. p. 106.

Cha: Houchins & Ann Towler a son William born May 4, 1782. Baptized July 21, 1782. p. 107.

ffrancis Houchins & Joyce Clements a son named Edward born feb: 28 1760. Baptized 1760 Ap: 8. p. 57.

ffrancis Houchins & Joicye Clements a Daughter named Eliza born Mar: 8 176—* Baptized 1762 Ap: 11. p. 62.

*Margin torn.

ffrancis Houchins & Joice Clements a son named ffrancis born feb: 17 1764. Baptized Ap: 1 1764. p. 67.

Francis Huchins & Joyce Clements a Daughter named Mary born feb: 9 1767. Baptized Mar: 29 1767. p. 76.

Francis Houchins & Joice Clements a son named Stephen born Mar: 19 1769. Baptized Ap: 23 1769. p. 84.

Francis Huchins & Joyce Clements a son named John born Jan. 25 1772. Baptized Aug 11 1771. p. 90.

Francis Houchins & Joyce Salmons a daughter named Susan born Jan 23, 1774. Baptized Mar. 13, 1774. p. 96.

Francis Huchins & Joyce Clements a daughter named Lucy born Sep 1, 1777. Baptized Oct. 19, 1777. p. 102.

Francis Houchins & Joice Clements a child Nancy born Nov. 15 1782. Baptized Ap: 19 1783. p. 109.

Da: Howard & Judith Lane a son Pleasants born Jan. 8, 1782. Baptized May 26 1782. p. 106.

Drury Howard & Mary Lane a son named David born Oct: 25, 1760. Baptized 1761 Jan 18. p. 58.

Drury Howard & Mary Lane a son named Allen born Mar: 23 1763. Baptized 1763 May 8. p. 64.

Drury Howard & Mary Lane a son named James born Jun: 16 1765. Baptized Jan: 19 1766. p. 72.

Drury Howard & Mary Lane a son named Thomas born Mar: 16 1768. Baptized Aug: 25 1768. p. 81.

Drury Howard & Mary Lane a son named Archie born May 13, 1771. June 2, 1773. p. 94.

James Howard & Jeanie Bowen a Daughter named Severa born Jun: 10 1768. Baptized Aug: 20 1768. p. 81.

James Howard & Jeanie Bowen a son named Benjamin born Nov: 31 1770. Baptized Feb: 21 1771. p. 89.

James Howard & Jeanie Bourn a daughter named Susannah born May 19, 1772. Baptized Aug 21, 1772. p. 92.

James Howard & Jeanie Bowen a daughter named Sarah born Nov. 15, 1773. Baptized Jun. 23, 1774. p. 97.

James Howard & Jeanie Bonds a son named Lindsay born Nov. 28, 1775. Baptized Ap. 11, 1776. p. 100.

Ja: Howard & Jean Bowen, twins Mally Vaughan & Jeansie Ann Sep. 22, 1782. Baptized Feb. 28, 1783. p. 108.

John Howard & Eliz: Stanley a son named James born Nov: 14 1765. Baptized May 17 1766. p. 74.

John Howard & Eliz: Stanley a Daughter named Molly born feb: 17 1769. Baptized Ap: 20 1769. p. 84.

Will: Howard & Rebekah Morgan a Daughter named Elizabeth born Oct: 19 1761. Baptized 1762 feb: 6. p. 61.

Will: Howard & Rebekah Morgan a Daughter named Susannah born dec: 2 1763. Baptized Mar: 3 1764. p. 66.

Will: Howard & Rebekah Morgan a son named Allen born Nov: 12 1766. Baptized Jan: 17 1767. p. 76.

Will: Howard & Judith Amos a Son named Alland born Mar: 13. 1756. Baptized 1756 May 16. p. 48.

William Howard & Judith Hemus a son named John born Aug: 20 1760. Baptized 1760 Sep: 28. p. 58.

William Howard and Judith Amos a daughter named Betty born Sep: 13 1766. Baptized Jun: 11 1767. p. 78.

Absolem Howel & Ann Holland a son named Absolom born Jul: 11 1770. Baptized Sep: 2 1770. p. 88.

John Howgens & Martha Orford a Daughter named Elizabeth born Jun: 14. 1763. Baptized 1763 Sep: 25. p. 65.

Rich: Howle & Ann Walker a daughter named Mally born Jan 16 1775. Baptized Ap. 16, 1775. p. 98.

Will: Howarton & Bathsheba Perry a son James, born June 8 1782. Baptized Oct: 23 1784. p. 113.

Will: Howverton & Barbara Perry, Barsheba Nov. 7 1784. Baptized Oct. 23 1785. p. 115.

Dan: Hubbard & Sar: Pasture a son named Joseph born Mar: 26. 1781. Baptized Jan. 4, 1782. p. 105.

John Hubbard & Elizabeth Clark a son named Jesse born feb: 11 1764. Baptized Ap: 8 1764. p. 67.

John Hubbard & Elizabeth Clark a Daughter named Judith born Jan: 2 1766. Baptized Ap: 13 1766. p. 73.

Thomas Hubbard & Margaret Kirk a Son named James born Nov: 17. 1756. Baptized 1757 feb: 27. p. 50.

Tho: Hubbard & Mary Kirk a son named William born Oct: 13 1758. Baptized 1758 Nov: 19. p. 53.

Thomas Hubbard & Margaret Kirk a son named Benjamin born Jul: 15 1760. Baptized 1760 Oct: 5. p. 58.

Thomas Hubbard & Margaret Kirk a son named Christopher born Aug: 5. 1762. Baptized 1763 Jun: 10. p. 64.

Thomas Hubbard & Margaret Kirk a Daughter named Anne-Kirk born Ap: 18 1764. Baptized Jul: 19 1764. p. 68.

Thomas Hubert & Margaret Kirk a Daughter named Winnifred born Jul: 15 1766. Baptized Aug: 15 1767. p. 78.

Tho: Hubbard & Marg: Kirk a son named Stephen: Shilton born Ap: 24 1770. Baptized Aug: 12 1770. p. 88.

Huckabee, John, & Ellis Camp a son named John born Mar: 4 1768. p. 81.

Ja: Huckstep & Eliz: Dobb a son David born May 7 1784. Baptized May 30 1784. p. 111.

Sam Huchstep & Nanny Harris a daughter named Rachel born Oct 14, 1771. Baptized 1772. p. 91.

Benjamin Hudlestone & Eliz: Pankie a son named Stephen born May 10 1766. Baptized Jul: 14 1766. p. 74.

Benjamin Hudlestone & Eliz: Pankie a son named Peyton born Jun: 11 1768. Baptized Aug: 19 1768. p. 81.

David Hudlestone & Sarah Easly a son named William born Jun: 8 1761. Baptized 1761 Jul: 12. p. 60.

Charles Hudlesey & Hannah Witt a son named Charles born Jul: 2 1756. Baptized 1756 Jul: 11. p. 49.

William Hudnel & ffanney Smith a Daughter named Susannah born Sep: 13 1758. Baptized 1759 Jan: 11. p. 54.

William Hudnel & Frances Smith a Daughter named Frankey born Sep: 20, 1760. Baptized 1761 Jul: 19. p. 60.

William H[u]dnell & ffrancis Smith a son named John born Jun: 29 1763. Baptized 1763 Jul: 3. p. 64.

William Hudnel & ffrances Smith a Daughter named Molly born Dec: 1 1765. Baptized Dec: 23 1765. p. 72.

William Hudnel & Frances Smith a Daughter named Joanna born Mar: 5 1768. Baptized Jun: 15 1768. p. 81.

Benjamin Hughes & Rebekah Cothan a Daughter named Mary born Jan: 11. 1757. Baptized 1757 Mar. 13. p. 50.

Ben: Hughes & Rebekah Cothan a Daughter named Eliz: born dec: 28, 1759. Baptized 1760 ffeb: 10. p. 56.

Benjamin Hughes & Rebekah Cothan a son named Tarlton born May 7. 1763. Baptized 1763 May 26. p. 64.

Benjamin Hughes & Rebekah Cauthon a son named Benjamin born Jul: 10 1767. Baptized Dec: 6 1767. p. 79.

John Hughes was baptized this day—born Jan: 24 1739. Baptized Jan: 15 1767. p. 76.

John Hughes & Judith Nevil a Daughter born Ap: 3 1758 named Judith. Baptized Jan: 15 1767. p. 76.

John Hughes & Judith Nevil a Daughter named Elizabeth born Sep. 25 1759. Baptized Jan: 15 1767. p. 76.

John Hughes & Judith Nevil a Daughter named Sally born May 24 1761. Baptized Jan: 15 1767. p. 76.

John Hughes & Judith Nevil a son named John born Aug: 11 1763. Baptized Jan: 15 1767. p. 76.

John Hughes & Judith Nevil a Daughter named Nancy born Nov: 13 1765. Baptized Jan: 15 1767. p. 76.

John Hughes & Judith Nevil a Daughter named Judith born Feb: 15 1768. Baptized Mar: 11 1768. p. 80.

John Hughes & Judith Nevil a daughter named Mary born Jul. 17. 1770. Baptized Jan. 23. 1772. p. 91.

John Hughes & Mary Grant a Daughter named ffrances born dec: 15 1763. Baptized Jan: 4 1764. p. 66.

John Hughes & Mary Grant a son named William born Jun: 12 1768. Baptized Jul: 27 1768. p. 81.

John Hughes & Mary Grant a daughter named Ann born Dec. 20 1769. Baptized Ap: 1 1770. p. 87.

John Hughes & Mary Grant a daughter named Elizabeth born Feb. 25, 1772. Baptized Jun. 7, 1772. p. 92.

John Hughes & Mary Grant a daughter named Sarah born Aug 28. 1773. Baptized Oct. 14, 1773. p. 95.

John Hughes & Mary Grant a son named Peter: Grant born May 17, 1775. Baptized Aug. 5, 1775. p. 98.

John Hughes & Mary Grant a daughter named Jeanie born Sep. 29, 1776. Baptized Oct 15, 1776. p. 100.

Jo: Hughes & Mary Grant a child Ann Gilbert born Mar: 1 1783. Baptized Nov: 4 1783. p. 110.

Joshua Hughes & Caroline Stringer a Son named David born Mar. 31, 1781. Baptized Jul. 15, 1781. p. 103.

Joshua Hughes & Caroline Stringer, Ruth-Watson, Jan. 17 1786. Baptized Aug: 6 1786. p. 117.

Rice Hughes & Lucy Gardner a son named Will-Gardener born May 16 1766. Baptized Jun: 15 1766. p. 74.

Rice Hughes & Lucy Gardner a son named Anthony born Nov: 14 1768. Baptized Feb: 5 1769. p. 83.

Rice Hughes & Christian Terrie a child named Ann born Ap. 21, 1781. Baptized Nov. 4, 1781. p. 105.

Rice Hughes & Christian Terry a son Thomas born Aug. 10 1783. Baptized Oct: 4 1783. p. 110.

Rice Hughes & Christian Tyrry a child Polly born Mar: .... 1785. Baptized May 1 1785. p. 114.

Sim: Hughes & Martha Biggars a son John born June 22 1783. Baptized Sep: 11 1783. p. 110.

Will Hughes & Susannah Bowles a daughter named Nancy born Jan. 21, 1776. Baptized Mar. 3, 1776. p. 99.

Will: Hughes & Susannah Bowles a daughter named Betsy born Feb. 10, 1776. Baptized Mar. 16. 1777. p. 101.

Will Hughes & Susannah Bowles a daughter named Sally born Mar: 25, 1778. Baptized May 10, 1778. p. 103.

Will Hughes & Susannah Bowles a Son Thomas born May 12. 1782. Baptized Sep. 1. 1782. p. 107.

Will: Hughes & Susannah Bowles a son William born Ap: 12 1784. Baptized May 9 1784. p. 111.

Will Hughes & Sarah Murray a son Jo: Murray born Aug. 26 1784. Baptized Oct. 3 1784. p. 113.

Will: Hughes & Sarah Murray, a son Antony, June 13; 1786. Baptized Jul: 16 1786. p. 117.

Billie Hughes & Sarah Murray a child Mary Ap: 11 1788. Baptized Aug. 11 1788. p. 121.

John Hulcher & Susannah George a daughter named Susannah born Jul: 22, 1776. Baptized Aug. 10, 1776. p. 100.

Charles Hulsey & Anna Witt a Daughter named Parthenia born Jul: 1. 1759. Baptized 1759 Sep: 29. p. 56.

John Humber & Eliz: Christian a son named John born Jan: 6 1764. Baptized Jan: 29 1764. p. 66.

David Humphrey & Jean Taylor a son named David born Dec: 18 1765. Baptized May 17 1766. p. 74.

Jo: Humphrey & Sally Young a child Nancy born June 12 1784. Baptized Sep: 12 1786. p. 117.

George Hunter & Mildred Miller a Son named Augustine born Jun: 6 1761. Baptized 1761 Jul: 5. p. 60.

George Hunter & Mildred Austine a Daughter named Lucy born Nov: 25 1763. Baptized Jan: 5 1764. p. 66.

George Hunter & Mildred Austine a Daughter named Ann born Aug: 9 1766. Baptized Sep: 20, 1766. p. 25.

George Hulton [Hunter] & Mildred Austine a son named David born Mar: 24 1769. Baptized May 21 1769. p. 84.

George Hunter & Mildred Austin a son named Samuel born Jan 12, 1773. Baptized May 9, 1773. p. 94.

Peter Hunter & Ann Cash in Louisa a Daughter named Delphe born Jul: 3 1765. Baptized Aug: 3 1765. p. 72.

Peter Hunter & Ann Cash a Daughter named Sarah born Nov: 20 1768. Baptized Jan: 28 1769. p. 83.

Peter Hunter & Ann Cash a daughter named Peggie born Aug. 31, 1773. Baptized Dec. 5, 1773. p. 95.

Peter Hunter & Ann Cash a son named Peter born Mar. 16, 1776. Baptized May 15, 1776. p. 100.

Stephen Hunter & Mary Steatum a son named Charles born Nov: 7 1766. Baptized Jun: 11 1767. p. 77.

Stephen Hunter & Mary Steatum a son named Will: born Oct: 18 1768. Baptized Nov: 10 1768. p. 82.

Stephen Hunter & Mary Statum a son named Samuel born Ap. 22, 1774. Baptized Jun. 6, 1774. p. 96.

Will: Hunter & Charity Loftus a son named John born Jun: 16, 1760. Baptized 1760 Jul: 25. p. 58.

William Hunter & Charity Loftus a son named William born Mar: 20 1765. Baptized Ap: 21 1765. p. 71.

William Hunter & Charity Loftis a son named George born Jul: 10 1768. Baptized Aug: 10 1768. p. 81.

Jo: Hutchison & Mary Steers a child Mary Lewis born Jul: 26 1783. Baptized Aug. 13 1784. p. 112.

Jo: Hutcheson & Mary Stears a child Jean Stears, born Nov. 21 1785. Baptized Mar: 8 1786. p. 116.

Rob: Hutchison & Phebe Carter, Rob: Waggoner born Sep. 13, 1782. Baptized Feb. 25, 1783. p. 108.

Rob: Hutchison & Phebe Carter, William, born Jul 6 1784. Baptized Oct. 23 1785. p. 115.

Will Hutcheson & Sarah Reid a child named Nancy born Dec. 20, 1780. Baptized May 13, 1781. p. 103.

Will Hutchison & Sarah Red a son Thomas, born Mar. 15 1783. Baptized Mar. 8 1786. p. 116.

Will Hutchison & Sarah Red a son Washington born Dec. 1 1783. Baptized Mar. 8 1786. p. 116.

Tho: Hutten & Susannah Green a son named William born Oct 4, 1775. Baptized Nov. 12, 1775. p. 99.

Thomas Imbry & Ann Jackson a Son named Joseph born Mar: 10 1758. Baptized 1758 Ap: 30. p. 52.

Tho: Imbry & Ann Jackson a son named William born feb: 14 1760. Baptized 1760 Ap: 4. p. 57.

John Ingle & Mary Huchins a Son named Joshua born May 10. 1758. Baptized 1758 Jun: 7. p. 52.

William Ingle & Ann Nash a Daughter named Elizabeth born Oct:
20 1766. Baptized Aug: 2 1767. p. 78.

Alexr Inglis & Mary Kavanaugh a Daughter named Jean born
Mar: 5. 1760. Baptized 1760 Mar: 12. p. 57.

Will: Ingram & Ann Hawkins a son Wyat born Aug. 13 1783.
Baptized Oct. 10 1783. p. 110.

Will: Ingram & Ann Hawkins a child Louisa born Jan: 19 1786.
Baptized Mar: 20 1786. p. 116.

Will Ingram & Hannah Hawkins, Amelia, June 19 1788.   Baptized Aug. 3 1789. p. 125.

Will Ingram & Hannah Hawkins, Matilda, May 21 1789.   Baptized Aug. 3 1789. p. 125.

James Isabel & Eliz: Coleman a daughter named Nancy born Nov.
2, 1776. Baptized Nov. 20, 1776. p. 101.

Lewis Isabel & Hannah Anderson a son named William born June
1s, 1777. Baptized July 26, 1777. p. 102.

William Isabel & Ann Dillard a son named Christopher born Mar:
5, 1757. Baptized 1757 Ap: 9. p. 50.

Will: Isabel & Ann Dillard a son named Henry born Oct: 3 1761.
Baptized 1762 Mar: 14. p. 62.

Will: Isabel & Ann Dilliard a son named Thomas: Dilliard born
Dec: 23, 1762. Baptized 1763 Ap: 17. p. 64.

William Isabel & Ann Dillard a son named Benjamin born Mar:
18 1764. Baptized May 20 1764. p. 67.

William Isabel & Ann Dillard a son named Zachariah born Dec: 1
1765. Baptized Feb: 9 1766. p. 73.

William Isabel & Ann Dillard a Daughter named Sarah born Jul:
26 1767. Baptized Nov: 1 1767. p. 79.

Will: Isabel & Ann Dillard a daughter named Mary born Dec:
3 1770. Baptized Mar: 24 1771. p. 89.

Cha: Jackson & Jean Anderson a sun Thomas born Jan: 20 1783.
Baptized May 18 1783. p. 109.

Cha: Jackson & Jean Anderson a son William born Nov. 9 1784.
Baptized Mar: 22 1785. p. 113.

Ch: Jackson & Jane Anderson a son John born Nov. 11 1786.
Baptized Ap: 15 1787. p. 118.

Jarvis Jackson & Helena Lee a Daughter named Helena born Aug:
21. 1758. Baptized 1758 Sep: 17. p. 53.

John Jackson & Eliz: Hodges a Daughter named Mary born feb:
17 1763. Baptized 1763 Ap: 24. p. 64.

John Jackson & Elizabeth Hodges a Daughter named Jeanie born
Nov: 3 1764. Baptized May 26 1765. p. 71.

John Jackson & Elizabeth Hodges a Daughter named Ann born
May 2 1766. Baptized Aug: 31 1766. p. 75.

John Jackson & Elizabeth Hodges a son named Joel born Dec: 9
1767. Baptized May 22 1768. p. 81.

John Jackson & Eliz: Hodges a Daughter named Elizabeth born feb: 23 1770. Baptized Jul: 29 1770. p. 88.

Joseph Jackson & Susannah Carter a son named William born Jan: 4 1765. Baptized Mar: 28 1765. p. 70.

Will Jackson & Susan Goodwin a child named Ann born Sep. 13, 1781. Baptized Oct 28, 1781. p. 105.

Will: Jackson & Susanna Goodwin a son Thomas born Feb. 24 1783. Baptized Aug: 10 1783. p. 110.

Richard James & Mary Turpine a son named ffrancis born Dec: 30 1761. Baptized 1762 Ap: 8. p. 62.

Richard James & Mary Turpine a Daughter named Polly-Fields born Nov: 6 1765 (sic). Baptized May 9 1765. p. 71.

Richard James & Mary Turpine a Daughter named Catie born feb: 28 1766. Baptized Jan: 15 1767. p. 75.

Richard James & Mary Turpine a son named Thomas born .... Baptized Oct: 31 1768. p. 82.

Will James & Mary Hinds a daughter named Ann born Feb. 24. 1777. Baptized Ap. 8, 1777. p. 101.

Will James & Mary Hinds a son William born Ap. 27, 1782. Baptized May 31, 1782. p. 106.

Will James & Mary Hinds a son Thomas born Dec. 14 1783. Baptized Apl. 17 1784. p. 111.

Isreal Jenkins & Ann Holland a son William, born May 18 1782. Baptized June 28 1783. p. 110.

Philip Johns & Eliz: Wright a Daughter named Mary born Ap: 22, 1760. Baptized 1760 May 25. p. 57. [See Jones.]

Benjamin Johnson & Susannah Pace a Daughter named Margaret born May 13. 1760. Baptized 1760 Jun: 8. p. 57.

Benjamin Johnson & Susannah Pace a son named Joseph born Nov: 9. 1761. Baptized 1761 Dec: 25. p. 61.

Benjamin Johnson & Susannah Pace a son named Benjamin born Nov: 18 1763. Baptized Jan: 1 1764. p. 66.

Benjamin Johnson & Susannah Pace a Daughter named Susannah born Oct: 17 1765. Baptized Dec: 25 1765. p. 72.

Benjamin Johnson & Susannah Peirce a son named William born dec: 16 1768. Baptized Feb: 19 1769. p. 83.

Ben: Johnson & Susannah Pierce a son named Curtis born Sep: 21 1770. Baptized Dec 23: 1770. p. 89.

Benjamin Johnson & Susan Pearse a daughter named Elizabeth born Nov. 25, 1776. Baptized Jan. 26, 1777. p. 101.

Benjamin Johnson & Martha Hughes a son named Thomas born Ap: 27 1767. Baptized Jun: 28 1767. p. 78.

Benjamin Johnson & Martha Hughes a Daughter named Jean born Oct: 14 1768. Baptized Feb: 5 1769. p. 83.

Ben Johnson & Martha Hughes a Daughter named Mary born Dec 1, 1770. Baptized May 12 1771. p. 89.

Ben: Johnson & Martha Hughes a daughter named Ffrances: Anderson born Sep. 23, 1772. Baptized Dec. 23, 1772. p. 93.

Ben Johnson & Martha Hughes a son named Benjamin born Sep. 10, 1774. Baptized Jan. 21, 1775. p. 97.

Ben Johnson & Martha Hughes a son named Isham born May 14, 1776. Baptized June 16, 1776. p. 100.

Ben: Johnson & Martha Hughes a child Charity born Oct. 21 1782. Baptized Ap: 18 1784. p. 111.

Ben: & Peggie Johnston a son Thomas born Aug. 19 1783. Baptized Jul: 8 1787. p. 119.

Ben: & Peggie Johnston Molly Thomson born Feb. 20 1786. Baptized Jul: 8 1787. p. 119.

Charles Johnston & Agnes Thomson a Daughter named Agnes born Mar: 30. 1757. Baptized 1757 May 8. p. 50.

Charles Johnson & Hannah Thompson a son named Benjamin born feb: 16 1761. Baptized 1761 Ap: 12. p. 59.

Cha: Johnson & Mary Ann Ferrar in Goochland, Ann, Dec. 16 1783. Baptized June 16 1787. p. 119.

Cha: Johnson & Mary Ann Ferrar in Goochland, Cha. Jones born Feb. 16 1788. Baptized Oct. 24 1788. p. 121.

Charles Johnson & Eliz. Edwards a daughter Mally born Dec. 7, 1772. Baptized Ap. 4, 1773. p. 94.

Daniel Johnson & Hannah Edwards a Daughter named Martha born Nov: 5, 1756. Baptized 1757 feb: 27. p. 50.

Daniel Johnson & Hannah Edwards a son named Jesse born Jul: 23. 1759. Baptized 1759 Sep: 9. p. 55.

Daniel Johnson & Hannah Edwards a Daughter named Ann born Oct: 23. 1761. Baptized 1761 Dec: 23. p. 61.

Daniel Johnstone & Hannah Edwards a son named Thomas born Jun: 15 1764. Baptized Aug: 12 1764. p. 68.

Dan: Johnson & Jean Woodie a Son named Stanhope born feb: 27, 1758. Baptized 1758 Ap: 25. p. 52.

David Johnson & Lucy Ellis a Daughter named Sarah born Mar: 14. 1763. Baptized 1763 Jun: 10. p. 64.

David Johnson & Lucy Ellis a Daughter named Ann born Oct 19 1764. Baptized Dec: 23 1764. p. 69.

David Johnson & Lucy Ellis a son named William born Dec: 11 1767. Baptized Ap: 5 1767. p. 77.

David Johnson & Lucy Ellis a Daughter named Susannah born Oct: 20 1769. Baptized Ap: 2 1770. p. 87.

David Johnson & Lucy Ellis a son named James born Ap. 2, 1772. Baptized Aug 30, 1772. p. 93.

David Johnson & Lucy Ellis a daughter named Lucy born Dec. 25, 1774. Baptized Mar. 21, 1775. p. 98.

David Johnson & Lucy Ellis a son named David born Sep. 11, 1777. Baptized Oct 14. 1777. p. 102.

Da: Johnson & Lucy Ellis a child Betty Ware born Sep: 25 1783. Baptized Ap: 18 1784. p. 111.

David Johnson —Mary Berryman a son named Thomas Jan: 11 1769. Baptized Mar: 6 1769. p. 83.

Drury Johnston & Hannah Clark a Son named Jacob born May 15. 1752. Baptized 1756 Aug: 22. p. 49.

Drury Johnston & Hannah Clark a Daughter named Jeanie born June 5th 1754. Baptized 1757 Mar. 6. p. 50.

Drury Johnson & Han: Clark a son named Elijah born Oct: 30, 1756. Baptized 1756 Dec: 26. p. 49.

Drury Johnson & Hannah Clark a Daughter named Ann born Jun: 23 1758. Baptized 1758 Jul: 23. p. 53.

Drury Johnson & Hannah Clark a Son named Clayborn born Jun: 17. 1760. Baptized 1760 Aug: 23. p. 58.

Drury Johnston & Hannah Clark a Daughter named Mary born Nov: 23 1762. Baptized Jul: 19 1764. p. 68.

Drury Johnson & Hannah Clark a daughter named Sarah born Ap. 28, 1765. Baptized Jul. 15, 1771. p. 90.

Drury Johnson & Hannah Clark a son named James born Jan 3, 1768. Baptized Jul. 15, 1771. p. 90.

Drury Johnson & Hannah Clark a son named Benjamin born Mar 15, 1771. Baptized Jul. 15, 1771. p. 90.

Drury Johnson & Hannah Clark a son named Isham born Feb. 24, 1773. Baptized Aug. 22, 1773. p. 94.

Geo: Johnson & Jean Roe [or Rowe] a child Sally, born Mar: 16 1786. Baptized Jul: 30 1786. p. 117.

Geo: Johnson & Jean Roe a son James born Aug: 4 1789. Baptized Aug. 24 1789. p. 125.

Henry Ashton Johnson & Ann Meekie, Elizabeth born May 7 1786. Baptized Jul: 15 1786. p. 117.

Henry Johnson & Ann Meekie a son Thomas born Jan. 7 1788. Baptized June 8 1788. p. 121.

James Johnston & Mildred Mims a Daughter named Sarah born Aug: 27 1755. Baptized 1756 May 16. p. 48.

James Johnson & Mildred Mims a Daughter named Martha born Aug: 2 1758. Baptized 1759 ffeb: 18. p. 54.

James Johnson & Mildred Mims a Daughter named Mary born Jul: 26 1760. Baptized 1761 Mar: 29. p. 59.

James Johnson & Mildred Mims a son named David born Mar: 17 1762. Baptized 1762 Ap: 11. p. 62.

Ja. Johnson & Mildred Mims, twins, named John & Benjamin born Mar: 17 1764. Baptized Jun: 3 1764. p. 67.

James Johnson & Mildred Mims a Daughter named Judith born Sep: 27 1765. Baptized Aug: 2 1767. p. 78.

James Johnson & Mildred Mims a son named James born Jan: 8 1767. Baptized Aug: 2 1767. p. 78.

James Johnson & Mildred Mims a Daughter named Nansy born Mar 6 1769. Baptized Jun: 4 1769. p. 85.

James Johnson & Rachel Street a son named Charles born Jun: 30. 1758. Baptized 1758 Jul: 30. p. 53.

James Johnston & Rachel Street a Daughter named Elizabeth born Ap: 29 1761. Baptized 1761 May 31. p. 60.

James Johnston & Rachel Street a son named William born Jul: 17. 1763. Baptized 1763 Aug: 21. p. 65.

James Johnson & Rachel Street a son named Jeremiah born Jul: 5 1766. Baptized Aug: 24 1766. p. 75.

James Johnson & Rachel Street a Daughter named Jean born Jan: 5 1769. Baptized Mar: 5 1769. p. 83.

James Johnson & Rachel Street a daughter named Mary born Jul: 23 1771. Baptized Oct: 27 1771. p. 90.

James Johnson & Rachel Haddin a Daughter named Ann born Nov: 29 1760. Baptized 1761 Mar: 22. p. 59.

James Johnson & Rachel Haden a Daughter named Mary born Ap: 19, 1763. Baptized 1763 May 25. p. 64.

James Johnson & Rebekah Martin a Daughter named Sarah born Nov: 4 1766. Baptized Jun: 11 1767. p. 77.

James Johnson & Rebekah Martin a son named William born Aug: 2 1768. Baptized Nov: 3 1768. p. 82.

Ja: Johnson & Rebekah Martin a Daughter named Judith born feb: 16 1771. Baptized Apl 8 1771. p. 89.

Ja: Johnson & Eliz: Clarkson a son William born Jan: 10 1781. Baptized Ap: 21 1783. p. 109.

Ja: Johnson & Eliz: Clarkson a child Jeanie More born Mar: 24 1783. Baptized Ap: 21 1783. p. 109.

Jeremiah Johnson & Susannah Cauthon a Daughter named Rebeckah born Dec. 25 1769. Baptized Ap: 23 1770. p. 87.

Jonathan Johnson & Ann Castle a son William born Dec. 24 1787. Baptized Ap: 27 1788. p. 121.

John Johnson & Hellender Thomson a Daughter named Winnifred born Sep: 19, 1757. Baptized 1757 Sep: 26. p. 51.

John Johnston & Hellender Thomson a Daughter named Hellender born Ap: 14. 1759. Baptized 1759 May 6. p. 55.

John Johnson & Pattie Perrie a Daughter named Mary born Jun: 19. 1760. Baptized 1760 Jun: 24. p. 57.

John Johnson & Martha Perry a Daughter, Margaret, born Jan: 4. 1762. Baptized 1762 feb: 5. p. 61.

John Johnson & Martha Perry a Daughter named Violette born Oct: 15 1763. Baptized Nov: 7 1763. p. 66.

John Johnson & Martha Perry a son named William born Sep: 16 1765. Baptized Mar: 29 1766. p. 73.

John Johnson & Martha Perry a son named John born May 11 1767. Baptized Jul: 5 1767. p. 78.

John Johnson & Martha Perry a son named Daniel born Jan: 18 1769. Baptized Feb: 6 1769. p. 83.

John Johnson & Mary Perry a daughter named Sally born Nov: 26 1770. Baptized Mar: 24 1771. p. 89.

Jo: Johnson & Judith Martin a Son Da: Harris born Dec: 10: 1779. Baptized Oct. 23, 1781. p. 105.

John Johnson & Molly Martin a child Judith Martin Jan 27, 1782. Baptized Nov. 24, 1782. p. 108.

Joseph Johnston & Sarah Harris a Daughter named Ann born Nov: 21 1757. Baptized 1758 Mar: 25. p. 52.

Joseph Johnson & Sarah Harris a son named David born Aug: 13 1760. Baptized 1761 Jul: 12. p. 60.

Joseph Johnson & Sarah Harris a Daughter named Joanna born feb: 19 1765. Baptized May 14 1768. p. 80.

Joseph Johnson & Sarah Harris a son named Thomas born Dec: 2 1767. Baptized May 14 1768. p. 80.

Joseph Johnson & Sar: Freeman a daughter Rebeck-Rollins Jul: 17 1790. Baptized Aug: 15 1790. p. 126.

Jos: Johnson & Sally Freeman a child Rosanna Jul. 20. Baptized Aug. 26 1792. p. 126.

Jos: Jonson & Sar: Freeman had a Letitia Freeman baptized born March 30 1795. Baptized May 26 1795. p. 127.

Richard Johnston & Ann Nichols a son named William born .... 1765. Baptized Jan: 1 1766. p. 72.

Richard Johnson & Ann Nuckols a Daughter named Jean born Ap: 10 1767. Baptized May 23 1767. p. 77.

Rich: Johnson & Ann Nichols a son named Nichols born May 17 1769. Baptized [June] 3 1769. p. 84.

Rich: Johnson & Ann Nichols 2 children christened viz. Baptized Mar. 6, 1774. p. 95.

Rich: Johnson & Ann Nicholas a child Rhoda born June 18. 1782. Baptized Nov. 3, 1782. p. 108.

Rich: Johnson & Dolly Powis [Powers] a son named Reuben Powis born Oct 7, 1772. Baptized Feb. 14, 1773. p. 93.

Richard Johnson & Dorothea Powers a son named Christopher born Oct 25, 1774. Baptized Mar. 24, 1776. p. 99.

Rich: Johnson & Dolly Power a son named Lewis born Feb 13, 1777. Baptized July 27, 1777. p. 102.

Rich: Johnson & Dorothy Powers a Son Francis born Mar. 19, 1782. Baptized June 16, 1782. p. 107.

Rich: Johnson & Susan Garret a Son named George born Nov. 1, 1780. Baptized Oct. 19, 1781. p. 104.

Rich: Johnson & Susanna Garret a child Susanna born Nov. 28 1782. Baptized June 1 1783. p. 109.

Rich: Johnson & Susanna Garret, Henry, born Dec. 23 1784. Baptized Oct. 2 1785. p. 115.

Rich: Johnson & Susanna Garret a daughter Kitty born Dec. 18 1786. Baptized May 17 1787. p. 119.

Rd: Johnson & Susanna Garrett a child John, born Oct: 20 1788. Baptized Oct. 27 1789. p. 122.

Stephen Johnson & Susan: Pierce [Pace] a son named John born Oct: 18 .... Baptized Feb: 15 1767. p. 76.

Stephen Johnson & Susanna Pace a Daughter named Elizabeth born Nov. 15 1768. Baptized Jan: 29 1769. p. 83.

Tho: Johnson & Eliz: Merriwether a Daughter named Elizabeth born Aug: 30, 1763. Baptized 1763 Sep: 14. p. 65.

Tho. Johnson & Eliz. Merriwether a daughter named Lucy born Feb. 27, 177... Baptized Ap. 12, 1773. p. 94.

Tho: Johnson & Eliz: Merriwether a son Thomas born Nov. 14 1783. Baptized Feb. 14 1784. p. 111.

Tho: Johnson & Betsey Merriwether a child born Oct: 10 1786 Ann Merriwether. Baptized Nov: 12 1786. p. 118.

Tho: Johnson & Ursley Green a daughter named Sally born Jan 21, 1774. Baptized Ap. 10, 1774. p. 96.

Maj: Tho: Johnson & Urcila Row, a child Lucy born July 14 1781. Baptized Aug. 21 1785. p. 115.

Maj: Tho: Johnson & Urcila Row, a son James born Sep: 29 1783. Baptized Aug. 21 1785. p. 115.

Maj: Tho: Johnson & Urcila Row, a child Alicia, born Jan: 25 1785. Baptized Aug. 21 1785. p. 115.

Townell Johnson & Jean Woodie a son named Edward born Jun: 28. 1760. Baptized 1761 Sep: 8. p. 61.

Will: Johnson & Christian Leek a Daughter named Judith born Ap: 13, 1751. p. 41.

Will: Johnson & Christian Leek a Son named William born Jun: 18, 1753. p. 41.

Will: Johnson & Christian Leek a Son named Walter born Sep: 23, 1755. p. 41.

Will: Johnson & Christian Leek a Son named Samuel born Nov: 17, 1757. p. 41.

Will: Johnson & Christian Leek a Son named Manoah born Jul: 13, 1759. p. 41.

Will: Johnson & Christian Leek a Son named Jeremiah born feb: 14, 1762. p. 41.

William Johnson & Christian Leek a son named Stephen born Sep: 20 1763. Baptized Nov: 20 1763. pp. 41, 66.

Will: Johnson & Christian Leek a Daughter named Christian born Feb: 15, 1767. p. 41.

William Johnson & Christian Leek a son named Josiah born Ap: 24 1769. Baptized Jul: 4 1769. pp. 41, 85.

Will: Johnson & Eliz: Huchison a Son named Thomas born Oct: 9 1756. Baptized 1757 Jan: 16. p. 49.

William Johnston & Eliz: Hutchison a son named William born Jun: 23. 1758. Baptized 1758 Aug: 13. p. 53.

William Johnson & Elizabeth Hutchison a Daughter name Betty born May 7. 1760. Baptized 1760 Jun: 24. p. 57.

William Johnson & Eliz: Mills a Son named Jeremiah born Jun: 15. 1757. Baptized 1757 Jul: 17. p. 51.

William Johnston & Eliz: Mills a Daughter named Judith born Jun: 2 1758. Baptized 1758 Aug: 13. p. 53.

Will: Johnson & Eliz: Mills a son named William born May 23. 1761. Baptized 1761 Jun: 28. p. 60.

Will: Johnson & Mary Weaver, a son named Daniel born Sep: 4 1771. Baptized Oct: 27 1771. p. 90.

Da: Jones & Betty Golson a Son named David born Feb. 12, 1782. Baptized Mar. 24, 1782. p. 106.

Godfred Jones & Mary McBride a son named Edward born Ap: 24 1767. Baptized June 8 1767. p. 77.

Godfrey Jones & Mary McBride a Daughter named Sally born Oct: 26 1768. Baptized Feb: 5 1769. p. 83.

Godfrey Jones & Mary McBride a Daughter named Elizabeth born Aug 10 1770. Baptized Oct 21 1770. p. 88.

Godfrey Jones & Mary McBride a son named Ben: Williamson born Jun 30, 1774. Baptized Mar. 21, 1775. p. 98.

Godfrey Jones & Mary McBride a .... Baptized Oct 13, 1777. p. 102.

Godfrey Jones & Mary McBride a .... Baptized Oct 13, 1777. p. 102.

[Harrison Jones] & Ruth Addison a Daughter named Ann born feb: 5, 1757. Baptized 1757 Mar. 20. p. 50.

Harrison Jones & Ruth Addison a Daughter named Susannah born Jan: 15 1—*. Baptized 1760 ffeb: 17. p. 56.

Harrison Jones & Ruth Addison a Daughter named Mary born Nov: 23 1761. Baptized 1762 feb: 14. p. 61.

Harrison Jones & Ruth Atterson a Daughter named Elizabeth born Jun: 9 1764. Baptized Jul: 15 1764. p. 68.

Harrison Jones & Ruth Addison a Daughter named Martha born Jan: 16 1767. Baptized May 31 1767. p. 77.

Harrison Jones & Ruth Addison a Daughter named Martha born Oct: 29 1768. Baptized Feb: 22 1769. p. 83.

Ja: Jones & Mary Golstone a child Elizabeth born Ap. 13, 1782. Baptized June 9 1782. p. 106.

Ja: Jones & Mary Golston a son Thomas born Ap: 19 1784. Baptized June 14 1784. p. 112.

John Jones & Lucy Mallory a Daughter named Lydia born Jan: 24 1761. Baptized 1761 Mar: 1. p. 59.

John Jones & Lucy Mallory a son named Jesse born Jun: 7 1764. Baptized Jul: 15 1764. p. 68.

Jo: Jones & Susanna Timberlick a child Frankie Norman born Dec. 28 1783. p. 111.

Philip Jones & Eliz: Wright a son named William born Mar: 14, 1758. Baptized 1758 Ap: 30. p. 52. [See Johns.]

Tho: Jones & Esther Thomas a Daughter named ffanny born May 17 1769. Baptized Jul: 16 1769. p. 85.

Thomas Jones & Esther Thomas a son named James born Jun. 27, 1772. Baptized Aug. 2, 1772. p. 92.

Tho: Jones & Sarah Partlow a child Lucy-Mary 1784. Baptized Jan: 14 1786. p. 116.

James Jordan & Sarah Stodghill a son named John born Jun: 15. 1761. Baptized 1761 Jul: 26. p. 60.

*Margin torn.

James Jordan & Sarah Stodgehill a son named James born May 8, 1763. Baptized 1763 Jun: 26. p. 64.

James Jordan & Sarah Stodghill a son named Charles-ffleming born Mar 28 1764. Baptized Jun: 17 1764. p. 68.

James Jordan & Sarah Stodghill a son named Samuel born Jun: 22 1766. Baptized Aug. 24 1766. p. 75.

James Jordan & Sarah Stodghill a son named Myles born Jan: 26 1769. Baptized Mar: 5 1769. p. 83.

James Jordan & Sarah Stodghill a Daughter named Elizabeth. Born May 13 1770. Baptized Jul 1. 1770. p. 88.

James Jordan & Sar: Stogehill a daughter named Sarah born Feb. 7, 1772. Baptized 1772. p. 91.

James Jordan & Sarah Stodghill a son named Reuben born Ap. 19, 1773. Baptized May 16, 1773. p. 94.

James Jordan & Sarah Stodghill a Son named John born Jan 21, 1775. Baptized Ap. 18, 1775. p. 98.

Mathew Jordan & Mary Stodghill a Daughter named Elizabeth born Jul: 21 1764. Baptized Sep: 3 1764. p. 69.

Mathew Jordan & Mary Stodghill a Daughter named Helena born Nov: 24 1766. Baptized Jan: 17 1767. p. 76.

Mat: Jordan & Mary Stodghill a son named Mathew born Mar: 24 1769. Baptized May 21 1769. p. 84.

Math: Jordan & Mary Stodghill a daughter named Mary born Jan. 19, 1772. Baptized Mar. 29, 1772. p. 93.

Math: Jordan & Mary Stodghill a son named Reeves born May 6 1775. Baptized June 25, 1775. p. 98.

William Jordan & Eliz. Woodson a son named Woodson born Dec. 27, 1772. Baptized Jun. 2, 1773. p. 94.

Eliz. Woodson about 17 years of age was christened this day now *Mrs. Jordan.* Baptized Dec. 15, 1771. p. 91.

John Ker & Eliz: Henderson a Daughter named ffrances born Jan: 23 1758. Baptized 1758 Ap: 23. p. 52.

John Ker & Eliz: Henderson a son named James born Ap: 11 1760. Baptized 1760 Jul: 27. p. 58.

James Kill & Morning Parish a Daughter named Dicea born Aug: 6, 1756. Baptized 1756 Sep: 5. p. 49.

James Kid & Morning Parish a Daughter named Sally born feb: 3 1761. Baptized 1761 Mar: 29. p. 59.

John Kid & Ruth Parish a son named Norman born Sep: 19 1758. Baptized 1758 Oct: 15. p. 53.

Lewis & Obedience Kids a Daughter named Nansie born Aug: 10, 1759. Baptized 1759 Sep: 30. p. 56.

Lewis Kid & Obedience Kid a Daughter named Patsie born Sep: 25 1767. Baptized Oct: 16 1768. p. 82.

Martin Kie & Ann Bibb a son named James born feb. 17 1768. Baptized Jun: 12 1768. p. 81.

Jo: Kilshaw & Sally Parish a child Catherine Feb: 8 1785. Baptized May 21 1787. p. 119.

Jo: Kilshaw & Sally Parish Elizabeth, July 8 1786. Baptized May 21 1787. p. 119.

Micajah Kimbro & Eliz: McNamara, a son named Nathaniel born Oct: 7 1770. Baptized Ap: 8 1771. p. 89.

Jos: Kimbrough & Eliz: Yauncey, a son William, born Jan. 6 1786. Baptized May 8 1786. p. 116.

Joseph Kimbrough & Eliz: Yauncey a child Unity-Yauncey Nov: 27 1787. Baptized Ap: 3 1788. p. 120.

Rob: Kimbro & Sally Smith a son William Smith, Nov: 20 1786. Baptized Mar: 28 1787. p. 118.

Robert Kimbrough & Sally Smith a child Sally born 3 Mch. 1791. Baptized Sept. 5 1791. p. 126.

Tho: Kimbro & Bettie Forster, Will: Forster, born Feb: 21 1786. Baptized Apl: 10 1786. p. 116.

Tho: Kimbrow & Eliz: Foster, James Chiles born Ap: 21 1788. Baptized Aug. 11 1788. p. 121.

Ambrose King & Sarah Brown a daughter named Ann: Chiles Dec 11, 1773. Baptized Feb. 14, 1774. p. 95.

James King & Winnifred Stokes a daughter named Nancy born Mar. 14, 1776. Baptized Sep. 1, 1776. p. 100.

John King & Mary Lipscum a Daughter named Patty born Ap: 6 1766. Baptized Feb: 2 1769. p. 83.

John King & Mary-Meak Lipscum a Daughter named Nunie born Oct: 2 1769. Baptized Mar: 2 1770. p. 87.

Martin King & Martha Guillam a son named Martin born Ap: 21, 1756. Baptized 1756 June 27. p. 49.

Martin King & Martha Gilliam a son named Herman born Ap: 9 1758. Baptized 1758 Ap: 11. p. 52.

Martin King & Martha Guillame a Son named Harman born May 22, 1759. Baptized 1759 Sep: 16 and Nov: 11. pp. 55-56.

Martin King & Martha Guillam a Son named Guillam born Mar: 29 1761. Baptized 1761 Aug: 30. p. 61.

Martin King & Martha Guillam a son named James born Nov: 2 1763. Baptized Mar: 11 1764. p. 67.

John Kirby & Sarah Morton a son named ffrancis born Nov: 4. 1757. Baptized 1758 Ap: 30. p. 52.

Will Kirby & Alley Seay a child named Nancy born Aug: 28, 1781. Baptized Oct. 21, 1781. p. 104.

James Knighton & Barbara Hall a son named Mordecai born Novr. 17th 1796. Baptized April 30 1797. p. 127.

Ja: Knighton & Molly Freeman a child named Moses born Sep: '95. Baptized Feb: 25 1796. p. 127.

Christopher Knowling & Mary Emmerson a daughter named Martha born Oct 28. 175... Baptized 1757 Ap: 11. p. 50.

David Knowling & Mary ffergusson a son named Joseph born May 8 1758. Baptized 1759 Sep: 29. p. 56.

David Knowling & Mary ffergusson a Daughter named Milley born Sep: 1, 1760. Baptized 1761 Jun: 6. p. 60.

David Knowling & Mary ffergusson a son named Abraham born May 3, 1763. Baptized 1763 Sep: 4. p. 65.

James Knowling & Sarah Webster a son named Samuel born Dec. 23, 1777. Baptized May 4, 1777. p. 101.

Ja: Knolling & Sarah Webster a child named Ann born Sep. 5, 1781. Baptized Nov. 18, 1781. p. 105.

John Knowling & Mary Paterson a son named James Pugh born Nov: 22 1765. Baptized Jun: 15 1766. p. 74.

John Knowling & Mary Peterson twins named Sarah & Susannah born Oct. 15 1767. Baptized Jan: 24 1768. p. 79.

Alexr. Lacy & Lucy Chetwood a son named Stephen born Oct: 5 1755. Baptized Mar: 9 1766. p. 73.

Charles Lacy & Eliz: Hudson a son named John born Dec. 9, 1776. Baptized Jul: 6, 1777. p. 102.

Cha: Lacy & Eliz: Hutson a son named Charles born Jan. 30, 1781. Baptized Mar. 17, 1782. p. 105.

Cha: Lacy & Eliz: Hutson Francis Hutson, a son, born Jan: 29 1784. Baptized Aug. 2 1785. p. 114.

Cha: Lacy & Eliz: Hudson a son Thomas born May 6 1788. Baptized Sep. 17 1788. p. 121.

Elkanah Lacy & Mary Brown a Son named Elliot born Oct: 24 1756. Baptized 1757 Jan: 16. p. 49.

Elliot Lacy & Eliz: Young a Daughter in fornication named Susan born Aug: 20 1757. Baptized 1758 Mar: 26. p. 52.

Elliot Lacy & Lucy Chitwood a son named Daniel born May 24. 1763. Baptized 1763 Jul: 24. p. 65.

Elliott Lacy & .... Baptized feb: 25 1770. p. 87.

Mat: Lacy & Susanna Rutherford, Susanna born Jul: .... 1785. Baptized Oct: 17 1787. p. 120.

Nathaniel Lacy & Mary Bootle a son named Jordan born May 2 1764. Baptized Jun: 17 1764. p. 68.

Noble Lad & Judah Damarel a son named Constant born Jan: 1753. Baptized 1758 Oct: 23. p. 53.

Will Ladd & Sarah Chowning a son Wilson, born Nov. 6 1785. Baptized Mar: 8 1786. p. 116.

Will: Loyd & Sar: Chowning twins, Willis & Sar: born Nov: 6 1782. Baptized Sep: 6 1783. p. 110.

Rene Laforce & Agnes Moseby a son named Robert born Aug: 27 1756. Baptized 1757 Jan: 30. p. 50.

Rene Laforce & Agnes Moseby a Daughter named Ann born Aug: 14 1758. Baptized 1758 Nov: 19. p. 53.

Rene Laforce & Agnes Moseby a Daughter named Agnes born Nov: 10 1760. Baptized 1761 May 4. p. 59.

Rene Laforce & Agnes Moseby a Daughter named Judith born Sep: 8 1765. Baptized Sep: 22 1765. p. 72.

Rene Laforce & Agnes Moseby a son named Monsire born Jul: 21 1768. Baptized Mar: 23 1769. p. 84.

Jo: Lancaster & Susan Singleton a child named Martha born Jan: 20, 1781. Baptized Ap. 15, 1781. p. 103.

Nathaniel Lancaster & Hope Walker a son named William born Aug: 2 1765. Baptized Aug: 25 1765. p. 72.

Nathaniel Lancaster & Hope Walker a Daughter named Ann born Oct: 19 1767. Baptized Dec: 13 1767. p. 79.

Samuel Landrum & Hannah Hawkins a son named Leving born Nov: 17 1765. Baptized Mar: 8 1766. p. 73.

Aires Lane & Mary Woodson a Son named Frederick born Ap: 15 1761. Baptized 1761 May 24. p. 59.

Aris Lane & Mary Woodson a Son named Robert born Jul: 11th 1759. Baptized 1760 ffeb: 17. p. 56.

Ayres Lane & Mary Woodson a son named Tarlton born Oct: 30 1764. Baptized Ap: 4 1765. p. 70.

Ayres Lane & Mary Woodson a son named John born Ap: 4 1767. Baptized Nov: 15 1767. p. 79.

Aires Lane & Mary Woodson a son named Woodson born Jul: 23 1769. Baptized Oct: 8 1769. p. 86.

Aires Lane & Mary Woodson a daughter named Betty born Oct 28. 1771. Baptized Dec. 18, 1771. p. 91.

Aires Lane & Mary Woodson a son named Lewis born Jan 25, 1774. Baptized May 15. 1774. p. 96.

Aires Lane & Mary Woodson a daughter named Mary born Sep. 5, 1776. Baptized Oct. 13, 1776. p. 100.

David Lane & Elizabeth Pryor had Twins named Eliz: & Martha born Mar: 30. 1757. Baptized 1757 Ap: 1st. p. 50.

David Lane & Eliz: Philpots a Daughter named Frankie born Oct: 5 1770. Baptized Ap: 8 1771. p. 89.

David Lane & Eliz: Philpot a son named James born Jan 15, 1776. Baptized Ap. 8, 1776. p. 100.

Da. Lane & Cat Fairies a son named Pryor born Jan 10, 1782. Baptized Nov. 24, 1782. p. 108.

Dumas Lane & Mary Dickens a child Mary born .... 1781. Baptized Ap: 12 1784. p. 111.

Dumas Lane & Mary Dickens a child Ann born .... 1783. Baptized Ap: 12 1784. p. 111.

Hen: Lane & Sarah Logan a son named Antony born Oct: 2 1759. Baptized 1759 Dec: 9. p. 56.

Henry Layne & Sarah Logan a Daughter named Ann born Sep: 29 1764. Baptized Nov: 18 1764. p. 69.

Henry Lane & Sarah Logan a daughter named Sarah, born Aug. 5 1770. Baptized Dec: 23 1770. p. 89.

Henry Lane & Sarah London a son named Richard born Jul. 27, 1774. Baptized Nov. 20, 1774. p. 97.

Henry Lane & Frances Spinner [Spiller] a child named Catherine born Jul. 18, 1781. Baptized Aug. 19, 1781. p. 104.

Henry Lane & Frances Spiller a son Thomas born Aug: 12 1786. Baptized Nov: 26 1786. p. 118.

Henry Lane & Frances Spiller a son Ben Spiller born June 5 1788. Baptized Mar: 28 1790. p. 122.

Jacob Lane & Mary Bradshaw a Daughter named Judah born Mar: 21. 1757. Baptized 1757 May 29. p. 51.

Jacob Lane & Mary Bradshaw a son named Samuel born Jan: 14 1760. Baptized 1760 Ap: 27. p. 57.

Jacob Lane & Mary Bradshaw a son named John born Mar: 3. 1762. Baptized 1762 May 23. p. 63.

Jacob Lane & Mary Bradshaw A Daughter named Molly born Sep: 10 1764. Baptized Oct: 30 1764. p. 69.

Jacob Layne & Mary Bradshaw a Daughter named Frances born feb: 17 1767. Baptized Jun: 21 1767. p. 78.

James Lane & Mary Bradshaw a son named Sherard born Sep: 10 1769. Baptized Oct: 29 1769. p. 86.

Jacob Lane & Mary Bradshaw a son named Jacob: Bradshaw born Aug. 15, 1772. Baptized Mar. 22, 1773. p. 93.

James Lane & Mary Craigwall a Daughter named Mally born Aug: 22, 1756. Baptized 1757 feb: 13. p. 50.

John Lane & Sarah Reems a Daughter named Eliz: born Jan: 5 1769. Baptized Mar: 5 1769. p. 83.

John Lane & Ann Garland a child Ann Garrit Nov. 11 1786. Baptized Ap: 19 1787. p. 118.

Jo: Lane & Agnes Garland a Son Thomas born Dec. 24, 1781. Baptized Ap. 13, 1782. p. 106.

Jo: Lane & Ann Garland a child Eliz: Bibb born Sep. 28 1784. Baptized May 9 1785. p. 114.

Jo: Lane & Nancy Garland a son Nath: Garland born Ap: 22 1790. Baptized Jul: 12 1790. p. 122.

Jo: Lane & Mary Owen a son James born May 4 1782. Baptized Oct: 17 1787. p. 120.

Jo: Lane & Mary Owen a child Patsy born Jan: 22 1785. Baptized Oct: 17 1787. p. 120.

Jo: Lane & Mary Owen a child Joyce Owen born Sep: 19 1787. Baptized Oct: 17 1787. p. 120.

Jo Lane & Susanna Jones a son William Jones born Jul: 10 1787. Baptized Nov. 18 1787. p. 120.

Rich: Lane & Sar. Yauncy, Marg: Yauncy born May 30, 1780. Baptized Oct 14, 1782. p. 108.

Tho. Lane & Mally Groom a son called Henry born May 2, 1774. Baptized Jun. 5, 1774. p. 96.

William Lane & Ruth Taylor a son named John born feb: 13 1765. Baptized Jul: 6 1765. p. 71.

Will: Layne & Ruth Taylor a Daughter named Concy born Ap: 18 1767. Baptized Jul: 17 1767. p. 78.

Will: Lane & Ruth Taylor a Daughter named Sally born Jun 17 1769. Baptized Jul: 10 1770. p. 88.

William Lane & Ruth Taylor a son named Taylor born Ap. 26, 1772. Baptized Mar. 22, 1773. p. 93.

Will Lane & Ruth Doss a daughter named Susannah born Sep. 27, 1774. Baptized Aug. 1, 1775. p. 98.

John Lansdown & ffrances Whirley a son named William born dec: 5, 1761. Baptized 1762 Mar: 6. p. 62.

Kimbrock Launders & Mary Branham a son Nathaniel born Jul: 24 1782. Baptized Oct. 5 1784. p. 113.

Kimbrock Launders & Mary Branham a son William born Nov. 16 1783. Baptized Oct. 5 1784. p. 113.

Aaron Laury & Ann Weldy a daughter named Betsy: Weldy born Oct 28. 1776. Baptized Ap. 27, 1777. p. 101.

Joseph Laury & Priscilla Fowler a son named Robert born Jun: 10 1765. Baptized May 17 1766. p. 74.

William Laury & Mary Pulleing a son named John born Mar: 14, 1763. Baptized 1763 May 1st. p. 64.

Tho: Lawless & Sarah Jones a Daughter named Sally born dec: 30 1760. Baptized 1761 Mar: 22. p. 59.

Thomas Lawles & Sarah Jones a son named John born Ap: 23. 1763. Baptized 1763 Jul: 10. p. 65.

Thomas Lawless & Sarah Jones a Daughter named Molly born .... Baptized Mar: 31 1765. p. 70.

Henry Laurence & Elizabeth Stanley a son named William born Mar: 11 1765. Baptized Ap: 14 1765. p. 70.

Jo: Lawrence & Mary Ann Powers a son John born July 2 1788. Baptized Sep: 17 1788. p. 121.

Aaron Lawrie & Penelope White a son named John born Jun: 30 1757. Baptized 1757 Dec: 25. p. 51.

Aaron Laurie & Penelope White a Daughter named Ann born Ap: 17. 1760. Baptized 1760 Jun: 22. p. 57.

Aaron Laury & Penelope White a Daughter named Mary born May 29 1761. Baptized 1761 Nov: 9. p. 61.

Aaron Laury & Penelope White a son named Aaron born Jun: 30 1763. Baptized 1763 Sep: 12. p. 65.

Aaron Laury & Penelope White a Daughter named Sarah born Sep: 19 1765. Baptized May 17 1766. p. 74.

Aaron Laurie & Penelope White a Daughter named Priscilla born Jul: 4 1768. Baptized Nov: 3 1768. p. 82.

Aaron Laurie & Maple Holland a son Overton born Feb. 23, 1782. Baptized Ap. 28, 1782. p. 106.

John Laury & Eliz: Beth [Davis] a Daughter named .... born Jun: 4. 1757. Baptized 1762 Ap: 12. p. 62.

Jo: Laury & Elizabeth Davis a Daughter named Mary born Mar: 11 1763. Baptized Mar: 31 1764. p. 67.

John Laury & Betty Davies a son named Edward Norcroft born Sep: 22. 1755. Baptized 1756 June 26. p. 49.

John Laurie & Betty Davis a son named Job born Ap: 20 1767. Baptized Nov: 11 1767. p. 78.

Matthew Laurie & Elizabeth Goss a son named Joel born Jan: 31. 1759. Baptized 1759 Ap: 1. p. 54.

Mathew Laury & Eliz: Goss a son named Thornton born Aug: 18, 1761. Baptized 1761 Nov: 8. p. 61.

Mathew Laurie & Elizabeth Goss a son named Mathew born Nov: 27 1764. Baptized Mar: 3 1765. p. 70.

Mathew Laurie & Elizabeth Goss a Daughter named Elizabeth born Jan: 25 1768. Baptized Ap: 11 1768. p. 80.

Mathew Laurie & Eliz: Goss a daughter named Nansy born Feb. 5, 1774. Baptized Jun. 5, 1774. p. 96.

Math: Laurie & Eliz: Goss a daughter named Lucy born Ap: 30, 1777. Baptized Aug 3, 1777. p. 102.

Math: Laury & Eliz: Goss a child named Sally born Jan. 29, 1781. Baptized Oct. 22. 1781. p. 105.

Moses Laurie & Elizabeth Clark a Son named William born Sep: 7 1756. Baptized 1757 Ap: 11. p. 50.

Moses Laury & Eliz: Clark a son named John-Clark born Aug: 18 1766 (sic). Baptized May 17 1766. p. 74.

Moses Laury & Eliz: Clark a son named Johnson born Jun: 8. 1776. Baptized Dec. 14. 1776. p. 101.

David Lawson & Ann Harvey a son named James born Jul: 31. 1760. Baptized 1760 Aug: 17. p. 58.

Jonas Lawson & Mary Nash a son named James born Aug: 3 1767. Baptized Nov: 15 1767. p. 79.

Jo: Lawyer & Mary Mallory a Son named Henry born Jul. 16, 1781. Baptized Sep. 9, 1781. p. 104.

Jo: Le May & Annas Branham a son John born May 14 1776. Baptized Oct. 5 1784. p. 113.

Jo: Le May & Annas Branham a son Thomas born Jul: 1777. Baptized Oct. 5 1784. p. 113.

John Lee & Betty Page a Son named Lewis born Aug: 9, 1757. Baptized 1757 Oct: 2. p. 51.

John Lee & Eliz: Page a Daughter named Mary born Ap: 27. 1759. Baptized 1759 May 27. p. 55.

John Lee & Elizabeth Page a Daughter named Ann born Oct: 13, 1760. Baptized 1760 Dec: 7. p. 58.

John Lee & Bettey Page a son named Philip born feb: 14 1762. Baptized 1762 May 9. p. 62.

John Lee & Betty Page a son named John born May 8 1764. Baptized Jun: 3 1764. p. 67.

John Lee & Betty Page a son named Edward born Jul: 7 1766. Baptized Aug: 31 1766. p. 75.

John Lee & Betty Page a son named Stephen born Nov: 26 1768. Baptized Jan: 29 1769. p. 83.

John Lee & Betty Page a son named Tarlton born Jan: 26 1771. Baptized Mar: 17 1771. p. 89.

Jo. Lee & Betty Page a son named William born Jan 28, 1774. Baptized Mar. 13, 1774. p. 96.

Molly Knight spouse to Joseph Lee was baptized this day. Baptized Dec: 13 1768. p. 83.

Stephen Lee & Ann Poor a son named Brackston born Aug: 2 1766. Baptized Oct: 12 1766. p. 75.

Elisha Leek & Joyce Thomason a Son named Geo: Thomson born Ap: 8 1781. Baptized May 20, 1781. p. 103.

Walter Leek & Winny Johnson a son named John born Aug. 22, 1774. Baptized Jan 21, 1775. p. 97.

Thomas Lenthicum & Jean Geather a Daughter named Rebekah-Geather born Jun: 6 1766. Baptized Nov: 23 1766. p. 75.

John Leonard & Mary Price a son named John born Jul. 13, 1775. Baptized Sep. 20, 1775. p. 99.

John Leprade & Temperance fferrar a Daughter named Joanna born Jan: 12 1749. Baptized 1758 ffeb: 12. p. 52.

John Leprade & Anna Williams a Daughter named Mary born feb: 10 1753. Baptized 1758 ffeb: 12. p. 52.

John Laprade & Susannah Waddly a son named John born Mar: 16 1766. Baptized Jul: 23 1766. p. 74.

John Laprade & Susannah Wadley, A Daughter named Susannah born May 14 1768. Baptized Aug: 28 1768. p. 82.

John Leprade & Susannah Wadley a Daughter named Betty born Jun: 23 1770. Baptized Sep: 22 1770. p. 88.

John Leprade & Susannah Wadley a Daughter named Martha born May 9. 1761. Baptized 1761 Jul: 12. p. 60.

John Leprade & Susan Wadely a daughter named Jeany born Mar. 16, 1773. Baptized Ap. 4, 1773. p. 94.

John Leprade & Susannah Wadlow a Daughter named Judith born Jul: 5, 1763. Baptized 1763 Aug: 1. p. 65.

Stephen Letcher & Elizabeth Perkins a son named Benjamin born .... Baptized Nov: 22 1767. p. 79.

Stephen Letcher & Eliz: Perkins a son named John born Oct: 24 1769. Baptized Dec: 19 1769. p. 86.

Stephen Letcher & Eliz: Perkins a daughter named Hannah, born .... Baptized Nov: 5 1771. p. 90.

Stephen Letcher & Eliz. Perkins a son named Stephen: Giles born Jan 26, 1774. Baptized Ap. 1, 1774. p. 96.

Stephen Giles Letcher & Eliz. Perkins had a Daughter named Mary born Ap. 23, 1776. Baptized 1778, Ap: 19th. p. 103.

Edward Lewis & Ann Meuse a son named Thaddeus Barber born Ap: 4 1764. Baptized Ap: 20 1764. p. 67.

Edward Lewis & Ann Muse a son named Patsey born May 27 1767. Baptized Jun: 14 1767. p. 78.

Edward Lewis & Ann Mews a son named Edward born Mar: 28 1769. Baptized May 28 1769. p. 84.

Edward Lewis & Ann Muse a son named William born Oct 6, 1773. Baptized Jan. 2, 1774. p. 95.

John Lewis & Judith Crouch a son named Richard born Nov: 26 1764. Baptized Dec: 22 1764. p. 69.

John Lewis & Judith Crouch a son named John born Sep: 7 1766. Baptized Oct: 27 1766. p. 75.

John Lewis & Judith Crouch a Daughter named Martha born Dec. 8 1768. Baptized Jan: 22 1769. p. 83.

John Lewis & Elizabeth mcBride a Son named Joseph born dec: 31 1758. Baptized 1759 ffeb: 14. p. 54.

John Lewis & Eliz mcBride a son named John born Ap: 5 1761. Baptized 1761 May 17. p. 59.

John Lewis & Elizabeth mcBride a son named William born May 16 1763. Baptized 1763 Jul: 10. p. 65.

John Lewis & Elizabeth McBride a Daughter named Mary born Mar: 21 1765. Baptized May 12 1765. p. 71.

John Lewis & Elizabeth McBride a Daughter named Sarah born June 4 1769. Baptized Sep: 24 1769. p. 86.

John Lewis & Eliz. McBride a daughter named Eliz born Ap. 20, 1771. Baptized Jul. 3, 1771. p. 90.

Joseph Lewis & Sarah Williamson a son named Robert-William-son born Nov: 13 1764. Baptized Mar: 10 1765. p. 70.

Joseph Lewis & Sarah Williamson a son named Richard born Nov: 25 1766. Baptized Dec: 25 1766. p. 75.

Joseph Lewis & Sarah Williamson a Daughter named Susannah born Ap: 14 1769. Baptized Jul: 23 1769. p. 85.

Will: Lewis & Sarah mcBride a son named Lewis born May 1756. Baptized 1756 Aug: 21. p. 49.

Will: Lewis & Hannah Underwood a son named Joseph born Ap: 22. 1760. Baptized 1760 May 25. p. 57.

Will: Lewis & Hannah Underwood a son named Nicholas born Jun: 8. 1762. Baptized 1762 Aug: 15. p. 63.

Will: Lewis & Hannah Underwood a son named Thomas born May 11 1765. Baptized Jun: 16 1765. p. 71.

William Lewis & Hannah Underwood a son named John born Jan: 1 1768. Baptized Jul: 31 1768. p. 81.

Will Lewis & Hannah Underwood a daughter named Sarah born Aug. 21, 1772. Baptized Nov. 22, 1772. p. 93.

Will Lewis & Hannah Underwood a son named John-Underwood born Nov. 4, 1774. Baptized Dec. 11, 1774. p. 97.

Will Lewis & Hannah Underwood a daughter named Ann born May 8. 1777. Baptized Aug. 1, 1777. p. 102.

Will: Lewis & Lucy Merriwether a daughter named Lucinda born Oct 31, 1772. Baptized Jan. 1. 1773. p. 93.

William Lewis & Sally Man a son named Jesse born Dec. 28 1774. Baptized March 5, 1775. p. 98.

Will Lewis & Sally Man a son named William born Jan. 19. 1777. Baptized Mar. 9, 1777. p. 101.

Zachariah Lewis & Ann Tyrril a son John born Feb. 25 1784 Baptized May 14 1784. p. 111.

Zachary Lewis & Anne Terrill a child Eliza born May 27 1786. Baptized Jul: 12 1786. p. 117.

Waller Lewis & Sarah Lewis a child Lucy born Oct. 6 1786. Baptized Nov. 15 1786. p. 118.

William Ligg & Elizabeth Webster a Daughter named Diana born Jun: 6 1758. Baptized 1758 Aug: 13. p. 53.

Thomas Lilly & Susannah* Smith a Son named Edmond born Oct: 28 1760. Baptized 1760 Dec: 7. p. 58.

Thomas Lilly & Susannah Smith a Daughter named Ann born Nov: 21 1764. Baptized Ap: 14 1765. p. 70.

Tho: Lilly & Susannah Smith a son named Joshua born feb: 17 1767. Baptized May 31 1767. p. 77.

Tho: Lilly & Susannah Smith a son named Robert born Sep: 7 1769. Baptized Jul: 29 1770. p. 88.

William Lilly & Elizabeth Pollet a Daughter named Ann born Sep: 26 1764. Baptized Jul: 6 1765. p. 71.

Tho: Lilsworth & Betsie .... a child Mary born .... Baptized July 3 1783. p. 110.

Caleb Lindsay & Sally Stevens a child Polly Nichols. Jan: 4 1786. Baptized Apl: 23 1786. p. 116.

Caleb Lindsay & Salley Stevens, a child Sallie Montague, June 2 1787. Baptized Feb: 16 1789. p. 122.

Caleb Lindsay & Sally Steven a child Landon born May 25 '89. Baptized Jul: 9 1790. p. 126.

Landie Lindsay & Cat: Quarles a son Nathaniel born Feb. 1, 1782. Baptized May. 26, 1782. p. 106.

Joseph Lipscomb & Frances Tandie a daughter named Mary born Dec. 24, 1774. Baptized June 6, 1775. p. 98.

Joseph Lipscomb & Frances Tandy a daughter named Frances born Mar. 26, 1777. Baptized Ap. 10, 1777. p. 101.

Jos: Lipscom & Frances Tandie a son Will: Tandie born Jan 9, 1782. Baptized Ap. 28, 1782. p. 106.

Joseph Lipscomb & Frances Tandie, Martha born Sep: 4 1786. Baptized Nov: 26 1786. p. 118.

Jo: Lipscomb & Mary Kimbro a son Joseph born Ap: 26 1782. Baptized May 4 1783. p. 109.

Jo: Lipscomb & Mary Kimbro a child Dianah Oct. 17 1784. Baptized Jan: 9 1786. p. 116.

Joseph Lively & Sarah Taylor a daughter named Jeanie born Oct 15, 1773. Baptized Nov. 5, 1773. p. 95.

Antony Logan & Agnes Curry a Daughter named Sally born Oct: 15. 1760. Baptized 1760 Dec: 7. p. 58.

Antony Logan & Agnes Curry a son named Alexr born born feb. 4. 1762. Baptized 1762 Ap: 25. p. 62.

Antony Logan & Agnes Currie a son named David born dec: 18 1763. Baptized Ap: 1 1764. p. 67.

*Marriage says Mary Smith.

Antony Logan & Agnes Currie a Daughter named Nannie born Mar: 1 1766. Baptized Ap: 27 1766. p. 73.

Antony Logan & Ann Currie a son named James born Ap: 27 1768. Baptized Jun: 12 1768. p. 81.

Antony Logan & Agnes Curry a son named Antony born Mar: 29 1770. Baptized Jan 13 1771. p. 89.

George Longmire & ffrances .... a son named John born Nov: 23 1765. Baptized Jan: 1 1766. p. 72.

Will: Longmyre & Hannah Britt a son named John born Ap: 6 1769. Baptized May 14 1769. p. 84.

George Lovel & Betty Burford a son named John born Nov: 25 1764. Baptized Dec: 9 1764. p. 69.

George Lovel & Betty Burford a son named George born Mar: 21 1766. Baptized May 18 1766. p. 74.

William Lovel & Mary Lovel a Daughter named Elizabeth born Dec: 21 1764. Baptized Mar: 3 1765. p. 70.

William Lovel & Mary Lovel a son named George born Ap: 3 1767. Baptized Ap: 19 1767. p. 77.

Will & Mary Lovels a daughter named Mally born Dec. 19, 1772. Baptized Jul. 25, 1773. p. 94.

William & Sarah Lovels a son named Billie born Feb. 19, 1776. Baptized Ap. 7, 1776. p. 99.

Geor: Lucas & Lucy Gerrard a Daughter named Martha born Jun: 18 1764. Baptized Jul: 10 1770. p. 88.

Jacob Lustre & Eliz: Bret a Son named Robert born Dec: 11 1769. Baptized May 27 1770. p. 87.

Alexr. McAlister & Eliz: Smith a child Patsie born .... Baptized Aug. 22 1783. p. 110.

Da: McAlister & Abigail Tate a son James born Dec. 4 1783. Baptized May 5 1784. p. 111.

Will McAlister & Eliz: Bib, a son named David born June 29, 1780. Baptized Jul: 29, 1781. p. 103.

Edward mcBride & Eliz: Williamson a Daughter named Betty born Ap: 10. 1757. Baptized 1757 Dec: 2. p. 51.

Edward mcBride & Eliz: Williamson a Daughter named Susannah born Jan: 22 1759. Baptized 1759 Jun: 6. p. 55.

Edward mcBride & Elizabeth Williamson a Daughter named Jean born Sep: 27. 1760. Baptized 1760 Nov: 19. p. 58.

Edward McBride & Elizabeth Williamson a Daughter named Sally born feb: 3 1765. Baptized June 2 1765. p. 71.

Edward McBride & Eliz: Williamson a Daughter named Patty born Nov: 23 1766. Baptized Dec: 29 1766. p. 75.

Edward McBride & Eliz: Williamson a Daughter named Julia born Jul: 15 .... Baptized Aug: 9 1769. p. 85.

John mcBride & Mary Curd, a D: born Sep: 29 1726 named Jane. p. 40.

Rich: McBride & Frances Moss a Son Jo. Hughes born Feb. 25, 1782. Baptized June 16, 1782. p. 107.

Stokes mcCawl & Mary Stratton a Son named William born Mar: 15 1756. Baptized 1756 May 10. p. 48.

Stokes McCawl & Agnes Williamson a Daughter named Mary born Dec. 29 1767. Baptized Jan: 29 1768. p. 79.

Stoakes McCawl & Agnes Williamson a son named Richard born dec. 13 1769. Baptized Jan: 2 1770. p. 86.

John Macomack & Susannah Bullington a son named Joel born Aug: 1 1765. Baptized Sep: 14 1765. p. 72.

Thomas mcCormack & Lucy Proft a Daughter named Ann born Jul: 14 1758. Baptized 1758 Jul: 23. p. 53.

Roderick McCrae & Mary Dudley a daughter named Ann born Sep. 26, 1771. Baptized Jul 3, 1772. p. 92.

Austin Mackghee & Mary Harris, Will-Graves, Jan. 19 1786. Baptized Jul: 9 1786. p. 117.

Augustine McGhee & Sarah Wyatt a son Wyatt born Nov. 11 1790. Baptized Mar: 20 1791. p. 126.

Augustine McGhee & Sarah Wyat a son Walter born Jan: 13 1793. Baptized May 7 1793. p. 122.

Augustin McGhee & Sar: Wyat a daughter Amie Chiles born Oct 3 1795. Baptized Apl. 22 1796. p. 138.

James McGhee & Lydia-Hansford Mullins a daughter named Marianne born Mar. 177... Baptized May. 7, 1775. p. 98.

Jo. McGehie & Mary Stewart a son Charles born Oct. 25. 1782. Baptized Dec. 25. 1782. p. 108.

Jo: McGhee & Mary Stewart a child Jeanie born Aug: 7 1787. Baptized Oct: 13 1787. p. 120.

Jo: McGhee & Molly Stewart a son Dillard born May 11 1790. Baptized Sep: 5 1790. p. 126.

Jo: McGhee & Molly Stewart a child Aggie born Jan: 25 1793. Baptized 1793-Ap: 18. p. 127.

Jo: McGhee & Mary Stewart a son named Carr born June 25 1795. Baptized Nov: 1 1795. p. 127.

Jos: McGehee & Ann Merriwether a son Carr born Aug. 5 1786. Baptized Nov. 15 1786. p. 118.

Jos: McGehee & Ann Merriwether a daughter Dorothy born Mar: 23 1784. Baptized Nov. 15 1786. p. 118.

Will: McGhee & Levina Smith a child Nancy Born Oct. 31 1783. Baptized Dec. 25 1783. p. 111.

ffrancis mcGuire & Hannah Jackson a Daughter named Mary born Jan: 4 1760. Baptized 1760 Ap: 4. p. 57.

Will: mcGuire & Ann Malory a Daughter named Ann born feb: 11 1758. Baptized 1758 Mar: 19. p. 52.

William mcGuire & Ann Mallory a Daughter called Sarah born Sep: 21 1760. Baptized 1760 Oct: 12. p. 58.

Will: mcGuire & Ann Mallory a son named William born Mar: 20. 1763. Baptized 1763 Ap: 10. p. 64.

William McGuire & Ann Mallory a son born Oct: 25 1762 named John. Baptized Sep: 29 1765. p. 72.

William McGuire & Ann Mallory a Daughter named Elizabeth born Aug: 19 1765. Baptized Sep: 29 1765. p. 72.

David McKay & Helen McClure a Daughter named Elizabeth born Mar: 10 1768. Baptized Mar: 25 1768. p. 80.

David McKay & Helen McClure a son named William born Jul: 29 1770. Baptized Sep: 6 1770. p. 88.

[Ben: McKenzie]* & Agnes Broadfoot a son named Charles born Jun: 12, 1772. Baptized Aug 2, 1772. p. 92.

Hugh McKie & Mary Lamkin a son named John born Jul: 14 1760. Baptized Jul: 29 1770. p. 88.

Hugh McKie & Mary Lambkin a son named William born Jan: 29 1765. Baptized Mar: 16 1765. p. 70.

Will Macon & Sally Woodson a son Henry born Mar. 2, 1782. Baptized June 17, 1782. p. 107.

Jo: Maddison & Mary Biggar a child Nancy born Aug: 6 1785. Baptized April 16 1786. p. 116.

John Madlock & Judah Witt a Son named Jesse born Sep: 27 1757. Baptized 1757 Oct: 30. p. 51.

John Madlock & Judah Witt a son named John born Sep: 27. 1758. Baptized 1758 Oct: 15. p. 53.

Henry Mallory & Sarah Dabney a child Rebeckah born June .... 1786. Baptized Aug: 20 1786. p. 117.

Jo: Mallory & Lucy Sutherland, a child Mary Coleman Sep: 25 1786. Baptized May 20 1787. p. 119.

William Mallory & Mary Tuggle a son named Charles born Ap. 16 1770. Baptized Jun: 17 1770. p. 88.

Will: Mallory & Ann Hoggan a son John born Nov. 21 1783. Baptized Dec. 25 1783. p. 111.

Will: Mallory & Ana Hoggan a son Henry Hickerson Mar: 18 1786. Baptized Apl: 20 1786. p. 116.

James Man & Betty Thomason a son named George born Dec: 2 1769. Baptized Mar: 25 1770. p. 87.

James Man & Betty Thompson a daughter named Martha born Ap. 29. 1772. Baptized Jun. 2. 1772. p. 92.

James Man & Betty Thomson a son named James born Oct 16, 1774. Baptized Nov. 20, 1774. p. 97.

John Man & Eliz: Davies a Daughter born dec: 21 1755. named Eve. Baptized 1756 Jan: 25. p. 48.

John Man & Eliz: Davis a Daughter named Annie born Nov: 24. 1759. Baptized 1760 ffeb: 3. p. 56.

John Man & Eliz: Davis a Daughter named ffrances born Sep: 17. 1761. Baptized 1761 Nov: 8. p. 61.

John Marks & Ann Collier a Daughter named Ann born Mar: 17 1766. Baptized Ap: 13 1766. p. 73.

*Marriage Record

John Marks & Ann Colier a son named John born Aug: 18 1768. Baptized Dec: 25 1768. p. 83.

Jo: Marks & Lucy Merriwether a son Jo: Hastings, Jan: 6 1786. Baptized June 9 1786. p. 116.

Peter Marks & Joanna Sydnor a son named Hastings born Sep: 12 1769. Baptized Jan: 19 1770. p. 86.

Peter Marks & Joanna Sydenham [Sydnor] a son named Fortunatus born Mar: 6 .... Baptized Aug 18, 1771. p. 90.

Bernard Markham & Mary Harris a Daughter named Martha born feb: 28 1768. Baptized Ap: 3 1768. p. 80.

Charles Marler & Sarah Brewer a Daughter named Jeanie born Jan: 16. 1760. Baptized 1760 May 8. p. 57.

Char: Marlow & Sar: Brewer a son named Char: Brewer born Jul: 20, 1762. Baptized 1762 Aug: 29. p. 63.

Charles Marlow & Sarah Brewer a Daughter named Elizabeth born Dec: 15 1764. Baptized Ap: 29 1765. p. 71.

Antony Martin & Sarah Holman a son named James born dec: 19 1761. Baptized 1762 feb: 6. p. 61.

Anthony Martin & Sarah Holman a Daughter named Jean born Sep: 9 1764. Baptized Nov: 11 1764. p. 69.

Antony Martin & Sarah Holman a Daughter named Sarah born Dec: 6 1766. Baptized Jan: 17 1767. p. 76.

Austine Martin & Ann fforsee a son named Stephen born Dec: 9 1765. Baptized Jun: 22 1766. p. 74.

Benjamin Martin & Dianah Harrison a son named Robert born Aug: 1st 1767. Baptized Sep: 13 1767. p. 78.

Benjamin Martin & Dianah Harrison a daughter named Sarah Meredith born .... Baptized Feb. 14, 1774. p. 95.

David Martin & Susannah Roberts [Robards] a Daughter named Mary born May 7 1758. Baptized 1758 Jul: 9. p. 53.

David Martine & susannah Roberts a Daughter named Judith born Ap: 1759. Baptized 1759 Oct: 28. p. 56.

David Martin & Susannah Robards a son named Mitchel born Mar: 26 1761. Baptized Jun: 11 1767. p. 77.

David Martin & Susannah Roberts a Daughter named Susannah born dec: 23 1760. Baptized Jan: 29 1767. p. 76.

David Martin & Susannah Roberts a son named David born Oct: 9 1763. Baptized Jan: 29 1767. p. 76.

David Martin & Susannah Roberts a son named William born Jun: 20 1765. Baptized Jan: 29 1767. p. 76.

David Martin & Susannah Roberts a Daughter named Nansy born dec: 18 1768. Baptized Ap: 21 1769. p. 84.

David Martin & Susannah Roberts a son named Thomas born Oct. .... 1770. Baptized Jan 2, 1772. p. 91.

Da: Martin & Susannah Roberts a son named John born Oct 11, 1773. Baptized Ap. 3, 1774. p. 96.

David Martin & Sus. Roberts a son named James born May 8, 1775. Baptized Feb. 25, 1776. p. 99.

David Martin & Susannah Roberts a son named Roberts born July 9, 1777. Baptized July 20, 1777. p. 102.

James Martin & Ann Ogilsvy a Son named Joseph born Ap: 8. 1763. Baptized 1763 May 6. p. 64.

Ja: Martin & Eliz: Clarkson a child Mary born Ap. 6, 1782. Baptized Nov. 24, 1782. p. 108.

Job Martin & Mary Clarkson a son named John born Mar: 18 1766. Baptized May 25 1766. p. 74.

Job Martin & Mary Clarkson a son named Valentine-Clarkson born dec. 1 1767. Baptized Mar: 2 1768. p. 80.

Job Martin & Mary Clarkson a Daughter named Nansy-Butts born May 14 1769. Baptized Jul: 22 1769. p. 85.

Job. Martin & Mary Clarkson a Daughter named Patsy Robinson born Ap. 25, 1771. Baptized 1772. p. 91.

Jo: Martin & Lucy Lane a child Judith born Jul 24. 1781. Baptized Aug. 27, 1781. p. 104.

Jo: Martin & Lucy Lane a child Sarah born Aug. 8 1783. Baptized June 26 1785. p. 114.

Jo: Martin & Lucy Lane a child Molly born Dec. 13 1785. Baptized July 8 1787. p. 119.

John Martin & Mary Rogers a son named John born Jun: 16 1764. Baptized Jul: 31 1764. p. 68.

John Martin & Rachel Pace a Daughter named Jean born Jul: 13, 1759. Baptized 1759 Sep: 2. p. 55.

John Martin & Rachel Pace a Daughter named Hannah born Ap: 11 1761. Baptized 1761 May 24. p. 60.

John Martin & Rachel Pace a son named Orston born Nov: 5 1764. Baptized Mar: 3 1765. p. 70.

John Martin & Rachel Pace a Daughter named Lucy born Oct: 6 1767 (sic). Baptized Feb. 11 1767. p. 76.

John Martin & Rachel Pace a Daughter named Rachel born Aug: 22 1768. Baptized Oct. 15 1768. p. 82.

John Martin & Ann Barbara Lewis a son named Peter born Mar: 16 1764. Baptized Ap: 20 1764. p. 67.

John Martin & Barbara Lewis a son named Edward born Dec: 30 1765. Baptized Ap: 20 1766. p. 73.

John Martin & Peter [Barbara] Lewis a Daughter named Nansie born Mar: 3 1768. Baptized May 15 1768. p. 81.

John Martin & Barbara Lewis a son named John born Dec: 26 1769. Baptized Dec: 24 1770. p. 86.

John Martin & Barbara Lewis a son named William born Feb. 20, 1773. Baptized Jun. 27, 1773. p. 94.

John Martin & Barbara Lewis a Son named Anthony born Jun. 17, 1775. Sep. 29, 1775. p. 99.

Jo: Martin & Sarah Hinds a child Dorothy born Aug: 11, 1781. Baptized Mar. 16, 1782. p. 105.

Jo: Martin & Sarah Hinds a son Tho: Duncan born Mar: 9 1783. Baptized Sep: 19 1784. p. 112.

Jo: Martin & Sarah Hinds a child Annie born Aug. 30 1784. Baptized Sep: 19 1784. p. 112.

John Martin & Mary Cairden a son named Jesse born Jan: 7 1769. Baptized Feb: 19 1769. p. 83.

John Martin & Mary Cairden a son named John born Oct 1, 1772. Baptized Oct 25, 1772. p. 93.

Mathew Martin & Molly Bullock a Daughter named Molly born Jul: 16 1764. Baptized Sep: 2 1764. p. 69.

Mat: Martin & Mary Bullock a Daughter named Elizabeth born Ap: 25 1766. Baptized Jun: 15 1766. p. 74.

Mathew Martin & Sarah Bullock a son named Mathew born Feb: 7 1768. Baptized Mar: 15 1768. p. 80.

Mitchel Martin & Mary Martin a child Molly Mitchel, Jul: 6 1783. Baptized June 20 1784. p. 112.

Samuel Martin & Susannah Jones a Son named Jacob born Ap. 9, 1764. Baptized Jul: 15 1764. p. 68.

Sam Martin & Susanna-Thomas-Jones a Daughter named Polly born Jul: 14 1765. Baptized May 18 1766. p. 74.

Sarah Martin was baptized this day aged 18 years in March last. Baptized 1763 Jul: 31. p. 65.

Tho. Martin & Susannah Walker a daughter named Betsy born Feb. 28. 1774. Baptized Jul. 25, 1774. p. 97.

Tho: Martin & Susan Walker a child Mary born July 2 1775. Baptized Oct 23, 1781. p. 105.

Tho: Martin & Susan Walker a child Will born Dec. 13, 1776. Baptized Oct 23, 1781. p. 105.

Tho: Martin & Susan Walker a child Dabney Amos born May 7 1778. Baptized Oct 23, 1781. p. 105.

Tho: Martin & Susan Walker a child Nancy born Apl. 26 1780. Baptized Oct 23, 1781. p. 105.

Tho: Martin & Susan Walker a child Hutson born May 21, 1781. Baptized Oct 23, 1781. p. 105.

Will: Martin & Judith Hemus a son named John born Sep: 3 1756. Baptized 1756 Oct: 2. p. 49.

William Martin & Eliz: Lockrum a son named David born May 14 1758. Baptized 1758 Jul: 9. p. 53.

Will: Martin & Jean Holman a Daughter named Nansie born Jan: 14, 1760. Baptized 1761 feb: 8. p. 59.

Will: Martin & Jean Holman a Daughter named Adna born Dec: 31 1766. Baptized Mar: 1 1767. p. 76.

Jos: Mason & Sarah Dunman had son named Benjamin born Jul: 5, 1753. p. 40.

Jos: Mason & Sarah Dunman a Daughter born Oct: 23 1754 named Elizabeth. p. 40.

Jos: Mason & Sarah Dunman had a Son born Jan: 9 1756 named Joseph. Baptized 1756 feb: 15. p. 48.

Joseph Mason & Sarah Dunman a son named Peter born Ap: 9, 1757. Baptized 1757 May 8. p. 50

Joseph Mason & Sarah Dunman a son named James born dec: 29 1758. Baptized 1759 ffeb: 25. p. 54.

Joseph Mason & Sarah Dunman a son named Reuben born dec: 25 1760. Baptized 1761 Mar: 1. p. 59.

Joseph Mason & Sarah Dunman a Daughter named Sarah born Dec: 24 1764. Baptized Mar: 17 1765. p. 70.

Peter Mason & Eliz: mcKoy a Son named Peter born Aug: 14. 1756. Baptized 1756 Sep: 26. p. 49.

Nathaniel Massie & Eliz. Watkins a son named Thomas born Jun. 2, 1772. Baptized Aug. 19, 1772. p. 92.

Nath: Massie & Ann Clark a daughter named Rebekah born Aug 28. 1777. Baptized Nov. 7. 1777. p. 103.

Nathaniel Massie & Ann Clark a child Ann born Mar. 5, 1779. Baptized July 20, 1782. p. 107.

Nathaniel Massie & Ann Clark a child Sarah born May 4, 1781. Baptized July 20, 1782. p. 107.

Thomas Massie & Mary Williams a Daughter named Martha born Ap: 1 1770. Baptized Jun: 5 1770. p. 87.

Thomas Massie & Mary Williams a daughter named Nansie born Feb. 19, 1772. Baptized May 11, 1772. p. 92.

Tho. Massie & Mary Williams a daughter named Suckie born Ap. 1774. Baptized Jul 1, 1774. p. 97.

Tho: Massie & Mary Williams a child Sally Christian born Ap: 11 1782. Baptized Ap: 26 1783. p. 109.

Tho: & Elizabeth Massies a Son named David born May 17, 1777. Baptized Aug 15, 1777. p. 102.

Tho: & Eliz: Massies a child named Eliz: Watkins born May 29, 1781. Baptized May. 18, 1781. p. 103.

Will: Massy & Frances Adams a Daughter named Molly born Aug: 5 1766. Baptized Nov: 2 1766. p. 75.

Will Massie & Frances Adams a daughter named Nancy born Jun. 16, 1775. Baptized Aug. 1. 1775. p. 98.

William Massie & Frances Adams a son named Benjamin born Jul: 13 1768. Baptized Aug: 14 1768. p. 81.

Will Massie & Frances Adams a daughter named Betty born Jun 22 .... Baptized Jul. 21, 1771. p. 90.

Will Massie & Frances Adams a daughter named Frankie born Feb 8. 1774. Baptized Ap. 24, 1774. p. 96.

Edward Mathews & Tabitha Hopson a son named William born Ap: 11. 1759. Baptized 1759 Jun: 24. p. 55.

Edward Mathews & Tabitha Hopson a Daughter named Betty born dec: 2 1760. Baptized 1761 Mar: 15. p. 59.

Edward Mathews & Tabitha Hopson a son named Edward born feb: 14. 1762. Baptized 1762 Jul: 4. p. 63.

Edward Mathews & Tabitha Dobson a Daughter named Fanny born Jan: 11 1764. Baptized Ap: 22 1764. p. 67.

Edward Mathews & Tabitha Dobson a Daughter named Nansy born Oct: 15 1765. Baptized Jan: 18 1767. p. 76.

Edward Mathews & Tabitha Hopson a son named Ben: Hopson born Oct: 19 1769. Baptized Mar: 18 1770. p. 87.

Richard Mathews & Agnes ffarmer a son named Gideon born Jan: 12 1762. Baptized 1762 Ap: 9. p. 62.

Sherard Mathews & Jean Byers a son Anderson Byers, born Feb. 21 1784. Baptized Nov: 12 1784. p. 113.

Will Mathews & Mary Holman in Goochland, a child Sar: Holman Apl. 27 1787. Baptized June 19 1787. p. 119.

Jo: Mathison & Mary Biggars a son James born May 24 1776. Baptized Sep: 11 1783. p. 110.

Jo: Mathison & Mary Biggars a child Jeanne born Feb: 22 1778. Baptized Sep: 11 1783. p. 110.

Jo: Mathison & Mary Biggars a child Polly born Ap: 28 1781. Baptized Sep: 11 1783. p. 110.

Jo: Mathison & Mary Biggars a child Pamela born May 20 1783. Baptized Sep: 11 1783. p. 110.

John Mathison & Mary Mathison in King William a son named Thomas born feb: 11 1759. Baptized 1759 May 2. p. 55.

Benjamin Mattox & Mary Moore a son named John Harris born Sep: 24, 1756. Baptized 1757 Jan: 13. p. 49.

David Mattox & Sarah Perkins a Daughter named Nansy born Jun: 14 176... Baptized Jul: 23 1769. p. 85.

David Mattox & Sarah Perkins a son named Tarlton born May 17, 1771. Baptized Jul. 7, 1771. p. 90.

Jacob Mattox & Susannah Clark [Clarkson]* a Son named Clai-born born Oct: 25. 1758. Baptized 1758 Nov: 17. p. 53.

Jacob Mattox & Lucy [Susannah?] Clarkson a Daughter named Mary born Sep: 17 1763. Baptized Jan: 29 1764. p. 66.

Jacob Mattox & Susanna Clarkson a son named John born Nov: 26 1765. Baptized Jan: 18 1766. p. 72.

John Maddox & Mary Boyd a Daughter named Judah born Ap: 24 1756. Baptized 1756 Aug: 28. p. 49.

John Mattox & Mary Boyd a son named Benjamin born Jun: 29 1758. Baptized 1758 Oct: 9. p. 53.

John Mattox & Mary Boyd a Daughter named Elizabeth born Jan: 5 1761. Baptized 1761 Mar: 22. p. 59.

John Mattox & Mary Boyd a son named Robert born Mar: 5 1765. Baptized Nov: 6 1766. p. 75.

John Maddox & Mary Boyd a son named Wilson born Jul: 11 1768. Baptized Sep: 17 1768. p. 82.

John Mattox & Mary Boyd a Daughter called Mary born May 11 1769. Baptized Jul: 23 1769. p. 85.

John Mattox & Mary Boyd a daughter named Ursley born Oct 23, 1771. Baptized Nov. 19, 1771. p. 91.

John Mattox & Mary Boyd a daughter named Sarah born Feb. 9, 1774. Baptized Jun. 1, 1774. p. 96.

*Marriage record.

John Mattox & Mary Boyd a son named Michal born May 27, 1776. Baptized Aug 4. 1776. p. 100.

William Mattox & Mary Sampson a Son named Benjamin born feb: 9. 1757. Baptized 1757 Jul: 17. p. 51.

William Mattox & Sarah Sampson a son named Michael born May 22. 1759. Baptized 1759 Sep: 29. p. 55.

William Mattox & Mary Sampson a Daughter named Joanna born Mar: 27 1765. Baptized Jun: 23 1765. p. 71.

William Mattox & Mary Sampson a Daughter named Sally born May 17 1768. Baptized Aug: 21 1768. ᵥp. 81.

Will Mattox & Mary Sampson a son named Joseph born Ap. 7, 1771. Baptized Jun. 8, 1771. p. 90.

William Maddox & Mary Ellis a son named Thomas born Jan: 22 1766. Baptized Feb: 16 1766. p. 73.

Ambrose May & Eliz: Baily a daughter named Eliz. born Aug. 7, 1771. Baptized Nov. 5, 1772. p. 93.

Ambrose May & Ann Chisholm a child Sally born Jan: 3, 1781. Baptized May 26, 1782. p. 106.

Jo: May & Chloe Chisom a son named Elijah born Mar: 2, 1779. Baptized Aug. 26, 1781. p. 104.

Jacob Mayo & Susanna Isbel a son named William-James born Aug: 21 1769. Baptized Sep: 12 1769. p. 86.

Jacob Mayo & Susannah Isabel a son named George born Dec. .... 1774. Baptized Feb. 19, 1775. p. 98.

Jacob Mayo & Susannah Isabel a son named Jacob born Nov. 25 1776. Baptized Feb. 2, 1777. p. 101.

Jacob Mayo & Susanna Isabel a Son Lewis born Jan. 29, 1783. Baptized Feb. 9, 1783. p. 108.

Jacob Mayo & Susanna Isabel a child Susanna Charlot born Aug. 27 1784. Baptized Mar: 22 1785. p. 113.

Jacob Mayo & Susanna Isabel, Stephen Gillard Mar: 12 1786. Baptized May 21 1787. p. 119.

Jac: Mayo & Susannah Isabel, Williamson, born Jan: 2. Baptized Oct. 20 1789. p. 122.

James Mayo & Martha Wiliamson a Daughter named Mary born Mar: 3 1764. Baptized Ap: 8 1764. p. 67.

Joseph Mayo & Jeany Richardson a daughter named Patty born Feb. 21, 1774. Baptized Ap. 21 1774. p. 96.

Rob: Mayo & Marg: Richardson a Daughter named Sally-Thomson born Jan: 30 1771. Baptized Mar: 24 1771. p. 89.

Robert Mayo & Margaret Richardson a son named James born Mar. 11, 1773. Baptized May 9, 1773. p. 94.

Valentine Mayo & Ann Paterson a Daughter named Mary born Jun: 2, 1760. Baptized 1760 Jun: 24. p. 57.

James Maydwell & Sarah Arp a Daughter named Sarah born Nov: 26 1756. Baptized 1758 Ap: 5. p. 52.

Henry Mede & Frances Young a Son Fielding-Lewis born Ap. 4, 1782. Baptized Sep. 2. 1782. p. 107.

Jo: Mead & Eliz: Meekie a child James Meekie born Nov: 23 1787. Baptized Jan: 5 1788. p. 120.

Isaac Meanly & Elizabeth Dennet a Daughter named Tabitha born Jan: 19. 1758. Baptized 1758 Jul: 9. p. 53.

Isaac Meanly & Eliz: Dennet a son named Richard-Millington born Nov: .... 1760. Baptized 1761 Mar: 9. p. 59.

Jacob [Isaac?] Meanley & Elizabeth Dennet a Daughter named Susannah born Mar: 26 1763. Baptized Jan: 31 1764. p. 66.

Isaac Meanley & Betty Dennet a Daughter named Frances born Aug: 28 1766. Baptized Sep: 3 1766. p. 75.

Geo: Meekie & Eliz: Meekie a son James born May 15 1783. Baptized Jul: 27 1783. p. 110.

Sam: Meredith & Mildred Bagby a son named Samuel born May 15 1760. Baptized 1762 Mar: 6. p. 62.

Ja: Meredith & Mildred Begby a son named Daniel born May 17 1762. Baptized 1762 Jul: 25. p. 63.

Will: Meredith & Ann Burns a son named James born Sep: 9 1765. Baptized Sep: 12 1765. p. 72.

Will: Meredith & Ann Bonds a Daughter named Fanny born Jan: 7 1767. Baptized May 16 1767. p. 77.

Will Merril & Sally Haden, a son Timothy born Apl. 31 1778. Baptized Nov. 27 1784. p. 113.

Will Merril & Sally Haden, a child Peggie Haden, born Feb. 4 1780. Baptized Nov. 27 1784. p. 113.

Will Merril & Sally Haden, a child Betsy Smith born Sep. 25 1782. Baptized Nov. 27 1784. p. 113.

Richard Merrin & Ann Conolly a son named samuel born sep. 21 1756. Baptized 1756 Nov: 14. p. 49.

Richard Merrine & Ann Conolly a son named Jesse born May 31 1758. Baptized 1758 Jul: 9. p. 53.

Richard Merrin & Ann Conway [Conolly?] a son named Hannah born feb: 27 1761. Baptized 1761 May 24. p. 60.

Richard Merrine & Ann Conolly a son named Mathew born Mar: 2 1765. Baptized May 5 1765. p. 71.

Richard Merrines & Ann Conolly a Daughter named Mary born Dec: 21 1767. Baptized Ap: 11 1768. p. 80.

Geor: & Martha Merriwethers a Daughter named Frances born Aug: 15 17..... Baptized Sep 22 1770. p. 88.

George Merriwether & Martha Merriwether a son named Reuben born Jul. 31, 1773. Baptized Oct. 5, 1773. p. 95.

Geo. Merriwether & Martha Merriwether a daughter named Mary born Ap. 10, 1777. Baptized July 31, 1777. p. 102.

James Merriwether & Elizabeth Pollard a Daughter named Ann born Jul: 13. 1763. Baptized 1763 Jul: 29. p. 65.

James Merriwether & Eliz: Pollard a son named Joseph born Ap: 23 1771. Baptized May 28 1771. p. 89.

Ja: Merriwether & Sally Merriwether a child Judith born May 14 1785. Baptized Sep. 18 1785. p. 115.

Nicholas Merriwether & Marg: Douglass a Son named William Douglas born Nov: 2. 1761. Baptized 1761 Nov: 7. p. 61.

Nicholas Merriwether & Margaret Douglass a son named Thomas born Ap: 24 1763. Baptized 1763 May 24. p. 64.

Mr. Nicholas Merriwether & Margaret Douglas a son named Nicholas born Jan: 9 1765. Baptized feb: 17 1765. p. 70.

Nicholas Merriwether & Marg: Douglas a son named Charles born Aug: 12 1766. Baptized Aug: 18 1766. p. 75.

Nicholas Merriwether & Marg: Douglas a son named Francis-Thornton born Nov 5 1768. Baptized Nov: 9 1782. p. 82.

Nic: Merriwether & Marg: Douglass, a Daughter born feb: 24 1771 named Elizabeth. Baptized Apl. 3 1771. p. 89.

Nicholas Hunter Merriwether & Beckie Tyrrel a son Douglas July 15 1788. Baptized Aug. 13 1788. p. 121.

Nic: Hunter Merriwether & Rebekah Tyrrel, yr son Charles born. Baptized Mar: 5 1790. p. 122.

Mr. Nic: Hunter Merriwether & Beckie Tyrrel a child called Anne Tyrrel born feb: 22 1792. Baptized Mar. 26 1792. p. 126.

Nic: Merriwether & Beckie Tyrrel a child Ann Tyrrell. Baptized Feb: 22 1791. p. 126.

Nicholas Hunter Meriwether & Becky Terrell his wife a son born February 9th Walker Gilmer Meriwether. Baptized March 16 1794. p. 127.

Nic: Hunter Meriwether & Beckie Tyrel a son Fountain [Fontaine] born 12 Jan: 1797. Baptized May 6 1797. pp. 127, 130.

Nicholas & Eliz. Merriwethers a daughter named Patty born Aug 4, 1772. Baptized Oct 20, 1772. p. 93.

Nic: Merriwether & Sar: Ragline a child Mary Ragline, Mar. 15 1787. Baptized May 9 1787. p. 118.

Nicholas Meriwether & Sar: Ragline a child Lucy Dec. 15 1788. Baptized Mar: 31 1789. p. 122.

Tho: Merriwether & Ann Minor a son Richard born May 11 1792. Baptized July 12 1792. p. 126.

Tho: Meriwether & Ann Minor a son Garret born as above (Ap: 20 1794) & baptized May 19 94. p. 127.

Tho: Meriwether & Ann Minor a son Peter Minor born Feb: 2 1796. Baptized Oct: 13 1796. p. 127.

Will: Merriweather & Martha Wood a Daughter named Martha born May 4. 1752. Baptized 1757 feb: 5. p. 50.

Will: Merriweather & Martha Wood a Son named David born Sep: 11. 1753. Baptized 1757 feb: 5. p. 50.

Will: Merriweather & Martha Wood a Daughter named Elizabeth born ffeb: 29. 1755. Baptized 1757 feb: 5. p. 50.

Will: Merriweather & Martha Wood a Son named William born Nov: 5. 1756. Baptized 1757 feb: 5. p. 50.

Cap: Will: Meriwether & Martha Wood a Daughter named Mildred born dec: 29 175..* Baptized 1758 Ap: 25. p. 52.

---

*Margin torn.

Capt Will: Merriwether & Martha Wood a son named Thomas born Ap: 14. 1759. Baptized 1759 Ap: 15. p. 55.

Cap: Will: Merriwether & Martha Wood a son named Valentine born Aug: 17. 1761. Baptized 1761 Sep: 8. p. 61.

Capt: Will: Merriwether & Martha Wood, twins, named James & Sarah born feb: 12 1764. Baptized Feb: 23 1764. p. 66.

William Merriwether & Martha Wood a Daughter named Ann born Oct: 12 1767. Baptized Nov: 19 1767. p. 79.

Will: Douglas Merriwether & Eliz: Lewis a son Nick: Lewis. Baptized Nov: 28 1788. p. 122.

James Meyhim & Martha Hatcher a Daughter named Susannah born Jul: 31 1765. Baptized Sep: 1 1765. p. 72.

Aventoun Mickleroy & Sarah Dawson a son named William born Feb. 6, 1773. Baptized Oct 17, 1773. p. 95.

Will: Miller & Mary Heath a Daughter born May 22, 1743 named Winnifred Jones. p. 40.

Will: Miller & Mary Heath a Son born Oct: 6, 1744 named John. p. 40.

Will: Miller & Mary Heath a Daughter born May 22 1746 named Elizabeth. p. 40.

Will: Miller & Mary Heath a Daughter born Oct: 15 1747 named Sarah. p. 40.

Will: Miller & Mary Heath a Son born Nov: 1 1749 named William Heath. p. 40.

Will: Miller & Mary Heath a Daughter born Nov: 11 1751 named Margaret. p. 40.

Will: Miller & Mary Heath a Son born Mar: 20 1754 named Thomas. p. 40.

Will: Miller & Mary Heath a Daughter born Mar: 8 1756 named Mary. Baptized 1756 Ap: 11. p. 48.

Will Miller & Mary Heath a son named Henry born Sep: 25 1758. Baptized 1758 Nov: 19. p. 53.

Will: Miller & Mary Heath a son named Heath-Jones born dec; 19 1761. Baptized 1762 feb: 20. p. 61.

William Miller & Joanna Leprade a son named John born May 1st 1773. Baptized Jun. 6, 1773. p. 94.

Will. Heath Miller & Joanna Leprade a son named John-Heath born Mar 10, 177... Baptized Ap. 18, 1775. p. 98.

William Miller & Joanna Leprade a daughter named Betsey born Jul, 8, 1776. Baptized Sep. 7, 1776. p. 100.

Nath: Mills & Frances Thomson, Nathaniel, born Oct. 31 1785. Baptized Dec. 28 1785. p. 115.

Nath: Mills & Frances Thomson a child Sarah born Dec. 14 1788. Baptized June 22 1788. p. 121.

Nathl. Mills & Frances Thomson a child Ceily born May 10 1790. Baptized Ap: 29 1792. p. 126.

Nathl. Mills & Frances Thomson a child Nancy born Febr. 1 1792. Baptized Ap: 29 1792. p. 126.

Nath: Mills & Frances Thomson a son Edmond born Oct: 27 1793. Baptized Mar: 30 1794. p. 127.

Will Mills & Peggie Swift a Son Richard born Feb. 7, 1782. Baptized Ap. 5, 1782. p. 106.

Will Mills & Peggie Swift a child Ann born Mar: 2 1784. Baptized Jul: 15 1784. p. 112.

Will Mills & Eliz. Fountain a Son George born Ap. 11, 1782. Baptized Feb. 9, 1783. p. 108.

David Milton & Constant Hog a Daughter named Sally born Ap: 16 1765. Baptized Jul: 6 1765. p. 72.

David Milton & Constance Hog a son named John born Mar: 10 1768. Baptized Ap: 11 1768. p. 80.

David Milton & Constant Hog a son named David born Jun. 15, 1774. Baptized Oct. 10, 1774. p. 97.

Will Milton & Keziah Lyne a child named Rebekah born June 22, 1781. Baptized Aug 5. 1781. p. 103.

Drury Mims & Elizabeth Woodson a son named Drury born Ap: 5 1761. Baptized 1761 May 24. p. 59.

John Mims & Sarah Horn a Son named Martin born Nov: 24 1756. Baptized 1757 Jan: 23. p. 50.

John Mims & Sarah Horn a Daughter named Aggie born May 25 1759. Baptized 1759 Jul: 8. p. 55.

John Mims & Sarah Horn a Daughter named Catie born Ap: 11 1761. Baptized 1761 Jun: 21. p. 60.

John Mims & Sarah Horn a son named Robert born Sep: 10 1763. Baptized Dec: 4 1763. p. 66.

John Mims & Sar: Horn a son named Jesse born Oct: 1 1765. Baptized Feb: 2 1766. p. 73.

John Mims & Sarah Horn a son named Randolph born Ap: 20 1768. Baptized Jun: 12 1768. p. 81.

John Mims & Sarah Horn a son named Lynch born Nov. 14, 1772. Baptized Feb. 7, 1773. p. 93.

John Mims & Mary Moss a son named Tarlton born Nov: 4 1765. Baptized Feb: 23 1766. p. 73.

Shadrach Mims & Elizabeth Woodson a son named Robert born Jun: 29 1764. Baptized Aug: 5 1764. p. 68.

Shadrach Mims & Elizabeth Woodson a Daughter named Mary born Jun: 18 1766. Baptized Jul: 20 1766. p. 74.

Shadrach Mims & Elizabeth Woodson a Daughter named Betty born Ap: 3 1769. Baptized May 14 1769. p. 84.

Shadrach Mims & Eliz: Woodson a daughter named Sally born Jul: .... Baptized Aug 27 1771. p. 90.

Shadrach Mims & Eliz. Woodson a daughter named Martha born Jan 17. 1774. Baptized Ap. 24, 1774. p. 96.

Shadrack Mims & Eliz. Woodson a daughter named Susannah born Jun. 24, 1776. Baptized Sep. 1, 1776. p. 100.

Thomas Mims & Mary Wright a son named David born Nov: 15 1760. Baptized 1761 Jan: 24. p. 58.

Thomas Mims & Mary Wright a Daughter named Judith born Jan: 12 1765. Baptized Mar: 3 1765. p. 70.

Thomas Mims & Mary Wright a son named Drury born Mar: 18 1767. Baptized Ap: 19 1767. p. 77.

Thomas Mims & Mary Wright a Daughter named Frankie born Ju— .... Baptized Aug. 6 1769. p. 85.

Tho. Mims & Mary Wright a son named John: Wright born Nov. 29, 1773. Baptized Mar. 13, 1774. p. 96.

Garret Minor & Mary Overton Tyrrell a daughter named Rebekah born Feb. 2. Baptized Feb. 13, 1775. p. 98.

Garret Minor & Mary Overton a daughter named Eliz: Lewis born Aug. 27, 1776. Baptized Nov. 6. 1776. p. 101.

Garret Minor & Mary Terril a child named Sarah born Aug 14, 1781. Baptized Sep. 20, 1781. p. 104.

Garret Minor & Mary Overton Terril a son Peter born June 30 1783. Baptized Aug: 5 1783. p. 110.

Col: Garrit Minor & Mary Terril a son James born Ap: 18 1785. Baptized Jul: 25 1785. p. 114.

Col: Garrit Minor & Mary Overton Tyrrill a child Louisa Aug. 13 1787. Baptized Sep. 7 1787. p. 119.

Col: Garret Minor & Mary Overton Tyrrel a son baptized named Sam Overton born June 3 1790. Baptized Aug: 18 1790. p. 126.

Tho: Ker Minor & Ann Reid, [Redd] a child Eliz: Louisa born May 27 1787. Baptized Aug. 27 1787. p. 119.

Tho: Carr Minor & Ann Redd a child named Caroline Feb: 17 1789. Baptized Ap: 12 1789. p. 122.

Thos. C. Minor & Ann Redd a child baptized (Frances) born 1 Dec. 1790. Baptized June 12 1791. p. 126.

Thomas Minor & Ann Redd a child John born Octo. 18 1792. Baptized April 12 1793. p. 122.

Thos. Minor & Ann Red a daughter Catherine born 29 May 1794. Baptized Sep: 6 1795. p. 127.

Richard Minter & Martha Scrugs a Daughter named Drusilla born Jan: 15 1758. Baptized 1758 Aug: 27. p. 53.

Archer Mitchel & Hannah Kirby a Daughter named Sally born Nov: 8 1761. Baptized 1762 May 9. p. 62.

Archilaus Mitchel & Mary Gregory a Daughter named Ann born Mar: 9 1766. Baptized Ap: 15 1766. p. 73.

Barnet Mitchel & Nancy Lane—Ann born .... Baptized Aug. 28. 1782. p. 107.

Barnet Mitchel & Eliz: Lane, Julius Cezar Augustus Lane, Jan. 26 1784. Baptized Jul: 15 1786. p. 117.

Benjamin Mitchel & Ann Holland Twins named William & David born Jan: 1757. Baptized 1757 Ap: 11. p. 50.

Benjamin Mitchel & Ann Holland a Daughter named Elizabeth born dec: 13 1759. Baptized 1760 Aug: 31. p. 58.

Benjamin Mitchel & Ann Holland a Daughter named Mary born Jun: 9 1762. Baptized 1763 Aug: 14. p. 65.

Benjamin Mitchel & Ann Holland a son named Pouncie born Mar: 23 1765. Baptized May 17 1766. p. 74.

Benjamin Mitchel & Ann Holland a son named Archilaus born Dec: 11 1768. Baptized Ap: 21 1769. p. 84.

Ben Mitchel & Ann Holland a daughter named Judith born Ap. 12, 1772. Baptized Aug. 21, 1772. p. 92.

David Mitchell & Sarah Moss a son named Reuben born dec: 5, 1756. Baptized 1757 Jan: 9. p. 49.

David Mitchell & Sarah Moss a son named Abner born May 30, 1762. Baptized 1762 Jun: 20. p. 63.

David Mitchel & Sarah Moss a Daughter named Annie born May 2 1764. Baptized Jun: 24 1764. p. 68.

David Mitchel & Sarah Moss a son named Edmund born Ap: 5 1767. Baptized May 10 1767. p. 77.

John Mitchel & Marianne Sinclair a daughter named Christian born Sep 7, 1775. Baptized Oct 26, 1775. p. 99.

Jo: Mitchel & Eliz: Snelson a child Catie born Jan. 2. 1782. Baptized June 2, 1782. p. 106.

Jo: Mitchel & Eliz: Snelson a child Garland born June 20 1787. Baptized Nov: 4 1787. p. 120.

Thomas Mitchel & Judith Moss a son named Charles born Mar: 13. 1759. Baptized 1759 Ap: 29. p. 55.

Thomas Mitchell & Judith Moss a son named Joel born Nov: 31 1761. Baptized 1762 Mar: 14. p. 62.

Thomas Mitchel & Mildred Merriwether a daughter named Barbara Milton born Dec. 6, 1775. Baptized Dec. 10, 1775. p. 99.

Tho: Mitchel & Isabella Jordan a child Frances Jordan born Mar: 10 1784. Baptized Ap: 14 1784. p. 111.

Tho: Mitchel & Isabella Jordan, Sarah Jordan, born Sep: 23 1785. Baptized Nov: 7 1785. p. 115.

Tho: Mitchel & Isabella Jordan, Alexr Williams born Nov. 26 1788. Baptized Dec. 1 1788. p. 121.

Will Mitchel & Sarah Letcher a son named Thomas born May 14, 1771. Baptized Jun. 16 1771. p. 90.

Amos Lad: More & Ann Rogers a son named John born Oct. 9, 1776. Baptized Dec. 1, 1776. p. 101.

Amos Lad More & Ann Rogers a child Pattie born Jan 1st. 1782. Baptized June 16, 1782. p. 107.

Amos Lad More & Ann Rogers a child Elizabeth born Mar: 12 1784. Baptized Ap: 18 1784. p. 111.

Charles More & Ann Wylie a son named Elisha born Jul: 3 1768. Baptized Nov: 3 1768. p. 82.

Charles More & Ann Wylie a Daughter named Patty born feb: 19 1770. Baptized Aug: 19 1770. p. 88.

Warren More & Anne Seay a son named Jesse born Sep. 5, 1779. Baptized Oct 21, 1781. p. 104.

William Moore & Sarah Perkins a son named David, born dec: 27. 1358. Baptized 1759 Sep: 29. p. 56.

Will: More & Sarah Perkins a son named Joseph born Sep: 13. 1761. Baptized 1762 May. 22. p. 63.

David Moracet & Jean Baker a son named Peter born Dec: 29 1768. Baptized Feb: 11 1769. p. 83.

John Moracet & Eliz: Blankenship a Daughter named Marey born Jul: 22 1757. Baptized 1757 Sep: 8. p. 51.

Jo: Moracet & Fanny fford Twins named John & Fanny born Ap: 4, 1763. Baptized 1763 May 29. p. 64.

John Moracet & Frances ffore a son named William born Oct: 31 1765. Baptized Jan: 25 1766. p. 73.

Drury Morel & Judah Sampson a Daughter named Martha born Nov: 18 1758. Baptized 1759 ffeb: 14. p. 54.

Drury Morell & Judith sampson a son named Stephen born May 28. 1760. Baptized 1760 Sep: 22. p. 58.

John Moreland & Ann Ogilvy a son named Jesse: Ogilvy born June 18, 1777. Baptized Aug. 17, 1777. p. 102.

Wright Moreland & Ann Wilson a son named Charles born Sep: 8 1764. Baptized Oct: 7 1764. p. 69.

Wright Morland & Ann Wilson a Daughter named Elizabeth born Dec: 24 1766. Baptized Feb: 15 1767. p. 76.

Wright Morning & Ann Wilson a Daughter named Lucy born Jan: 8 1769. Baptized Feb: 19 1769. p. 83.

Wright Moreland & Ann Wilson a daughter named Ann born Nov. 17, 1771. Baptized Jan. 5 1772. p. 91.

John Morgan & Mary Rogers a Daughter named Kesiah born dec: 21 1758 [sic]. Baptized 1758 Jun: 11. p. 52.

John Morgan & Mary Rogers a Daughter named Mary born Oct: 9 1760. Baptized 1760 Nov: 22. p. 58.

Gerard Morgan & Eliz: Milton a son named Gerard born Oct. .... 1772. Baptized Dec. 13, 1772. p. 93.

Da. Morris & Eliz: Guthry a son David, born Jan: 20 1784. Baptized June 26 1785. p. 114.

Geo: Morris & Sally Biggars a child Patsy Oliver born Jul: 2 1784. Baptized Dec. 1 1784. p. 113.

Is: Morris & Ann Dickerson Smith, a son Dickerson born Nov. 3 1785. Baptized Dec. 27 1785. p. 115.

Jo: Morris & Sar: Periere a child Francis born Oct. 17 1782. Baptized Ap: 21 1783. p. 109.

Jo: Morris & Linney Brown, a child Nancy-born Oct: 12: 1786. Baptized Jan: 30 1787. p. 118.

Joseph Morris & Annie Potter a daughter named Susannah born May 24 17..... Baptized Jun. 30, 1771. p. 90.

Joseph Morris & Ann Potter a son named William born Dec. 24, 1773. Baptized Mar. 13, 1774. p. 96.

Joseph Morris & Mary Ffarrar a son named Joseph Royal born Oct 13, 1773. Baptized Dec. 26, 1774. p. 95.

Sam: Morris & Mary Jones a son Sam: Timberlick born Oct. 18 1783. Baptized Aug: 29 1784. p. 112.

Sam Morris & Mary Jones a son George born Aug. 8 1783. Baptized June 26 1785. p. 114.

William Morris & Sarah McComack a son named Edward born Mar: 25 1765. Baptized May 1 1765. p. 71.

Will Jordan Morton & Martha Pryor a child Sarah born Nov: 10 1781. Baptized Sep. 18 1785. p. 115.

Will Jordan Morton & Martha Pryor a child Rebeckah born May 21 1783. Baptized Sep. 18 1785. p. 115.

Will Jordan Morton & Martha Pryor a child Frances born Mar: 9 1785. Baptized Sep. 18 1785. p. 115.

Jo: Morton & Mary Tandie a son Clegat born Mar: 28 1789. Baptized Aug. 23 1789. p. 125.

Da: Moseby & Ann Coke a Son Micajah born Sep. 3, 1781. Baptized Feb 28, 1783. p. 108.

Rob: Moseby & Ann Lewis a son named Samuel born Nov. 9 1770. Baptized Jan: 10 1771. p. 89.

Sam: Moseby & Jerusha Bowles a Daughter named Mary born Oct: 2. 1755. Baptized 1757 feb: 5. p. 50.

Sam: Moseby & Jerusha Bowles a son named Joseph born Jan: 27 1756. Baptized 1757 feb: 5. p. 50.

Samuel Moseby & Jerushah Bowles a Daughter named Eliz: born Nov: 20 1758. Baptized 1759 Ap: 15. p. 55.

Capt: Sam: Moseby & Jerusha Bowls a Daughter named Sybylla born May 10 1762. Baptized 1762 Jun: 6. p. 63.

Sam: Moseby & Jurisha Bowles a son named Thomas born feb: 13 1764. Baptized Feb: 23 1764. p. 66.

Arthur Mosely & Martha Camp a son named Arthur born July 31, 1763. Baptized 1763 Sep: 18. p. 65.

Arthur Mosely & Martha Camp a Daughter named Susannah born Nov: 30 1766. Baptized Jan: 17 1767. p. 76.

Elijah Mosely & Nivine Garner a Daughter named Judith born Jun: 14 1768. Baptized Aug: 7 1768. p. 81.

John Mosely & Ann Williams a Son named Jesse born feb: 13, 1757. Baptized 1757 Mar. 20. p. 50.

John Mosely & Ann Williams a son named James born dec: 25. 1759. Baptized 1760 Jan: 26. p. 56.

John Mosely & Ann Williams a Daughter named Mary born Jun: 15 1765. Baptized May 23 1766. p. 74.

John Mosely & Ann Williams a Daughter named Nancy born Jan: .... 1769. Baptized Jul: 5 1769. p. 85.

John Mosely & Sarah Walker a Daughter named Martha born Jun: 14 1764. Baptized Aug: 5 1764. p. 68.

Joseph Mosely & Ann Graves a Daughter named Mary born Dec: 31 1768. Baptized Ap: 1 1769. p. 84.

Joseph Mosely & Anna Graves a daughter named Susannah born Jan 14, 1772. Baptized May. 30, 1772. p. 92.

John [Joseph?] Mosely & Ann Graves a son named Marvel: Adams born Feb 25, 1775. Baptized May 7 1775. p. 98.

Rob: Mosely & Magdalen Garren [Gerrand?—now Guerrant] a Daughter named Esther: Garren born Jun: 20: 1762. Baptized 1762 Jul: 25. p. 63.

Rob: Mosely & Magdalen Garren [Gerrand?—now Guerrant] a son named Arthur born Nov: 7. 1760. Baptized 1762 Jul: 25. p. 63.

Robert Mosely & Magdalen Gerran a Daughter named Sarah born Jul: 26 1764. Baptized Sep: 9 1764. p. 69.

Robert Mosely & Magdalene Gerran a son named John born Jan: 7 1766. Baptized Mar: 8 1766. p. 73.

Robert Mosely & Magdalene Gerrand a son named Robert born Jan: 23 1768. Baptized Mar: 12 1768. p. 80.

Sam: Mosely & Martha Hodges a Daughter named Jeanie born May 15. 1762. Baptized 1762 Aug: 15. p. 63.

Samuel Mosely & Martha Hodges a Daughter named Annie born Jul: 29 1765. Baptized May 17 1766. p. 74.

William Mosely & Keziah Overstreet a daughter named Betsy born Jan 10, 1773. Baptized May. 3, 1773. p. 94.

Will Mosely & Kesiah Overstreet a son named Samuel born May 11, 1775. Baptized Jul. 21. 1775. p. 98.

Will Mosely & Keziah Overstreet a Daughter named Evice born Dec: 26, 1776. Baptized June 1, 1777. p. 102.

Will Mosely & Ann Lewis a son named Edward: Hawk born Oct: 7. 1776. Baptized Nov. 10, 1776. p. 101.

Will: Mosely & Ann Lewis a child Betsy Lewis born Mch. 10 1784. Baptized June 22 1784. p. 112.

Alexr Moss & Ann Thurmond a Daughter named Jean born Nov: 24 1761. Baptized 1762 Ap: 12. p. 62.

Alexr Moss & Ann Thurman a son named Philip born May 21, 1763. Baptized 1763 Sep: 12. p. 65.

Alexander Moss & Ann Thurmond a son named Fleming born Ap: 20 1765. Baptized Jul: 6 1765. p. 71.

Alexr Moss & Ann Thurmond a daughter named Susannah born Jun. 18, 1773. Baptized Sep. 5, 1773. p. 95.

Gideon Moss & susannah Richardson a Daughter named Sally born dec: 29 1762. Baptized 1763 Mar: 31. p. 64.

Gideon Moss & Susannah Richardson a son named John born Mar: 10 1765. Baptized May 26 1765. p. 71.

Gideon Moss & Susannah Richardson a Daughter named Susannah born Jul: 9 1766. Baptized Ap: 19 1767. p. 77.

Gideon Moss & Susannah Richardson a son named Gideon, born Mar: 19 1768. Baptized Nov: 3 1768. p. 82.

Hugh Moss & Jeanie fford a Daughter named Sally-Winn born Ap: 17 1769. Baptized May 11 1769. p. 84.

John Moss & Charity Hughes a Daughter named ffrances born Ap: 1, 1763. Baptized 1763 Sep: 12. p. 65.

John Moss & Charity Hughes a son named Anderson born Sep: 12 1766. Baptized Mar: 29 1767. p. 76.

John Moss & Charity Hughes a son named Hugh born Sep: 19 1768. Baptized Nov: 3 1768. p. 82.

John Moss & Charity Hughes a son named Alexr born Feb. 24. 1771. Baptized Jun. 30, 1771. p. 90.

John Moss & Charity Hughes a daughter named Elizabeth born May 20, 1773. Baptized Sep. 5, 1773. p. 95.

John Moss & Charity Hughes a daughter named Jean born Nov. 5, 1775. Baptized Feb. 17, 1777. p. 101.

Samuel Moss & Eliz: Tisdale a son named Samuel born May 23 1764. Baptized Jul: 15 1764. p. 68.

Samuel Moss & Eliz: Tisdale a daughter named Sarah born Nov: 19 1765. Baptized May 17 1766. p. 74.

Samuel Moss & Susan: Powel a son named William, born Jan: 7. 1777. Baptized June 23, 1777. p. 102.

Harry Mullins & Mary Tony a Son named Archer born Oct: 3. 1760. Baptized 1763 Jun: 19. p. 64.

John Mullen & Betty Connerly [Conolly] a Daughter named Elizabeth born May 16 1756. Baptized 1756 Jun: 13. p. 48.

John Mullens & Elizabeth Conolly a son named David born May 11 1758. Baptized 1758 June 25. p. 53.

John Mullens & Elizabeth Conolly a Daughter named Mary born feb: 1st 1760. Baptized 1760 Ap: 27. p. 57.

John Mullens & Betty Conolly a son named Joel born Jul: 23 1762. Baptized 1762 Aug: 29. p. 63.

John Mullens & Elizabeth Conoly a son named William born Mar: 6 1764. Baptized Ap: 22 1764. p. 67.

John Mullens & Betty Conolly a Daughter named Frances born Dec: 5 1766. Baptized Feb: 3 1767. p. 76.

Will Mullin & Eliz. Hooten* a daughter named Susannah born Nov. 24, 1775. Baptized Ap. 28 1776. p. 100.

Abram Munday & Molly Burrows, a son, Henry, born Ap: 3 1786. Baptized Oct. 9 1786. p. 117.

Abram Monday & Molly Burress a child Polly Mar .... 1788. Baptized Sept. 22 1788. p. 121.

Abraham Monday & Mary Burrows a child, Burrows, born Jan: 2 1793. Baptized Mar: 21 1793. p. 122.

Samuel Mylom & Sarah Kemp a son named Jordan born feb: 28 1764. Baptized Jul: 29 1764. p. 68.

Archibald Napier & Mary Hubbard a Daughter called Jean born May 19 1766. Baptized Jan: 8 1768. p. 79.

Arch: Napier & Mary Hubbard a son named Ja: Kirk born Jul: 14 1768. Baptized Aug: 12 1770. p. 88.

Booth Napier & Christian Norvil a son named Will: Parsons born Oct: 19 1765. Baptized Feb: 9 1766. p. 73.

*Hutton in Marriage record.

John Napier & Mary Champion a son named Moses Champion born May 1 1764. Baptized Jul: 15 1764. p. 68.

Rene Napier & Rebekah Hurt a Daughter named Lucy born Jan: 19 1766. Baptized Aug: 17 1766. p. 74.

Rene Napier & Rebekah Hurt a son named Shelton born May 29 1767. Baptized Dec: 22 1767. p. 79.

Rene Napier & Rebekah Hurt a son named Thomas born Nov: 1 1768. Baptized Mar: 19 1769. p. 84.

Rene Napier & Rebekah Hurt a Daughter named Sarah Garland born Jan: 22 1771. Baptized May 24 1771. p. 89.

Rene Napier & Rebecca Hurt a son named Rene born Ap. 11, 1772. Baptized May 1, 1774. p. 96.

Rene Napier & Rebekah Hurt a daughter called Chloe born Jan 12, 1774. Baptized Feb. 27, 1774. p. 95.

Rene Napier & Susannah Horn a child Betsie Booth, Oct: 17 1781. Baptized Sep: 21 1784. p. 112.

Arthur Nash & Sarah Abrey had a Son baptised dec: 31 1755 [sic] called .... Baptized 1756 Jan: 1st. p. 48.

Mr. Arthur Nash & Sarah Avery had a son named John born Dec 31, 1755. p. 105.

Henry Nash & Alice Holland a daughter Betsy: Holland born May 23, 1773. Baptized Jul. 4, 1773. p. 94.

John Nash & Mary Basket a Daughter named Suckie born Jun: 7, 1762. Baptized 1762 Aug: 15. p. 63.

John Nash & Mary Basket a Daughter named ffrances born Jan: 20 1764. Baptized Ap: 22 1764. p. 67.

John Nash & Mary Basket a Daughter named Mary born Sep: 27 1766. Baptized Nov: 2 1766. p. 75.

John Nash & Mary Basket a son named William born Nov 5 1768. Baptized Jan: 29 1769. p. 83.

Marvel Nash & Agnes Hodges a son named William born Jul: 26 1766. Baptized Nov: 2 1766. p. 75.

Ja. Nelson & Lucy Robinson a child Agnes born Feb 6, 1782. Baptized Ap. 5, 1782. p. 106.

Ja: Nelson & Lucy Robinson a son William born Oct. 18 1783. Baptized Jul: 15 1784. p. 112.

Jo: Nelson & Lucy Robinson, Elizabeth born Oct. 18 1785. Baptized Mar: 26 1786. p. 116.

Jo: Nelson & Rebekah Woodley a child named Lucy Eppes born Nov. 3, 1781. Baptized Mar. 13, 1782. p. 105.

John Nelson & Rebecca Woodleif a daughter named Rebecca: Woodleif born Jan 1st 1773. Baptized Jun. 15, 1773. p. 94.

Jo: Nelson & Rebeccah Woodliff a son John born Mar 4 1786. Baptized Sep: 17 1786. p. 117.

Jo: Nelson & Rebekah Woodlif, Catherine Griffin, born June 14 1783. Baptized Nov. 15 1784. p. 113.

Jo: Nilson & Rebecca Woodlief a son Salmon Hugh Jan. 2 1788. Baptized Jul: 13 1788. p. 121.

Jo: Nelson & Susanna Coleman a child Elizabeth. Baptized Jul: 15 1784. p. 112.

Jo: Nelson & Susanna Coleman a child Francis born Oct: 10 1786. Baptized Jan: 8 1787. p. 118.

Jo: Nelson & Agatha Winslow, Catherine-Winslow Sep: 20 1785. Baptized Oct. 23 1785. p. 115.

John Nelson & Agatha B. Winslow Mariah 2 Feby. 1787. Baptized Mar: 2 1788. p. 120.

Joseph Nelson & Lucy Tate a child Lucy born May 18 1783. Baptized June 9 1783. p. 109.

Jos: Nelson & Lucy Tate a child Sarah born Ap: 1 1785. Baptized Aug: 12 1785. p. 114.

Jo: Nelson & Lucy Tait a child Mary-Ann born Mar: 26 1787. Baptized May 3 1787. p. 118.

Col: Jo: Nelsons family Feb. 18 1789. p. 135.

Jo: Nelson & Fanny Armstead were maried.

Sep. ....65 Francis Anderson yr daughter was born

Jo. Nelson & Rebekah Woodley were maried.

Sarah Philip yr child was born.

Ann yr child was born.

Hepzibah yr child was born.

Rebekah Woodley yr child was born.

Mary yr child was born.

Elizabeth yr child was born.

Mary yr child was born, now dead.

Lucy Eppes yr child was born.

William yr son was born.

Catherine Griffin yr child was born.

John yr son was born.

Salmon Hughes yr son was born.

Wade Netherland & Ann Williamson a Daughter named ffrances born Oct: 21 1765. Baptized Feb: 1 1766. p. 73.

Wade Netherland & Ann Williamson a son named Wade born Nov: 4 1767. Baptized Dec: 26 1767. p. 79.

Will: Neves & Christian Mask a Daughter named Mary-Mask born Ap: 16 1759. Baptized Jun: 23 1765. p. 71.

Will: Neves & Christian Mask a son named Daniel born feb: 7 1761. Baptized Jun: 23 1765. p. 71.

Will: Neves & Christian Mask a son named John-Mask born Jan: 7 1753. Baptized Jan: 13 1764. p. 69.

Will: Neves & Christian Mask a son named William born Oct: 8 1755. Baptized Jan: 13 1764. p. 69.

Will: Neves & Christian Mask a Daughter named Elizabeth born Oct: 26 1764. Baptized Jan: 13 1764. p. 69.

Edward News & Susannah Rogers a Daughter named Sukie born Jul 3 1763. Baptized Jul: 31 1764. p. 68.

Sam. Newton & Agnes Chiles a Son Henry born Jul. 3, 1781. Baptized Ap. 9, 1782. p. 106.

Sam: Newton & Agnes Chiles a son Thomas born Mar: 5 1785. Baptized June 13 1785. p. 114.

Sam Newton & Agnes Chiles a child Fannie born Jan: 12 1788. Baptized Ap: 11 1789. p. 122.

Samuel Newton & Agnes Chiles a son Samuel born Oct. 7 1789. Baptized Ap: 2 1791. p. 126.

William Nichols & Mary Peek deceased a son named Charles born May 16. 1760. Baptized 1760 Jun: 24. p. 57.

Mathew Nightingale & Lucy Cothan a Daugh: named Mary born Jan: 20 1761. Baptized 1761 Ap: 5. p. 59.

Mat: Nightingale & Lucy Cauthon a Daughter named Catherine born Jun: 22 1762. Baptized 1762 Aug: 8. p. 63.

Mathew Nightengale & Lucy Cothan a Daughter named Lucy born Jan: 22 1765. Baptized Ap: 7 1765. p. 70.

Jacob Noon & .... a Daughter born Jan: 26 1739 named Susannah. p. 40.

Christopher Norden & Mary Emmerson a son named William born Jun 13. 1754. 1756 June 26. p. 49.

Joseph Norman & Eliz: Sled a son Nelson, born Dec. 7 1785. Baptized 1785. p. 115.

Joshua Normand & Eliz: Slate, Molly, born Ap: 3 1786. Baptized Oct. 9 1786. p. 117.

Thomas Norvil & Mary Dawson a Daughter named Sarah born Oct: 29 1768. Baptized Jan: 29 1769. p. 83.

Tho: Norvil & Mary Dawson a daughter named Martha born Aug. 24, 1771. Baptized Dec. 15, 1771. p. 91.

Thomas Norvil & Mary Dawson a daughter named Jeanie born Oct 2, 1774. Baptized Jan. 22, 1775. p. 97.

Tho: Norvil & Mary Dawson a son named Spencer Dawson born Mar 5, 1777. Baptized Aug. 10, 1777. p. 102.

Isaac Oakes & Rachel Crane a daughter named Sarah born Feb. 17. 1775. Baptized May. 28, 1775. p. 98.

Jacob Ogilsvey & Ann Bailey a Son named Thomas born Jan: 5. 1761. Baptized 1761 May 24. p. 60.

Jacob Oglisby & Ann Bailey a son named Jesse born Nov: 15 1763. Baptized Aug: 12 1764. p. 68.

[Jacob Ogilsby] & Ann Bailey a son named Pleasants-Bailey born Mar: 15 1766. Baptized May 10 1767. p. 77.

Richard Ogilsby & Sarah ffergusson deceased a Son named James born dec: 17. 1756. Baptized 1757 Ap: 9. p. 50.

Richard Ogilsby & Eliz: Price a son named Jesse born Mar: 24 1759. Baptized 1759 May 2. p. 55.

Will: Ogilsby & Ann Perkins a son named Joseph born May 6. 1756. Baptized 1756 Jul: 14. p. 49.

William Ogilsby & Ann Perkins a Daughter named Hannah born
Oct: 8 1764. Baptized Dec: 13 1764. p. 69.

Will. Ogilvy & Martha Ellis a daughter named Lucy born Feb.
4, 1774. Baptized Jan. 29, 1775. p. 97.

Charles Ominet & Dianah Hudson a Daughter named Martha born
feb: 2, 1763. Baptized 1763 May 1st. p. 64.

John Oliver & Ann Sharp a Daughter named Lucy born May 15.
1758. Baptized 1758 Jun: 24. p. 52.

Thomas Oliver & Agnes Boyd a Daughter named Elizabeth born
May 20 1765. Baptized Dec: 13 1769. p. 86.

Thomas Oliver & Agnes Boyd a Daughter named Eleanor born
Mar: 14 1767. Baptized Dec: 13 1769. p. 84.

Thomas Oliver & Ann Boyd a son named William born Ap: 5
1769. Baptized May 2 1769. p. 84.

Tho: Oliver & Agnes Rollins a Daughter named Sarah born Mar:
16 1758. Baptized Jun: 22 1766. p. 74.

Tho: Oliver & Agnes Rollins a son named James born ye same
time, being twins. Baptized Jun: 22 1766. p. 84.

Marg: Daughter to Tho: Oliver & Aggie Rolins, aged ....
was baptized. Baptized Aug: 5 1768. p. 81.

Ja: Orford & Lucy Bailey a Daughter named Mary born Aug: 1.
1756. Baptized 1756 Sep: 5. p. 49.

James Orford & Lucy Bailey a Daughter named ffanny born Jan:
15 1759. Baptized 1759 Mar: 4. p. 54.

.... Eliz: *Orford a daughter named Ann born Feb. 13, 1771.
Baptized May. 11, 1772. p. 92.

Michael Osburn & Mary Hanson a son named Randolph born Jul:
18. 1759. Baptized 1759 Sep: 30. p. 56.

James Overstreet & Frances Ewbank a Daughter named Mary born
Jul: 1 1768. Baptized Aug: 14 1768. p. 81.

James Overstreet & Frances Eubank a son named Charles born
feb: 10 1770. Baptized Ap: 15 1770. p. 87.

James Overstreet & Frances Eubank a son named William born
Feb. 8. 1772. Baptized May 11, 1772. p. 92.

James Overstreet & Frances Eubank a son named John born Ap.
1, 1774. Baptized Jun. 5, 1774. p. 96.

James Overstreet & Frances Hewbank a daughter named Frances
born Feb. 3, 1777. Baptized Mar. 30, 1777. p. 101.

Ja: Overstreet & Nancy Lewis a child Milly May 18 1786. Baptized Jul: 9 1786. p. 117.

Tho: Overstreet & Zillas Yeamie a child Nansie born Oct. 19 1784.
Baptized 1785. p. 115.

Tho: Overstreet & Zellah Yeamans a child Jean Mar: 1 1787.
Baptized June 10 1787. p. 119.

---

*[Elizabeth Taylor—m—Ja: Orford 30 May 1771].

Barnet Owen & Mary Walker a Daughter named Mary born Mar: 22 1757. Baptized 1757 Jun: 12. p. 51.

Barnet Owen & Mary Walker a Daughter named Joyce born feb: 24 1759. Baptized 1759 May 27. p. 55.

Barnet Owen & Eliz. *Orton a daughter named Sally born Sep. 3, 1772. Baptized Oct. 20, 1772. p. 93.

Barnet Owen & Eliz. Orton a daughter named Mally born Jan. 21. 1774. Baptized Ap. 27, 1774. p. 96.

James Owen & Eliz: Rusel a daughter Sally Baugh born Jul. 30, 1777. Baptized Oct 19, 1777. p. 102.

Joel Owen & Eliz: Gilbert a Daughter named Cecily born in fornication feb: 28 1765. Baptized Sep: 15 1765. p. 72.

Joel Owen & Mary Wilkerson a Daughter named Susannah born Nov 14 1766. Baptized Mar: 8 1767. p. 76.

Joel Owen & Mary Wilkerson a Daughter named Jeanie born Oct: 20 1768. Baptized Jan: 29 1769. p. 83.

Joel Owen & Mary Wilkerson a son named James born Nov. 14, 1771. Baptized Jun. 8. 1771. p. 90.

Joel Owen & Mally Wilkerson a daughter named Mally born Mar. 23, 1772. Baptized May 11, 1772. p. 92.

Joel Owen & Mary Wilkerson a daughter named Nelly born Aug. 4. 1776. Baptized Sep. 8. 1776. p. 100.

Joel Owen & Sarah Fenwicks a son named James born Oct: 5 1768. Baptized Ap: 23 1769. p. 84.

William Owen & Agnes Wilkerson a son named Barnet born Jul: 29 1769. Baptized Sep: 24 1769. p. 86.

Jesse Pace & Frances Hill a Daughter Hannah Boutle born Mar: 15, 1777. Baptized Jul: 13, 1777. p. 102.

John Pace & susannah Huchins a Daughter called Elizabeth born May 3. 1759. Baptized 1759 Jun: 10. p. 55.

John Paces & susannah Hutchins a son named Edward born May 27 1761. Baptized 1761 Jun: 21. p. 60.

John Pace & Susannah Houchins a son named Francis born Nov: 23 1764. Baptized Ap: 14 1765. p. 70.

John Pace & Susannah Huchins a Daughter named Rachel born dec: 21 1766. Baptized Mar: 8 1767. p. 76.

John Pace & Susannah Huchins a son named Charles born Oct: 24 1768. Baptized Jan: 29 1769. p. 83.

John Pace & Susannah Houchins a son named Stephen born Oct: 2 1770. Baptized Nov. 11 1770. p. 88.

John Pace & Susannah Huchins a son named James born Nov. 25, 1772. Baptized Jan. 8. 1773. p. 93.

Axelheath Page & Christian Page a Son named Joseph born Ap: 22. 1756. Baptized 1756 May 16. p. 48.

*Rachel Horton in marriage record.

Ben: Page & Ann Wright a son named William born Mar. 5, 1773. Baptized Ap. 11, 1773. p. 94.

Ben: Page & Anna Wright a daughter named Frances born Jul. 23, 1775. Baptized Aug 20, 1775. p. 99.

James Page & Mary England a Daughter named Elizabeth born Mar: 26 1766. Baptized Jun: 29 1766. p. 74.

James Page & Mary England a son named Anderson born Jul 27 1768. Baptized Sep: 4 1768. p. 82.

Ja: Page & Mary England a Daughter named Mary born Jan: 21 1771. Baptized Ap: 10 1771. p. 89.

James Page & Mary England a son named Benoni born Oct 1, 1772. Baptized Oct 25, 1772. p. 93.

James Page & Mary England a son named James born Sep 10, 1774. Baptized Nov. 3, 1774. p. 97.

James Page & Mary England a son named William born Oct 26. 1776. Baptized Dec. 25, 1776. p. 101.

James Page & Sarah Welburn a daughter named Judith born Sep. 14. 1771. Baptized Jan. 5, 1772. p. 91.

John Page & Unity Harris a son named William born Jul: 5 1758. Baptized 1758 Aug: 6. p. 53.

John Page & Unity Harris a son named John born feb: 6 1760. Baptized 1760 Ap: 8. p. 57.

John Page & Unity Harris a son named Venson born feb: 6. 1762. Baptized 1762 Ap: 25. p. 62.

John Page & Unity Harris a son named Absalom born Mar: 22 1764. Baptized Ap: 22 1764. p. 67.

John Page & Edie Cothan a son named Jesse born May 2 1765. Baptized May 26 1765. p. 71.

John Page & Edith Cauthon a Daughter named Betty born Jun: 24 1767. Baptized Jul: 19 1767. p. 78.

John Page & Edith Cauthon a son named James born Nov: 12 1769. Baptized Nov: 18 1769. p. 86.

John Page & Evie Cothan a daughter named Sally born Mar. 15, 1773. Baptized May 2, 1773. p. 94.

Joseph Page & Isabel Steventon a son named John born Ap: 7 1764. Baptized May 13 1764. p. 67.

Joseph Page & Elizabeth Steventon a Daughter named Betty born May 16 1767. Baptized Jun: 21 1767. p. 78.

William Page & Ann England a daughter named Mary-Anderson born Ap: 5 1767. Baptized May 10 1767. p. 77.

Will: Page & Ann England a Daughter named Elizabeth born feb: 10 1771. Baptized Mar 24 1771. p. 89.

Will: Page & Ann England a daughter named Nansy born Nov. 4. 1772. Baptized Dec. 13, 1772. p. 93.

Will Page & Ann England a son named Dabney: Anderson born Nov. 24. 1776. Baptized Jan. 26, 1776. p. 101.

Will: Page & Agnes Houchins a Daughter named Jean born Sep: 12 1758. Baptized 1758 Oct: 15. p. 53.

Will: Page & Agnes Houchins a son named Robert born Jan: 26. 1762. Baptized Mar: 14 1762. p. 62.

William Page & Agnes Houchins a Daughter named Susannah born feb: 17 1764. Baptized Ap: 1 1764. p. 67.

William Page & Agnes Hutchins a Daughter named Elizabeth born May 11 1769. Baptized Jun: 25 1769. p. 85.

Will: Page & *Sarah Wetherspoon a daughter named Fanny born Sep: 17 1771. Baptized Oct: 13 1771. p. 90.

William Page & Mary Wetherspoon a son named Jesse born Oct 29, 1774. Baptized Jan. 22, 1775. p. 97.

William Page & Mary Wetherspoon a son named Reuben born .... 1776. Baptized Nov. 3. 1776. p. 101.

Will Page & Mary Wetherspoon a child Patsy born Sep: 22 1782. Baptized Ap: 19 1783. p. 109.

Will: Page & Jeanie Stevens a Son born dec: 23. 1755 named Joseph. Baptized 1756 Jan: 17. p. 48.

William & Jean Pages a son named William born dec: 27 1757. Baptized 1758 Jan: 22. p. 51.

Will: Page & Jeany Steventon a son named Melchisideck born Aug: 6 1761. Baptized 1761 Sep: 13. p. 61.

William Page & Jean Steventon a son named Hezekias born dec: 23 1763. Baptized Mar: 11 1764. p. 67.

Samuel Pankie & Betsey Belford a son named Philip born feb: 16. 1763. Baptized 1763 May 29. p. 64.

Aaron Parish & Sarah *Binns a Daughter named Salley born Mar: 13 1764. Baptized Jun: 24 1768. p. 68.

Aaron Parish & Sarah Barns a Daughter named Charity born Mar: 12 1766. Baptized Jul: 28 1766. p. 74.

Aaron Parish & Sarah Barns a Daughter named Elizabeth born Jan: 26 1768. Baptized Feb: 10 1768. p. 79.

Abraham Parish & Martha Holland a Daughter named Ann born Nov: 4 1764. Baptized Mar: 22 1765. p. 70.

Abram Parish & Sarah Clark a Daughter named Nansy born Nov: 10 1768. Baptized Ap: 20 1769. p. 84.

Bowker Parish & Constancy Massie a Daughter named Susannah born Nov: 13 1767. Baptized Feb: 10 1768. p. 79.

Booker Parish & Constance Massie a daughter named Ann born Oct 12, 1769. Baptized Aug 21, 1772. p. 92.

Booker Parish & Constance Massie a son named David born Jan. 12. 1772. Baptized Aug 21, 1772. p. 92.

Booker Parish & Constancy Massie a daughter named Peggie born Mar. 18, 1774. Baptized Sep. 15, 1775. p. 99.

David Parish & Judith Holland a Daughter named Martha: Holland born dec: 26. 1758. Baptized 1759 ffeb: 21. p. 54.

---

*Mary in marriage record.
*Barnes in marriage record.

Umphah* Parrish & Eliz: Lane a Daughter named Elizabeth born Jan: 30 1756. Baptized 1756 Jun: 3. p. 48.

Humphrey Parish & Eliz: Lane a son named Humphrey born Jan: 10 1761. Baptized 1761 Jul: 2. p. 60.

Humphrey Parish & Elizabeth Lane a son named George born Jun: 16 1763. Baptized Feb: 17 1764. p. 66.

Humphrey Parish & Elizabeth Lane a Daughter named Mary born Dec. 22 1766 (sic). Baptized Aug. 16 1766. p. 74.

Humphrey Parish & Eliz: Lane a Daughter named Sally born Oct 22 176... Baptized Sep: 7 1770. p. 88.

Humphrey Parish & Eliz: Lane a son named Dabney born Feb. 25, 1772. Baptized Ap. 16, 1772. p. 92.

Humphrey Parish & Eliz. Lane a son named David born Ap. 25, 1775. Baptized May. 28, 1775. p. 98.

Isham Parish & Elizabeth Atkinson* a son named Benjamin born May 24 1766. Baptized Jun: 27 1766. p. 74.

Isham Parish & Elizabeth Atkinson a son named Meredith born Feb. 30 1768. Baptized Mar: 27 1768. p. 80.

Isham Parish & Eliz: Atkins a son named Major born Feb: 20 1769. Baptized Ap: 9 1769. p. 84.

Isham Parish & Eliz: Atkins a Daughter named Mary born Mar: 7 1770. Baptized Ap: 22 1770. p. 87.

Isham Parish & Eliz: Atkins a daughter named Elizabeth born Dec. 12, 1771. Baptized Ap. 26, 1772. p. 92.

Ja: Parrish & Sarah Timberlick a son Waddy born Mar: 27 1785. Baptized Sep. 18 1785. p. 115.

Ja: Parish & Sar: Timberlake a Son Lewis born Oct. 31, 1781. Baptized Ap. 12, 1782. p. 106.

Joel Parish & Eliz: Hill a son named Nathaniel born Oct: 23. 1758. Baptized 1758 Dec: 29. p. 53.

Joel Parish & Elizabeth Hill a Daughter named Nansie born May 24. 1760. Baptized 1760 Sep: 14. p. 58.

Joel Parish & Elizabeth Hill a Daughter named Mary born Sep: 22 1764. Baptized Oct: 22 1764. p. 69.

Joel Parish & Elizabeth Hill a son named Joel born feb: 11 1767. Baptized Jun: 21 1767. p. 78.

Joseph* Parish & Eliz: Hill a son named Samuel born May 26 1769. Baptized Sep: 13 1769. p. 86.

Joel Parish & Eliz. Hill a son named Parks born Mar. 3. 1772. Baptized Nov. 6, 1772. p. 93.

John Parish & Susannah Green a Daughter named Ann born May 18, 177... Baptized Sep 30 1770. p. 88.

Jolly Parish & Ann Powis a son named Corbin born Dec. 8 1767. Baptized Feb: 10 1768. p. 79.

*Humphreh in marriage record.
*Atkins in marriage records.
*Evidently mistake—should be Joel.

Jo: & Mary Parishes a son named Ephraim born Jan. 26, 1769. Baptized May 18, 1781. p. 103.

Joseph Parish & Mary Pretty a son named Bartlet born May 6, 1777. Baptized June 23, 1777. p. 102.

Moses Parish & Sarah Martin a son named Billie: Parish born Jan: 28 1759. Baptized 1759 Mar: 4. p. 54.

Moses Parish & Mary Hill............a Daughter named Suckie born Jan: 22 1764. Baptized Feb: 23 1764. p. 66.

Moses Parish & Mary Hill a Daughter named Frankie Parish born Aug: 4 1767. Baptized Feb: 10 1768. p. 79.

Moses Parish & Mary Hill a son named Mathew born Jan: 16 1769. Baptized May 29 1771. p. 89.

Moses Parish & Mary Hill a son born Mar: 2 1771 named Nicholas. Baptized May 29 1771. p. 89.

Moses Parish & Mary Hill a daughter named Tabath born Sep. 11, 1773. Baptized Nov. 20, 1773. p. 95.

Nelson Parish & Mary Parish a son named Sherard born May 7, 1776. Baptized June 29, 1776. p. 100.

Nimrod Parish Ann Williams a child Lucy born June 2 1787. Baptized Jul: 8 1787. p. 119.

Rob: Parish & Sarah Beaks a child Eliz: born Ap: 17 1785. Baptized June 26 1785. p. 114.

Rob: Parish & Sarah Bowles a child Polly born Aug. 21 1788. Baptized Sep: 16 1788. p. 121.

Harry Parker & Joanna Thomas a son Charles, Sep: 22 1787. Baptized Nov. 11 1787. p. 120.

Rich: Parker & Hannah Cave a child named Fanny born June 2, 1781. Baptized Jul. 29, 1781. p. 103.

Winslow(?) Parker & Mary Thomas a son Harvey born Ap. 22, 1782. Baptized July 15, 1782. p. 107.

Winston Parker & Mary Thomas a child Jean More born Mar: 28 1784. Baptized Jul: 15 1784. p. 112.

Will Parker & Susanna Winslow, Benjamin Winslow, Aug. 10 1785. Baptized Oct. 23 1785. p. 115.

Will Parker & Susanna Winslow, Catherine Oct: 25 1787. Baptized Dec: 13 1787. p. 120.

Rich: Paulet & Cat: Smith a child Patsy Home born Ap. 8, 1782. Baptized Dec. 2. 1782. p. 108.

Rich: Paulet & Catie Smith a son Alexander born Oct: 19 1783. Baptized Dec: 2 1783. p. 110.

Rich: Paulet & Catherine Smith, Lewis-Meriwether & Lucy Smith, twins, June 8 1786. Baptized Sep: 24 1786. p. 117.

Richard Paulett & Caty Smith a child Henry born Jany. 28 1789. Baptized June 13 1789. p. 122.

Richard Paulett & Caty Smith a child Thomas born 18 Mch. 1791. Baptized Sept. 5 1791. p. 126.

Archer Payne & Martha Dandridge a son named John Dandrige born Nov: 20 1770. Baptized Jan: 3 1771. p. 89.

Archy Payne & Martha Dandrige a daughter named Ann: Spotswood born Ap. 19—. Baptized May 26, 1772. p. 92.

Arch Payne & Martha Dandrige a daughter named Martha born Nov. 8, 1773. Baptized Jan. 1. 1774. p. 95.

Archer Payne & Martha Dandrige a son named Archer born Nov. 29, 1775. Baptized Jan. 4, 1776. p. 99.

Archer Payne & Martha Dandridge a daughter named Dorothea Dandrige born Jul 10. 1777. Baptized July 31, 1777. p. 102.

Archer Payne & Pattie Dandridge a child Elizabeth born Oct: 29 1782. Baptized Ap: 20 1783. p. 109.

Archer Payne & Martha Dandridge a child America, Nov. 5 1786. Baptized May 21 1787. p. 119.

George Payne & Mary Woodson, a S: born Oct: 30 1705 named Josias. p. 40.

Geor: Payne & Mary Woodson a Son born Nov: 21 1707 named George. p. 40.

Geor: Payne & Mary Woodson a Son born Nov: 16 1709 named Robert. p. 40.

George Payne & Mary Woodson a Son born dec: 4 1713 named John. p. 40.

Geor: Payne & Judith Burton a Son named Joseph born Mar: 23 1758. Baptized 1758 Ap: 16. p. 52.

George Payne & Judith Burton a Daughter named Elizabeth born Sep: 19 1760. Baptized 1760 Dec: 6. p. 58.

George Payne & Judith Burton a son named Richard born Ap: 29 1765. Baptized May 26 1765. p. 71.

Geor: Payne & Agatha George a Son born Mar: 14. 1756 named Jesse. Baptized 1756 Ap: 18. p. 48.

George Payne & Agatha George a Daughter named Anna born Ap: 25 1762. Baptized 1762 Jun: 6. p. 63.

Geor: Payne & Agatha George a daughter named Mary: Watts born Jan: 29 1771. Baptized Mar: 17 1771. p. 89.

Geor: Payne & Agatha George a daughter named Susannah: Woodson born Ap. 1, 1775. Baptized Ap. 22. 1775. p. 98.

George Payne & Agatha George a son named Will: George born Ap: 24. 1777. Baptized June 23, 1777. p. 102.

Geor: Payne & Betty Morton a daughter named Mary: Barnes born Aug. 27, 1772. Baptized Jan 8, 1773. p. 93.

Geo: Payne & Betty: McCarty: Morton a daughter named Lucy: Hubbard born May 14. Baptized Aug. 1, 1777. p. 102.

Geo: Payne & Eliz: Morton a son Mathew Montjoy born Jan: 17 1784. Baptized Ap: 18 1784. p. 111.

Jesse Payne & Frances Morton a son named George-Morton born Jun: 28 1768. Baptized Jul: 11 1768. p. 81.

Jesse Payne & ffrances Morton a son named Richard-Baylor born Sep: 16 1769. Baptized Dec: 19 1769. p. 86.

Jesse Payne & Frances Morton a son named Jesse-Burton born Jun. 27, 1771. Baptized Aug. 11, 1771. p. 90.

Col: Jo: Payne & Jean Smith had a daughter Ann born Oct. 7 1758. Baptized Nov. 7 1758. p. 129.

Col: Jo: Payne & Jean Smith had a son Philip born Mar: 29 1760. Baptized May 10 1760. p. 129.

Col: Jo: Payne & Jean Smith had a daughter Jean born Ap: 30 1762. Baptized May 29 1762. p. 129.

Col: Jo: Payne & Jean Smith had a son named Smith born Jan: 18 1764. Baptized Feb: 25 1764. p. 129.

Col: Jo: Payne & Jean Smith had a son Geo-Woodson born Oct: 9 1767. Baptized Dec: 1 1767. p. 129.

Col: Jo: Payne & Jean Smith had a daughter Mildred-Mathews born Mar: 27 1769. Baptized Ap: 10 1769. p. 129.

Col: Jo: Payne & Jean Smith had a son named Robert born Oct: 30 1770. Baptized Dec: 3 1770. p. 129.

Col: Jo: Payne & Jean Smith had a daughter named Eliz: Woodson born. Baptized Nov: 26 1772. p. 129.

Col: Jo. Payne their father died Jul: 28 1784. aged .... p. 129.

John Payne & Jane Smith a Daughter named Ann born Oct: 7, 1758. Baptized 1758 Nov: 7. p. 53.

Mr. John Payne & Jean Smith a son named Philip born Mar: 29 1760. Baptized 1760 May 10. p. 57.

John Pain & Jean Smith a Daughter named Jean born Ap: 30 1762. Baptized 1762 May 29. p. 63.

Colo: John Payne & Jean Smith a son named Smith born Jan: 18 1764. Baptized Feb: 25 1764. p. 66.

John Payne & Jean Smith a son named George Woodson born Oct: 9 1767. Baptized Dec: 1 1767. p. 79.

John Payne & Jean Smith a daughter named Mildred-Mathews born Mar: 27 1769. Baptized Ap: 10 1769. p. 84.

John Payne & Jean Smith a son named Robert born Oct. 30 1770. Baptized Dec: 3 1770. p. 88.

Jo: Payne Sen. & Jean Smith a daughter named Eliz: Woodson born. Baptized Nov. 26, 1772. p. 93.

John Payne & Mary Chichester a son named John Chichester born feb: 5 1767. Baptized Feb: 12 1767. p. 76.

John Payne & Mary Chichester a Daughter named Anna-Ball born ffeb 16 1769. Baptized Mar: 19 1769. p. 84.

John Payne & Mary Chichester a Daughter named Mary-Chichester born .... 1770. Baptized May 21 1770. p. 87.

John Payne & Mary Chichester a daughter named Mally born Ap. 3, 1774. Baptized Jun. 11, 1774. p. 96.

Jo: Payne & Mary Jones a son Rhoderick born Jan: 5 1782. Baptized Oct. 23 1788. p. 121.

*Joseph Payne & Eliz: ffleming a son named Tarleton born febr: 21 1758. Baptized 1758 Ap: 16. p. 52.

Eliz: ffleming & Josiah Payne a Daughter named Sally born Sep: 16. 1759. Baptized 1759 Nov: 25. p. 56.

*Josias in marriage record.

Josias Payne & Elizabeth ffleming a Son named Josias born Ap: 25 1761. Baptized 1761 May 22. p. 59.

Josias Payne & Eliz: ffleming a son named William born Jun: 1 1764. Baptized Jun: 29 1764. p. 68.

Josias Payne & Elizabeth Fleming a son named Fleming born Jun: 26 1766. Baptized Aug: 2 1766. p. 74.

Josias Payne & Elizabeth Fleming a son named Charles-ffleming born Jan: 8 1768. Baptized Mar: 1 1768. p. 80.

Josias Payne & Eliz: Fleming a Daughter named Eliz: Chichester born Nov: 29 1769. Baptized Dec: 25 1770. p. 86.

Robert Payne & Ann Burton a Daughter named Betsey born Mar: 31. 1763. Baptized 1763 Ap: 7. p. 64.

Robert Payne & Ann Burton a Daughter named Keturah born jan: 2 1765. Baptized feb: 17 1765. p. 70.

Robert Payne & Ann Burton a Daughter named Ann born Nov: 13 1766. Baptized Dec: 14 1766. p. 75.

Rob. Payne & Marg: Sydenam Morton a daughter named Lucy Morton born. Baptized May 7, 1775. p. 98.

Rob: Payne & Mary Sydenham: Morton, a son named Rich: Beckwith born Aug: 9 177... Baptized Aug. 1. 1777. p. 102.

Rob. Burton Payne a Marg: Sydenham Morton a son Rob: Burton July .... Baptized Oct 22, 1781. p. 104.

Rob: Burton Payne & Marg Sydenham Morton a child Molly Jordan born Aug 21, 1780. Baptized Oct. 22, 1781. p. 105.

Tarleton Payne & Eliz: Winston a son Jo. Winston-born June 28 1784. Baptized Ap: 10 1785. p. 114.

Will: Payne & Mary Barret a Daughter named Sally born dec: 9 1760. Baptized 1761 Mar: 22. p. 59.

Will: Payne & Mary Thomson a Daughter named Susannah born Jan: 24 1768. Baptized May 22 1768. p. 81.

Edward Peacock & Mally Underwood a son named Richard: Davis born Mar. 9, 1774. Baptized Ap. 1, 1774. p. 96.

Edward Peacock & Mally Underwood a daughter named Sally born Sep. 5, 1775. Baptized Oct 19, 1775. p. 99.

Richmond Pearson & Sarah Haden a daughter named Betsey born Aug. 10, 1773. Baptized Nov. 29, 1773. p. 95.

Jo: Peik & Sally Sneed, Pattie Perry born Dec. 19 1785. Baptized Jul: 8 1787. p. 119.

George Pey & Mary Eubank a son named John born Mar: 28 1767. Baptized Ap: 19 1767. p. 77.

Geor: Pea & Mary Eubank a son named Ambrose born Aug: 29 1769. Baptized Oct: 8 1769. p. 86.

Anderson Peers & Ann Powers a daughter named Dorothea born Aug 17, 1772. Baptized Nov. 8, 1772. p. 93.

Anderson Peers & Ann Powers a son named John born Jul. 20, 1774. Baptized Sep. 11, 1774. p. 97.

Anderson Peers & Ann Powers a son named Anderson born May 19, 1776. Baptized Jul. 21, 1776. p. 100.

Anderson Peers & Judith Leprade a son Thomas born Aug 4, 1781. Baptized June 16, 1782. p. 107.

Anderson Peers & Judith Laprade, a son Jo: Leprade born feb: 7 1783. Baptized Ap: 21 1783. p. 109.

Henry Pendleton & Ailcy Ann Winston a son Edmond, Oct: 24 1786. Baptized Ap: 15 1787. p. 118.

Henry Pendleton & Ann Winston, John Bickerton Feb. 16 1788. Baptized Ap: 13 1788. p. 120.

Hezekiah Periere & Mary Ellis a son named Ellis born Mar: 15 1766. Baptized Ap: 20 1766. p. 73.

Obadiah Periere & Mary Miller a son named Peter Miller born Feb. 16. 1782. Baptized Feb. 21, 1782. p. 105.

Obediah Periere & Mary Miller a son Tho: Heath born Jan. 9 1784. Baptized Ap. 18 1784. p. 111.

Thomas Perriere & Mary Bowles a son named John born Jul: 27 1767. Baptized Jul: 27 1768. p. 81.

Abraham Perkins & Sicily Turpine a Daughter named Elizabeth born Nov: 28. 1756. Baptized 1757 Ap: 9. p. 50.

Abraham Perkins & Cecily Turpine a Daughter named Martha born Jul: 22 1759. Baptized 1759 Sep: 29. p. 56.

Abraham Perkins & Cecily Turpine a Daughter named Lucy born Jun: 24 1765. Baptized Aug: 25 1765. p. 72.

Abraham Perkins & Cecily Turpine a son named Jesse born Sep: 13 1768. Baptized Oct: 23 1768. p. 82.

Abraham Perkins & Eliz: Williams a son named Zachariah: Williams born May 2, 1776. Baptized June 30, 1776. p. 100.

Antony Perkins & Aggie Pulham a child Betsie born Jul: 30 1781. Baptized Aug. 29 1784. p. 112.

Antony Perkins & Aggie Pulham a child Polly Antony born June 14 1784. Baptized Aug. 29 1784. p. 112.

Archilaus Perkins & Ann Mitchel, a child Lucy born Mar 7 1788. Baptized Sep: 14 1788. p. 121.

Benjamin Perkins & Mary Curd a Daughter named Marianne born May 6 1770. Baptized May 30 1770. p. 87.

Ben Perkins & Mary Curd a son named Stephen born Dec. 21, 1771. Baptized 1772. p. 91.

Ben. Perkins & Mary Curd a son called Edmond born Aug. 15, 1773. Baptized Sep. 11, 1773. p. 95.

Ben: Perkins & Mary Curd a daughter named Elizabeth born Feb. 19, 1777. Baptized May 4, 1777. p. 101.

Ben: Perkins & Mary Curd a child Frances Curd born Sep: 16 1783. Baptized Ap: 18 1784. p. 111.

Ben Perkins & Mary Curd a son Ben: Hughes born Sep: 15 1785. Baptized Oct. 17 1787. p. 120.

Constant Perkins & Mary Walker a son named Stephen born Ap: 22. 1760. Baptized 1760 Jun: 10. p. 57.

Hardine Perkins & Sar: Price a Daughter named Sarah born Aug: 15 1756. Baptized 1756 Aug: 28. p. 49.

James Perkins & Judith Whitlow a Daughter named Martha born Oct: 30 1765. Baptized Feb: 9 1766. p. 73.

James Perkins & Judith Whitlow a Daughter named Ann born Sep. 27 1767. Baptized May 7 1768. p. 80.

James Perkins & Judith Whitlow a Daughter named Elizabeth born Nov: 28 1770 [sic]. Baptized Feb: 18 1770. p. 86.

James Perkins & Judith Whitlow a son named Henry born Feb. 11, 1772. Baptized Ap. 5, 1772. p. 92.

James Perkins & Judith Whitlow a son named John born Ap 26. .... Baptized Jun 12, 1774. p. 96.

Joel Perkins & Ann Bailey a Daughter named Sally born Oct: 23 1768. Baptized Mar: 12 1769. p. 83.

Joel Perkins & Ann Bailey a son named Will: Bailey born Aug. 17, 1771. Baptized .... 16, 1772. p. 91.

John Perkins & Rachel ffergusson a Son named Richard born Sep: 6. 1757. Baptized 1757 Nov: 15. p. 51.

John Perkins & Rachel ffergusson a Son named Abraham born Mar: 1. 1760. Baptized 1760 Oct: 5. p. 58.

John Perkins & Rachel ffergusson a son named Jesse born Jun: 26 1764. Baptized Nov: 1 1764. p. 69.

John Perkins & Rachel ffergusson a son named Martin born Mar: 10 1767. Baptized Jul: 19 1767. p. 78.

John Perkins & Mary Anthony a son named Jesse born Oct: 13 1765. Baptized May 17 1766. p. 74.

John Perkins & Ursley Richardson a son named Thompson born Aug: 18 1769. Baptized Sep: 24 1769. p. 86.

John Perkins & Ursley Richardson a son named Pleasants born Feb. 24, 1772. Baptized Jun 25, 1772. p. 92.

John Perkins & Ursley Richardson a daugnter named Lucy born Dec 11, 1774. Baptized Ap. 30 1775. p. 98.

John Perkins & Lucy Mitchel a son named Jesse born Sep: 2 1766. Baptized Oct: 22 1766. p. 75.

John Perkins & Lucy Mitchel a son named John born Sep: 13 1769. Baptized Oct: 29 1769. p. 86.

John Perkins & Lucy Mitchel a son called Grief born Sep. 11, 1772. Baptized Oct 25, 1772. p. 93.

John Perkins & Lucy Mitchel a son named Mitchel born Dec. 1, 1775. Baptized Jan. 1, 1776. p. 99.

Jo: Perkins & Lucy Mitchel a child Ann born Feb 25, 1782. Baptized July 21, 1782. p. 107.

Jo: Perkins & Sarah Sned, Suckie Crumpton born July 15 1788. Baptized Oct: 12 1789. pp. 122, 125.

Joseph Perkins & Hellender Taylor a son named George born Jun: 29 1765. Baptized Aug: 4 1765. p. 72.

Joseph Perkins & Ellis Taylor a Daughter named Frances-Ann, born Jun: 21 1767. Baptized Jul: 19 1767. p. 78.

Joseph Perkins & Allice Taylor a son named Robert born Dec: 13 1768. Baptized Feb: 5 1769. p. 83.

Joseph Perkins & Eliz. Taylor a son named Joseph born Dec. 12, 1771. Baptized 1772. p. 91.

Joseph Perkins & Betty Price a son named Jesse born Oct 9, 1776. Baptized Feb. 20, 1777. p. 101.

Jos: Perkins & Eliz: Price a son named Stephen born Feb 23, 1781. Baptized May 19, 1781. p. 103.

Jos: Perkins & Eliz: Price a son Price born Aug. 15 1783. Baptized Oct. 5 1783. p. 110.

Mich. Perkins & Winifred Rae a son named Dabney born June 8, 1781. Baptized Sep. 20, 1781. p. 104.

Michael Perkins & Winnifred Rae a child Mary born Jan. 27 1783. Baptized Ap: 12 1784. p. 111.

Michael Perkins & Winnifred a son William born Feb. 4 1785. Baptized Ap: 11 1785. p. 114.

Michael Perkins & Winnifred Rae a son Pleasants born Mar: 30 1788. Baptized Oct. 13 1788. p. 121.

Michael Perkins & Winnifred Rae, Tho: Wright born Feb. 15 (or 14) 1789. Baptized Oct: 12 1789. pp. 122, 125.

Rich: Perkins & Jane .... a Son born Sep: 29 1725 named Richard. p. 40.

Richard Perkins & Susannah Coleman a Son named Richard born Nov: 30 1756. Baptized 1757 Ap: 9. p. 50.

Richard Perkins & susannah Coleman a Daughter called Mary born Ap: 13, 1759. Baptized 1759 Jun: 10. p. 55.

Rich: Perkins & susannah Coleman a son named Philemon born Sep: 17 1761. Baptized 1762 Ap: 10. p. 62.

Richard Perkins & Susannah Coleman a son named Samuel born Ap: 14 1764. Baptized Oct: 29 1764. p. 69.

Richard Perkins & Susannah Coleman a son named John born Dec: 6 1766. Baptized Oct: 6 1767. p. 79.

Samuel Perkins & Jean Johnson a son Joseph born Nov. 27 1784. Baptized Ap: 11 1785. p. 114.

Sam: Perkins & Jean Johnson, a child Nancy, born Mar: 13 1786. Baptized April 10 1786. p. 116.

William Perkins & Susannah Holland a Son named Christian born Aug: 7. 1757. Baptized 1757 Sep: 23. p. 51.

William Perkins & Susannah Holland a son named William born Aug: 22. 1759. Baptized 1759 Oct: 28. p. 56.

Will: Perkins & susannah Holland a Daughter named Sally born Aug: 9. 1763. Baptized 1763 Sep: 12. p. 65.

William Perkins & Susannah Holland a Daughter named Mary born May 5 1765. Baptized Jun: 16 1765. p. 71.

Edmond Perry & Eliz: Lockinton a Son named Edmond born Sep. 29. 1780. Baptized May. 13, 1781. p. 103.

Ja: Perrie & Nansie Tandy a child Henry Tandy born feb: 18 1792. Baptized Aug: 12 1792. p. 126.

Ja: Perry & Ann Tandie a girl Paty Mills born Aug: 28 1793. Baptized Mar: 30 1794. p. 127.

Larkin Perry & Isabel Collins a son Harry born Jan: 11 1782. Baptized Oct. 13 1784. p. 113.

Larkin Perry & Isabel Collins a son Thomas born Dec. 31 1783. Baptized Oct. 13 1784. p. 113.

Roderick Perry & Jean Randolph a child Nancy born Mar: 10 1783. Baptized Ap; 12 1784. p. 111.

Samuel Perry & Agnes Johnson a son named Thomas born Sep: 3 1764. Baptized Sep: 30 1764. p. 69.

Will: Perry & Ann Beazly a son Benjamin born Oct. 8 1783. Baptized Oct. 13 1784. p. 113.

Rich: Philips & Ann Johnson a Son Richard born June 15. 1782. Baptized Aug. 4. 1782. p. 107.

Rich: Philips & Eliz: Waddy a son Will: Ballard born Jan: 20 1788. Baptized Ap: 13 1788. p. 120.

John Philpot & Eliz: Man a Daughter named Sally born Ap: 1 1770. Baptized May 6 1770. p. 87.

John Philpots & Eliz. Man a daughter named Mary born Mar. 24, 1772. Baptized May 10, 1772. p. 92.

John Philpots & Eliz Man a son named Paul born Feb. 2, 1774. Baptized Mar. 13, 1774. p. 96.

John Philpot & Eliz. Man a daughter named Elizabeth born Jan 14, 1776. Baptized Feb. 25, 1776. p. 99.

Ben: Phop [See Fop] & Mary Reeve a son named Benjamin born Dec. 15, 1780. Baptized May. 20, 1781. p. 103.

Joseph Pierce & Marianne Page a son named Robert born Oct: 19 1763. Baptized Nov: 20 1763. p. 66.

Joseph Peace & Marianne Page a Daughter named Ann born Ap: 29 1766. Baptized June 8 1766. p. 74.

Joseph Pearse & Marianne Page a son named Joseph born May 28 1768. Baptized Jul: 3 1768. p. 81.

Joseph Pearse & Marianne Page a Daughter named Jean born Aug: 24 1770. Baptized Sep 30 1770. p. 88.

Joseph Pearse & Maryanne Page a son named John, born Sep. 26, 1773. Baptized Nov. 7, 1774. p. 95.

Joseph Pierce & Marianne Page a son named Josiah born Sep. 23, 1776. Baptized Nov. 3, 1776. p. 101.

Josias Pierce & Eliz: Britt a Daughter named Susannah born Mar: 7 1759. Baptized 1759 Ap: 15. p. 54.

Muray Pierce & Mary Bragg a son Joseph born Jul: 27 1785. Baptized May 14 1787. p. 118.

William Pierce & Hannah Bowden a son named Jesse born Sep: 21 1756. Baptized 1756 Nov: 14. p. 49.

Richard Pleasants, a young man was christened, wt three of his children, viz, as follows: Baptized Jul: 5 1767. p. 78.

Richard Pleasants & *Jeanie Laprade a Daughter named Jeanie born Nov: 2 1763. Baptized Jul: 5 1767. p. 78.

---

*Ann Leprade in Marriage Record.

Richard Pleasants & *Jeanie Laprade a Daughter named Martha born Ap: 26 1765. Baptized Jul: 5 1767. p. 78.

Richard Pleasants & *Jeanie Laprade a son named John born Jan: 10 1767. Baptized Jul: 5 1767. p. 78.

Archy Pledge & Christian Fferrar a son named John born Sep. 15, 1774. Baptized Sep. 22, 1774. p. 97.

Archer Pledge & Ann Woodson, a Son Archer born Jan. 1, 1782. Baptized June 16, 1782. p. 107.

Francis Pledge & Eliz: Poindexter a Daughter named Mildred born Sep: 3 1769. Baptized Nov: 26 1769. p. 86.

Francis Pledge & Eliz. Poindexter a daughter named Nanny born Dec 22, 1774. Baptized Feb. 23, 1775. p. 98.

Francis Pledge & Eliza Poindexter a daughter named Betsey Bor. Nov 27, 1778 [sic]. Baptized Aug. 9, 1778. p. 103.

Francis Pledge & Eliz: Poindexter a son Pascal Paoli born Aug. 10, 1781. Baptized Feb. 21, 1782. p. 105.

Will Pledge & Ursula Woodson a son named William born Mar. 4, 1776. Baptized Aug 31, 1776. p. 100.

Will Pledge & Ursley Woodson a son named Francis born Aug 15, 1781. Baptized Feb. 21, 1782. p. 105.

Jo: Poindexter & Eliz: Johnson a Son Tho: Poindexter born dec. 31, 1782. Baptized Mar. 1, 1783. p. 108.

Jo: Poindexter & Eliz: Thornton Johnson, Eliz: Merriwether, Mar: 16 1784. Baptized May 8 1784. p. 111.

Jo: Poindexter & Eliz: Thornton Johnson, Nicholas-Johnson born Sep: 17 1786. Baptized Dec. 27 1786. p. 118.

Jo: Poindexter & Eliz: Hunter Johnson a child Lucy Jones, born feb: 2 1789. Baptized Ap: 4 1790. p. 125.

Nimrod Poindexter & Ann Rocket a son named Patrick-Henry born Sep: 17 1769. Baptized Oct: 27 1769. p. 86.

Thomas Pindexter & Elizabeth Pledge a Daughter named Ann born dec: 18. 1760. Baptized 1761 Jan: 31. p. 58.

Thomas Poindexter & Elizabeth Pledge a son named ffrancis born Dec: 9 1764. Baptized feb: 17 1765. p. 70.

Tho: Poindexter & Eliz: Pledge a son named William-Pledge born Dec: 7 1766. Baptized Jan: 28 1767. p. 76.

Tho: Poindexter & Eliz: Pledge a Daughter named Patty-Milner born Dec: 18 1768. Baptized Mar: 27 1769. p. 84.

Tho: Poindexter & Eliz: Pledge a son named Tho: Wentworth born Jan: 3 .... Baptized Nov. 5 1771. p. 90.

Will Poindexter & Marg. Daniel a child .... born June 9. 1782. Baptized July 28. 1782. p. 107.

John Pointer & Dolly Davis a Daughter named Betsey born Jan: 27 1767. Baptized Jul: 5 1767. p. 78.

John Pollock & Marg: Jones a daughter named Sally born Feb: 11 1769. Baptized Jun: 25 1769. p. 85.

---

*Ann Leprade in marriage record.

John Pollock & Marg: Jones a Daughter named Nansy born Jan: .... 1770. Baptized May 22 1770. p. 87.

John Pollock & Margaret Jones a son called William born. Baptized May 24. 1777. p. 102.

John Pollock & Margaret Jones a son called John born. Baptized May 24. 1777. p. 102.

John Pollock & Margaret Jones a daughted named Mary born. Baptized May 24. 1777. p. 102.

Peter Pollock & Mary Poor a son William born Ap: 16 1782. Baptized Ap: 20 1783. p. 109.

Tho: Pollock & Susanna Curd a child Eliz: Smith born Dec. 20 1782. Baptized Sep: 15 1783. p. 110.

Tho: Pollock & Susannah Curd, Catherine Curd born Sep: 6 1784. Baptized Sep: 20 1784. p. 112.

Abraham Poor & Judah Gardener a son born Mar: 20 named Thomas. Baptized 1756 Ap: 19. p. 48.

Abraham Pore & Judah Gardener a Daughter named Kesiah born Sep: 29 1758. Baptized 1758 Oct: 29. p. 53.

Abraham Pore & Judith Gardener a Daughter named sarah born feb: 20 1761. Baptized 1761 Mar: 29. p. 59.

Abraham Pore & Judith Gardener a son named Robert born Jun: 18. 1763. Baptized 1763 Jul: 31. p. 65.

Abraham Poor & Judith Gardener a son named James born Oct: 30 1765. Baptized Dec: 22 1765. p. 72.

Abraham Poor & Judith Gardener a son named Will-Gardener born dec. 18 1768. Baptized Feb: 17 1769. p. 83.

Abram Poor & Judith Gardener a daughter named Lucy born Jan 13, 1772. Baptized Mar. 29, 1772. p. 92.

Rob: Pore & Judith Walker a son named Thomas born Jan: 5 1762. Baptized 1762 feb: 20. p. 61.

Robert Pore & Judith Walker a Daughter named Ann born Aug: 31 1765. Baptized Dec: 16 1765. p. 72.

Robert Poor & Judith Walker a Daughter named Susannah born May 11 1769. Baptized Jun: 11 1769. p. 85.

Robin Poor & Judith Walker a son named Robin born Feb. 19, 1772. Baptized 1772. p. 91.

Robert Poor & Judith Walker a daughter named Sally born Feb. 17, 1774. Baptized Ap. 1, 1774. p. 96.

Thomas Pore & Eliz: Mosely a Daughter named Lucy born dec: 23. 1756. Baptized 1757 feb: 20. p. 50.

Tho: Pore & Elizabeth Mosely a Daughter named Judith born Oct: 29 1759. Baptized 1759 Dec: 23. p. 56.

Thomas Poor & Elizabeth Mosely a son named William born Nov: 1 1765. Baptized Dec: 22 1765. p. 72.

Thomas Poor & Elizabeth Mosely a son named Thomas born Jul: 12 1768. Baptized Sep: 4 1768. p. 82.

Will Poor & Mally Sampson a daughter named Sally born Jan 24, 1773. Baptized Feb. 21, 1773. p. 93.

William Poor & Mally Sampson a daughter named Judith born Dec. 6, 1774. Baptized Jan. 29, 1775. p. 97.

Will: Poor & Mary Sampson, Ann, born Aug .... 1784 in Goochland. Baptized June 15 1787. p. 119.

Tho: Pope & Mary Sneed a son named Archibald born June 3, 1781. Baptized Oct 21, 1781. p. 104.

John Porter & Sarah Watkins a son named Thomas born Ap: 26 1765. Baptized Jun: 9 1765. p. 71.

John Porter & Sarah Watkins a son named John born Mar: 16 1767. Baptized May 3 1767. p. 77.

John Porter & Sarah Watkins a Daughter named Margaret born feb: 5 1769. Baptized Mar: 24 1769. p. 84.

William Porter & Rebekah Burner a son named Josiah born Dec: 10 1764. Baptized Mar: 16 1765. p. 70.

William Porter & Magdalene Chastain a son named Stephen born Dec: 21 1765. Baptized Jan: 25 1766. p. 73.

William Porter & Magdalene Chastain a son named Thomas born Jun: 14 1767. Baptized Jul: 26 1767. p. 78.

Tho: Potter & Diana Alsop a son named John born May 8 1764. Baptized Jun: 3 1764. p. 67.

John Potter & Diana Alsop a Daughter named Delilah born Jul: 10 1766. Baptized Aug: 10 1766. p. 74.

Tho: Potter & Dianah Alsop a son named Hugh-Ryan born Jan: 15 1769. Baptized Jul: 16 1769. p. 85.

Thomas Pouckeet & Mary Franklin a son named Joel born Aug: 12 1766. Baptized Feb: 8 1767. p. 76.

Rob: Povall & Winnifred-Jones Miller a Daughter named Mary-Heath born Jan: 22, 1762. Baptized 1762 feb: 20. p. 61.

Charles Povel & Winnifred-Jones Miller a son named Charles born Sep: 23 1763. Baptized Nov: 13 1763. p. 66.

Dan: Powis & Ann Laurence a child Ann born Oct. 22. 1781. Baptized Mar. 19, 1782. p. 106.

Daniel Powers & Ann Laurence a son Daniel born May 30 1784. Baptized June 7 1784. p. 112.

Major Powis & Dorothea Mathison a Daughter named Jeanie-Major born Aug. 9 1767. Baptized Oct: 22 1767. p. 79.

Thomas Powis & Mary Trammel a Daughter named Kesiah born May 13 1767. Baptized Oct: 16 1768. p. 82.

Will: Powis & Judah Mattison a Son called Mattison born Mar: 20 1758. Baptized 1758 May 10. p. 52.

William Powis & Judith Mathison a Daughter named Kesiah born Sep: 30 1763. Baptized Feb: 5 1764. p. 66.

William Powis & Judith Mathison a son named John born Sep: 20 1765. Baptized Feb: 15 1766. p. 73.

Will: Powis & Judith Mathison a Daughter named Molly born Jan: 19 1768. Baptized May 8 1768. p. 80.

William Powers & Judith Mathison a Daughter named Sally born feb: 3 1770. Baptized Mar: 2 1770. p. 87.

William Powers & Judith Mathison a son named Major born Ap. 2. 1773. Baptized Oct 14, 1776. p. 100.

William Powers & Judith Mathison a daughter named Jeanie born Sep. 5 1776. Baptized Oct 14, 1776. p. 100.

Jo: Powell & Eliz: .... a Son named ffrances born feb: 21. 1756. Baptized 1756 Jun: 7. p. 48.

Samuel Powel & Sarah Nuckols a daughter named Mally born Feb. 2, 1774. Baptized Nov. 13, 1774. p. 97.

William Powell & Elizabeth Liggins a Daughter named Elizabeth born Jul: 2 1767. Baptized Aug: 15 1767. p. 78.

William Powell & Eliz: Liggins a son named William born Aug: 7 1769. Baptized Oct: 1 1769. p. 86.

William Powel & Eliz: Liggins a son named John: Sampson born Ap. 25, 1776. Baptized Jun. 2. 1776. p. 100.

Thomas Pretty & Eliz: Harlow a Daughter named Molly born Jun: 21 1768. Baptized Jul: 27 1768. p. 81.

William Pretty & Jean Hunter a son named George born Ap: 27 1764. Baptized Jun: 10 1764. p. 68.

William Pretty & Jean Hunter a Daughter named Sally born Oct. 1 1766. Baptized Nov: 9 1766. p. 75.

William Pretty & Jean Hunter a son named William born Jan: 8 1768. Baptized Ap: 17 1768. p. 80.

Will: Pretty & Jean Hunter a son named Littleberry born Ap: 9, 1762. Baptized 1762 May 22. p. 63.

Jo: Price & Mary Johnson a Son William born Oct 19, 1782. Baptized Mar. 23, 1783. p. 108.

Jo: Price & Mary Johnson a son James, born Dec. 27 1785. Baptized May 9 1785. p. 114.

John Price & Mary Johnston a son Daniel born Oct. 12 1786. Baptized July 8 1787. p. 119.

Meredith Price & Eliz: ffox a son named John-ffox born May 31 1764. Baptized Jun: 21 1764. p. 68.

Meredith Price & Elizabeth ffox a Daughter named Ann-ffox born Oct: 12 1766. Baptized Nov: 14 1766. p. 75.

Meredith Price & Eliz: Fox a son named Nathaniel West born Oct: 25 1768. Baptized Nov: 19 1768. p. 82.

Meredith Price & Elizabeth ffox a son named John ffox born Jun: 1 1770. Baptized Jul: 9 1770. p. 88.

Meredith Price & Eliz: Fox a daughter named Caty-Fox born Dec. 5, 1772. Baptized Jan. 1, 1773. p. 93.

Meredith Price & Eliz: Fox a daughter named Jean: Ballard born Feb. 27, 1777. Baptized Ap. 26, 1777. p. 101.

Samuel Price & Elizabeth Perriere a son named John White born May 31 1763. Baptized Oct: 19 1763. p. 66.

William Price & Susannah Burton a daughter named Nansy born Mar 7, 177..... Baptized Mar. 28, 1774. p. 96.

William Price & Susannah Burton a daughter named Patsy born Jun. 21, 1776. Baptized Jul. 21, 1776. p. 100.

Geor: Priddy & Penelope Davis a son named Lewis born Jan 19, 1774. Baptized Feb. 14, 1774. p. 95.

Geo: Priddy & Penelope Davis a son John born June 12 1781. Baptized Ap: 26 1783. p. 109.

Geo: Priddy & Penelope Davis a son George born Ap: 1 1783. Baptized Ap: 26 1783. p. 109.

David Profit & Eliz: Smith a son named John born Jul: 9, 1760. Baptized 1760 Oct: 12. p. 58.

John Profit & Susannah Arrington a son named Sylvester born Ap: 18 1758. Baptized 1758 May 14. p. 52.

John Prophet & Susannah Arrington a Daughter named Mary born Jan: 31 1764. Baptized Ap: 22 1764. p. 67.

John Proft & Susannah Arrington a son named James born Jan: 26 1768. Baptized Ap: 1 1768. p. 80.

Jo: Profit & Susannah Arrington a son named David born May 31 1769. Baptized Jul: 16 1769. p. 85.

Jo: Prophet & Susan Arrington a daughter named Martha born Aug 20 1771. Baptized Sep: 22 1771. p. 90.

Will: Prophet & Sarah Thurston a son named Samuel born Jun: 3, 1763. Baptized 1763 Sep: 12. p. 65.

Will: Prophet & Sarah Thurstone a son named Jesse born Mar: 22 1766. Baptized May 17 1766. p. 74.

Will: Profit & Sarah Thurston a son named George born Jul: 21 1768. Baptized Nov: 3 1768. p. 82.

Will Profit & Sarah Thurston a daughter named Judith born Dec. 31, 1771. Baptized Nov. 15, 1772. p. 93.

David Pruit & Rachel Vinninghame a Daughter named Rachel born feb: 5, 1763. Baptized 1763 May 1st. p. 64.

John Pruit & Ellis Addison a son named Obadiah: Addison born Aug: 9 1758. Baptized 1759 Ap: 1. p. 54.

John Pruit & Ellis Atterton [Addison] a son named Meredith-ffield born May 27 1764. Baptized Jul: 15 1764. p. 68.

John Pruit & Allice Addison a son named Meredith-field born Ap. 12 1767. Baptized May 7 1767. p. 77.

John Pruit & Allice Addison a Son named Harold born Jun: 12 1769. Baptized Aug: 27 1770. p. 86.

Rich: Pryor & Mary Mooncy in Albemarle a son named Richard born Dec: 11 1763. Baptized Jun: 28 1764. p. 68.

Sam: Pryor & ffrances Morton a son named Samuel born Jan: 12 1762. Baptized 1762 Mar: 19. p. 62.

Cap: William Pryor & Sara Wood a Daughter named Elizabeth born ffeb: 10 1757. Baptized 1757 Ap: 11. p. 50.

Cap: Will: Pryor & Sarah Wood a son named John born ffeb: 21 1759. Baptized 1759 Ap: 15. p. 54.

Will: Pryor & Sarah Wood a Daughter named Patty born Ap: 6. 1761. Baptized 1761 Jun: 8. p. 60.

Major Will: Pryor & Sarah Wood a Daughter named Mary born feb: 4 1764. Baptized Feb: 23 1764. p. 66.

William Pryor and Martha Wood a son named Mathew born feb. 16 1765. Baptized feb: 20 1765. p. 70.

Major William Pryor & Sarah Wood a Daughter named Ann born Jun: 5 1766. Baptized Jul: 18 1766. p. 74.

William Pryor & Sarah Wood a son named Valentine-Wood born Jan: 18 1768. Baptized Feb: 10 1768. p. 79.

William Pryor & Sarah Wood a son named Luke born Jun: 25 1769. Baptized Jun: 25 1769. p. 85.

Will Pryor & Eliz: Hughes a child Martha born Mar: 31. 1782. Baptized May. 30, 1782. p. 106.

Will: Pryor & Eliz: Hughes a son William born Jan: 21 1784. Baptized Jul: 29 1784. p. 112.

Willoughby Pugh & Martha Landrum a Daughter named Martha born Nov: 2 1763. Baptized Jan: 8 1764. p. 66.

David Pulham & Bettie Dickerson a son William born Sep: 7 1786. Baptized Oct: 19 1786. p. 117.

Ja: Pulham & Agnes Matlock a child named Lucy born Mar. 5, 1781. Baptized Ap. 9. 1781. p. 103.

Joseph Pulham & Betty Holyday a child Winny born Sep: 26 1785. Baptized Dec. 25 1785. p. 115.

Joseph Pulham & Eliz: Holladay a son Joseph born Dec. 18 1787. Baptized Ap: 28 1788. p. 121.

Tho: Pulham & Jeanie Rae* a child named Nancy born Oct: 21, 1780. Baptized Ap. 9, 1781. p. 103.

Tho: Pulham & Jean Rae a child Polly born Oct: 1 1782. Baptized Ap: 14 1783. p. 109.

Tho: Pulham & Jeanie Ray a child Jeanie born Feb. 26 1783. Baptized Ap: 12 1784. p. 111.

Tho: Pulham & Jean Ray a child Winny, born May 17 1786. Baptized Aug: 14 1786. p. 117.

Zachariah Pulham & Sarah Black a child Nancy born Nov. 9 1783. Baptized Ap: 12 1784. p. 111.

John Quarles & Rebecca Minor a daughter Maria Terrell born 12 Feb. 1794. Baptized Sep: 6 1795. p. 127.

John Quarles & Rebekah Minor a daughter born Feb. 2 1796. Baptized Oct: 13 1796. p. 127.

Robt. Quarles & Patsey Minor a child born 18 Aug. 1792 named Pryor. Baptized Aug. 26 1792. p. 126.

Rob: Quarles & Patsie Minor a son Pryror born Aug: 18 1792. Baptized Oct: 3 1792. p. 122.

Robert Quarles & Patsey Minor a daughter named Louisa Anna born May 20th 94. Baptized July 18 1794. p. 127.

Rob: Quarles & Martha Minor twins Garret Green & Da: Lewis born Ap: 11 1796. Baptized Oct. 13 1796. p. 127.

Tunstal Quarles & Susannah Edwards a son Tunstal born May 11, 1781. Baptized Aug 26, 1781. p. 104.

*Ray in marriage record.

Will: Quarles & Frances Evans a son James born Sep: 10 1782. Baptized Ap: 26 1784. p. 111.

Will: Quarles & Frances Vivians a child Jeanie born Ap. 25 1785. Baptized Oct. 11 1785. p. 115.

Will: Quarles & Frances Vivain a child Patey born Mar: 19 1788. Baptized June 22 1788. p. 121.

Aaron Quissenbury & Rachel Shilton a son David born Mar: 28 1781. Baptized 1783 .... p. 110.

Aaron Quissenbury & Rachel Shilton a child Winnifred born June 11 1783. Baptized 1783 Jul: 13. p. 110.

George Quisenberry & jean Daniel a child Jean born June 21 1784. Baptized Oct. 22 1785. p. 115.

Geo. Quisenberry & Jane Daniel, George Sep. 23 1786. Baptized Aug. 16 1787. p. 119.

Edward Radford & Ann Curd a son named William born May 16. 1763. Baptized 1763 May 31. p. 64.

Edward Radford & Ann Curd a son named Richard born Sep: 20 1765. Baptized Dec: 29 1765. p. 72.

Edward Radford & Ann Curd a Daughter named Sally: Downer born Dec: 8 1767. Baptized Jan: 19 1768. p. 79.

Edward Radford & Ann Curd a Daughter named Mary born feb: 12 1770. Baptized Mar: 22 1770. p. 87.

Edward Radford & Ann Curd a son named John born Jan. 26, 1773. Baptized Mar. 28, 1773. p. 94.

Edward Radford & Ann Curd a daughter named Lucy born May 22, 1775. Baptized Aug. 27, 1775. p. 99.

Edward Radford & Ann Curd a daughter named Nansy born Sep. 1, 1777. Baptized Sep. 3, 1777. p. 102.

Edward Radford & Ann Curd a son Francis Will: born Feb. 21 1783. Baptized Dec. 16 1783. p. 110.

Milner Radford & Eliz: Pollock a Daughter named Lucy born Aprile 5 1761. in fornication. Baptized 1761 Aug: 6. p. 60.

Millener Radford & Sarah Lewis a son named Robert born Aug: 21 1767. Baptized Dec: 18 1767. p. 79.

Milner Radford & Sarah Lewis a Daughter named Elizabeth born Ap: 24 1769. Baptized Jul: 23 1769. p. 85.

Milner Radford & Sarah Lewis a daughter called Mary born Dec: 27, 1773. Baptized Feb. 27, 1774. p. 95.

Millener Radford & Sarah Lewis a son named William born Jul: 10, 1777. Baptized Sep. 3. 1777. p. 102.

Milner Redford & Sarah Lewis a son named William Bor. Oct 28, 1778 [sic]. Baptized Aug 9, 1778. p. 103.

Milliner Radford & Sarah Lewis a son William born May 25 1783. Baptized Dec. 16 1783. p. 110.

David Rae & Elizabeth Rice a Daughter named Sucky born Dec: 20 1768. Baptized Jun: 4 1769. p. 85.

Isaac Raglin & Eliz: Thomson a Son named Isaac born May 23 1757. Baptized 1757 Jul: 3. p. 51.

Isaac Ragline & Eliz: Thomson a Son named James born Jun: 22. 1759. Baptized 1759 Jul: 29. p. 55.

Isaac Raglin & Elizabeth Thomson a son named John born Oct: 14. 1761. Baptized 1761 Nov: 15. p. 61.

Capt John Raley & Eliz: Randolph in Cumberland a Daugh: born Jan: 25 1756 named Susannah. Baptized 1756 Mar. 14. p. 48.

John Raily & Eliz: Randolph a Son named Isham born July 15. 1759 [sic]. Baptized 1759 Jul: 6. p. 55.

John Raily & Eliz: Randolph a Daughter named Annie born Sep: 17 1759. Baptized 1759 Dec: 14. p. 56.

Capt Jo: Really & Eliz: Randolph a son named William born dec: 26 1760. Baptized 1761 Dec: 19. p. 61.

John Really & Eliz: Randolph a son named James born Ap: 16 1762. Baptized 1762 Jun: 3. p. 63.

John Railey & Elizabeth Randolph a Daughter named Jean born Aug: 9 1763. Baptized Nov: 9 1764. p. 69.

John Railey & Elizabeth Randolph a son named Martin born Oct: 27 1764. Baptized Nov: 9 1764. p. 69.

Capt. John Realy & Elizabeth Randloph a son named Charles born Nov: 24 1766. Baptized Jan: 15 1767. p. 76.

John Railey & Eliz: Randolph a son named Randolph born May 14 1770. Baptized Jul: 18 1770. p. 88.

Isham Raily & Susanna Woodson a son John born Jul: 18 1785. Baptized April 2 1786. p. 116.

John Rain & Susannah Mitchel a Daughter named Eliz: born Oct: 26. 1755. p. 41.

John Rain & Susannah Mitchel a Son named Nathaniel born dec: 4 1757. Baptized Dec: 25 1757. p. 51.

John Rain & Susannah Mitchel a Daughter named Mary born May 21, 1760. Baptized 1760 Jun: 8. p. 57.

John Rains & Eliz: Whitlow a Son named William born Ap: 26 1758. Baptized 1758 Jul: 16. p. 53.

Nathaniel Raine & Judith Blackwell, Eliz: Blackwell, Ap: 7 1783. Baptized Sep: 16 1783. p. 110.

Col: Tho: Randolph of Tucahoe his family. p. 143.

Tho: Randolph of Tuckahoe & Ann Carey a son William born Jun: 16 '70. Baptized Jan: 23. 1770. p. 143.

Col: Tho: Randolph & Ann Carey a daughter named Judith born Aug: 24 '71. Baptized Sep: 6: 71. p. 143.

Tho: Randolph & Ann Carey a daughter named Ann born Sep: 16, '74. Baptized Nov: 29: 72. p. 143.

Tho: Man Randolph & Ann Carey a daughter named Jean Carey born Dec: 17. '76. Baptized Jan: 19: 77. p. 143.

Tho. Man Randolph & Ann Carey a son named Tho. Man. born Oct. 1. 68. Baptized Oct: 26: 68. p. 143.

Capt Isham Randolph & Jane Rogers a Daughter born Sep: 25 1738 named Susannah. p. 40.

Tho: Randolph & Jane Cary, Twins, viz: Isham & Thomas born Mar: 27 1771. Baptized Ap: 15 1771. p. 89.

Mr: Tho: Randolph & Mrs. Ann Cary of Tuckahoe a Daughter named Mary born Aug: 9 1762. Baptized Jan: 22 1764. p. 66.

Mr: Tho: Randolph & Mrs. Ann Cary of Tuckahoe a son named Henry-Cary born Jan: 8 1764. Baptized Jan: 22 1764. p. 66.

Tho: Randolph & Nansy Cary a son named Tho-Man born Oct: 1 1768. Baptized Oct: 26 1768. p. 82.

Col: Tho: Randolph & Ann Cary a son named William born Jan. 16 1770. Baptized Dec: 23 1770. p. 86.

Tho: Man Randolph & Ann Carey, a son named Archibald Carey born Aug 2 1771. Baptized Sep: 6 1771. p. 90.

Tho: Man: Randolph & Ann Cary a daughter named Judith born Nov. 24, 1772. Baptized Nov. 29, 1772. p. 93.

Tho. Man Randolph & Ann Carey a daughter named Ann: Carey born Sep. 16, 1774. Baptized Sep. 21, 1774. p. 97.

Tho: Man Randolph & Ann Carey a daughter named Jane-Carey born Dec: 17, 1776. Baptized Jan. 19. 1777. p. 101.

Will: Ratcliff & Elizabeth Harrison a son named William born Jan: 14 1764. Baptized Mar: 4 1764. p. 66.

Benja: Rawlings & Betty Holladay a son Lewis Dec. 9 1786. Baptized Jany. 11 1786. p. 118.

Ben: Rawlings & Eliz: Holladay twins James & Sarah, Jan: 25 1788. Baptized Ap: 27 1788. p. 121.

Jo: Rawlings & Nancy Holliday, Mary-Stevens, Ap: 14 1785. Baptized Nov. 10 1785. p. 115.

Jo: Rawlins & Nancey Holladay a son Ben: Holladay born Aug. 29 1786. Baptized Sep: 28 1786. p. 117.

Jo: Rawlings & Ann Holladay a son Levi born Feb: 29 1788. Baptized Ap: 28 1788. p. 121.

Abraham Redman & Eliz: Slater a child Marieanne, Dec. 14 1785. Baptized June 4 1786. p. 116.

Abram Redman & Catie Brown a child Elizabeth Ap: 20 1789. Baptized July 3 1789. p. 125.

Abram Redman & Cath: Brown a child Catie born Sep: 10 1790. Baptized Dec: 5 1790. p. 122.

John Rees & Judith Watson a Son named Thomas born Jan: 10 1749. Baptized 1756 June 26. p. 49.

John Rees & Judith Watson a Daugh: named Charity born Jan: 25 1751. Baptized 1756 June 26. p. 49.

John Rees & Judith Watson a Daugh: named Lydia born feb: 12 1754. Baptized 1756 June 26. p. 49.

John Rees & Judith Watson a Daughter named Sally Austine born Ap: 21. 1757. Baptized 1757 May 21. p. 50.

John Rees & Judith Watson a Daughter named Judith born Mar: 26. 1759. Baptized 1761 Ap: 27. p. 59.

John Royal Reid & Frances Morton a daughter named Lucy: Franklin born Oct 31. 1773. Baptized Jan. 12, 1774. p. 95.

John Royal Reid & Ffrances Morton a daughter named Martha Royal born Jun. 20, 1775. Baptized Oct 26 1775. p. 99.

Charles Rice & Mary Toney a daughter named Mally born Feb. 15, 1777. Baptized Ap. 27, 1777. p. 101.

Charles Rice & Mary Holman a Daughter named ffranky born Ap: 3 1756. Baptized 1756 May 30. p. 48.

Clayborn Rice & Mary Rice a daughter named Susannah born Oct 6, 177..... Baptized Sep. 10, 1772. p. 93.

Edward Rice & Ann Ryan a Daughter named Patty born Jul: 16 1758. Baptized 1758 Aug: 6. p. 53.

Edward Rice & Ann Ryan a Daughter named Mary born Jul: 9 1759. Baptized 1759 Aug: 5. p. 55.

Edward Rice & Ann Ryan a son named Peter born Nov: 9 1761. Baptized 1761 Nov: 22. p. 61.

Edward Rice & Ann Ryan a Daughter named Ann born Nov: 4 1763. Baptized Jan: 15 1764. p. 66.

Edward Rice & Ann Ryan a Daughter named Elizabeth born Jan: 27 1767. Baptized Ap: 19 1767. p. 77.

Edward Rice & Ann Ryan a Daughter named Patty born May 24 1768. Baptized Jul: 3 1768. p. 81.

Edward Rice & Ann .... a son named Ja: Buchanan born Ap. 21, 1770. Baptized Mar. 25, 1773. p. 93.

Ed: Rice & Ann Ryan a child Sarah born Oct 15, 1771. Baptized Aug 25, 1781. p. 104.

Hez: Rice & Mary Saunders a sun Jo: Saunders born Mar 16 1783. Baptized May 18 1783. p. 109.

Jo: Rice & Mary Johnson a child Nancy born Sep. 22. 1780. Baptized June 17, 1782. p. 107.

Jo: Rice & Mary Johnson a child Nancy born Sep. 22, 1780. Baptized Sep. 30, 1782. p. 107.

Tandy Rice & Sarah Sampson a Daughter named Mary born Jun: 26 1766. Baptized Aug: 17 1766. p. 74.

Tandie Rice & Sarah Sampson a Daughter named Elizabeth born Jul: 15 1768. Baptized Jul: 31 1768. p. 81.

Tandie Rice & Sarah Sampson a Daughter, Catherine Smith born Oct: 5 1770. Baptized Ap 10 1771. p. 89.

Tandie Rice & Sarah Sampson a daughter named Nansy born May 17, 1772. Baptized Jun. 19, 1772. p. 92.

Jeremiah Rich & Mary Hunter a son named Jesse born Nov: 24 1758. Baptized 1759 ffeb: 18. p. 54.

Jeremiah Rich & Mary Hunter a Daughter named Judith born Jan: 2, 1761. Baptized 1761 Jan: 31. p. 58.

Charles Richards & Susannah Ryan a Daughter named Elizabeth born Mar: 29 1760. Baptized 1760 Jun: 22. p. 57.

Charles Richards & Susannah Ryan a son named William born Mar: 27, 1763. Baptized 1763 Jun: 5. p. 64.

Jo: Richards & Ursly Rutherford a child Mary born July 2, 1781. Baptized June 1. 1782. p. 106.

Will Richards & Sarah Smith a Son named Dickie born Nov. 14, 1780. Baptized Ap. 15, 1781. p. 103.

George Richardson & Elizabeth Miller a Daughter called Agnes born Jan: 31 1768. Baptized 21 feb: 1768. p. 80.

George Richardson & Eliz: Miller a son named William Miller born May 2 [176]9. Baptized Jul: 31 1769. p. 85.

Geor: Richardson & Eliz: Miller a daughter named Sarah born feb. 5 1771. Baptized Apl 3 1771. p. 89.

George Richardson & Eliz: Miller a daughter named Mary-Heth born Oct 20 1772. Baptized Feb. 28. 1773. p. 93.

George Richardson & Eliz: Miller a daughter named Betsy Jones born Mar 25. 1777. Baptized May 11, 1777. p. 102.

Geo: Richardson & Eliz. Miller a child Marg: Frizel born Oct. 22, 1782. Baptized July 21, 1782. p. 107.

Landy Richardson & Sarah Underwood a Daughter named Martha born Mar: 17 1759. Baptized 1759 Sep: 29. p. 56.

Landy Richardson & Sarah Underwood a Son named James born Ap: 21 1761. Baptized 1761 Jun: 6. p. 60.

Landie Richardson & Sarah Underwood a Daughter named Sally born Aug: 6 1764. Baptized Sep: 2 1764. p. 69.

Rob: Richardson & Sarah ffurbish a son named Robert born Sep: 14 1758. Baptized 1758 Oct: 29. p. 53.

Rob: Richardson & Sarah ffurbish a Daughter named Nannie born Ap: 6. 1760. Baptized 1760 May 11. p. 57.

Rob: Richardson & Mary Bibb, Mary, Dec. 3 1784. Baptized Apl: 23 1786. p. 116.

Rob: Richardson & Mary Bibb a child Sarah born Oct. 1783. Baptized May 17 1785. p. 114.

Sam: Richardson & Susannah Hales a daughter named Agnes born Dec. 20, 1767. Baptized Oct. 21, 1777. p. 102.

Sam: Richardson & Susannah Hales a son named Samuel born Aug. 23, 1777. Baptized Oct. 21, 1777. p. 102.

Turner Richardson & Ann Allen a son named Nathaniel born Nov: 22 1766. Baptized Jun: 11 1767. p. 78.

Will Richardson & Ffrances Harrison a daughter named Sarah born M. .... Baptized Jul 21, 1771. p. 90.

Will Richardson & Nancy Arnot a son James born Mar. 10 1785. Baptized May 17 1785. p. 114.

Tho: Riddel & Agnes Mims a Daughter named Martha born Sep: 12 1756. Baptized 1756 Oct: 17. p. 49.

Tho: Riddel & Agnes Mims a Daughter named Annie born Mar: 10. 1758. Baptized 1758 Ap: 30. p. 52.

Tho: Riddle & Agnes Mims a son named John born Oct: 11, 1760. Baptized 1760 Nov: 22. p. 58.

Tho: Riddel & Agnes Mims a son named Archibald born May 14. 1762. Baptized 1762 Jul: 4. p. 63.

Tho: Riddel & Agnes Mims a Daughter named Betty born feb: 24 1765. Baptized Ap: 4 1765. p. 70.

Thomas Riddel & Agnes Mims a son named Thomas born Jan:
13 1767. Baptized Feb: 11 1767. p. 76.

Thomas Riddle & Agnes Mims a son named David born Oct: 3
1768. Baptized Jan: 28 1769. p. 83.

James Roach & Mary Hardine a son named Joseph born Jul: 19,
1763. Baptized 1763 Sep: 4. p. 65.

John Robards & Sarah Marshal twins viz: William & Marshal
born Jan. 24. 1774. Baptized Feb. 20, 1774. p. 95.

John Roberts & Sarah Marshal a daughter named Mary born
May 16, 1776. Baptized Aug. 11, 1776. p. 100.

Jo: Robarts & Sally Marshall a Son John born Aug: 19, 1781. Baptized July 21, 1782. p. 107.

Will Robards* & Eliz: Cocke a son named George born Feb. 28,
1777. Baptized Ap. 27, 1777. p. 101.

Will Robards & Eliz. Cocke a daughter named Elizabeth born Ap.
25 177... Baptized June 18, 1775. p. 98.

James Roberts & Mary Massie a daughter named Jeanie born
Dec. 17, 1775. Baptized Ap. 8, 1776. p. 100.

Will: Roberts & Eliz: Lewis a son named Lewis born dec: 18
1758. Baptized 1759 Jan: 20. p. 54.

William Roberts & Elizabeth Lewis a son named George born
Aug: 5 1760. Baptized 1760 Aug: 31. p. 58.

William Roberts & Eliz: Lewis a son named Jesse born Ap: 7.
1762. Baptized 1762 May 10. p. 62.

Will: Robards & Eliz: Lewis a Daughter named Sally born Jan:
25 1765. Baptized Mar: 21 1765. p. 70.

William Roberts & Elizabeth Lewis a son named Joseph born Dec.
11 1766. Baptized Dec: 14 1766. p. 75.

William Roberts & Eliz: Lewis a Daughter named Eliz: Lewis
born Ap: .... 1771. Baptized May 18 1771. p. 89.

Will Robards & Eliz: Lewis a son named Robert born Dec. 7,
1773. Baptized Jan. 4, 1774. p. 95.

Will Roberts & Eliz: Lewis a child Nansie Sep. 24, 1782. Baptized Feb 28. 1783. p. 108.

John Robertson & Judah Brier a Son named John born dec: 7
1758. Baptized 1759 Jan: 15. p. 54.

Ben: Robinson & Catherine Parker, Ann-Parker Mar: 22 1785.
Baptized June 16 1785. p. 114.

Benjamin Robinson & Catherine Parker a child Eliz: Winslow
Parker born June 6 1789. Baptized Aug. 3 1789. p. 125.

John Robertson† & Elizabeth Parish a son named John born May
23 1764. Baptized Jun: 25 1764. p. 68.

John Robison‡ & Eliz: Parish a son named George born feb: 17
1766. Baptized Ap: 27 1766. p. 73.

John Robinson & Elizabeth Parish a Daughter named Annie born
Dec: 13 1767. Baptized Ap: 11 1768. p. 80.

*Roberts in marriage records.
†Robinson in marriage records.
‡Robinson in marriage records.

John Robertson* & Eliz: Parish a daughter named Eliz: Perkins born Nov: 30 1770. Baptized feb: 21 1770. p. 87.

Jo. Robertson & Eliz. Parish a son named Michal born Mar. 21, 1772. Baptized Ap. 22, 1772. p. 92.

John Robertson & Eliz. Parish a son named William-Parish born Ap. 1, 1774. Baptized Jun. 6. 1774. p. 96.

Thomas Robertson & Agnes Hill a daughter named Lucy born feb: 19 1769. Baptized Mar: 19 1769. p. 84.

John Robison & Ann fford a Daughter named Marianne born Jun: 11 1758. Baptized 1758 Jul: 23. p. 53.

Will Robinson & Agnes Smith a child Agnes born Oct. 28, 1781. Baptized Ap. 5, 1782. p. 106.

George Rogers & Frances Pollard a Daughter named Ann born Jul: 12 1764. Baptized Aug: 16 1764. p. 68.

John Rogers† & Ann Lewis a son named William born Aug: 19 1769. Baptized Sep: 17 1769. p. 86.

John Rogers & Ann Lewis a daughter named Betty born Mar. 24, 1771. Baptized Jun. 30. 1771. p. 90.

Will: Rogers & Judah Bradshaw a son born Sep: 25 1755 Named David. Baptized 1756 feb: 29. p. 48.

Will: Rogers & Judith Bradshaw a Daughter named Ann born feb: 22 1758. Baptized 1758 Mar: 25. p. 52.

William Rogers & Judith Bradshaw a son named William born Jun: 27 1760. Baptized 1761 May 17. p. 59.

Will: Rogers & Judith Bradshaw a son named Charles born feb: 22 1763. Baptized 1763 Ap: 17. p. 64.

William Rogers & Judith Bradshaw a Daughter named Elizabeth born May 12 1765. Baptized Jul: 14 1765. p. 72.

Will Rogers & Mary Callifax a daughter named Susannah born Jan 10, 1772. Baptized Ap. 17, 1772. p. 92.

Alexr. Ross & Morning Woody a daughter named Eliz. born Aug. 15, 1773. Baptized Nov. 7, 1773. p. 95.

Turner Rowntree & Sarah Woodson a .... named bor....born Dec: 30 1769. Baptized feb: 22 1770. p. 87.

Turner Rountree & Sarah Woodson a daughter named Mally born Aug 23, 1771. Baptized Dec. 18, 1771. p. 91.

Will: Royster & Prudence Watkins a son named Thomas born feb: 12 1761. Baptized 1761 Mar: 22. p. 59.

Will: Royster & Prudence Watkins a son named David born May 10 1762. Baptized 1762 Jun: 13. p. 63.

William Royster & Prudence Watkins a Daughter named Mary born Jan: 17 1764. Baptized Mar: 4 1764. p. 67.

William Royster & Prudence Watkins a son named William born Dec: 17 1765. Baptized Jan: 25 1766. p. 73.

William Royster & Prudence Watkins a son named Joel born Aug: 4 1768. Baptized Sep: 17 1768. p. 82.

*Robinson in marriage records.
†Rodgers in marriage record.

Will: Royster & Prudence Watkins a Daughter named Frances born Sep: .... Baptized Oct: 14 1770. p. 88.

Will Royster & Prudence Watkins a son named Anderson born Ap. 26, 1773. Baptized Jun. 27, 1773. p. 94.

Will Royster & Prudence Watkins a daughter named Ann born Dec. 7, 1775. Baptized Jan. 28. 1776. p. 99.

Will: Royster & Prudence Watkins a son named John born Dec. 28, 1781. Baptized Mar. 17, 1782. p. 105.

Will Royster & Prudence Watkins a son Francis Watkins Oct: 27 1785. Baptized Aug: 22 1786. p. 117.

Thomas Russel & .... [Mary Gardener]. Baptized Jun: 3 1769. p. 85.

Tho: Russel & Mary Gardener a son named James born Nov. 5, 1776. Baptized Nov. 20, 1776. p. 101.

Larkin Rutherford Rachel Morgan a son named Robert born Jan: 22. 1758. Baptized 1758 Mar: 12. p. 52.

Larkin Rutherford & susannah Morgan a Daughter named Sally born dec: 17 175—*. Baptized 1760 ffeb: 10. p. 56.

Will: Rutherford & Ursley Parish a son named Archelaus born Aug. 14 1766. Baptized Oct: 2 1766. p. 75.

William Rutherford Ursley Parish a son named Archibald born feb. 21 1768. Baptized Jun: 20 1768. p. 81.

Edward Ryan & Susan. Whit a son named Edward born Sep. 22, 1774. Baptized Aug 27, 1775. p. 99.

Philip Ryan & Jean Bullington a Daughter named Ann-Morning born Ap: 24 1768. Baptized May 22 1768. p. 81.

Philip Ryan & Eliz Milns† a daughter named Elizabeth born May 26, 1773. Baptized Mar. 31, 1776. p. 99.

Philip Ryan & Eliz Milns† a son named Thomas born Dec. 10, 1775. Baptized Mar. 31, 1776. p. 99.

Whitehead Ryan & Elizabeth ffulcher a Daughter named Elizabeth born Mar: 29. 1757. Baptized 1757 May 15. p. 50.

Whitehead Ryan & Elizabeth ffulsha a son named Andrew born May 20, 1763. Baptized 1763 Aug: 28. p. 65.

Will: Ryan & Sarah Swanson a Daughter named Mary born Mar: 3 1761. Baptized 1761 Ap: 26. p. 59.

William Ryan & Sarah Swanson a daughter named Martha born May 30 1766. Baptized Jul: 20 1766. p. 74.

Benjamin Sadler & Ann Taylor a Son named Benjamin born Mar: 15 1756. Baptized 1756 May 11. p. 48.

Benj: Sadler & Anna Taylor a Daughter named susannah born Jun: 13. 1759. Baptized 1759 Sep: 29. p. 56.

John Sadler & Susanna Atkinson a Daughter named Jeanie born Sep: 18 1769. Baptized Dec: 10 1769. p. 86.

John Sadler & Susannah Atkins a daughter named Mildred born Mar 5 1772. Baptized May 17, 1772. p. 92.

*Margin torn.
†Mills in marriage record.

Will Sadler & Ann Brown a son named Benjamin born Jul. 20, 1771. Baptized Aug. 8, 1771. p. 90.

William Sadler & Ann Brown a daughter named Polly born Ap. 5, 1773. Baptized May. 9, 1773. p. 94.

Will Sadler & Ann Brown a daughter named Betsey born Mar. 12, 1775. Baptized May 6, 1775. p. 98.

Will Sadler & Ann Brown a son named Isham born Dec. 13, 1776. Baptized Mar. 13, 1777. p. 101.

Peter Sage & Eliz Stewart, a child Nansie Stewart born. May 25, 1782. Baptized Mar. 25, 1783. p. 108.

Abraham Sally & Elizabeth Woodson a Daughter named Judith born Mar: 21. 1763. Baptized 1763 May 1st. p. 64.

Abraham Sally & Eliz: Woodson a Daughter named Lucy-Charlotte born Jan: 19 1765. Baptized Ap: 7 1765. p. 70.

Abraham Sallee & Eliz: Woodson a son named Isaac born May 23 1766. Baptized Jun: 1 1766. p. 74.

Abraham Salley & Eliz: Woodson, a son named John born Jul: 5 1768. Baptized Aug: 28 1768. p. 82.

Benjamin Samons & Priscilla Potter a Daughter named Nannie born Aug: 6, 1756. Baptized 1756 Sep: 5. p. 49.

Benjamin Salmons & Priscilla Potter a son named Thomas born Nov: 17 1758. Baptized 1759 ffeb: 18. p. 54.

Ben: Salmons & Priscilla Potter a Daughter named Priscilla born feb: 3 1762. Baptized 1762 Mar: 14. p. 62.

Benjamin Salmons & Priscilla Potter a Daughter named Mary born feb: 6 1765. Baptized May 5 1765. p. 71.

Benjamin Salmons & Priscilla Potter a Daughter named Judith born Jun: 28 1767. Baptized Aug: 23 1767. p. 78.

Benjamin Salmons & Priscilla Potter a Daughter named Jeanie born Ap: 23 1771. Baptized May 19 1771. p. 89.

Ben. Salmons & Priscilla Potter a daughter named Patty born Ap. 7, 1775. Baptized May 28, 1775. p. 98.

John Salmons & Naomie Depriest a son named Jacob born Jun: 6 1759. Baptized 1759 Sep: 16 & Nov: 11. pp. 55-56.

John Salmons & Naomi Depriest a Daughter named Mally born feb: 6 1762. Baptized 1762 May 9. p. 62.

John Salmons & Naomi Depriest Twins named John & Sally born Sep: 28 1764. Baptized Jun: 16 1765. p. 71.

John Salmons & Naomi Depriest a son named Joel born Mar: 17 1767. Baptized May 10 1767. p. 77.

John Salmons & Naomi Depriest a son named Robert born Aug: 19 1770. Baptized Oct: 21 1770. p. 88.

Jo: Salmons & Judith Cairden, a son Thomas born Jul: 26 1783. Baptized June 20 1784. p. 112.

Charles Sampson & Ann Porter a Daughter named Eliz: Barbarah born Aug: 26 1768. Baptized Sep: 18 1768. p. 82.

Rich: Sampson & Ann Curd a son named Robert born Nov. 1, 1772. Baptized Dec. 13, 1772. p. 93.

Richard Sampson & Ann Curd a son called Richard born May 23, 1774. Baptized Jul 3, 1774. p. 97.

Richard Sampson & Ann Curd a Daughter named Elizabeth: Ann born Mar: 9, 1777. Baptized June 15. 1777. p. 102.

Stephen Sampson & Mary Woodson a Son born Aug: 16 1729 named Stephen. p. 40.

Stephen Sampson & Mary Woodson a D: born Oct: 6 1731 named Mary. p. 40.

Stephen Sampson & Sarah Johnson a Daughter named Sarah born Jan: 10. 1757. Baptized 1757 May 29. p. 51.

Stephen Sampson & Sarah Johnson a Daughter named Eliz: born Sep: 17. 1759. Baptized 1759 Dec: 3. p. 56.

Stephen Sampson & Sarah Johnson a Daughter named Ann born Jun: 11. 1763. Baptized 1763 Jul: 25. p. 65.

Stephen Sampson & Sarah Johnson a Daugh: named Judith born Nov: 21. 1761. Baptized 1762 Ap: 4. p. 62.

Stephen Sampson & Mary Johnston a son named William born Jan: 13 1765. Baptized Mar: 8 1765. p. 70.

Sep. .... 1753—Old Stephen Sampson & Sarah Johnson were maried. p. 135. [See Marriages, p. 42, supra.]

Jan: 10 57 Sarah Sampson was born.

Sep: 17 59 Eliz: Sampson was born.

June 11 63 Ann Sampson was born.

Jan: 13 65 Will: Sampson was born.

Feb 7 68 Jean Sampson was born.

Oct: 8 69 Stephen Sampson was born.

Jan: 9 72 Ja: Johnson Sampson was born.

Dec: 12 73 their old very honest Grandfayr Stephen Sampson was buried, who if now alive would be vexed that his son should pursue his old Min. to another county to burden him wt ye repairs of Goochland glebe after ye Vestry had driven him out of it against ye laws both of God & Man & against ye good will of almost ye whole parish. p. 135.

Stephen Sampson & Sarah Johnson a Daughter named Jean born feb: 7 1768. Baptized Mar: 27 1768. p. 80.

Stephen Sampson & Sarah Johnson a son named Stephen born Oct: 8 1769. Baptized Oct: 31 1769. p. 86.

Stephen Sampson & Sarah Johnson a son named Ja: Johnson born Jan 9, 1772. Baptized 1772. p. 91.

Stephen Sampson & Sarah Johnson a daughter named Martha born Sep. 27, 1773. Baptized Dec. 12, 1773. p. 95.

Geo: Saunders* & Patty Rice a daughter named Mally Holman born Jan 16. 177..... Baptized Ap. 11, 1773. p. 94.

John Sanders & Betty Hancoke a Son named Joseph born Mar: 1. 1759. Baptized 1759 Ap: 5. p. 54.

John Sanders & Elizabeth Hancoke a son named William born born dec: 8. 1760. Baptized 1761 Jan: 26. p. 58.

---

*Sanders in Marriage records.

John Saunders & Elizabeth Hancoke a son named John born Nov:
13 1764. Baptized Ap: 5 1765. p. 70.

John Saunders & Elizabeth Hancoke a Daughter named Mary born
Jun: 13 1767. Baptized Mar: 27 1768. p. 80.

John Saunders & Eliz: Hancoke a son named Jacob born Ap: 19
1769. Baptized May 21 1769. p. 84.

John Saunders & Eliz: Hancock a daughter named Winnifred born
May 27 17......... Baptized Jul. 7, 1771. p. 90.

John Saunders & Eliz. Hancoke a daughter named Susannah born
Sep 29, 1773. Baptized Nov. 14, 1773. p. 95.

John Saunders & Eliz Hancoke a son named Benjamin born Sep.
16, 1775. Baptized Oct. 25, 1775. p. 99.

Jo: Saunders & Mercy .... a child Jemima Glen born
Feb. 13 1783. Baptized May 18 1783. p. 109.

Julius Sanders & Jemima Wooward in Albemarle a Son born Oct:
1755 named Clayburn. Baptized 1756 Jan: 27. p. 48.

Julius Saunders & Jemima Woodward a son named Pleasants born
Mar: 15. 1763. Baptized 1763 May 6. p. 64.

Nath: Sanders & Sally Patty a child named Sally born Mar. 15,
1781. Baptized Mar: 7. 1782. p. 105.

Will Sanders & Judith Lane a daughter named Ann born Oct 27,
1771. Baptized Nov. 17, 1771. p. 91.

Will Saunders & Judith Lane a daughter named Eliz. born Feb.
19, 1774. Baptized Oct. 10, 1774. p. 97.

Will Saunders & Judith Lane a son named Reuben born Ap. 17,
1776. Baptized Jul. 28, 1776. p. 100.

Will Sanders & Judith Lane Mary born Jul. 26, 1781. Baptized
June 16, 1782. p. 106.

Abram Sandiford & Joanna Branch a Daughter named Susannah
born Aug: 5 1764. Baptized Sep. 9 1764. p. 69.

Abram Sandiford & Joanna Branch a daughter named Diana born
Nov: 30 1766. Baptized Jan: 17 1767. p. 76.

Ja: Sandige & Patsie Bronaugh* a child Polly born Ap: 14 1788.
Baptized Jul: 31 1788. p. 121.

Alexander Sasseen & Sally Banton, Twins named Susannah &
Jean born Mar: 31 1769. Baptized May 7 1769. p. 84.

David Sasseene & Eliz: Harris† a son named John born May 13
1769. Baptized Jun: 18 1769. p. 85.

Ja: Scot & Ann Gray, a child Elizabeth, born Feb. 24 1780. Baptized Jany. 25 1783. p. 108.

Ja: Scot & Ann Gray, a son James born June 25 1782. Baptized
Jany. 25 1783. p. 108.

Ja: Scot & Nancy Gray a child Frances born Nov. 14 1786. Baptized Ap: 3 1787. p. 118.

John Scot & Judith Atkins‡ a son named Cosbie born Oct: 18 1768.
Baptized Dec: 25 1768. p. 83.

*Benaugh in marriage records.
†Parish in marriage record.
‡Atkinson in marriage record.

John Scot & Judith Atkins a son named William born Ap 14 1770. Baptized Jun: 24 1770.   p. 88.

Walter Scot & Agnes Martin a Daughter named Martha born feb: 21 1767.   Baptized Mar: 1 1767.   p. 76.

John Scrimjour & Ann Lyon a Son named Robert born May 24 1762.   Baptized 1762 Jul: 22.   p. 63.

Julius Scrugs & Sarbery Frinch a son named Richard born .... Baptized Nov: 10 1766.   p. 75.

Richard Scrugs & Rachel Wright a Daughter named Mary born Nov: 19 1765.   Baptized Dec: 22 1765.   p. 72.

Richard Scrugs & Rachel Wright a son named William born feb: 4 1769.   Baptized Ap: 2 1769.   p. 84.

Rich. Scrugs & Rachel Wright a daughter named Elizabeth born Jan 5, 1772.   Baptized 1772.   p. 91.

Rich. Scrugs & Rachel Wright a daughter named Nancy born Nov. 30, 1775.   Baptized Feb. 25, 1776.   p. 99.

Abraham sea & Naomi Lovine a son named Austine born dec: 25 1759.   Baptized 1759 Oct: 28.   p. 56.

Josiah Seay & Prudence Utley a daughter named Lockley born May 1, 1778.   Baptized Aug. 9, 1778.   p. 103.

Jo: Seay & Rebekah More a son named Warran born Feb. 28, 1781.   Baptized Oct 21, 1781.   p. 104.

Stephen Seay & Ann Ryan a Son named Abraham born Dec. 3, 1780.   Baptized Oct 21, 1781.   p. 104.

Roger Shakine & Ann Carter, a son named William born Nov: 13 1770.   Baptized Ap: 10 1771.   p. 89.

Thomas Shambles [Chambliss?] & Million Wells a Son named Travis born May 13. 1757.   Baptized 1757 July 31.   p. 51.

William Sharp & Susannah Childers a Daughter named Mary born feb. 24 1767.   Baptized Mar: 5 1769.   p. 83.

William Sharp & Susannah Childers a Daughter named Sicily born feb: 17 1769.   Baptized Mar: 5 1769.   p. 83.

Will Sharp. & Susannah Childers a daughter named Lucy born Mar 1, 1772.   Baptized Mar. 7, 1774.   p. 96.

Tho: & Judith Sharps a child named Melinda born Dec. 13, 1781. Baptized Jan. 10, 1782.   p. 105.

John Shastine & ffrances Branch a Daughter named Charlotte born Jun: 10 1762.   Baptized 1762 Jul: 25.   p. 63.

John Shasteen & Eliz: Logwood a son named William born Jul: 16 1768.   Baptized Aug: 28 1768.   p. 82.

Samuel Sheets & Susannah Langford a son named William born Jul. 21, 1773.   Baptized Sep. 6, 1773.   p. 95.

Samuel Sheets & Susannah Langford a .... Baptized Aug 3, 1775.   p. 98.

John Shilton & Eliz: Lawson a son named David born Jun: 11. 1761.   Baptized 1761 Jul: 5.   p. 60.

John Shilton & Elizabeth Lawson a Daughter named Elizabeth born feb: 28. 1763.   Baptized 1763 Ap: 10.   p. 64.

John Shilton & Elizabeth Lawson a son named William born Mar: 9 1765. Baptized Ap: 14 1765. p. 71.

John Shilton & Elizabeth Lawson a Daughter named Nannie born Oct: 29 1767. Baptized Nov: 15 1767. p. 79.

Peter Shilton & Frances Nichols a son named Peter born Jul: 23. 1763. Baptized 1763 Sep: 4. p. 65.

Peter Shilton & ffrances Nichols a Daughter named Lucy born Dec: 3 1764. Baptized Jan: 31 1764. p. 69.

Peter Shilton & Frances Nichols a Daughter named Frances born Jul: 5 1766. Baptized Aug: 17 1766. p. 74.

Peter Shilton & Frances Nichols a son named Thomas born Mar: 2 1768. Baptized Ap: 17 1768. p. 80.

Peter Shilton & ffrances Nichols a Daughter named Judith born Oct: 8 1769. Baptized Dec: 17 1769. p. 86.

Tho: Ship. & Jediah Moor a son named Lemuel born Oct 15, 1776. Baptized Mar. 30, 1777. p. 101.

ffrancis Shodoang [Chadouin] & Sarah Weaver a son named John born Nov: 16 1761. Baptized 1762 feb: 6. p. 61.

ffrancis Shadwin [Chadouin] & Sarah Weaver a son named Jesse-Weaver born Sep: 18 1763. Baptized Oct: 1763. p. 66.

ffrancis Shadrone [Chadouin] & Sarah Weaver a son named David born feb: 15 1766. Baptized Mar: 8 1766. p. 73.

Augustine Shepherd & Sarah Shilton a Daughter named ffrances born Dec: 21 1760. Baptized 1761 Jan: 18. p. 58.

John Shepherd & Mary Lilly a Son named David born Jun: 9 1761. Baptized 1761 Nov: 9. p. 61.

John Shepherd & Mary Lilly a Daughter named Ann born Nov: 7 1764. Baptized Jul: 6 1765. p. 71.

John Shepherd & Mary Lilly a Daughter named Frances born Dec: 2 1766. Baptized Jun: 11 1767. p. 77.

John Shepherd & Mary Lilly a son named John born May 1, 1771. Baptized Jun. 16, 1771. p. 90.

Philip Shepherd & Susan Thomson a son Lewis born May 3 1786. Baptized June 4 1786. p. 116.

Rob: Shepherd & Eliz: Baxter a son named Thomas born Nov: 15 1766. Baptized Jan: 18 1767. p. 76.

Robert Shepherd & Eliz: Blackstone a Daughter named Elizabeth born Ap: 9 1769. Baptized Jun: 11 1769. p. 85.

Rob: Shepherd & Eliz: Blackstock a son named Benjamin born Jan: 6 1771. Baptized Mar: 24 1771. p. 89.

Samuel Shepherd & Eliz: Blackstone a daughter named Mildred born Jul 18, 1773. Baptized Aug 22, 1773. p. 94.

Will: Shepherd & Martha Arrington a Daughter named Annas born Ap: 7 1762. Baptized 1762 Aug: 8. p. 63.

Evan Shoemaker & Judith Burks a Daughter named Sally-Winston born Oct: 2, 1756. Baptized 1759 Sep: 29. p. 56.

John Shoemaker & Sarah Jerrat a son named Randolph born Mar: 3 1758. Baptized 1758 June 25. p. 53.

John Shoemaker & Sarah Jerrat a Daughter named Sally ffox born Ap: 11. 1760. Baptized 1761 Nov: 9. p. 61.

John Shoemaker & Sarah Jerrat a son named John born Dec: 13 1761. Baptized 1762 Ap: 12. p. 62.

John Shoemaker & Sarah Jerrat a son named Tarlton born dec: 17 1763. Baptized Mar: 31 1764. p. 67.

John Shoemaker & Sarah Jarret a Daughter named Jeanie born Jan: 7 1766. Baptized May 17 1766. p. 74.

John Shoemaker & Sarah Gerrard a Daughter named Judith born feb: 1 1768. Baptized Ap: 11 1768. p. 80.

John Shoemaker & Sarah Gerrat a son named Thomas born Dec: 7 1769. Baptized Aug: 14 1770. p. 88.

Tho: Shoemaker & Sarah Hicks on Tuckahoe a Daugh: born Jan: 30 1756 named Angelica. Baptized 1756 Mar 14. p. 48.

Tho: Shoemaker & Sarah Hicks a Daughter named Judah born Nov: 22, 1757. Baptized 1758 ffeb: 12. p. 52.

Tho: Shoemaker & Sarah Hicks a Daughter named Mary born Dec: 17 1763. Baptized Oct: 7 1768. p. 82.

John Short & Olive Sassine a son named William born feb. 29 1768. Baptized May 15 1768. p. 81.

Thomas Short & Ann Payne a Daughter named Judith born feb: 5 1765. Baptized May 19 1765. p. 71.

Young Short & Mary Bilboa a Daughter named Elizabeth born Mar: 7 1764. Baptized Ap: 15 1764. p. 67.

Young Short & Mary Bilboa a Daughter named Mary born .... Baptized Sep: 14 1766. p. 75.

Young Short & Mary Bilboa a son named Reuben born Jan: 10 1769. Baptized Mar: 4 1769. p. 83.

James Sims & Eliz: Saunders a Daughter named Ann born Ap: 1 1767. Baptized May 10 1767. p. 77.

James Sims & Eliz: Sanders a son named Mathew born Dec: 29 1768. Baptized Jan: 29 1769. p. 83.

John Slaydon* & Susannah Hodges a Daughter named Sarah born Jan: 8 1758. Baptized 1758 ffeb: 19. p. 52.

John Slaten & susannah Hodges a son named James born Mar: 22, 1760. Baptized 1760 May 11. p. 57.

John Slaten & Susannah Hodges a Daughter named Martha born Aug: 13 1768. Baptized Sep: 25 1768. p. 82.

John Slayden & Susannah Hodges a son named John born Sep. 12, 1773. Baptized Jul. 15 1775. p. 98.

Jo: Slaydon* & Susanna Groom a child Mary born May 19 1788. Baptized Sept 17 1788. p. 121.

William Slaton* & Sarah Groom a daughter name Jeanie born Nov. 30 1770. Baptized Feb: 21 1771. p. 89.

Will [Slaydon] & Sarah Grooms a daughter named Mally born Jan. 13, 1772. Baptized Aug. 2, 1772. p. 92.

*Sladen in marriage record.

Will Slyden & Sarah Groom a son named Arthur born Oct 29, 1773. Baptized Jul. 15, 1775. p. 98.

Will Slaton & Sarah Groom a child named Sarah born Dec. 24, 1780. Baptized Mar. 16, 1782. p. 105.

Jo: Sladon & Susannah Groom a Son Daniel Born June 22. Baptized Sep. 30, 1782. p. 107.

Will: Sladen & Sar: Groom a son Will: Douglas born Feb: 3 1783. Baptized Sep: 16 1783. p. 110.

Will: Slaydon & Sarah Groom a son Major born June 18 1789. Baptized Oct: 20 1789. p. 122.

Cha:. Slaughter & Eliz: Poindexter, Ann Poindexter July 17. 1782. Baptized Aug. 9, 1782. p. 107.

Cha: Slaughter & Eliz: Poindexter; Jo: Poindexter, born Mar: 7 1784. Baptized June 3 1784. p. 111.

Cha: Slaughter & Eliz: Poindexter, Polly-Smith born Jan. 2 1786. Baptized Feb. 2 1786. p. 116.

Champness Smith & Eliz: Hubbard a son Austine born Feb. 18 1785. Baptized Aug. 16 1785. p. 114.

Christopher Smith & Mary Anderson a son Christopher Lewis May 26 1787. Baptized May 25 1788. p. 121.

Childers Smith & ffrances ffield a Daughter named Elizabeth born Dec: 25 1763. Baptized Jan: 7 1764. p. 66.

David Smith & Mary Byers a child Roxana born Ap: 15 1784. Baptized May 6 1784. p. 111.

David Smith & Frances Dickerson a son Elisha Dickerson born dec. 5 1789. Baptized ap: 1 1791. p. 126.

Edward Smith & Sally Rice a .... Baptized Aug: 5 1764. p. 68.

Edward Smith & Sarah Rice a Daughter named Betty born .... Baptized Feb: 2 1766. p. 73.

Edward Smith & Sally Rice a Daughter named Sally born Nov: 4 1767. Baptized Dec: 6 1767. p. 79.

Edward Smith & Sally Rice a Son named William born Sep: 23 1769. Baptized Oct: 8 1769. p. 86.

George Smith & Ann [Caroline] Tribue a Daught: named Mary born feb: 7 1762. Baptized 1762 Ap: 4. p. 62.

George Smith & Caroline Tribue a son named Thomas born dec: 7 1763. Baptized Mar: 3 1764. p. 66.

George Smith & Caroline Tribue a Daughter named Martha-Ann born Jan: 19 1767. Baptized Ap: 12 1767. p. 77.

George Smith & Caroline Tribue a son named Antony-Tribue born Mar: 24 1769. Baptized May 28 1769. p. 84.

George Smith & Caroline Tribue a daughter called Nansy Clark born Dec. 13, 1772. Baptized Jan. 24, 1773. p. 93.

George Smith & Judith Gerran a Daughter name Marianne born Ap: 16 1767. Baptized May 24 1767. p. 77.

George Smith & Judith Gerrand a Daughter named Esther born Ap: 13 1768. Baptized May 15 1768. p. 81.

Jesse Smith & Malley Henley a daughter named Lucy born Feb. 11, 177..... Baptized May 6, 1774. p. 96.

John Smith & Susannah Raison a daugh: born Oct: 7 1736 named ffrances. p. 40.

John Smith & Susannah Raison. a Son born feb: 24 1740 named Robert. p. 40.

John Smith & Susannah Raison. a Son born Aug: 3 1742 named Philemon. p. 40.

John Smith & Susannah Raison. a Son born Aug: 7 1745 named Thomas. p. 40.

John Smith Major & Susannah Raison Twins named Philemon & Nanny born Nov: 29. 1756. Baptized 1756 Dec: 26. p. 49.

John Smith & Eliz: Hopkins a Daughter named Elizabeth born Ap: 4 1758. Baptized 1758 Jun: 7. p. 52.

John Smith & Eliz: Hopkins a son named Bowker born Aug: 19, 1760. Baptized 1760 Sep: 23. p. 58.

John Smith & Caroline Short a son named William born Oct: 17 1764. Baptized Jan: 12 1764. p. 69.

John Smith & Mary Storey a Daughter named Mary born Ap: 1764. Baptized Nov: 2 1766. p. 75.

John Smith & Mary Story a son named James born Jun 16 1766. Baptized Oct: 12 1766. p. 75.

John Smith & Mary Storey a Daughter named Sarah born Mar: 8 1769. Baptized Jun: 4 1769. p. 85.

John Smith & Mary Story a son named Robert born Oct 27, 1771. Baptized Jan. 26, 1772. p. 91.

Jos: Smith & Eliz: Smith [*Edwards] a son Rollins born May 21 1790. Baptized Oct. 4 1790. p. 126.

Leonard Smith & Eliz. Hollanhead a daughter named Elizabeth born Oct 7, 1774. Baptized Nov. 11, 1774. p. 97.

Leonard Smith & Eliz: Hollinshed a son names James born Sep. 16, 1776. Baptized Oct 23, 1776. p. 100.

Michael Smith & Judith Rice a Daughter named Milley born Jun: 15. 1759. Baptized 1759 Sep: 30. p. 56.

Michal Smith & Judith Rice a son named Reuben born Aug: 15, 1761. Baptized 1761 Sep: 27. p. 61.

Moses Smith & Biddy Alexander a Daughter named Sally born Ap: 12 1764. Baptized Jun: 24 1764. p. 68.

Moses Smith & Biddy Alexander a son named Thomas born .... Baptized Oct: 25 1767. p. 79.

Nathan: Smith & Unity Dickerson a child named Unity born Nov. 30, 1780. Baptized Ap. 8, 1781. p. 103.

Obadiah Smith & Mary Burk a Son named Luke born 1744 Aug: 23. p. 41.

Obadiah Smith & Mary Burk a Daughter named Susannah born 1746 Ap: 28. p. 41.

*See marriage.

Obadiah Smith & Mary Burk a Son named Peartree born 1748 June 13. p. 41.

Obadiah Smith & Mary Burk a Daughter named Elizabeth born 1750 Nov: 28. p. 41.

Obadiah Smith & Mary Burk a Son named William born 1752 Nov: 15. p. 41.

Obadiah Smith & Mary Burk a Son named Obadiah born 1755 May 7. p. 41.

Obadiah Smith & Mary Burk in Tuckahoe a Daughter named Lucy born dec: 8 1756. Baptized 1757 Mar. 12. p. 50.

Obadiah Smith & Mary Burks a son named Joseph born Nov: .... 1761. Baptized 1761 Dec: 14. p. 61.

Obadiah Smith & Lucy Poor a daughter named Betsey born Aug. 30, 1775. Baptized Nov. 12, 1775. p. 99.

Obadiah Smith & Lucy Poor a daughter named Sally born Dec. 20. 1776. Baptized Ap. 6. 1777. p. 101.

Payton Smith & Judith Wadley a Daughter named Sally born Dec: 17 1763. Baptized Jan: 8 1764. p. 66.

Peyton Smith & Judith Wadly a son named Peyton-Thomas born Ap: 11 1767. Baptized Jul: 5 1767. p. 78.

Rob. Smith & Susan Barnet a son named Daniel Johnson born Jul: 22, 1780. Baptized Aug 26, 1781. p. 104.

Rob. Smith & Susanna Barnet, Jane Ware born June 22, 1782. Baptized Nov. 24, 1782. p. 108.

Will: Smith & Eliz: Watkins a son named William born May 4 1762. Baptized 1762 Jul: 25. p. 63.

William Smith & Elizabeth Watkins a son named Samuel born feb: 13 1764. Baptized May: 6 1764. p. 67.

Will Smith & Sar: Pryor a son Will: Thornton, born Feb. 2 1785. Baptized Aug. 14 1785. p. 114.

Will Smith & Sarah Pryor .... Baptized 17 Oct. 1787. p. 120.

Will Smith & Sally Pryor a child Dorothy born June 2 1788. Baptized Sep. 17 1788. p. 121.

William Smith & Mary Rose a daughter named Lucy born Jul. 23, 1773. Baptized Oct 9, 1773. p. 95.

Will Smith & Mary Rhodes a son named Nelson born Sep. 17, 1781. Baptized Oct. 8, 1781. p. 105.

Will: Smith & Mary Rhodes a son Clifton Rhodes born Ap: 12 1784. Baptized June 13 1784. p. 112.

Will Smith & Eliz. Young a daughter named Ann: Merriwether born Mar 15, 1774. Baptized Mar. 15, 1774. p. 97.

Will Smith & Frances McGhee a child Susannah born Ap. 7, 1782. Baptized June 2, 1782. p. 106.

Will Smith & Frances [McGhee] Smith a child Polly Wharton born Jul: 7 1784. Baptized Jul: 3 1785. p. 114.

Billie Smith & Cat Bibb a Son Billie born. Baptized Sep. 15, 1782. p. 107.

Rob: Smithy & Rebekah Shepherd a Son named John born Oct: 6. 1756. Baptized 1756 Nov: 7. p. 49.

Arch: Sneed & Sally Pope a child Matilda born Jul: 24, 1780. Baptized Oct 21, 1781. p. 104.

Charles Sneed & Mary Guillam a Daughter named Sally born Sep: 5 1768. Baptized Oct: 23 1768. p. 82.

Charles Sneed & Mary Guillam a daughter named Judith born Mar. 16, 1772. Baptized Nov. 25, 1772. p. 93.

John Sneed & Sarah Woodrum a son named Benjamin born feb: 9 1764. Baptized Mar: 18 1764. p. 67.

John Sneed & Sarah Woodrum a son named Clayburn born Dec: 28 1765. Baptized Jan: 26 1766. p. 73.

John Sneed & Sarah Woodrum a Daughter named Elizabeth born Oct: 16 1767. Baptized Nov: 29 1767. p. 79.

Jo: Snead & Sarah Johnson, a child Cynthe Mims born Jan: 10 1784. Baptized May 30 1784. p. 111.

Will: Snead & Catherine Sharp a Daughter named Catherine born Ap: 6 1748. Baptized Oct: 19 1763. p. 66.

Will: Snead & Catherine Sharp also a Daughter named Martha born Jun: 18 1750. Baptized Oct: 19 1763. p. 66.

Will: Snead & Catherine Sharp also a son named Robert born Mar: 27 1754. Baptized Oct: 19 1763. p. 66.

Nathaniel Snelson & Sar: Spier a child Ann Mar: 22 1788. Baptized Ap: 27 1788. p. 120.

Turner Southall & Martha Vandeval a son named William born Ap 27 1765. Baptized May 7 1765. p. 71.

Stephen Southall & Martha Wood a child Mary Wood Ap: 9 1787. Baptized May 21 1787. p. 119.

Da: Spier & Eliz: Wash a son David born Nov. 15 1784. Baptized Oct. 9 1785. p. 115.

Capt Will: Stamps & Elenor Brent a Daughter named Catherine born Oct: 17, 1757. Baptized 1757 Nov: 4. p. 51.

Capt: William Stamps & Helen Brent a son named James born Jan: 6. 1760. Baptized 1760 Jan: 29. p. 56.

David Standford & Elizabeth Fulcran* a son named David born May 8 1765. Baptized Jul: 21 1765. p. 72.

David Stanford & Eliz: Furcran a son named James born May 25 1767. Baptized Jul: 26 1767. p. 78.

David Staples & Christian fford a son named John born Sep: 14, 1757. Baptized 1757 Dec: 4. p. 51.

Ben: Stark & Ann Chace twins Fielding & Delphe born Oct 11, 1782. Baptized May 19, 1782. p. 106.

Ben Starks & Annie Chace a son Thomas, born Mar: 5 1785. Baptized June 14 1785. p. 114.

Cap: Thomas Stark & Jean Williams a Daughter named Jean born feb: 15, 1757. Baptized 1757 Mar. 28. p. 50.

---

*ffurkerant in marriage record.

Capt. Tho: Stark & Jean Williams a son named Reuben born Aug: 21. 1759. Baptized 1759 Sep: 30. p. 56.

Thomas Stark & Jean Williams a son named John born May 15 1762. Baptized 1762 Jun: 6. p. 63.

Tho: Stark & Martha Price a Daughter named Mary born Apl: 27 1763. Baptized Oct: 19 1763. p. 66.

Joseph Starkie & Eliz: Leprade a son named William: Jacobson born Ap: 5, 1760. Baptized 1760 Jun: 1. p. 57.

Will Steers & Sara Halliday, a son James born Oct. 7 1783. Baptized Sept. 13 1785. p. 115.

Will Steers & Sara Halliday, a son Holliday, born Feb. 13 1785. Baptized Sept. 13 1785. p. 115.

Will: Steers & Sar: Hollowday, Philadelphia born Oct. .... 1786. Baptized Jan: 8 1787. p. 118.

Henry Stevens & Eliz: Davis a son Jeremiah born Nov: 13 1786. Baptized Mar: 14 1787. p. 118.

Henry Stevens & Eliz: Davis a son Thomas born June 3 1788. Baptized Dec. 7, 1788. p. 121.

Rob: Stewart & Jean Wright a son John born June 27 1788. Baptized Sep 5 1788. p. 121.

Ambrose Stodghill & Susan: Denton a son named William born Ap: 5 1770. Baptized May 20 1770. p. 87.

Ambrose Stogehill & Susannah Fenton a son named James born Jul. 5, 1772. Baptized Aug. 16, 1772. p. 92.

Ambrose Stodgill & Susanna Denton a son named Ambrose born Aug 26, 1780. Baptized Aug. 25, 1781. p. 104.

Ambrose Stoghill & Susanna Denton a son David born May 23 1783. Baptized Oct. 5 1783. p. 110.

Abram Strange & Mary More a son named Archeleus born Jul. 12, 1780. Baptized Oct. 21, 1781. p. 104.

Abram Strange & Mary More anoyr Son named Jo: Walker born Sep: 27, 1781. Baptized Oct. 21, 1781. p. 104.

John Strange & Ann Mitchell a Daughter named Patty born Sep: 22 1756. Baptized 1756 Oct: 31. p. 49.

John Strange & Ann Mitchel a son named Abner: Alloa born Mar: 7. 1761. Baptized 1761 May 24. p. 60.

William Street & Judith Bryant a son named Isaac born Mar: 12 1764. Baptized May 6 1764. p. 67.

Nathan Strong & Catherine Callichan a son named John born Dec. 10, 1776. Baptized Mar. 30, 1777. p. 101.

William Strong & ffrances Johnson a son named Isham born Ap: 22 1764. Baptized Jun: 10 1764. p. 68.

William Strong & Frances Johnson a son named John born Ap: 12 1768. Baptized May 29 1768. p. 81.

Will Strong & Frances Johnson, twins named .... Baptized Sep: 22 1770. p. 88.

Joseph & Ann Stuarts a daughter Betsie Purvis born May 12 1788. Baptized Sep: 5 1788. p. 121.

Henry Stubblefield & Frankie Smith a son George born June 25 1786. Baptized Oct: 19 1786. p. 118.

Rob: Stubblefield & Susanna Parker a son Beverly born Mar: 11 1783. Baptized Aug: 1 1783. p. 110.

Rob: Stubblefield & Susan Parker, a son Benjamin, born Jul: 5 1785. Baptized Aug. 30 1785. p. 115.

Rob: Stubberfield & Susanna Parker a child named Eliz: Beverly born Ap. 30, 1781. Baptized Aug. 19, 1781. p. 104.

Benjamin Sublet & Elizabeth Jordan a Daughter named Sarah born Dec: 26 1763. Baptized Jan: 22 1764. p. 66.

Benjamin Sublet & Betty Jordan a son named Charles-Jordan born Jul: 31 1766. Baptized Sep: 3 1766. p. 75.

Ben: Sublet & Eliz: Jordan a Daughter named Ursley born Mar: 24 1769. Baptized May 21 1769. p. 84.

Ben Sublet & Eliz. Jordan a daughter named Elizabeth born. Baptized Dec. 21, 1771. p. 91.

Ben Sublet & Eliz Jordan a daughter named Elizabeth born Oct 14, 1771. Baptized May 25, 1775. p. 98.

Ben Sublet & Eliz. Jordan a daughter named Elizabeth born Oct 14, 1771. Baptized May 28, 1775. p. 98.

Benjamin Sublet & Eliz. Jordan a son named Ben: Branch born Mar. 29, 1774. Baptized Jun. 1, 1774. p. 96.

Benjamin Sublet & Eliz: Jordan a son named Samuel born Aug: 29, 1776. Baptized Mar. 31. 1777. p. 101.

Lewis Sublet & Frances Hillason a son named Abraham born May 28, 1763. Baptized 1763 Jul: 24. p. 65.

Tho: Summers & Martha Wetherspoons a son James, born Sep: 23 1782. Baptized 14 Sept. 1788. p. 121.

Tho: Summers & Martha Wetherspoons a son John born Sep. 6 1786. Baptized 14 Sept. 1788. p. 121.

Christopher Sumpter & Eliz: ffarmer a Daughter named Sally born Ap: 29 1762. Baptized 1762 May 30. p. 63.

Sanders Sutherland* & Martha Davis a son named William born Sep: 23 1759. Baptized 1760 Ap: 27. p. 57.

Alexr Sutherland & Martha Davis a son named George born Aug: 16, 1761. Baptized 1762 Jul: 4. p. 63.

Joseph Sutherland & Judith Appleberry a Daughter named Sally born Ap: 12 1761. Baptized 1761 Sep: 13. p. 61.

Joseph Sutherland & Judith Appleberry a Daughter named Betty born Jan: 11 1769. Baptized May 14 1769. p. 84.

Will: Sutton & Tabitha Wisdom, a son Frances, born Mar: 18 1786. Baptized May 20 1786. p. 116.

Will: Swanson & Mary mcGuire a Son named John born Oct: 7 1757. Baptized 1758 Ap: 30. p. 52.

William Swanson & Mary mcGuire a Daughter named ffanny born Ap: 15. 1760. Baptized 1760 Jun: 8. p. 57.

---

*Southerland in marriage record.

Rich: Swift & Eliz: Rice a son William born Mar: 16 1783. Baptized Ap: 15 1783. p. 109.

William Swift & ffrances Waddy a Son named William born dec: 30. 1756. Baptized 1757 feb: 20. p. 50.

Will: Swift & ffrances Waddy a son named Anthony born Jan: 9 1761. Baptized 1761 feb: 19. p. 59.

William Swift & Francis Waddie a son named Richard born Ap: 2 1767. Baptized May 7 1767. p. 77.

William Swift & Frances Waddy a son named Will-Park born Jan: 3 1769. Baptized Feb: 17 1769. p. 83.

James Symes & Eliz: Sanders a son named James born Oct: 18 1770. Baptized Jan: 13 1771. p. 89.

James Symes & Eliz. Sanders a son named John born Dec 25, 1772. Baptized Jan. 17, 1773. p. 93.

Fenton Symes & Keziah Hill a child Molly born Oct. 20 1782. Baptized Ap: 14 1783. p. 109.

Moses Symens & .... Baptized Feb: 11 1770. p. 86.

Nick: Taliferrar & Ann Taliferrar a child Lucy: Mary born Aug 6, 1782. Baptized Jan 18, 1783. p. 108.

Geo: Tally & Lydia* Cole a son Richard born dec. 17 1794. Baptized Ap: 5 1795. p. 127.

Story Tally & Ann Hagart a son Nathaniel born Nov. 10 1784. Baptized Dec. 19 1784. p. 113.

Story Tally & Ann Harger a child Mary baptized, born Jul. 6 1787. Baptized Aug. 12 1787. p. 119.

Will: Tally & Lydia Cole a child Joseph born Jan. 18 1792. Baptized June 3 1792. p. 126.

Henry Tandie & Ann Mills a son named Ralph born Nov. 6, 1781. Baptized Jan. 23, 1782. p. 105.

Henry Tandy & Ann Mills a son Jackson born Aug. 28 1784. Baptized Nov. 10 1784. p. 113.

Henry Tandie & Ann Mills a son Nathaniel born Jul. 1 1789. Baptized Aug. 23 1789. p. 125.

Ja. Tate and Frances Hutson a son John born May 8, 1781. Baptized Nov. 11, 1782. p. 108.

Ja. Tate & Frances Hutson a child Abigail born dec. 22, 1782. Baptized Jan. 25, 1783. p. 108.

Ja: Tate & Frances Hutson, a child Matilda born Jul. 23 1784. Baptized Dec. 29 1785. p. 115.

Ja: Tate & Francis Hutson a son James, Mar: 5 1786. Baptized June 26 1786. p. 117.

Ja: Tate & Frances Hutson a child Euphan born Oct. 25 1787. Baptized Oct. 12 1788. p. 121.

Ja: Tate & Frankie Hudson Bobbie a son born July 15 1789. Baptized Jan: 6 1790. p. 126.

Ja: Tate & Rebekah Hutson a child Rebekah born Ap. 18. 1782. Baptized Aug. 28, 1782. p. 107.

*Sally in marriage record.

Rob: Tate & Susanna Bibb, a son Ja: Bibb born Jul: 3 1780. Baptized Aug. 12 1786. p. 117.

Rob: Tate & Susanna Bibb, a son Nathan born Oct: 29 1782. Baptized Aug. 12 1786. p. 117.

Rob: Tate & Susanna Bibb, a son Benjamin, born Nov: 11 1783. Baptized Aug. 12 1786. p. 117.

Rob: Tate & Susanna Bibb, a daughter Abigail born Jan: 20 1785. Baptized Aug. 12 1786. p. 117.

Rob: Tait & Susannah Bibb twins, Eliz: & Mary Feb: 23 1787. Baptized Ap: 3 1787. p. 118.

Rob: Tate & Susanna Bibb a child Nansie born Feb. 11 1789. Baptized 1789 Ap: 14. p. 122.

Rob: Tate & Susanna Bibb, Will: Arnet born May 13 1790. Baptized Jul: 8 1790. p. 125.

Will Tate & Eliz: Hutson a Son Cha: Hutson born Feb 17, 1782. Baptized Ap. 10, 1782. p. 106.

Will: Tate & Eliz: Hudson, a son William born Oct. 13 1782. Baptized June 5 1784. p. 111.

Will: & Marg: Tates a child Elizabeth born Mar: 25 1783. Baptized May 19 1783. p. 109.

Will: Tate & Margaret Tate a child Elizabeth born Mar: 25 1783. Baptized June 26 1786. p. 117.

Will: Tate & Margaret Tate a son Nathan born Ap: 24 1786. Baptized June 26 1786. p. 117.

Will: & Marg: Tates a child Euphan born Sep: 29 1788. Baptized Apl: 14 1789. p. 122.

Zimri Tate & Martha Mayfield a child Martha born Aug. 6 1782. Baptized May 19 1783. p. 109.

And: Mintellet Tayloe & Lucy Fletcher a son Washington Taloe Ap: 25 1787. Baptized Ap: 3 1787. p. 118.

Absolom Taylor & Sarah East a son named Edie born Feb 1, 1769. Baptized May, 18, 1781. p. 103.

Edward Taylor & Judith Coleman a daughter called Ann born Feb. 13. 1776. Baptized Nov. 20, 1776. p. 101.

John Taylor & .... a Daughter named Dianah born .... Baptized Sep: 18 1768. p. 82.

Richard Terrell & Lucy Carr a daughter born named Mary Jefferson. Baptized 1793, July 17. p. 127.

Joel Terrel & Lucy Ragline a child named Mary born Aug: 24 1781. Baptized 20 Feb. 1782. p. 105.

Chiles Tyrrill & Margt. Douglas a son Ja: Hunter born Sep: 8 1784. Baptized Oct. 5 1784. p. 113.

Will Tyrril & Martha Winston a child named Ann born May 14. 1781. Baptized May. 18, 1781. p. 103.

Will: Tyrrill & Martha Winston a child Emily born March 18 1786. Baptized Sept. 7 1787. p. 119.

Da: Terry & Nelly Biggar a child Catie born Feb. 24 1777. Baptized May 29 1783. p. 109.

Da: Terry & Nelly Biggar a child Nelly born Mar: 3 1783. Baptized May 29 1783. p. 109.

Da. Tyrrie & Hellender Biggar a son Champ Biggar Jany. 14 1786. Baptized Nov: 6 1786. p. 118.

Manuel Tyrrie & Eliz: Thomson a son Thomson, born Aug. 7 1785. Baptized Oct. 12 1785. p. 115.

Emanuel Terry & Eliz: Thompson a son Overton Feb: 28 1786. Baptized Ap: 9 1787. p. 118.

Emanuel Terry & Betsy Thomson a child Sally born Oct. 3 1790. Baptized Dec: 24 1790. p. 126.

Benjamin Thacker & Ruth Bowls a Daughter named Marianne born Jul: 2. 1757. Baptized 1757 Aug: 21. p. 51.

Benjamin Thacker & Ruth Bowles a son named Benjamin: Aker born Jan: 14. 1759. Baptized 1759 Jul: 8. p. 55.

Benjamin Thacker & Ruth Boas a son named Nathaniel: Pettice born Mar: 8 176....* Baptized 1761 Jun: 21. p. 60.

Benjamin Thacker & Naphena Emmerson a Daughter named Milley born Aug. 30 1768. Baptized Jun: 26 1769. p. 85.

Nathaniel Thacker & Kesiah Evans a son named Joel born feb: 27 1767. Baptized Jun: 11 1767. p. 78.

William Thacker & Mary Evans a Daughter named Elizabeth born Sep: 12 1756. Baptized 1757 Ap: 11. p. 50.

James Thacston [?] & Eliz: Clark a Son born feb: 7 1756 named David. Baptized 1756 May 24. p. 48.

James Thactston & Elizabeth Clark a son named Peter born dec: 10 1758. Baptized 1759 ffeb: 25. p. 54.

James Thactston & Eliz: Clark a son named William born Nov: 8 1760. Baptized 1761 May 17. p. 59.

James Thackston & Elizabeth Clark a Daughter named Peggie born dec: 17 1763. Baptized Jul: 19 1764. p. 68.

James Thackston & Elizabeth Clark a son named James born Sep: 12 1767. Baptized Dec: 10 1768. p. 83.

James Thactstone & Eliz. Clark a son named John born. Baptized Dec. 22, 1771. p. 91.

Charles Thomas & Frances Amson a son named Charles born Feb. 26, 1781. Baptized Oct 19, 1781. p. 104.

Cha: Thomas & Frances Anson a child Polly born Sep. 22. 1782. Baptized Mar. 23, 1783. p. 108.

Cha: Thomas & Frances Ampson a son Christopher John, Jan: 30 1785. Baptized June 26 1785. p. 114.

Cha: Thomas & Francis Armstead a son James Nov: 13 1786. Baptized May 17 1787. p. 119.

Daniel Thomas & Sally Weldie† a son named George born Jul. 19, 1776. Baptized Oct. 30, 1776. p. 100.

Geo. Thomas & Sarah Payne a daughter named Mally: Ward born Dec. 14. 1771. Baptized 1772. p. 91.

---

*Margin torn.
†Welday in marriage record.

Geo: Thomas & Mary White a daughter named Mildred born Dec 9, 1775. Baptized Ap. 29, 1776. p. 100.

James Thomas & Mary White a son named Joel born Jul: 4 1769. Baptized Aug: 6 1769. p. 85.

James Thomas & Mary White a son named Daniel born Feb. 22, 1772. Baptized May. 10, 1772. p. 92.

James Thomas & Mary White a son named Rich: White born Ap. 15, 1775. Baptized May. 28, 1775. p. 98.

Jesse Thomas & Jean Bowles a Son Hen: Hughes born Feb 16, 1782. Baptized Mar. 29, 1782. p. 106.

Nathan Thomas & Mary Jones a child named Fanny born Oct 23, 1781. Baptized Sep. 7, 1781. p. 104.

Rowland Thomas Sr. & Jane Thurston Jo: More born Ap. 22, 1782. Baptized July 15, 1782. p. 107.

Rowland Thomas & Mary Parker a Son Ben: Parker born June 3, 1782. Baptized July 15, 1782. p. 107.

Rowland Thomas & Mary Parker a child Eliz: Winston, May 22 1785. Baptized Aug. 17 1785. p. 114.

Byers Thomason & Sally White, Eliz: Henderson born Jan: 2 1785. Baptized Mar: 28 1785. p. 113.

Byres Thomason & Sar: White a child Nancy Chapman, Jan: 7 1787. Baptized Ap: 9 1787. p. 118.

Fleming Thomason & Ann Smith Martha, born Ap: 18 1785. Baptized May 1 1785. p. 114.

Fleming Thomason & Ann Smith a child Ann born Aug: 30 1783. Baptized Sep: 28 1783. p. 110.

Fleming Thomason & Ann Smith a child Sally born Feb. 29 1789. Baptized June 6 1789. p. 122.

Fleming Thomason & Ann Smith, Lipscome Bibb, May 28 1787. Baptized Jul: 1 1787. p. 119.

Fleming Thomason & Ann Smith a son Pollard-Smith born Ap. 5 1791. Baptized May 17 1791. p. 126.

GEORGE THOMASON was born 10 Nov. 1703 and died 22 August 1783, aged 80. MARY POLLARD, his wife, was born 6 Nov. 1706. p. 28.

Their children were as follows:
Elizabeth Thomason was born February 27th 1735.
Thomas Thomason was born February 25th 1737.
Richard Thomason was born December 24 1739.
John Thomason was born October 20 1741.
Gorge Thomason was born February 18, 1743.
Ann Thomason was born April 4th 1749.
Fleming Thomason was born September 19 1751.
Christiana Thomason was born August 31 1754.
Sally Thomason was born November 2nd 1758.

Geo. Thomason & Eliz. Timberlick, a son George born Aug. 1782. Baptized Nov. 17, 1782. p. 108.

Geo: Thomason & Eliz: Timberlick, a son Wylie, born Oct. 16 1784. Baptized June 12 1785. p. 114.

Geo: Thomason & Eliz: Timberlick a son John Oct: 18 1786. Baptized Jan: 7 1787. p. 118.

Geo: Thomason & Eliz: Timberlick Betsy Fleming Feb. 28 1789. Baptized Jul: 17 1789. p. 125.

Geo. Thomason & Eliz: Timber[lick] had a child Presly. Baptized Jul: 24 '91. p. 140.

Geo: Thomason & Sarah Payne a son named Landie born Jan. 5 1776. Baptized Ap. 28, 1776. p. 100.

Jo: Thomason & Susanna .... a son Will-Robins, Sep. 24 1785. Baptized Dec. 12 1785. p. 115.

Jo: Thomason & Frances Cook a child Betsie Day born dec. 17, 1782. Baptized Jan. 30, 1783. p. 108.

Jo: Thomason & Frances Cook a son Tho: Cook born Jul: 30 1784. Baptized Mar 31 1785. p. 114.

Jo: Thomason & Francis Cook a child Jemima Day born Mar. 3 1787. Baptized May 20 1787. p. 120.

John Thomason & Frances Cook a child John Poindexter born Jany 31 1787. Baptized March 6 1788. p. 120.

Nath: Thomason & Patty Wood a child Nansie Burton born dec. 28. 1782. Baptized Mar. 23. 1783. p. 108.

Nathaniel Thomason & Martha Wood a child Sally born Jan. 3 1785. Baptized Mar: 14 1785. p. 113.

Nath: Thomason & Patsy Wood, James born .... 29 1786. Baptized Feb: 12 1787. p. 118.

Nath: Thomason & Pattie Wood a child named Ritter Mar: 12 1789. Baptized Apl. 13 1789. p. 122.

Nath: Thomason & Martha Wood a son William born Jan: 23 1791. Baptized Ap: 8 1791. p. 126.

Nathl. Thomason & Betty Wood his wife had a child Lucy born Mch. 24 1793. Baptized 1793 July 4. p. 127.

Rich: Thomason & Sarah Terry a son Sam: Gentry June 29 1788. Baptized Jul: 28 1788. p. 121.

Rich: Thomason & Sar: Tyrie [Terry] a son Richard born Jul: 24 1790. Baptized Oct: 4 1790. p. 126.

Sam Thomason & Ann Payne a son named Nilson born Sep. 4, 1774. Baptized Oct 10, 1774. p. 97.

Thomas Thomason & Eliz: Lodan had Twins named Lucy & Sarah born May 28 1758. Baptized 1758 Oct: 1. p. 53.

Tho: Thomason & Mary Wright a daughter named Patsy born May 10. 1777. Baptized Jul. 19, 1777. p. 102.

Tho: Thomason & Mary Wright a child named Sally Stark born Aug 23, 1781. Baptized Oct 3, 1781. p. 104.

Tho: Thomason & Mary Wright a son Will-Byers Feb: 1 1788. Baptized Mar: 26 1788. p. 120.

Tho: Thomason & Eliz: Waldy*, a son named William born Jul: 18 1771. Baptized Aug 11, 1771. p. 90.

Tho: Thomason & Elizabeth Weldy a daughter named Rebekah born Mar 20, 1777. May 11, 1777. p. 102.

Will Thomason & Basset Umphrah [Humphrey] Rebekah born Dec. 23, 1781. Baptized Mar. 24, 1782. p. 106.

[Will Thomason] & Basset Humphrey a child Lydia born Ap: 15 1783. Baptized Jul: 4 1784. p. 112.

Will: Thomason & Eliz: Hallom a child Winny Wright born Dec. 2 1783. Baptized Ap: 12 1784. p. 111.

Anderson Thomson & Ann Anderson a child Frances Jackson, Dec. 24 1785. Baptized June 13 1786. p. 117.

Anderson Thomson & Ann Anderson Alexr. Spotswood Jan: 26 1787. Baptized May 20 1787. p. 119.

Cha: Thomson & Agnes Wood a Son Daniel born. feb. 11, 1783. Baptized Mar. 15, 1783. p. 108.

Cha: Thomson & Agnes Wood, a child Lettie born June 16 1785. Baptized Sep: 11 1785. p. 115.

Da: & Hellender Thomsons a Son named Waddy born Sep. 28, 1780. Baptized Ap. 8. 1781. p. 103.

Ja: Thomson & Tempe Mooney a child Susanna born Aug. 16 1783. Baptized Sep: 21 1783. p. 110.

Jo: Thomson & Lucy Epperson a Son Littleberry born June 8. 1777. Baptized Oct 12, 1781. p. 104.

Jo: Thomson & Lucy Epperson a Son named William born June 18, 1781. Baptized Oct 12, 1781. p. 104.

Math: Thomson & Sarah Wyat a son John born Oct: 3 1783. Baptized Dec. 18 1783. p. 111.

Rodger Thomson & Ann Crenshaw Elizabeth born Sep: 19 1785. Baptized Dec. 15 1785. p. 115.

Stephen Thomson & Mary Armstead, Armstead Thomson, Aug. 4 1785. Baptized Feb: 2 1786. p. 116.

Waddy Thomson & Mary Lewis a daughter named Mildred born Sep. 21, 1775. Baptized Oct. 11, 1775. p. 99.

Will: Thomson & Frances Quarles a child Mary Ann born Nov: 4 1782. Baptized Ap: 5 1783. p. 109.

Will Thurley & Eliz. Applebery a Son named Benjamin born Ap. 1. 1781. Baptized Aug 26, 1781. p. 104.

Benjamin Thurmond & susannah Moss a Daugh: named Betsey born May 16, 1761. Baptized 1761 May 24. p. 60.

Ben Thurmond & Susan: Moss a child named Judith born Feb. 7, 1778. Baptized Oct. 20, 1781. p. 104.

John Thurmond & Mally Dickerson a son named William born Jan: 1, 1761. Baptized 1761 Mar: 15. p. 59.

Philip Thurmond & Judith Tucker a son named William born feb: 28 1766. Baptized Ap: 10 1766. p. 73.

*Weldie in marriage record.

Philip Thurmond & Judith Tucker a son named Elisha born Dec: 15 1767. Baptized Ap: 11 1768. p. 80.

Will: Thurmond & Mackie Norvil a son named Jamie born Aug: 22 1767. Baptized Nov: 20 1767. p. 79.

Will: Thurmond & Mackie Norvil a son named William born Oct: 14 1769. Baptized feb: 21 1770. p. 87.

ffrancis Thurstane & Hester Richards a Daughter named Sally born Jan: 4. 1757. Baptized 1757 Ap: 17. p. 50.

ffrancis Thurstane & Esther Richard a Daughter named Massey born Sep: 4 1759. Baptized 1760 Ap: 13. p. 57.

John Thurston & Patty Wetherspoon a daughter named Betsy born Dec. 15, 1774. Baptized Jan. 22, 1775. p. 97.

Jo: & Thurston & Martha Wetherspoon a child Molly born Jan: 9 1783. Baptized Ap: 19 1783. p. 109.

Reuben Thurston & Marianne Laury a daughter Sally born Feb. 19, 1775. Baptized Oct 26, 1775. p. 99.

William Thurstane & Jean Jones a son named Archer born Feb: 18 1765. Baptized Ap: 14 1765. p. 71.

Bailey Thurston & Jean Jones a son named Merriwether born Aug: 6 1767. Baptized Sep: 13 1767. p. 78.

Will: Thurstane & Jean Jones a Daughter named Annie born Jul: 30 1769. Baptized Mar: 25 1770. p. 87.

Will Thurston & Jean Jones a daughter named Susannah born Jun. 10, 1773. Baptized Sep. 26, 1773. p. 95.

Jo: Timberlick & Christina Thomason a child Polly born Dec. 22 1782. Baptized Nov. 4 1784. p. 113.

Jo: Timberlick & Christina Thomason a child Nancy born Oct. 10 1784. Baptized Nov. 4 1784. p. 113.

Philip Timberlick & Jean Fears [Peers] a child Mary born Dec. 29 1782. Baptized Ap: 14 1783. p. 109.

Philip Timberlick & Jean Peers a child Nancy Oct: 12 1786. Baptized Jany. 8 1786. p. 118.

Philip Timberlick & Jean Fears 2 children James & Jean twins Nov. 7 1790. Baptized Mar: 26 1791. p. 126.

Philip Tinsley & Kesiah Stodghill a son named Ambrose born Oct: 4 1765. Baptized Jan: 5 1766. p. 72.

Philip Tinsley & Keziah Stodghill a son named Cornelius born Ap: 18 1769. Baptized May 28 1769. p. 84.

Philip Tinsley & Keziah Stodghill twins James & David born Ap. 19, 1774. Baptized Jun. 19, 1774. p. 97.

John Todd & Mary Williams a son named John born Aug. 7, 1775. Baptized Nov. 12, 1775. p. 99.

John Tod & Mary Williams a Daughter named Ann born Dec: 23 1764. Baptized Jan: 25 1764. p. 69.

John Tolliver & Eliz: Symer a Daughter named Lucy born May 23 1768. Baptized Jul: 3 1768. p. 81.

Will: Tomkins* & Mary Meekins† a child Elisabeth Watkins born Dec. 5 1787. Baptized Jan: 5 1788. p. 120.

Aaron Tony & Ann Weildy a son Solomon born Jan: 20, 1782. Baptized May. 26, 1782. p. 106.

Bishop Tony & Sarah Ashly a son named John born Mar: 20. 1756. Baptized 1756 June 26. p. 49.

Bishop Tony & Sarah Ashlan a son named Jesse born Sep: 13. 1760. Baptized 1761 Nov: 8. p. 61.

Bishop Tonier & sarah Ashley a Daughter named Ann born feb: 25 1763. Baptized 1763 Mar: 31. p. 64.

Charles Tony & Ann Steventon a Daughter named Jean born Nov: 28. 1761. Baptized 1762 Mar: 14. p. 62.

Sherard Tony & Laurinia England a Daughter named Caroline born Jun: 7 1767. Baptized Jul: 12 1767. p. 78.

Sherwood Tony & Lucy England a son named Micajah born .... Baptized Dec: 27 1767. p. 79.

Sherard Tony & Lorana England a son named John born Aug. .... 1770. Baptized Oct: 21 1770. p. 88.

Cornelius Towler & Nanny Grubs a son named John born Nov. 10, 1775. Baptized Feb. 25, 1776. p. 99.

Geo: Towler & Fannie Bourns a son William born Sep: 3 1787. Baptized Nov. 18 1787. p. 120.

James Towler & Mary Jones a son named Godfrey born Sep: 29 1768. Baptized Nov: 13 1768. p. 82.

James Towler & Mary Jones a son named William born Aug 25, 1775. Baptized Dec. 2. 1775. p. 99.

John Toller [Towler] & Sarah Thomas a son named John born Jan: 2 1762. Baptized 1762 feb: 24. p. 61.

John Towler & Sarah Thomas a Daughter named Elisabeth born Aug: 28 1763. Baptized Nov: 6 1763. p. 66.

John Towler & Sarah Thomas a Daughter named Kesiah born Ap: 18 1765. Baptized May 26 1765. p. 71.

John Towler & Sarah Thomas a son named Benjamin born .... Baptized Jan: 25 1767. p. 76.

John Towler & Sarah Thomas a Daughter named Sally born May 6 1768. Baptized May 22 1768. p. 81.

John Towler & Sarah Thomas a Daughter named Frances born Mar: 22 1770. Baptized May 6 1770. p. 87.

Limmard Towler & Hellender Churchill twins Limmard & Agathy born dec. 21 1767. Baptized Mar: 8 1768. p. 80.

Stokely Towles & Elizabeth Downman a son named Portues born Jan. 3, 1777. Baptized Feb. 9, 1777. p. 101.

Stokely Towles & Eliz: Dunman [Downman] a child Mildred born Oct. 13 1782. Baptized Ap: 25 1783. p. 109.

David Tribue & Mary Sallee a son named Joseph born Jan: 30 1765. Baptized Ap: 28 1765. p. 71.

*Tompkins . . . †Meekie in marriage record.

David Tribue & Mary Sallee a son named David born Oct: 9 1768. Baptized Mar: 4 1769. p. 83.

John Tribue & Ollan Dupuy a son named Stephen born feb: 23 1766. Baptized Mar: 31 1766. p. 73.

Jo: Trice & Pattie Smith, Nancy Dickerson, born Sep. 27 1784. Baptized Ap: 24 1785. p. 114.

Henry True & Jane Hatter, a son Benjamin, born Dec. 10 1785. Baptized Sep: 14 1786. p. 117.

Joseph True & Sarah Wheeler, a son William born December 1 1785. Baptized Sep: 14 1786. p. 117.

Martin True & Betsie Snead a child Delphie born Jan: 17 1784. Baptized Oct: 19 1786. p. 117.

Martin True & Betsie Snead a child Keturah born June 19 1786. Baptized Oct: 19 1786. p. 117.

Simpson Tucker deceased & Mary Kent a Daughter named Ann born Jan 3 1757. Baptized 1757 Ap: 11. p. 50.

Henry Tuggle & Hellender Conolly a son named William born Ap: 27 1759. Baptized 1759 May 27. p. 55.

Henry Tuggle & Hellender Conolly a Daughter named Elizabeth born Jul: 4 1761. Baptized 1761 Aug: 16. p. 60.

Henry Tuggle & Helleneder Conolly a Daughter named ffrances born Jan: 28 1764. Baptized Ap: 1 1764. p. 67.

Henry Tuggle & Ellender Conolly a son named Thomas born Oct: 10 1766. Baptized Dec: 14 1766. p. 75.

Henry Tuggle & Hellender Conolly a Daughter named Jeanie born feb: 23 1769. Baptized Ap: 23 1769. p. 84.

John Tuggle & Mary Huchen [Houchens] a son named James born Sep: 19. 1756. Baptized 1756 Oct. 17. p. 49.

John Tuggle & Mary Houchins a Daughter named Seela born May 17 1764. Baptized Jul: 15 1764. p. 68.

John Tuggle & Nansy Cawley a daughter named Nannie born Dec: 30 1770. Baptized Feb: 3 1771. p. 89.

John Tuggle & Ann Cawley a daughter named Mally born Aug. 31, 1774. Baptized Oct. 10, 1774. p. 97.

Bartholomew Turner & Mary Johnston a son named James born Jul: 18 1765. Baptized Sep: 15 1765. p. 72.

Bartholomew Turner & Mary Johnson a son named Charles born Dec: 11 1766. Baptized Ap: 5 1767. p. 77.

Bartlet Turner & Mary Johnson a son named Reuben born Jul: 21 1768. Baptized Nov: 13 1768. p. 82.

Bartley Turner & Mary Johnson a son named Henry born Ap. 5 1770. Baptized Mar: 24 1771. p. 89.

Bartholomew Turner & Mary Johnson a son named John born Jan 22. 1773. Baptized May 29, 1773. p. 94.

Bartholomew Turner & Mary Johnson a son named Pleasants born Nov. 29, 1774. Baptized Jan. 21, 1775. p. 97.

Bartholomew Turner & Mary—Johnson a son named William born Mar. 6, 1777. Baptized July 27, 1777. p. 102.

Henry Turner & Susannah Johnson a Son named Benjamin born Oct: 4. 1756. Baptized 1757 Ap: 9. p. 50.

Henry Turner & Susannah Johnson a Daughter named Mary born May 16 1758. Baptized 1758 Nov: 19. p. 53.

Henry Turner & Jane Godby, Richard, August 25 1787. Baptized Mar: 10 1788. p. 120.

Thomas Turpine & Martha-Ward Gains a son named Thomas born Nov: .... 1768. Baptized May 7 1769. p. 84.

Rich: Tyrie & Tamar Hilliard a son named Benskin born Jan. 1, 1772. Baptized 1772. p. 91.

Dickie Tyrrie & Tamar Hillyard a daughter named Nancy born Sep 5, 1776. Baptized Oct 27, 1776. p. 100.

George Underwood & Betty Curd a son named Richard born Ap: 5 1769. Baptized May 21 1769. p. 84.

Geor: Underwood & Eliz: Curd a son named Thomas born Mar: 17 1771. Baptized Mar 24 1771. p. 89.

Geo: Underwood & Eliz: Curd a son named Francis born Mar. 18, 1773. Baptized Mar. 23, 1773. p. 94.

Geo. Underwood & Eliz. Curd a son named James born Feb. 6, 1775. Baptized Ap. 30, 1775. p. 98.

George Underwood & Eliz: Curd a son named Edmond born Ap. 1, 1777. Baptized May 4, 1777. p. 101.

Geo: Underwood & Eliz: Curd a son named George born Nov. 21, 1781. Baptized Mar. 17, 1782. p. 105.

Geo: Underwood & Eliz: Curd, William, born Jan: 23 1784. Baptized Sep. 19 1785. p. 115.

Geo: Underwood & Eliz: Curd, In Goochland John Curd Mar: 20 1786. Baptized June 15 1787. p. 119.

Thomas Underwood & Ann Taylor a son named William born Oct: 2 1765. Baptized Jan: 1 1766. p. 72.

Thomas Underwood & Ann Taylor a son named John born feb: 22 1767. Baptized Ap: 17 1767. p. 77.

Tho: Underwood & Ann Taylor a son named Thomas born Mar: 31 1768. Baptized May 8 1768. p. 80.

Thomas Underwood & Ann Taylor a son named Alexander, born Aug: 1 1769. Baptized Sep: 24 1769. p. 86.

Thomas Underwood & Ann Taylor a .... Baptized Dec: 30 1770. p. 89.

Tho: Underwood & Ann Taylor a daughter named Mary born Sep 2, 1772. Baptized Nov. 24, 1772. p. 93.

Tho. Underwood & Ann Taylor a son named Francis born Mar. 18, 1775. Baptized May 14, 1775. p. 98.

Tho: Underwood & Ann Taylor a son named James born Oct 10, 1776. Baptized Feb. 2. 1776. p. 101.

Jacob Utley & Dinah Hilsman a son named John born Aug. 28, 1775. Baptized Dec. 17, 1775. p. 99.

Jo: Utley & Alice Woodrum a son named John born Jun: 8 1770. Baptized Aug: 12 1770. p. 88.

John Utley & Ann Lewis a Son born decr. 26 1755 named Josiah. Baptized 1756 feb: 15. p. 48.

John Utley & Ann Lewis a Son named Obadiah born Oct: 3, 1757. Baptized 1757 Nov: 6. p. 51.

John Utley & Ann Lewis a Son named Hezekiah born Nov: 13 1759. Baptized 1759 Dec: 16. p. 56.

John Uttley & Ann Lewis a Daughter named Lillie born Dec: 4. 1760. Baptized 1761 Ap: 12. p. 59.

John Utley & Nanny Clarkson a son named Josiah born Feb. 26, 1774. Baptized Sep. 11, 1774. p. 97.

John Utley & Ann Clarkson a son named John born Nov. 27, 1776. Baptized Aug. 4. 1776. p. 100.

John Utley & Nancy Clarkson a daughter named Elizabeth born Mar. 4. 1777. Baptized May 18, 1777. p. 102.

Josiah Utley & Eliza: Gordon had a son named Reuben Bor. Ap. 3d. 1778. Baptized Aug. 9, 1778. p. 103.

William Utley & Mary Ragline a son named John born Oct: 26 1767. Baptized Nov: 29 1767. p. 79.

James Vaughan & Amelia Broomfield a Daughter named Sarah born Aug: 23, 1763. Baptized 1763 Sep: 25. p. 65.

James Vaughan & Amelia Broomfield a son named John born May 29 1766. Baptized Oct: 19 1766. p. 75.

Ja: Vaughan & Judith Hopkins a son Ja: Martin born Dec. 29 1783. Baptized Ap: 17 1784. p. 111.

Joseph Vaughan & Ann Payne a Daughter named Jeany born May 9 1770. Baptized Jul: 29 1770. p. 88.

Joseph Vaughan & Ann Payne twins Eliz: Payne & Ann Tucker, born Aug 9, 1772. Baptized Oct 4, 1772. p. 93.

Joseph Vaughan & Ann Payne a daughter named Clara born May 19, 1776. Baptized Sep. 1, 1776. p. 100.

Mathew Vaughan & Mary Martin a Daughter named Eliz: Shields born Jul: 23 1767. Baptized Nov: 4 1767. p. 79.

Mathew Vaughan & Mary Martin a Daughter named Ann born Ap: 28 1769. Baptized Jun: 22 1769. p. 85.

Mat Vaughan & Mary Martin a daughter named Martha: Martin born Oct 7. 1771. Baptized Ap. 12, 1772. p. 92.

Mathew Vaughan & Mary Martin a son named John born Oct 11, 1773. Baptized Aug. 19, 1774. p. 97.

Math: Vaughan & Mary Martin a daughter named Clariss born Jul. 25, 1775. Baptized Aug. 25, 1776. p. 100.

Mat Vaughan & Mary Martin a son named Henry: Hutson born Sep. 13, 1777. Oct 13, 1777. p. 102.

Shadrach Vaughan & Mary Merriwether a son named Merriwether born .... Baptized Oct: 23 1771. p. 90.

Shadrack Vaughan & Mary Merriwether a daughter named Ann born Ap. 5, 1779. Baptized May 26, 1773. p. 94.

Shadrack Vaughan & Mary Merriwether a son named Nick: Merriwether born Mar 17......., Baptized May 9. 1775. p. 98.

Hugh: Lewis Venable & Mary Martin a Daughter named Martha born May 27. 1760. Baptized 1760 Sep: 28. p. 58.

Hugh-Lewis Venable & Mary Martin a Daughter named Elizabeth born Dec: 8 1764. Baptized Jul: 6 1765. p. 71.

Hugh-Lewis Venable & Mary Martin a son named Nathaniel born feb: 22 1767. Baptized June 11 1767. p. 77.

Hugh-Lewis Venable & Mary Martin a daughter named Frankie born Mar. 1, 1773. Baptized Nov. 29, 1773. p. 95.

Hugh Lewis Venable & Mary Martin a son named Abraham born Aug. 26. 1780. Baptized Aug. 25, 1781. p. 104.

William Venable & Ann Clark a son named William born Mar: 12 1767. Baptized Jun: 11 1767. p. 77.

William Venables & Ann Clark a son named James born Dec: 20 1768. Baptized Ap: 20 1769. p. 84.

Jo: Vest & Lucy Chandler a son Charles born Sep. 27 1784. Baptized June 16 1785. p. 114.

Dan Wade & Delphe Green a Son William born Mar. 4 1782. Baptized June 16, 1782. p. 107.

Daniel Wade & Delphe Green a child .... born Apl: 11 1787. Baptized Oct. 17 1787. p. 120.

David Wade & Eliz: Price a daughter named Sally, born Jan: 18 1771. Baptized Aug 11 1771. p. 90.

John-Utley Wade & Ellis Woodrum a son named Castletoun born Jan: 1 1765. Baptized Mar: 17 1765. p. 70.

John Utley Wade & Ellis Woodrum a son named Ryal born Jul: 10 1766. Baptized Oct: 16 1766. p. 75.

John Utley-Wade & Ellice Woodrum a Daughter named Susannah born Oct: 25 1768. Baptized Mar: 26 1769. p. 84.

Nath: & Mary Wades a Son Daniel born Ap. 27, 1782. Baptized July 28, 1782. p. 107.

Nathaniel Wade & Mary Taylor a son John born Mar: 7 1784. Baptized May 30 1784. p. 111.

Richard Wade & Betty Barker a Son named William born Mar: 4. 1757. Baptized 1757 May 22. p. 51.

Richard Wade & Betty Barker a son named Hood born Jun: .... 1759. Baptized 1762 feb: 21. p. 61.

Richard Wade & Betty Barker a Daughter named Elizabeth born Nov: 24 1761. Baptized 1762 feb: 21. p. 61.

Richard Wade & Betty Barker a son named Obadiah born Ap: 15 1764. Baptized Jun: 17 1764. p. 68.

Richard Wade & Betty Barker a son named Michael born Sep: 14 1766. Baptized Oct: 16 1766. p. 75.

Richard Wade & Betty Barker a Daughter named Patty born Dec. 24 1768. Baptized Mar: 26 1769. p. 84.

Rich: Wade & Betty Barker a son named Joseph born May 11, 1771. Baptized Jul. 14, 1771. p. 90.

Rich. Wade & Betty Barker a son named Reuben born Dec. 20, 1773. Baptized Mar. 28, 1774. p. 96.

Richard Wade & Betty Barker a daughter named Lucy born Sep. 1, 1776. Baptized Oct 20, 1776. p. 100.

Richard Wade & Judah Hancoke a son named Elisha born Sep. 30, 1773. Baptized Nov. 5, 1773. p. 95.

Rich: Wade & Judith Hancoke a daughter named Rosanah born Jun. 26. 1776. Baptized Oct 15, 1776. p. 100.

Will: Wade & Ann Cothan a Daughter named Joanna born Jun: 23. 1757. Baptized 1757 Oct: 9. p. 51.

Will: Wade & Ann Baily a son David born Feb. 17 1784. Baptized Jul: 18 1784. p. 112.

Samuel Waddy & Mary Cook a child Sarah born Sep: 15 1783. Baptized Ap: 25 1784. p. 111.

Sam Waddy & Mary Cook a child Mildred born Sep: 23 1785. Baptized Nov. 11 1786. p. 118.

David Walker & Sarah Sladen a Daughter named Martha born Jan: 10 1759. Baptized 1759 ffeb: 18. p. 54.

David Walker & Ann Horn a Daughter named Sarah born Aug. 16 1767. Baptized Ap: 11 1768. p. 80.

John Walker & Lydia Gilbert a Daughter named Susannah born Dec: 17 1769. Baptized Jun: 17 1770. p. 88.

Jo: Walker & Lydia Gilbert a daughter named Agnes born Jun: 26 1771. Baptized Sep: 22 1771. p. 90.

John Walker & Lydia Gilbert a daughter named Judith born Nov. 16, 1776. Baptized Jan 18, 1776. p. 101.

Joseph Walker & Mary Howard a son named Pleasants born Sep: 23 1764. Baptized feb: 20 1765. p. 70.

Joseph Walker & Mary Howard a son named Charles born Mar: 20 1766. Baptized May 17 1766. p. 74.

Peter Walker & Eliz: Harris a son named Shadrach born Jul: 1. 1759. Baptized 1759 Sep: 29. p. 56.

Peter Walker & Elizabeth Harris a Daughter named Milley born Ap: 7. 1761. Baptized 1761 Jun: 6. p. 60.

Peter Walker & Elizabeth Harris a Daughter named Elizabeth born Mar. 3 1764. Baptized Ap: 29 1764. p. 67.

Peter Walker & Eliz: Harris a son named Jesse-Harris born feb: 8 1766. Baptized Ap: 20 1766. p. 73.

Peter Walker & Elizabeth Harris a son named Jesse Harris born Mar: 7 1766. Baptized Oct: 14 1766. p. 75.

Philip Walker & susannah Hilton a son named Jacob born Sep: 26, 1759. Baptized 1760 ffeb: 3. p. 56.

Shadrach Walker & Hannah Shepherd a son Sam: Shepherd, Ap: 12 1783. Baptized Dec. 17 1783. p. 110.

Tho: Walker, surgeon, & Mildred Thornton a son named ffrancis born Jun: 22 1764. Baptized Jun: 27 1764. p. 68.

Sam: Wardrop & Jean Foster a child Frances, born Oct: 14 1784. Baptized Dec. 19 1784. p. 113.

Sam: Waldrup & Jane Foster a child Jane born Feb. 7 1787. Baptized Ap: 15 1787. p. 118.

John Ware & Ann Harrison a Son named James born dec: 27, 1756. Baptized 1757 Ap: 8. p. 50.

John Ware & Ann Harrison a Son named Andrew born May 24 1758. Baptized 1758 June 25. p. 53.

John Ware & Ann Harrison a son named John born Jun: 10. 1762. Baptized 1762 Jul: 18. p. 63.

John Ware & Ann Harrison a Daughter named Betty born May 27 1764. Baptized Jun: 24 1764. p. 68.

John Ware & Ann Harrison a Daughter named Milley born Sep. 27 1766. Baptized Nov: 2 1766. p. 75.

John Ware & Hannah Harrison a Daughter named Jeanie born Dec: 14 1768. Baptized Jan: 29 1769. p. 83.

Jo: Ware & Ann Harrison a daughter named Anne born Jun: 30 1771. Baptized Sep: 22, 1771. p. 90.

.... Ware & Betsy Brown a child Betsie born Feb. 20 1783. Baptized June 3 1783. p. 109.

Malachi Ware & Bettie Brown a child Nansie, born Aug. 22 1785. Baptized Oct. 16 1785. p. 115. [See Waugh.]

Tho: & Henleey Wash a son William born Nov. 14 1786. Baptized May 20 1787. p. 120.

Charles Watkins & Lucy Curd a son named Edward born Oct 3, 1773. Baptized Nov. 14, 1774. p. 95.

Charles Watkins & Lucy Curd a daughter named Nancy born Oct 24. 1776. Baptized Nov. 10, 1776. p. 101.

Geo: & Eliz: Watkins a son Fielding Lewis born Feb. 13. Baptized Ap. 23, 1782. p. 106.

John Watkins & Sarah Turner a son named James born Aug: 22 1764. Baptized Dec: 2 1764. p. 69.

Sarah Turner spouse to John Watkins was baptised this day. Baptized Nov. 26 1775. p. 99.

Joel Watkins & Barbara Overton Harris a son Joel Merriwether, born Jan: 12 1784. Baptized Jul: 22 1784. p. 112.

Thomas Watkins & Dorothy Dickson a son named George: Cheeseman born May 27 1761. Baptized 1761 Jul: 26. p. 60.

Thomas Watkins & Dorothy Dick[son], twins named Joseph & Benjamin born Mar: 26 1764. Baptized May 6 1764. p. 67.

Thomas Watkins & Dorothy Dickson a Daughter named Mildred born Jun: 16 1766. Baptized Jul: 27 1766. p. 74.

Tho: Watkins & Dorothy Dickson a .... Baptized May 21 1769. p. 84.

John Watson & Ann Jones a son named John born Ap. 5 1773. Baptized May. 18 1773. p. 94.

Jo: Watson & Nancy Anderson a son named Josiah born June 20. 1781. Baptized Feb. 20, 1782. p. 105.

Will: Watson & Patty Pleasants a Daughter named Nansy born dec. 21 1767. Baptized Jan: 24 1768. p. 79.

Patty Pleasants spouse to Will: Watson was this day baptized Jan: 24 1768. p. 79.

Malachi Waugh & Betty Brown a son named Wilson born Feb. 20, 1781. Baptized Ap. 8, 1781. p. 103. [See Ware.]

Daniel Weaver & Sarah Durham a Daughter named Mary born dec: 4 1761. Baptized 1762 feb: 6. p. 61.

Daniel Weaver & Sarah Durham a Daughter named Elizabeth born Jan: 18 1764. Baptized Mar: 3 1764. p. 66.

Dan: Weaver & Sarah Durham a son named Daniel born Mar: 22 1766. Baptized May 11 1766. p. 73.

David Weaver & Massenburg Shoemaker a son named Peter born May. 17, 1771. Baptized Jun. 23, 1771. p. 90.

Sam: Weaver & Eliz: Williams a Son named John born Sep: 9 1756. Baptized 1756 Oct: 24. p. 49.

Sam: Weaver & Eliz: Williams a son named Samuel born Sep: 9 1758. Baptized 1758 Oct: 8. p. 53.

Isham Web & Ann ffarmer a daughter named Patty born Aug: 17 1771. Baptized Oct: 13 1771. p. 90.

Isham Webb & Ann Ffarmer a daughter named Eliz: born Oct: 31, 1772. Baptized Feb. 28. 1773. p. 93.

Ja. Web & Agnes Hughes a daughter named Susannah born Dec. 6, 1770. Baptized Jun. 16, 1771. p. 90.

Will Web & Marg: Ffarmer a daughter named Ann born Dec. 6, 1774. Baptized Jul. 25, 1774. p. 97.

Will: Webb & Marg: Farmer a son named Farmer born Oct 26 1777. Baptized July 20, 1777. p. 102.

Will: Webb & Marg: Farmer a son named William born June 20, 1777. Baptized July 20, 1777. p. 102.

Will: Webb & Mourning Pruit a Daughter born Ap: 12 1756 named Mary Ann. Baptized 1756 Ap: 19. p. 48.

William Webb & Morning Pruit a Daughter named Morning born feb: 14 1762. Baptized 1762 Jun: 20. p. 63.

Philip Webber & Tahpenes Ward a son named Richard born May 24. 1756. Baptized 1756 Jul: 4. p. 49.

Philip Webber & Tahpenes Ward a son named Philip born Ap: 30. 1758. Baptized 1758 Jul: 16. p. 53.

Philip Webber & Talipenas Ward a son named Benjamin born Oct: 6 1760. Baptized 1761 Ap: 12. p. 59.

Philip Webber & Tahpanhes Ward a son named Seth born Mar: 20 1766. Baptized Aug: 24 1766. p. 75.

William Webber & Anne Win a Daughter named Susannah Win born Aug: 1 1764. Baptized Sep: 2 1764. p. 69.

William Webber & Annie Winn a son named Charles born Nov: 26 1766. Baptized Mar: 1 1767. p. 76.

William Webber & Ann Winn a son named Archer born .... Baptized May 12 1769. p. 84.

David Webster & Judith Carter a daughter named Betsie born Dec. 23, 1774. Baptized May 1, 1774. p. 96.

David Webster & Judith Carter a son named John Carter born Nov. 11, 1776. Baptized May 4. 1777. p. 101.

Geo: Webster & Ann Humphreys a child Catherine Lewis May 8 1787. Baptized Sep. 10 1787. p. 119.

John Webster & Ann Knowling* a Daughter named Sarah born Ap: 15. 1763. Baptized 1763 Sep. 25.   p. 65.

John Webster & Ann Knowline a son named Jacob born feb: 2 1767. Baptized Mar: 13 1767. p. 76.

John Webster & Ann Knowling a son named James born May 28 1769. Baptized Jun: 30 1769. p. 85.

Luke Webster & Sally Begbie a son named John: Begby born Oct 13, 1772. Baptized Nov. 27, 1772. p. 93.

Luke Webster & Sarah Begby a daughter named Lucy born Feb 16, 1775. Baptized Ap. 2, 1775. p. 98.

Luke Webster & .... Baptized Dec. 15, 1782. p. 108.

Math: Webster & Marg: Steel a Son named Jacob born Jul: 19. 1756. Baptized 1756 Sep: 26. p. 49.

Nathaniel Webster & Marg: Steel a Daughter named Aggie born May 22. 1760. Baptized 1760 Jul: 27. p. 58.

Daniel Weiseger & Mary Bell a son named John born May 17. 1763. Baptized 1763 May 30. p. 64.

Will: Weldie & Ann Baily a child Mary Whitehead born June 4 1782. Baptized Oct 13 1782. p. 108.

Gunnery Welburn & Judith Owen a daughter named Sally born Sep. 14. 1771. Baptized Jan 5, 1772. p. 91.

Lewis Wellburn & Mary Ship a son named Robert born Ap: 23. 1760. Baptized 1760 May 25. p. 57.

Lewis Wilburn & Mary Ship a son named Richard born Jan: 8 1758. Baptized 1758 Mar: 19. p. 52.

Lewis Welburn & Mary Ship a Daughter named Sarah born Sep: 9 1765. Baptized Dec: 22 1765. p. 72.

Thomas Wilburn & Christian Page a Daughter named Elizabeth born Sep: 12. 1760. Baptized 1760 Nov: 9. p. 58.

Tho: Welburn & Christian Page a Daughter named Nannie born Mar: 24. 1763. Baptized 1763 Ap: 24. p. 64.

Thomas Welburn & Christian Page a son named Robert born Oct: 7 1765. Baptized Dec: 22 1765. p. 72.

Will Welburn & Jane Alsome a Daughter named Eliz: Ann born Dec. 15, 1773. Baptized Ap. 3, 1774. p. 96.

Jo: Wharton & Rachel Schooler a son, Reuben born Sep. 6 1785. Baptized Mar: 8 1786. p. 116.

Sam: Wharton & Lucy Schouler a son Garrit, May 12 1785. Baptized Aug. 18 1785. p. 114.

Mark Wheeler & Frances Hutson, a son Nathaniel, born Oct. 22 1781. Baptized Oct. 14 1782. p. 108.

Mark Wheeler & Francis Hutson, Jo: Hutson, born Oct. 22 1783. Baptized April 10 1786. p. 116.

---

*Knowline in marriage record.

Mark Wheeler & Francis Hutson, a child, Sarah, born Jan: 25 1786. Baptized April 10 1786. p. 116.

George White & Marg: Adrian [Orren] a son named John born Sep: 13 1763. Baptized Oct: 23 1763. p. 66.

George White & Margaret Orren a Daughter named Sarah born Sep: 3 1765. Baptized Dec: 22 1765. p. 72.

Rich: White & Lucy Richardson a son named Richardson born Oct 29, 1773. Baptized Nov. 18, 1773. p. 95.

Will White & Cattie Chapman, a son Pendleton born Oct. 20 1785. Baptized Feb: 9 1786. p. 116.

Will: White & Catherine Chapman a son Pendleton born May 26 1788. Baptized June 10 1788. p. 121.

Will White & Ann Overstreet a son named Garland born Ap. 20, 1772. Baptized May. 10: 1772. p. 92.

Will Whitefield & Mary Toller* a son named George born Sep. 20, 1773. Baptized Oct 17, 1773. p. 95.

Will: Whitefield & Mary Towler a son James: Towler born May 17. 1777. Baptized June 22, 1777. p. 102.

Will: Whitefield & Mary Towler a child Mary born Mar. 21, 1782. Baptized July 21, 1782. p. 107.

Will Whitefield & Mary Towler a son William born Aug. 4 1783. Baptized Ap: 17 1784. p. 111.

Joseph Whithead & Grisheld Rogers had a daughter born 1751 May 8. named Bettey. p. 40.

Joseph Whitehead & Grishild Rogers a Daugther born Nov: 11th 1755 named Mally. Baptized 1756 Jan: 26. p. 48.

Henry Whitloe & Martha Radford a son named Radford born Jan: 6 1769. Baptized Feb: 12 1769. p. 83.

John Whitlock & Ann Logan a Son named Thomas born Jun: 15, 1757. Baptized 1757 Aug: 7. p. 51.

John Whitlock & Ann Logan a son named John born Oct: 19 1759. Baptized 1759 Dec: 9. p. 56.

John Whitlock & Ann Logan a Daughter named Sarah born Jan: 14 1762. Baptized 1762 Ap: 11. p. 62.

John Whitlock & Ann Logan a son named James born Jul: 3 1764. Baptized Aug: 26 1764. p. 69.

John Whitlock & Ann Logan a Daughter named Sally born Oct: 25 1766. Baptized Nov: 23 1766. p. 75.

John Whitlow & Ann Logan a son named Michel born Ap. 29, 1772. Baptized Aug. 25, 1772. p. 92.

John Whitlock & Catherine Barnet a Daughter named Ursley born Aug: 1. 1756. Baptized 1756 Sep: 12. p. 49.

John Whitlow & Cat: Barnet a Daughter named ffanny born Mar: 7 1758. Baptized 1758 Ap: 9. p. 52.

John Whitloe & Catherine Barnet a son named Jordan born Ap: 22. 1760. Baptized 1760 Jun: 1. p. 57.

*Towler in Marriage records.

John Whitlow & Catherine Barnet a Daughter named Jean born Nov: 15 1764. Baptized Mar: 17 1765. p. 70.

John Whitlock & Sarah Edwards a daughter named Milley born Oct 28, 1774. Baptized Dec. 12. 1774. p. 97.

Nathan Whitlow & Diana Hicks a son named Goulder born Jan: 22 1759. Baptized 1759 Ap: 7. p. 54.

Nathan Whitloe & Diana Hicks a Daughter named Aggie born Oct: 23 1760. Baptized 1760 Dec: 14. p. 58.

Nathan Whitlow & Diana Hicks a son named Solomon born Ap: 28 1762. Baptized 1762 May 22. p. 63.

[Robert Whitlock]* & Agnes Alford a Daughter named Nannie born .... 1763. Baptized Nov: 14 1763. p. 66.

Thomas Whitlock & Sarah Henderson a Daughter named Elizabeth May. 2. 1777. Baptized June 22, 1777. p. 102.

Tho: Whitlock & Sar: Henderson a child Sar: Thomason born Dec. 3, 1781. Baptized Mar. 17, 1782. p. 105.

Thomas Whitlock & Mary Williamson a Daugh: named Elizabeth born may 6. 1756. Baptized 1756 Jul: 25. p. 49.

Tho: Whitlock & Mary Williamson a Daughter named Lucy born feb: 19 1758. Baptized 1758 Ap: 30. p. 52.

Tho: Whitlock & Mary Williamson a son named John born feb: 14. 1760. Baptized 1760 Mar: 30. p. 57.

Tho: Whitlock & Mary Williamson a son named Thomas born Nov: 16. 1762. Baptized 1763 Ap: 17. p. 64.

Will: Whitlock & Mildred Gentry a son Euclid born June 23 1783. Baptized Sep: 8 1783. p. 110.

Will: Whitlock & Milly Gentry, Betsie Major Sep: 12 1786. Baptized Oct: 9 1786. p. 117.

Will: Whitlock & Mildred Gentry a girl named Jean born June 30 1790. Baptized Ap. 12 1791. p. 126.

Will: Whitlock & Milley Gentry a son Jesse born Mar: 1 1793. Baptized May 2 1793. p. 122.

Henry Whitler† & Martha Radford a Daughter named Delilah born Dec 14, 1775. Baptized Sep. 4, 1777. p. 102.

Henry Whitler† & Martha Radford a Son named Andrew; Straiton born Jun 6. 1777. Baptized Sep. 4, 1777. p. 102.

Gerard Wilkerson & Ann Perkins a son named William born Ap. 15, 1781. Baptized Oct 19, 1781. p. 104.

Jerrat Wilkison & Ann Perkins a son Meredith born Feb. 1784. Baptized Jul: 18 1784. p. 112.

Richard Wilkerson & Mary Woosnam [Worsham] a Daughter named Martha born Aug: 3 1759. Baptized 1759 Sep: 23. p. 55.

Richard Wilkerson & Mary Worsham a Daughter named Ann born dec: 4 1761. Baptized 1762 Jan: 24. p. 61.

Richard Wilkerson & Mary Osenum [Worsham] a Daughter named Lucy born Jan: 16 1764. Baptized Feb: 12 1764. p. 66.

*Marriage records.
†Whitlow in Marriage Records.

Townsend Wilkison & Mally Carter a son named Will: Carter born Oct 13, 1771. Baptized 1772. p. 91.

Will: Wilkerson & Lurana Perkins a Daughter born Mar: 2d. 1756. Named Betty: Ann. Baptized 1756 May 22. p. 48.

Will: Wilkerson & Lurana Perkins Twins named Richard & Jeanie born Ap: 30 1759. Baptized 1759 Jul: 15. p. 55.

Wyat Wilkerson & Mary Brett a Daughter named Sally born Oct: 25 1766. Baptized Nov: 23 1766. p. 75.

Wyat Wilkinson & Mary Brit a Daughter named Hannah born Jun: 16 1769. Baptized Jul: 16 1769. p. 85.

Wyat Wilkerson & Mary Bret a Daughter named Mary born feb: 15 1771. Baptized Mar: 29 1771. p. 89.

Drury Williams & Tabitha Marshal a son named Will: Marshal born Nov. 8. 1771. Baptized Dec. 15, 1771. p. 91.

Drury Williams & Tabitha Marshal a daughter named Nansy born Ap. 1. 1774. Baptized May 15, 1774. p. 96.

Drury Williams & Tabitha Marshal a daughter named Mary born July 12, 1776. Baptized Oct 13, 1776. p. 100.

Elias Williams & Agatha Mosely a son named James born May 24 1761. Baptized 1761 June: 21. p. 60.

Elias Williams & Agathy Mosely a Daughter named Jean born Ap: 15 1764. Baptized Jun: 24 1764. p. 68.

Eliezer Williams & Martha Strong a Daughter named Elizabeth born Sep: 30 1767. Baptized Nov: 15 1767. p. 79.

Eliezer Williams & Martha Strong a Daughter named Sarah born Jul: 30 1769. Baptized Aug: 27 1769. p. 86.

Henry Williams & Ann Lightfoot a Daughter named Lightfoot born Dec. 2 1769. Baptized Jun: 4 1770. p. 87.

James Williams & Eliz Mullins a child Sarah born Aug 31, 1781. Baptized July 21, 1782. p. 107.

Ja: Williams & Eliz: Mullins, Francis Taylor born Dec. 21 1783. Baptized June 20 1784. p. 112.

John Williams & Susannah Ellis a son named Cutbird born Ap: 5 1765. Baptized Jul: 6 1765. p. 71.

John Williams & Susannah Ellis a Daughter named Sally born feb: 27 1767. Baptized Jun: 11 1767. p. 77.

John Williams & Eliz: Fickland a son named John born Nov: 24 1769. Baptized Ap: 23 1770. p. 87.

Jo: Williams & Mary Marshal a child Frankie born May 17, 1780. Baptized July 21, 1782. p. 107.

Jo: Williams & Mary Marshal a daughter Elizabeth born Dec: 23, 1781. Baptized July 21, 1782. p. 107.

Philip Williams & ffrances Taylor two Daughters named Eliz: Taylor, & Ann: Christian both born Aug: 17. 1759. Baptized 1759 Sep: 29. p. 56.

Philemon Williams & Ann Lancaster a Son named Charles born ffeb: 22 1757. Baptized 1757 feb: 27. p. 50.

Powel Williams & Lucy Haines a Daughter named susannah born Mar: 23 1760. Baptized 1760 May 4. p. 57.

Powel Williams & Louisa Haines a son named John born Sep: 3. 1761. Baptized 1761 Oct: 4. p. 61.

Powel Williams & Lucy Haines a son named Williams born Sep: 27 1764. Baptized Dec: 2 1764. p. 69.

Powel Williams & Lucy Haynes a Daughter named Eliz: born Jul: 9 1767. Baptized Aug: 16 1767. p. 78.

Powel Williams & Lucy Haynes a son named Powel born Feb: 4 1770. Baptized Ap: 8 1770. p. 87.

Solomon Williams & Lucy Holland a son Jack Philemon born May 20 1782. Baptized Ap: 26 1783. p. 109.

Will: Williams & Elizabeth Comber a son named John born feb: 7 1764. Baptized Mar: 9 1764. p. 67.

William Williams & Betty Comber a son named Williams born May 28 1766. Baptized Sep: 20 1766. p. 75.

William Williams & Ann Mayo a Daughter named Marianne born dec: 7 1768. Baptized Mar: 19 1769. p. 84.

Zach: Williams & Mary Pore a son named John Oct: 1 1756. Baptized 1756 Oct: 31. p. 49.

Zachariah Williams & Mary Pore a Daughter named Elizabeth born Jan: 13 1758. Baptized 1758 Mar: 19. p. 52.

Zachariah Williams & Mary Pore a Daughter named Mary born Jan: 1st 1760. Baptized 1760 ffeb: 17. p. 56.

Zachar: Williams & Mary Pore a Daughter named Joanna born Dec: 4. 1761. Baptized 1761 Dec: 14. p. 61.

Zachariah Williams & Mary Pore a Daughter named Fanny born Nov: 25 1763. Baptized Jan: 2 1764. p. 66.

Zachariah Williams & Mary Poor a Daughter named Sally born dec. 24 1765. Baptized Feb: 2 1766. p. 73.

John Williamson & Lucy Hog a son named John born May 26 1765. Baptized Jul: 6 1765. p. 71.

John Williamson & Lucy Hog a son named Elisha born Sep: 14 1767. Baptized Ap: 11 1768. p. 80.

Jo: Williamson & Lucy Hog, twins Susannah & Benjamin born feb: 16 1771. Baptized Ap: 9 1771. p. 89.

Pat Williamson & Nannie Champion a child named Elizabeth born Aug. 8 .... Baptized Oct 21, 1781. p. 104.

Will: Williamson & Ann Mayo a Daughter named Martha-Williamson, born Mar: 2 1767. Baptized May 17 1767. p. 77.

Edward Willis & Catherine Barker a Daughter named Elizabeth born Nov: 6 1765. Baptized Jan: 26 1766. p. 73.

Edward Willis & Catherine Barker a Daughter named Mary born Jan: 5 1767. Baptized Feb: 8 1767. p. 76.

Henry Willis & Mary Watkins a daughter born Nov: 3 1755 named Mary. Baptized 1756 feb: 15. p. 48.

Henry Willis & Mary Watkins a Daughter named Eliz: born feb: 11, 1758. Baptized 1758 Ap: 23. p. 52.

Henry Willis & Mary Watkins a Daughter named Christiana born Sep: 6 1761 [sic]. Baptized 1761 Ap: 5. p. 59.

Pleasants Willis & Sally Reid a daughter named Nancy born Sep 11, 1775. Baptized Oct 26, 1775. p. 99.

Rob: Willis & Hellender Nailine a Son named Edward born Jul: 12. 1756. Baptized 1756 Aug: 22. p. 49.

Robert Willis & Hellender Nailine a Daughter named Lucy born Aug: 20 1758. Baptized 1758 Nov: 19. p. 53.

William Willis & Susannah ffreeman a Daughter named Sally born Aug: 31 1764. Baptized Mar: 17 1765. p. 70.

Henry Willoughby & Jean Lipscomb a son Will: Tandie Feb: 1 1788. Baptized Mar: 31 1788. p. 120.

Jonathan Wilson & Marg. Stewart a daughter named Mary born Nov. 13, 1773. Baptized Mar. 13, 1774. p. 96.

Jo: Wily & Jean Johnson a son John born Nov: 12 1783. Baptized July 11 1784. p. 112.

Jo: Wylie & Jean Johnson a son, Scot born Jan. 12 1786. Baptized May 17 1787. p. 118.

Rich: Windrow & Millender Antony a child Eliz: born Oct 17, 1781. Baptized Mar. 24, 1782. p. 106.

Rich: Windrow & Millener Antony a child Nancy born Dec. 31 1783. Baptized Ap: 12 1784. p. 111.

Rich: Windrow & Millender Antony, Henry Brent, Apl. 3 1786. Baptized June 12 1786. p. 116.

Peter Wimphrey & Betty Moon a Daughter named Mary born dec: 30. 1759. Baptized 1760 Jul: 10. p. 58.

John Winfrey & Mary Turpine a Daught named Sally born feb: 13 1762. Baptized 1762 Ap: 4. p. 62.

Mathew Wingfield & Sarah Hinds a Daughter called Mary born Oct. 9, 1776. Baptized Dec. 1, 1776. p. 101.

Robert Wingfield & Frances Jordan a Daughter named Elizabeth born Ap: 26 1768. Baptized May 29 1768. p. 81.

Tho: Wingfield & Eliz: Nelson a son Charles born Ap: 13 1784. Baptized June 27 1784. p. 112.

Tho: Winn & Eliz: Dabney Anderson a child named Eliz: Pledger born Mar 9, 1781. Baptized Oct 21, 1781. p. 104.

Ja: Winston & Sarah Marks a son Jo: Hastins born Aug. 20 1783. Baptized Oct: 19 1783. p. 110.

John Winston & Tabitha Cocke a Daughter named Sarah born May 14 1761. Baptized 1761 Jun: 8. p. 60.

John Winston & Tabitha Cocke a Daughter named Ann born Ap: 12. 1763. Baptized 1763 May 23. p. 64.

Jo. Winston & Mary Johnson a Son Thomas born Oct 11, 1781. Baptized 21 Ap: 1782. p. 106.

Jo: Winston & Mary Johnson a son John born May 1 1783. Baptized Sep: 13 1783. p. 110.

Jo. Winston & Mary Johnson, Will Overton, born Oct. 24 1785. Baptized Nov. 20 1785. p. 115.

Jo: Winston & Mary Johnston a son Bickerton born Ap: 3 1788. Baptized May 4 1788. p. 121.

Tarleton & Eliz: Winston a child Ann Overton born July 14 1788. Baptized Sep: 28 1788. p. 121.

William Winston & Marianne Curd a son named Edward born Sep: 4 1770. Baptized Dec: 18 1770. p. 89.

John Witt & Mary Bullington a Daughter named Ann born 1753 Aug: 30. p. 41.

John Witt & Mary Bullington a Son named John born 1756 Dec: 25. p. 41.

John Witt: & Mary Bullington a Daughter named Mary born Nov: 18 1760. Baptized 1761 Jan: 31. p. 58.

John Witt & Mary Bullington a Daughter named Jeanie born Mar: 7. 1763. Baptized 1763 May 27. p. 64.

John Witt & Mary Bullington a son named Jesse born Jan: 15 1766. Baptized Mar: 2 1766. p. 73.

Ja: Wood & Nancy Lipscomb a son William born May 10 1786. Baptized Jul: 16 1786. p. 117.

John Wood & Sarah Byrd a son named Stephen born Jan: 23 1762. Baptized 1762 Ap: 12. p. 62.

Samuel Wood & Elizabeth Marion a son named William born Sep: 29 1763. Baptized Dec: 4 1763. p. 66.

Samuel Wood & Elizabeth Merrine a Daughter named Mary born Mar: 28 1765. Baptized May 26 1765. p. 71.

Samuel Wood & Eliz: Merrine a son named Jesse born Dec. 5 1766. Baptized May 31 1767. p. 77.

Samuel Wood & Elizabeth Mariot a son named Samuel born Ap: 9 1769. Baptized Jun: 25 1769. p. 85.

Sam Wood & Eliz. Marianne a daughter named Jeanie born Aug. 27, 1771. Baptized Jan. 5 1772. p. 91.

Tho: Wood & Ellender Johnson a child named Sally born Nov: 26, 1781. Baptized Mar. 24. 1782. p. 106.

Tho: Wood & Hellender Johnson a son George born Feb. 3 1783. Baptized Ap: 1783. p. 109.

Tho: Wood & Helender Johnson a son William born Nov. 6 1784. Baptized Jan: 28 1785. p. 113.

Tho: Wood & Nelly Johnson, Elizabeth, born Jan: 10 1786. Baptized Jul: 16 1786. p. 117.

Tho Wood & Mary Hope a son Thomas born June 9, 1781. Baptized Aug. 26, 1781. p. 104.

Major Valentine Wood & Lucy Henry a son named Henry born feb: 7 1765. Baptized Mar: 22 1765. p. 70.

Valentine Wood & Lucy Henry a Daughter named Sarah born Mar: 1 .... Baptized May 10 1767. p. 77.

Valentine Wood & Lucy Henry a Daughter named Mary born May 8 1769. Baptized Jun: 25 1769. p. 85.

Valentine Wood & Lucy Henry a son named Valentine born. Baptized 1772. p. 91.

Valentine Wood & Lucy Henry a daughter named Lucy born Jan. 7, 1774. Baptized Mar. 16, 1774. p. 96.

Valentine Wood & Lucy Henry a son named John born Jan 18, 1776. Baptized Ap. 30, 1776. p. 100.

William Wood & Martha Cate a Daughter named Betty born Jul: 27 1760. Baptized 1761 Mar: 1. p. 59.

Will Wood & Sarah Hall a son John, Oct: 28 1785. Baptized Jan: 9 1786. p. 116.

Will: Wood & Sarah Hall, Betsie born Feb. 23 1788. Baptized May 12 1788. p. 121.

Charles Woodhall & Eliz: Black a son named William born Ap: 30 1768. Baptized Jul: 27 1768. p. 81.

Charles Woodhall & Eliz. Black a son named John born Mar. 5, 1773. Baptized Jun. 27, 1773. p. 94.

Charles Woodhall & Eliz. Black a .... born June 24, 1775. Baptized Aug. 7, 1775. p. 98.

Jacob Woodhall & Agnes Hicks a son named Absalom born Oct: 5 1763. Baptized Oct: 30 1763. p. 66.

Jacob Woodhall & Aggie Hicks a son named James born May 1st 1765. Baptized Jun: 2 1765. p. 71.

John Woodhall & Dorothea Pledge a Son named Mathew born May 14, 1757. Baptized 1757 Jul: 31. p. 51.

John Woodhall & Dorothea Pledge a son named Robert born feb: 7 1759. Baptized 1759 Ap: 29. p. 55.

John Woodhall & Dorothy Pledge a Daughter named Aggie born Mar: 15 1761. Baptized 1761 Jun: 6. p. 60.

John Woodhal & Jemima Willis a son named David: Willis born Jun: 27 1758. Baptized 1758 Aug 13. p. 53.

John Woodhall & Jemima Willis a Daughter named Eleanor born Sep: 5. 1760. Baptized 1760 Oct: 5. p. 58.

John Woodhall & Jemima Willis a son named John born Nov: 27 1763. Baptized Jan: 22 1764. p. 66.

John Woodhall & Jemima Willis a son named William born Ap: 28 1769. Baptized Jul: 30 1769. p. 85.

Sampson Woodhal & Sarah Steen [Steel] a Daughter named Sally born Mar: 24 1756. Baptized 1756 Aug: 28. p. 49.

Samson Woodhal & Sarah Steel a son named John born Oct: 5 1758. Baptized 1759 Sep: 23. p. 55.

Sampson Woodhall & Sarah Steel a son named Samuel born Mar: 20 1761. Baptized 1761 Jun: 6. p. 60.

Sampson Woodhall & Sarah Steel a son named Jacob born Jul: 10, 1763. Baptized 1763 Sep: 25. p. 65.

William Woodhal & Mary ffielder a son named Jacob born dec: 13, 1759. Baptized 1760 Jun: 1. p. 57.

Will: Woodhall & Mary ffielder a son named Michal born Mar: 27 1762. Baptized 1762 May 22. p. 63.

Will: Woodhall & Marianne Hancock a Daughter named susannah born Ap: 25 176—* Baptized 1761 Jul: 12. p. 60.

William Woodhall & Marianne Hancoke a Daughter named Sarah born Jun: 14. 1763. Baptized 1763 Sep: 25. p. 65.

William Woodhall & Marianne Hancoke a son named Benjamin born Jun: 10 1765. Baptized Sep: 15 1765. p. 72.

Will: Woodhall & Marianne Hancocke a Daughter named Susannah born Jan: 5 1768. Baptized May 8 1768. p. 80.

Henry Woodie & Susannah Martin a son named John born Mar: 12 1764. Baptized Aug: 28 1765. p. 72.

William Woodie & Lucy Barnet a Daughter named Biddie born Jan: 21 1765. Baptized Aug: 28 1765. p. 72.

Morning Woody a young woman was this day baptized. Ap. 8. 1772. p. 92.

John Woodrum & Mary Bays a Daughter named Catie born Mar: 24 1764. Baptized Jun: 17 1764. p. 68.

John Woodrum & Mary Bayse a son named John born Mar: 29 1767. Baptized May 3 1767. p. 77.

John Woodrum & Mary Bays a son named Richard born Nov: 5 1768. Baptized Jan: 22 1769. p. 83.

John Woodrum & Mary Bayes a daughter named* Baptized Jun. 1771. p. 90.

John Woodrum & Mary Bays a son named Balty born Jun. 10, 1774. Baptized Jul 24, 1774. p. 97.

John Woodrum & Mary Bays a son named Baltie born June. 10, 1774. Baptized Aug. 28, 1774. p. 97.

John Woodrum & Mary Barker twins, Richard & Bartlet born Jan 3, 1776. Baptized Jan 9, 1776. p. 99.

William Woodram & Martha More a son named John born Mar: 4. 1756. Baptized 1756 Oct: 24. p. 49.

William Woodrum & Martha More a son named William born Nov: 5, 1759. Baptized 1759 Jul: 15. p. 55.

Will: Woodrum & Martha More a Son named Stephen born feb: 5. 1761. Baptized 1761 Jun: 6. p. 60.

Will: Woodrum & Martha More a Daughter named Eliz: born feb: 14. 1763. Baptized 1763 Ap: 17. p. 64.

William Woodram & Martha More a Daughter named Jean born May 31 1765. Baptized Aug: 25 1765. p. 72.

William Woodrum & Martha More a son named Jacob born Sep: 3 1767. Baptized Nov: 1 1767. p. 79.

Benjamin Woodson & Rebekah Cock a son named Booth born Dec: 4, 1757. Baptized 1758 Jul: 25. p. 53.

Benjamin Woodson & Rebekah Cox a Daughter named ffrances born dec: 17. 1759. Baptized 1760 Jun: 24. p. 57.

Benjamin Woodson & Rebekah Cocke a Daughter named Tabitha born Jul: 12 1763. Baptized Oct: 30 1763. p. 66.

*Margin torn.

Benjamin Woodson & Rebekah Cocke a Daughter named Rebekah born Mar: 29 1766. Baptized Jun 15 1766. p. 74.

Benjamin Woodson & Rebekah Cocke a Daughter named Sarah born Jul: 6 1768. Baptized Jan: 27 1769. p. 83.

Benj: Woodson & Rebekah Cocke a son named Benjamin born Jul 8, 1772. Baptized Sep. 27, 1772. p. 93.

James Woodson & Eliz: Whitlock a son named James born Mar: 10. 1758. Baptized 1758 Ap: 30. p. 52.

James Woodson [&] Elizabeth Whitlock a Daughter named Jeanie born May 2. 1760. Baptized 1760 Aug: 27. p. 58.

James Woodson & Elizabeth Whitlock a Daughter named Gillie born Jan: 13 1765. Baptized feb: 17 1765. p. 70.

James Woodson & Elizabeth Whitlock a son named Thomas born Feb: 28 1767. Baptized May 17 1767. p. 77.

James Woodson & Eliz: Whitlock a Daughter named Sally born May 25 .... Baptized Aug: 6 1769. p. 85.

James Woodson & Eliz: Whitlock a son named Cary, born May 11 1771. Baptized Aug 11 1771. p. 90.

John Woodson & Thia [Durothea] Randolph a Daughter named Elizabeth born Nov: 1756. Baptized 1756 Dec: 19. p. 49.

Jo: Woodson & Dorothea Randolph a son named Josiah born Jan: 16. 1758. Baptized 1758 May 9. p. 52.

John Woodson & Dorothea Randolph a Son named Isham born Sep: Baptized 1760 Mar: 30. p. 57.

John Woodson & Dorothea Randolph a Daughter named susannah born Jun: 26 1761. Baptized 1762 feb: 21. p. 61.

John Woodson & Dorothea Randolph a son named John born feb: 28. 1763. Baptized 1763 May 15. p. 64.

John Woodson & Dorothea Randolph a Daughter named Martha born Jul: 6 1764. Baptized Sep: 9 1764. p. 69.

John Woodson & Dorothea Randolph a Daughter named Judith born feb: 16 1767. Baptized Ap: 10 1767. p. 77.

John Woodson & Dorothea Randolph a Daughter named Lucy born Oct: 13 1768. Baptized Mar: 26 1769. p. 84.

John Woodson & Dorothea Randolph a daughter named Sarah born Nov. 14, 1770. Baptized Dec. 26, 1773. p. 95.

Of COL: JO: WOODSON Children I Baptized—12—*

Arch: Pleasant & Jeanne Woodson maried Aug: 5 75. p. 129.

Nansie Woodson was born Oct. 12, 77. p. 129.

Josiah Woodson age 20 maried to Betsie Woodson age 19 Decr. 3 78. p. 129.

Jo: Woodson maried to Mary Anderson Mar: 30 86. p. 129.

I Baptized 2 grandchildren to him too. p. 129.

His son Isham was born Sep: 60. p. 129.

His daughter Elizabeth was born Nov. 56. p. 129.

Col: Jo. Woodson & Bethia Randolph were maried Oct. 51. p. 129.

---

*These entries are printed here just as they appeared in the Birth Register. The marriages are noted elsewhere in proper order.

Of Col: Jo: Woodsons family I have baptized 12 and maried 4, he is now dead Feb: 15 '90. p. 137.

His daughter Jeane to Arch: Pleasant is maried Aug. 5 1775. p. 137.

his daughter Nansy to Jo: Stephen Woodson is maried Oct. 12 1777. p. 137.

his son to Eliz: Woodson is maried Dec 3 1778. p. 137.

his son John to Mary Anderson Mch 30 1786. p. 137.

I baptized likewise to him 2 grandchildren.

Will: Douglas.

John Woodson & Eliz: Baily a Daughter named Susannah born feb: 11. 1756. Baptized 1756 May 30. p. 48.

John Woodson & Elizabeth Bailey a son named Tarlton born Mar: 22 1758. Baptized 1758 Jun: 25. p. 52.

John Woodson & Ann Harris a Daughter named Sarah born Dec: 25 1764 [sic.] Baptized Ap: 15 1764. p. 67.

John Woodson & Mary Mims a Daughter named Jeanie: Booth born Oct: 25 1760. Baptized 1761 Jul: 19. p. 60.

John Woodson & Mary Mims a Daughter named Elizabeth born May 22 1764. Baptized Aug: 12 1764. p. 68.

John Woodson & Mary Mims a son named: Sam: Tucker born Sep: 1769. Baptized Oct: 31 1770. p. 88.

John Woodson & Mary Mims a son named Booth born Aug. 28, 1771. Baptized Sep. 1773. p. 95.

Jos: Woodson & Sarah Crouch a son Le Tyatte born Oct: 12 1783. Baptized Nov: 6 1783. p. 110.

Mathew Woodson & Betty Villain a son named John: Stephen born Aug: 17. 1757. Baptized 1757 Sep: 25. p. 51.

Mathew Woodson & Betty Villain a Daughter named Elizabeth born May 12 1759. Baptized 1759 Jun: 17. p. 55.

Mathew Woodson & Elizabeth Villaine a Daughter named Mary born May 28. 1763. Baptized 1763 Jun: 26. p. 64.

Mathew Woodson & Elizabeth Villaine a son named Samuel born Jul: 24. 1761. Baptized 1761 Sep: 6. p. 61.

Mathew Woodson & Elizabeth Villain a Daughter named Frances born Oct: 22 1764. Baptized Dec: 2 1769. p. 69.

Mathew Woodson & Elizabeth Villaine a son named Jacob born May 25 1766. Baptized Jun: 22 1766. p. 74.

Mathew Woodson & Elizabeth Villain a son named Philip born Aug. 7 1767. Baptized Sep: 6 1767. p. 78.

Mathew Woodson & Eliz: Villain a son named Daniel born Ap: 29 1769. Baptized May 28 1769. p. 84.

Pat Woodson & Nancy Cloof a child named Mally born Jul. 25, 1771. Baptized Oct 21, 1781. p. 104.

Pat Woodson & Nancy Cloof a child named Nancy born Aug: 16. 1781. Baptized Oct 21, 1781. p. 104.

Rene Woodson & Mary Thomson deceased a Daughter named Eliz: Booth born feb: 16 1759. Baptized 1759 May 2. p. 55.

Rene Woodson & Martha Johnson a child Fanny born Aug. 23, 1780. Baptized Aug. 26. 1781. p. 104.

Samuel Woodson & Sar: Mills, twins Will Fontain & Jo: Le Villaine Jan. 30. 1783. Baptized Feb 9, 1783. p. 108.

Shadrach Woodson & Susannah Walker a son named David born Ap: 8 1770. Baptized Ap: 23 1770. p. 87.

Stephen Woodson & Lucy fferrar a son named Stephen born Jan: 11 1759. Baptized 1759 Mar: 25. p. 54.

Stephen Woodson & Lucy fferrar a Daughter named Mary born Oct: 27 1760. Baptized 1761 feb: 8. p. 59.

Tho: Woodson & Mary Woodson a Daughter named Elizabeth born Jun: 3 1758. Baptized 1758 Oct: 22. p. 53.

Mary Woodson Spouse to Thomas Woodson on Janito. was baptized. Baptized 1761 Aug: 9. p. 60.

Thomas & Mary Woodsons a Son named Jacob born Mar: 29. 1761. Baptized 1761 Aug: 9. p. 60.

Thomas Woodson & Mary Woodson a son named Stephen born Nov: 2 1768. Baptized Mar: 19 1769. p. 84.

Tho. Woodson & Mary Woodson a daughter named Judith born Mar. 7, 1771. Baptized Nov. 19, 1771. p. 91.

Tho: Woodson & Elizabeth Woodson a Daughter named Susannah born Nov: 19 1763. Baptized Mar: 4 1764. p. 67.

Thomas & Elizabeth Woodsons a Daughter named Mary born Jun: 15 1766. Baptized Sep: 14 1766. p. 75.

Tucker Woodson & Mary Netherland a Daughter named Sarah born Sep: 22 1764. Baptized Dec: 28 1764. p. 69.

Tucker Woodson & Mary Netherland a son named John-Pleasants born May 21 1766. Baptized Dec: 29 1766. p. 75.

Tucker Woodson & Mary Netherland a son named Benjamin born Aug: 21 1768. Baptized Nov: 23 1768. p. 82.

Tucker Woodson & Mary Neyrland [Netherland] a son named Henry-Macon born Mar: 22 1770. Baptized May 4 1770. p. 87.

Tucker Woodson Sarah Knolling a son named Charles Woodson born Dec 29, 1774. Baptized Jan. 15, 1775. p. 97.

John Woodward & Susannah Tilman a Daughter named Mary born Mar: 22. 1757. Baptized 1757 Ap: 24. p. 50.

John Woodward & Susannah Tilman a Daughter named Lucy born Oct: 24 1758. Baptized 1758 Nov: 19. p. 53.

John Woodward & susannah Tilman a son named Samuel born Nov: 3, 1760. Baptized 1760 Dec: 14. p. 58.

John Woodward & Susannah Tilman a son named John born Mar: 31 1764. Baptized May 27 1764. p. 67.

John Woodward & Susanna Tilman a Daughter named Sarah born dec: 8 1766. Baptized Jan: 18 1767. p. 76.

John Woodward & Susannah Tilman a son named Charles born Aug. 20 1769. Baptized Oct: 1 1769. p. 86.

John Woodward & Susannah Tilman a son named Richard born Jun. 22, 1772. Baptized Jul: 26, 1772. p. 92.

John Woodward & Susannah Tilman a son named Nathaniel born Oct 7, 1774. Baptized Dec. 25, 1774. p. 97.

Jer: Woodward & Elizabeth Morris a Daughter named Jeany-Williams born Jun: 7 1770. Baptized Jul: 1 1770. p. 88.

Warwick Woodward & Ann Hamler a son named William born Oct 21, 1773. Baptized Dec. 12 1773. p. 95.

John Woolams & Eliz. Cawley a daughter named Sally born Feb. 2, 1774. Baptized Ap. 10, 1774. p. 96.

Richard Woolbanks & Priscilla Hewet a son named Berryman born Mar: 14 1767. Baptized Ap: 19 1767. p. 77.

John Wooton & Ann Harris a son named John born Mar: 14 1769. Baptized [June] 3 1769. p. 84.

Tho: Word & Frances Henderson a son William born May 11 1783. Baptized June 28 1783. p. 109.

Tho: Worthy & Sar: Gannonay [Gannoway] a son named Jo: Gannonay born Dec 12, 1771. Baptized Mar. 29, 1772. p. 92.

Tho. Worthy & Sarah Ganny [Gannoway] a son named Peyton born Jun. 13, 1774. Baptized Oct 10, 1774. p. 97.

Agustine Wright & Mary Pucket a Son named Moses born feb: 15. 1757. Baptized 1757 Ap: 1st. p. 50.

Cha: Wright & Sallie Jarvis a child born named Ann Minor. Baptized Aug. 19 1793. p. 122.

Cha: Wright & Sarah Gergis [Jarvis?] a daughter Martha. Baptized Dec: 21 1795. p. 127.

Cha: Wright & his wife Sally a child Molley. Baptized Dec. 21 1795. p. 138.

John Wright & Judith Barns a son named Benjamin born Mar: 22. 1759. Baptized 1759 Ap: 29. p. 55.

John Wright & Judah Easly on Lickinhole a Daugh: born feb: .... 1756 named Betty. Baptized 1756 Mar. 21. p. 48.

Jo: Wright & Eliz: Frazer an excellent child Margaret Sep: 11 1777. Baptized Jan: 15 1787. p. 118.

John Wright & Eliz: Frazer a child Sarah born Ap: 7 1784. Baptized Oct. 14 1784. p. 113.

John Wright & Mary Pace* a son named John born Aug: 1. 1759. Baptized 1759 Sep: 2. p. 55.

John Wright & Mary Pace a Daughter named Ann born Nov: 14 1765. Baptized Dec: 22 1765. p. 72.

John Wright & Mary Pace a Daughter named Mary born Jan: 13 1768. Baptized Ap: 1 1768. p. 80.

John Wright & Mary Pierce a son named Joseph born Mar: 17. 1757. Baptized 1757 Ap: 17. p. 50.

John Wright & Mary Pierce a Son named James born Mar: 5, 1761. Baptized 1761 Ap: 12. p. 59.

Jo: Wright & Fanny Thomason a child Polly born Dec. 9 1783. Baptized Jan: 25 1784. p. 111.

*Pierce in Marriage records.

Jo: Wright & Fanny Thomason a son Moses born Dec. 20 1785. [sic] Baptized Mar: 28 1785. p. 113.

Jo: Wright & Fanny Thomason a child Betsie Jul: 26 1786. Baptized Aug: 14 1786. p. 117.

Jo: Wright & Jeanie Thomason a son John born Mar: 17 1788. Baptized May 12 1782. p. 121.

Roderwick Wright & Hannah [Cawley] a Daughter named Nansie born Sep: 20 1770. Baptized Nov: 11 1770. p. 88.

Roderick Wright & Hannah Cawley a daughter named Betsey born Jul: 3, 1773. Baptized Sep. 5, 1773. p. 95.

Roderick Wright & Hannah Cawley a daughter named Judith born Dec. 16, 1774. Baptized Mar 5, 1775. p. 98.

Rhoderick Wright & Hannah Cawley a son named John born Aug: 13, 1776. Baptized Dec. 25, 1776. p. 101.

Tho: Wright & Betsie Groom a child Lucy born Jan. 19 1779. Baptized Oct. 2 1784. p. 113.

Tho: Wright & Betsie Groom a son Richard, born May 8 1782. Baptized Oct. 2 1784. p. 113.

Tho: Wright & Betsie Groom a child Sally born Mar: 20 1784. Baptized Oct. 2 1784. p. 113.

Tho: Wright & Elizab: Groom, Jean Dec. 17 1786. Baptized June 30 1787. p. 119.

Will Wright & Martha Cawley a daughter named Chicely born June 5, 1773. Baptized Jun 13, 1773. p. 94.

John Yarborough & Bathsheba Harris a son named Daniel born Jul: 27. 1763. Baptized 1763 Aug: 28. p. 65.

Thomas Griggs Yarborrough & Mary Spurlock a son named Randolph Norman born Jun: 15. 1756. Baptized 1756 Jul: 11. p. 49.

Thomas: Griggs Yarborough & Mary Spurlock a son named Richard born feb: 1 1759. Baptized 1759 Mar: 4. p. 54.

Tho: Grigs Yarborough & Mary Spurlock a son named James born Dec: 20 1764. Baptized Mar: 3 1765. p. 70.

Will Yates & Sarah Harris a child Patsie Marshal born Nov: 11 1786. Baptized Oct: 17 1787. p. 120.

Cha: Yauncey & Mary Crawford a child Mary born Oct. 13 1784. Baptized Jan. 1 1785. p. 113.

Jo: Yauncey & Eliz: Cosbie .... June 25 1783. Baptized Dec. 25 1783. p. 111.

Stephen Yauncey & Jean Bond a son John born May 29 1783. Baptized Sep: 10 1784. p. 112.

Hakely Young & Susanna Lane a child Susanna born Oct: 8 1787. Baptized Ap: 27 1788. p. 120.

Lewis Young & Eliz: Smith a child Eliz: Lewis born Sep. 10 1785. Baptized Dec. 27 1785. p. 115.

John Younger & Ann Moss a Daughter named Elizabeth born Oct: 20. 1758. Baptized 1759 Ap: 1. p. 54.

John Young & Ann Moss a Daughter called Mary born Jul: 29 1760. Baptized 1760 Oct: 12. p. 58.

John Young [Younger] & Ann Moss a Daughter named Susannah born feb: 6 1764. Baptized Mar: 31 1764. p. 67.

John Younger & Ann Moss a son named John born Dec: 30 1767. Baptized Ap: 11 1768. p. 80.

John Younger & Ann Moss a daughter named Jean born Mar: 4 1769. Baptized feb: 21 1770. p. 87.

LIST OF BIRTHS
NAME OF ONE PARENT ONLY BEING ENTERED

.... Eliz: Almond, a child Eliz: born Ap: 24 1787. Baptized Aug. 13 1787. p. 119.

.... & Lucy Barly a son Nathaniel. Baptized Aug. 25, 1781. p. 104.

.... Barbara Beven a child Martha born Oct. 2. 1775. Baptized Sep. 30, 1782. p. 107.

.... Hellender Black a Daughter named Annie born Nov: 24 1769. Baptized Ap: 23 1770. p. 87.

.... & Mary Cowley a Son named John: Hill born Oct: 22. 1761. Baptized 1761 Nov: 8. p. 61.

.... Mary Cowley a Daughter named Peggie born Oct: 4 1766. Baptized Jan: 29 1767. p. 76.

.... Mary Cowley a daughter named Betsy: Adams born Mar. 29, 1772. Baptized Jul. 31, 1775. p. 98.

.... Salley Crutchfield a son named Rob: George born Jun. 3, 1775. Baptized Sep. 15, 1775. p. 99.

.... Sally Crutchfield a child Nancy Feb. 9. 1782. Baptized July 21, 1782. p. 107.

.... & Mally Curry a .... Baptized Sep. 5, 1773. p. 95.

.... Judith Emmerson a Daughter named Elizabeth-Campbell born Jan: 15 1767. Baptized Ap: 11 1768. p. 80.

.... & Letty Faries a son named Littleton Ayres born Sep. 26, 1772. Baptized Jan 1, 1773. p. 93.

.... Pattie Fairies a child Jean born May 27, 1782. Baptized June 20, 1782. p. 107.

.... Ann ffarmer a son named Zachariah born Sep: 1 1764. Baptized Oct: 7 1764. p. 69.

.... Mary Fits a child Elizabeth born Sep. 7 1783. Baptized May 30 1784. p. 111.

.... Francis Gill a son named Ikekizedeck: Bricken born Jun. 1776. Baptized Mar. 23, 1776. p. 101.

.... Penelope Goodman a child Mary born Jan: 1784. Baptized Oct. 5 1784. p. 113.

.... & Nannie Green a son named Jesse born May 1775. Baptized May 18, 1781. p. 103.

.... Sarah Haley a son named Pleasants: Wade born Jun: 10. Baptized Jul. 22, 1771. p. 90.

.... Mary Holbrook, a child Bettie born Dec. 22 1782. Baptized Ap: 19 1783. p. 109.

.... & Mary Holt a Daughter named Ursley-Caroline about 9 years old. Baptized Aug: 25 1765. p. 72.

.... Hughes .... a child. Baptized Dec. 18 1783. p. 110.

James .... & Frances Hughland a son in fornication names James born .... 1765. Baptized Aug: 18 1765. p. 72.

.... Hutchison a son named Shadrack born Dec. 8, 1766. Baptized Nov.* 1771. p. 91.

.... Hutchison a daughter named Nansy born May 22 1771. Baptized Nov.* 1771. p. 91.

.... & Lucy Johnson a Daughter named Sarah born Ap: 30 1764. Baptized Nov: 4 1764. p. 69.

.... & Margaret Jones a Daughter called Patty-Cannon born Sep: 12 1765. Baptized Mar: 2 1766. p. 73.

Rebekah Jones a son named William Jones born Nov. 7. Baptized 1772. p. 91.

.... Nancy Laurie a son named Overtorn born. Baptized Oct 22, 1781. p. 105.

.... Martha Loftus a son named James born Sep: 14 1767. Baptized May 29 1768. p. 81.

Eliz: mcBride a Daughter born Mar: 29 1756 named Ann Lewis. Baptized 1756 May 11. p. 48.

........................Nanny McBride a son named John born Jan. 10, 1775 or 1772. Baptized Aug 27, 1775. p. 99.

.... Mary Man a son named Jesse born Decr. 5. 1755. Baptized 1763 Sep: 6. p. 65.

........................Sarah Overstreet twins named Will & Mary born Jan. 22, 1772. Baptized May 10, 1772. p. 92.

.... & Mary Owen .... Baptized Ap. 8, 1781. p. 103.

.... Mary Acorn Owen a Son Seigneur born July 14, 1782. Baptized Dec. 5: 1783. p. 108.

.... Mary Paulet a child Jane Smith born Jul: 12 1783. Baptized Jan: 14 1785. p. 113.

.... Aggie Pool a son named John-Scot born Mar: 23 1763. Baptized Oct: 16 1763. p. 66.

Judith Potter a Son named John born decr. 27 1761. Baptized 1762 Ap: 11. p. 62.

.... Susannah Railstock a child Sally Garland Jan: 28 1782. Baptized Aug: 20 1786. p. 117.

.... Susannah Railstock a child Ursley Anderson Sep: 28 1785. Baptized Aug: 20 1786. p. 117.

.... Bettie Robinson, a child Lucy, Sep: 9 1784. Baptized June 4 1786. p. 116.

.... Eliz. Row a son named James born Aug. 17, 1774. Baptized Dec. 12, 1774. p. 97.

.... Mary Shepherd a son named Charles: Cottrel born Jan. 23, 1777. Baptized Ap. 13, 1777. p. 101.

*Margin torn.

.... Betsie Sladon a child Betsie born May 19 1788. Baptized Sep: 17 1788. p. 121.

.... Mary Taylor a son named Patrick born Sep 21, 1774. Baptized Aug. 7, 1775. p. 99.

.... Caroline Tony a son named Aaron born Jan: 18 1771. Baptized Ap 22 1771. p. 89.

.... Patsie Turner, a child named Catie Dickson, born Sep: 20 1783. Baptized Jul: 24 1785. p. 114.

.... Judith Ward a son named John born Jun: 5 1760. Baptized May 5 1765. p. 71.

.... Judith Ward a daughter named Sally born .... Baptized Jun: 25 1769. p. 85.

.... & Lucy West a son named John born Nov: 12 1767. Baptized Jan: 31 1768. p. 79.

.... Linsey Wharton a child Polly born Nov: 20 1782. Baptized Mar: 25 1783. p. 109.

.... Biddy Wilson a daughter named Patty: Wilson born Mar. 9, 1775. Baptized Oct 3, 1775. p. 99.

.... Mally Wood a Son Francis Giddon born June 1782. Baptized Aug. 18, 1782. p. 107.

......................Rebekah Woodward a son named Joshua Woodward born May 5, 1773. Baptized Aug 6, 1773. p. 94.

.... & Ursley Woody a Daughter named Martha born Mar: 28 1757. Baptized 1761 Ap: 26. p. 59.

.... Sarah Woolbanks, a daughter named Molly born feb: 10 .... Baptized Aug 27 1771. p. 90.

.... Mary Yarbrough a Daughter named Elizabeth born Sep: 5 1764. Baptized Oct: 7 1769. p. 69.

DEATHS AND FUNERALS.

May 26 1782—Mr Alford in Fluvannas fun: Ser: Heb: 4.9.—
p. 38.

May 26 1782—Ja: Alfords fun: Powhatan. p. 123.

Nov: 3 1774—Wyat Andersons & Rob: Cairdens childrens funeral Sermon on 2 Kings 4.25, 26.—p. 36.

Ap: 8 1781—Jo: Andersons fun Louisa. p. 123.

Ap: 8 1781—Mr. Is: Andersons ˏfun: Ser. on Ps: 17.15.—in Louisa. p. 37.

Sep: 19 1782—Col: Andersons wifes fun: Ez: 24.16. in Louisa—
p. 38.

Sep: 19 1782—Col. Andersons wifes fun: Louisa. p. 124.

Dec: 19 1790—Mr Rob: Armsted died aged about 64. p. 39.

——p: 7 1775—Thomas Baileys fun: Sermon. on Dan: 12.13 in Goochland—p. 36.

Mar: 19 1780—Da: Bailey fun: Ser: on Ps: 88:18. in—in Fluvanna. p. 37.

Mar: 19 1780—Da: Bailies fun: Albemarle. p. 125.

Feb: 5 1762—John Barrets fun: Sermon on Ja: 4.1.—in Gooch. p. 35.

Feb. 5 1762—Jo Barnets fun. Goochland. p. 125.

Jul: 13 1783—Mrs. Beadles fun: Ser: 1 Cor: 3.22. in Louisa—
p. 38.

Jul: 13 1783—Mr. Beigles wifes fun: Louisa. p. 125.

Feb: 8. 1784—Mr. Beadles child fun: Ser: Job 1.18-22 in Louisa. p. 38.

feb: 8 1774—Mrs. Beigles childs fun: Louisa. p. 124.

Jun: 3 1769—John Bibbs fun: Sermon. on 1 Thess: 4-13.—
p. 36.

June 3 1769—Mr. Bibbs fun: Goochland. p. 125.

Ap: 9 1790—Mrs. Bibb died. p. 39.

1789—Mrs. Bibb in Louisa died. p. 137.

Jan: 1. 1774—John Bradshaws fun: Sermon on Luke 7.12. in Gooch. p. 35.

Jany: 1 1774—Jo: Bradshaws fun: Goochland. p. 123.

Jany: 1 1774—Preached Jo: Bradshaws fun: p. 128.

Jul: 27 1777—Mrs Ann Bradshaws fun: Ser: Mat: 24.44.—ye widow. in Gooch: p. 37.

Jul. 27 1773—Widow Bradshaws fun: p. 123.

Aug: 31 1777—Mary Bradshaws fun: Ser: 2 Chr: 34.3—her daughter:* in Gooch: p. 37.

Aug: 31 1777—Molly Bradshaws fun: Goochland. p. 124.

---

*Daughter of Mrs. Ann Bradshaw.

Jul: 3 1759—Mr. Bromfields fun: Sermon on Mat: 24-44. in Gooch. p. 35.

Jul: 3 1759—.................Bromfields fun. Goochland. p. 123.

Nov: 16[?] 1787—Preached at old Mrs. Bryans fun: in Goochland on Ps: 23.4. p. 38.

Mar: 10 1777—Tho: Bryants fun: Sermon. 1 Cor: 15.54.—in Gooch: p. 37.

Mar: 10 1777—Tho: Bryans fun: p. 124.

May 11 1776—Mrs. Bullocks fun: Sermon in Hanover on Rev: 14.13.—p. 37.

Ap. 11th 1776—Mrs. Bullocks funeral Ser. p. 100.

May 11 1776—Mrs. Bullocks fun: Hanover. p. 123.

May 31 1769—Noel Burtons fun: Sermon on Heb: 11.13.—p. 36.

May 31 1769—Noel Burtons fun: Goochland. p. 125.

Dec: 23 1781—Jo: Byers fun: Ser: on Jo: 14.28.—in Louisa. p. 37.

Dec. 23 1781—Jo: Byres fun: Louisa. p. 123.

Aug: 7 1785—Byres daughters fun: Ser: 1 Thes: 4.18. in Louis [sic]. p. 38.

Aug. 7 1785—Mrs. Byars daughters fun: Louisa. p. 125.

Nov: 3 1774—Rob: Cairdens* & Wyat Andersons* Childrens funeral Sermon on 2 Kings 4, 25, 26.—p. 36.

Nov: 3 1774—Cairden & Wilkersons fun: Goochland (Dodge). p. 124.

Dec: 18 1761—Dr Chastines fun: Sermon. in Manikentown on 1 Cor: 15.54.—p. 36.

Dec. 19 1761—Dr. Chastines fun: Maniken. p. 124.

Dec: 23 1763—Capt: Childers fun: Sermon in Albemarle. on Ecc: 12.7.—p. 36.

Dec. 23 1763—Capt. Childers fun: Albemarle. p. 124.

Dec: 6. 1769—Rev. Sam: Clark died aged 42. p. 134.

May 26 1780—Mrs. Clarks fun: Ser: in Fluvanna on Ez: 24.16—p. 37.

May 26. 1780—Mrs. Clarks fun: Fluvanna. p. 124.

Jul: 8 1787—Is: Clarks fun: Ser: Gen: 5-24, in Louisa. p. 38.

Mar: 13 1772—Mrs Cobbs fun: Sermon in Buckingham. on Ps: 17-15—p. 36.

Mar: 12 1772—Mrs. Cobbs fun: p. 124.

Oct—30 1778—Mr Colemans daughters fun: Ser: 2 Kings 4.25, 26. —in Spot. p. 37.

Oct. 30 1778—Mr. Colemans daughters fun: Spotsylvania (Dodge). p. 124.

Jul: 23 1780—At Mr Cosbies childs fun: 2 Kings 4.25, 26—in Louisa. p. 37.

Jul: 23 1780—Jo: Cosbies ....fun: Louisa (Dodge). p. 124.

*Transposed.

Jul: 11 1784—Mrs. Cosbies fun: Ser: at Sheriff Thoms. Ex: 9.10 in Louisa. p. 38.

July 11 1784—Mrs. Cosbies fun: Louisa. p. 124.

May 18 1776—Francis Cowleys fun: Sermon on Rev: 14.13.—in Gooch. p. 37.

May 18. 1776—Frank Cowleys funeral Ser. p. 100.

May 1776—Frank Cowlys fun: Gooch: p. 123.

Mar: 9 1777—Mrs Crouchers fun: Sermon on Ps: 34.12-15.—in Gooch: p. 37.

Mar: 9 1777—Mrs. Crouchers fun: Goochland. p. 123.

Oct: 8 1774—Mrs. Curds fun: Sermon on Ps: 102.23, 24.—in Gooch. p. 36.

Oct. 8 1774—Ja: Curds wifes fun: p. 123.

Jul: 17 1779—Mrs. Jo: Daniels, fun: 2 Cor: 5.2—in Louisa. p. 37.

Jul: 17 1779—Mrs. Daniels fun: Louisa. p. 124.

Dec: 17 1780—At Beven Daniels Sons. fun: 1 Cor: 15.54—in Spot: p. 37.

Dec: 2 1781—Mrs. Daniels fun: Ser: on Ez: 24.16.—in Louisa. p. 37.

dec: 2 1781—Jo: Daniels wifes fun: Louisa. p. 124.

Aug: 27 1785—Cha: Daniels Daughters fun: Ser: on Ps: 23.4 in Louisa. p. 38.

Aug. 27 1785—Cha: Daniels daughters fun: Louisa. p. 123.

Jan: 1 1786—Jo: Daniels daughters fun on Jer: 28.16 in Louisa. p. 38.

Jan: 1 1786—Jo: Daniels daughters fun: in Louisa. p. 124.

June 4 1786—Jo: Daniels fun: on Mat: 24-44, in Louisa. p. 38.

June 4 1786—Jo: Daniels fun: Louisa. p. 123.

Dec. 17 1790—Beven Daniels sons fun: Orange. p. 124.

Oct: 11 1778—Jo: Delanys fun: Ser: Ps: 27.10.—in Spot. p. 37.

Oct. 11 1778—Jo: Delaineys fun: Spotsylvania. p. 125.

May 9, 1779—Delaineys children Job 1. 18-22 in Spotsyl—p. 37.

May 9 1779—Wid: Delaineys sons fun: Louisa. p. 124.

May 21 1780—Delainey child 2 Kings 4.25, 26 in Spot:—p. 37.

May 21 1780—Wid: Delaineys childs fun: Spotsylvania. p. 124.

Nov: 20 1751—Isaac Dittnay Broyr to Mrs. Porter fun: Sermon on Job 31.2.—in Maniken town. p. 37.

Nov. 20 1751—Isaac Dittnay fun. Maniken. p. 123.

Nov: 20 1751—Preached Is: Dittrich fun: Sermon. p. 26.

Nov: 20 1751—Is: Dittriahs fun: Ser: Job 31.2, 3—in Manickentown. p. 35.

Jan: 21 1781—Rob: Douglasses fun: Ser: Rev: 14.13.—in Louisa. p. 37.

Jan: 21 1781—Rob: Douglas fun: Louisa. p. 123.

Jan: 20 1782—Mrs. Douglasses fun: Ser: Deu: 32.29 by Mr. Murray—p. 37.

Mar: 17 1782—I preached at Beaverdam my dear wifes fun: Ser: on Ps: 88. 18.—p. 35.

Nov: 14 1763—Geo: Drumwrights fun: Sermon on 2 Chron: 34.3. p. 36.

Nov: 14 1762—Geo: Drumrights fun: Goochland. p. 124.

Ap: 23 1780—Mrs Duets fun: Ser: on Ps: 88.18 in Louisa—p. 37.

Ap: 23 1780—Mrs. Duets fun: Louisa. p. 125.

Ap: 27 1772—James Dunns fun: Sermon on 2 Cor: 5.9.—in Gooch. p. 36.

Ap: 27 1772—Ja: Duns fun: Goochland. p. 124.

Ap: 8 1790—Mrs. Edwards died. p. 39.

May 8 1790—Mrs. Slade Edwards died aged 64. p. 137.

May 10 1768—Capt Edwards fun: Sermon. on Jo: 11.26.—in Gooch. p. 35.

May 10 1768—Cap: Edwards fun: Goochland. p. 123.

Oct. 14 1766—Mrs. Tho: Ellis fun: Henrico. p. 123.

Feb: 17 1772—Dr Ellices fun: Sermon in Gooch: p. 37.

Feb: 17 1772—Honest Dr. Ellis died a youth. p. 128.

Aug: 5 1773—Preached Mrs. Ellis funeral ser: in Henrico. p. 128.

Aug: 7 1773—Mrs Ellis fun Sermon in Henrico on Job 1-21.—p. 36.

Aug: 7 1773—Capt. Ellis wifes fun: Henrico. p. 124.

Oct: 28 1775—Thomas Ellis's funeral Sermon in Henrico on Jo: 14-28.—in Henrico [sic]. p. 37.

Oct 28 1775—Tho: Ellis fun: in Henrico. p. 123.

Ap: 24 1783—Mrs Ellis in Henricos fun: Ser: Ps: 39.12.—p. 38.

Sep: 7 1768—Mrs. Tabitha Evans fun: Sermon. on Job 5.26—in Gooch: p. 35.

Sept. 7 1768—Tabitha Evans fun: Goochland. p. 125.

Aug: 10 1776—Mrs. Fulchers fun: Goochland. p. 123.

Mar: 18 1787—Jack Freemans fun: Ser: on Mat: 24.44—in Louisa. p. 38.

May 2 1789—Mrs. Sara Freeman died aged 89, an honest old woman. p. 125.

Aug: 10 1776—Mrs. Fulchers fun Sermon. on Ps: 17.15.—in Gooch: p. 37.

Ap: 27 1788—Mrs. Garrets fun: Louisa. p. 125.

Nov: 27 1773—Leonard Georges fun: Sermon. on Ps: 88.18.—p. 36.

Nov. 27 1773—Leonard Georges fun: p. 123.

May 18 1781—Ja: Georges fun: Ser: Jo: 14.28—in Gooch. p. 37.

May 18 1781—Ja: Georges fun: Goochland. p. 123.

Jun: 20 1784—Mrs. Georges fun: Ser: Ex: 9.10 in Goochland—p. 38.

June 20 1784—Mrs. Georges fun: Goochland. p. 124.

Dec: 2 1795—Dr. Geo: Gilmour died age. p. 39.

Jul: 18 1760—Mr Goodwins Buckingham on Job 3.17.—Buckingham. p. 35.

July 18 1760—Mr. Goodwin's ....fun: Albemarle. p. 125.

Mar: 29 1778—Alexr. Grants childrens fun: Ser: Mat: 2.18—in Fluvanna. p. 37.

Mar: 29 1778—Alexr: Grants childs fun: Albemarle. p. 124.

Oct: 18 1772—Mrs Graves's fun: Sermon on Ps: 23.4.—in Gooch: p. 36.

Oct: 18 1772—Mrs. Graves fun: Goochland. p. 123.

Nov: .... 1752—Mrs Grayson Col: Monroes Sister died. p. 39.

Oct—10 1779—Billie Grooms fun: Ser: on Jo: 11.26. in Spot:—p. 37.

Oct 10 1779—Billie Grooms fun: Louisa. p. 123.

Sep: 15 1794—Jo: Guillam died. p. 39.

Sep: 32 1794—his *son Taylor Guillam died. p. 39.

.... 1753—Sar: Harris's fun: p. 27.

Sar: Harris's funeral in Maniken town. p. 32.

May 15 1753—Mrs. Sarah Harris's fun: Sermon on Job 3.17.—in Maniken town. p. 35.

May 15, 1753—Sar: Harris' fun: at Maniken. p. 124.

Feb: 3. 1769—Col: Henrys two Daughters fun: Sers. at Col: Henrys in Hanover on 2 Chron: 34.3.—p. 36.

Feb: 3 1769—Col: Henrys daughters fun: Hanover. p. 124.

Jun: 14 1760—James Hiltons wifes funeral Sern. on Job 3.17.—p. 36.

June 14 1760—Ja: Hiltons wifes fun: Goochland. p. 125.

Oct: 20 1777—Randolph Holbrooks fun: Ser: Gen: 5.24.—in Gooch: p. 37.

Feb. 15 1778—Ran: Holbrooks fun; Goochland. p. 125.

.... 1750—Mrs. Hollands fun: Sermon on. p. 35.

Jun: 12 1759—Capt Holmans fun: Sermon on Job 5.26—in Gooch. p. 35.

June 12 1759—Cap. Holmans fun: Goochland. p. · 123.

Nov: 20 1761—Mr Ja: Holmans funeral Sermon on 2 Kings 4.25, 26.—in Maniken town. p. 36.

Nov: 20 1761 Ja: Holmans fun: Maniken. p. 124.

Jul: 18 1773—Mrs Holmans fun: Sermon on Pro: 16.31.—in Gooch: p. 36.

July 18 1773—Mrs. Holmans fun: Goochland. p. 125.

.... 1769—Col: Arthur Hopkins died in Goochland. died. p. 38.

Mar: 28 1778—Ja: Howards fun: Ser: Job 5-26—in Goochland. p. 37.

Mch. 27 1778—Ja: Howards fun: Goochland. p. 125.

Jan: 5 1761—Peggie Huddlestone died. p. 128.

*Jo: Guillam's son.

Nov: 27 1755—Jos: Hughes in Cumberlands. fun: Ser: 1 Thes: 4.18. p. 35.

Nov: 27 1755—Mr Jos Hughes fun: Sermon in Cumberland on 1 Thes: 4.18.—p. 35.

Nov: 5 1773—Mr Hughes's childs fun: Sermon in Hanover on 2 Kings 4. 25, 26. p. 36.

Nov: 5 1773—Jo: Hughes childs fun: Hanover. p. 124.

Nov: 16 1782—Died Mrs Hughes in Hanover, aged 72. p. 38.

Aug: 21 1759—Dr. Jo: Hunter died. p. 128.

Oct: 14 1766—Dr Will: Hunters fun: Sermon on Gen: 5.24.— in Gooch. p. 35.

Oct: 2 1766—Dr. Will: Hunter died. p. 128.

Oct: 14 1766—Dr. Will: Hunters fun: Goochland. p. 123.

May 13 1781—Mrs Hutchisons fun: in Spotsyl: Jo: 14.28—p. 37.

May 13 1781—Hutchisons wifes fun: Spotsylvania. p. 123.

Dec. 18 1787—Soame Jennings died aged 83—a pious man. p. 143.

Aug: 12 1761—Josephs Johnsons funeral Sermon his Child on Mat: 2.18—p. 36.

Aug: 12 1761—Jos: Johnsons childs fun: Goochland. p. 124.

Feb: 13 1773—Mrs Johnsons fun: Sermon on Jo: 14.28.—in Gooch: p. 36.

feb: 13 1773—Jo: Johnsons wifes fun: Goochland. p. 124.

May 29 1773—David Johnsons Childs fun: Sermon—on Is: 46.4.—p. 25.

......p: 15 1775—Aggie Johnsons fun: Sermon. on Ps: 37, 37.— p. 36.

Ap: 15 1775—Aggie Johnsons fun: Goochland. p. 123.

June 16 1782—Ja: Johnstons fun: in Goochland Jo: 14.28:—p. 38.

June 16 1782—Ja Johnsons fun. Goochland. p. 123.

[F]eb: 26 1775—Mrs Johnsons fun: Sermon old James's wife on Dan: 12.13.--p. 36.

May 9 1769—Harrison Jones's wifes fun: Sermon. on Heb: 11.13. —in Gooch. p. 35.

May 9 1769—Gab: Jones wife's fun: Goochland. p. 125.

Oct: 30. 1779—Mr Jordans on Jo: 11. 35. in Gooch: p. 35.

Oct. 30 1779—Ja: Jordans fun. Goochland. p. 123.

Novr: 6 1773—Charles Jordans fun: Ser: on Ps: 23.4.—in Gooch: p. 35.

Nov. 6 1773—Cha: Jordans fun: Goochland. p. 123.

Oct: 30 1778—Mr Jordans fun: Sermon. On Jo: 11. 35.—p. 36.

.... 1789—Mrs. Ker in Louisa died. p. 137.

Aug: 25 1781—Is: Knights fun: Ser: in Fluvanna, Ps: 102.23, 24. —p. 37.

Aug. 25 1781—...........................Knights sons fun. Powhatan. p. 123.

Ap: 16 1780—Hemus Lads fun: Sermon on Rev: 2.10. in Goochland—p. 37.

Ap: 16 1780—Hemus Lads fur: Goochland. p. 124.

Oct: 20 1769—Betty Leprades funeral Sermon. on Jo: 11.35.—p. 36.

Oct. 20 1769—Betty Laprades fun. Goochland. p. 123.

Oct: 22 1781—Moses Lauries sons fun: in Fluvanna on 2 Kings 4.25—p. 37.

Oct: 22 1781—Moses Lauries sons fun: Fluvanna. p. 124.

Nov: 24 1775—Walter Leeks fun: Sermon on Pet: 3.14.—in Goochland. p. 37.

Nov. 24 1775—Wal: Leeks fun: Goochland. p. 123.

Oct: 13 1770—John Lees fun: Sermon on Job 30.23.—in Gooch. p. 36.

Oct. 2 1770—Jo: Lees fun. Goochland. p. 123.

Jul: 24 1771—Mrs Lees funeral Sermon. on Luke 10.41, 42—Gooch: p. 36.

Aug: 24 1764—Edward Lewis's fun: Sermon on 2 Chron: 34.3. p. 36.

Aug: 24 1764—Ed: Lewis' Goochland. p. 124

Sep: 12 1771—Susannah Lewis's fun: Sermon. on 1 Cor: 15.57. —in Gooch. p. 36.

Sep: 12 1771—Miss Suckie Lewis fun. Goochland. p. 123.

1779—Col: Cha: Lewis in Goochland died. p. 38.

1783—Mrs Lewis died. ye Colonels* widow died in Goochland. p. 38.

Aug: 6 1774—Mrs mcBrides fun: Sermon. on Ps. 92.14.—Grannie in Gooch: p. 36.

Sep: 30 1766—Mrs mcCawls funeral Sermon on Ps: 17.15.—in Gooch: p. 36.

Sep: 30 1766—Mrs. McCawls fun. Goochland. p. 123.

Jul: 23 1773—Mr. McLaurines fun: Cumberland. p. 124.

Jul: 5 1773—The Revd. Mr. Robt. McLaurine died. p. 128.

Jul: 23 1773—Rev: Mr mcLaurines fun: Ser: in Cumberland on 1. Pet: 5-4.—once my scholar for many years. p. 36.

Jun: 5 1774—John Mattax's Daughters fun: Sermon Job 1: 13:22. in Gooch: p. 36.

May 28 1774—Jo: Mattox childs fun: Sermon on Job 1.18-22—in Gooch: p. 35.

Jan: 21 1775—Jo: Maddox's childs fun: Goochland. p. 124.

Mar: 25 1783—Mr Mannins fun: Ser: Ps: 88.18 in—. p. 38.

Mar: 25 1783—Mr. Mannins fun: Spotsylvania. p. 125.

Nov: 24 1782—Mr Martin in Goochland wife & Sons fun: Job 1. 21.—p. 38.

Nov; 24 1782—Mrs. Martins and her grandsons fun: Goochland. p. 124.

*Col. Charles Lewis.

May 29 1755—Tho: Massies fun: Sermon. on 1 Thes: 4-18. p. 35.
May 29 1755—Tho: Massies wifes fun: Goochland. p. 125.
Nov: 4 1774—Mrs Massies fun: Sermon on Ezek: 24.16.—p. 36.
Nov: 4 1774—Nat: Massies wifes fun: Goochland. p. 124.
Jul: 1 1770—Ned Matthews wifes fun: Goochland. p. 124.
Jul: 1 1770—Ed: Mathews wifes fun: Ser: on Ez: 24.16. p. 12.
Jul. 1. 1770—Mrs Matthews fun: Sermon. on Ezek: 24.16.—Neds
wife. p. 36.
Feb. 28 1760—At Mr Mainards in Albemarle on Mat: 2.18. a
Childs fun.—p. 35.
feb: 28 1760—Maynards childs fun: Albemarle. p. 124.
June 13 1733—Rev. Daniel Mayo died. p. 134.
Dec: 9 1773—Mrs Mayos fun: Sern: in Cumberland on Ps. 88-18
—p. 36.
Nov: 28. 1773—Madam Mayo in Cumberland died. p. 134.
dec. 9 1773—Mrs. Mayos fun: Cumberland. p. 125.
Jun: 1 1776—Isaack Meanleys fun: Sermon, on 2 Cor: 5-2—in
Gooch. p. 37.
Jun: 1 1776—Is: Meanleys fun Goochland. p. 124.
.... 1750—Mr Millers Broyrs fun: Sermon. p. 35.
.... 1751—Jo: Millers funeral. p. 26.
Jan 7. 1787—Mrs Miltons fun: Ser: on Pro: 16:31. p. 38.
Feb: 8 1777—Mrs Mims's fun: Sermon on Ps: 88.18.—in Gooch:
p. 37.
Mar: 8 1777—Mrs Mims fun: Ser: Ps: 88.18—in Gooch: p. 38.
feb: 8 1777—Mrs. Mims fun: Goochland. p. 125.
Nov: 7 1779—Jo: Mims fun: Ser. on Ps: 23.4, in Goochland—
p. 37.
Nov. 7 1779—Jo: Mims fun: Goochland. p. 123.
Oct: 3 1776—Tho: Mitchels fun: Sermon on Ja: 4. 14.—in
Gooch: p. 35.
Oct: 3 1776—.....................Mitchells fun Goochland. p. 125.
May 30 1782—Mrs. Mitchel in Goochland fun: No Ser: p. 38.
Feb: 5 1767—Jo: Monroe ye Collonels Son died. A pious young
man. p. 39.
Ap: 11 1773—Mrs Moseleys fun: Sermon on Jo: 11.26 in Gooch:
p. 35.
Ap: 11 1773—Mrs. Moseleys fun: Goochland. p. 123.

Oct: 13 1763—Ann Napiers fun: Sermon. Albemarle on 2 Cron:
34, 3.—p. 36.
Oct: 13 1762—Ann Napiers fun: Goochland. p. 124.
Ap: 23 1770—Booth Napiers fun: Sermon on Mat: 25.13.—
Junior. p. 35.
Ap: 23 1770—Booth Napier-Junr. fun Goochland. p .123.
Mar: 13 1773—Mrs Napiers fun: Sermon, on Jo: 11.26.—in
Gooch. p. 35.
Mar: 13 1773—Mrs. Napiers fun: Goochland. p. 123.

Jan 2 1790—Col: Jo: Nilson* died aged 47—in Louisa. p. 39.
Jan: 2 1790—Col: Jo: Nelson in Louisa died aged 48. p. 137.
Jun: 24 1760—Mrs. Nichols funeral Sermon on Job 3.17.—p. 36.
June 24 1760—Mrs. Nicholas fun. Goochland. p. 125.

Sep: 23 1774—Mrs. Ogilvys fun: Sermon on Philip: 1.22—24.—
in Gooch. p. 36.
Sep: 23 1774—Mrs. Ogilvys fun: Goochland. p. 124.
Sep: 27 1774—Preached at Mrs. Ogilvys fun: p. 128.
Mar: 16 1782—Barnet Owens fun: Ser: Gen: 5-24.—in Gooch:
p. 37.
Mch. 16 1782—Barnet Owens fun: Goochland. p. 125.

Jan: 23 1773—Rob: Paisleys fun: Sermon on Ecc: 12.7.—in
Gooch. p. 36.
Jan: 23 1773—Robin Paisleys fun: Goochland. p. 124.
Mar: 19 1786—Rich: Pawlets childrens fun: on Mat: 2.18, in
Louisa. p. 38.
Mar: 19 1786—Mr. Paulets childrens fun: Louisa. p. 124.
Oct: 31 1770—Jesse Paynes fun: Sermon. on Job 1-18—22, in
Gooch. p. 36.
Oct: 31 1770—Jesse Paynes fun: Goochland. p. 124.
Nov: 5 1774—Geo: Paynes childs fun: Sermon. on Mat: 2-18.—
in Gooch. p. 36.
Nov: 5 1774—Geo: Payne Jnr. fun: Goochland. p. 124.
Sep. 30 1779—Maj. Payne's wifes fun: Goochland. p. 125.
Oct: .1 1779—Mrs Paynes fun: Ser: on Rev: 14.13. in Gooch-
land—p. 37.
Jul: 28 1784—Col: Jo: Payne in Goochland died. pp. 129, 137.
Jul: 29 1784—Col: Jo: Payne in Goochland died. p. 39.
.... 1785—Major Payne died. p. 38.
May 29 1780—Anderson Peers's wifes fun: Ser: Ez: 24.16 in
Goochland—p. 37.
May 29 1780—Anderson Peers wifes fun: Goochland. p. 124.
Dec: 18 1770—Constant Perkins fun: Sermon on Job 5.26.—in
Gooch. p. 36.
Jul: 25 1772—Stephen Perkins fun: Sermon on 2 Tim: 4.7, 8.—
in Gooch. p. 36.
Jul: 25 1772—Steph: Perkins fun: Goochland. p. 123.
Jun: 8 1776—Nicholas Perkins fun: Sermon on Ecc: 9.10.—in
Gooch. p. 37.
Jun: 8 1776—.................Perkins fun: Goochland. p. 124.
May 19 1781—Walker Perkins fun: Ser: Jo: 11-26. & his Moyr—
in Gooch: p. 37.
May 19 1781—Widow Perkins sons fun: Goochland. p. 123.
Jan: 14 1785—Mrs. Philips fun: Ser: on Jo: 14.28.—in Louisa.
p. 38.

*Nelson.

Jan. 14 1785—Mrs. Philips fun: Louisa. p. 123.

Nov: 24 1779—Will: Pledges fun: Ser: on Ecc: 12.7. in Goochland—p. 37.

Nov: 24 1779—Billie Pledges fun: Goochland. p. 124.

Dec: 3 1773—Two Mrs Pledges fun: Sermon. on Ps: 88-18.— p. 36.

dec. 9 1773—Pledges .... fun: Goochland. p. 125.

June 21 1798—Elizabeth Meriwether Poindexter, daughter to John Poindexter, Junior aged seven years last March died with the inflamitary fever supposed after an illness of about 23 days. [In another handwriting.] p. 137.

dec: 26 1791—Mr Joseph Pollard died aged about. p. 39.

May 24 1777—Mrs & John Pollocks fun: Sermon on Gen: 5.24.— p. 37.

May 24 1777—Jo: Pollocks fun Goochland. p. 125.

Feb: 1 1788—Tho: Poor in Goochland died a worthy good man. p. 38.

.... 21 1775—John Pruits Sons fun: Sermon. p. 36.

Jun: 9 1777—Col: Pryors fun: Sermon in Gooch. p. 37.

Feb: 14 1779—Mrs Quales fun: Ser: Ps: 17.15 in Spotsylvania. p. 37.

Feb. 14 1779—Mrs. Quarles fun: Spotsylvania. p. 123.

Jul: 12 1783—Mrs Quisenberrys fun: Ser. Gen: 5.24 in Spotsyl— p. 38.

Jul: 12 1783—Mrs. Quisenberry's fun: Orange. p. 125.

1751—Billie Radfords funeral. p. 26.

Jun: 17 1752—Billie Radfords fun: Goochland. p. 125.

Jan: 17 1752—Mr Radfords fun: Ser: on Ps: 27.10, in Gooch: p. 35.

Dec: 3 1774—Ned Radfords Childs fun: Sermon on 2 Kings 4.25, 26. in Gooch. p. 35.

Dec. 3 1774—Ned Radfords childs fun: Goochland (Dodge). p. 124.

Jan: 7 1758—Allan Ramsay died. p. 39.

Nov: 20 1793—Mr Tho: Randolph of Tuckahoe died aged. p. 39.

Nov. 20 1793—Mr. Thomas Randolph of Tuckahoe died aged. p 142.

Mar: 6 1789—Mrs. Randolph of Tuckahoe in Goochland died aged. p. 39.

Sep: 11 1782—Mrs. Realy died Sep: 11.82. p. 38.

Oct: 4 1784—Mr. Realy died. Oct: 4, 84. p. 38.

Sep: 8 1756—Billie Robards wifes fun: Sermon on Ezek: 24.16. —in Gooch: p. 35.

Sept. 8 1756—Billie Roberts wifes fun: Goochland. p. 124.

Aug: 13 1789—Mrs Susanna Robinson Spouse to Col: Winslow died aged. p. 39.

June 3 1764—Sexton Ryans fun: Goochland. p. 125.
Jun: 3 1764—Philip Ryans fun: Sermon on Job 5.26.—& his wife
buried together ye Same day in Goochland. p. 35.

Dec: 12 1773—Stephen Sampsons daughters fun: Sermon on Ps:
88.18.—p. 36.
dec. 12 1773—Steph: Samsons oldest: fun: Gooch:—a worthy
good old man. p. 125.
[Oc]t: 20 1775—Stephen Sampsons daughters fun: Sermon on
Job 1-21.—p. 36.
Oct: 20 1775—Steph: Samsons daughters fun: Goochland. p. 124.
Jun: 23 1755—Hannah Smiths fun: Sermon on Mat: 2-18.—in
Gooch. p. 35.
June 23 1755—Hannah Smiths fun: Goochland. p. 124.
.... 1775—Col: Jo: Smith in Goochland died. p. 38.
Ap: 26 1783—Will: Smith in Goochlands fun: Ser: Pro: 16.31—
p. 38.
Ap: 26 1783—Billie Smiths fun: Goochland. p. 125.
.... 1757—John Stark in Westmorland died. p. 39.
Mar: 2 1783—Billie Steels fun: Ser: Ps: 37.37. In Louisa—
p. 38.
Mar: 2 1783—Billie Steels fun: Goochland. p. 123.
May 16 1773—John Stodghills fun: Sermon on Mat: 24-44—
in Gooch. p. 35.
May 16 1773—Jo. Stodghills fun: Goochland. p. 123.
Jan 27 1782—Mr Suttles Moyrs fun: Ser: in Louisa. p. 37.
Feb: 27 1789—Will: Suttles of Louisa a pious man died. p. 39.

Sep: 7 1776—Mrs Thomasons fun: Sermon, on Jo: 14.28.—in
Gooch: p. 37.
Sep: 7 1776—Mr. Thomasons wifes fun: Goochland. p. 123.
Nov: 29 1778—Geo: Thomasons Grandchildren fun: Ser: Mat: 2,
18—in Louisa. p. 37.
Dec: 6 1778—Mr Thomasons childs fun: Ser: Mat: 2.18 in
Louisa. p. 37.
dec: 6 1778—Mr. Thomasons childs fun: Louisa. p. 124.
Ap: 24 1785—Sam: Thomasons daughter fun: 2 Kings 4.25, 26.
—in Louisa. p. 38.
Ap: 24 1785—Sam Thomasons daughters fun: Louisa. p. 124.
Aug: 25 1771—Mrs Thomsons fun: Sermon, on Job: 30.23—in
Gooch. p. 36.
Aug: 25 1771—Mrs. Thomsons fun. Goochland. p. 123.
Aug. 25 1771—Mrs. Thomsons fun: Goochland. p. 125.
Mar: 16 1789—Mr Will: Thurston in Louisa died. p. 39.
May 5 1763—Mrs Tilmans fun: Ser: in Albemarle on 1 Thess
4.13.—p. 36.
May 5 1763—Tho: Tilmans wifes fun: in Amherst. p. 125.
Jul: 27 1793—R: Mr Jo: Tod died. p. 39.

Mar: 29 1766—Mrs Turners fun: Sermon on Job 5.26—in Gooch: Bartley turners Moyr. p. 36.

Mch. 29 1766—Bartley Turners Moyr [mother] fun: Goochland. p. 125.

Sep: 22 1752—............... Vaughans fun: Ser: on Luke 10.42. p. 35.

Jan: 21 1775—Math: Vaughans Childs fun: Sermon on Job 1.18-22—in Hanover. p. 35.

1775—Mat: Vaughans childs fun: Ser: on Job 1.18-22 in Hanover. p. 38.

Jan: 21 1775—Mat: Vaughans childs fun: Goochland. p. 124.

Oct: 3 1776—Ja: Vaughans wifes fun: Sermon on Luke 10.41, 42. in Gooch: p. 35.

feb: 13 1768—John Villaines fun: Sermon in Maniken town on Jo: 11.26—feb: 13-68. p. 36.

Feb. 12 1768—Jo: Villains fun: Maniken. p. 123.

Feb: 25 1773—Mr Wadleys fun: Sermon on Jo: 14.28.—in Gooch: p. 36.

Feb: 25 1773—Thos: Wadleys fun: in Goochland. p. 123.

Feb: 22 .... —Mrs Wadleys fun: at Jo: Leprades—in Gooch: p. 35.

Feb: 22 1777—Mrs Wadleys fun: Sermon on Ps: 34, 12—15—in Gooch: p. 37.

Feb. 22 1777—Mrs. Wadleys fun: Goochland. p. 123.

Aug: 30 1772—David Walker Junr. fun: Sermon on Philip: 1.21.—in Gooch: p. 25.

Aug: 30 1772—Da: Walker Junr. fun: Goochland. p. 124.

Feb: 26 1774—David Walkers fun: Sermon. on 1 Cor: 15-49—ye old man in Gooch: p. 36.

Feb. 26 1774—Da: Wakers fun Goochland. p. 123.

Sep. 21 1777—Mrs Walkers fun: Ser: at Beverdam Luke 10.41, 42 —in Gooch: p. 37.

Nov—25 1775—Tho: Watkins fun: Sermon on Ps: 27.10—in Gooch: p. 37.

Nov. 25 1775—Tho. Watkins fun: Goochland. p. 125.

Feb: 1762—Will: Watkins wifes fun: Ser: in Cumberland on Ezek: 24.16.—p. 36.

feb: 3 1762—Billie Watkins wifes fun: Cumberland. p. 124.

Mar: 10 1753—Capt: Jo: Watts in Westmorland died. p. 39.

Dec: 23 1761—Mr Webbers fun: Sermon. on Mat: 24, 44.—p. 36.

Dec: 23 1761—Mr. Phil Webbers fun: Goochland. p. 123.

Mar: 18 1781—Mrs Websters fun: Ser: on Heb: 4.9.—in Gooch: p. 37.

Mar: 18 1781—Mrs. Websters fun: Goochland. p. 123.

.... Mrs. White in Louisa died. p. 137.

Jul: 31 1769—Honest Jo: Williamson died. p. 128.

[F]eb: 13 1785—Mr Wilsons fun: Ser: on Heb: 9.27. p. 23.

Feb. 13 1785—Mr Wilsons fun: Ser: in Louisa on Heb: 9.27.—in Louisa. p. 38.

Feby. 13 1785—Mr. Wilsons fun: Louisa. p. 124.

Jul: 12 [17]93—Col: Beverly Winslow died age 60. p. 39.

Jul: 12 1793—Col: Beverly Winslow died aged 60.—p. 142.

[Ja]n: 13 1775—John Woodrums Childs fun: Sermon on Job 21.23-26.—p. 36.

.... 4 1775—John Woodrums fun: Sermon. on Job 30.23.—p. 36.

Jan: 13 1775—Woodrums childs fun: Goochland. p. 124.

Nov. 4 1775—Molly Woodrums fun.'Goochland. p. 123.

Dec: 12 1775—Mrs Woodsons fun: Sermon on Ps: 17.15, Tuckers wife—in Gooch: p. 37.

Dec. 12 1775—Mrs. Tuck: Woodsons fun: Goochland. p. 123.

Mar: 1 1778—Mrs Mally Woodsons fun: Ser: on Heb: 11.13.—in Gooch: p. 37.

Mar: 1 1778—Robin Woodson's wife Mollys fun: Goochland. p. 125.

Dec: 2 1789—Col: Jo: Woodson in Goochland died aged. p. 39.

Dec: 2 1789—Col: Jo: Woodson in Goochland died. p. 39.

Dec: 2, 1789—Col: Jo: Woodson in Goochland died. p. 137.

Feb: 2 1794—[Woodson] Dorothea Randolph his wife died. p. 39.

Feb. 2 1794—Col: Jo: Woodsons widow Bethia Randolph died. p. 137.

Oct: 23 1794—Mat: Woodson died. p. 39.

Oct. 23 '94—Mat: Woodson died. p. 137.

Oct: 7 1780—Stephen Yaunceys Wifes fun: Job 1-21—in Louisa. p. 35.

Oct: 7 1780—Mr. Yaunces daugh: fun: Louisa. p. 124.

Oct: 7 1780—Mr Yaunceys daughr fun: Ser: Job 1.21 in Louisa. p. 37.

Aug: 21 1785—Mr Char: Yaunceys Daughters fun: Ser: on Ps: 23.4 in Louisa. p. 38.

Aug. 21 1785—Mr. Yaunceys daughters fun: Louisa. p. 123.

Mar 12 1752—Mr Youngs fun: Sermon in Maniken town on Job: 21.23—26.—p. 35.

Mar. 12 1752—................Youngs fun: Maniken. p. 124.

MARRIAGE, BIRTH & DEATH RECORDS OF COLORED PERSONS

COLORED MARRIAGES

Aug: 29 1775—Jacob Banks & Susannah Jones Mulattoes both in ys. p. 16.

Dec: 15 1759—Francis Cousins & Mary Martin Mulattoes both of Maniken town. p. 4.

Oct: 27 1769—Drury fferrar & .... Mulattoes in this parish. p. 11.

Sep: 23 1773—Jo: Ferrar & Mally Gantlet Molattoes in Goochland. p. 14.

Oct: 2 1778—Da: Grantum, & Elizabeth, Mulattoes in Goochland. p. 18.

Jun: 18 1775—Charles Howel & Abbie Scot Mulattoes both in ys. p. 16.

Nov: 7 1776—James Johnson & Mary Banks both of ys parish, & Mulattoes. p. 17.

Sep: 25 1775—Bristol Mathews & Nanny Lynch Mulattoes both of ys parish. p. 16.

Dec: 24 1761—William Lansford & Elizabeth Scot Mulattoes, he in this parish and she in Hanover. p. 6.

Nov: 10 1773—Stephen Scot & Mally fferrar Molattoes. p. 14.

COLORED BIRTHS

James Holman a Negroe child born 1721 Aug: 15 named Susannah .... Negroe. p. 40.

James Holman a Negroe child born 1725 Nov: 27 named Judith .... Negroe. p. 40.

Will: Miller a Negroe boy born 1751 feb: 18 named James. p. 40.

Will: Miller a Negroe Girl born 1753 feb: 27 named Sue. p. 40.

A Negroe boy born 1755 feb: 16 named York. p. 40.

Jos: Evans a Negroe child named Jeahie born 1755 Jul: 4. p. 40.

Dick a negroe boy belonging to Capt Stamps born 1756 feb: 29. p. 48.

Betty Colo-fflemings Negroe wench had a Daughter born Aug: 1748 named Phillis. Baptized 1756 Mar. 7. p. 48.

Ruth Mathews a free Mulattoe a Daughter born Oct 1748 named Elizabeth. Baptized 1756 Mar. 7. p. 48.

Lucy Howel a free Mullattoe a Daughter born Jun: 10 1755 named Judah. Baptized 1756 Mar. 7. p. 48.

Nelly .... Colo Lewis's negro wench a Daughter born named Hannah. Baptized 1756 Mar. 7. p. 48.

Negroe Grissy of Colo. Lewis's a Daughter named ffanny born dec: 14 1755. Baptized 1756 May 30. p. 48.

Mary Begs a Negroe w Wal: Leek a Daughter named Agnes born Jan: 1756. Baptized 1756 Jun: 13. p. 48.

Negroe Stephen belonging to Colo Lewis born 1741. Baptized 1756 Jun: 13. p. 48.

Ja: Mathews a Negroe & susannah fford white, a son named Richardson born Ap: 17 1760. Baptized 1760 Jun: 24. p. 57.

William Lansford & Eliz: Scott Mulattoes a Daughter named Milley born May 28 1762. Baptized 1762 Aug: 8. p. 63.

Negroe Ben & Molly Cockran a Daughter named Betsy born Oct: 31 1765. Baptized Jan: 19 1766. p. 72.

Negroes, John & Dorcas belonging to Mary Allen, a Daughter named Nanny born Jun: 18 1769. Baptized Sep: 17 1769. p. 86.

Tho: Lynch was born Whitsunday 1772 a mulatto of Co: Paynes. Baptized Ap. 22, 1775. p. 98.

Negroe Frankly a free woman a Girl named Lucy Barnet born June 13 1778. Baptized 1779 June 17.

Negroe Bridget a Son named York, then baptized & about 8 years old.

Negroe Bridget a Son James, then about 6 years old.

Negroe Bridget a Son Thom, then about 2 years old.

Negro Bridget a Daughter named Jean then about 9 moneths old.

N. B. The above 5 Negroes children & their Moyr all belong to Mr. David Ross and were all baptized at the parents desire the above date by me W. Douglas. p. 41.

PERSONAL FAMILY ENTRIES. p. 33

I, William Douglas, was born Aug: 3. 1708 in·ye Shire of Gallo-way, Parish of Penningham, Scotland, [In another handwriting] his mothers' name Grishild McKeand.

Nicholas Hunter, my excellent wife, was born Sep: 1715 in Niths-dale county, Glencairn Parish, Scotland, We were married Nov: 27. 1735.

We came to Virginia Oct: 6 1750. She was seized wt. a palsy Oct: 19 & died dec: 31. 1781 by 6 of ye clock Monday. She was a Sincere Christian on earth & most certainly is now a glorified Saint in heaven.

Apr: 2, 1737—Peggie Douglas was born. [Elsewhere recorded Tuesday Aug. 30 1737.]

Dec: 31 1760—Peggy Douglas was married to Nic. Merriwether. He died dec: 19.72, aged 36.

----v. 2 1761—Will: Douglas Merriwether was born, her oldest child.

Apl: 24 1763—Tho: Merriwether was born. her 2d child.

--n: 9. 65—Nic. Hunter Merriwether was born her 3d child.

Aug: 12. 66—Cha: Merriwether was born her 4th child.

Nov: 5 68—Francis Thornton Merriwether was born her 5th child.

Feb: 24 71. Elizabeth Merriwether was born her 6th child.

Feb: 20 83—Peggie Douglas was married to Chiles Tyrril.

Sep: 8- 84—Chiles Tyrril & Mary Douglas had a son called Ja: Hunter her 7th child.

My Fayr Will: Douglas died aged 77.

My Moyr Grishild McKeand died aged 70.

My sister Mary Douglas died aged 21 maried.

My sister Janet Douglas died aged 20 unmaried.

Nov: 1. 61—My Broyr John: died aged 64. left 6 children viz: 5 boys & one girl.

May 12 63—My Broyr. Ja: Douglas died aged 52. left 6 chil-dren, 2 sons & 4 girls.

June 15 59—My sister Elizabeth died aged 47½ [In another hand-writing:] she was the wife of ....Heron[?]

Aug: 21 59—My wifes cousin Dr. Jo: Hunter died. Single.

----ch. 2 66—My wifes Broyr. Dr. Will: Hunter died aged 33. Single.

Dec: 16 71—My wifes Fayr. died aged 84.

Feb: 15 58—My wifes Broyr Ja: Hunter died.

1703—My sister Mary Douglas was born.............& died May 1786.

Jan: 27. 81—Lady Cossencarry died aged 90, whose son I tutored 2 years.

Sep. 3 83—Her son, My Pupil, died Geo: Muir Esq: principal Clerk of Justiciary.

Apl: 10 66—My wifes Uncle Hunter of Lochrinney died.

Apr: 66—My wifes Aunt Mary Hunter died.

Mar: 9 64—My wifes sister Eliz: died & left 6 children, Agnes, Marg: Nic: & Eliz:

Nov: ---5—My wifes Uncle Will: Hunter died aged 77 had never a child.

Dec: 28 ....—My wifes Uncle Mr. Rob: Hunter died aged 86. Never married.

.... 47—Broyr James' Betty was born.

.... 48—Broyr James' Matty was born.

May 12 51—Broyr James' William was born.

.... 55—Broyr James' Jeanie was born.

June 28 56—My broyr James' son James was born.

Mar: 20 59—Broyr James' Peggie was born.

Broyr John's Son William was born.

Broyr Johns' Son James was born.

Broyr Johns' Son George was born.

.... 57—Broyr Johns' daughter Peggie was born.

60—Broyr Johns' son Samuel was born.

78—Broyr. Johns' widow Martha Heron died.

79—Broyr Johns' Peggie had a child Bettie.

81—Do......................anoyr. daughter called Douglas.

63—Niece Laurie had a Daughter Lydia born Agst. 29 1763.

1780—My Broyr in law Geo. McCrae died. p. 34.

1775—My niece Margaret Laurie was married to McMillan of Barwhinnock, worth 300£ a year. p. 21.

1782—My niece Mary Laurie was married to Rev: Mr. McWhay of St: Quibbox. p. 21.

1780—My Broyr. p. 21.

1784 -Dec:—Geo: Douglas in New York & Mary Carne aged 21 were married. p. 21.

My Peggie was married to Chiles Tyrril feb: 20 '83. p. 22.

1783 Feb: 20—Chiles Tyrell & my Peggie were married. p. 28.

1786. May—Marg: Douglas my sister in Galloway died aged 84. p. 38.

p. 146.

Descendants of Parson Douglas's Brother, JAMES.
Betty.
Molly.
William, married a Selden and died without issue.
Jeanie.
James, died a bachelor.
Peggy.

Mrs. G. D. & her daughters M. & H. arrived at James H. Terrell's on Thursday 11th of November 1824 & departed after a most heartfelt visit to their newly discovered cousins—the descendants of Parson Douglas, departed for Jas. Madison's 13th same month.

(signed) Harriet Douglas, the humble instrument under Providence of discovering this branch of the Family tree.

(Note in lead pencil) Jas. Madison born March 16 1751.

Jas. Madison died June 28 1836.

He was 73 yrs. in 1824 & 85 when he died.

p. 147.

An Account by Harriet Douglas of New York of the Children of Parson Douglas' brother John as put down by him in P. 33.

WILLIAM DOUGLAS died a Baronet in 1809 after founding a Castle in Kivenbright instead of a family.

James Douglas died at Orchardton April 1821 leaving William Douglas; Sarah, Mary & Matilda.

W. D. of Alnierness died a bachelor three months after his Father. Sarah married Col. Maxwell, no children, which will deprive them of the intailed Estate of Gretna Green willed by her father to her eldest son. Mary married William Rose Robinson, S'hriff of Lanerkshire. They have six children. Matilda married to William Maitland of Dalskeith.

John Douglas died a Bacheloe at the age of nineteen.

George Douglas died at the age of 50 leaving six children; the eldest Elizabeth died at 14 ten minutes after him. George, William, Margaret, Harriet & Elizabeth Mary all single but the last who married in 1822 to James Monroe Jr. of Albemarle Virginia. Their son Douglas Monroe was born 7 April 1823 & their daughter Frances the 14 do 1824.

Margaret Haffie died in 1898 leaving two daughters, Elizabeth who married at the instigation of her uncle, Sir William, & at his Castle, Adam Thomson Mims, a gentle man much older who left her a widow in 1822. Margaret D. Haffie married at the Castle Mr. Brown of Liverpool who died in 1823 leaving her the mother of two sons Douglas & George.

Samuel Douglas died 14 April 1824 leaving a daughter Mrs. Abercromby who has 5 daughters and one son—called for its two grandfathers George.............................

p. 149.

Aunt Peggie Douglas McCrae Her husband George McCrae died 1780.*

Loose Memo. in Register, made by Mr. Robt. Lewis.

Memorandum furnished me at Farmington, Albemarle Co. Va. by
Marcia Louise Margaret Meriwether, wife of Charles James Meri-
wether, d. of .... Miller of Goochland & ....
Guerrant.

Grandfather was Heath Jones Miller, Lickinghole Church.

Charles J. Meriwether was son of Capt. Wm. Douglas Meriwether
of Cloverfields, Albemarle county, Va., who was son of Nicholas Meriwether & Peggy Douglas; son of David; son of Thomas; son of
Nicholas, first of his name in America.

Two brothers Meriwether, buried on a knoll near the eastern end
of the Free Bridge over the Rivanna.

Marcia Louise Margaret Meriwether & her husband Chas. J., vis-
ited the three great-nieces of Parson Douglas of Virginia, daughters of
Sir William Douglas of Castle Douglas, near Firth of Solway, viz:
Mrs. Maitland of Castle Douglas; Mrs. Maxwell of Orchardton and
Mrs. Robinson, all widows. The address of Mrs. Maitland was c/o
Sir William Douglas, Douglas Castle, Castle Douglas, Douglas Arms.
(This was probably the nephew taught by Parson Douglas, who re-
turned to Scotland & inherited a title. The ladies acknowledged them
as cousins. Reference was made to their ages recorded in Goochland
Parish register in possession now of Robert W. Lewis, which record
was made by Harriet Douglas in 1824 at Music Hall.

p. 128.

Anectdotes of my own family

Sep: 21.57—Doctor Jo: Hunter another physician came to lodge
wt me.

Aug: 21.59—Doctor Hunter died a young man.

Nov: 2. 61—My grandson Billie Douglas was born.

Jan: 25 63—Dr. Will: Hunter arrived here, an eminent physician.

Oct: 2 66—The excellent Dr. Will: Hunter died a young man.

Feb: 5 64—Preached at Beaver Dam.

Jan: 9 65—My grandson Nic: Hunter Meriwether was born.

June 5 69—Mr. Alex: McCawl sailed from Richmond.

Feb: 24 71—Betty Merriwether was born.

Dec. 18 71—I bought Goldmine of Landie Richardson.

year 69—I made tobacco at Fork creek by 4 hands 4196.

Dec: 19 72—Mr. Nic: Merriwether my son in law died aged.

Ap: 18. 74—I bought Lickinghole plantation of Mr. Temple.

---

*Pencil note: Their daughter maried a Lanie who left a daughter Lydia who married
Charles Meriwether.

p. 130—

Sep: 5 1777—Mr. Douglas was voted by Vestry out of his Parish of Goochland against the will of almost the whole parish & ye laws, both of God and man, after having served ye parish most acceptably as minister above 27 years & Manikentown 19 years at ye same time & Buckingham county 4 years, all most acceptably & what is a scandal to be heard in a Christian country, his old parish is now prosecuting him for ye repairs of ye glebe out of wch they had driven him 12 or 14 years agoe & had deprived him of ye benefit of them. Oh! Tempora! Oh Mores!

Will: Douglas.

Mar. 9 1795—Mrs Nancie Tyrrel died aged 70. p. 46.

Jul. 12. 1793—Col. Beverly Winslow died aged 60. p. 45.

Aug. 15 1788—Mr. Jo. Bevens in Orange died aged 74. p. 38.

Aprile 14 1771—Mr. Sam Gordon Mercht. in Blandford died. p. 38.

Oct. 10 1787—Ja. Buchanan died in Richmond. p. 38.

1786—Rev. Alex. Gordon at Petersburg died. p. 38.

Mr. Will: Monroes family on Potomack have come to nothing. p. 137.

Jan. 20 1758—Col. Turner & Harry Ashton died last fall. p. 39.

1788—Dr. Ja. Bankhead died, he had 6 children, 3 sons & 3 daughters. The two oldest, ye eldest a Doctor died about 3 years agoe, leaving 2 children and a daughter. The 2nd James died about 3 years agoe, leaving 3 children. The 3d son, John is still alive. Of his daughters one married Mr. Rob. Talliferrar and has 8 children. The second Elizabeth maried to Peter Thornton and is now a widow wt. 4 children. The 3d Martha about 36 years old is still single. p. 137.

Jan. 24 1785—R more from Jesse Grubs 2 Silver Dollars. p. 20.

1757—Capt. Rich. Henry Lee to Miss Elliot Col. Washington's Sisterinlaw. p. 20.

1757—Tho. Jett married then to Mrs. Vaulx. p. 20.

1767—Sir Rob. Lawries eldest son to Lord Rutherfords eldest daughter. p. 20.

Sep. .... 1787—Will. Black & Jeanie Douglas in Kilsture were married—both in Scotland. p. 25.

May 4 1788—The Earl of Glasgow to Lady Ann Hay daughter to ye Earl of Errol not by me. p. 25.

MISCELLANEOUS MEMORANDA

(Miscellaneous Memoranda made by Rev. Wm. Douglas)

p. 29.

JOHN SIMPSON, professor of Divinity of Glasgow died January 1740.

July 1 1749—Mr. Rob: Jardine Minr. of Glencairn died.

June 16 1752—Col: Will: Maxwell of Cardoness, aged 95.

History of Jacque le Fevre, Grelincourt Vol: 3.48. age 100.

History of Le Duc de la Force who died in 1652 aged 94, Drelin: 53 Vol: 3.

History of Mr. Moulin aged 90 who died in 1658, page 53 Drelin: Vol: 3.

p. 30.

.... died, being burnt ....

Feb: 14 1540—Martin Luther died aged 63.

May 27 1564—Jo: Calvin died aged 55.

Feb: 18 1687—Mary of Scotland died, beheaded, aged 45.

Oct: 23. 1605—Theodore Beza died aged 86.

Jan: 9. 1649—King Charles 1st beheaded.

Nov: 24 1572—Jo: Knox died aged 62.

Mar: 21 1655—Mr. Usher died aged 85.

Dec: 8 1691—Mr. Baxter died aged 76.

Nov: 25 1748—Dr. Watts died aged 75.

Mar: 28 1661—Mr. Rutherford died.

June 1658—Mr. Durham died.

June 1 1661—Mr. Guthrie executed.

May 27 1661—Argyle was beheaded.

Jan: 26 1686—Mr. Pedin died aged 60.

Sep: 28 1687—Mr. Francis Turretin died aged 63 yrs. 11 months 17 days—a great man.

Oct. 22 1708—Dr. Herman Witsius died aged 72: 8: 10 days.

1726—Mr. Whitby died aged 88.

1724—Mr. Will: Woolaston died aged 65.

Sep: 3. 1658—Oliver Cromwel died aged 59.

Oct: 24 1703—Mr. Will: Burkit died aged 53. yrs. 3 m.

Mar: 10 1658—Peter du Moulin died aged 90.

Sep: 23 1712—Mr. Tho: Halyburton died aged 37 yrs. 9 m.

June 4 1752—Mr. Rich: Burnham died aged 41.

Nov: 22. 1761—Dr. Jo: Guyse died aged 81.

Ap: 22. 1785—Dr. Tho: Gibbons died aged 87.

Feb: 4. 1761—Mr. Sam: Davis died aged 36.

Aug: 27. 1758—Dr. Ben: Grosvenor died aged 83.

Aug: 28. 1645—Grotius died 71 :4 months—his age. "Be serious" was his last advice.

Aug: 11 1786—Frederick King of Prussia died aged 74.

1622—Dr. David Parcus died aged 74. an eminent Divine & Writer.

Oct: 28 1704—Mr. Jo: Lock ye Philosopher died aged 73.

Mar: 17. 1715—Bishop Gil: Burnet died aged 72.

1713—Archbishop Sharp died aged 69.

Aug: 4. 1723—Mr. Will: Fleetwood died aged 67.

Dec. .... 1732—Mr. Jo: Gay, ye Poet died.

Nov: 15 1632—Gustavus Adolphus was Slain aged 38.

Mar: 26. 1729—Mr. Rob: Moss died aged 63.

Mar: 20 1726—Sir Is: Newton died aged 85.

1718—Will: Penn ye Quakers Bulwark died aged 74.

Jan: 28 1725—Czar Peter ye Great of Moscovy died Aged 53.

Feb: 1695—Mr. Jo: Scot author of ye Xtian life died aged 57.

Dec: 4. 1779—Mr. Tho: Hobbs died, aged 91.

June 20. 1743—Mr. Geo: Keysler a notable traveller died aged 55.

Aug: 25 1776—Mr. Da: Hume ye Historian died a meer Sceptist.

1724—Mr. Will: Woollaston an eminent Writer died aged 65.

1658—Mr. Ja: Durham, Minr. of Glasgow died aged 36.

June 26 1691—Mr. Jo: Flavel a great writer died aged 64.

1671—Mr. Tho: Vincent died.

Feb: 7. 1716—Dr. Dan: Williams died aged 72.

Oct: 29 1720—The great Mr. Will: Dunlap died aged 28.

Apr. 17. 1790—Benjamin Franklin of Philadelphia Esqr. & L. L. Dr. died aged 84. p. 35.

Feb. 20 1790—Joseph 2d Emperor of Germany died. p. 35.

Nov. 2 1726—Princess of Zell Spouse to King George ye first died aged. p. 35.

(17)85—Dr. Geo. Wishart died aged 83 a flaming preacher in his youth. p. 35.

Jan. 25 (17)84—Dr. Alexr. Webster of Edinr died aged 76 my colledge fellow. p. 35.

Feb. .... 1761—Revnd Mr. Sam Davis died aged 37. p. 38.

Jan. 2 1788—Ch. Wesley his broyr died aged 80. p. 38.

Nov. 1788—Jo. Wesley yet alive aged 86. he died Mar. 2 (178)9. p. 38.

June 28 1788—The Rev. Mr. Adam Gibb an eminent associate Minr. in Scotland died at Edinburgh aged 75. p. 38.

Oct. 3 1788—Mr. Tho. Burrows died aged 66.   p. 38.

Jan. .... 1788—Jo. McKeand Ackerside my old Schoolmaster died aged 82. p. 38.

Dec. 3 1785—Dr. Will. Leechman professor of Divinity in Glasgow died. p. 38.

Dec. 3 1785—Will. Leechman of Glasgow died aged 79. p. 39.

Mar. 2 1735—Master Ja. Murrary Minr of Penpont died aged 63 now in heaven. p. 39.

May 12. 1753—Pricll Will. Wishart at Ednr. died. p. 44.

June 12. ......85—Dr. Geo. Wishart of Edinr. died 83. p. 44.

Oct. 10 1665—Mr. Will Guthrie Minr of Finwick died aged 45. p. 44.

May 8. ....66—Dr. Sam. Chandler of London died aged 73. p. 44.

June 4 ....44—Rev. Mr. Kirby Reyner of Bristol died. p. 44.

May .... 1683—Dr. Ben. Whichcote Rector of St Laurence died aged 74. p. 44.

Jan. 25 ....84—Dr Alexr Webster of Edinr. died aged 76. p. 44.

June 1. 1661—Rev. Mr Ja. Guthrie of Stirling was executed for ye truth age. p. 44.

Nov. 24. 1572—Rev. Jo. Knox of Edinr. aged 62 an eminent Reformer died. p. 44.

June .... 1658—Rev. Mr. Ja. Durham of Glasgow died. p. 44.

Jan. 26 1686—Rev. Mr. Alexr. Peden of Glenluce died aged 60. p. 44.

1770—Rev. Mr. Ja. Dickson New Luce & Mr. Henderson of Portpatrick. p. 44.

Ap. 5 ......61—Rev. Mr. Alexr. Robison of Tinwald aged 87 died. p. 44.

Jul. 17 ....61—Bishop Sherlock of London died aged ....ordained Rev. Wm. Douglas. p. 44.

Mar. 26 ....29—Rev. Rob. Moss Dean of Ely died aged 63. p. 44.

1713—Archbishop Jo. Sharf died. p. 44.

June 26 1691—Rev. Mr. Jo. Flavel of Exeter died aged 64. p. 44.

Mar. 22 ....54—Rev. Mr. Sam. Bourn died aged 65 of Birmingham. p. 44.

Ap. 22 ....85—Rev. Dr. Tho. Gibbons of London died aged 87. p. 44.

Nov. 22 ....61—Dr. Jo. Guyse of London died aged 81. p. 44.

....26—Dr. Dan. Whibby Rector of Salisbury died aged 88. p. 44.

Feb. 4. ....61—Rev. Sam. Davis of Provincetown died aged 36. p. 44.

Jan. 23 ....72—Rev. Mr. Will. Moodie of Glencairn died. p. 44.

Jan. 28 ....55—Rev. Mr. Isaac Kimber of London died aged 62. p. 44.

Mar. 21. 1655—Archbishop Ja. Usher died aged 85. died. p. 44.

May 27 1564—Rev. John Calvin aged 55 died. p. 44.

Oct. 13. 1605—Theodore Beza aged 86 died. p. 44.

p. 45.

Mar: 1661—Mr. Samuel Rutherfoord died.

June 15th 1769—Mr. William Hamilton Minister of Douglas died.

1658—Mr. James Durham died aged 36.

Feb: 7th 1758—Doctr. Jos: Stennet died aged 66.

June 20 1743—Mr. Jno. Keysler died aged 55.

June 2d 1772—Mr. Jno. Robertson Mins of Alyth died aged 64.
Next day Mrs. Robertson his wife died.
July 17th 1786—Mr. William Notcut died aged 85.
Mar: 9 1770—Mr. William Guthry died aged 62.
Dec: 31 1731—Revd. Mr Jno. Hurrison died aged 56.
Jan: 26 1713—Revd. Daniel Burgess died aged 67.
Mar: 14 1759—Revd. Risdon Darracot died aged 43.
Apl: 19 1560—Melancton died aged 63.
Feb: 18 1546—Mr. Luther died aged 63.
Dec. 8 1691—Revd. Richard Baxter died aged 76.
June 24 1696—Revd. Philip Henry died aged 65.
June 26 1714—Revd. Matthew Henry his son died aged 52.
Sepr. 28th 1687—Revd. Francis Turretine died aged 63.
Sepr. 10th 1759—Revd. Tho: Bradbury died aged 82.
Octr: 22d 1708—Revd. Harmen Witsius died aged 83.
Sepr. 8 1756—Bishop Hall died aged 82.
Aug: 3 1768—Bishop Secker died aged 75.
Sepr: 18th 1788—Revd. Ebenezer Stott died aged.
July 16 1757—Mr. Maitland the Historian died.
Aug: 28 1788—Revd. Chs. Wesley Methodist died.
Mar: 2 1791—Revd. Jno. Wesley died. his brother.
Sepr. 30 1770—Mr. Geo: Whitefield died aged 56.
Feb: 13 1767—Mr. Tho: Boston relief Minsr died.
May 30 1766—Doctr. Jno. Jardine Minr. in Edinh. died.
Sepr. 27 1766—Jean Drummond Jno. Jardines widow died.
July 9 1778—Jno: Jas: Rouseau died aged 72.
Jan: 25 1784—Dr. Alexr. Webster Minr. died aged 76.
Nov: 5 1753—Dr. Jas: Foster died aged 56.
June 17 1754—Mr. David Brown Minr. of Port Glasgow died.
Apl. 3 1760—Dr. Jas. Winslow Anatomist died aged 92.
Decr: 25 1758—Mr. Jas. Hervey of Weston Favel died aged 45.
Apl. 17th 1761—Mr. Ben: Hoadly Bishop of Winchester died.
July 17 1761—Dr. Tho: Sherloch Bishop of London died.
Nov: 22 1761—Dr. Jno Guyse a dissent: Minr died aged 81.

p. 46.

Dec: 29 1717—Mrs Dorcas Billinsly died.
May 13 1722—R: Mr Jo: Billingsly her husband died.
Oct: 8 1781—Mrs Mary Wesly Jo: Wesleys wife died aged 71.

p. 131.

List of Scots & British Kings from James ye First of Scotla.id.

Feb: 21 1436—James 1, died aged 44.
Aug: 3 1460—James 2, died aged 30.
June 11 1487—James 3 died aged 35.
Sep: 9 1513—James 4 died aged 41.

Dec: 23 1587—James 5 died aged 30.

Feb: 8 1587—Queen Mary was beheaded aged 45.

Mar: 27 1625—James 6 died aged 59.

Jan: 30 1649—Charles I, was beheaded aged 49.

Sep: 3 1658—Oliver Cromwell died aged 60.

Feb: 6 1685—Charles 2 died aged 54.

Sep: 6 1701—King James 7 died aged 66.

Mar: 8 1702—King William died aged 51 yrs. 4 mos. 4 ds.

Aug: 1. 1714—Queen Ann died aged 50.

Dec: 28 1694—Queen Mary died aged 33.

1694—Archbishop Tillotson died aged 65.

June 11 1727—King George died aged.

Oct: 25 1760—King George died aged 77.

Nov: 20 1737—Queen Caroline died aged 55.

Oct: 12 1753—Prince Frederick of Denmark born ye old King.

Jan: 18. 1749—King of Denmark Christian 6 was born his son.

Jul: 22 1751—Caroline Matilda Queen of Denmark was born & died May 10 '75.

Nov: 30 1719—Augusta Princess of Wales was born & died feb: 3 1772 aged 52.

Ap: 27 1736—She was maried to Frederick Prince of Wales aged 17.

Mar: 20 1751—Frederick Prince of Wales died & left issue as follows:

Aug. 11 1737—Augusta maried to ye prince of Brunswick Jan. 16 1764.

June 4 1738—Her son George ye third born.

Aug. 11 1737—Her daughter Augusta was born Maried to ye Prince of Brunswick.

Mar: 14 1739—Edward Duke of York was born & died Sep: 1767.

Dec. 30: 1740—Eliz: Caroline was born & died Sep: 4 1750.

Nov. 14: 1743—Will: Henry Duke of Gloucester was born.

Oct: 17 1745—Henry Frederick Duke of Cumberland was born.

Mch. 8 1749—Louisa Ann was born & died May 13 1768.

May 13 1750—Frederick William was born & died dec: 29 1765.

Jul: 11. 1751—Caroline Matilda was born & died in exile May 10 1775.

1722—Dr. Will: Robertson was born, author of Lewis ye 5th of Spain's history.

Mar: 24 1603—Queen Elizabeth died aged 70.

Aug: 1 1714—Queen Ann died aged 50.

Nov: 20 1737—Queen Caroline died aged 55.

Dec: 28 1694—Queen Mary a pious Christian died aged 33.

Sep: 10 1662—Mr. Rich: Baxter & Mary Charleton were maried.

June 14 1681—Mrs. Baxter a most pious woman died.

Nov: 17 1558—persecuting Mary of England died aged.

Oct: 31 1735—Mrs. Housman died.

June 4 1752—Mr. Rich: Burnham died aged 41.
May 3 1679—Archbishop Sharp was slain.
1415—John Huss one of ye first reformers was burnt.
Dec: 13 1788—Charles 3d King of Spain died aged 73.
Dec. 28 1694—King Williams wife Queen Mary died aged 33.
Sep. 28 1688—Francis Turretine, Divinity Professor at Geneva died aged 67.
Sep: 4 1719—Queen Julia Maria of Denmark was born & maried in 1752.

p. 132.
Oct: 25. 1760—King George 2d died aged 77.
Sep. 8. 61—King George 3d maries Charlote princess of Meckingburg Strelitz born 19 May '44.
Aug: 12 62—Prince of Wales born, George Augustus Frederick.
Aug: 16. 63—Prince Frederick born, Elected Bishop of Osnaburg
.... 64—Royal Family of Britain &c.
Aug: 21. 65—Prince William Henry born.
Sep: 29 66—Princess Charlote Augusta Matilda born.
Nov: 2. 67—Prince Edward was born.
Nov: 8. 68—Augusta Sophia was born.
May 22 70—Princess Elizabeth was born.
June 5 71—Prince Ernest Augustus was born.
Jan: 27. 73—Augustus Frederick was born.
Feb: 24. 74—Adolphus Frederick was born.
Dec: 20. 78—Queen of France bore Maria Theresa Charlotte.
Ap: 25. 76—Princess Mary was born.
Nov: 4 77—Princess Sophia was born.
Feb: 23 79—Prince Octavius was born. May 3 '83 he died aged 3.
Sep: 22 1780—Prince Alphred died Aug: 20, 83.
Oct: 22 81—Queen of France bore a Prince.
Jul: 2 1752—Frederick King of Denmark maried to Princess of Brunswick.
Aug: 7 83—Princess Amelia born.
Oct: 12 63—Frederick King of Denmark has a son Frederick.
Jan: 14 66—Frederick King of Denmark died aged 43.
Oct: 4 66—Christian King of Denmark was maried to Princess Caroline Matilda born Jul. 22. 51.
Jan: 28 68—Queen of Denmark delivered of Prince Frederick.
Aug. 12 68—King of Denmark lands at Dover returns home Oct: 8.
June 71—Queen of Denmark bore Princess.
Jan: 17 72—Queen of Denmark sent to prison.
Aug: 12 72—Queen of Denmark leaves Denmark.
May 10 75—Queen of Denmark dies in exile aged 24.
Feb: 2 69—Pope Clement 13 is dead aged 75.
Sep: 21 74—Pope Clement 14 died aged 69.
May 10 74—King Lewis 15 of France died aged 64.

Feb: 8 72—Princess of Wales Moyr. to King George died aged 53.

Ap: 26 78—Catherine Grand Duchess of Russia died.

July 78—Grand Duke and Princess of Wirtemburg were maried.

Jan: 5. 62—Elizabeth Empress of Russia died aged 57.

July 11 44—Peter the 3 & Princess Catherine Alexeuna of Anhalt Zerbst were maried.

Oct 1 54—Peter 3d & Catherine Alexiena had Paul Petroville.

Jan: 5 62—Peter 3d succeeded to be Emperor; The Empress 33 years old.

Jul: 9 62—Peter 3 dethroned by his wife & murdered Jul: 17 1762.

June 6 1509—Jo: Calvin one of ye great reformers of ye Church was born at Noyon in Picardy and died May 27 1564 aged 55.

Feb: 16 1495—Philip Melancthon anoyr great Reformer was born at Bretton in ye Palatine & died Ap: 19. 1560 aged 64.

Martin Luther anoyr reformer died in 1546 being born 1483, aged 63.

Theodore Beza one of ye principal pillars of ye reformed church in 1703 aged 86 being born in 1619.

July 17 1756—Rev: Will: Notcutt, Minr. at Ipswich died aged 84.

Nov: 24 1572—Mr. Jo: Knox died aged 62.

Oct: 24 1703—Mr: Will: Burkit died aged 53.

Dec: 22 1666—Mr: Hugh McKail was executed for ye truth aged 26.

Sep: 23 1712—Mr: Tho: Halyburton died aged 38.

p. 134.

July 12 1536—Erasmus died aged 69.

Dec: 1732—Mr. Jo: Gay ye famous poet died.

Nov: 15. 1632—Gustavus Adolphus of Sweden was killed age 33.

Sep: 15 1656—Bishop Joseph Hall died aged 82½.

May 12. 1788—Prince Lewis of Brunswick died suddenly aged 70.

Oct: 11. 1771—Frederick ye King of Denmarks half brother by Queen Juliana then completed his 18th year.

Sep: 4. 19—Queen Julia Maria of Denmark was born.

52—She maried Frederick King of Denmark.

Oct: 12. 53—Her son Frederick was born.

Jan: 18. 49—Christian King of Denmark was born.

July 22. 51—Carolina Matilda Queen of Denmark was born.

June 27. 1682—Charles 12 of Sweden was born.

Oct: 1718—Charles 12 of Sweden was killed aged 36½.

Nov. 15 1632—Gustavus Adolphus of Sweden was killed aged 38.

Feb: 10 1763—Mr. Hen. Miles d. d. died aged 65.

Feb: 10. 1763—Mr. Jo. Mason, M: A: died aged 58.

Oct: 27. 1722—Revnd. Mr. Will Lorimer died aged 82.

Oct: 22. 1727—Rev. Jo. Nesbit died aged 67.

June 13. 1733—Rev. Daniel Mayo died.

Oct: 26. 1751—Dr. Doddrige died aged 50 preached by Job Orton his fun. ser.

Mar: 2. 1752—Mrs. Mary Slater died aged 30 preached by Mr. Amory fun. ser.

Sep: 16 1762—Mr. Da. Jennings d: d: died aged.

Ap: 28 1760—Rob: Tilling was executed. An eminent convert; his fun: ser: preached by Rev: Jo: Stevens.

Jul: 10 1762—Rev: Jo: Auther died aged 74 preached by Mr. Wallin.

June 9. 1572—Joan Queen of Navarre died aged 44 an eminent christian.

Jan: 7 1651—Dr And: Rivet died.

Mar: 25 1655—Archbishop Usher died aged 75.

June 1657—Mr. Jo: Janeway a pious Minr. died aged 24.

Mar: 10. 1658—Pet: de Moulin an eminent Minr. died aged 90.

May 27 1661—The noble Marquis of Argyle was unjustly beheaded.

June 5 1661—Mr. Ja. Guthrie a pious Minr. was hanged aged.

Aug: 28. 1645—The great statesman and scholar Grotius died aged 62.

Mar: 1 1661—Pious Mr. Sam: Rutherford died aged.

Feb: 19. 1671—Mr. Cha: Chancey a pious Minr. died aged 82, leaving six sons all Minrs. Isaac: Ichabod; Barabas; Nathaniel; Elnathan & Israel.

Feb: 1679—Dr. Tho. Goodwin died a renowned Minr. aged 80.

Ap: 26. 1682—Mr. Hen: Dorney a Minr., died aged 69.

Dec: 8. 1691— Mr. Rich: Baxter died aged 76 a firm protestant.

Jul: 25 1694—Pious Mr: Rob: Fleming died aged 64.

Ap: 2. 1705—Mr. Jo. Howe died aged 75.

Feb: 13. 28.—Dr. Cotton Mather died aged 65.

p. 127.

Mar. 23 1760—Will Dalyrymple of Waterside Esqr. died.

Apr. 9 1788—The Rev. Charles Wesley died lately aged 81 and his brother John now in perfect health at 86. They were ye original founders of ye rug sect of ye Methodists wh. have now branched out into innumerable Independent Congregations, each supporting its own Pastor. The meetings they have at London are supposed to contain more than all Churches put together.

p. 137.

Dec. 7 1542—Queen Mary of Scotland was born.

Feb. 8 1587—Mary is beheaded.

Mch 27 1625—King James 6 died aged 59.

Mch 24 1603—Queen Elizabeth died aged 70.

Jan. 30 1649—King Charles 1st was beheaded aged 48.

July 15 1685—Duke of Monmouth was beheaded aged 36.

Dec 28 1694—Mary King Williams Queen died aged 33.

Mar. 8 1702—King William died aged 51.

Sep. 6 1701—King James 7 died aged.

Nov. 11 1708—Prince George of Denmark husband to Queen Ann died aged 56.

Aug. 1 1714—Queen Ann died aged 50. daughter to King James 2.

June 8 1714—Princess Sophia of Hanover died aged 24.

A...... 24 1572—was ye General Massacre.

An instructive anecdote for more impressive on dying mortals who are going not to Cantuck but to a world of immortality, which I had from himself viz: I near Rich. Thomas formerly in my neighborhood.

Apl. 14 1761—Maried at Edinburgh Will: Earl of Sutherland aged 26 & Miss Mary Maxwell eldest daughter of Dr. Maxwell of Preston aged 21.

May 26 1764—Countess of Sutherland of a daughter.

June 1, 1766—Mary Maxwell Countess of Sutherland died aged 26.

June 16, 1766—William Earl of Sutherland died aged 31.

Their fine Epitaphs are in Scots Magazine 66.

Their eldest....................died an infant. p. 140.

Jan. 28, 1686—Mr. Alex. Peden died a non such Scots minister. p. 143.

p. 141.

Ages and deaths of several renowned old worthys famous for their holy useful writings & zeal for ye reformation.

1415—Jo: Huss was burnt.

1546—Mr Geo Wishart was burnt.

Feb: 18. 1546—Luther died aged 63.

May 27 1564—Calvin died aged 55.

1705—Theodore Beza died 86 born 1619.

Nov: 15. 1632—Gustavus Adolphus was slain aged 37.

Mar: 28. 1661—Mr Sam: Rutherford died.

June 1 1661—Mr. Ja: Guthrie suffered, an excellent Minr.

Mar: 21 1655—Mr. Ja: Usher died.

Dec: 8. 1691—Mr. Rich: Baxter died aged 76.

Nov: 22 1694—Dr. Jo: Tillotson died aged 65.

Dec: 28. 1694—Queen Mary wife to King William died aged 33.

Dec. 22. 1666—Mr. Hugh McKail suffered aged 26.

Ap: 2 1705—Mr. Jo: Howe died aged 75.

Sep: 23 1712—Mr. Tho: Halyburton died aged 38.

Nov. 25. 1748—Mr. Isaac Watts died aged 75.

Oct: 31 1735—Mrs Houseman died aged.

Mar: 22 1754—Mr. Sam: Bourn died aged 65.

Jul: 17 1756—Mr. Will: Notcut died aged 84.

Feb: 7 1758—Dr Joseph Stennit died aged 65.

Aug: 27 1758—Dr. Geo: Grosvenor died aged 83.

Jan: 2 1761—Mr. Innes Pearse died aged 62.

June 17 1768—Dr Nath: Lardner died aged.

Oct: 9 1729—Sir Rich: Blackmore died aged 76.

Ap: 19 1560—Philip Melankton died aged 64.
Ap. 22 1785—Dr. Tho: Gibbons died aged.
Jul: 14 1699—Dr. Will: Bates died aged 74.
Feb: 10 1763—Mr. Jo: Mason died aged 63.
May 20 1755—Mr Will: May died aged 49.
Nov 1572—Mr. Jo: Knox died aged 67.
Feb: 4 1761—Mr. Sam: Davis died aged 36.
Sep: 30 1770—Mr. Whitefield died aged 56.
Nov: 5 1753—Dr. Ja: Foster died aged 56.
Oct: 29 1720—Mr. Will: Dunlap died aged 28.
Jul: 17 1761—Dr. Thomas Sherlock, Bishop of London died, aged 82. (Ordained Parson Douglas).
June 17 1768—Dr. Nath: Lardner died aged.
Nov: 22 1761—Dr Jo: Guyse died aged 81.
June 27 1777—Dr Will: Dodd suffered at Edinb. aged 49.
May 8 1766—Dr Sam: Chandler died aged 73.
Sep: 8 1656—Dr. Joseph Hall, Bishop of Norwich died aged 82.
Feb .... 1695—Mr. Jo: Scot died aged 57.
Aug 25 1776—Mr. David Hume died an Historian.
Mar: 9 1770—Will: Guthrie Esqr., the Historian died aged 62.

WILL OF REUBEN SKILTON.

In the name of God Amen.   I Reu: Skilton of Goochland County make this my last will & testament in manner following first I devise that all my Just debts be paid out of my Estate by the Executor hereinafter mentioned.   Item I give & devise unto my dear wife Elizabeth my whole Estate both real & personal to her & her heirs forever.   But in case I should survive my said wife, & not have any knowledge of her death as I intend for Great Brittain, whereby my Estate would descend according to the Rules of Law to my elder Brother, whom I do not intend to prefer.   In such case I give & devise my whole estate both real & personal to my younger Broyr & his Heirs forever.   Item I hereby apoint my friend Colo Will: Randolph my whole & sole Executor hereby revoking all other Wills by me heretofore made.   In witness whereof I have hereunto Set my hand and ,affixed my Seal this 15 day of May 1759.

Reuben Skilton

Signed Published & declared
as his last Will & testament
in presence of us.

Note: This will seems not to have been executed, as the witnesses did not sign.

Reuben Skilton was Burgess from Goochland, 1759.

Pasted to the back of the Douglas Register.

KING WILLIAM PARISH, or "MANAKIN TOWN"
The Huguenot Settlement on the James River

While there had been, almost since the foundation of the Colony, many individual refugees who sought safety in the Colonies, those referred to in these notes were part of a body of some five hundred immigrants who came to Virginia in 1700 under the Marquis de la Muce, and who landed in this country in four successive debarkations. (Beverley's History of Virginia p. 244) (Baird, C.W., II, p. 177.)

"Three ministers of the Gospel and two physicians were among their number. The ministers were Claude Phillipe de Richebourg, Benjamin de Joux and Louis Latane. The physicians were Castaing and La Sosse.

"Among the ministers who served the Parish of King William (Manakin-Town) were the following: Benjamin de Joux until his death in 1704; Claude Phillipe de Richbourge, who removed to South Carolina in 1707; Jean Cairon, who died in 1716; Peter Fontaine 1720-1721; Francis Fontaine 1722-1724; William Finney, 1722 and later; William Murdaugh of St. James Northam, Goochland, and Zachariah Brooke of Hanover in 1727; Mr. Neirn 1727-1728; David Mossom, of St. Peters Parish, New Kent, 1727; Mr. Swift and Danl. Taylor of Blissland Parish, New Kent, 1728-1729; James Marye 1731-1735; Anthony Gavain 1739 and later; Rev. William Douglas from 1750 to 1777 and subsequently Rev. Mr. Hopkins of Goochland."

The above list is given by Dr. R. A. Brock in the introduction to his work on the Huguenot immigration to Virginia, in "Collections of the Virginia Historical Society," vol. V, published in 1886, from which most of these notes have been obtained.

As there were constant inter-marriages between the French Refugees and the colonist already in Virginia, the records as contained in the Douglas Register can be more readily understood when read in connection with the records of King William Parish, and for that reason they are included in this publication.

For a similar reason we are publishing an index which will give ready reference to the wills, inventories, estate divisions, marriage agreements, etc.

These notes are not claimed to be full and complete, but are only given as an aid to the better understanding of the various names which the Rev. William Douglas, like many other of our early scribes, has spelled as the fancy moved him. In some cases he has spelled the same name three or four different ways.

By way of an introduction to the whole subject the following extracts from Bishop William Meade's "Old Churches, Ministers and Families in Virginia", will prove of interest.

"This parish was originally in Henrico county, which extended thus far and beyond it on either side of James River. It is now in Powhatan county, whose name is taken from the ancient name of the river and the old King Powhatan. By Act of Assembly in 1790, it was assigned to the French refugees who were driven from their country by the persecutions of Louis XIV., and sought an asylum in Virginia as hundreds of thousands did in all the various countries of Protestant Christendom."

"As early as the year 1660 some few came over fleeing from the earlier persecutions. They were sufficient in number to induce an Act of Assembly granting them the privilege of citizens. Toward the close of the century some of them settled themselves on the Rappahannock. In the year 1790, so many had settled on the south side of the James River, in Henrico county (which was then on both sides of the river) that the Assembly passed an act giving them a large tract of land along the river as their possession, exempting them from all county and State taxes for seven years, and then extending the privilege indefinitely. They were required to support their own minister in their own way. Accordingly, in dividing the grant into farms, all running down to the river in narrow slips, a portion of the most valuable was set apart for the minister, and continued for a long time to be in the possession and use of the minister, while one was resident in the parish, and after that to be rented out and the proceeds paid for such occasional services as were rendered by neighbouring ministers. At length, as it could not be seized and alienated by the act for selling glebes, it got into private hands, and has thus been held for many years. * * * * * I mention the names of those families still remaining in Virginia who derive their descent from the Huguenots. From information obtained from books and from individuals, they are as follows: Marye, Fontaine, Dupuy, Harris, Sublett, Watkins, Markham, Sully, Chasteen, Duvall, Bondurant, Flournoy, Potter, Michaux, Pemberton, Munford, Agie, Hatcher, Jacqueline, Bernard, Barraud, Latane, Moncure, Amouet, Chadouin, Dibrell, Farrar, Jeter, Jordan, Jouette, LeGrand, Ligon, Maupin, Maxey, Pasteur, Perrou, Thweatt, Maury, Boisseau, Fouche, Lanier, Le Neve. Concerning a few of these it may be questioned whether they be not of Welsh descent, while their are doubtless others who might be added."

"Goochland County was cut from Henrico in 1727. In the year 1744 the parish of St. James Northam, was restricted to the north side of the river, and that on the south side was called St. James Southam, both of them being in Goochland, which still lay on both sides of the river, and extended from Louisa line to Appomattox River. Albemarle county and Parish were also in this year taken from Goochland by a line from Louisa to the Appomattox. * * * * (The Rev. Anthony Gavin preceded Rev. Wm. Douglas as minister.)

"Immediately after his (Mr. Gavin's) death the Rev. Mr. Douglas was chosen. He entered on his duties in 1750. His history and character deserve some notice, and must be acceptable to his numerous and respectable descendants. They are gathered chiefly from a large register of baptisms, funerals, marriages, sermons, &c., interspersed with other notices, throwing some light upon the peculiarities which distinguished him. The Rev. William Douglass was from Scotland. In the year 1735 he married Miss Nicholas Hunter, by whom he had an only child,—a daughter named Margaret. In the year 1748 or 1749 leaving them behind, he came over as teacher in the family of Colonel Monroe of Westmoreland, father of President Monroe, who was one of his pupils, as was also Mr. Jefferson afterward, in Goochland. After some time, returning to England, he was ordained, and brought back his wife and daughter in the year 1750, and in the same year settled himself in Goochland. His daughter Margaret, whom he always called Peggy, married Mr. Nicholas Meriwether of Albemarle, and they were the ancestors of many of that name in Virginia. He brought with him or had sent to him, two nephews from Scotland, whom he adopted, educated, and called his children. He had a brother James, who settled in New York and left a numerous posterity there. Perhaps some of that name who have ministered in our Church may be his descendants. A few years since a Mr. George Douglass and two daughters from this family in New York paid a visit to Albemarle to see their relatives in that county, when a happy family meeting occurred. One of the adopted sons of Mr. Douglass (William) returned to Scotland and inherited a title. The other (James) went to New York and became a successful merchant. One of his daughters married James Monroe (the nephew and adopted son of President Monroe), who some years since represented the city of New York in Congress. After this biographical notice of himself and family, I return to his register, from which we learn some things concerning the early history of this parish nowhere else to be found. He states, as coming to him from good authority, that the church at Dover was undertaken by Mr. Thomas Mann Randolph in 1720; that it was finished in 1724 at a cost of fifty-four thousand nine hundred and ninety pounds of tobacco; that it was fifty by twenty-four feet in size that the Rev. Mr. Finnie was employed during these four years to preach once a month; that the Rev. Mr. Murdaugh was then received as a minister; that he was to preach the last Sunday in every month alternately at the plantation of Mr. Robert Carter, on the south side of James River, and of Major Bolling, on the northside of James River. We learn that in the year 1727 the Rev. Mr. Brooke preached once per month for them; and that in the same year the Rev. Mr. Beckett was received into the parish as a Minister. We learn also, from his diary kept in this register, that ministers were very scarce in the surrounding counties, so that Mr. Douglass had much to perform in the way of funerals, marriages, etc. He records one thousand and three hundred and eighty-three marriages, and four thousand and sixty nine baptisms. His views of doctrine and ministerial character may be seen from the favourable notice taken of Turretine, Doddridge, Walker, Hill and Whitefield, also of Showers Sacramental Discourses. In one of Doddridge's works—his Sermon to Young Men—he has written on a blank leaf these lines to his children:

"This, with all Doddridge's other writings, I leave as my best legacy to my dear children, to supply my deficiencies in your education, which I now sadly remember has been shamefully neglected. Part with none of his works for gold or silver, but let your children enjoy them, if you will not.

I am your loving father,
WILLIAM DOUGLASS."

To this I add an extract from a letter to one of his nephews, just married, not long before his death:—

"Industry, frugality, good contrivance, with the divine blessing, are the only scheme to make us happy for this world and another. That was your father's and grandfather's scheme; and oh, Billy and Martha, make it yours! Set up, by all means, the worship of God in your family; and let others about you do what they will, and heap up riches by every method, but as for you and your family, do you serve God. As for me, I am quite unfit for this world, and am daily waiting till my change come."

As to the time in which the churches were completed, with the exception of that at Dover, it is not easy to determine. The three churches at which Mr. Douglass officiated were Dover, Beaver Dam and Licking Hole. In the year 1777, after a ministry of twenty seven years, he resigned his charge, and settled on a farm in Louisa, where he spent the remainder of his years, which were not many."*

---

*NOTE: In this last statement the good Bishop was mistaken. as he lived until 1798, and entries appear in his hand writing in the Register until 1797, which show that he continued to act as a minister for over forty years from the time he entered the Parish in Goochland, or twenty years after he severed his connection with the vestry of Northam Parish. Furthermore he did not resign from St. James' Northam Parish—but was dismissed by his Vestry—See page 353 supra.

"A LIST OF YE FRENCH REFUGEES THAT ARE SET-TLED ATT YE MANNACHIN TOWN ARE AS FOLLOWS:

In ye first Shipp.

Mr. Phillip* (1) and his wife	2
Mr. Peter Chalin, his wife and 3 chil'n	5
Mr. Abrah. Nicod	1
Mr. Char. Saillee	1
Theph. Mallott and his wife	2
Gulte	1
Mullin	1
John ffarcy and his wife	2
Steph. Chastaine and his wife	2
Peter Tuly and his wife	2
John Joacmi and his wife	2
Minst and his wife	2
Gawey and his wife	2
Bilbun and his wife	2
ffaur, his brother and sister	3
Parcule and his wife	2
Leverre	1
Gillan	1
Voyer and his wife	2
Peter Gaway and his wife	2
John Saye	1
Pantier	1
Chambures and his wife	2
Morret and his wife	2
Peter Perry	1
Mallon, his wife and father	3
Brouse and one child	2
Corun	1
Cabarnis (now Cabiness) and wife	2
Imbart and his wife	2
Sasin	1
Vigue	1
Garrén	1
Chalagenie, his wife and one child	3
Debart	1
Bernard and his wife	2
Cath. Billet	1

*The full name of the minister thus modestly designated was Claude Phillipe de Riche-bourg. He was a relative of Isaac Porcher de Richebourg, the ancestor of a prominent Huguenot family of South Carolina, but being descended from the Counts of Richbourg, of St. Severe. Owing to disputes in his parish, which were referred to the Council of Virginia, September 2, 1707, M. Phillipe, with numerous followers, left Virginia, soon after this date, and settled in the Carolinas.

Sublet, his wife and four children.. 6
Moroll and his wife and one child... 3
Cocuelguic 1
Veras and his wife... 2
Isaac Verey 1
John Buffe, Du Clue, La Cadon.. 3
                                                                                                         ——
                                                                                                         81

The names of such as came in ye second ship:

Mr. Benj'n. De Joux... 1
Barel, his wife and one child.. 3
Govin, his wife and Joshua Pettit... 3
Alocastres, John Gunn and Timothy Russ... 3
Isaac Lefavour and his wife and Meshall... 3
John Owner and his wife, Gavand and his wife................................... 4
Remy and his wife, Gavand and his wife.. 4
Villam and his wife and Shabron.. 3
Abrate Befour, his wife and 4 children.. 6
Jasper Subus, his wife and 4 children.. 6
                                                                                                         ——
                                                                                                         35

All and every ye persons herein before mentioned are seated between ye creeks (except Duclow and Snadow) who came also in ye first ship and are settled on ye other side ye said creek.

And these that follow are likewise seated between ye said creeks but came in the third ship, (vizt.) :

Rapine, his wife and 2 children.. 4
ffran Benon and Gillaum... 2
Treyon, his wife and 1 child below ye creek.. 3
                                                                                                         ——
                                                                                                         9

The names of those y't came in ye fourth ship and are also settled between ye creeks:

Buffo, Shulo, and his wife and 3 children.. 6
Tumar and his wife, Chevas and 2 children... 5
Vallant, ffasant, John Pastour... 3
Mary Legraund 1
Robert, his wife and one child.. 3
Mocks, his wife and one child.. 3
Lamas 1
                                                                                                         ——
                                                                                                         23

A list of such as came in ye second and fourth shipps, and that are seated below ye creeks are as follows:

Greordocaso 1
Jno. Boshard, his wife and 3 children.. 5

Dan'l. Bluet and 2 children... 3
Pet'r Musset and his wife, and Misar Brock........................... 3
Jos. Oliver, Po. Leaseo, and Jno. Marsarae......................... 3
ffr'a. Clapy-and Legraund and 3 children............................. 5
Nicti Mar, his wife and 2 children....................................... 4
Sam'l Huntteeker, his wife and 2 children............................ 4
ffra Duacon, Anth. Bonion, and Provo................................. 3
Muller and 1 child... 2
Dufontaine, his wife and one child...................................... 3
Jasper Gardner, his wife and 3 children............................... 5
                                                                                      —
                                                                                      41

In ye fourth Shipp:

John Leroy, booker and his wife and one child..................... 4
Coullon and his wife... 2
                                                                                      —
                                                                                      6

below ye Creek:

Merchant Suillee, his wife and 2 children, and one negro woman.... 5
Anthony Obray between ye Creeks...................................... 1
                                                                                      —
                                                                                      6

These two persons last mentioned came from New York.
David Ministres and his wife not gone up falling creek............ 2
                                                                                      6
                                                                                      6
                                                                                      41
Nov. 10, 1701   23
   WM. BYRD   9
     Copia   35
      Testa   81
DIONISIUS WRIGHT   —
    Total...203

* * * * *

In 1715 the London Society for Promoting Christian knowledge
(Vol. V, p. 56) sent to Virginia:
  Philip Gouiran and Claude de Boire.

* * * * *

The Vestry of "Monacantown Parish" (Vol. V., p. 70)

Jacob Amonner	Jean Guerin	Pierre Chastain
Abra. Soblet	Jacque Lacaze	Jean Farcy
Jacques Brousse	Abra. Remy	Jean Foniuelle
Louis Outartre	Andre Aubry	Abra. Salle.

* * * * *

LISTE GENERALLE DE TOUS LES FRANCOIS PROTES-TANTS REFUGIES ESTABLYS DANS LA PAROISSE DU ROY GUILLAUME D'HENRICO EN VIRGINIA, Y COM-PRES LES FEMMES, ENFANS, VEUSES, ET ORPHELINS.

(From original Mss. as published by Wm. Stevens Perry, D.D. in "Papers Relating to the History of the Church in Virginia," A. D. 1650-1776. Privately printed 1870. The Mss. is undated but may be assigned to the period 1714.)

NOMS DES HOMMES	Femmes	ENFANS Garcons	Filles.	TOTAL
[1]Jean Cairon, Ministre	....	3	....	4
[2]Abraham Salle	....	5	1	7
Pierre Chastain	1	2	4	8
Charles Perault	1	1	3	6
Jean Forquerand	1	2	....	4
Anthoine Matton	1	5	....	7
Isaac Lesebure	1	1	3	6
Jacques Bilbaud	1	1	....	3
Jacob Amonnet	....	3	2	6
Michel Cantepie	1	....	....	2
Jean Voyé	1	2	2	6
Francois Dupuy	1	....	1	3
Daniel Guerrand	1	2	2	6
Barthelemy Dupuy	1	3	2	7
Jacques Sobler	1	1	1	4
Pierre Trauve	1	1	1	4
Mathieu Agé	1	....	....	2
Thomas Briaus	1	2	3	7
Jean Chastain	1	....	....	2
Francois De Clapie	1	....	2	4
Louis Sobler	1	1	....	3
Tho. D'allizon	1	....	....	2
Pre. Dutoit	1	....	2	4
Jean Calver	1	3	2	7
Jean Farcy	1	3	....	5
Estienne Chastain	1	....	....	2
Estienne Bonard	1	2	1	5
Abra. Sobler, lesué	....	....	....	1
Abra. Sobler, le jeune	1	....	....	2
Gedeon Chambon	1	1	....	3
Pre. Morisser	1	1	3	6
31	27	45	35	138

[1]Jean Cairon, né á Figeac, ci-cevant ministre de Cajarc dans la Haute Guyenne, was one of the French pastors who in 1688 had taken refuge in Zurich. (Baird, II, 145). His will is recorded in Henrico County Court, Feb. 1715 (1716)—Sons: Peter, Daniel, Isaac.
[2]His will probated Henrico county court, Mch. 1719 (1720).

FRANCOIS PROTESTANTS REFUGEES—*Continued*

NOMS DES HOMMES	Femmes	ENFANS Garcons	Filles.	TOTAL
Isaac Lafuitte	1	2	....	4
Jean Panetie	1	1	....	3
Jean Joanis	1	....	2	4
Jacq. Bioret	1	1	....	3
Jean Solaigre	1	1	....	3
Daniel Maubain	1	....	....	2
Isaac Parenteau	....	1	2	4
Andre Aubry	....	....	....	1
Gillaume Genin	1	....	....	2
Jean Fonuiele	1	1	....	3
Joseph Cailland	1	....	1	3
Joseph Bernard	....	....	....	1
David Bernard	1	4	1	7
Estienne Regnault	1	....	2	4
Pierre Oliver	....	....	....	1
Pierre Viet	....	....	....	1
Anthoine Giraudan	1	1	1	4
Jean Levillain	1	2	2	6
Jean Filhon	1	....	....	2
Abra. Michaux	1	4	6	12
Adam Vique	1	....	1	3
Abra. Remy	1	1	2	5
Anthoine Trabue	1	3	....	5
Jean Martin	1	3	1	6
Moize Leneveau	1	2	....	4
Jacob Cappon	1	....	....	2
Pierre Dalaunay	....	....	....	1
Francois Lassin	1	1	2	5
Jean Powell	1	2	....	4
Jean Dupre	1	....	1	3
Jean Gorner	....	....	....	1
Gaspard Gorner	1	1	....	3
Mathieu Bonsergent	....	....	....	1
[8]Jacques LeGrand	1	....	....	2
Pierre David	1	....	....	2
Claude Garry	1	....	....	2
Nicollas Souille	....	....	....	1
Anthoine Rapinne	1	....	1	3
Gillaume Martin	1	3	....	5
Pierre Deppe	....	....	....	1
40	30	34	25	129

[8]Will of James Le Grand, "late of La Haye, Holland," recorded in Henrico county court September 1716. Legal portion of his estate to his wife Elizabeth, residue to his brother John.

FRANCOIS PROTESTANTS REFUGEES—*Continued*

FEMMES VEUVES ET LEURS ENFANS	Femmes	ENFANS		TOTAL
		Garcons	Filles.	
Lavenne Souillé	....	....	2	3
Lave. Lorange	....	....	....	1
Lave. Gorry	....	....	....	1
Lave. Mallet	....	1	1	3
Lave Launay	....	....	1	2
5 Femmes Veuves	....	1	4	10

ENFANS ORPHELINS	Femmes	ENFANS		TOTAL
		Garcons	Filles.	
Jean Fauve	....	....	....	1
Estienne Mallet Suzane Mallet Marie Mallet	....	....	....	3
Isaac Gorry Jean Gorry	....	....	....	2
Anthoine Berin	....	....	....	1
Pre. Sobriche Jeanne and Suzanne	....	....	....	3
Jean Loncadou Pierre Loncadou	....	....	....	2
Suzanne Imbert Jeanne Imbert	....	....	....	2
	....	....	....	14

RECAPITULATION DU TOUT	Femmes	ENFANS		TOTAL
		Garcons	Filles.	
Page 4 31	27	45	35	138
" 5 40	30	34	25	129
71	57	79	60	267
Veuves et leurs Enfans	5	1	4	10
Enfans Orphelins	....	....	....	14
71	62	80	64	291

A LIST OF KING WILLIAM PARISH—June 1744.
(Vol. 5, Va. His. Col., p. 112 et seq.)

The estate of John James Flournoy, viz: Jos. Akin, Yarmouth, Charles, Will, Sue, Sara	6
John James Dupuy, Dick, Betty	3
John James Levilin, Betty	2
James Ford, Stephen Ford	2
Thos. Bradley	1
Stephen Mallet, Robin, Lucy, May	5
John Levilin, Jack, Dick, Mary, Nan	5
James Cocke, Henry Godsie, Jack, Dick, Sarah, Hannah, Betsy, Jane	8
Wm. Salle, George, Betty, Jenny, John Proan	5
Peter Salle, Jemine	2
Peter Bondurant	1
John Bondurant	1
Joseph Bondurant, Thomas Miles	2
Richard Annis, Constable	2
William Meginson, Tom, Abram, George	4
Peter Ford, Daniel Ford, Jogg	3
Peter Soblet	1
John Young	1
John Harris, Demetius, Young, Bob, Chloe, Phillis, Moll	6
Peter Lewis Soblet	1
Thomas Porter, Isaac Dutoy, Hamton, Joe, Caesar, Judy, Sarah	7
John Peter Bilbo, John Gory, Sara, Will	4
John Porter, Judy	2
John Chandler, Jos. Chandler	2
Stephen Forssee, Sam	2
Thomas Smith, James Smith, Will	3
Peter Guerrant, John J	0
Tom, Betty	0
John Burner	1
For Mrs. Elize Bernard: Will'm Howard, James, Charles, Will, Adam, Essex	6
Edmund Goin	1
Stephen Reno, Jno. Weaver	2
Mattie Ayce, Jas. Ayce, Francis Hilguro, Ege Edins	4
John Butler: George, Jack, Betty	0
David Lesueur, Dick, Philis	3
Thomas Kemp	1
John Ford	1
Benjamin Harris, Ben, Harry, Matt, Lasey	5
David Thomas, Betty	2
James Robinson, Moll	0

John Carner, William Carner	2
For Am't. Bennj: Matt. Bingley, Am't. Debril, Betty, Cassy, Jenny, Jack	6
Peter Depp, Peter Orange	2
James Drowen	1
Andrew Ouinet, Jno. Ford	2
Eliza Hampton, Left	0
John Sullavant, Phillis, Sarah, Moll	4
Jno. Pankey, Lucy	2
	126

Daniel Gory	1
For Rene Chastain: Thos. Godsee, Betty	2
Sam Weaver, Sam'l. Weaver Jr., Wm. Young, Sam Robin	0
Henry Trent, Jno. C'k	0
Dilsey Aggy	0
Chastain, Jno. Chastain Jun., Charles, Prince, Belinda	5
Charles, Ominett	2
William Platt, Charles, Stannad, Phillis	4
Mrs. Anne Scott: Dan'l. Scott, Thomas Mansfield, Sampson, Jerry, Cooper, Jupiter, Pope, Dick	8
Talb Dillery	0
Anthony Ayce	1
John Edins	1
Wm. Banton	1
John Young	1
Peter Lookado	1
Peter Ford, Jr.	1
Clarke Trabue: June	1
Joseph Bingley, Butler, Judy	3
James Bryant, Sec'y	2
Jeremiah Rasceine	1
James Stelman, Jr., Watt, Jonathan, Caesar, Lucy, Effe	6
Widow Martin: Wm. Kemp, Peter, Daniel, Jack, Dick, Jenny, Kate	7
Peter, David, Dick, Manowa, Dina	5
John Jas. Flornoir	6
John Young	1
Giles Ford	1
Stephen Reno	1
Samuel Wever	0
Antony Benin	6
Peter Loucadou	1
Daniel Peros	3
Louis Soblet	1
Jno. Bartholomew Dupuy	1
Charles Pean	2
Jean Faure	5

Richard Sumpter	1
Richard Sumter	1
Jean Moriset	1
Isaac Robinson	3
Wm. Guettle	1
Eli Sassin	1
Jacob Trabue	4
Jaque Martain	4
Janne Dupres Tevis	2
Antoine Bernard	1
Samuel Jordins	3
Pierre Forqueran	1
Richard Deen	1
Magdelaine Salle	2
Abraham Salle	2
	113

A LIST OF YE REFUGEES

(From Va. Historical Collections, Vol. VI, p. 65 et seq.)

Pierre Delome, et sa femme.
Magdelaine Mertle, Jean Vidau.
Pierre Lauret, Jean Roger.
Philippe Duvivier.
Francois Clere, Symon Sardin.
Pierre du Loy, Abraham Nicod, Jean Oger, sa femme et trois enfants.
Jean et Claude Mallefant, avec leur mere.
Isaac Chabanas, sou fils, et Catherine Bomard.
Estienne Chastain, Adam Vignes.
Jean Menager et Jean Lesnard.
Estienne Badouet, Pierre Morriset.
Jean Farry et Jerome Dumas.
Jean Chevas, et sa femme.
Jacques Roy, et sa femme.
Quintin Chastatain et Michael Roux.
Henry Cabinis, sa femme et un enfant.
Francois Bosse, Jean Fouchie.
Jean Gaury, sa femme et un enfant.
Jaques Hulyre, sa femme et quatre enfants.
Isaac Penetier, Jean Parransos, sa seur.
Antoine Trouillard, Jean Bourru et Jean Bouchet.
Catherine Godwal, Pierre la Courru.
Abraham Moulin et sa femme.
Jaques Broret, sa femme et deux enfants.
Etienne Guevin, Rene Massoneau.
Jean Parmentier, David Thonitier et sa femme.
Marie Lavesque, Jean Constantin.
Jean Imbert, sa femme.
Jaques Richard, et sa femme.

Jaques Viras, et sa femme.
Pierre Cornu, Louiss Bon.
Jean Gaillard, et son fils.
Jean Lucadou, et sa femme.
Daniel Taure, et deux enfants.
Pierre Grelet, Jean Jovany, sa femme deux enfants.
Pierre Ferrier, sa femme un enfant.
Pierre Chatanier, sa femme et son pere.
Catherine Billot, Marie et Symon Jourdon.
Abraham Menot, Timothy Moul, sa femme un enfant.
Jean Sargeaton, sa femme, un enfant.
Gabriel Sturter, Pierre de Corne.
Marguerite See, et sa fille.
Tertulien Sehult, et sa femme et deux enfants.
Pierre Chastain, sa femme et cinq enfants.
Pierre Nace, sa femme et Leur deux filles.
Soubragon, et Jacques Nicolay.
Pierre Mallet, Francoise Coupet.
Jean Saye, Elizabet Angeliere.
Estienne Chastain, Adam Vignes.
Jean Menager et Jean Lesnard.
Jedron Chamboux, et sa femme.
Joseph Bourgoian, David Bernard.
Jean Tardieu, Jean Moreau.
Abraham Sablet, et des deux enfants.
Jean Quictet sa femme et trois enfants.
Jaques Sayte, Jean Boisson.
Francoise Sassin, Andre Cochet.
Pierre Gaury, sa femme et un enfant.
Pierre Perrut, et sa femme.

Elie Tremson, sa femme, Elizabet Tignac.
Jaques Voyes, Elizabet Mingot.
Jean et Michell Cautepie, sa femme et deux enfants.
Francois Billot, Pierre Comte (?).
Francois du Tartre, Isaac Verry.
Moyses Lewreau, Pierre Tillou.
Claud Bardon, sa femme.
Elizabet Fleury, Loys du Pyn.
Adam et Marie Prevost.
Jaques Brousse, sou enfant.

Isaac Fordet, Jean Pepre.
Anthonie Matton, et sa femme.
Louiss Orange, sa femme et un enfant.
Pierre Cupper, Daniel Roy, Magdelain Gigou.
Isaac Arnaud, et sa femme.
La vefve faure et quatre enfants.
Jean Fonasse, Jaques Bibbeau, Jean March, Helen Trubyer.
Jean Savin, sa femme, un enfant.
Claude Philipe, et sa femme.

59 femmes ou filles.
38 enfants.
108 hommes.
———
205 personnes.
Messrs De la Muce et de Sailly fout en tout 207 personnes.

VIRGINIA: James Town, July 31, 1700.
This is a true Copy.

Olivier De La Muce
Ch. De Sailly

Received of ye hon'ble Marquis de la Muce and Chas. de la Sailly, ye summe of nine hundred, fourty five pounds in full for ye passage of two hundred and five people aboord ye ship Mary Ann, bound for Virginia. I say receiv'd this 19th April 1700.

£ 945—   GEO. HAWES

Witness: ALEXANDER CLEERE.
(A true copy, the original being in the custody of FFras. Nicholson.)

KING WILLIAM PARISH RECORDS
(Alphabetically Arranged)

20 Sept.   1730—Judith, dau. Andre and Janne Amonet.
15 June   1732—Jacob, son Andre and Janne Amonet.
 6 Aug.   1734—Jean, son Andre and Janne Amonet.
 9 Mch.   1736—Charle, son Andre and Janne ·Amonet.
29 Feb.   1753—Jean, son Charle and Diane Amonet.
 6 Nov.   ....—Antoine, son William and Anne Apperson.

 9 Aug.   1729—Isac, son of Antoine and Elizabeth Benin.
 7 Sept.   1731—Judith, dau. of Antoine and Elizabeth Benain.
10 Feb.   1734—Joseph, son of Antoine and Elizabeth Benin.
 7 Sept.   1736—Elizabet, dau. of Antoine and Elizabet Benin.
10 Sept.   1737—Antoine, son of Antoine and Elizabet Benin.
30 June   1730—Jaque, son of Jean and Susane Billiebo.
23 Dec.   1733—Maria, dau. Jean Pierre and Susane Bilbo.
26 Nov.   1735—Jean, son Jean and Susane Bilbo.
13 Feb.   1739—Elizabet, dau. Jean Pierre and Susane Bilbo.
 5 Dec.   1740—Elizabet, dau. Jean Pierre and Susane Bilbo.
 8 Mch.   1731—Marie, dau. of David and Anne Bernard.
 9 Apl.   1734—David, son of David and Anne Bernard.
 8 June   1735—Magdelaine, dau. of David and Anne Bernard.
27 Oct.   1731—Judith, dau. Jean and Anne Bernard.
24 Apl.   1734—Rebecca, dau. Jean and Anne Bernard.
 4 Apl.   1736—Jean, son Jean and Anne Bernard.
 6 Oct.   1738—Anne, dau. Jean and Anne Bernard.
21 Sept.   17....—David, son Jean and Anne Bernar.
24 Jan.   1743—Francoi, son Jean and Anna Bernar.
14 Sept.   1742—Ester, dau. Antoine and Sara Bernar.
 9 May   1731—Jean, son Edward and Sara Bryer.
25 July   1734—Sarah, dau. Edward and Sara Bryers.
29 Dec.   1736—Alexander, son Edward and Sara Bryers.
12 Nov.   1739—Lataus, son Edward and Sara Bryers.
27 May   1742—Edmond, son Edward Bryer.
 5 Oct.   1738—Willeam, son of Willeam Bantan.
12 Aug.   1739—Isaac Brian, son of Jaque and Elizabet Brian.
15 May   1746—Marie, dau. Jaque and Clere Brian.
15 Oct.   17....—Thomas, son Jaque and Clere Brian.
12 Jany.   1754—Marte, dau. Jaque and Cleet Brian.
 1 Oct.   1737—Jean, son of Jean Bonduran.
22 Aug.   1740—Richard, son of Jean Bonduran.
10 Nov.   1745—Anne, dau. Joseph and Agnes Bonduran.

26 Sept.   1721—Jean, son of Jean and Marianne Chastain.

10 May	1727—Judith, dau. Jean and Charlot Chastain.
24 Feb.	1728—Pierre, son, Jean and Charlote Chastain.
5 Jany.	1732—Magdelaine, dau. Jean and Charlote Chastain.
9 Nov.	1737—Estiene, son Jean and Charlote Chastain.
3 Oct.	1734—Janne, dau. Jean and Judith Chastain.
23 Jany.	1744—Magdelaine, dau. Jean and Judith Chastain.
23 Aug.	1727—Marie Magdelaine, dau. Mr. Estiene and Martha Chastain.
3 Nov.	1728—......................, son Etienne Chastain.
1 Mch.	1729—Estiene, son Estiene and Martre Chastain.
15 Mch.	1734—Isaac, son Rene and Judith Chastain.
6 Nov.	1736—Pierre, son Rene and Judith Chastain.
17 May	1738—Mariane, dau. Rene and Judith Chastain.
30 June	17....—Rene, son Rene and Judith Chastain.
12 Jany.	1728—Antoine, son Antoine and Anrietta Chaveron.
24 Dec.	1734—Anne Elizabet, dau. Gedeon and Janne Chambon.
13 Oct.	1743—Chastain, son of Jamse and Marie Cocke.
10 May	1722—Anne, dau. of Pierre and Anne David.
15 Jany.	1738—Anne, dau. of Pierre and Elizabet David.
1 July	1748—Pierre, son of Pierre and Elizabet David.
3 June	1727—Jean, son of Jean and Elizabeth Dyker.
15	1728—Jean Antoine, son of Christoffe and Mariana Dubreil.
12 Feb.	1728—Pierre, son of Pierre and Judith Dupuy.
20 Feb.	1731—Marie, dau. of Pierre and Judith Dupui.
7 Feb.	1732—Isaac, son of Pierre and Judith Dupuy.
11 Oct.	1734—Judith, dau. of Pierre and Judith Dupuy.
28 Sep.	1738—Marie Magdelaine, dau. of Pierre and Judith Dupuy.
12 Nov.	1729—Olimpe, dau. Jean Jaque and Susane Dupui.
25 Apl.	1734—Susane, dau. Jean Jaque and Susane Dupuy.
26 Feb.	1736—Marie, dau. Jean Jaque and Susane Dupuy.
17 Mch.	1738—Jean, son Jean Jaque and Susane Dupuy.
4 Sept.	1740—Elizabet, dau. Jean Jaque and Susane Dupuy.
28 Jany.	1745—Jaque, son Jean Jacque and Susane Dupuy.
21 May	1747—Marie, dau. Jean Jaque and Susane Dupuy.
21 Aug.	1732—Jean, son of Francoi Dupuy.
8 Oct.	1734—Judith, dau. of Francoi and Marie Dupuy.
13 July	1734—Francoise, dau. of Thomas and Anne Dilkins.
4 May	1739—Frederick, son of Nathanael and Elizabet Don.
13 Mch.	1733—Elizabet, dau. of Jean Edmon.
22 Nov.	1736—Samuel, son of Jean Edmon.
31 July	1738—Susane Elizabet, dau. Thomas and Elizabet Elson.
3 Sept.	1746—Mariane, dau. of Daniel and Anna Esley [Easley].
12 Dec.	1728—......................, son of Jean Faure.
2 Sept.	1730—Marie, dau. Jaque and Anne Faure.
6 Sept.	1732—Judith, dau. Jaque and Anne Faure.

11 Jany.   1734—Pierre, son Jaque and Anne Faure.
20 Aug.   1736—Magdelaine, dau. Jaque and Anne Faure.
24 Feb.   1738—Anne, dau. Jaque and Anne Faure.
27 Aug.   1739—Rachel, dau. Jacque and Anne Faure.
14 Mch.   1743—Jaque, son Jaque and Anne Faure.
14 Feb.   1745—Ruth, dau. Jaque and Anne Faure.
31 May   1729—Joseph, son of Pierre and Judith Faure.
 3 Nov.   1742—Judith, dau. of Pierre and Marie Faure.
31 May   1744—Joseph, son of Pierre and Marie Faure.
25 Nov.   1745—Pierre, son of Pierre and Marie Faure.
22 June   1747—Archeleus, son of Pierre Faure.
 2 May   1749—William, son of Pierre Faure.
11 April   1730—Lousi, dau. of Daniel Faure.
10 Feby.   1728—Pierre, son of Jean and Susane Farsi.
 9 Sept.   1734—Mariana, dau. Estiene and Mariana Farsi.
 7 Mch.   1736—Anne, dau. Estiene and Marie Farsi.
29 Aug.   1739—Jane, dau. Estiene and Marie Farsi.
25 Nov.   1741—Elizabet, dau. Ethiene and Marie Farci.
19 Oct.   1744—Sara, dau. Estienne and Marie Farci.
 2 Nov.   1750—Estiene, son Estine and Marie Farci.
15 Mch.   1736—Jean, son of Moyse and Susane Forqueran.
24 Sep.   1737—Janne, dau. of Moyse and Susane Forqueran.
 7 Oct.   1739—Elizabeth, dau. of Moyse and Susane Forqueran.
 2 June   1749—Boos, son of Jaque Ford.

18 Augt.   1721—Daniel, son of Daniel and Francoise Guerrant.
12 Oct.   1728—Francoise, dau. of Daniel Guerand.
17 July   1733—Jean, son Pierre and Magdelaine Gueran.
 2 Dec.   1735—Ester, dau. Pierre and Magdelaine Guerrant.
17 Dec.   1737—Pierre, son Pierre and Magdelaine Gueran.
31 Aug.   1740—Magdelaine, dau. Pierre and Magdelaine Gueran.
17 Oct.   1745—Judith, dau. Pierre and Magdelaine Gueran.
23 Apl.   1748—Daniel, son Pierre and Magdelaine Gueran.
21 Feb.   1721—Jean, son Jean Casper and Susanne Gilmer.
21 May   1727—Jean, son of Eglan and Jeane Gori.
25 Oct.   1728—Elizabet, dau. of Jamse and Mariana Gore.
 1 Mch.   1729—Jean, son of Thommas and Judith Girodan.
 3 Aug.   1740—Sara, dau. James and Mariana Gase.
 6 Apl.   1746—Jerusha, dau. Thomas and Febe Godsy.
11 Feb.   17.....—Henry, son .... Godsey and Febe, his wife.
14 June   1741—Jesse, reputed son of John Harris and Elizabet
                 Roberd.

28 Apl.   1743—Jean, dau. William and Rebecca Howard.
21 Dec.   1744—Marie, dau. William and Rebecca Howard.

 2 Oct.   1742—Binjamen, son of James and Mariane Joss.

28 Mch.   1742—Anne, dau. Thomas and Mary Kemp.

28 Apl.   1741—David, son of William Lacy.
16 Nov.   1743—Henry, son of William and Elizabeth Lacy.
 1 Apl.   1750—Elize, son of Thomas and Caterine Lacy.
29 May   1751—Louica, dau. of Nathaneal and Marie Lacy.
25 July   1729—Elizabet, dau. Jean and Catherine Legrand.
 9 Nov.   1728—Elizabet, dau. David Le Seur.
25 Nov.   1733—David, son David and Elizabet Lessueur.
12 Nov.   1735—Catrine, dau. David and Elizabeth Lessueur.
 4 Oct.   1738—David, son David and Elizabeth Lesueur.
25 Dec.   1740—Jaque, son David and Elizabet Lesueur.
24 Dec.   1744—Chastain, son David Le Sueur and Elizabeth, his wife.
15 Oct.   1747—Samuel, son David and Elizabeth Lesueur.
23 Oct.   1750—Peter and John, sons David and Elizabeth Lesuer.
 5 Nov.   1736—Elizabet, dau. of Pierre and Elizabet Loucadou.
27 Sept.   1738—Jean, son of Pierre and Elizabeth Loucadou.
 2 Apl.   1743—Guillieaume, son of Pierre and Elizabeth Loucadou.
 2 Oct.   1731—Marye, dau. of Jean and Philipe (Le) Villain.
28 May   1733—Susane, dau. of Jean and Philipe (Le) Villain.
12 Oct.   1735—Jean, son of Jean and Philipe (Le) Villain.
28 Nov.   1737—Elizabet, dau. of Jean Levilain.

 1 Mch.   1721—Elizabeth, dau. of Pierre and Elizabeth Morriset.
29 Oct.   1726—John, son of Etienne and Elizabeth Monford.
 4 May   1729—Jacob, son of Etiene Monfor.
 8 Sept.   1727—Jacque Martin ....
 2 July   1730—Jean Pierre, son of Jaque and Janne Martain.
24 May   1735—Guillieaume, son of Jaque and Janne Martain.
27 Sep.   1737—Antoine, son of Pierre and Mariane Martain.
11 July   1740—Jean, son of Pierre and Mariane Martain.
 8 Mch.   17....—Marie, dau. Etiene and Olive Mallet.
29 Nov.   1731—Estiene, son Estiene and Olive Malet.
28 Jan.   1734—Guillieaume, son Eliene and Olive Malet.
 2 Sep.   1736—Judith, dau. Etiene and Olive Malet.
27 Nov.   1738—Ester, dau. Etiene and Olive Malet.
20 Jany.   1741—Elizabet, dau. Etiene and Olive Malet.
10 Nov.   1742—Marie Magdelaine, dau. Etiene and Olive Malet.
28 Feb.   1746—Martain Goouge, son of Andrew Martin and Marie
                Goouge.

20 Nov.   1735—Estiene, son of David and Marie Perault.
 5 Sept.   1728—Charle, son of Daniel and Marie Peroe.
19 Oct.   1728—..................., a dau. of Roger Prot.
12 Apl.   1731—Joseph, son of Jean and Elizabeth Peen.
10 Oct.   1737—Jean, son of Charle and Marie Pene.
17 Dec.   1747—Charle Peane.
 4 Mch.   1730—William, son of Thomas and Elizabet Porter.
22 Oct.   1734—John, son of Thomas and Elizabet Porter.

20 May 1736—Elizabet Porter was born.
17 Feb. 1738—Dutoy, son of Thomas and Elizabeth Porter.
27 Nov. 1740—William, son of Thomas and Elizabeth Porter.
7 Feb. 1744—Sara, dau. of Thomas and Elizabet Porter.
25 Dec. 1751—Marie, dau. of Thomas and Elizabeth Porter.
23 July 1753—Isaac, son of Thomas and Elizabet Porter.
30 Mch. 1738—Marie, dau. Jean and Marie Porter.
14 Jany. 1746—Mike, son of Richard and Elizabeth Pembreton.
30 Jany. 1749—William, son of Richard and Elizabeth Paimbreton.
17 Oct. 1752—Marthe, dau. of Richard and Elizabeth Pimbreton.

23 Oct. 1738—Jean, son of Jean and Janne Roberd.
28 June 1732—Alexandre Robinson was born.
15 Dec. 1733—Zacarie, son of Jaque and Susane Robinson.
8 Oct. 1736—Thomas, son of Isaac and Anne Robinson.
25 Mch. 1739—Diane, dau. of Isaac and Anne Robinson.
15 Mch. 1741—Lucy and Magdelaine, daus. of Isaac and Anne Rob-
          inson.
12 Apl. 1731—Anne, dau. Jamse and Susane Robinson.
7 June 1735—Jamse, son Jamse and Susane Robinson.
20 May 1739—Marie, dau. Jamse and Susane Robinson.

9 Nov. 1726—Judith, dau. of Abraham and Magdelaine Salle.
13 Mch. 1728—Elizabeth, dau. of Abraham and Magdelaine Salle.
20 Aug. 1731—Marriane, dau. of Maglaine Salle.
4 July 1728—Elizabeth, dau. Guillaume and Elizabeth Salle.
21 Feby. 1729—Elizabeth, dau. guillaume and Elizabeth Salle.
17 Apl. 1732—Guillieaume, son, Guillieaume and Elizabet Salle.
8 May 1734—Guilieaume, son, Guillieaume and Elizabet Salle.
27 July 1739—Isaac, son Guillieaume and Elizabet Salle.
22 Apl. 1741—Isaac, son Guillieaume and Magdelaine Salle.
13 July 1743—Pierre, son Guillieaume and Magdelaine Salle.
2 Nov. 1745—Jean, son Guillieaume and Magdelaine Salle.
5 Nov. 1749—Olive, son Guillieaume and Magdelaine Salle.
5 Oct. 1734—Isaac, son of Pierre and Francoise Salle.
18 Nov. 1736—Abraham, son of Pierre and Francoise Salle.
1 Oct. 1741—Marie, dau. of Pierre and Francoise Salle.
9 Feb. 1744—Jacob, son of Pierre and Francoise Salle.
9 Mch. 1746—Joseph, son of Pierre and Francoise Salle.
29 Oct. 1749—Judith, dau. of Pierre and Francoise Salle.
21 Dec. 1729—Pierre, son of Elie Sassain.
4 Oct. 1732—Jean, son of Eli and Susanne Sassain.
11 Apl. 1735—Louy, son of Elie and Susane Sassain.
31 Aug. 1740—David, son of Eli and Susanne Sassain.
9 Apl. 1728—Louis, son of Pierre Louis and Marte Soblet.
14 Mch. 1730—Jaque, son of Pierre Louis and Marie Soblet.
23 Apl. 1732—Beinjamain, son of Pierre Louis and Marie Soblet.
12 Oct. 1728—................., a son of Nicolas Soullie.

19 June   1735—Nanni, a dau. of Nicolas and Francoise Soulie.
21 Jany.   1736—George, son of George and Anne Smith.
29 Aug.   1732—David, son of William and Caterine Stanford.
20 May   1733—Francoise, dau. of Edward and Anne Scot.

 1 Sept.   1731—Sarah, dau. of Jaque and Marye Teller.
 7 Oct.   1737—Mary, dau. of Chas. Taller.
 4 Jany.   1733—Joseph, son of Jacob and Marie Trabue.
28 Aug.   1735—Jean, son of Jacob and Marie Trabue.
10 Dec.   1737—David, son of Jacob and Marie Trabue.
23 Mch.   1739—William, son of Jacob Trabue.
24 Mch.   1742—Elizabet, dau. of Jacob Trabue.
29 Nov.   1744—Marie, dau. of Jacob and Marie Trabue.
 4 Nov.   1747—Josue, son of Jacob and Marie Trabue.
14 Oct.   17....—Daniel, son of Jacob and Marie Trabue.
10 May   1752—Thomas, son of Jacob and Marie Trabue.

 1 Apl.   1740—Marie, dau. of Stephen and Judith Watkins.
22 Sep.   1742—....................., dau. of Estiene and Judith Watkins.
19 Oct.   1744—Judith, dau. of Estienne and Judith Watkins.
19 Mch.   1732—Mariane, dau. of Benjamin and Mariane Witt.
28 July   1732—Sabary, dau. of Jean and Sara Williamson.
20 Oct.   1734—Mathiew, son of Jean and Sara Williamson.
20 Oct.   1732—Jean, son of John and Sara Williamson.
 6 May   1739—Daniel, son of Samuel and Francoise Wever.

FRAGMENT OF DEATH RECORDS

Janne La Fitt, wife of Tobit Lafitt 15 Dec. 1722, aged ....teen years, daughter of Estienne Malet and of Marie Malet her father and mother.

J. Soblet, Clerk.

The 12 January 1722 (1723) died Janne Chastain, daughter of ....ieur Chastain and of Anne Chastain her father and mother, aged about 6 years; was buried the 13th of the month on Sunday at 3 o'clock in the afternoon.

9 April 1723, died Anne Soblet the ....sieur Pierre Chastain aged about .... years; was buried the 4th of the month.

January 1723 (1724) died Sieur Anthony (Trabue?) aged about 56 or 7 years; was buried the 30th of the same.

J. Soblet, Clerk.

Died, Francois de Clapie, aged about 61 years. Was buried ....of the year 1724.

J. Soblet, Clerk.

.... Magdelaine LeFevre daughter of Isaac LeFevre and of Magdelaine LeFevre her father and mother; ....was buried on Sunday the 26th of the month.

.... August 1724, died Mariane............n Chastain, aged 28 years; .... was buried the 21st of the month at 5 o'clock in the afternoon.

The 26th February 1724 (1725) died Jeanne—wife of Francois La Fitt, aged 69.

The 24th December 1725, died Marthe........, wife of Monsieur Estiene Chastain, aged about fifty two or three years.

The 9th of January 1725 (1726) died Daniel................; aged about 44 years, was buried the ....of the month............Sunday.

The 24th January 1725 (1726) died ....wife of................ Chastain, aged ....; buried the 25th of the month.

19 January 1720 (?) died Jean .... about .... was buried.

The 5th 8ber died Jacob Amonnet.

William Porter son of Thomas Porter died ....
Elizabeth Benin, daughter of Antoine Benin died the 20th 8ber.

Jean Chastain.

AN INDEX
Of the Older Wills, Inventories, Divisions, Etc.
Of Goochland County, Va.

NAME	YEAR	BOOK	PAGE
BIBB, John	1769	9	213
BIRCH, Samuel	1739	3	249
BLACKWELL, John	1780	13	96
BLANKALL, William	1831	29	262
BLAYLOCK, Jeremiah	1824	25	543
BOLLING, James	1730	1	269
BONDURANT, John Peter	1734	2	56
BOSTICK, John	1761	8	116
BOURNE, Stephen	1829	28	221
BOWDEN, Elizabeth	1840	32	266
BOWLES, Elizabeth	1840	32	252
BOWLES, Gideon	1799	17	464
BOWLES, Judith	1823	25	407
BOWLES, Richard C.	1812	21	327
BOWLES, Seth F.	1833	29	207
BOWLES, William	1761	8	117
BOWLES, Zachariah	1761	8	170
BOYCE, Daniel	1804	19	140
BOYCE, Daniel	1818	23	140
BRADLEY, Daniel S.	1732	29	323
BRADLEY, William	1734	3	165
BRADSHAW, Ann	1777	12	36
BRADSHAW, Benjamin	1753	8	178
BRADSHAW, Benjamin	1761	8	179
BRADSHAW, Benjamin	1732	29	406
BRADSHAW, John	1777	12	47
BRADSHAW, Larner	1750	6	120
BRIGGS, George	1734	2	5
BRITT, Geo. H.	1814	23	78
BRITT, John	1778	17	163
BRITT, John	1803	18	508
BRITT, William	1787	14	373
BROOKS, Fielding	1829	28	429
BROOKS, Mary	1806	19	580
BROOKS, Thomas	1838	31	388
BRUCE, James	1817	23	69
BRUMFIELD, Moses	1760	8	68
BRYANT, Thomas	1777	12	35
BURGAME, John	1736	1	234
BURGAMY, Peter	1735	2	95
BURNER, David	1736	3	145
BURTON, Robert	1748	5	487
BUSH, Francis	1795	16	232
BUSH, William	1840	32	304
BUTLER, Edmond	1747	5	342
BYBE, Thomas	1729	1	161

NAME	YEAR	BOOK	PAGE
CAMBBELL, Benjamin	1805	19	343
CANNON, Jeremiah	1767	9	85
CARDEN, Robert	1785	14	157
CARR, Dabney	1773	10	369
CARROL, William	1734	2	31
CARROL, William	1797	17	152
CARROLL, Booker	1831	29	150
CARROLL, Roger	1796	17	65
CARTER, Charles	1777	12	57
CARTER, Daniel W.	1840	32	233
CARTER, Edward	1749	5	534
CARTER, James	1820	24	396–425
CARTER, Robert	1794	16	350
CARTER, Thomas	1738	3	138
CARTER, Thomas	1763	8	313
CARVER, Henry	1819	24	100
CAUSBY, David (Cosby)	1804	19	80
CAWLEY, Nathaniel	1796	17	31
CAWTHON, Robert	1755	7	1
CAWTHORN, Gideon	1799	17	515
CHADELL, Frances	1739	3	268
CHAMBOONS, Gideon	1737	3	236
CHANDLER, John	1747	5	353
CHASTAIN, Martha	1744	3	285–421
CHASTAIN, Peter	1728	1	43
CHEATHAM, John	1839	32	195
CHESHIRE, William	1737	3	2
CHILDRESS, Philip	1812	21	305
CHILDRESS, William	1833	29	668
CHISMANS, ———?	1736	2	258
CHRISTIAN, Charles	1784	13	359
CHRISTIAN, Thomas	1737	3	32
CHRISTIAN, Thomas	1743	4	316
CHRISTIAN, Thomas	1744	4	403
CLARK, Joseph	1814	21	471
CLARK, William	1779	13	15
CLARKE, Edward	1778	12	169
CLARKE, Joseph	1743	4	462
CLARKSON, John	1759	8	15
CLEMENT, Jesse	1803	22	138
CLEMENTS, James	1822	25	240
CLEMENTS, Joseph W.	1822	25	205
CLEMENTS, Stephen	1746	5	147
CLOPTON, Agnes	1809	20	416
CLOPTON, Benjamin	1791	15	449
CLOUDAS, George	1789	15	253
COCK, Richard	1815	22	44

NAME	YEAR	BOOK	PAGE
COCKE, David P.	1837	31	229
COCKE, Frances	1799	17	410
COCKE, Haney	1809	2–	395
COCKE, James	1819	24	540
COCKE, James	1831	29	380
COCKE, Barbara	1832	29	409
COLE, Mary	1770	10	62
COLEMAN, Grissell	1739	3	264
COLEMAN, Samuel	1748	5	481
COLEY, Sally	1808	20	201
COLEY, Susanna	1803	18	600
COLEY, Molly	1828	27	593
COLLEY, Frances	1776	11	136
COLLEY, Frances	1820	24	379
COLLINS, Matthew	1760	8	78
COLQUHON, Charles	1778	12	165
CONE, John	1730	1	201
CONLY, Bryant	1784	14	43
COOKE, John	1737	3	36
COOPER, Aggie	1832	29	325
COOPER, Page	1821	24	329
COOPER, Samuel	1838	31	44
COOTS, Isaac	1761	8	238
COUCH, Samuel	1800	17	545
COX, Bartholomew	1730/1	1	298–299
COX, Edward	1811	21	76
COX, George	1728	7	22
COX, John	1785	14	182
COX, Matthew	1734	2	71
COX, Nicholas	1731	1	343
COX, Sarah	1747	5	365
COX, Winney	1738	3	156
CRADDOCK, Thomas	1752	6	262
CRAWFORD, James	1767	9	44
CRENSHAW, Benjamin	1803	18	553
CRENSHAW, John, Sr.	1815	22	40
CRENSHAW, Reuben	1818	23	224
CRENSHAW, Susan	1828	28	150
CREW, Joseph	1740	3	348
CROOM, Daniel	1735	2	96
CROON, Daniel	1735	2	189
CROSS, Joseph	1814	21	598
CROSS, Sarah	1830	28	418
CROUCH, John	1780	13	30
CROUCH, Richard	1765	9	47
CROUCH, Stephen	1818	23	147–198
CROUCH, William	1832	29	547

NAME	YEAR	BOOK	PAGE
CROW, John	1773	10	381
CRUTCHFIELD, Stapleton	1831	29	620
CRUTCHFIELD, William	1789	15	247
CRUTCHFIELD, William	1817	22	365
CUNNINGHAM, Edward	1836	30	517
CURD, James	1792	16	26
CURD, John	1752	6	240
CURD, John (Divn. Est.)	1759	7	336
CURD, John	1819	24	46
CURD, Richard	1778	12	194–225
CURD, Sarah	1792	16	445–482
DANDRIDGE, Alexander	1822	25	195
DANDRIDGE, Henry M.	1828	27	596
DANIEL, Ezekiel	1790	15	386
DANIEL, Ezekiel (Div. Est.)	1812	21	297
DANIEL, George A.	1833	29	245
DANIEL, James	1734	2	251
DANIEL, Moseley	1795	16	539
DANIEL, Obediah	1774	12	147
DAVID, Nicholas	1745	5	26
DAVID, Peter	1730	1	214
DAVIDSON, Nathaniel	1816	22	164
DAVIS, John	1828	26	39
DAVIS, Richard	1839	31	511
DAVIS, Robert	1782	13	249
DAVIS, Sarah	1782	13–163	......
DAVIS, William	1730	1	232
DEMENT, Timothy	1747	5	308
DENNIS, John	1788	15	165
DEPRIEST, William	1749	6	15
DESASY, James	1737	3	49
DICKINS, Thomas	1741	3	435
DILLON, Thomas	1744	4	412
DILLON, William	1744	4	355
DIMMUNO, Eliza	1834	30	124
DOWDY, John	1786	14	347
DRAKE, Edward	1785	14	480
DRAKE, Eliza	1826	26	391
DRAKE, Jonathan	1793	16	229–451
DRAKE, Sarah	1831	29	578
DRUMWRIGHT, George W.	1763	8	374
DRUMWRIGHT, George	1832	29	243
DRUMWRIGHT, William	1752	6	223
DRUMWRIGHT, William	1830	28	491
DUPEY, Bartholemew	1743	4	173
DUMAS, Jeremiah	1734	2	57
DUNMORE, Lorous	1826	27	6

NAME	YEAR	BOOK	PAGE
EARLY, John	1746	5	159
EAVANS, John	1754	6	422
EDWARDS, Thomas	1768	9	171
EDWARDS, Robert	1834	30	12
ELLETT, Benjamin	1835	30	477
ELLIET, William	1772	10	188
ELLIS, Stephen	1819	24	39
ENGLAND, William	1768	9	159
EVANS, John	1755	7	3
EVANS, John	1781	13	109
EVANS, Joseph	1782	13	200
EVANS, Tabitha	1768	9	174
FARGUSON, James	1741	3	429
FARISH, Betty	1809	20	415
FARLEY, Francis	1731	1	269
FARMER, Henry	1835	29	263
FARRAR, Francis	1811	21	179
FARRAR, Wm.	1812	21	303
FARROW, Joseph	1749	6	28
FARROW, John	1782	13	183
FARROW, Mary	1757	7	186
FARROW, Thomas	1742	3	561
FARROW, William	1744	4	374
FARROW, Thomas	1761	8	190
FERRESS, William	1745	4	524
FIFE, Elizabeth	1828	27	590
FLEMING, Tarleton	1750	6	113
FLEMING, Tarleton	1778	12	83
FLEMING, Thomas	1777	12	14
FLEMING, Thomas M.	1801	18	252
FLEMING, Wm. R.	1831	29	210
FONTAINE, Abraham	1832	29	463
FONTAINE, Maria	1838	31	379
FORD, John	1782	13	191
FORD, Peter	1745	4	525
FORD, William	1751	6	179
FORD, Tom	1816	22	193
FORD, Reuben	1817	22	410–445
FORD, Wm. F.	1828	27	643
FORD, Wm. F.	1830	31	412
FORRISTER, John	1757	7	189
FOWLER, Alex.	1821	25	36
FOWLER, Thomas	1818	24	37
FRANCKLING, Thomas	1737	3	33
FRENCH, Hugh	1800	18	104
FRENCH, Mason	1827	27	305
FREEMAN, Titus	1801	18	155

NAME	YEAR	BOOK	PAGE
GARLAND, Eliza	1838	31	449
GARLAND, Susan E.	1836	31	9
GARTHRIGHT, William	1819	24	221
GARTHRIGHT, William	1828	27	414–437
GARY, Claudius	1737	3	57
GAY, Judith	1828	27	477
GEORGE, James	1805	19	253
GEORGE, Leonard	1774	10	476
GEORGE, Nancy	1838	31	397
GEORGE, William	1828	27	283–424
GEORGE, William	1837	31	199
GILL, John	1795	17	7
GILLIAM, Jacob	1809	20	389
GILLIAM, John	1794	16	362
GILLIAM, John	1794–5	19	803
GILLIAM, John	1825	26	160
GILLIAM, Taylor	1795	16	373
GILLIAM, Sarah	1809	20	400
GLASS, David	1826	26	371
GLASS, James	1837	31	222
GLASS, John	1827	27	336
GORDON, Ann	1799	17	370
GRANT, Alex.	1808	20	240
GRANTHAM, David	1804	19	64
GRANTHAM, Catherine	1808	20	53
GRAVES, Judith	1773	10	344
GRAVES, Mary	1800	18	101
GRAVES, Ralph	1762	8	243
GRAY, John	1838	31	409
GRAY, Thomas	1815	21	705
GRAVES, Rice	1822	25	97
GRESHAM, Elizabeth	1762	8	268
GRESHAM, James	1770	10	44
GRISKENS, Richard	1746	5	208
GROOM, Nancy	1806	19	568
GRUBBS, Andrew	1780	13	69
GRUBBS, Daniel	1800	18	94
GRUBBS, Mary	1809	20	299
GUERRANT, Daniel	1730	1	279
GUERRANT, Elizabeth	1820	24	392
GUERRANT, John	1813	21	368
GUERRANT, Peter	1744	4	412
GUN, John	1735	2	98
HADON, Zachariah	1792	16	75
HALE, William	1797	17	175
HAMPSHIRE, Henry	1737	2	123

NAME	YEAR	BOOK	PAGE
HANCHELWOOD, John	1754	6	403
HARDING, Sarah	1797	17	84
HARDING, William	1768	9	154
HARRIS, Frances	1822	25	260
HARRIS, Henry	1776	11	120
HARTAN, Thomas	1751	6	140
HARRIS, Samuel	1818	23	223
HARRISON, Thomas R.	1833	30	10
HATCHER, Gideon	1817	19	640
HATCHER, Josiah	1762	8	232
HATCHER, Josiah	1800	18	112
HATCHER, Josiah	1830	28	322
HATCHER, Priscilla	1734	2	55
HATCHER, Sarah	1798	17	279
HATCHER, Thomas	1797	17	124–250
HEDSPETH, Geo.	1736/7	4	486
HENDERSON, John	1793	16	150
HENDERSON, Richard	1748	5	424
HERNDON, Benjamin	1778	12	205
HERNDON, Benjamin	1778?	13	197
HERNDON, John	1821	24	515
HERNDON, Valentine	1799	17	500
HICKS, John	1772	10	242
HICKS, John	1821	22	163
HICKS, Meshack	1826	27	19
HILL, Luke	1743	4	340
HILL, Watt	1817	22	418–419
HINES, Richard	1778–1792	15–16	361–183
HINSHELWOOD, John	1754	6	409
HIX, Daniel	1735	2	111
HIX, David	1784	14	25
HIX, John	1748	5	457
HIX, Nathaniel	1735	2	89
HODGES, Welton W.	1772	10	244
HODGES, William	1807	19	694
HODGES, Wm.	1827	27	19
HOLLAND, Judith	1751	6	179
HOLLAND, John	1773	10	387
HOLLAND, Michael	1746	5	222
HOLLAND, Nathaniel	1828	27	325
HOLMAN, Henry	1740	3	345
HOLMAN, James	1823	25	390
HOLMAN, Susanna	1817	22	364
HOLMAN, William	1799	17	48
HOLMAN, Wm. M.	1838	31	421–426
HOPKINS, Elizabeth	1820	24	408
HOPKINS, Charles	1807	20	21

NAME	YEAR	BOOK	PAGE
HOPKINS, John	1807	19	714
HOPKINS, John	1807	20	52
HOPKINS, James	1816	22	443
HOPPER, James	1765	8	464
HOPPER, John	1792	15	537
HOPPER, Mildred	1796	17	30
HOPPER, Paterson	1816	22	278
HORSLEY, Robert	1734	2	58
HOUCHINS, Charles	1782	13	266
HOUTCHINS, ...?	1765	8	456
HOUTCHINS, Elizabeth	1836	31	79
HOUTCHINS, John	1829	28	150
HOUTCHINS, James	1833	29	579
HOUTCHINS, Mary	1836	31	81
HOWARD, Allen	1732	1	392
HOWARD, Allen	1761	8	164
HOWARD, Elizabeth	1776	11	20
HOWARD, James	1778	12	161
HOWELL, Charles	1831	29	163
HOWLE, William	1729	1	108–200
HUDGORS, Benjamin	1768	9	148
HUDGORS, Jesse	1820	24	247
HUDGORS, Jesse	1822	25	71
HUDGORS, Jesse	1822	25	80
HUGHES, Benjamin	1816	22	256
HUGHES, Sarah	1730	1	188
HUGHSON, John	1829	28	186
HUMBAR, Elizabeth	1836	30	206
HUNNICUTT, Elizabeth	1834	25	505
HUNNICUTT, John	1825	30	575
HUNNICUTT, Thomas	1823	25	376
HUNTON, Austia	1837	31	150
HURST, William	1765	8	525
HUTCHESON, Matthew	1750	6	75
ISBELL, William	1807	20	10
ISBELL, William	1832	30	55
ISBELL, William	1830	31	480
JAMBON, Gideon	1737	3	34
JAMES, Francis, Jr.	1746	5	194
JAMES, William	1809	19	725
JAMES, William	1832	29	492
JARRATT, Archalaus	1794	16	336
JARRATT, Christain	1837	31	148
JARRATT, David	1801	18	292
JARRATT, Deurieux	1820	24	81

NAME	YEAR	BOOK	PAGE
JARRATT, Jas.	1761	8	114
JENNINGS, Kelly	1773	10	294
JOHNS, Phillip	1787	14	482
JOHNS, Sudith	1735	2	97
JOHNS, Wm. C.	1784	15	5
JOHNSON, Benjamin	1744	4	405
JOHNSON, Benjamin	1785	14	160
JOHNSON, Benjamin	1813	21	400
JOHNSON, Benjamin	1824	25	518
JOHNSON, Benjamin	1840	32	314
JOHNSON, Daniel	1754	6	369
JOHNSON, Daniel	1834	30	186–406
JOHNSON, Isham	1798	17	202
JOHNSON, Isham	1798	18	376
JOHNSON, James	1822	25	95
JOHNSON, Jacob	1830	28	442–462–463
JOHNSON, John	1750	6	121
JOHNSON, John	1789	15	274
JOHNSON, John	1796	17	39
JOHNSON, Jos.	1781	13	152
JOHNSON, Margaret	1840	32	232
JOHNSON, Obediah	1840	32	318
JOHNSON, Stephen	1805	19	293
JOHNSON, William	1782	13	210
JOHNSON, Wm.	1796	17	26
JOHNSON, Wm.	1827	27	111
JOHNSON, Wm.	1833	29	634
JONES, Harrison	1813	21	302
JORDAN, Charles	1774	10	437
JORDAN, James	1781	13	145
JORDAN, John	1810	20	538
JORDAN, Miles	1817	23	145
JORDAN, Phoebe	1839	32	193
JORDAN, Robt.	1779	12	234
JORDAN, Reuben	1839	32	194
KARN, Andrew	1837	31	284
KARN, Martha W.	1839	32	190
KARN, William	1743	4	246
LACY, Elliott	1809	20	372
LACY, Sarah	1794	16	342
LACY, Stephen	1772	10	234
LADD, Constantine	1766	9	17
LA FORCE, Rene	1728	1	37
LA FORCE, Sarah	1757	7	143
LANE, Daniel's wife	1805	19	345

NAME	YEAR	BOOK	PAGE
LANG, John H.	1836	30	519
LAPRADE, John	1784	14	84
LAPRADE, John's wife	1795	16	495
LAPRADE, Susanna	1816	22	244
LAWLESS, Thomas	1765	8	527
LAYNE, David	1791	16	34
LAYNE, Henry	1812	21	265
LAYNE, John	1755	7	5
LEAKE, Elisha	1806	19	591
LEAKE, Josiah	1795	16	475
LEAKE, Samuel D.	1808	20	276
LEAKE, Walter	1758	7	279
LEE, John	1771	10	110
LEE, John	1779	12	254
LE GRAND, Peter	1737	3	45
LEMAY, Samuel	1815	22	7
LEMAY, William	1827	27	134
LeVILLAIN, Jean (John)	1746	5	138
LEWIS, Charles	1779	13	13
LEWIS, Elizabeth	1784	14	77
LEWIS, Howell	1804	19	342
LEWIS, Howell & Elizh. McLein, Marriage Agreement	1831	....	......
LEWIS, John	1746	5	158–360
LEWIS, John	1796	17	45
LEWIS, Joseph	1783	13	325
LEWIS, Robert	1803	18	54
LEWIS, William	1791	16	14
LIGGAN, William	1765	9	10
LINDSAY, Curtis	1815	22	36
LOCKETT, Thomas	1745	5	90
LOVETT, George	1778	12	146
LOVETT, John	1780	14	27
LOWRY, Joseph	1799	17	492
LOWRY, Matthew	1794	16	313
LUMSDEN, William	1743	4	261
LYNCH, John	1839	32	33
LYNCH, Polly	1817	22	350
McBRIDE, Ann	1830	28	519
McCAUL, Stokes	1818	23	415
McDEARMAN, James	1816	22	184
McDONALD, Angus	1804	19	87
MacLACHLAN, John	1752	7	253
McLAUGHLIN, Hugh	1805	19	241
McLEIN, George W.	1833	29	694
McMICKING, William	1794	16	252

NAME	YEAR	BOOK	PAGE
MADDOX, Benjamin	1798	15	332
MADDOX, John	1749	6	12
MADDOX, John	1789	15	331
MADDOX, Michael	1748	5	430-465
MADDOX, Martha A.	1830	28	486
MAN, Mary	1794	16	323
MANGUM, Lucy Ann	1840	32	218
MARRON, Daniel	1749	6	13
MARTIN, Gilbert	1738	3	140
MARTIN, John	1739	3	210
MARTIN, John	1787	15	87
MARTIN, Matthew	1786	14	357
MARTIN, Peter	1743	4	174
MARTIN, Samuel	1790	15	369
MARTIN, William	1794	16	75
MARTIN, William	1797	17	50
MARKHAM, John	1801	18	279
MASSIE, Charles	1817	22	463
MASSIE, David	1755	7	28
MASSIE, Mary R. and Jos. S. Leake. Marriage Agreement—			
MASSIE, Nathaniel	1802	18	382
MASSIE, Susanna	1818	23	227
MASSIE, Susan	1820	24	393
MASSIE, Thomas	1755	7	26
MASSIE, William	1804	19	6
MATTHEWS, Ailcy	1821	24	424
MATTHEWS, Benj.	1833	29	619
MATTHEWS, Edward	1785	14	153
MATTHEWS, John	1740	3	399
MATTHEWS, Thomas	1824	25	635
MATTHEWS, William	1816	22	227
MAY, Samuel L.	1815	22	7
MAYO, John	1772	10	189
MAXEY, Susanna	1743	4	212
MEANLEY, Isaac	1776	11	149
MECHUM, Thomas	1754	6	345
MEGEHE, Abraham	1743	4	246
MERRIN, Elizabeth	1838	31	481
MERION, Richard	1777	12	38
MERIWETHER, Nich.	1744	4	437
MERIWETHER, Nich.	1758	7	307
MILLER, Henry	1752	6	189
MILLER, Heath J.	1819	24	27
MILLER, John	1807	19	19
MILLER, Mary	1796	16	16
MILLER, Mary A.	1827	27	366

NAME	YEAR	BOOK	PAGE
MILLER, Thomas	1742	4	60
MILLER, Thomas	1819	24	27
MILLER, William	1815	12	21
MILLER, Wm. H.	1825	26	119
MIMS, David	1781	13	142
MIMS, David	1786	14	324
MIMS, Frances	1821	24	537
MIMS, Shadrach	1777	12	68
MITCHELL, David	1816	22	278
MITCHELL, Edmond	1815	26	300
MITCHELL, Thomas	1776	11	148
MITCHELL, William	1777	12	21
MOLIM, Thomas	1730	1	190
MOORE, Amos L.	1836	31	10
MOORE, John	1785	14	196
MORGAN, Robert	1753	6	291
MORGAIN, Robert	1746	5	196
MORRISETT, William	1797	17	166
MORRISON, Malcolm	1806–	22	293
MOSBY, William C.	1830	28	501
MOSS, Hugh	1780	13	28
MOSS, Samuel	1818	23	372
MULLINAX, John	1745	5	71
MULLINS, Conelly	1826	26	386
MULLINS, Henry	1798	17	233
MULLINS, Henry	1814	21	682
MULLINS, John	1783	13	302
MULLINS, William	1804	19	117
MURRELL, Joseph	1740	3	418
NAPIER, Rene	1751	6	180
NELSON, Wright	1793	16	186
NETHERLAND, Sarah	1745	5	91
NEVES, Christian	1790	16	67
NEVES, William	1763	8	324
NEWBURN, Wm. C. R.	1835	30	299
NICHOLAS, Nicholas	1733	1	469
NICHOLSON, Joshua	1796	17	28
NORVELL, Thomas	1810	20	637
NOWLIN, David	1777	11	171
NOWLING, James	1749	6	34
NUCKOLS, Pouncey	1815	22	119
NUCKOLS, Saumel	1833	29	333
NUCKOLS, Thomas	1815	21	691
NUCKOLS, Thomas	1833	30	147
NUCKOLS, William	1796	16	533
NUCKOLS, William	1821	21	545

NAME	YEAR	BOOK	PAGE
OGELBE, Richard	1731	1	306
OWEN, Barrett	1782	13	211
PACE, John	1790	15	398
PACE, Joseph	1765	8	384
PACE, Joseph	1815	22	17
PACE, Wingfield	1790	15	403
PAGE, Annah	1824	25	529
PAGE, Elizabeth	1816	22	290
PAGE, James	1797	17	148
PAGE, John	1804	19	98
PAGE, Robert	1787	14	422
PAGE, William	1811	21	21
PAGE, William	1815	22	6
PARRISH, Aaron	1833	29	590
PARRISH, Dabney	1834	30	141
PARRISH, George	1823	25	340
PARRISH, Henry	1753	6	324
PARRISH, Humphrey	1743	4	176
PARRISH, Humphrey	1773	10	390
PARRISH, Humphrey	1800	18	64
PARRISH, Humphrey	1823	25	313
PARRISH, James	1792	16	78
PARRISH, John	1752	6	214
PARRISH, John	1786	14	266
PARRISH, John N.	1834	30	107
PARRISH, Mildred	1829	28	202
PARRISH, Nelson	1781	13	95
PARRISH, Sherod	1824	26	10
PARRISH, Susanna	1837	31	238
PARRISH, William	1790	15	402
PAYNE, George	1744	4	484
PAYNE, George	1784	14	8
PAYNE, Jean	1807	19	703
PAYNE, Jesse	1771	10	122
PAYNE, Margaret	1815	22	10
PAYNE, Robert	1764	8	410
PAYNE, Robert	1770	10	95
PAYNE, Robert	1905	19	378
PAYNE, Tarleton	1817	23	56
PATE, Thomas	1747	5	270
PATTERSON, Charles	1738	3	145
PEARMAN, Edward	1733	1	448
PEERS, Anderson	1793	16	176
PEERS, Anderson	1831	29	734
PEERS, George	1811	21	146
PEERS, John M.	1797	17	67

NAME	YEAR	BOOK	PAGE
PEERS, John L.	1809	20	427
PEERS, M. L.	1829	29	166
PEERS, Thomas	1837	31	112
PENNINGTON, Paul	1730	1	218
PERKINS, David	1769	9	206
PERKINS, James	1785	14	122
PERKINS, John	1805	19	283
PERKINS, Mary	1797	17	172
PERKINS, Nicholas	1777	12	67
PERKINS, Obedience	1771	10	122
PERKINS, Philemon	1769	9	204
PERKINS, Polly	1823	25	389
PERKINS, Stephen	1772	10	262
PERKINS, Walker	1782	13	174
PEMBERTON, Thomas	1826	27	622
PHELPS, John	1747	5	389
PHILPOTTS, John	1838	31	450
PLEASANTS, Archibald	1826	31	51
PLEASANTS, Isaac W.	1826	26	422
PLEASANTS, James	1826	26	91
PLEASANTS, James	1831	31	119
PLEASANTS, Mary	1798	17	230
PLEASANTS, Margaret	1806	19	623
PLEASANTS, Richard	1778	12	178
PLEASANTS, Thomas	1775	11	38
PLEASANTS, Thomas	1775	11	103
PLEASANTS, Thomas	1804	19	40
PLEDGE, Archer	1804	19	604
PLEDGE, Francis	1784	14	129
POOR, Abraham	1792	16	43
POOR, Thomas	1788	15	12
POOR, Thomas	1830	28	486
POINDEXTER, Wm. C.	1819	24	124–126
POLLARD, Joseph	1792	56	16
POLLACK, John	1755	6	449
POLLACK, Mayer	1823	25	432
POPE, Levenia	1834	30	39
POWELL, Samuel	1799	17	465
POWELL, William	1817	22	427
POWER, Major	1792	16	23
POWERS, William	1807	19	601
POWERS, John	1833	30	64
POWERS, Keziah	1825	26	93
POWERS, Major	1840	32	270
PRATS, Roger	1730	1	191
PREWIT, John	1788	16	346
PRICE, Elizabeth	1814	21	638

NAME	YEAR	BOOK	PAGE
PRICE, Leonard	1772	10	190
PRITCHETT, John	1735	2	144
PROPHET, Silvestra	1767	9	70
PRYOR, David	1746	5	218
PRYOR, John	1756	7	77
PRYOR, Nicholas	1746	5	206
PRYOR, Samuel	1766	10	392
PRYOR, Samuel	1773	10	394
PRYOR, William	1777	12	12
PRYOR, William	1800	18	407
PURKINS, Abram	1742	4	151
PURYEAR, Ann	1815	22	81
PURYEAR, Hezekiah	1796	17	32
PURYEAR, Noblin	1815	27	22
PURYEAR, Rebecca	1834	30	9
PURYEAR, Thos. H.	1813	21	572
QUARLES, James	1824	25	615
RAGLAND, Dudley	1832	29	375
RAGLAND, Elizabeth	1808	20	242
RAGLAND, Finch	1835	30	372
RAGLAND, Isaac	1796	17	27
RANDOLPH, Benjamin	1801	18	277
RANDOLPH, Isham	1742	4	110
RANDOLPH, Jane	1761	8	168
RANDOLPH, Jediah	1816	22	215
RAPPAN, Anthony	1737	3	62
RAWLEY, William	1748	5	525
REDD, Ann C.	1834	30	600
REDD, Jesse	1817	22	317
REDFORD, Edward	1804	18	741
REDFORD, Francis W.	1814	21	573
REDFORD, Jesse E.	1818	23	413
REDFORD, Milner	1805	19	284
REDFORD, Richard	1823	25	123–327
REDFORD, William	1752	6	188
REDFORD, William	1824	26	58
REYNOLDS, James	1820	24	300
RICE, Charles	1785	14	207
RICE, Edward	1770	10	67
RICE, Michael	1731	3	83
RICH, Timothy	1736	2	253
RIDDLE, David	1802	18	481
RIDDLE, John	1771	10	111
ROACH, Patrick	1789	15	184
ROANE, Spencer	1835	30	229

NAME	YEAR	BOOK	PAGE
ROBARDS, John	1755	7	2
ROBARDS, William	1783	13	347
ROBERTSON, Eliz'h.	1831	29	266
ROBINSON, James	1745	5	514
ROBINSON, Thomas	1743	4	245
ROGERS, Adaston	1749	6	20
ROGERS, Robert	1740	3	374
ROGERS, William	1777	12	32
ROYSTER, Anderson	1808	20	191
ROYSTER, Henry	1804	19	74
ROUNTREE, Randal	1788	15	166
ROUNTREE, William	1766	9	38
ROUNTREE, William	1776	11	133
RUNALS, William	1730	1	194
RUSSELL, Benjamin	1801	18	185
RUTHERFORD, William	1814	21	620
RYAN, Philip	1764	8	402
SADLER, Benjamin	1794	15	566
SALLE, Isaac	1730	1	282
SALLEE, Jno. F. G.	1836	30	580
SALMONS, Benjamin	1794	16	333
SALLMONS, Nancy	1815	22	85
SAMSON, Francis	1744	4	499
SAMPSON, Bridgett	1757	7	157
SAMPSON, Charles	1776	11	79
SAMPSON, Mary	1774	10	471
SAMPSON, Saml. S.	1825	26	269
SAMPSON, Stephen	1768	9	131
SANDERS, John	1825	26	269
SATTERWHITE, James	1801	18	128
SCOTT, Edward	1738	3	107
SCOTT, John	1730	1	205
SCOTLAR, Nicholas	1739	3	225
SCRUGGS, Edward	1787	14	388
SCRUGGS, James	1817	22	467
SCRUGGS, Richard	1824	25	527
SCRUGGS, Susanna	1819	24	51
SCRUGGS, William	1795	17	37
SEACOR, Squire	1817	23	1
SEVILLE, Nicholas	1735	2	143
SEVILLEY, Nicholas	1735	2	252
SHELTON, William A.	1824	25	521
SHELTON, William P.	1778	12	211
SHEPHERD, Wm. B.	1779	12	236
SHEPHERD, Robert	1797	17	147
SHOEMAKER, Thomas	1803	18	706

NAME	YEAR	BOOK	PAGE
SHOMAKER, Judith	1827	27	307
SLAYDEN, Arthur	1787	14	436
SLAYDEN, John	1817	23	54
SMITH, Elizabeth	1840	32	253
SMITH, George	1816	22	172
SMITH, Granville	1826	26	373
SMITH, James	1839	31	489
SMITH, John	1755	6	449
SMITH, John	1806	19	478
SMITH, John	1826	27	420
SMITH, John	1832	29	267
SMITH, Marcellas	1829	28	492
SMITH, Robert	1794	16	275
SMITH, Thomas	1817	22	377
SMITH, Wm. Sharp	1783	15	32
SOBLET, James	1741	3	533
SOULI, Nicholas	1741	3	159
SPURLOCK, Ann	1759	8	52
SPEARE, James	1732	1	340
SPEARS, John	1743	4	343
SPEARS, Robert	1740	3	348
STAMPS, William	1746	5	115
STEPHEN, John	1738	5	140
STEPHEN, Joshua	1735	5	13
STEPHEN, Newton	1822	25	231
STODGHILL, Edward	1773	10	376
STONEBANK, John	1749	6	25
STOVALL, William	1736	2	225
SYME, Martha T.	1824	26	12
TAURMAN, Thomas	1810	20	621
TAURMAN, Saly	1823	25	488
TAYLOR, Charles	1742	4	112
THACKER, Reuben	1814	21	655
THOMASON, George	1801	18	182
THOMASON, James	1801	18	291
THOMPSON, George	1767	9	122
THOMPSON, Mary	1771	10	166
THOMPSON, Mary	1774	10	495–500
THOMPSON, Richard	1778	12	191
THURSTON, Daniel	1777	12	71
THURSTON, Elizabeth	1803	17	440
THURSTON, Francis	1774	10	455
THURSTON, James	1829	28	120
THURSTON, John	1818	23	324
THURSTON, Meriwether	1803	18	627
THURSTON, Pleasants	1824	25	577

NAME	YEAR	BOOK	PAGE
THURSTON, Reuben	1786	14	311
THURSTON, William	1817	23	77
TINDALL, Thomas	1742	4	87
TINSLEY, Ann	1836	31	11
TINSLEY, John	1814	21	511
TOLER, George	1823	25	420–423
TOLER, James	1781	13	146
TOLER, John	1780	13	124
TOLER, William	1838	32	323
TONY, Charles	1776	11	124
TRABUE, Anthony	1743	4	321
TRACY, Prince	1812	21	298
TRICE, William	1775	11	51
TRUEHEART, Mary	1779	13	15
TUGGLE, John	1793	16	225
TURNER, Henry	1735	2	91
TURNER, Henry	1760	8	93
TURNER, James	1734	2	15
TURPIN, Obedience	1745	5	139
TUTTLE, Ichabod	1832	30	1
UTLEY, John	1762	8	222
UTLEY, Josiah	1826	27	73
UTLEY, Lilly	1821	24	434
UTLEY, Obediah	1824	25	513
UTLEY, William	1810	19	691
VAIDEN, John	1781	13	139
VAUGHAN, Mary	1820	24	299
VAUGHAN, Matthew	1798	17	265
VAUGHAN, N. M.	1833	29	665
VAUGHAN, Nicholas W.	1833	29	604
VAUGHAN, Patrick	1816	22	121
VIGNE, Adam	1729	1	8
WADE, Ambrose	1831	29	73
WADE, Dabny	1805	19	295
WADE, Daniel	1829	28	......
WADE, Gisle	1768	9	132
WADE, Keturah	1839	32	137
WADE, Lucy	1826	27	102
WADE, Richard	1795	11	514
WADE, Robert	1708	20	212
WADE, William	1772	10	200
WADE, William	1779	12	279
WADE, William	1832	29	324
WADLOW, Thomas	1773	10	319

NAME	YEAR	BOOK	PAGE
WAFFORD, Thomas	1817	23	127
WAFFORD, Eliz'h.	1823	25	325
WALKER, Agnes	1798	17	322
WALKER, David	1740	3	434
WALKER, David	1772	10	283
WALKER, David	1774	10	435
WALKER, Eliz'h.	1822	25	143
WALKER, John, Jr.	1740	3	365
WALKER, John	1767	9	74
WALKER, John	1794	16	361
WALKER, Mary	1777	12	46
WALKER, Peter	1800	18	24
WALKER, Peter	1806	19	399
WALKER, Philip	1798	17	219
WALKER, William	1806	19	553
WALDROP, Thomas	1838	31	437
WALMACK, Henry	1790	15	377
WALTON, William	1747	5	379
WARE, James	1819	24	16
WARE, John	1816	22	211
WARE, Peter	1741	3	526
WATKINS, Benjamin	1753	6	307
WATKINS, Benjamin	1794	16	277
WATKINS, Benjamin	1799	17	524
WATKINS, Benjamin	1816	22	204
WATKINS, Benj. P.	1824	25	542
WATKINS, David	1838	31	450
WATKINS, James	1803	18	621
WATKINS, Jane	1778	12	91
WATKINS, Joseph	1734	2	72
WATKINS, Joseph	1805	19	159
WATKINS, Mary	1829	28	96
WATKINS, Mayo C.	1813	21	442
WATKINS, Thomas	1776	11	74
WATKINS, Thomas	1783	17	404
WATKINS, William	1779	12	257
WEATHERSPOON, Francis	1837	31	173
WITHERSPOON, Reuben	1793	16	172
WORTHERSPOON, Reuben	1791	16	94
WEBB, William	1814	21	519
WEBBER, Augustine	1751	8	31
WEBBER, William	1794	16	311
WEBBER, William	1808	20	210
WEBBER, William	1833	30	323
WEBSTER, David	1834	30	184
WEBSTER, John	1733	1	432
WEBSTER, Mary	1805	19	223

NAME	YEAR	BOOK	PAGE
WEBSTER, Nathaniel	1801	18	139
WEST, George and wife	1747	5	360
WHARTON, Austin	1834	30	106
WHARTON, Jno. G.	1839	32	10
WHITLOCK, Grizil	1759	7	342
WHITLOCK, John	1775	11	7
WHITLOW, Henry	1788	15	116
WHITLOW, William	1768	9	139
WIDRON, John	1761	8	125
WIGHT, Hezekiah L.	1832	31	219
WILDY, George	1821	24	477
WILDY, Nancy	1827	27	233
WILDY, Rebecca	1770	10	56
WILLISS, Daniel	1749	6	84
WILLIS, Ellender	1795	16	374
WILLIS, Edward	1805	19	234
WILLIS, Robert	1755	7	16
WILLIS, Samuel	1825	26	356
WILLIAMS, Edward	1730	1	283
WILLIAMS, Eleazer	1789	15	324
WILLIAMS, Francis	1797	17	155
WILLIAMS, James	1812	21	221
WILLIAMS, James	1817	22	324
WILLIAMS, John	1740	3	348
WILLIAMS, John	1806	19	537
WILLIAMS, Jno. Powell	1803	18	584
WILLIAMS, Philip	1792	16	139
WILLIAMS, Philemon	1760	8	95
WILLIAMS, William	1783	13	329
WILLIAMS, William C.	1832	29	465
WILLIAMS, Womack	1762	8	235
WILLIAMS, Zachariah	1766	9	35
WILLIAMS, Zachariah	1771	10	202
WILLIAMSON, George	1742	4	154
WILMORE, Cecelia	1740	3	277
WILSON, David	1752	6	220
WILLSON, Richard	1735	2	96
WINGFIELD, Robert	1791	15	539
WIXON, Daniel	1742	4	350
WOOD, Henry	1757	7	165
WOOD, Sarah	1757	7	234
WOOD, Valentine	1781	13	124
WOOD, Valentine	1799	17	508
WOODALL, John	1754	6	130
WOODALL, William	1797	17	104
WOODSON, Benjamin	1738	3	160
WOODSON, Benjamin	1750	6	78

NAME	YEAR	BOOK	PAGE
WOODSON, Benjamin	1809	20	328
WOODSON, Bouth	1757	7	178
WOODSON, Elizabeth	1803	18	568
WOODSON, Jacob	1762	8	203
WOODSON, Jno. & Robt.	1742	3	544
WOODSON, John	1734	2	71
WOODSON, John	1754	6	635
WOODSON, John	1790	15	335
WOODSON, John	1803	18	673
WOODSON, John	1823	25	391
WOODSON, John's heirs	1803	19	4-13
WOODSON, Joseph	1734	2	14
WOODSON, Joseph, Sr.	1734	2	73
WOODSON, Joseph	1784	14	25
WOODSON, Joseph	1817	22	343
WOODSON, Josiah	1736	2	267
WOODSON, Lewis	1771	10	128
WOODSON, Matthew	1795	16	480
WOODSON, Robert	1729	1	104
WOODSON, Robert	1750	6	100
WOODSON, Robert	1778	10	469
WOODSON, Robert	1784	14	42
WOODSON, Robert	1823	25	339
WOODSON, Robt. H.	1807	19	596-636
WOODSON, Samuel	1810	20	530
WOODSON, Samuel	1829	28	113
WOODSON, Sarah	1818	23	132
WOODSON, Stephen	1736	2	249
WOODSON, Susanna	1757	7	209
WOODSON, Susanna	1800	18	98
WOODSON, Tarleton	1774	10	493
WOODSON, Thomas	1803	18	582
WOODSON, Thos. heirs		18	747
WOODSON, Thos. heirs	1803	19	5-412
WOODSON, Tucker	1795	16	484
WOODSON, Tucker	1796	17	140
WOODSON, William	1815	22	113
WOODSON, William	1817	23	2
WOODWARD, John	1771	12	9
WOODWARD, Mary	1753	6	265
WRIGHT, James D.	1825	26	300
WRIGHT, John	1729	1	194
WRIGHT, Maridy	1735	2	163
YOUNGHUSBAND, Mary	1812	13	301

www.ingramcontent.com/pod-product-compliance
Lightning Source LLC
Chambersburg PA
CBHW020452030426
42337CB00011B/89